Roots of Justice

A History of Race and Racism in Nebraska

Edited by Kevin Abourezk

and with an Introduction by

M. Dewayne Mays and Paul A. Olson

ROOTS OF JUSTICE

Truth and Reconciliation Nebraska

2025

ISBN 978-1-60962-354-8 paperback
ISBN 978-1-60962-355-5 ebook
doi:10.32873/unl.dc.rj0

Copyright © 2025 Truth and Reconciliation Nebraska.

This work is openly licensed via CC BY 4.0.
Some illustrations are copyright by their original creators or publishers who may require additional permission for re-use.

This edition produced and distributed by
Zea Books, Lincoln, Nebraska.

Cover images:
Omaha Mural Project, photographs by Patricia A. Saldaña

Epigraph

"I believe that if a person reads all the chapters, there's going to be something that will touch their soul."
—M. Dewayne Mays

Contents

Foreword 7
Bill Arfmann

Introduction 9
M. Dewayne Mays and Paul A. Olson

Native Americans I 31
Gabriel Bruguier

Native Americans II 61
Kevin Abourezk

African Americans
A History of African Americans in Nebraska 88
Preston Love, Jr., with Adam Fletcher Sasse and Heather Fryer

Latinos
**Voices of Latinidad: A Truth and Reconciliation Movement to Preserve
    Latino and Latina History** 175
J.S. Onésimo (Ness) Sándoval

Asian Americans
**Exclusion from the Good Life: The Impact of Anti-Asian Racism on
    Asian Nebraskans** 215
Heather Fryer and Sharon Ishii-Jordan

Recent Arrivals: Refugee Resettlement in Nebraska 259
Emira Ibrahimpašić and Julia Reilly

Contributors 297

Acknowledgments 299

Foreword

by Bill Arfmann

There is much to understand about the history of Nebraska and how the past shapes the present. This book attempts to bring into clearer focus the triumphs and trials of five broad groups whose lives have often been overlooked when the state's history is told. The authors know some of this history of racism firsthand: Most of them have lived as people of color in Nebraska. They've experienced "the good, the bad and the ugly" that makes up our state story.

Many readers will turn first to the chapter that resonates with them, to read how Sin Goon was driven out of North Platte by the KKK or how Rowena Moore won jobs for Black women in the Omaha meatpacking plants. There is power, though, in considering these chapters as a whole. What historical themes bridge these chapters? What stories overlap? Native Americans and African Americans, Asian Nebraskans, Latinos and refugees all have faced struggles and traumas, and have shown remarkable resilience. What did they face and what did they overcome? Where did this racism come from?

Readers, whether black, white or brown, may wish to delve into their own family histories and discover similar struggles and trauma. How do our histories differ? What might distinguish the traumas of white folks from those of color? Beyond that, what common threads tie together Nebraskans of different races? And what's the difference between individual racist attitudes and historical racism that permeates policies and institutions?

Not everyone will be eager to explore such questions. Some might prefer to challenge, to downplay, or to ignore this history. For those who may want to challenge the historical accuracy in these chapters-- please do so based upon documented facts. And let us ask ourselves, what would be the impact of burying this integral part of Nebraska history?

This book can only serve as a beginning of a discussion about race and racism in Nebraska, as author Ness Sándoval suggests. He and the other authors have sought in these chapters to document the truths of our history, but there is so much more to tell. Many vital stories are yet to be found and brought to light.

We encourage educators, scholars and family historians to continue to dig, to document and to tell these stories. And then to ask:

How can we best acknowledge the racism that is part of our history?

How might Nebraskans remedy the wrongs of the past and create a future in which racism is no longer a divisive issue? Can we imagine a culture in which differences and stereotypes do not rule the future for our children and grandchildren?

How is it possible for all Nebraskans, through what organizations and institutions, to work for the common good in Nebraska?

May this history compel us all to imagine a better future – and then to take action to make it happen!

Introduction[1]

M. Dewayne Mays and Paul A. Olson

Nebraska has made racism a way of life through most of its history. It is still the way of life for many. In 2020, a Nebraska columnist wrote the following about Nebraska: "[T]he issues stemming from racism can seem like foreign concepts, confined to the larger cities (or the American South) and relics of a distant past."[2] The column goes on to show that these issues were not confined to large cities or to the South; they rested on our back door in Nebraska. Yet, one often heard back as far as one could remember that Nebraska is not and was never a racist state. The chapters in this study do not allow this perception to stand.

Nebraska's land was stolen from the Native American nations that preceded the United States. In 1879, a federal court had to tell Nebraska that a Nebraska Native American, Standing Bear, was a person in the "full meaning of the law."[3] Less than seventy years ago a person of color and a white person did not have the right to marry one another under Nebraska law.[4] Until the 1960s, federal housing rules applied in Nebraska with respect to lending practices did not allow financial institutions to lend to people of color who were mostly Blacks who wished to buy a house in most neighborhoods in Nebraska.[5] The state accepted the situation; hence perpetuating segregated housing in many of its cities and towns. Three Blacks and two Hispanics during the late 1800s and early 1900s were among the fifty-seven total lynchings accounted for in Nebraska.[6] Hispanic people worked "to the bone" in the fields of Nebraska without serious governmental labor protections until the mid-twentieth century.[7]

The American perception of racial difference tied inextricably to ideologies of white supremacy, allowing these racist developments and actions to take place. It was only recently the Human Genome Project of the National Library of Medicine has "helped to inform us about how remarkably similar all human

---

1. This chapter was visualized by several members of the Steering Committee of the Roots of Justice Project; Paul Olson, following Mr. Mays' outline generally, wrote the chapter. It was, thereafter, edited and corrected by Kathleen Rutledge, Kathleen Johnson, and Jeannette Eileen Jones.
2. Jordan Martin, "Confronting racism's legacy, from town to country," Civic Nebraska Writer's Group, June 19, 2020, https://www.civicnebraska.org/legacy-racism-town-country/.
3. Jennifer David, "Chief Standing Bear and His Landmark Civil Rights Case," *Library of Congress Blogs*, November 21, 2019, https://blogs.loc.gov/law/2019/11/chief-standing-bear-and-his-landmark-civil-rights-case/.
4. Nebraska Legislature, "Sen. Edward Danner," Nebraska Legislature, n.d., https://nebraskalegislature.gov/education/danner.php.
5. North Omaha Information Support Everyone, "Omaha Redlining Resource Guide," July 23, 2019, https://www.noiseomaha.com/resources/2019/7/12/redlining-resources.
6. James E. Potter, "'Wearing the Hempen Neck-Tie': Lynching in Nebraska, 1858-1919," *Nebraska History* 93 (2012): 138-53.
7. Bryan Winston, "Mexican Community Formation in Nebraska: 1910-1950," *Nebraska History* 100 (2019): 2-19.

In *Roots of Justice: A History of Race and Racism in Nebraska*. Edited by Kevin Abourezk, with an Introduction by M. Dewayne Mays and Paul A. Olson (Lincoln, Nebraska: Truth and Reconciliation Nebraska, 2025). Copyright © 2025 by the authors; CC-BY. DOI: 10.32873/unl.dc.rj1

beings are—99.9% at the DNA level" and that "[t]hose who wish to draw precise racial boundaries around certain groups will not be able to use science as a legitimate justification."[8] Yet, the realities of racism, despite our understanding of the social construction of race, continue to plague our nation and the State of Nebraska. The mistaken idea of sharp racial boundaries and "white superiority" has played a significant role in our history, as the chapters in this book demonstrate, because the perceived differences between groups of people in Nebraska are the products of unique histories and cultures. Racism grows out of where groups lived, how they adapted to where they lived; who and what forces governed their lives, and what group antagonisms their leaders cultivated for social, political, and economic advantage. To overcome our prejudices and our unequal treatment of one another, we need to understand how racism became part of the Euro-American creation of Nebraska Territory and the foundation of the state of Nebraska.

Nebraska emerged out of the crucible of the state's antebellum, Civil War, and immediate post-Civil War struggles. This means that issues having to do with the perception of race were by no means settled when the state came into being in 1867, just two years after the Civil War and the constitutional abolition of slavery. As the African American chapter shows, though Nebraska was admitted as a so-called "free state", in territorial times slaveholders brought enslaved African Americans with them along the Missouri River. These men and women brought with them the racial assumptions that undergirded slavery, the dispossession of Native American land, and Indigenous removal. Though territorial Nebraskans sided with the North during the Civil War, many of its residents acted in ways that did not reflect Civil War abolitionist sentiment or the Reconstruction era's Constitutional amendments XIII, XIV, and XV. The amendments prohibited slavery, required that all citizens, including African Americans, receive "equal protection under the laws," and forbade denying the right to vote to men based on race.[9]

As an illustration of the fact that racist ideas survived the Civil War, one may cite the ideas of J. Sterling Morton, the founder of Arbor Day and one of the most prominent political leaders in early Nebraska. Morton favored the South and slavery during the Civil War and in its aftermath as Nebraska was seeking admission to the Union, he stated in 1866 that black people in Nebraska should not be given suffrage as the state's price of admission to the Union: "It will be more manly to accept negro suffrage by legal enforcement than to humiliate ourselves by its voluntary adoption as the price of admission to the Union... We take n—-r [Morton's epithet] only when forced to it by Congress and therefore are for remaining at present a territory."[10] Morton's statement flew in the face of the Civil Rights Act of 1866 that recognized African Americans as natural-born citizens. It also anticipated that Black men would receive universal suffrage in the near future. Later Morton modified his views. As editor of the Nebraska City newspaper, he received criticism for his past proslavery views and present anti-Black sentiment. Over time he backed away from those positions.

Many of Nebraska's heroes, after which many places in the state are named, approved of slavery. Stephen Douglas, after whom early Nebraskans named Douglas County and Douglas Street in Omaha, argued, in an appeal to Southerners and proslavery people, that each state should decide whether it wished for the institution of slavery or not. His defense of popular sovereignty relied on the ability of voting white men to make decisions about the legality of slavery in any given state. Stephen F. Nuckolls, a co-founder of Nebraska City, was a slaveholder and is the person after whom Nuckolls County is named.[11]

Native Americans were also treated unequally from the beginning of the state's founding. General George

---

8. Francis S. Collins and Monique K. Mansoura, "The Human Genome Project." *Cancer* 91 (1 Suppl) (2001):221-5, doi: 10.1002/1097-0142(20010101)91:1+<221::aid-cncr8>3.3.co;2-0. PMID: 11148583.

9. Eric Foner, "The Reconstruction Amendments: Official Documents as Social History," *History Now: The Journal*, Issue 2 (Winter 2004), https://www.gilderlehrman.org/history-resources/essays/reconstruction-amendments-official-documents-social-history. See also Adam Fletcher Sasse, "A History of Enslavement in Nebraska," in North Omaha History, January 22, 2023, https://northomahahistory.com /2023/01/22/a-history-of-slavery-in-nebraska/.

10. David L. Bristow, "Was J. Sterling Morton a racist? Here's what the Arbor Day founder said and did," *Nebraska History* (blog), March 29, 2019, https://history.nebraska.gov/was-j-sterling-morton-a-racist-heres-what-the-arbor-day-founder-said-and-did/.

11. Tyler Ellyson, "Journey to Freedom: Graduate thesis addresses slavery in Nebraska Territory," *UNK News*, April 12, 2021, https://unknews.unk.edu/2021/04/12/journey-to-freedom-graduate-thesis-addresses-slavery-in-nebraska-territory/; Lilian Fitzpatrick, "Nebraska Place Names," *University of Nebraska Studies in Language, Literature, and Criticism* 6 (1925): 13-147.

Custer, after whom Custer County was named and who fought many battles reaching out from Fort Robinson, wrote harshly of the foes from which he was seizing land: "Throughout his memoir, Custer consistently describes Indians as savage, violent, and uncivilized. Establishing Indians as "savage" and impossible to civilize is central to Custer's construction of Indians as the "enemy."[12] Even the judge who decided that Ponca head chief, Standing Bear, was a full human being in the meaning of the law, and thus a person deserving the protection of the U. S. laws, did not respect Native Americans. He also said, in his famous 1879 opinion, that Native Americans are a "weak, insignificant, unlettered, and generally despised race."[13] All the treaties with Nebraska tribes negotiated by the U.S. federal government were broken, as if America's word to Native Americans did not matter.[14]

Though Lincoln, as capital of Nebraska, was named after the "Great Emancipator," and Nebraska entered the union as a state on March 1, 1867, the badges and indices of discrimination that existed across our history dictated Nebraska policies governing housing, labor, individual rights, education, public accommodations, and even sports. To understand why this was the case, we need to unpack the history of the ideas of race and of racial superiority as they existed during Nebraska's settlement period and after.

Admittedly, most cultures have a sense of "us" and "them," a set of practices or criteria that defined "our group" as over against "other groups." In the past, human beings of almost all groups have tended to believe that their group of people was better than others. Racism, however, is more than just group pride and arose relatively recently in human history, dating back to the seventeenth century. Race is a conception of *superior and inferior inherited characteristics* based on the idea that people having a darker skin color or other "different" physical characteristics are a species – different in genetics or natural characteristics.[15]

Contemporary scholars argue that the idea of race involves the construction of "pseudo-species" groups based on skin color and insignificant differences in body type.[16] For the idea of racial superiority to exist, one must have an idea that certain parts of humankind are similar by nature because they have the same or similar inherited characteristics not shared by other groups: skin color, facial appearance, bodily frame, intelligence or skill. Before genetics and the idea of inherited characteristics came to be, in some parts of the world, broad divisions of humankind were thought to exist because of religious ideas that fed into later ideas of inherited racial superiority or inferiority. For instance, the flood-surviving "sons of Noah" in the *Bible* – Ham, Shem, and Japheth – were sometimes said to present three groups of humankind: Ham, dark-skinned people; Shem, Jewish and Arabic peoples; and Japheth, other "white" people having success as rulers of others.[17] This division, made popular in assorted religious circles until at least the 1940s, left out Asian peoples and ignored many other groups who did not fit the threefold division.

When the biological idea of race — that different species of creatures having differing inherited characteristics — appeared in the 18th and 19th centuries, race as a pseudo-scientific idea was born, superimposed on the extant religious ideas and used to justify colonialism, slavery, and general exploitation. Groups that held power in colonial and slave-holding states at the time, all white, were said — by the "pseudo-scientific" community made up of phrenologists, craniologists, and ethnologists — to be superior. "Pseudo-science" served to give an apparent objectivity to exploitation. Those social groups who gained from believing that people of a different color or skeletal type were born to serve them tried to separate people whom they wished to be in the underclasses based on skin color or on the basis of skull configuration through the "science" of phrenology.[18]

---

12. Danielle Johannesen, "Depictions of American Indians in George Armstrong Custer's 'My Life on the Plains.'" *Humanities* 8, no. 1 (2019), 2, https://doi.org/10.3390/h8010056.
13. Gillian Brockell, "The civil rights leader 'almost nobody knows about' gets a statue in the U.S. Capitol," *Washington Post*, September 20, 2019, https://www.washingtonpost.com/history/2019/09/20/civil-rights-leader-almost-nobody-knows-about-gets-statue-us-capitol/.
14. Helen Hunt Jackson, *A Century of Dishonor* (Boston: Roberts, 1888 [c1885]).
15. Hussein Mohsen, "Race and Genetics: Somber History, Troubled Present," *Yale J. Biol Med.* 93 (2020): 215–219.
16. George Kelsey, "The Racist Search for the Self," *The Journal of Religious Ethics* 6 (1978): 240-241.
17. Benjamin Braude, "The Sons of Noah and the Construction of Ethnic and Geographical Identities in the Medieval and Early Modern Periods," *William and Mary Quarterly* 54 (1997): 103-42.
18. Paul Wolff Mitchell, "The fault in his seeds: Lost notes to the case of bias in Samuel George Morton's cranial race science," *PLOS Biology* 16 (2018), doi: 10.1371/journal.pbio.2007008.

The prejudices that Europeans held against all people who looked different from them or who practiced different customs emerged during the ages of exploration and colonization (15th-18th centuries) to justify conquest and exploitation.[19] These pre-scientific ethnic prejudices were reinforced by the pseudo-scientific ones mentioned above and used to justify colonialism, slavery, Indian removal, Chinese exclusion, Jim Crow, and the denial of equal rights under the law to people of color over the course of the history of colonial America and the United States. Many of these views of racialized minorities were held by the highest-ranked political leaders in the nation. For example, Teddy Roosevelt – considered by his contemporaries to be a progressive president—justified the subjugation of African American people in the South and Indigenous people everywhere based on the pseudoscience of eugenics. Roosevelt shaped much of early twentieth century American imperialist policy and justified Southern policies that subjugated people of color.[20] Woodrow Wilson followed in his footsteps,[21] proclaiming the film Birth of a Nation to be a masterpiece in its racist depiction of African Americans and celebration of the Ku Klux Klan. If American leaders displayed such prejudices from George Washington to Wilson and beyond, it is not surprising that many ordinary white people both foreign-born and native-born who settled Nebraska from the Civil War to the present embraced these prejudices. Many revered white Nebraskans certainly did. As this book makes clear, many prominent Nebraska leaders whose names receive honor on maps and public monuments supported the idea of white superiority and an ethos of discrimination. Popular beliefs about racial difference and hierarchy were buttressed by the racial "sciences" of the nineteenth and twentieth centuries. Phrenology, the discipline that theorized that African skulls indicated that they were made to be subservient and that Native American skulls revealed that they were "adverse to cultivation, slow in acquiring knowledge," was taught in Nebraska schools and colleges.[22] Eugenics, a pseudoscience that advocated for the peopling of the nation and world with the "higher" races through exclusionary immigration laws and white propagation, had a following in Nebraska.[23]

Racism and the Peoples of Nebraska

In Nebraska, the broad categories of groups that were subjected to clearly "race-based" discrimination, as explored in the *Roots of Justice* project, were Native Americans, African Americans, Latinos, Asian Americans, and post-1965 immigrants.[24] Given the massive amount of research that remains to be done on these populations, we have barely scratched the surface in this project and thus, encourage others to conduct fuller and deeper research.[25] In examining the histories of ordinary people of color in our state, one notices a number of commonalities among the groups experiencing racism:

---

19. John R. Pittenger, "'What Good Can There Be In This Kind of Human?' Spanish Justification for the Conquest of the Americas," *Gettysburg Historical Journal* 7 (2020): 58-73, https://cupola.gettysburg.edu/cgi/.
20. Christopher Klein, "How Teddy Roosevelt's Belief in a Racial Hierarchy Shaped His Policies," History, accessed December 2023, https://www.history.com/news/teddy-roosevelt-race-imperialism-national-parks.
21. Dick Lehr, "The Racist Legacy of Woodrow Wilson," *The Atlantic*, https://www.theatlantic.com/politics/archive/2015/11/wilson-legacy-racism/417549/.
22. History Nebraska, "Phrenology: Science or Entertainment?" *History Nebraska Publications*, accessed December 2023, https://history.nebraska.gov/publications_section /phrenology-science-or-entertainment/; "Skulls in print: scientific racism in the transatlantic world," University of Cambridge, 19 March 2014, https://www.cam.ac.uk/research/news/skulls-in-print-scientific-racism-in-the-transatlantic-world.
23. Paul A. Lombardo, "'We Who Champion the Unborn': Racial Poisons, Eugenics, and the Campaign for Prohibition," *Journal of Law, Medicine & Ethics* 50 (2022), https://www.cambridge.org/core/journals /journal-of-law-medicine-and-ethics/article/we-who-champion-the-unborn-racial-poisons-eugenics-and-the-campaign-for-prohibition/.
24. We use the Immigration and Nationality Act of 1965 to mark this period but also pay particular attention to the end of the Vietnam War when the United States accepted a large number for refugees into the nation.
25. The great periods of civil rights struggle and of many great civil rights warriors came in earlier periods, their lives often largely undocumented and their work, if noticed at all, often chronicled by publications that did not support equal rights. This is particularly true of the period from the fifties through the seventies when a great civil rights ferment in this state and nation occurred. A few biographies and autobiographies of significant Nebraska civil rights leaders do exist in book form or online, those for Malcolm X, Reuben Snake, Norma Elia Cantú, Robert Navarro, Ernie Chambers, Leola and Hugh Bullock, Hughes and Lela Shanks, and Ben Kuroki. These deserve study (see Appendix I). However, the story of most of the leaders in the movement toward equality largely remains to be told.

1. All groups of color – including most Native American groups — moved, or were forced to move, from their traditional lands, homes, and cultures to profit European-based groups that took over their resources, including the products of their labor.
2. Groups of color were, until recently, forced by law and social codes to live in separate enclaves and denied important legal rights and education, health, and employment opportunities.
3. Groups of color received unequal legal treatment in matters relating to wealth creation and retention from the federal government, from state and local agencies, and often from financial institutions.
4. Groups and individuals of color were threatened with lynching, bullying, and private abuse if they got "out of line."
5. The intellectual justification for the racism was white superiority (or supremacy), but its actual motor was, in most cases, economic and social advantage.
6. The system was partially maintained, after the Civil Rights movement and Civil Rights legislation of the 1950s-1970s, by unequal enforcement of the law, particularly drug laws, and punitive policies directed against people of color in the justice system.
7. Recent immigrant groups, because of their recent appearance on the American scene (after the passage of the Civil Rights acts) did not experience items 1-6 above in the same way as other groups but they did experience some of the vestiges of our racist past.

While these commonalities exist, we must examine each of these patterns separately.

All groups of color – including most Native American groups — moved, or were forced to move, from their traditional lands, homes, and cultures to profit European-based groups that took over their resources.

One scholarly source addresses the legacies of forced Indigenous removal in modern times, stating:

> While most migrants do not experience mental health problems, people displaced as a result of conflicts, violence, fear of persecution and human rights violations can [be] at increased risk of mental health problems. This is particularly true for persons who have experienced violence and trauma, including exploitation, torture or sexual and gender-based violence. Issues can range from low to moderate levels of anxiety and depression through to more severe mental disorders…. When individuals and families seek safety by leaving their homes, cultures, and communities because of the threat of violence and persecution, emotional distress can be heightened. About one third of displaced persons will experience high rates of depression, anxiety, and post-traumatic stress disorders (PTSD) as a result of the circumstances they faced during their migration, which can significantly affect the quality of their life.[26]

This is obviously true for Native American and African American groups forcibly removed from their homes and homelands. Garland Blaine, a historian of the Pawnee tribe, speaks of the depression experienced by the Pawnee when they were moved from Nebraska to Oklahoma and experienced white diseases and the depopulation of their tribe:

> The Pawnees in the 1870s moved to Indian Territory. Now after they settled at what is now around and near Pawnee, Oklahoma, due to change of climate, water, environment, and due to sicknesses that followed, the Pawnees dwindled from many people to as low as in the-1880s — I think it was in the late 1880s — as low as eight hundred and fifty probably or down to maybe six hundred, plus or minus a few. There were a few years that they did not hold their ceremonies, only superficially, only got together and, the seats not being filled, went on ahead and went as far as they could, due to the fact that they knew that the rest of them that could be there were probably at home sick.[27]

---

26. D. Silove, P. Ventevogel, and S. Rees, "The contemporary refugee crisis: an overview of mental health challenges" *World Psychiatry* 16 (2017):130-9.
27. Garland Blaine, "Religion Among the Pawnee After the Removal to Oklahoma in the 1870s," in *The Pawnee Experience: From Center Village to Oklahoma*, (ERIC Document 235934, 1978), 44. https://files.eric.ed.gov/fulltext/ED235934.pdf.

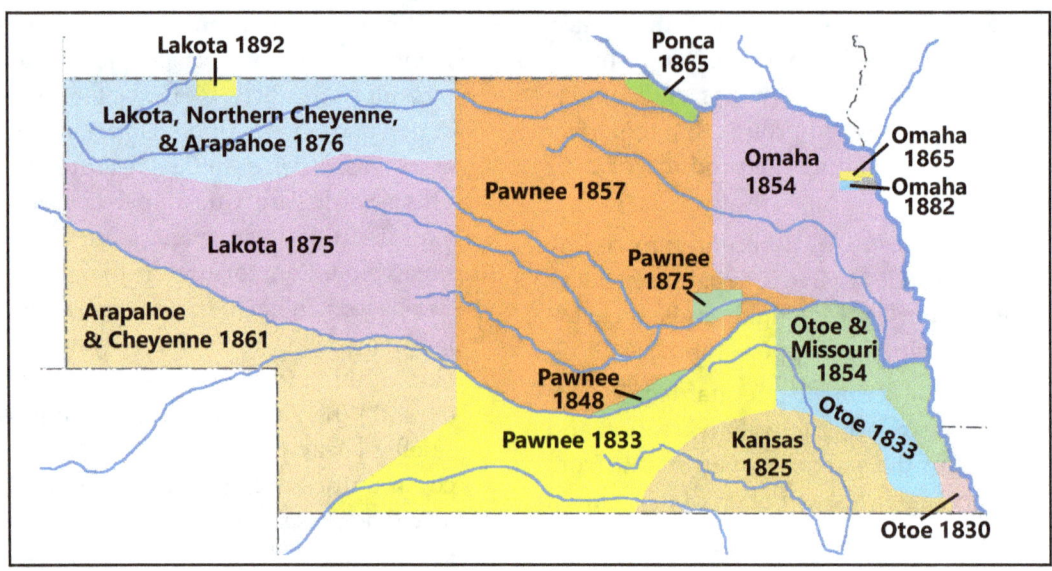

Nebraska Tribe Cessions.

The changes in place and loss of life required religious changes and changes in everything else in Pawnee life; hence, the discouragement and anomie. Even the Omaha nation, whose modern reservation still includes part of the territory where the Omaha traditionally farmed and hunted, have only a small part of their original agricultural lands and hunting grounds.[28] Their original Nebraska lands included some of the richest grazing and riverside agricultural lands in the world. They gave a part of their reservation to Winnebago, 1864 refugees from the Crow Creek area where they had been confined and were slowly dying of hunger and disease in South Dakota. The remainder of their farmlands have largely been purchased or taken under adverse legal conditions by white farmers. Other Nebraska nations such as Otoe-Missouria and Ponca were moved from their original territories to inferior land in Oklahoma, the Lakota from their lands in South Dakota and Nebraska to bad land on reservations in South, and North Dakota, and the Arapaho and Cheyenne from their western Nebraska lands to similarly limited reservations in Oklahoma, Wyoming, and Montana, in each case to territory inferior to Nebraska for agriculture and hunting.[29] Moreover, the bison herds were systematically destroyed by the 1880s by hunting and other factors to deprive the Nebraska nations of much of their protein source.[30] The tribes located into Nebraska, the Santee Sioux, the Winnebago, and the Sac/Fox-Iowa (this latter group assigned a reservation no longer recognized in Nebraska) were given marginal land in this state save for some Omaha tribal land, most of that eventually allotted and sold or leased from under the tribe.[31]

To cite another example: African Americans who came to Nebraska were descended from Africans kidnapped from their homelands in Africa and then enslaved in the American colonies and/or the United

---

28. Judith A. Boughter, *Betraying Their Trust: The Dispossession of the Omaha Nation, 1790-1916* (master's thesis, University of Nebraska at Omaha, 1995). https://digitalcommons.unomaha.edu/studentwork/503/.
29. Jackson 1888.
30. Pekka Hämäläinen, "The First Phase Of Destruction Killing The Southern Plains Buffalo, 1790-1840," *Great Plains Quarterly* 21 (2001): 101-114.
31. "Nebraska Tribe Cessions" is based on the map on Plate CXLVIII in *Eighteenth annual report of the Bureau of American Ethnology to the Secretary of the Smithsonian Institution, 1896-'97*, by J. W. Powell, Director. Part 2. Washington, Government Printing Office, 1899. https://archive.org/details/annualreportofb1896smit_0/mode/2up Part 2 includes a "Schedule of Treaties and Acts of Congress Authorizing Allotments of Land in Severalty" on pages 645-647 and the "Schedule of Indian Land Cessions" on pages 648-949, which provides details by "Date, Where or how concluded, Reference, Tribe, Description of cession or reservation, Historical data and remarks, Designation of cession on map." The "Designation of cession on map" includes "Number" and "Location." The Plates are located following page 949 and are found by Roman numerals, not by page numbers. Plate CXLVIII shows the entire state of Nebraska. Other sources for complete images of the map may be found on an Internet search for "map of Indian land cessions Nebraska". See also Nebraska Studies, "Taking Indian Land," accessed December 2023, https://www.nebraskastudies.org/en/1850-1874/native-american-settlers/taking-indian-land/

States. Enslaved Blacks did not receive legal freedom until after the Civil War, only then to be denied education, rights, and a place as full citizens in the South after the Civil War. In moving to Nebraska, some found homes using the Homestead Act, but others were gradually moved into segregated areas in cities and towns by lawmakers and restrictive covenants.

Something similar has happened, mostly in the last hundred years, to Latino citizens in towns where large numbers of Latinos have settled (see Latinos chapter). Almost all Latino citizens had to leave their traditional homes in Mexico, Central or South America because of economic or political conditions that prompted their leaving, but they retained much of their cultural tradition in their new locations.[32] Omaha had its own Chinatown.[33] Japanese groups in Nebraska have been small. As far as we know, the refugees who came to Nebraska after World War II have not been confined to one section of Nebraskan cities or towns.

Groups of color were often forced by law and social codes to live in separate enclaves and denied important legal rights and education, health, and employment opportunities.

Forced movement separated people from their traditional human communities and the ecosystems they had learned how to manage, and, in modern circumstances, often led to their "ghettoization," the creation of separate enclaves for them where, compared to other citizens, they experienced inferior education, justice system services, and employment/trade opportunities compared to people descended from Europeans. Such segregated areas were often created by Federal Housing Authority sponsored "redlining" implemented from 1934 until the 1960s and continued by custom and local prejudice thereafter.[34] The cordoning off of people of color began with the removal of Native Americans from the lands that their nations had occupied and their confinement to limited reservations; the dates of these treaties for Nebraska tribes are as follows: Oto, 1830 and 1833; Pawnee, 1833 and 1848; Omaha, 1854; Oto and Missouri, 1854; Pawnee, 1857; Arapaho and Cheyenne, 1861; Omaha, 1865; Lakota, 1875; Pawnee, 1875; Lakota, Northern Cheyenne and Arapaho, 1876; Omaha, 1882; and Lakota 1892. (See map, page 14). Through these treaties virtually all the productive grazing or farming land controlled by the Native American nations was taken from them, sometimes in return for federal guarantees or protection or some goods. That some of the Nebraska nations were fully fledged nation states and not simply somewhat disorganized wandering tribes has been argued persuasively by Pekka Johannes Hämäläinen of Oxford University.[35]

This removal of people of color into resource-poor areas continued with the forcing of African Americans in Nebraska into separated parts of such cities as Omaha and Lincoln, beginning in Omaha in 1902 and in Lincoln in 1916.[36] and continued with the development of separated enclaves in other Nebraska white towns or with the development of "sundown" towns where no person of color was supposed to be within the town limits after dark. Though sundown towns often enforced the rule through silent cultural pressure rather than open enforcement, James Loewen has a citation of Plattsmouth, Nebraska as openly a sundown town; his informant says,

> I remember being shocked to learn soon after moving there [Plattsmouth] that blacks were not allowed to even work in that town after 5 or 6 pm. I had never heard of such a thing at that time… Not only did I never see a black student at Plattsmouth High, only once do I recall ever seeing a black person in the town of Plattsmouth. He was working on a construction crew shortly after I moved there [1961], and that's when I was told (I can't recall by whom) that he would have to be out of Plattsmouth by 5 p.m. because of a town ordinance that did not allow blacks who remain beyond that hour… I would not describe the kids that I knew as more racist than many of the average white kids that I knew in Florida or California. But they imbibed a form of racism based on not having

---

32. Ralph Grajeda, "Chicanos: the Mestizo Heritage," in *Broken Hoops and Plains People*, ed. Paul A. Olson, (Lincoln: Nebraska Curriculum Development Center, 1976), 47-98.
33. Ryan Roenfeld, "A History of Omaha's Chinatown," in North Omaha History, March 5, 2019, https://northomahahistory.com/2019/03/05/a-history-of-omahas-chinatown-by-ryan-roenfeld/.
34. Jonathan Rose, "Redlining," June 22, 2023, Federal Reserve History, https://www.federalreservehistory.org/essays/redlining#
35. Pekka Johannes Hämäläinen, *Lakota America: A New History of Indigenous Power* (New Haven, CT: Yale University Press, 2019).
36. Jennifer Hildebrand, "The New Negro Movement in Lincoln, Nebraska," *Nebraska History* 91 (2010): 168.

much if any normal contact with blacks in their daily lives. Increasing their fear and hatred of blacks were the stories of sex and mayhem . . . that they heard in regard to blacks in Omaha. During the daily course of events, however, the Plattsmouth people that I knew rarely talked about race at all, reflecting the absence of blacks in their daily lives. But when they did, they were likely to express fear and loathing, and to use the 'N' word freely.[37]

North Platte, Nebraska drove out its black residents in 1929,[38] and many other Nebraska towns or counties seems to have had formal or informal sundown provisions.[39]

As large numbers of Hispanic migrants came to Nebraska, they also were, in Lincoln and Omaha, assigned to separated portions of the town.[40] This continues to this day. Our Hispanic chapter represents increasing numbers of small Nebraska towns becoming largely Hispanic or retaining separated Hispanic enclaves. Those Japanese American women who studied at the University of Nebraska during World War II were segregated by the assistant dean of women, Elsie Ford Piper.[41] Only the immigrants of color who came after the Vietnam War were not confined egregiously to separate residential areas not of their own choosing. The effect of forced separation on those so forced has been, in general, inferior housing and financing for housing, less competent educational institutions for their children, inferior work opportunities that left the residents with physical labor jobs, and inferior protection under the law.[42]

Groups of color received unequal legal treatment in matters relating to wealth creation and retention from the federal government, from state and local agencies, and often from most financial institutions.

Since the publication of Thomas Piketty's book on wealth creation and its effects on American and other societies,[43] people have begun to pay more attention to how much accumulated wealth groups of people have — how much they can pass from generation to generation; inequality in wealth creation and transmission, as Piketty argues, has created devastating differences among groups that go back many centuries. Looking at the disparity between black and white family wealth is an extension of Piketty's argument into racial history as Francisco Pérez indicates in the *Non-Profit Quarterly*.[44] Pérez summarizes from William "Sandy" Darity and Darrick Hamilton—two leading economists studying racial inequality, who "assert in a 2018 paper that the racial wealth gap is the best measure of the burden that historic and ongoing racism has imposed on Black Americans." Pérez also reports that The Urban Institute reported "that in 1983, the median white family had eight times the wealth of the median Black family" and that "[i]n 2019, the gap was the same."[45]

Pérez also notes that "Black Americans make up 13 percent of the population but own an estimated 2.6 percent of US wealth," and that the wealthiest one percent of Americans are over 96% white and only a little over 1% Black.

This intergenerational disparity in wealth was created partly because, as Piketty shows, people who

---

37. James W. Loewen, "Plattsmouth." History and Social Justice, accessed December 2023, https://justice.tougaloo.edu/sundowntown/plattsmouth-ne/
38. David G. Dales, "North Platte racial incident: Black-white confrontation, 1929," *Nebraska History* 60 (1979): 424–446.
39. James W. Loewen, "Historical Database of Sundown Towns," History and Social Justice, accessed December 2023, https://justice.tougaloo.edu/sundown-towns/using-the-sundown-towns-database/state-map/
40. Ana-Mari Gonzalez Wahl, Steven Gunkel, Bennie Shobe, Jr. "Becoming Neighbors or Remaining Strangers? Latinos and Residential Segregation in the Heartland," *Great Plains Research* 15 (2005), https://digitalcommons.unl.edu/greatplainsresearch/789/
41. Andrew B. Wertheimer, "Admitting Nebraska's Nisei: Japanese American Students at the University of Nebraska, 1942-1945," *Nebraska History* 83 (2002): 58-72. See also Nebraska Studies, "Japanese Americans," accessed December 2023, https://www.nebraskastudies.org/en/1925-1949/the-war-nebraska-stories/japanese-americans/
42. Margery Austin Turner and Karina Fortuny, "Residential Segregation and Low-Income Working Families," Low-Income Working Families, Paper 10, The Urban Institute, February 2009, https://www.urban.org/research/publication/residential-segregation-and-low-income-working-families
43. Thomas Piketty, *Capital in the Twenty-First Century* (Cambridge, Mass.: Cambridge University Press, 2014).
44. Francisco Pérez, "How Do We Build Black Wealth? Understanding the Limits of Black Capitalism," *Nonprofit Quarterly* (2022), https://nonprofitquarterly.org/how-do-we-build-black-wealth-understanding-the-limits-of-black-capitalism/
45. Urban Institute, "Median Family Wealth by Race/Ethnicity, 1963-2019, https://www.urban.org/sites/default/files/2021-02/wealthbyrace-med.png

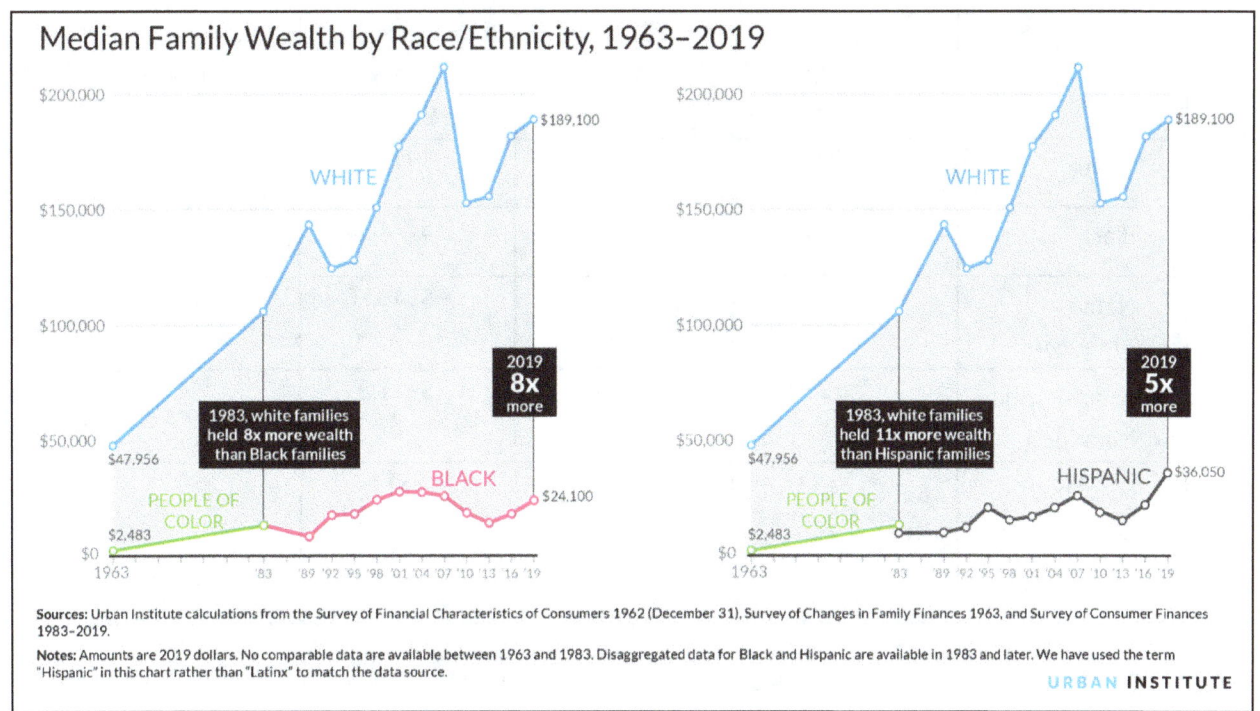

Median Family Wealth by Race/Ethnicity 1963-2019. (See Note 45, which references https://www.urban.org/sites/default/files/2021-02/wealthbyrace-med.png.

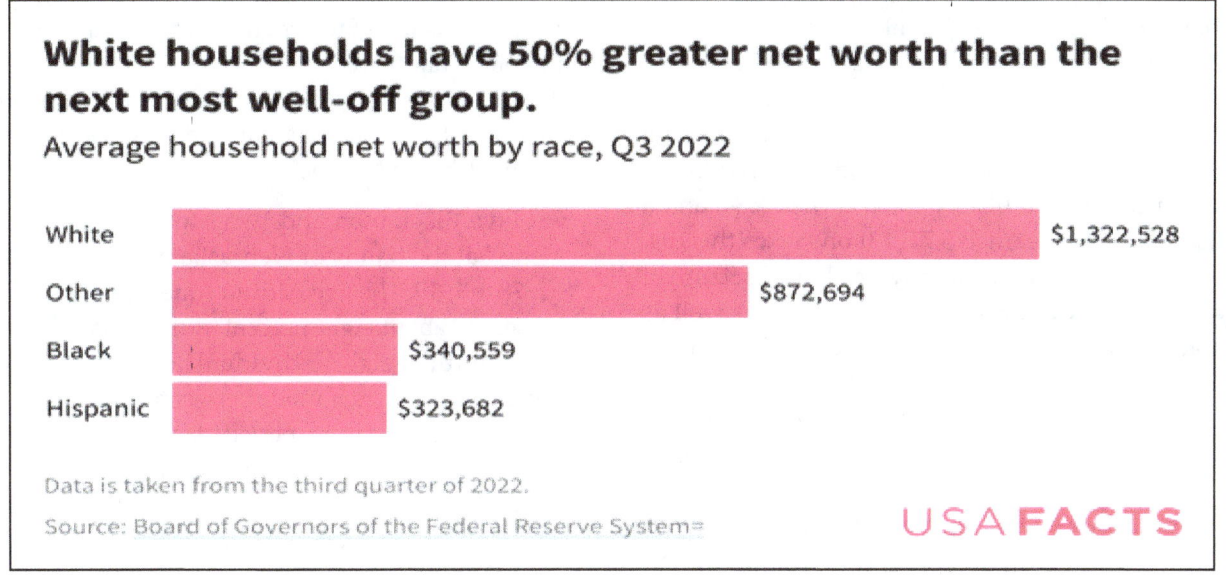

Average household net worth by race, Q3 2022. (See Note 46, which references USA Facts. 2023.)

have capital can grow it faster than economies grow, but also because former slaves and people of color began with very little and received unequal treatment in loans, farm support, and Federal Housing Authority support, as well as a whole range of government support systems that assisted white middle class people in the acquisition of wealth. If one extends this search to all groups of color, the disparity in net worth remains. A Federal Reserve Board chart shows this for 2022.[46]

The "Other" category in the chart above contains Asian, Native Hawaiian or Pacific Islander, American Indian or Alaska Native, and multi-racial households.

46. USA Facts. 2023, "Wealth inequality across race: what does the data show?" Updated on April 6, 2023, https://usafacts.org/articles/wealth-inequality-across-races-what-does-the-data-show/.

Race or Ethnicity	Number of Workers	Share of Workers	Average Weekly Earnings	Earnings per Dollar
White	809,601	81.21%	$917.39	$1.00
Black	33,181	3.33%	$774.00	$0.84
Native American	5,485	0.55%	$548.76	$0.60
Asian-Pacific Islander	26,360	2.64%	$915.23	$1.00
Hispanic/Latino	110,116	11.05%	651.66	$0.71
Multiracial	12,143	1.22%	681.18	$0.74

Earning comparisons by race in Nebraska, January 2017-December 2019. (See Note 48, which references Office of Federal Compliance Programs 2020.)

While we do not have data for the wealth accumulation of each group-of-color in Nebraska, we do have, from the Office of Federal Contract Compliance Programs, earning comparisons by race in Nebraska for the January 2017 – December 2019 period.[47]

This means that for every dollar that a Nebraska white worker earned in that period, a Native American earned $.60, a Black person earned $.84, and a Hispanic person earned $.71.[48] If one takes this disparity in salary and the legally sanctioned seizure of Native American property into account, as well as what should be equal wages for African American and Hispanic and then couple that with government sanctions for denying home purchases to people of color for decades, one can understand why the racial wealth gap exists. Differences in family wealth not only affect family stability and housing but even such matters as ACT and SAT scores that collectively are closely correlated with wealth.[49]

Groups of color were threatened with lynching, bullying, and private abuse if they got "out of line." Violence is a tool that creates social subordination and fear of rebellion.

All persons, under the Constitution, are entitled to equal protection under the Constitution's XIVth Amendment's Equal Protection Clause and to the presumption of innocence. Lynching does not afford such protection or presumption. The lynching of people of color was not common in Nebraska, as James Potter writes In *Nebraska History*:

> Five Black men and two Mexicans perished at the hands of Nebraska mobs from 1878 to 1919. The five African Americans represented about eight percent of the probable total of fifty-eight individuals dispatched by Nebraska lynch mobs between 1859 and 1919. During the same period, African Americans never exceeded one percent of the state's population.[50]

Some newspapers in Nebraska condoned lynching as suitable for its victims, and many of them justified lynching of persons of color on racist grounds. Though lynching was the most egregious of the intimidation tactics used against persons of color, they were also subjected to other forms of violence, name-calling, and intimidation, a feature of public

---

47. Office of Federal Contract Compliance Programs, "Earnings Disparities by Race and Ethnicity: Nebraska," (2020), U. S. Department of Labor, accessed December 2023, https://www.dol.gov/agencies/ofccp/about/data/earnings/race-and-ethnicity
48. Office of Federal Contract Compliance Programs, "Earnings Disparities by Race and Ethnicity: Nebraska," (2020).
49. Abigail Johnson Hess, "Rich students get better SAT scores—here's why." *Penn Social Policy and Practice*, Oct. 3, 2019, https://sp2.upenn.edu/press/rich-students-get-better-sat-scores-heres-why/
50. Potter 2012, 144.

cultural life against which 1997 Nebraska Revised Statute 28-110 was designed to protect people; the statute reads:

> A person in the State of Nebraska has the right to live free from violence, or intimidation by threat of violence, committed against his or her person or the destruction or vandalism of, or intimidation by threat of destruction or vandalism of, his or her property regardless of his or her race, color, religion, ancestry, national origin, gender, sexual orientation, age, or disability.[51]

This statute was passed to prevent the kind of experience that a Black family had in the arson of their home that occurred in the Lincoln suburb of Havelock in April of 1958. The Brown family, after it rented a dwelling in white Havelock, was cursed and abused by people in the neighborhood whenever they did yard work; eventually its house was broken into and fire set in two places that gutted the interior. After the fire, Mrs. Brown said, "I never dreamed it would be like this. We were so glad to get a place to live I never thought about any trouble. I pray to God every night that He will help me understand them" [i.e., the racist arsonists that burned down her house].[52]

As Hazel Adams explained when interviewed in 2007, "You couldn't live in Havelock." Half a century after the event, the memory of a Black family "being burned out" of Havelock, possibly by members of the Ku Klux Klan, remained fresh in the minds of Adams and other interviewees.[53] Albert Maxey said at the November 20, 2023, listening session of the *Roots of Justice* project that when he was a police officer on the beat in Havelock, he'd walk into a bar and they'd say, "Nigger, get out of here." His boss took him out of Havelock because "they were planning on killing me." (Rutledge, African American Listening Session, Christ Temple Church, 2023). Interviewees recall being forced by realtors and community pressure to live in particular areas of town, most notably the area surrounding the Malone Community Center. African Americans were acutely aware of areas in which they were especially unwelcome.

Many of the expressions of hate based on race seem to be minor slights, but, when these may appear constantly and in many forms and when the specter of violence lurks in the background, they are used to enforce white superiority and supremacy. When Juanita McWilliams took care of a white family's children, she overheard the father complain one day, "I worked just like a nigger." She said she made a point of walking by him, so he knew she had heard him. "I have learned to ignore the stupid people," she said. (Rutledge, African American Listening Session, Christ Temple Church, 2023) In the May 27, 1997, hearing on LB90, a hate crimes bill, Senator Ernie Chambers elicited an example of the kind of slight that threatens and intimidates without doing bodily harm.

> There has been an outbreak of overt racist activity in this state recently. A few days ago, there were cards, hundreds of them, spread through two of the largest retail stores in Omaha. One was Baker's supermarket; the other was Albertson's supermarket. These skinheads had put these cards with their racist and anti-Semitic messages throughout the store. They put them in packages of goods, hid them behind other items. Put them in containers which held a number of cans of pop or bottles of pop. So I guess it might have been designed to give the impression that this was the store's point of view.[54]

Again, recently the governor of Nebraska dismissed a report concerning pollution on his hog farms by a local news reporter of Chinese descent because of her Chinese background; he did not speak to question of her evidence on the issue.[55] The authors of this chapter have experienced or witnessed work and retail situations where racist bullying and name calling were standard fare or where

---

51. Nebraska Legislature, *Laws* 1997. LB 90, § 2, Nebraska Revised Statute 28-110, https://nebraskalegislature.gov/laws/statutes.php?statute=28-110
52. Anon., "Negro Home Fire Definitely Arson," *Lincoln Star*, April 14, 1958: A1.
53. Brianna Jo Theobald, "'By Any Means Necessary': The Lincoln, Nebraska, YWCA Confronts Racism, 1970-1984" (master's thesis, University of Nebraska Lincoln, 2010), 35, https://digitalcommons.unl.edu/historydiss/28/.
54. Nebraska Legislature Transcriber's Office, "Transcript prepared by the Clerk of the Legislature," Floor Debate transcripts for the 95th Legislature (May 27, 1997), 8392, https://nebraskalegislature.gov/transcripts/view_page.php?page=8392&leg=95
55. Gloria Oladipo, "Nebraska governor's remarks about Chinese reporter spark outrage," *Guardian*, Oct 19, 2023, https://www.theguardian.com/us-news/2023/oct/19/nebraska-governor-chinese-reporter-remarks-outrage

retailers and agents selling things made clear that they were willing to sell persons of color inferior or spoiled goods.

In the period from June 2020-December 2023, Race/Ethnicity/Ancestry accounted for 61% of the hate crimes reported in Nebraska.[56]

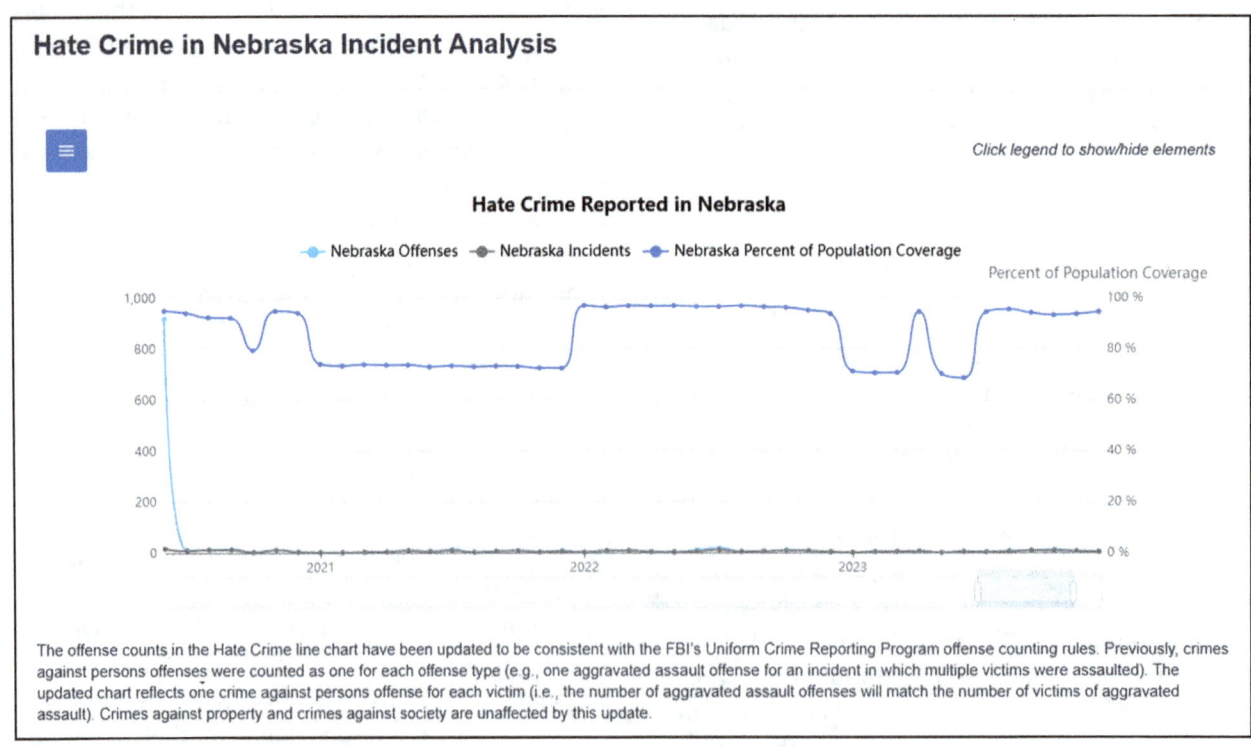

Hate Crime in Nebraska Incident Analysis.[57] See Note 57, which references FBI Crime Data Explorer. Hate Crime Reported in Nebraska, June 2020-December 2023.]

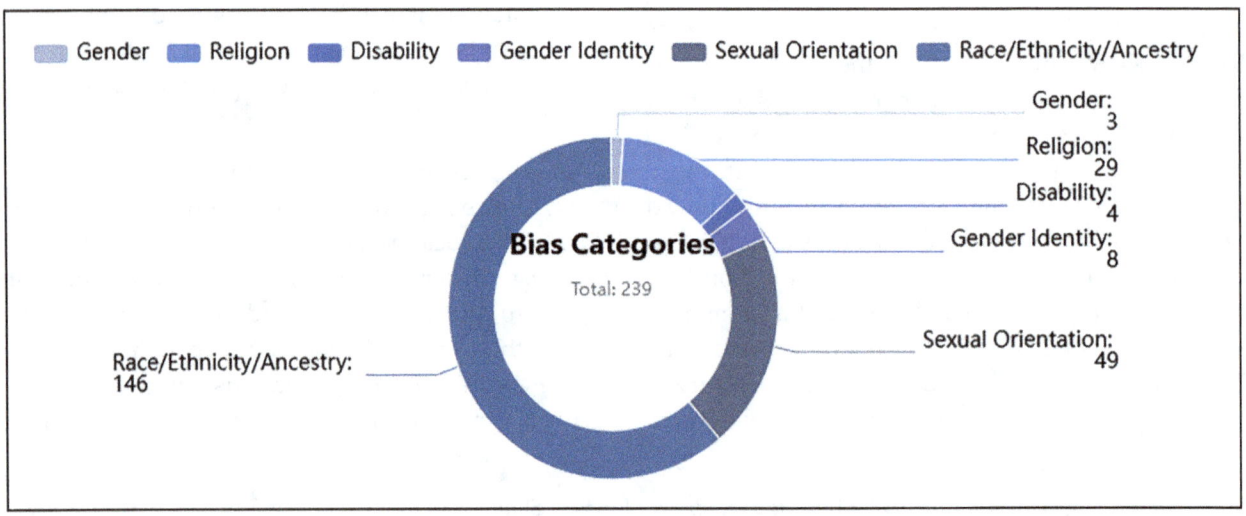

Hate Crime Reported in Nebraska, June 2020-December 2023. Bias Categories.[58] See Note 58, which references FBI Crime Data Explorer. Hate Crime Reported in Nebraska, June 2020-December 2023. Bias Categories.

---

56. FBI Crime Data Explorer, [Location Select: Nebraska], Hate Crime in Nebraska Incident Analysis, accessed in June 2025, https://cde.ucr.cjis.gov/LATEST/webapp/#/pages/explorer/crime/hate-crime
57. FBI Crime Data Explorer, [Location Select: Nebraska], Hate Crime in Nebraska Incident Analysis.
58. FBI Crime Data Explorer, [Location Select: Nebraska], Hate Crime in Nebraska Bias Categories.

Though the intellectual justification for the racism was the assumption of white superiority (or supremacy), the actual motor seems to have been economic and social advantage.

The seizure of virtually all productive lands in Nebraska from Native Americans was prompted by a desire for economic advantage though it was justified as good for both Native American and white people; as Andrew Jackson, the first president to implement Native American removal to the West, stated:

> [Removal] will separate the Indians from immediate contact with settlements of whites; free them from the power of the States; enable them to pursue happiness in their own way and under their own rude institutions; will retard the progress of decay, which is lessening their numbers, and perhaps cause them gradually, under the protection of Government and through the influence of good counsels, to cast off their savage habits and become an interesting, civilized, and Christian community. What good man would prefer a country covered with forests and ranged by a few thousand savages to our extensive Republic, studded with cities, towns, and prosperous farms embellished with all the improvements which art can devise or industry execute, occupied by more than 12,000,000 happy people, and filled with all the blessings of liberty, civilization and religion?... How many thousands of our own people would gladly embrace the opportunity of removing to the West on such conditions! If the offers made to the Indian were extended to them, they would be hailed with gratitude and joy.[59]

When Jackson implemented his removal policy with the Cherokee, they did not embrace removal but called the trek to new lands "the Trail of Tears."

Native American culture was also regarded by white leaders in early Nebraska as primitive, unproductive, and "uncivilized," even though the indigenous nations of this state had learned methods to harvest the bison and other game and edibles native to the plains in an environmentally sensitive way, even though their agriculture was possible with minimal manipulation of the environment in the riparian valleys of Nebraska, even though corn, beans and squash were effectively grown, and even though the Indigenous period did not produce the global climate change threatened at present but actually captured carbon in the heavy native grasses at a record rate.

Clearly persons who employed Hispanic field workers or African American manual laborers at minimal salaries profited economically from their "Jim Crow" conditions. The same may be said of the employment of Native American workers in Nebraska on reservation-adjacent farms and potato farms and in other contexts where they were desperate for employment and employers sought low-cost labor after the 1930s. This was also the impulse behind the initial importation of Chinese service industry workers.

The system has been partially maintained, after the Civil Rights Movement and Civil Rights legislation of the 1950s-1970s, by unequal enforcement of the law, particularly drug laws, and punitive policies directed against people of color in the justice system[60]

This point is obvious and does not need discussion after the events since 2020, particularly the George Floyd murder. A white policeman in Minneapolis held his knee on the neck of Floyd, a black man convicted of no crime, in the presence of black people filming his actions, until Mr. Floyd died, even though he was warned by the spectators that he was doing harm.

Recent Arrivals: Post-Vietnam war immigrant groups, because of their recent appearance on the American scene (after the passage of the Civil Rights acts) did not experience items 1-6 above in the same way or to the same degree as other groups.

Setting aside this discussion for the moment as this topic is largely covered in the "Recent Arrivals" chapter, it may be useful to observe here that some of the difference in their experiences from that of historically

---

59. Andrew Jackson, "President Andrew Jackson's Message to Congress 'On Indian Removal' (1830)," May 10, 2022, *National Archives Milestone Documents*, https://www.archives.gov/milestone-documents/jacksons-message-to-congress-on-indian-removal/

60. Cf. Michelle Alexander. *The New Jim Crow: Mass Incarceration in the Age of Colorblindness* (New York, NY: New Press, 2012).

older U.S. groups of color may derive from protections offered by the civil rights acts and court decisions of the 1950s-1970s and some may derive from the fact that many of the new arrivals were our allies in our various wars, especially in Asia.

* * * * *

Race and "Nebraska Nice"

Some critics may argue that Nebraska racism is no different from racism in other parts of the country particularly the North, and some of this idea may be true, as reflected in a 1999 account to the *Daily Nebraskan* by Leola Bullock, a Lincoln Civil Rights leader:

> [Leola Bullock] rode 30 miles across county lines because the high school in her (Mississippi) county didn't let Black folks in. Racism. Mockery. Colored-only rest rooms. Name-calling. By 1950 Leola Bullock was fed up. At 21 years old, she left the South and all its dirty prejudice behind. But what she found in Lincoln was not the promised land that Martin Luther King Jr. would later talk about Americans someday finding.
>
> [After] Rosa Parks, a 43-year-old black seamstress, is arrested in Montgomery, Ala., for refusing to give up her seat on a bus to a white man and [the] Montgomery Bus Boycott ensues with the help of . . . Martin Luther King Jr. [in] 1955[,] Bullock had a dream to escape the deep-rooted racism of the South. She doesn't regret leaving the South, but her northern refuge was not much better. "I came here in the pursuit of finding freedom from racial discrimination," said the 69-year-old Bullock. 'It was interesting that we had so much hope and belief - that Americans really believed in justice and believed in democracy.' And here in 1999, Nebraska is more racist than Mississippi was in the 1940s when I was there."[61]

The 1950s in Lincoln still brought dirty looks, sub-standard housing and a black ghetto for Bullock:

> "We don't hire Negroes here," was what she was told when she applied at her neighborhood Laundromat near 23rd and T streets. Three months later she was the first Black salesperson at Gold's Galleria department store downtown. By 1960, she was president of the Lincoln chapter of the National Association for the Advancement of Colored People. She went on to head countless freedom marches in Lincoln as a response to violations of civil rights across the country. She staged lunch counter sit-ins and picketed Woolworth's, drawing attention to racist hiring and serving practices.[62]

One of the myths in Nebraska in the 1950s, communicated to one of the writers of this chapter, was that Nebraska did not suffer from racial prejudice, or, if it did, it was the prejudice against Native Americans against which Governor Robert Crosby and Governor Norbert Tiemann had begun a process with study groups and commissions. This myth was confronted when Comedian Dick Gregory spoke in Lincoln at the University of Nebraska in 1967; a report by Don Pieper in the *Omaha World-Herald* from Oct. 26, 1967, quotes Gregory saying, "This area treats its Negroes very well — all three hundred of them. It's the Indians you have got to worry about." One assumes that Gregory was speaking ironically about how the area "treats its Negroes" and referring to the widespread Nebraska belief that it was without racism.[63]

The chapters in this book suggest intense satire in Dick Gregory's remark. What needs to be understood is that Nebraska came into being on a great wave of hope for a different, less racist future. Nebraska had been clearly a free state under the Kansas-Nebraska Act of 1854. It had chosen, as the name for its capital "Lincoln," the great emancipator and the power behind Constitutional amendments XIII, XIV and XV. The town of Union was probably named in defiance of the Southern rebellion. Yankee Hill was named in honor of early anti-slavery settlers. One of the towns near Lincoln, Seward, was named for President Lincoln's Secretary of State, and the small town of Grant for the most successful of the Northern generals. Kearney, Sheridan, Hooker, Howard, McPherson, McCook, Crook, Sheridan, Thayer – all county or town place names In Nebraska— took their titles from Northern Civil War officers.[64] One would assume then that Nebraska began with anti-slavery and anti-racist traditions and that the idea that the state was without racism, voiced by some Nebraska citizens until recently, was true. However, human nature does not change suddenly, and the curse of racism was

---

61. Jessica Fargen, "King's legacy continues in Lincolnites' lives," *Daily Nebraskan,* Jan. 14, 1999: 1.
62. Fargen 1999.
63. Don Pieper, "Gregory Tells N.U. Crowd 'Drastic' Change is Needed," *Omaha World-Herald,* October 26, 1967: 28.
64. Cf. Fitzpatrick in Bibliography for examples.

inherited not only by white Southerners but by the nation. Indeed, customary social practice in housing, employment, public accommodations, credit and banking, the popular media, and bullying invective made clear that the no-racism bromide was not true.

The issues recounted may seem surprising in a state born out of Civil War struggles, one with the Civil War-based motto, "Equality before the law."[65] However, they are typical for racism internationally and especially in the United States where efforts to form a pseudo-species of peoples of color in America are endemic. Although much Nebraska racism is like racism anywhere, there also exist historical differences among the experiences of the various groups of color in Nebraska and differences that the interaction between "white privilege" and the need to subordinate a specific group created in Nebraska. These differences need to be recognized if we are to "redeem the time" or escape from what has been called "truly our nation's original sin," by author Jim Wallis.[66] We cannot treat all problems as one. Some of the differences that occur to us as we read the five chapters of this book are as follows.

Historical differences among the experiences of the various groups of color

1. Differences in Native American treatment: Two major factors differentiate racism directed against Native Americans, from that directed against other groups. First, The United States was bound to Nebraska Indian nations by its several treaties with them as it was not to other groups, and these treaties were supposed to have the force of law; yet, as Helen Hunt Jackson wrote, in her 1880s *Century of Dishonor*, "The history of the United States Government's repeated violations of faith with the Indians convicts us, as a nation, of having outraged the principles of justice, which are the basis of international law; and of having laid ourselves open to the accusation of both cruelty and perfidy."[67] In particular, she describes dishonest dealings by the U.S. and Nebraska with seven U.S. groups, four of which are Nebraska tribes: the Cheyenne, the Sioux, the Ponca, and the Winnebago. Subsequently, scholars have further recognized — in the making and breaking of laws covering Native Americans, their confinement to reservations, and the history of imposed disease, poverty, and dispossession — something akin to the genocide or cultural genocide we condemn in others.[68] If one adds to this, Nebraska Native American struggles with outsider-introduced addictive substances, mainstream Nebraska indifference to the desperation, poverty, and cultural suppression created, and mainstream mockery of Native Americans based on stereotypes — one has a picture of an effort to wipe out a series of people physically or culturally that tends to the genocidal, all in the pursuit of free land. That effort did not succeed largely because of over a century of Nebraska civil rights resistance in the Native American community and more recently in many communities.

2. Differences in African American treatment: Nebraska policies directed against African American people were not in most cases genocidal in that they never sought to wipe them out. The dominant culture depended on African American household and manual labor so genocide would have been counterproductive. Subordination was wanted. As the African American chapter demonstrates, mobs of whites were sometimes lethal or very harsh to individual African American persons as they lynched, segregated, intimidated, and otherwise marginalized them to secure their obedience. Civil War era African Americans in Nebraska mostly began as people who had been rural, kept by slave-masters, and restricted from formal education. Much of their early migration was to rural Nebraska because they had farmed on the plantations of the South — under differing conditions but farmed, nonetheless.

African Americans in the early days of Nebraska sometimes founded their own successful farming communities such as DeWitty.[69] They made a go of it until a combination of factors drove them out – Nebraska drought, lack of support from the U. S. Department of Agriculture, from local authorities and from credit agencies, and the appearance of a number of rural Nebraska sundown towns that did not permit African American people to be in the said towns after sundown or around 6:00 p.m. or to feel safe in the

---

65. James E. Potter, "'Equality Before the Law': Thoughts on the Origin of Nebraska's State Motto," *Nebraska History* 91 (2010): 116-121.
66. Jim Wallis, "America's Original Sin: The Legacy of White Racism," *CrossCurrents* 57 (2007): 197-202.
67. Jackson 1888, 29.
68. For a bibliography of studies of whether the destruction of the Indian nations constitutes genocide and in what sense, see Samuel Totten and Robert K. Hitchcock (eds.) *Genocide of Indigenous Peoples Genocide: A Critical Bibliographic Review* (New Brunswick: Transaction Publishers, 2011).
69. National Park Service, "DeWitty Nebraska," accessed December 2023, https://www.nps.gov/places/dewitty-nebraska.htm

countryside.⁷⁰ Finally, the growth of the Ku Klux Klan in Nebraska in the 1920s suppressed African American rural populations. For example, "[o]n April 24, 1924, crosses ... burned in Beatrice, Milford, Seward, Beaver Crossing, Barneston, and Hebron."⁷¹

As Native Americans were forced into the reservations when most of their good land was stolen, African Americans were after the turn of the twentieth century— and especially in the period of, and after, World War I — forced from rural communities and the general residence areas of towns and cities into the segregated parts of the larger towns and cities, especially after the Omaha lynching of William Brown in 1919. As we have mentioned, all African American residents in North Platte, numbering between a few dozen and two hundred, were "invited" (i.e. forced) to leave in 1929 after a Black man shot a white police officer there.

While racism against Native Americans centered on the theft of land and removal of the indigenous nations from resources permitting the groups to make a life for themselves, racism directed against African Americans in Nebraska centered on keeping them as a laboring underclass, a source of cheap labor segregated in districts where existed the poorer housing, education, infrastructure and social opportunity that was set them apart as an underclass. Dr. Harry A. Burke, after whom Omaha Burke High School is named, ran the Omaha Public Schools along racist lines from 1946 to 1962 and "proclaimed that as long as he was superintendent, there would not be a black educator in the school system, other than the two schools that served the black community," because he opposed having black teachers in authority over white children. Omaha was instructed to submit a court ordered plan to desegregate its schools as late as January 1, 1976.⁷²

3. Differences in Latino treatment: Whereas African American people in Nebraska came to be largely urban, Latino people were forced to settle not only adjacent to the South Omaha stockyards as workers there but also as rural laborers in the beet fields and other large agricultural layouts of Western Nebraska. Later when the Omaha stockyards were replaced by meat packing plants in smaller Nebraska towns, their companies hired substantial amounts of Latino labor. The forms of racism directed against Latinos in Nebraska were a combination of those visited upon Native American people and those pushed on African Americans with the addition of religious prejudice against Catholics.

The very earliest European expeditions into Nebraska's territory or territory nearby such as Kansas, the Villasur 1720 expedition, was Latino led, but the majority of Latinos in Nebraska came recently and presently form our state's largest community of color.⁷³ Latinos did not always identify as people of color because Latin American heritages included a considerable admixture of European, Native American, and African or African American lineages, but increasingly Latinos see themselves – and are seen— as a community of color. The *Los Angeles Times* observes the following about the national situation:

> Strikingly, the share of Latinos who identified their race as white in the 2020 census fell from about 53% in 2010 to about 20% in 2020; the share who identified as "other" rose from 37% to 42%, and the share identifying as two or more races jumped from 6% to 33% ... changes ... that cannot be explained just by intermarriage and that challenge a narrative that Latinos will eventually assimilate into whiteness.⁷⁴

Clearly about 75% of Latinos in the US identify as partly people of color, and Nebraska's dominant culture has treated them as such. Latino people have had field agriculture jobs like Native Americans, meatpacking jobs like African Americans, and railroad jobs like Asian peoples in other states. They have increasingly been settled in separated communities, some of which have lost most of their white populations, because of their culture and work and because of white prejudice. The signs that said "No Indians or Dogs Allowed" were easily switched in racist Nebraska into signs that said "No Mexicans or Dogs allowed."⁷⁵ White prejudice against Latinos is

---

70. James Loewen, *Sundown Towns: A Hidden Dimension of American Racism.* (New York: Touchstone, 2006).
71. Michael W. Schuyler, "The Ku Klux Klan in Nebraska, 1920-1930," *Nebraska History* 66 (1985): 236.
72. Adam Fletcher Sasse, "A History of Segregated Schools in Omaha, Nebraska," in North Omaha History, February 6, 2018, https://northomahahistory.com/2018/02/06/a-history-of-segregated-schools-in-omaha-nebraska/
73. Thomas E. Chávez, "The Segesser Hide Paintings: History, Discovery, Art." *Great Plains Quarterly*, 10 (1990): 96-109.
74. Manuel Pastor and Pierrette Hondagneu-Soto, "Why did so few Latinos identify themselves as white in the 2020 census?" *Los Angeles Times*, Sept. 9, 2021, https://www.latimes.com/opinion/story/2021-09-09/south-los-angeles-immigration-displacement-latinos-blacks-2020-census
75. Such signs were seen in Scottsbluff in earlier times by Professor Marty Ramirez. A study needs to document how widespread their use was before laws concerning public accommodations forbade them.

not greatly different from that which applies to African Americans peoples and Native American ones, save that the efforts to strip language and culture from Latinos have seemingly been less strenuous and less violent than those that took slaves from their African culture or Native Americans from that of their nations to the deculturalization of the boarding schools.[76] If land was the primary thing desired and taken from Native Americans and free, or cheap, labor from African-Americans in Nebraska, cheap labor on the land or in the slaughterhouse was what was most desired and taken from Latinos.

4. *Differences in the treatment of Asian peoples*: Asian immigrants to Nebraska, initially primarily Chinese and Japanese persons, were treated to the usual racist memes that greeted other groups of color. They were "dangerous hordes" that would take away jobs and land from proper Nebraska citizens – i.e., white ones. Under law, they could not own land in Nebraska as they might take it all; they could not marry "white" people; they were confined in towns and cities where they settled to "Chinatowns" or like settlements. Indeed, they were, in some cases, labeled as uncivilized though Chinese "civilization," including urban settlements and agriculture, is almost 5000 years old and Japanese goes back about three thousand years. Initially Asian peoples were also largely confined to physically difficult railroad and agricultural work. World War II changed matters in that the U.S. was an ally of China, and public relations vehicles, such as comic strips and editorial columns, in some cases endeavored to change stereotypes about China and the Chinese.

The Japanese internment camps created by Roosevelt were not established in Nebraska, and some Nebraskans from that period and before, had a high regard for Japanese people and argued for their rights —William Jennings Bryan in earlier times, Reverend Charles Drew, University Director of Admissions George W. Rosenlof, and Chancellor C.S. Boucher of the University of Nebraska during World War II.[77] Indeed, one foundation of the civil rights movement in Nebraska — in the white community — may be some gestures toward the just treatment of Asian peoples during World War II. Ambiguity is also evident in the treatment of Filipino peoples in Nebraska – racism against them because they were Asian, openness to them because they were from 1898-1946 an American colony and our allies in World War II. Still, prejudice remained. One of the writers of this chapter remembers that a Japanese psychology Ph. D. student and his fiancé, a Euro-American woman, had to go to Iowa for their marriage in the late 'fifties because Nebraska still had a law against so-called "mixed-race" marriages.[78] They also had to make special arrangements for their housing.

5. *Treatment of Recent Arrivals*: "Recent Arrivals" are persons who have come to Nebraska since the end of the war in Vietnam in 1975 – Vietnamese, Yugoslavs, Iraqis, Burmese, and Sudanese groups; some of these groups are not victims of racism directed against people of color in the classic sense but groups who may have suffered religious prejudice because of Islamic or Karen Christian beliefs, especially Yugoslav, Iraqi, and Burmese immigrants (though the Burmese are also perceived as people of color). Most of the recent arrivals came to Nebraska during and after the 1960s civil rights struggle when open racism ceased to be a calling card in elite circles in the state. Yet, as the chapter notes, Vietnamese refugees, most of whom had favored the American side during their country's civil war, still suffered from racism. Though Nebraska has a good reputation for welcoming recent refugees, most of it is due to the efforts of certain groups of concerned citizens and it is undermined by the rhetoric and actions of some state policy makers, the "Recent Arrivals" chapter reports. The authors also note that resources for refugee support are not keeping pace with increasing need in Nebraska. They say the state's record, though a legitimate source of pride, is also a mixed record because much of the welcoming tradition stems from members of refugee communities themselves. Even in the area where Nebraskans legitimately feel pride in, our record of resettlement of recent immigrants, the record is mixed and much of our positive record has been made by a few organizations or by the refugee groups, themselves.

The Way Forward

To return to the beginnings of our argument: Nebraska was born amid the idealism of the North in the Civil War, its capital named Lincoln, its motto,

---

76. Grajeda 1976.
77. Wertheimer 2002.
78. Nebraska Legislature, "Sen. Edward Danner"

"Equality Before the Law,"[79] and the names of war heroes scattered across its landscape. Still, it did not live out the war's putative ideals. The architecture of its state capitol building celebrates many heroes and many ethnic groups, but its history does not embody that celebration. Nebraska's distinguished sculpture near the west entrance of the capitol, a statue of Abraham Lincoln created by Daniel Chester French with the Lincoln Gettysburg Address carved into the granite backdrop, has been disowned by our history. The Address begins "Four score and seven years ago our fathers brought forth on this continent, a new nation, conceived in Liberty, and dedicated to the proposition that all men are created equal."

We have not acted, as a state and as towns and neighborhoods, as if all people are created equal. Partly, European-based people carried with them, to the Americas and into the Great Plains, religious (i.e., the "Ham" part of the Noah story), ethnic, and xenophobic prejudices against other people who looked "different." Added to that, they were told by pseudo-sciences such as phrenology ("craniology") that white people were superior and all races of color inferior. They were influenced by some immigration of people from the slaveholding South, especially from Missouri, before and after the Civil War who held on to the racial assumptions that allowed them to be complacent about their part in slavery. Many important Nebraska leaders from the 1860s – witness J. Sterling Morton of Arbor Day— to the present have espoused white supremacist views and justified racist dishonor in the state's behavior.

Some of our failure may derive from imperfect civic education in what our foundational ideas are; some from imperfect scientific education. Some certainly derives from greed; stealing land from Native American nations, paying poor wages to African American, Latino and other workers of color, and providing people with poor educations to keep them as manual laborers satisfied greed. On the other hand, much of the action directed toward Asian people and recent arrivals grew out of fear of competition in the labor market or national security issues, however incorrectly analyzed.

Federal and local officials developed ways of enforcing inequitable policy as if it were equitable, justifying the treatment of Native Americans as "civilizing" them, rationalizing the mistreatment of African Americans as making them "separate but equal," arguing that rules giving opportunity to persons of color in the face of historic wrongs were "illegal quotas" and so on.

Some apologists for the old system have indicated that the European-based ancestors did not know that land was stolen from Native Americans, or that African Americans remained virtually without rights under Jim Crow, or that Hispanics involved in hard labor in Nebraska had few labor rights or rights of appeal for justice. This argument contains some truth. Clearly many European-based immigrants did not know the history of slavery and Jim Crow or the seizure of Native American lands; one of the writers of this chapter had a grandfather who had two successive farms in northern Nebraska carved out of what, by treaty, had been Omaha and then Santee Sioux land. The grandfather was an unlettered man who clearly did not know where his land came from as the myth of an "empty continent" had been taught him. However, ignorance is not an excuse for injustice in present circumstances. Science, law, and history tell us of our equality as human beings. It is not clear how one can undo history. Much of the task requires that one recognize what the past has been and move toward fairness. Some of the task involves our recognizing the truth and undertaking reconciliation processes — studying the truth and doing what is possible to right our wrongs and heal the wounds we have inflicted on ourselves as a people. A Brown University Steering Committee charged with studying what we should do about historic wrongs, such as we have discussed, developed the following statement:

> Human history is characterized not only by slavery but also by genocide, "ethnic cleansing," forced labor, starvation through siege, mistreatment of prisoners of war, torture, forced religious conversion, mass rape, kidnapping of children, and any number of other forms of gross injustice. Different civilizations at different historical moments have developed their own understandings of such practices, specifying the conditions under which they were allowed or forbidden and against whom they might legitimately be directed. Jews, Christians, and Muslims all devised rules for slavery, the conduct of war, and the treatment of prisoners and civilian populations. Our era is hardly the first to grapple with humanity's capacity for evil.
>
> The idea that certain actions were inherently illegitimate and should be universally

---

79. Potter 2010.

prohibited, no matter the circumstances or the particular target group, emerged in the eighteenth century. At the root of this belief was the idea of shared humanity, the belief that all human beings partook of a common nature and were thus entitled to share certain basic rights and protections. This conviction, which animated the early movement to abolish the slave trade, received its classic expression in the preamble to the American Declaration of Independence, with its invocation of "self-evident" truths about equality and inalienable rights to "life, liberty, and the pursuit of happiness." Obviously, these rights have not been extended to all people at all times. As we have already seen, the idea of race, also a product of the eighteenth century, has played a particularly key role in blunting the claims of certain groups to full equality. Yet there is no question of the historical importance of the idea of shared humanity, which undergirds the whole edifice of international humanitarian law.

In bequeathing us the ideas of shared humanity and fundamental human rights, the eighteenth century also left us with a series of practical and philosophical problems. How are human rights to be enforced and defended? Do nation-states have the right to treat their own citizens as they please, or are there occasions when the demands of humanity trump national sovereignty? How are perpetrators of human rights abuse to be held to account? Such questions are obviously most pointed in the midst or immediate aftermath of atrocities, but they have longer-term implications as well, for great crimes inevitably leave great legacies. Are those who suffered grievous violations of their rights entitled to some form of redress, and, if so, from what quarter? Do such claims die with the original victims, or are there occasions when descendants might also deserve consideration? How do societies move forward in the aftermath of great crimes?[80]

These are not merely academic questions. On the contrary, the global effort to define, deter, and alleviate the effects of gross historical injustice represents one of the most pressing challenges of our time. The modern era will go down in history as, among other things, the age of atrocity, an age in which the fundamental human rights that most societies profess to cherish have been violated on a previously unimaginable scale. It is not the business of this study to say how we as a society can remedy past wrongs described here. That they must be remedied is undeniable. How they might be remedied remains for the government and people of Nebraska.

Reconciliation is the next step.

Appendix I

Some biographies of midcentury and after Nebraska civil rights leaders are as follows:

1. For Reuben Snake, see Jay C. Fikes. *Reuben Snake: Your Humble Serpent: Indian Visionary and Activist.* Santa Fe, N.M.: Clear Light Publishers, 1996.
2. For Norma Cantú, see Google and her Wikipedia entries.
3. For a brief biography of Robert Navarro, see https://www.ops.org/Page/1896.
4. For Ernie Chambers, see Tekla Agbala Ali Johnson. *Free Radical: Ernest Chambers, Black Power, and the Politics of Race.* Lubbock: Texas Tech University Press, 2012.
5. For Ben Kuroki, see Ralph G. Martin, *Boy From Nebraska: The Story of Ben Kuroki.* New York London, Harper & Brothers, 1946 and Carroll Stewart, *The Most Honorable Son, Ben Kuroki: WWII gunner, 4 Air Forces, 8th, 12th, 9th, 20th*. Alexandria, Va.: Distributed by PBS.org, 2007.
6. For the Bullock and Shanks families, see JoAnne Young, *Lincoln Journal Star*, Column June 7, 2020, Updated June 17, 2021 (https://journalstar.com/news/local/legends-among-lincoln-civil-rights-activists-stood-up-for-justice/article).

Bibliography

Alexander, Michelle. *The New Jim Crow: Mass Incarceration in the Age of Colorblindness.* New York, NY: New Press, 2012.

Anon. "Negro Home Fire Definitely Arson." *Lincoln Star*, April 14, 1958: A1.

---

80. Brown University Steering Committee on Slavery and Justice, "Confronting Historical Injustice: Comparative Perspectives," Brown University's Slavery and Justice Report, 2006, https://slaveryandjusticereport.brown.edu/sections/confronting-historical-injustice-comparative-perspectives/

Blaine, Garland. "Religion Among the Pawnee After the Removal to Oklahoma in the 1870s." In *The Pawnee Experience: From Center Village to Oklahoma*. (ERIC Document 235934, 1978): 44-45. https://files.eric.ed.gov/fulltext/ED235934.pdf

Boughter, Judith A. *Betraying Their Trust: The Dispossession of the Omaha Nation, 1790-1916*. Master's thesis, University of Nebraska at Omaha, 1995. https://digitalcommons.unomaha.edu/studentwork/503/

Braude, Benjamin. "The Sons of Noah and the Construction of Ethnic and Geographical Identities in the Medieval and Early Modern Periods." *William and Mary Quarterly* 54 (1997): 103-42.

Bristow, David L. "Was J. Sterling Morton a racist? Here's what the Arbor Day founder said and did." *Nebraska History* (blog). 2019. https://history.nebraska.gov/was-j-sterling-morton-a-racist-heres-what-the-arbor-day-founder-said-and-did/

Brockell, Gillian. "The civil rights leader 'almost nobody knows about' gets a statue in the U.S. Capitol." *Washington Post*, September 20, 2019. https://www.washingtonpost.com/history/2019/09/20/civil-rights-leader-almost-nobody-knows-about-gets-statue-us-capitol/

Brown University Steering Committee on Slavery and Justice. "Confronting Historical Injustice: Comparative Perspectives." Brown University's Slavery and Justice Report. 2006. https://slaveryandjusticereport.brown.edu/sections/confronting-historical-injustice-comparative-perspectives/

Chávez, Thomas E. "The Segesser Hide Paintings: History, Discovery, Art." *Great Plains Quarterly*. 10 (1990): 96-109.

Collins, Francis S. and Monique K. Mansoura. "The Human Genome Project." *Cancer* 91 (1 Suppl) (2001): 221-5. DOI:10.1002/1097-0142(20010101)91:1+3.0.CO;2-0

Dales, David G. "North Platte racial incident: Black-white confrontation, 1929." *Nebraska History* 60 (1979): 424–446.

David, Jennifer. "Chief Standing Bear and His Landmark Civil Rights Case." *Library of Congress Blogs*. Nov. 2019. https://blogs.loc.gov/law/2019/11/chief-standing-bear-and-his-landmark-civil-rights-case/

Ellyson, Tyler. "Journey to Freedom: Graduate thesis addresses slavery in Nebraska Territory." *UNK News*. April 12, 2021. https://unknews.unk.edu/2021/04/12/journey-to-freedom-graduate-thesis-addresses-slavery-in-nebraska-territory/

Fargen, Jessica. "King's legacy continues in Lincolnites' lives." *Daily Nebraskan*, Jan. 14, 1999: 1.

FBI Crime Data Explorer. [Nebraska]. Accessed December 2023. https://cde.ucr.cjis.gov/LATEST/webapp/#/pages/explorer/crime/hate-crime

Fitzpatrick, Lilian. "Nebraska Place Names." *University of Nebraska Studies in Language, Literature, and Criticism* 6 (1925): 13-147.

Foner, Eric. "The Reconstruction Amendments: Official Documents as Social History." *History Resources*. 2004. https://www.gilderlehrman.org/history-resources/essays/reconstruction-amendments-official-documents-social-history

Grajeda. Ralph. "Chicanos: the Mestizo Heritage." In *Broken Hoops and Plains People*, edited by Paul A. Olson, 47-98. Lincoln: Nebraska Curriculum Development Center, 1976.

Hämäläinen, Pekka. "The First Phase Of Destruction Killing The Southern Plains Buffalo, 1790-1840." *Great Plains Quarterly* 21 (2001): 101-114.

Hämäläinen, Pekka Johannes. *Lakota America: A New History of Indigenous Power*. New Haven, CT: Yale University Press, 2019.

Hess, Abigail Johnson. "Rich students get better SAT scores—here's why." *Penn Social Policy and Practice*, 2019. https://sp2.upenn.edu/press/rich-students-get-better-sat-scores-heres-why/

Hildebrand, Jennifer. "The New Negro Movement in Lincoln, Nebraska." *Nebraska History* 91 (2010): 166-189.

History Nebraska. "Phrenology: Science or Entertainment?" *History Nebraska Publications* (blog). Accessed December 2023. https://history.nebraska.gov/publications_section/phrenology-science-or-entertainment/

Jackson, Andrew. "President Andrew Jackson's Message to Congress 'On Indian Removal' (1830)." *National Archive Milestone Documents*,

2022. https://www.archives.gov/milestone-documents/jacksons-message-to-congress-on-indian-removal/

Jackson, Helen Hunt. *A Century of Dishonor*. Boston: Roberts, 1888 [c1885].

Johannesen, Danielle. "Depictions of American Indians in George Armstrong Custer's 'My Life on the Plains.'" *Humanities* 8 (2019). https://doi.org/10.3390/h8010056

Kelsey, George. "The Racist Search for the Self." *The Journal of Religious Ethics* 6 (1978): 240-256.

Klein, Christopher. "How Teddy Roosevelt's Belief in a Racial Hierarchy Shaped His Policies." *History*, 2023. https://www.history.com/news/teddy-roosevelt-race-imperialism-national-parks

Lehr, Dick. "The Racist Legacy of Woodrow Wilson." *The Atlantic*, Nov. 27, 2015. https://www.theatlantic.com/politics/archive/2015/11/wilson-legacy-racism/417549/

Loewen, James. *Sundown Towns: A Hidden Dimension of American Racism*. New. York: Touchstone, 2006.

Loewen, James W. "Historical Database of Sundown Towns." *History and Social Justice*. 2023. https://justice.tougaloo.edu/sundown-towns/using-the-sundown-towns-database/state-map/

Loewen, James W. "Plattsmouth." *History and Social Justice*. 2023. https://justice.tougaloo.edu/sundowntown/plattsmouth-ne/

Lombardo, Paul A. "'We Who Champion the Unborn': Racial Poisons, Eugenics, and the Campaign for Prohibition." *Journal of Law, Medicine & Ethics* 50 (2022). https://www.cambridge.org/core/journals/journal-of-law-medicine-and-ethics/article/we-who-champion-the-unborn-racial-poisons-eugenics-and-the-campaign-for-prohibition/

Martin, Jordan. "Confronting racism's legacy, from town to country." *Civic Nebraska Writer's Group*. June 19, 2020. https://www.civicnebraska.org/legacy-racism-town-country/

Mitchell, Paul Wolff. "The fault in his seeds: Lost notes to the case of bias in Samuel George Morton's cranial race science." *PLOS Biology* 16 (2018). doi: 10.1371/journal.pbio.2007008

Mohsen. Hussein. "Race and Genetics: Somber History, Troubled Present." *Yale J. Biol Med.* 93 (2020): 215–219.

National Park Service. n.d. "DeWitty Nebraska." *National Park Service*. n.d. https://www.nps.gov/places/dewitty-nebraska.htm

Nebraska Legislature. *Laws* 1997. LB 90, § 2. https://nebraskalegislature.gov/laws/statutes.php?statute=28-110

Nebraska Legislature. "Sen. Edward Danner." *Nebraska Legislature*. n.d. https://nebraskalegislature.gov/education/danner.php

Nebraska Legislature Transcriber's Office. "Transcript prepared by the Clerk of the Legislature, U.S. Department of Justice January 9, 1997": 8392. *Nebraska Legislature*. https://nebraskalegislature.gov/transcripts/view_page.php?page=8392&leg=95

Nebraska Studies. "Japanese Americans." n.d. http://Nebraskastudies.org/netwagtaildev.unl.edu/nebstudies/en/1925-1949/the-war-nebraska-stories/japanese-americans/

Nebraska Studies. "Taking Indian Land." n.d. https://www.nebraskastudies.org/en/1850-1874/native-american-settlers/taking-indian-land/

North Omaha Information Support. *Omaha Redlining Resource Guide*. 2019. https://www.noiseomaha.com/resources/2019/7/12/redlining-resources

Oladipo, Gloria. "Nebraska governor's remarks about Chinese reporter spark outrage." *Guardian*. Oct 19, 2023. https://www.theguardian.com/us-news/2023/oct/19/nebraska-governor-chinese-reporter-remarks-outrage

Office of Federal Contract Compliance Programs. "Earnings Disparities by Race and Ethnicity: Nebraska." 2020. *U. S. Department of Labor*. Accessed December 2023. https://www.dol.gov/agencies/ofccp/about/data/earnings/race-and-ethnicity

Pastor, Manuel and Pierrette Hondagneu-Soto. "Why did so few Latinos identify themselves as white in the 2020 census?" *Los Angeles Times*, Sept. 9, 2021. https://www.latimes.com/opinion/story/2021-09-09/south-los-angeles-immigration-displacement-latinos-blacks-2020-census

Pérez, Francisco. "How Do We Build Black Wealth? Understanding the Limits of Black Capitalism." *Nonprofit Quarterly* (2022). https://nonprofitquarterly.org/how-do-we-build-black-wealth-understanding-the-limits-of-black-capitalism/

Pieper, Don. "Gregory Tells N.U. Crowd 'Drastic' Change is Needed." *Omaha World-Herald*, Thursday, October 26, 1967: 28.

Piketty, Thomas. *Capital in the Twenty-First Century*. Cambridge, Mass.: Cambridge University Press, 2014.

Pittenger, John R. ""What Good Can There Be In This Kind of Human?' Spanish Justification for the Conquest of the Americas." *Gettysburg Historical Journal* 7 (2020): 58-73. https://cupola.gettysburg.edu/cgi/

Potter, James E. "'Equality Before the Law': Thoughts on the Origin of Nebraska's State Motto." *Nebraska History* 91 (2010): 116-121.

Potter, James E. "'Wearing the Hempen Neck-Tie': Lynching in Nebraska, 1858-1919." *Nebraska History* 93 (2012): 138-53.

Powell, J. W. *Eighteenth annual report of the Bureau of American Ethnology to the Secretary of the Smithsonian Institution, 1896-'97*, by J. W. Powell, Director. Part 2. Washington, Government Printing Office, 1899. https://archive.org/details/annualreportofb1896smit_0/mode/2up

Roenfeld, Ryan. "A History of Omaha's Chinatown." *North Omaha History*. March 5, 2019. https://northomahahistory.com/2019/03/05/a-history-of-omahas-chinatown-by-ryan-roenfeld/

Rose, Jonathan. "Redlining." *Federal Reserve History*. 2023. https://www.federalreservehistory.org/essays/redlining#.

Sasse, Adam Fletcher. "A History of Segregated Schools in Omaha, Nebraska." *North Omaha History*. Feb. 6, 2018. https://northomahahistory.com/2018/02/06/a-history-of-segregated-schools-in-omaha-nebraska/

Sasse, Adam Fletcher. "A History of Enslavement in Nebraska." January 22, 2023. *North Omaha History*. https://northomahahistory.com/2023/01/22/a-history-of-slavery-in-nebraska/

Schuyler, Michael W. "The Ku Klux Klan in Nebraska, 1920-1930." *Nebraska History* 66 (1985): 234-256.

Silove, D., P. Ventevogel, and S. Rees. "The contemporary refugee crisis: an overview of mental health challenges." *World Psychiatry* 16 (2017): 130-9.

"Skulls in print: scientific racism in the transatlantic world" University of Cambridge. 19 March 2014. https://www.cam.ac.uk/research/news/skulls-in-print-scientific-racism-in-the-transatlantic-world

Theobald, Brianna Jo. "'By Any Means Necessary': The Lincoln, Nebraska, YWCA Confronts Racism, 1970-1984." Master's thesis, University of Nebraska-Lincoln, 2010. https://digitalcommons.unl.edu/historydiss/28/

Totten, Samuel and Robert K. Hitchcock (eds.). *Genocide of Indigenous Peoples: A Critical Bibliographic Review*. New Brunswick: Transaction Publishers, 2011.

Turner, Margery Austin and Karina Fortuny. "Residential Segregation and Low-Income Working Families." *Low-Income Working Families, Paper 10*. 2009. https://www.urban.org/sites/default/files/publication/32941/411845-Residential-Segregation-and-Low-Income-Working-Families

Urban Institute. "Median Family Wealth by Race/Ethnicity, 1963-2019. https://www.urban.org/sites/default/files/2021-02/wealthbyrace-med.png

USA Facts. "Wealth inequality across race: what does the data show?" 2023. https://usafacts.org/articles/wealth-inequality-across-races-what-does-the-data-show/.

Wahl, Ana-Mari Gonzalez, Steven Gunkel, Bennie Shobe, Jr. "Becoming Neighbors or Remaining Strangers? Latinos and Residential Segregation in the Heartland." *Great Plains Research* 15 (2005). https://digitalcommons.unl.edu/greatplainsresearch/789/ .

Wallis, Jim. "America's Original Sin: The Legacy of White Racism." *CrossCurrents* 57 (2007): 197-202.

Wertheimer, Andrew B. "Admitting Nebraska's Nisei: Japanese American Students at the University of Nebraska, 1942-1945." *Nebraska History* 83 (2002): 58-72.

Winston, Bryan. "Mexican Community Formation in Nebraska: 1910-1950." *Nebraska History* 100 (2019): 2-19.

A History of Native People in Nebraska Part I

By Gabriel Bruguier

On September 28, 2024, I gave an invited talk about the Genoa Indian Industrial School as part of the United Methodist Church's Day of Remembrance service. To prepare, I reviewed a transcript of an interview that my Grandma Dora Bruguier gave in July of 1994, when she was seventy-four years old.[1] She recounts her experience of being taken from the Cheyenne River Reservation to boarding school, near Gettysburg, South Dakota, when she was around ten years old. Her story was not atypical. She didn't speak English; her hair and newly made dress were stripped off her and taken away forever; she was afraid and alone. Some older girls who were familiar with the school talked to her in Lakota, comforted her, and told her to just speak all the English she knew. Since she only knew "yes" and "no," she joked that she just said "yes" to everything at first. She eventually got accustomed to the routine at the school, but nevertheless she would gather with other girls in the middle of night to cry for their folks, and their life back home.

That same summer of 1994, I took a car trip from Vermillion, South Dakota, down to Stillwater, Oklahoma, to go to my father, Leonard Bruguier's, graduation ceremony. He had earned a Ph.D. in American History from Oklahoma State University. Grandma Dora assisted with his doctoral hooding at the commencement; she wore a traditional dress. On the long, hot drive down, he and my grandma listened to the tapes from which that transcript was made. They discussed

Dora Bruguier, March 2000. Courtesy of Drake Hokanson.

her experience and visited about other relatives who had gone to boarding school with her. Thirteen-year-old me had no idea about the importance of her story, or those stories she told about her long-passed relatives. I'm ashamed to admit that I would have preferred they put on a station that played rap music.

---

1. Dora Shoots Off-Bruguier, interview by Greg Huff and Bev Barkowsky, Cheyenne River Reservation, July 15, 1994.

In *Roots of Justice: A History of Race and Racism in Nebraska*. Edited by Kevin Abourezk, with an Introduction by M. Dewayne Mays and Paul A. Olson (Lincoln, Nebraska: Truth and Reconciliation Nebraska, 2025). Copyright © 2025 by the authors; CC-BY. DOI: 10.32873/unl.dc.rj2

At the commencement and reception I remember I felt proud of my father, and remember being impressed by all the important-looking people who came and congratulated him. And that the food at the party was great. But I didn't really understand the significance of his accomplishment and the legacy of his work until around thirty years later.

From 1990 to 2003, my father was the Director of the Institute of American Indian Studies at the University of South Dakota (USD). His journey there had taken him from the village of Greenwood on the Yankton Sioux Reservation, to the city of Yankton, South Dakota, where he excelled academically and athletically in high school but was the constant recipient of racist insults and segregation from the white student body; to the United States Marine Corps, where he served two combat tours in Vietnam; then as a "non-traditional student" to university studies at USD, and later at Oklahoma State University.[2] Above all the numerous services that the Institute offered at USD, he judged that its most important function was as a sacred home for the oral history of the plains tribes. In 2002 he wrote of the Institute:

Leonard Bruguier, c. 1987. Herbert T. Hoover and Leonard R. Bruguier, *The Yankton Sioux*, (Chelsea House Publishers, 1988).

> South Dakota Oral History Center serves as the heart of the Institute of American Indian Studies. The Center is important because it preserves the voices and life experiences of thousands of individuals from various locations throughout our universe. Because many of those people who shared themselves for posterity have departed from this life, the Institute's director and staff view the recorded interviews as a repository of information and as a memorial to what these people accomplished and contributed to humanity. In the words of the Nakota Oyate, the South Dakota Oral History Center is *nina wakan*, very sacred.[3]

Elsewhere, he said of his role at the Institute, "I've been put in charge of keeping the voices. Many of the people are no longer with us. I consider it a very spiritual place."[4]

Oral history, and especially Native oral history, was at the time a contested source of evidence for historians. It was dismissed by scholars as folklore, myth, or legend; not valuable to the historical record. Native historians pushed back against this; my father's view was that "All history is built on oral history. Books and newspaper articles are just written oral history, but they are taken as fact."[5] The oral history that shaped him as a person, and consequently as a scholar, is as urgent then as it is now. It has come down to me, and I proceed as an extension of that legacy.

We are descendants of Chief *Padaniapapi*, or Struck By the Ree, a signatory of the 1858 Treaty of Washington, and the leader of the Yankton Sioux Tribe as they transitioned to reservation life. *Padaniapapi* was troubled by the encroachment of white settlers on the borders of the Yankton's territory, on the east by what are now the states of Minnesota and Iowa, and on the south by what is now the state of Nebraska.

---

2. It brought me to tears to read about aspects of his student years in Yankton, which he never told me about, but were recorded by one of his mentors, Dr. Herbert Hoover, who featured my father as an exemplar of a modern day Native man who is rooted in both traditional practices and the "modern" world. Herbert T. Hoover and Leonard R. Bruguier, *The Yankton Sioux* (New York: Chelsea House Publishers, 1988), 95-7.
3. Leonard R. Bruguier and Scott E. White, "The Institute of American Indian Studies: A Tradition of Scholarly Pursuit," *Indigenous Nations Studies Journal* 2 no. 1 (Spring 2001): 5. Online: https://kuscholarworks.ku.edu/server/api/core/bitstreams/0e90ee11-54af-479b-ae60-301bc45eb964/content
4. Marjane Ambler, "History in the First Person: Always Valued in the Native World, Oral History Gains Respect among Western Scholars," *Tribal College Journal of American Indian Higher Education* 6, no 4 (Spring 1995): https://tribalcollegejournal.org/history-person-valued-native-world-oral-history-gains-respect-western-scholars/
5. Ambler, "History in the First Person"

Chief Struck by the Ree, circa 1858. South Dakota State Historical Society.

Though there was dissent among the other headmen of the Yankton, *Padaniapapi* was resigned to treaty negotiations with the United States government in order to secure a permanent homeland for his people. Though he worked tirelessly to live in the new way and encouraged the new way of life for the Yankton people, his efforts were hampered by the government's failure to uphold their end of the treaty. In 1865 he testified,

> When I went to make my treaty, my grandfather [i.e., the U.S. President] agreed, if I would put three young men to work, he would put one white laborer with them to learn them; that I should put three young men to learn ploughing, and he would put one white man to learn them; also, three to sow, three to learn the carpenter's trade, three to learn the blacksmith's trade, and such other trades as we should want; and my great grandfather was to furnish one white man for each trade to learn the young men. My grandfather also said that a school should be established for the nation to learn them to read and write; that the young boys and girls should go to school, and that the young men who worked should have the same pay as the whites. My grandfather told me if my young men would go to work that the money going to those who would not work should be given to those who would work. None of these things have been fulfilled... .
>
> My friend, I think if my young men knew how to sow, farm, carpenter, and do everything else, I could send the white men away; we ourselves should have the money paid the white men, and we should have plenty of money. If we had been learned all these things we could support ourselves, have plenty of money, have schools, and I could have written my great grandfather, and have got a letter from him; I could have written him myself what I wanted.
>
> ... If I had understood from what my grandfather told me that I was to be treated as I have been, I would never have done as I have done; I never would have signed the treaty.... The Great Spirit knows that I have spoken the truth; knows what I say"[6]

These are the stories my father grew up with. The same stories have been told within countless families on the reservations of Nebraska and among those tribes that were relocated from their homelands. The larger historical reality that emerges is of the betrayal of sacred, binding agreements, of broken promises to be welcomed into a new nation, of prosperity that never came.

By the time of my father's childhood, conditions on the reservation had barely improved. He recalled hard times and a people still struggling as the state around them prospered. Later in life he recalled of his childhood,

> In the late 1940s, I can remember going hungry for two or three days at a time. It was hot ... seemed like it never rained. We'd spend a lot of time at the river. We ate plants ... Sheep Showers (Sheep Sorrel). They looked like four leaf clovers and tasted kinda [*sic*] sour ... could make your nose wrinkle. We ate plums, rosebuds, and wild onions. I still

---

6. Palaneapope, "How the Indians Are Victimized by Government Agents and Soldiers," in *When Sorry Isn't Enough: The Controversy Over Apologies and Reparations for Human Injustice*, ed. Roy L. Brooks (New York: New York University Press, 1999),, 254-256. https://doi-org.libproxy.unl.edu/10.18574/nyu/9780814739471.003.0046

eat Sheep Showers and plums ... to renew my acquaintance with them. *Our stories are the same. We carry them on because what they're for... to draw strength from. When I remember how my relatives lived through hard times, I can cope with today, even though today...it's not that much better.*[7] (emphasis mine)

For me, my father's story is a significant part of the oral history of the Yankton people. It is an intermediate point between my relatives of early Yankton reservation life and our own time. I've started here to tell you where I come from, and why it is important to look back to the recent past to understand where we are now. While reflecting on the historical material that I present in this chapter, while comparing past times against the current political culture, I am often led to conclude as my father did so many years ago, that things are not much better than they were when he was recalling his childhood on the reservation. A difference, however, is that from my vantage point, I can qualify the thought to say that *certain* things are not much better. It is undeniable that material conditions have improved on reservations, and in the towns and cities in which the majority of Natives within the state of Nebraska live; that tribal communities in Nebraska, despite being located in food deserts, have been empowered (and fed) by Indigenous Food Sovereignty movements; and that we no longer have to fear unchecked naked aggression against us.[8] Nevertheless, culturally, there is still an inside/outside line drawn between the white majority class and Native populations, with Natives still outside; and among the general population there exists a widespread ignorance and occlusion of Native history and culture. And so the work must go on.

I am going to cover the historical period of 1831 to the 1930s. This encompasses the period immediately preceding the passage of the Indian Trade and Intercourse Act of 1834, which established Indian Territory as a permanent home for Native peoples, to the Wheeler-Howard Act of 1934, more commonly known as the Indian Reorganization Act. My discussion will serve as a starting point for the second part of the chapter which covers Native activism. Nebraska Territory was created under the guise of popular sovereignty, the main proponent of which, Stephen Douglas, conceived of as being a government for white people, by white people. Despite popular sovereignty eventually giving way to a representative form of government that recognized equal rights, after the creation of the State of Nebraska in 1867, the Native population within lacked important rights. The result was a voiceless, unprotected people.

My discussion will also serve as a complement to the introduction for this book, contextualizing portions dealing with land displacement for settlers' gain, physical isolation, generational wealth, and white superiority.

I: 1831 – 1854: Prelude to Nebraska Territory

Indian Country, De Tocqueville's Prediction, and Big Elk's Warning

The following isn't a comprehensive history; the aim is to highlight important events and the ideas of those whose actions brought forth the history of the region and eventually the state of Nebraska. Using an analogy from the book *The Nebraska State Constitution*, we can think of how the state developed as a sort of fence, a way of separating what is "mine" and "yours", who is "us" and "them," and who the "insiders" and "outsiders" are.[9] In examining the period leading up to the formation of Nebraska Territory, it is instructive to point to how outside forces desired and then claimed the land, though it was rightfully inhabited by several Indigenous nations, and how the relation of inside/outside was quickly reversed as white settlers became established within the territory.

Neither is this chapter a historical examination of each Nebraska tribe during this historical period. For a definitive treatment of this time period, I urge readers to consult David Wishart's *An Unspeakable Sadness: The Dispossession of the Nebraska Indians*.[10] Wishart comprehensively covers the histories of the Omaha, Otoe-Missouria, Pawnee, and Ponca Tribes, detailing all the treaties, the deaths resulting from the introduction of disease and alcohol, and the corrupt and

---

7. Renee Sansom-Flood, *Lessons From Chouteau Creek: Yankton Memories of Dakota Territorial Intrigue*, (Hills, MN: Crescent Publishing, Inc., 1986), 82.
8. I want to thank Dewayne Mays for helping me appreciate this point. Dewayne Mays, "National Day of Racial Healing Conversation with Dr. DeWayne Mays" (Presentation, University of Nebraska Libraries, Love Library, January 28, 2025).
9. Robert D, Miewald, Peter J. Longo, and Anthony B. Schutz, *The Nebraska State Constitution: A Reference Guide*, 2nd ed. (Lincoln: University of Nebraska Press, 2009), 2-3.
10. David J. Wishart, *An Unspeakable Sadness: The Dispossession of the Nebraska Indians* (Lincoln: University of Nebraska Press, 1994).

unscrupulous Indian agents who were sent to "care for the Indians." The title of the book is taken from a portion of a speech by White Horse, an Omaha, delivered on August 13, 1912. He lamented, "Now the face of all the land is changed and sad. The living creatures are gone. I see the land desolate, and I suffer unspeakable sadness. Sometimes I wake in the night and feel as though I should suffocate from the pressure of this awful feeling of loneliness."[11]

How could such unchecked destruction occur over such a short period? The treaties signed in the lead-up to territorial status were a major mechanism by which these devastating changes occurred.

In Appendix I, I have compiled treaty information from the Oklahoma State University Library website, *Tribal Treaties Database*.[12] This wonderful, comprehensive resource gathers texts from treaties, agreements, and other documents between Indigenous tribal nations and the United States government. It also provides resources to help interpret the language used in the treaties and understand their importance. This resource puts in the readers' hands the understanding of those tribal leaders who, in the interest of their people, exchanged rights and land for a promise of survival in a new way of life. But those promises were never kept.

It is well-known and discussed among Native people that of the 368 treaties signed between tribal nations and the US government, most were either broken or not entirely honored. From the tribal signatories' point of view, each condition within the treaty was a sacred promise made to them. Vine Deloria Jr. explains the difference in understanding treaty obligations between tribes and the US Government. He observes, "When Indians gave their word and smoked the pipe, they sent the smoke to the Creator. It was sacred, and the treaty was good in the eyes of all. The white men had to go back and ask other white men if they could keep their promises and make good on their word."[13] Deloria's suggestion is that white treaty negotiators made promises in bad faith. It is often difficult for non-Native people to appreciate the sense of betrayal and alienation involved. I encourage a thoughtful exploration of the treaties signed in the years prior to the formation of Nebraska Territory, and an accompanying text such as *Behind the Trail of Broken Treaties: An Indian Declaration of Independence* by Vine Deloria Jr. and *Nation to Nation: Treaties Between the United States and American Indian Nations*, edited by Suzan Shown Harjo.[14]

In December 1831, the French nobleman Alexis de Tocqueville, who later authored *Democracy in America*, was at the Mississippi River in northeastern Louisiana. He was observing the forced removal of the Choctaw Nation as they marched westward on the Trail of Tears. He described the pitiful scene the following way. "The Indians had their families with them, and they brought in their train the wounded and the sick, with children newly born and old men on the verge of death. They possessed neither tents nor wagons, but only their arms and some provisions."[15]

> As the ragged columns boarded the boats that would take them forever from their ancestral home, there was "[N]o cry, no sob... all were silent. Their calamities were of ancient date, and they knew them to be irremediable." Of the situation he shrewdly observed that the people *"have been ruined by a competition which they had not the means of sustaining. They are isolated in their own country, and their race constituted only a little colony of troublesome strangers in the midst of a numerous and dominant people."*[16] (emphasis mine)

De Tocqueville predicted that the ambition and greed of the American people, aided by the complicity of the US government, would push through to the inevitable conclusion that the Native peoples would vanish from the land. That prediction almost became reality, but more interesting to me is his observation about Native peoples "being ruined by competition." This proves as illuminating as it is foreshadowing of

---

11. Cited in Wishart, *An Unspeakable Sadness*, v.
12. "Tribal Treaties Database," Oklahoma State University Libraries, accessed April 8, 2025. https://treaties.okstate.edu/.
13. Vine Deloria Jr., quoted in, Suzan Shown Harjo, "Introduction", in *Nation to Nation: Treaties Between the United States and American Indian Nations*, ed. Suzan Shown Harjo (Washington, D.C. and New York: Smithsonian Institution, 2014), 3
14. Vine Deloria Jr., *Behind the Trail of Broken Treaties: An Indian Declaration of Independence* (Austin: University of Texas Press, 1985); *Nation to Nation: Treaties Between the United States and American Indian Nations*, edited by Suzan Shown Harjo. Washington, DC: Smithsonian Books, 2014).
15. Both de Tocqueville's recollection and the Choctaw Trail of Tears is cited on, "Trail of Tears, Indian Removal Act, Andrew Jackson, Native American Displacement, Cherokee, Forced Migration, 1830s, U.S. Government Policy." *Bill of Rights Institute*, accessed October 30, 2024, https://billofrightsinstitute.org/essays/the-trail-of-tears/
16. "Trail of Tears"

American Progress by John Gast, circa 1872. Library of Congress.

what was to come. White greed and the US government were foes that no Native nation could conquer.

At this time, the conception of the land west of the Mississippi was a savage wilderness, not fit for American agriculture. In 1820, Stephen Long had coined the description "The Great American Desert," to describe it.[17] Generations of Nebraska writers would later spill much ink to dispel this misconception.

However, the land would do for the Natives, the US government concluded, and in 1834 the Indian Trade and Intercourse Act, which established a congressionally designated refuge for displaced tribes, was passed. This act prohibited white settlement west of the Mississippi River, and was seen as a benevolent act to protect from further encroachment on Indigenous lands.[18] In the following text, 'Indian title' refers to a tribal nation's "right of occupancy and use" of land, and protects against the sale of such land without the tribal nation's—a sovereign political entity—involvement.[19] 'Aboriginal title' or 'title' are variants of this term. Section 1 of the 1834 Indian Trade and Intercourse Act states,

> That all that part of the United States west of the Mississippi, and not within the states of Missouri and Louisiana, or the territory of Arkansas, and, also, that part of the United States east of the Mississippi River, and not within any state to which the Indian title has not been extinguished, be taken and deemed to be Indian country.[20]

---

17. Martyn J. Bowden, "Great American Desert," *Encyclopedia of the Great Plains*, ed. David J. Wishart (Lincoln: University of Nebraska Press, 2004): http://plainshumanities.unl.edu/encyclopedia/doc/egp.ii.032

18. The process of displacement for many tribes was not a one-and-done affair. Once a tribe had been displaced to Indian Country, its tenure there was uncertain. I would suggest the history of the Sauk and Fox Tribe as a case study: "Sac and Fox," *Oklahoma Historical Society*, accessed October 31, 2024, https://www.okhistory.org/publications/enc/entry?entry=SA001

19. Claire Blumenthal, " 'We Hold the Government to Its Word': How *McGirt v. Oklahoma* Revives Aboriginal Title," *The Yale Law Journal* 131, no. 7 (May 2022): 2331-2.

20. Cited in William Unrau, *The Rise and Fall of Indian Country, 1825-1855* (Lawrence: University of Kansas Press, 2007), 2.

Tribal leaders were led to believe that the land was to be for the Native peoples "as long as the sun shines, and the rain falls," according to Lewis Cass, a US Senator from Michigan who favored relocation.[21] Cass's assurances certainly qualify as being offered in bad faith. Cass is well-known to history as being the Secretary of War under Andrew Jackson, being instrumental in implementing the latter's Indian Removal Policy, and as a main proponent of *manifest destiny,* the belief that the United States were destined by God to expand westward across the continent.

Historian William Unrau has persuasively argued that the benevolence of protecting Indigenous nations in a land of their own was a smokescreen.[22] The myth of the Great American Desert was just that—a myth—and enterprising individuals were aware of the many natural resources available on the sprawling continent for the burgeoning country to exploit. In our region in particular, there was a golden road leading to the West Coast along the Platte River Valley. Overland travel was entering into the American consciousness as a possibility and a promise to a better life. Already by the 1830s, land boosters and opportunists were advertising the ease of crossing the Rocky Mountains, going so far as saying that even "delicate females" could cross with ease.[23] No act of Congress could hold back the "trappers, traders, farmers, religious groups, gold seekers, and assorted pilgrims [who] began their quests for something and somewhere new."[24] Overland travel opened the door to white encroachment on to Indian Country.

For tribes living in what would become Nebraska, a different sort of competition arose as a result of the displacement of Eastern tribes being relocated onto their traditional lands. In the 1830 Treaty of Prairie du Chien, we find the first federal acquisition of land from Nebraska tribes. This treaty ceded hunting grounds east of the Missouri River, in what is now Iowa, of the Omaha and Otoe-Missouria tribes, land that was also claimed in part by Santee Dakota,

> I did not know who to believe. The white people have too many chiefs. They do not understand each other. They do not all talk alike.
>
> Chief Joseph

Iowa, Sauk and Fox, and Yanktons.[25] The cession was to tribes to the northeast, including eastern bands of the Dakota (Sisseton, Wahpeton, and Medawakonton), Sauk and Fox, Menominee, Iowa, Ho-Chunk, and the Council of Three Fires, who were rapidly being displaced due to white settlement.

These newcomers to the territory increased the occurrence of inter-tribal skirmishes and violence. Though they were often characterized as "treaties of friendship," so-called due to the formalization of friendly relations between tribal nations and the US government, the treaties of the 1820s also contain clauses detailing submission to the government. Typical of these is the *1825 Treaty with the Pawnee Tribe,* which will be discussed here as an example.[26] Containing six articles, the first article has the Pawnee tribe admit US supremacy, and admit that the US has the right to "regulate all trade and intercourse with them."[27] Article 2 is the agreement of the US government to receive the tribe into their friendship, and extend "benefits and acts of kindness as may be convenient," at the discretion of the US president.[28] Articles 3 and 4 limit "trade and intercourse" with the tribe to designated locations, stipulate who is authorized to trade with the tribe, and lay out the conditions of such trade. Article 5 denies tribes the ability to administer justice according to their own code of justice and requires compliance with the "laws of the United States" and its legal system. This article also charges Pawnee chiefs with the

---

21. Cited in Unrau, *The Rise and Fall,* 61.
22. Unrau, *The Rise and Fall,* 61.
23. John D. Unruh Jr., *The Plains Across: The Overland Emigrants and the Trans-Mississippi West, 1840-1860* (Urbana: University of Illinois Press, 1979), 29
24. Robert D. Miewald, Peter J. Longo, and Anthony B. Schutz, *The Nebraska State Constitution: A Reference Guide,* 2nd ed. (Lincoln: University of Nebraska Press, 2009), 3.
25. Wishart, *An Unspeakable Sadness,* 59.
26. "Treaty with the Pawnee Tribe," *Tribal Treaties Database,* accessed April 8, 2025, https://treaties.okstate.edu/treaties/treaty-with-the-pawnee-tribe-1825-0258
27. "Treaty with the Pawnee Tribe"
28. "Treaty with the Pawnee Tribe"

responsibility to recover property stolen from US citizens, and finally, promises for repayment for property stolen from Pawnees if the property cannot be recovered, and it is proven that a US citizen stole it. Finally, in Article 6, it is prohibited for the Pawnee to provide tribal nations who have not signed treaties of friendship with the US, with "guns, ammunition, or other implements of war" and charges chiefs to return property stolen from white citizens to its proper owners, else the perpetrator face punishment. An early example of "mine" and "yours."

Nebraska Indian Country began shrinking as a result of land cessions by the Otoe-Missouria Treaty of 1833. The land itself was becoming depleted of game and timber, and a desperate people were resigned to "give up the hunt" in exchange for agricultural and educational provisions. Wishart writes that, "In total, the Otoe-Missouria were given almost forty thousand dollars' worth of goods and services for relinquishing their title to about one million acres of land, or 4.1 cents an acre. Thus began in earnest the process whereby the Nebraska Indians sold their lands for a living."[29]

Chief Big Elk of the Omaha could sense the coming intrusion of whites into Indian Country. He visited Washington, DC in 1837-38 and upon his return, he delivered the following speech, as a warning to other Omahas.

> My chiefs, braves, and young men, I have just returned from a visit to a far-off country toward the rising sun, and have seen many strange things. I bring to you news which it saddens my heart to think of. There is a coming flood which will soon reach us, and I advise you to prepare for it. Soon the animals which *Wakon'da* has given us for sustenance will disappear beneath this flood to return no more, and it will be very hard for you. Look at me; you see I am advanced in age; I am near the grave. I can no longer think for you and lead you as in my younger days. You must think for yourselves what will be best for your welfare. I tell you this that you may be prepared for the coming change. You may not know my meaning. Many of you are old, as I am, and by the time the change comes we may be lying peacefully in our graves; but these young men will remain to suffer. Speak kindly to one another; do what you can to help each other, even in the troubles with the coming tide. Now, my people, this is all I have to say. Bear these words in mind, and when the time comes think of what I have said.[30]

This powerful speech stands as an interesting complement to de Tocqueville's prediction. Big Elk could see that the traditional way of life was losing out to the outsider's way of life. He was urging unification for his people. He predicted that would be the best defense against the coming tide's culture of selfish individualism.

Extinguishing Land Titles and Pioneers

James Malin, a Kansas historian writing in the 1950s, argued that the extinguishing of land titles that took place in the 1830s prepared the way for a grand appropriation of land by means of the Nebraska-Kansas Act.[31] Among the many actors who contributed to this, Malin focuses on how in 1853, Thomas Hart Benton, a white supremacist senator from Missouri, made a study of all the land titles created by dispossessed eastern tribes, and those titles re-negotiated in the 1830s. In a series of speeches he gave in 1853 Benton argued, "Nearly thirty years ago the United States made a general extinction of the Indian titles west of the Missouri, to be assigned in parcels to emigrant tribes. Part has been assigned, part not; and this unassigned part I hold to be United States Territory, now open to settlement without objection from the Indians."[32] There was no legality to his claim; his position was meant to sway those in Congress who also wanted the land, but who were moved to block the Kansas-Nebraska Act on account of the land titles held by the tribes. Benton was campaigning hard to eliminate the reluctance of a Congress that was lagging behind a land-hungry public.

On the surface, while Benton's interest in acquiring land was for the creation of a trans-continental railroad, at bottom his interest was asserting the racial superiority of whites, and the rights to the land which followed from this. In an 1846 speech before Congress, he said,

---

29. Wishart, *An Unspeakable Sadness*, 62.
30. "Chief Big Elk." *Sarpy County Museum*, accessed October 28, 2024, https://sarpycountymuseum.org/2014/09/chief-big-elk/
31. James C. Malin, *The Nebraska Question, 1852-1854* (Ann Arbor: Edwards Brothers, Inc, 1953), 128-32.
32. Malin, *The Nebraska Question.*, 132.

It would seem that the White race alone received the divine command, to subdue and replenish the earth! for it is the only race that has obeyed it — the only one that hunts out new and distant lands, and even a New World, to subdue and replenish. Starting from western Asia, taking Europe for their field, and the Sun for their guide, and leaving Mongolians behind, they arrived, after many ages, on the shores of the Atlantic, which they lit up with the lights of science and religion, and adorned with the useful and elegant arts. Three and half centuries ago, this race, in obedience to the great command, arrived in the New World, and found new lands to subdue and replenish.... The van of the Caucasian race now top the Rocky mountains, and spread down to the shores of the Pacific. In a few years a great population will grow up there, luminous with the accumulated lights of European and American civilization. Their presence in such a position cannot be without its influence upon eastern Asia.... Civilization, or extinction, has been the fate of all people who have found themselves in the track of the advancing Whites, and civilization, always the preference of the Whites, has been pressed as an object, while extinction has followed as a consequence of its resistance. The Black and the Red races have often felt their ameliorating influence.[33]

Even before this push for Western expansion, which included Nebraska land, in 1848 limited reservations were desired by self-interested whites: "It is indispensably necessary that they be placed where they can be controlled and finally compelled by stern necessity to resort to agriculture or starve."[34] This reflects a cynical view that many politicians held. Couched in benevolent terms as aiding tribes in gaining agricultural skills that will guide them to self-sufficiency, it is plausible to read deeper below the surface and realize that the previous quote probably reflects the desire of many for the eventual starvation of the Native people. In the context of settlement, Native extinction was a means to that end, a view that was accepted not only by politicians, but also by the society at large.

> The White man does not understand the Indian for the same reason he does not understand America. He is far too removed from its formative processes. The roots of his tree of his life have not yet grasped the rock and soil. The white man is still troubled with primate fears; he still has in his consciousness the perils of the frontier continent, some of its fastnesses not yet having yielded to his questing footsteps and inquiring eyes. He shudders still with the memory of the loss of his forefathers upon its scorching deserts and forbidding mountaintops. The man from Europe is still a foreigner and an alien. And he still hates the man who questioned his path across the continent.
> But in the Indian the spirit of the land is still vested; it will be until other men are able to divine and meet its rhythms. Men must be born and reborn to belong. Their bodies must be formed of the dust of their forefathers' bones.
>
> Chief Luther Standing Bear, 1933

A typical expression of that view from that time saw the replacement of the rightful inhabitants of the land by a new tenant—the pioneer. In the following text we see the author claiming the right of pioneers to take over the land on account of their character, which is intimately connected to race and colonial legacy. Traits of the pioneer were contrasted against the received view of Natives as savage and unwilling to settle the land, and the argument advanced was that the pioneers are better suited to populate the plains. In this text we see elements of the racism espoused by Benton, though it is toned down. He

---

33. Benton, T. Hart. (1846). *Speech of Mr. Benton, of Missouri, on the Oregon question: delivered in the Senate of the United States, May 22, 25 & 28, 1846.* [Washington?: s.n.], 29-30. https://hdl.handle.net/2027/aeu.ark:/13960/t2h71hg65
34. J. Sterling Morton, Albert Watkins, and George L. Miller, *Illustrated History of Nebraska: A History of Nebraska from the Earliest Explorations of the Trans-Mississippi Region with Steel Engravings, Photogravures, Copper Plates, Maps, and Tables, Volume 2* (Lincoln: Jacob North and Company, 1907), 246.

begins by claiming that that the land is "untried ... through permanent settlement by civilized men." He continues to extol the character of the pioneers over that of the Native, arguing that

> [m]en and women who had the courage, spirit, and ambition to give up agreeable environments in an old home for the purpose of founding a new one. From the days of the colonies in Virginia, New England, and New York, the best types of mankind, physically and mentally, and the strongest individuals of those types—those gifted with self-reliance and inspired by the spirit of self-denial—have penetrated new countries and opened them to the institutions of civilization. . . . Self-reliance, self-control, and stability among savages are merely sporadic; consequently we find no traces of voluntary migrations for establishing permanent sovereignty and settlements by the Indians who preceded us upon these plains. The strong characteristic of the pioneer is his ambition and zealous, enthusiastic work for tomorrow, his willingness cheerfully to endure hardships in the present that others may enjoy consummate satisfactions in the future—satisfactions which he himself may never experience. There were genuine heroes among the openers and testers of the vast crust of soil which stretched from the river to the mountains.[35]

In a tragic, persistent oversight, this writer ignores any actual improvements that Native people have made to the land, such as the widespread cultivation of crops like the "three sisters" (corn, beans, and squash), deep knowledge of foodstuffs and medicinal plants throughout the plains or controlled burning practices that maintained the grassland ecosystem. Indigenous agricultural and hunting practices were small-scale and sustainable rather than large-scale and commercial. In the big picture, their agricultural and hunting patterns had developed over centuries to be self-sustaining and harmonious with nature, in contrast to those maximized for the greatest yield to feed a burgeoning population located in a distant part of the country, the land of which had been used up by massive settlement and industrialization. Viewed in this light, the pioneers were the salvation of the republic.

> The love of possessions is a disease in them. These people have made many rules that the rich may break, but the poor may not! They have a religion in which the poor worship, but the rich will not! They even take tithes from the poor and weak to support the rich and those who rule. They claim this mother of ours, the earth, for their own use, and fence their neighbor away. ... If America had been twice the size it is, there still would not have been enough.
>
> Sitting Bull

According to Morton, George Manypenny, Commissioner of Indian Affairs, "[b]y the act of Congress of March 3, 1852. . . was authorized to conduct negotiations with the Indians west of the states of Iowa and Missouri to obtain their permission for white people to settle on their lands, and to procure extinguishment of the Indian title."[36] "Permanent Indian Country" was a distant, forgotten promise.

> To the white man untilled land, an absence of towns or houses, is "empty." As nature abhors a vacuum, the white man abhors what he perceives as an empty void and hastens to "fill it up" with fields, houses, barns, towns, people. The vast emptiness of what was called the "great American Desert" was strangely unsettling to the white pioneers.
>
> Robert Bunge, 1984

---

35. J. Sterling Morton, Albert Watkins, and George L. Miller, *Illustrated History of Nebraska: A History of Nebraska from the Earliest Explorations of the Trans-Mississippi Region with Steel Engravings, Photogravures, Copper Plates, Maps, and Tables, Volume 1*, 3rd. ed (Lincoln: Jacob North and Company, 1911),192-3.
36. Morton, *Illustrated History of Nebraska*, vol. 2, 247.

In 1853, land boosters in Iowa were eager for the settlement of Nebraska. In contrast to pioneers, land boosters' interests were to claim land to serve as hubs in transportation networks joining the east and west coasts. An example of a land booster's viewpoint is expressed by Hadley Johnson from Council Bluffs. With an eye towards Western development, Johnson had established residence there in the expectation that the city would be the eastern terminus of the Pacific railroad. He observed,

> The people will watch with intense anxiety the transaction of Congress during the approaching session, and, if the territory of Nebraska is not organized and opened to settlement within a year, they will wait no longer for the action of Congress, but settle it themselves, as the pioneer did Oregon and California, and leave Congress 'alone in its glory' to follow in the rear.[37]

Johnson captures the impatience of both pioneers and boosters. Congress's move to nullify the promise of a permanent territory for tribes was not proceeding at the pace of "progress." On the other hand, progress had had a most deleterious effect on the Nebraska tribes during this period.

The influx of pioneers brought epidemics of smallpox, cholera, dysentery, and measles to Nebraska tribes, greatly diminishing their populations. Major movements of people from the east, such as the Mormon Exodus, which traveled through the territories of the Omaha, Pawnee, and Ponca, severely depleted game and timber. And inter-tribal relations, strained by hardship and competition for disappearing resources, were at an all-time low. Reports from the Omaha reservation at this time stated that people were surviving on roots, the occasional stray racoon or muskrat, and the reservation superintendent feared that without emergency rations, the tribe would go extinct. Around 1847 or 1848, an Omaha chief (unnamed in the historical record) lamented to a Presbyterian missionary, "We have had a dark time. The clouds came down alone to us. They pressed on our heads."[38] Indeed dark times had fallen upon each of the tribes of Nebraska. Each had suffered serious losses of population due to the rapid spread of disease, starvation, and a heightened threat of aggression from other tribal nations.

In reviewing early histories of Nebraska Territory, most assessments of the pioneers follow along the same lines as above—patriotic, selfless heroes who open up the wilderness for civilization. This early historian's candidness about the first territorial legislature is quite progressive for the period:

> Neither the dominant spirit nor the general work of this first legislature may be commended or admired. It worked under abnormal conditions and without the restraints of organized society. There could be no appeal to public sentiment through public discussion ... because there was as yet no public. ... Our first handful of pioneers had come the very year of the first session to spy out the land while it was still in possession of its original occupants. Ten years before, Douglas had served unequivocal notice—in his bill of 1844—of the intention of the stronger to 'go in and possess the land' of the weaker race. This was no new departure, but the natural process and the immemorial rule of the progress of civilization, and never perhaps pursued by the strong nations of the earth with such unanimity and aggressiveness as in the last quarter century.[39]

They continue,

> As a token of the refinement of civilization nineteen centuries after Christ in contrast to the barbarism of fifteen centuries before Christ, unlike the Israelitish summary dealing with the Canaanites, our pioneers offered the people the grace of peaceful , as the alternative of enforced surrender of their homes! But the difference was merely conventional, and there was the same notion and spirit of conquest and force in the one case as in the other. The chief difference between these beginning years of Nebraska and those of the easterly territories was that while, owing chiefly to the legal barrier against gradual occupation of this forbidden "Indian Country," our invasion was sudden and comparatively artificial and superficial, their settlement was the result of steady purpose, and their institutions, accommodating themselves to these conditions, were more the product of growth and development. In short

---

37. Quoted in James Potts, "Nebraska Territory, 1854 – 1867: A Study of Frontier Politics," Ph.D. Diss., (University of Nebraska, 1973), 57.
38. Quoted in Wishart, *An Unspeakable Sadness*, 83–87.
39. Morton, *Illustrated History of Nebraska*, vol. 1, 244-5.

the differentiation of Nebraska Territory was that it did not grow but was made.[40]

And so it was. In 1854, Commissioner of Indian Affairs Manypenny made another round of treaties with the tribes of Nebraska, ceding ever more land, constricting freedoms and rights to a greater extent, and opening the door for the legislation that would create the Nebraska Territory.

II: 1854 – 1867 : Nebraska Territory, and the Government of Popular Sovereignty.

After Nebraska became a territory, the question of slavery dominated political discourse. The Kansas-Nebraska Bill contained a clause that superseded the Missouri Compromise and allowed the question of slavery to be decided within the territory by a vote of the people. This was known as popular sovereignty. I will direct the reader to other parts of this collection for a discussion of the topic of slavery. Popular sovereignty at the time was limited to white males.

The treaties within this time period, compiled in Appendix II, are characterized by further land cessions, provisions of agricultural and educational services, and, in the case of the Treaty with the Otoe and Missouria of 1869, removal from the territory. The period is marked by a steady growth in white settlement, and the concurrent growth of a political culture that demonized and constrained Native people even further.

The Nebraska territorial motto "Popular Sovereignty" was favored by the Democratic Party, which held the political majority in the first election of the territory. A brief consideration of Illinois Senator Stephen A. Douglas's speeches of the time will reveal the racist doctrines underlying the political sentiment during the formation of Nebraska Territory. The following is from Douglas's speech, "Ours A White Man's Government—Negroes Not Citizens," delivered in Springfield, Illinois on June 15, 1858 (I have retained the crowd's approval in the text, indicated in parentheses throughout):

> I am free to say to you that in my opinion this government of ours is founded on the white basis. (Great applause.). It was made by white men, for the benefit of the white man, to be administered by white men, in such a manner as they should determine. (Cheers.) It is also true that a negro, or any other man of an inferior race to a white man, should be permitted to enjoy, and humanity requires that he should have all the rights, privileges and immunities which he is capable of exercising consistent with the good of the society in which he lived ("Bravo."). *But you may ask me what are these rights and these privileges. My answer is that each State must decide for itself the nature and extent of these rights.* ("Hear, hear" and applause.) [41] (emphasis added)

The emphasized text signals the promotion of popular sovereignty. During the same campaign, Douglas delivered a similar message in his "Speech at Bloomington," delivered in Indiana on July 16, 1858:

> I believe that this government of ours was formed on the white basis. (Prolonged cheering.). I believe that it was established by white men—(applause)—by men of European birth and descended of European races, for the benefit of white men and their posterity in all time to come. ("Hear, hear."). I do not believe that it was the design or intention of the signers of the Declaration of Independence of the framers of the Constitution to include negroes or other inferior races with white men as citizens. (Cheers.)[42]

The racist rhetoric against BIPOC (Black, Indigenous, and People of Color) individuals is sadly familiar to us at the time of writing in Fall 2024. The rhetoric attending the 2024 Republican presidential campaign cleaved upon many of the same racial lines, and pursued a wide-ranging, white supremacist agenda.[43]

In Nebraska, this type of white supremacist message found its voice in J. Sterling Morton, a towering figure in early Nebraska politics. In a speech delivered during the Territorial fair in 1860, Morton said,

> Royalty has always been an unconscious but all-consuming goal of the European immigrant.
>
> Vine Deloria Jr., 1971

---

40. Morton, *Illustrated History of Nebraska*, vol.1, 245.
41. H. M. Flint, *Life of Stephen A. Douglas: To Which Are Added His Speeches and Reports* (Philadelphia: John E. Potter Publisher, 1865), 111.
42. Flint, *Life of Stephen A. Douglas*, 121.
43. "Trump on DEI and Anti-Discrimination Law," ACLU, accessed April 8, 2025, https://www.aclu.org/trump-on-dei-and-anti-discrimination-law

The Anglo-Saxon race are being driven by the hand of God across the continent of America and are to inhabit and have dominion over it all himself, are intended for the abiding place of the pioneers in the progress of the world. The American Indian, in whom there are none of the elements of thrift, held a tenancy upon these fertile plains for centuries, but there was neither labor in his arm nor progression in his spirit. He was an unworthy occupant of so goodly a land, and he has been supplanted. He has gone, and his race is fast becoming extinct; the world is too old for its aborigines. Their destiny is completed as they are Journeying to their fate; they must die, and in a few years hence only be known through their history as it was recorded by the Anglo-Saxon while he pushed them before him in his onward tread. [44]

This passage is important not simply because it ties the political sentiment of the leaders of Nebraska to a larger racist political system that was proceeding westward, but because of the observation Morton made about the Anglo-Saxon writing of history. In what would become the history of the state, and particularly of the fate of the Native people, there was Anglo-Saxon control of the narrative. This was a deliberate strategy that connected prevailing political views to the education of the youth of the state. It became the accepted narrative that Indigenous people were a dying race, to be replaced by a superior white one. And how better to control that narrative than to make it the official story of the state.

The Indigenous people of the newly-created Nebraska Territory were suffering under the federal reservation system. While the settlers around them were building wealth and capital, they were withering under the lack of promised support. Depredations increased, as families became desperate. The extent to which is unknown, as there is reason to be skeptical of reports as they were used as a scare tactic. Further, there is evidence that that majority of crime was committed by squatters and white marauders:

> From facts which have come to the knowledge of this department , it is deemed certain that these Indian depredations and disturbances were the result of combined action between several tribes, instigated, aided and counseled

Big Chief Killahun sheet music, c.1918. Bowling Green State University Libraries.

> by lawless white men who hoped to share in the plunder which would result from their robberies and massacres. It is by no means certain that these coadjutors of the savages were not the emissaries of the rebel government, prompted to their inhuman work by the hope of creating a diversion in favor of their waning cause in the South. Portions of the Sioux, Cheyennes, Arapahoes, Kiowas, Comanches, and Apaches, were evidently confederated for the purpose of attacking the frontier settlements and emigrant trains in Nebraska, Kansas, Colorado, and southeastern Idaho. Suddenly and almost simultaneously, without the slightest warning, ranchmen and emigrants were attacked at no less than four different points, remote from each other, thus proving, beyond the possibility of doubt, that the plan had been matured and the coöperation of different tribes secured in the work of destruction.[45]

Nevertheless, the image of the vicious and thieving savage was what dominated the fears of the Nebraska pioneers.

44. "Territorial Governors," accessed April 8, 2025, https://usgennet.org/usa/ne/topic/resources//OLLibrary/collections/volIV/pages/v4s2p027.htm
45. "History of Nebraska," accessed April 8, 2025, https://usgennet.org/usa/ne/topic/resources//OLLibrary/MWHNE/mwhne340.htm

It is interesting to note that the danger of Indian depredation was likely overplayed by governors in their quest to build the economic base of the territory. One argument for that position is given by Howard Lamar in his landmark study of South Dakota territorial politics. Lamar argued that, for a territory in desperate need of revenue, government contracts that accompanied forts and infantrymen were a way in which to build territorial wealth.[46] Given the supplies and infrastructure required by garrisoning officers and infantrymen, demand for local farmers and ranchers' products is driven up, and the development of the land and building of infrastructure is needed, engaging local industries. Fighting Indians—real or imagined—was good for business.

Along these lines, we find in the first message from acting Territorial Governor Thomas Cuming on January 16, 1855, a plea to the newly formed legislature to push for "'Telegraphic and Letter Mail Communication with the Pacific,' including the protection of emigrants and formation of settlements along the route through Nebraska, Utah, California and Oregon; the promotion of amicable relations with the Indians, and facilitating intercourse across the American continent."[47] To establish this, he calls for increased military garrisons and personnel. In the same speech, he also calls for a mobilization of civilians against the Native people:

> We have reason to believe that bands of the Sioux, Poncas, and other Indians, stimulated by poverty and rapacity, and emboldened by previous success, will renew their depredations upon immigrants, in the coming spring, or may, this winter, descend upon the frontier settlement. I therefore respectfully renew the recommendations of a late proclamation, that volunteer companies be organized for self protection, in every neighborhood, ready to move at any moment, wherever their services may be needed.[48]

Elsewhere in the address, Cuming calls for unity among the citizens of the territory, admonishing that though the citizenry be composed of Northerners and Southerners, all are united under the common identity of the Constitution and the principles of the founding fathers; a subtle nod toward the racial bond that all share.

> These Indians are fierce, they wear feathers and grunt. Most of us don't fit this idealized figure since we grunt only when overeating.
> Vine Deloria Jr., 1971

The subject of Native depredations—the myth versus the facts—is taken up in the first published history of Nebraska, written by A. T. Andreas and published in 1882. Andreas's own favorable attitude toward Native people is evident early on in the following passage:

> Notwithstanding the fact that, at the early settlement of the county, the country was infested and overrun by numerous bands of Indians belonging to various tribes, yet, contrary to expectation, in a place so new and so little civilized, the settlers suffered but little from them. Their relations with the whites, were, from the beginning, with but few exceptions, friendly and peaceable.

Andreas does record one incident in 1864 in which a small party from an unnamed tribe raided the Patton family farm, but he continues,

> Scares of this kind were frequent, but not general. Individual families were often startled by some causes, which at first, were thought to be hostile tribes, but which, in most cases, were unnecessary fright…
>
> With acquaintance with the Indians and their habits, the settlers became less fearful of them. And, although large bands continued to roam about the country, the settlements did not suffer from them, except in petty thefts at times. The presence of these bands became less frequent each year; still, even at the present day, small squads make periodical hunting excursions through the settled districts, but are perfectly peaceable and harmless. It is the return of the children to behold their inheritance, the hunting-grounds of their

---

46. Howard R. Lamar, *Dakota Territory 1861-1889: A Study of Frontier Politics* (New Haven: Yale University Press, 1956), 100-1.
47. *Messages and Proclamations of the Governors of Nebraska 1854-1941, Volume 1: 1854-1887,* ed. Addison Sheldon (Lincoln: Work Projects Administration and University of Nebraska, 1941), 10.
48. *Messages and Proclamations,* 12.

fathers, which the superior law of the whites says belongs to us who discovered it, rather than those who lived upon the soil centuries before the existence of the country was known to the claimants.

Lo, the poor Indian! Where is he? Driven from his possessions by a superior race—a Christian people—to become a homeless, wandering vagabond. Forced upon the territory of neighboring tribes, whose hostility must be resented in slaughter and the decimation of tribes. Such is the policy of a boasted civilization, such are the plans of a Christian people, as to bring about the extinction of a race by inciting internal destruction and annihilation. The idea is perhaps more forcibly put by the rural poet in his plain and homely phrase thus—
Onst the wild Injuns hyar tuk their delight;
Fisht, fit and bled.
Now the inhabitants is mostly white,
With nary a red.[49]

Andreas's conclusion hearkens back to the idea of racial replacement that we've seen throughout. His closing remarks highlight a popular sentiment that a preferable solution to the Indian Problem is to let them fight out amongst themselves and bring about their own extinction.

The general alarm from Cuming's speech contrasted with Andreas's favorable historical account, suggests that depredations by Native people were considered more significant when they threatened the larger economic interests of the territory. Though as the territory moved toward statehood, and population increased, hostility toward Natives grew in the population. With increased political and legal power, Nebraska Natives became even more marginalized.

III: 1867 – 1887: Statehood and Equality Before the Law [sic]

This period marks an intensified erasure of Native culture and history. As statehood is achieved, a creation narrative emerges; as the institutions of statehood grow they are inextricably linked to education. Generations of new Nebraskans must learn about and be proud of their state.

A state motto is a useful starting point to understand that entity's political culture and is meant to express the dominant beliefs or ideals within it. By "political culture," I adopt Lucian Pye's definition that "Political culture is the set of attitudes, beliefs, and sentiments, which give order and meaning to a political process and which provide the underlying assumptions and rules that govern behavior in the political system."[50] In this discussion, I will be addressing the political culture of Nebraska state government. And within the definition, the elements about *underlying assumptions* and *rules that govern behavior* will be germane to the discussion in what follows. A state motto projects to outsiders how the territory or state thinks about and acts towards its citizens.

Just months after statehood was achieved, on June 14, 1867, Nebraska's first governor, David Butler, signed into law H.R. 41, "An Act to Provide for Procuring a Seal for the State of Nebraska," which specified the motto, "Equality Before the Law," be included upon the seal.[51]

The motto was certainly in accordance with national political sentiment; Congress had passed the 14th amendment in June of 1866. Butler and Albert Wiles, the author of the bill, were Nebraska Republicans, the majority party in the state legislature. In April 1866, the Republicans adopted a party philosophy that expressed: "Resolved, that the party which has triumphantly sustained and vindicated the government of the United States and carried it safely through four years of sanguinary war, waged by the enemies of civil and religious liberty, owes it to itself, to its cherished principles, and to humanity to secure liberty and *equality before the law* to all men."[52] When the State of Nebraska was admitted to the Union on March 1, 1867, citizenship was open to recently liberated African American adults, and suffrage was granted to all males.[53]

The Nebraska State motto interests me for two reasons. First, "Equality before the law" meant different things to different people. Second, among the

---

49. A. T. Andreas, *History of the State of Nebraska,* Kansas Collection Books, Alice Vosika, ed., accessed April 8, 2025, https://www.kancoll.org/books/andreas_ne/saline/saline-p1.html#indian
50. "Political Culture." *International Encyclopedia of the Social Sciences. Encyclopedia.com.* (May 5, 2025). https://www.encyclopedia.com/social-sciences/applied-and-social-sciences-magazines/political-culture-0
51. James E. Potter, "'Equality Before the Law': Thoughts on the Origin of Nebraska's State Motto," *Nebraska History* 91 (2010): 117.
52. Quoted in Potter, "Equality Before the Law," 119.
53. Potter, "Equality Before the Law," 119.

> If the white man wants to live in peace with the Indian, he can live in peace... Treat all men alike. Give them all the same law. Give them all an even chance to live and grow. All men were made by the same Great Spirit Chief. They are all brothers. The Earth is the mother of all people, and all people should have equal rights upon it.
>
> White Elk

various interpretations of the motto, none of them applied to the Native population of the state. They were excluded from Nebraska's political culture. At least, as we will see, in any positive sense.

An important point in this discussion is the fact that, through the passage of a state constitution, under the provisions of the United States Constitution, inhabitants of the state *ought to be* recognized as free, with equal access to all provisions provided by the Constitution, and equal protection under the law. This precedent was argued by Charles Sumner in his landmark case, *Roberts v. Boston,* of 1850. Sumner presented that argument to demonstrate that racial discrimination in education was unconstitutional. He argued that under the concept of equality shared by the US Constitution and the Massachusetts State Constitution that there is an obligation upon the state for equal treatment of all.[54] Sumner was certainly not unknown to Nebraska Republicans of the time and an affinity is apparent in their sentiments about equality before the law.

It is clear that the lawmakers in Nebraska did not view the matter as Sumner did. Governor David Butler was in favor of removing Native people from the state —in violation of their property rights granted through treaties, and upheld by the Constitution. In his Third Inaugural Message, delivered on January 6, 1871, he made the argument that the high cost of bringing Natives to trial justified their removal to Indian Country—which by this time had shrunk considerably, being restricted to what is now the state of Oklahoma. The high cost of trial is certainly a flimsy argument; Butler's remark about choice agriculture land betrays his actual desire for removal. Butler says,

> Within the borders of our State are several Indian Reservations, embracing some of the choicest agricultural lands in the State, I am fully satisfied it would be better for both whites and Indians, could these titles be extinguished and the Indians removed, either to the Indian Territory, or some other place designated by the general government. Many depredations have been committed by members of the tribes occupying these reservations, and it has been found very difficult to bring the guilty parties to trial. A crime is committed in one of our newly organized counties; the United States courts decide they have no jurisdiction; as a result, this new county, with little or no money in its treasury, must at a heavy expense, arrest the parties, indict and bring them to trial, and in event of either conviction or discharge, find its treasury sadly depleted, perhaps entirely bankrupt. Some remedy should be devised, and I recommend that you memorialize Congress to remove, as soon as practicable, all Indians from our State, and that in the interval, jurisdiction be given the United States courts to try all cases of crime committed by members of the tribes in treaty with the Government within the limits of our State.[55]

The duration between Butler's promotion of "Equality Before the Law" as the state motto and this address was less than four years. Butler's observations about jurisdictional issues and the high cost of a trial for Native defendants were likely due to one high profile case—*The United States v. Yellow Sun et al.*—in which four Pawnee men were charged with murder-ing a settler, and was tried in federal court in Omaha.[56] As we will soon see in the discussion of this case, the high cost of the trial was likely attributable more to the prejudicial and unjust treatment of the Native defendants than anything else. This suggests that Butler might have been exaggerating the issue of cost as a reason for removal. The cherished principles of 1866 seem to have been pushed aside for economic growth.

---

54. Charles Sumner, *His Complete Works* (Boston: Lee and Shepard, 1900), 54. https://hdl.handle.net/2027/uc1.a0002683779
55. *Messages and Proclamations of the Governors of Nebraska*, 314.
56. James Riding In, "*The United States v. Yellow Sun et al.* (The Pawnee People): A Case Study of Institutional and Societal Racism and U.S. Justice in Nebraska from the 1850s to 1870s," in *Native Historians Write Back: Decolonizing American Indian History,* eds. Susan A. Miller and James Riding In (Lubbock: Texas Tech University Press, 2011), 152

Nebraska's second governor was likewise in favor of Native removal for economic reasons. In Robert Furnas's inaugural message, delivered on January 13, 1873, he said,

> With great earnestness I call your attention to the new settlements on our western border — the rapid extension of civilization in that direction. The people who are making efforts and sacrifices to open and populate that portion of our state, look to you with interest and great confidence for such legislation as will aid them in their noble work. In considering their wants, not least in the many, is the question of continuing the Indians on their present reservations. The class of our citizens to whom I now refer are enduring a multitude of privations incident to the settlement of all new countries, and exhibiting a commendable degree of pioneer enterprise. They should no longer be subjected to the additional and perplexing embarrassment produced by the presence of the nomadic race. In addition, the valuable lands now held by these aborigines should be permitted to pass into the hands of intelligent, enterprising citizens, who would render them productive; and further, they being exclusively the wards of the general government, we having no control over or management of them whatever, should not be subjected to their retarding influences. The commendable policy indicated by the government could be more successfully, satisfactorily, and expeditiously accomplished by locating them elsewhere, and to themselves.[57]

In this selection, as in the previous one, the rights and protections of the Native people are viewed as obstacles toward further growth. Therefore, Furnas echoes Butler in urging state government to intervene with the law of the land for the economic benefit of a certain segment of society.

A final illustration of the failure to recognize the equal status of Native peoples in Nebraska comes from Nebraska State Historical Society Superintendent Addison Sheldon's school textbook, *Nebraska Civil Government*, published in 1924.[58] Sheldon's

> *Maka ke wakan* — the land is sacred. These words are at the core of our being. The land is our mother, the rivers our blood. Take our land away and we die. That is, the Indian in us dies.
>
> Mary Brave Bird

omissions underscore the power inherent in being in control of the historical narrative. He traces the following "principles of free government" from their English origin to the Nebraska Territory:

> The Principles of Free Government:
> No human being shall be deprived of freedom, except upon a fair trial for offences against society.
> Every person shall enjoy freedom of speech, of the press, of peaceable public assembly, and of religious worship, being responsible for abuse thereof.
> No person shall be deprived of his private property except for public purposes upon payment of its value.
> The people have the right to govern themselves in an orderly manner.[59]

It escaped Sheldon's treatment that confinement to reservations with the inability to leave them without punishment was a frequent reality for Nebraska tribes. That the Code of Indian Offenses of 1883 made traditional religious practices illegal and was not repealed until 1978.[60] That Native people had been dispossessed of their land and were under constant threat of being removed. The dominance of Anglo-Saxon history earlier noted has thus left a distorted view of political life in Nebraska — and indeed, across the United States — in the minds of generations of Nebraska students. The principles listed above have not been consistently applied to all inhabitants throughout the history of the state, and many are still struggling to achieve the ideals contained therein.

---

57. *Messages and Proclamations of the Governors of Nebraska*, 389.
58. Addison E. Sheldon, *Nebraska Civil Government* (Lincoln: The University Publishing Company, 1924).
59. Sheldon, *Nebraska Civil Government*, 30-33.
60. Fund, Native American Rights. "Healing from the Dark Period of Religious and Cultural Persecution." *Native American Rights Fund,* 13 May 2024, https://narf.org/history-religious-persecution/

I will now turn my discussion to three court cases that demonstrate the extent to which courts deviated from the ideal of equality before the law when Native individuals and rights were in question. These cases occurred in Nebraska Courts during the formative years of statehood, with ramifications that affected Native peoples across the nation. We will begin with the 1869 case *The United States v. Yellow Sun et al.*, then discuss the 1879 case of *U.S. ex Rel. Standing Bear v. Crook,* and conclude with the 1880 case, *Elk v. Wilkins.*

The case of *The United States v. Yellow Sun et al.,* (hereafter *Yellow Sun*) is one that exemplifies inequality in the administration of justice in the burgeoning State of Nebraska. Though the *Yellow Sun* case is now relatively unknown, Pawnee historian James Riding In argues that at its time, 1869, it was "the most important Indian trial to date in Nebraska."[61] Newspapers and public opinion at the time showed bias against the Native population at the time, though Riding In notes that the *Omaha Weekly Herald* frequently published items critical of the injustices carried out at the indigenous population of the state. Nevertheless, systemic racism affected all stages of the investigation and subsequent trial.

On May 8, 1869, Polk County homesteader Edward McMurty mysteriously disappeared. He had set off to the northeast from his homestead for Columbus, but neither made it to his destination, nor returned home. His route necessitated crossing the Platte River, and several days after his disappearance, neighbors went out in search of him, and near where he would have crossed the Platte, on an island typical of that shallow sandy river, they encountered an encampment of Pawnee men, women, and children. One of the men, Yellow Sun, had what appeared to be a swollen jaw and drops of blood on his shirt. The neighbors accused him of murdering their friend, which Yellow Sun denied, and a search of the island turned up no trace of McMurty. Over the next month, the search intensified, carried out by armed vigilantes, and on June 19th, McMurty's body was found on the same island, weighed down in a shallow pond. News of the discovery spread rapidly, with Yellow Sun and the other men blamed as the perpetrators, and the majority public opinion called for their swift death without a trial, that is, vigilante justice.[62]

> Owing to the prejudice that exists in the minds of the people here, I believe it is impossible to secure justice in any case in which the rights of the Indian [are] involved in the U.S. or state courts, he has no representation in either, no voice in the government under which he is tried.
>
> Pawnee Superintendent
> Samuel M. Janney, 1870

Vigilante justice for the men was avoided, but in the court trial that ensued, the procedures were so grossly unjust that the experience brought about the deaths of many of the defendants, as suggested by Riding In.[63] To begin with, the men were coerced into a confession under extreme duress, without any actual evidence presented against them. In a council of Pawnee Chiefs, Pawnee Agents, assorted lawmen, and armed citizens, an ultimatum was presented that annuities and cash payments owed to the Pawnee by treaty rights, would be withheld until the "guilty" men were handed over. The Pawnee at this time were already demoralized, experiencing starvation and severe economic hardship, and the external threat by both pioneers and the Lakota kept them confined to their reservation. The meager annuities were their main source of sustenance. Under these circumstances, Pawnee chiefs acquiesced and surrendered Yellow Sun and seven other men: Horse Driver, Little Wolf, Great Traveler, Man Scared of Horses, Lucky Man, Lame Man, and Young Fox.[64] These men were transferred to a jail in Omaha, and subsequently, Pawnee Agent "Janney sent the annuity goods to the starving Pawnees."[65]

The accused men first appeared in court during preliminary hearings to obtain evidence against the suspects, during which only white homesteaders were allowed to testify, essentially repeating the highly circumstantial stories previously told, and only being able to identify three of the eight Pawnees on trial—Yellow Sun, Horse Driver, and Little

---

61. Riding In, "*The United States v. Yellow Sun,*" 140.
62. Riding In, "*The United States v. Yellow Sun,*" 145-6.
63. Riding In, "*The United States v. Yellow Sun,*" 155.
64. Riding In, "*The United States v. Yellow Sun,*" 149.
65. Riding In, "*The United States v. Yellow Sun,*" 149.

Wolf. None of the prisoners were allowed to speak on their own behalf. Next, Pawnee Chiefs and other tribal members were subpoenaed to Omaha and kept there, in an attempt to coerce the accused men to confess. They were detained from June to early August, when the Pawnees would normally be on their summer buffalo hunt. Riding In suggests that this was a tactic to increase the pressure upon the men to confess.[66]

After the preliminary hearings, five of the men were released, and the three who had been identified by the homesteaders, and an additional suspect implicated in the hearings, named Blue Hawk, proceeded to trial. The trial was heard in a federal circuit court in Omaha, beginning on November 5th, with Judge Elmer Dundy presiding. Defense attorney Chase tried to neutralize the white jurors' prejudices by pleading to them to "consider the evidence as they would in the trial of a white person," and questioned the legality of the trial, as the U.S. Constitution requires a jury of one's peers, and an all-white jury did not meet that requirement.[67] One concession to fairness was the allowance of interpreters for the defendants and Pawnee witnesses. The jury heard witnesses including the same friends and neighbors who had originally accused Yellow Sun; Pawnee Chiefs, who explained Yellow Sun had removed an infected tooth, thus resulting in a swollen jaw; and even a fellow prisoner, a white man who shared a cell with the accused, who claimed that the men had made gestures and sounds such as "pow-pow" that indicated having committed the murder. On November 9th, attorneys offered their closing arguments, and while white protestors chanted outside, jurors took just five hours to return a guilty verdict for each man.[68] Chase filed a motion for an arrest of judgment and a new trial, which was granted on the grounds of the inconclusive evidence. The *Herald* published a story charging "that the defendants had been convicted by mob pressure."[69]

What followed was a roundabout legal maneuvering to ensure the new trial would be heard in a federal court. The defense's fear was that if the trial

> When I lay down to sleep I have to lay my head on my revolver to save my life and property… We are surrounded by pale-faces and cannot go out and kill game, and we want to go south and be free.
>
> Pitaresaru, Pawnee Chief, 1874

was heard in a state court, racial prejudices would be even greater. Furthermore, the defense was encouraged by then President Grant's more favorable views on Indian policy, with assurances of support.[70] Nevertheless, judges Dillon and Dundy ruled that the trial would be heard in a state court, and in November 1870, the four men were indicted on charges of murder.[71] Janney, the Pawnee agent, advocated on behalf of the men, pleading for release on bond while they awaited their trial. And in June 1871, after *twenty-two* months of "tortuous confinement," the men were released on a $5000 bond.[72] Pioneer jails were crude and miserable. The men were emaciated and near death. Each man had attempted suicide at some point during their imprisonment, despite the practice being prohibited by their religion. Yellow Sun died several months after release, and the remaining men soon after.[73] Their trial, scheduled to be heard at a Lancaster County court, was removed from the docket on October 23, 1871, thus ending this legal saga.[74]

To conclude the discussion of the *Yellow Sun* case, the words of an editorial, published in the *Herald* on April 30, 1871, reflect a progressive view that condemns the racism that pervaded the case, "This Pawnee Indian case is a wretched, almost cruel farce. It is a burning disgrace to the law, and to those officers of it who are responsible for one of the most wicked mockeries that ever blackened our criminal jurisprudence.[75]

---

66. Riding In, "*The United States v. Yellow Sun,*" 150.
67. Riding In, "*The United States v. Yellow Sun,*" 152.
68. Riding In, "*The United States v. Yellow Sun,*" 154.
69. Riding In, "*The United States v. Yellow Sun,*" 154.
70. Riding In, "*The United States v. Yellow Sun,*" 155.
71. Riding In, "*The United States v. Yellow Sun,*" 156.
72. Riding In, "*The United States v. Yellow Sun,*" 156.
73. Riding In, "*The United States v. Yellow Sun,*" 157.
74. Riding In, "*The United States v. Yellow Sun,*" 156.
75. Riding In, "*The United States v. Yellow Sun,*" 158.

Our discussion continues with the case of the Trial of Chief Standing Bear. This case is probably the most famous of the three discussed here, gaining national attention in 2019 when a bronze statue of the chief by artist Benjamin Victor was installed in the National Statuary Hall in Washington DC.[76] The surrounding discussion brought Standing Bear's story back into the public consciousness, raising awareness of the injustices endured by the Ponca Tribe as the United States consolidated territory through tribal land dispossession. In 1877, the Poncas were forcibly removed from their reservation, their homelands, located along the Niobrara River in northeast Nebraska, to Indian Territory in Oklahoma. During the 600-mile Trail of Tears, and subsequent settlement in a harsh, unfamiliar environment, it is estimated that around one-third of the Ponca's population died.[77] In 1879, after the death of Standing Bear's son Bear Shield, Standing Bear and twenty-nine others fled back to Nebraska to bury his son in their homelands. They journeyed over 600 miles in the dead of winter, traveling by night and hiding by day, making it as far as the Omaha reservation, where they were arrested by the U.S. Army that March. Standing Bear was interviewed by Thomas Henry Tibbles, assistant editor of the *Omaha Daily Herald*, and the story brought forth national support for the cause, with attorneys John Lee Webster and A. J. Poppleton stepping in to defend the chief in court. The trial concluded on May 12, 1879 when Judge Elmer Dundy ruled that noncitizen Natives, "were defined as persons in terms of federal law and entitled to review under habeas corpus protections," in this case, "a constitutionally based appeal used to determine whether a person is restrained or imprisoned without due process."[78] Standing Bear and his relatives were subsequently released from custody.

The Standing Bear case is often heralded as a landmark decision insofar as Dundy's opinion stated, "That an *Indian* is a PERSON within the meaning of the laws of the United States,"[79] the first such recognition under U.S. law. Nevertheless, other features

> I want to go back to my old place.... I want to save myself and my tribe. If a white man had land, and someone should swindle him, that man would try to get it back, and you would not blame him.
>
> Standing Bear, 1879

of Dundy's ruling are less discussed, and invite critical scrutiny. First, As Frances Kaye points out, "most other American Indians and Standing Bear's 'personhood' depended upon his explicit assimilation and renunciation of his Indian status."[80] In other words, tribal members must give up their language and culture in order to be considered a person. This underscores a widespread inequality insofar as in the eyes of the law, Natives *as* Natives were still considered an inferior race. Next, Dundy's ruling may have set Standing Bear and his relatives free, but the ruling upheld that tribal members needed permission from the United States government to enter reservations established for other tribes, violations of which were punishable by arrest.[81] Standing Bear could not in

> This hand is not the color of yours, but if I pierce it, I shall feel pain. If you pierce your hand, you also feel pain. The blood that will flow from mine will be of the same color as yours. I am a man. The same God made us both.
>
> Standing Bear, 1879

---

76. "Chief Standing Bear Statue," Architect of the Capitol, accessed February 21, 2025, https://www.aoc.gov/explore-capitol-campus/art/chief-standing-bear-statue
77. Kevin Abourezk," Ponca Chief Standing Bear completes one last journey of triumph," *indianz.com*, September 23, 2019, https://indianz.com/News/2019/09/23/ponca-chief-standing-bear-makes-one-last.asp
78. Dennis J. Smith, "Trial of Standing Bear," *Encyclopedia of the Great Plains*, ed. David J. Wishart, accessed February 21, 2025, http://plainshumanities.unl.edu/encyclopedia/doc/egp.pd.053
79. Jennifer Davis, "Chief Standing Bear and His Landmark Civil Rights Case," *Library of Congress Blogs*, November 21, 2019, https://blogs.loc.gov/law/2019/11/chief-standing-bear-and-his-landmark-civil-rights-case/
80. Frances W. Kaye, *Goodlands: A Meditation and History on the Great Plains* (Edmonton, CA: Athabasca University Press, 2011), 181.
81. "What does it mean?," *nebraskastudies.org*, Accessed February 25, 2025, https://www.nebraskastudies.org/en/1875-1899/the-trial-of-standing-bear/what-does-it-mean/

fact return to his homelands to fulfill his son's wish to be buried there. Additionally, this puts an undue restriction upon the personal liberties of tribal members, many of whom, for instance the Ponca and the Omaha, are related to one another and accustomed to freely pass between the reservations. Finally, it is a common misperception that Dundy's ruling made the Poncas, or Native Americans generally, citizens of the United States. It would be another forty-five years until the Indian Citizenship Act of 1924 before Natives were recognized as US citizens. Interestingly, an important legal case in that long process was heard in the State of Nebraska.

The case of *Elk v. Wilkins* followed soon after Standing Bear's victory. In fact, the plaintiff John Elk was represented by A.J. Poppleton and John L. Webster, the same attorneys who defended Standing Bear.[82] Elk was a Winnebago man who lived off the reservation, in a wigwam near Omaha. On April 6, 1880, Elk registered to vote for an Omaha city council election, and was denied by Charles Wilkins, the registrar for the fifth ward in the city. In the court records for the case, it is established that Elk had severed ties with his tribe, was employed, and was a resident of Douglas County for more than forty days, which met the qualifications under the laws of the State of Nebraska to be registered as a voter.[83] On April 14, 1880, at the U.S. circuit court in Omaha, Elk filed a petition for citizenship and sued Wilkins, demanding $6,000 to compensate for Wilkins' denial of his right to vote and for violating his constitutional rights. On November 8, 1880, Wilkins' attorneys filed their response, asserting that Elk's petition did not provide sufficient evidence to justify the need for compensation in that amount, and asserted that the court did not hold jurisdiction over Elk and his petition.[84] In January 1881 the case was heard, ruling in favor of Wilkins by sustaining that even if the facts of the complaint are true, there are not sufficient facts for a cause of action, in other words, Elk would not be compensated in any amount. The court also filed a writ of error, which referred the case to the Supreme Court.[85] Nebraska was reluctant

> I want you to help us keep this thing citizenship, away from us.
>
> Unknown Omaha man petitioning Congress after allotment, 1887

to decide on the issue of whether Natives are U.S. citizens.

It would prove that the Supreme Court was likewise reluctant to grant citizenship to Native Americans. *Elk v. Wilkins* was argued April 28, 1884, and decided on November 3, 1884, ruling in favor of Wilkins. Justice Gray wrote the opinion of the court, declaring "that there were only two categories of U.S. citizens, those by birth and those by naturalization, and naturalization could not occur without federal action."[86] Although Elk had been born in the United States, in a geographical sense, he had been born within a tribal nation, which in the opinion of the court, was akin to be born in a foreign country, or to "ambassadors or other public ministers of foreign nations."[87] The opinion detailed many scenarios in which Natives might be considered birthright citizens, or made citizens through federal action, but the conclusion for Elk was, "absent federal action, an Indian born in tribal relations could not become a citizen simply by living apart from his tribe."[88] Jeanette Wolfley summarizes the situation Elk and many other tribal members were in this way, "Indians were neither citizens nor aliens; they were not white under the naturalization laws, or slaves, or persons in a previous condition of servitude. Barring special acts, treaties, or a constitutional amendment, many Indians appeared to exist in a legal vacuum."[89]

The ruling also rested on racist views that were to have devastating effects on Native nations across the United States.

Gray's decision upheld the view that Natives were childlike and savage; they were classified as an

---

82. Bethany R. Berger, "Birthright Citizenship on Trial: Elk v. Wilkins and United States v. Wong Kim Ark," Cardozo Law Review 37, no. 4 (April 2016): 1210.
83. Berger, "Birthright Citizenship on Trial," 1215.
84. Berger, "Birthright Citizenship on Trial," 1233.
85. Berger, "Birthright Citizenship on Trial," 1233
86. Berger, "Birthright Citizenship on Trial," 1235.
87. Justice Gray's opinion, cited in Berger, "Birthright Citizenship on Trial," 1235.
88. Berger, "Birthright Citizenship on Trial," 1235.
89. Jeanette Wolfley, "Jim Crow, Indian Style: The Disenfranchisement of Native Americans," American Indian Law Review 16, no. 1 (1991): 175.

inferior race. In his opinion, Gray wrote that Natives "were in a dependent condition, a state of pupilage, resembling that of a ward to his guardian."[90] Gray was in favor of governmental control to bring Natives to a higher level of civilization. Reformers on the East Coast, who were closely watching this case unfold, saw this as an opening to push legislation that would "promote" Native autonomy. Bethany Berger writes that Senator Henry Dawes attempted and failed to overturn the Elk decision, and soon after passed a bill, The Dawes Act, to allot Native land individually and force tribal members to live on their individual plots, and sell off surplus land, thus preventing communal farming and hunting.[91] Tribal members who fulfilled the conditions would eventually become citizens. The guiding idea was that by owning property and living individualistically, Natives would be taught "selfishness, which is at the bottom of civilization" which would "lift him up into citizenship and manhood."[92] Furthermore, the surplus land sold to white settlers would surround tribal members with upstanding, enterprising citizens, thus providing an ideal to which Natives could aspire.

While reformers acted with what they considered good intentions, "the allotment era that the [Dawes] act ushered in is today universally viewed as one of the darkest chapters in the annals of federal-Indian relations."[93] The imposed way of life eroded traditional beliefs and practices. Since most tribal members could not handle the immense cultural shift—a terrible burden forced upon them— their farms failed, and their land was sold off or foreclosed upon. And millions of acres of land were lost when surplus land was sold or leased by the government. As Mark Scherer concludes, "the ultimate effect of the allotment program was to separate the Native Americans from millions of acres of their lands without accomplishing any of the 'reforms' intended by the act's proponents."[94] Readers are encouraged to consult Judith Boughter's book, *Betraying the Omaha Nation, 1790-1916*, for an in-depth coverage of the effects of the Dawes Act upon the Omaha Nation.[95]

IV: Recovering Native Voices

The preceding sections have provided a glimpse into the developing political culture in the State of Nebraska. Despite the dire conditions that existed on Nebraska reservations, exceptional individuals grew up and out of their conditions. Here I will introduce four of them. The four were among the first generations of children born on Indian Country reservations. This means that they had contact with pre-reservation culture. However, secondly, they were all products of Western education through boarding schools and American institutions of higher education. Therefore, their perspective is unique; they were able to convey culture, but more importantly the need for change, to a wider audience for the first time. In spite of their immersion in white culture, they were able to maintain their Native identity and fought in important ways for their relatives.

- Susette La Flesche (1854 – 1903)
- Charles Eastman (1858 – 1939)
- Angel De Cora (1871 – 1919)
- Henry Roe Cloud (1884 – 1950)

Susette La Flesche, *Inshata Theumba* ["Bright Eyes"] (1854–1903)

Susette LaFlesche was born in Bellevue, Nebraska, in 1854 and grew up on the Omaha Indian Reservation. She was the oldest daughter of Joseph La Flesche, the last recognized chief of the Omaha. "From 1862 to 1869 she attended the Presbyterian Mission Boarding Day School on the reservation, where she learned to read, write, and speak English, as well as to cook and sew." La Flesche continued her education at "the Elizabeth Institute for Young Ladies, a private school in New Jersey." There she became known for her writing ability: an essay written during her senior year was published by the *New York Tribune*. After graduation, La Flesche returned home to her reservation and later began work as a teacher at the government school on the reservation, where she taught for several years.[96]

---

90. Elk v. Wilkins, 112 U.S. 94 (1884)
91. Officially titled the General Allotment Act of 1887. Mark R. Scherer, "Dawes Act," *Encyclopedia of the Great Plains*, ed. David J. Wishart, last modified March 2025, http://plainshumanities.unl.edu/encyclopedia/doc/egp.law.015#:~:text=Formally%20titled%20the%20General%20Allotment,individual%20members%20of%20each%20tribe.
92. Dawes, cited in Berger, "Birthright Citizenship on Trial," 1237.
93. Scherer, "Dawes Act."
94. Scherer, "Dawes Act."
95. Judith Boughter, *Betraying the Omaha Nation, 1790-1916* (Norman: University of Oklahoma Press, 1998).

Susette La Flesche. Nebraska State Historical Society.

La Flesche met Thomas Tibbles, an editor with the *Omaha World-Herald,* and together they began to publicize the forced removal of the Ponca, and the poor conditions on the southern Ponca reservation in Oklahoma.[97] La Flesche came to national prominence while serving as Chief Standing Bear's interpreter during the *Standing Bear v Crook* case in 1879.[98] Following the trial, La Flesche joined her half-brother Francis La Flesche (also a writer and anthropologist of note), Standing Bear, and Tibbles on a speaking tour of the East Coast,[99] eventually testifying in Washington, DC, before a congressional committee about the Ponca removal.[100] Throughout her life, she continued to do speaking tours, write, and illustrate work with Tibbles, whom she married in 1881. La Flesche's ability and poise inspired many activists in her time, most prominent among them Helen Hunt Jackson.[101] Her voice brought attention to the unjust treatment of Nebraska Natives during a period of upheaval and rapid change.

Further reading for Susette La Flesche:

La Flesche, Susette. "The Plight of the Ponca Indians." Faneuil Hall, Boston MA. November 25, 1879. https://speakingwhilefemale.co/indigenous-la-flesche1/

La Flesche, Susette. "Nedawi," In *The Singing Spirit: Early Short Stories by North American Indians,* ed. Bernd C. Peyer. Tucson: The University of Arizona Press, 1989. https://pages.ucsd.edu/~rfrank/class_web/ES-110/ETHN110articles/Plains/peyer_ps.pdf

Charles Eastman, *Ohiyesa* (1858–1939)

Eastman was born to a mixed-blood mother and a Santee father on the Santee Dakota reservation in Redwood Falls, Minnesota. After the US-Dakota War of 1862, the Santee were exiled from Minnesota, eventually settling in north-central Nebraska, but Eastman's family went to North Dakota and Canada. At the insistence of his father, Eastman pursued higher education at Kimball Union Academy, Beloit College, Knox College, and he graduated from Dartmouth College. He then attended medical school at Boston University, earning a medical degree in 1890.[102]

University of Oregon philosophy professor Scott Pratt presents a reading of Eastman that contextualizes him within the worlds of Indigenous and white civilization, and within the intellectual current of

> I have said "a conquered people." I do not know that I have the right to say that. We are helpless, it is true; but at heart we do not feel that we are a conquered people. We are human beings; God made us as well as you.
>
> Susette La Flesche, 1879

---

96. Emma Rothberg, "Susette La Flesche Tibbles ("Bright Eyes") (1854-1903)," National Women's History Museum, https://www.womenshistory.org/education-resources/biographies/susette-la-flesche-tibbles-bright-eyes. This website provided both paraphrased and directly quoted information in the preceding paragraph.
97. "Susette La Flesche," Wikipedia, accessed spring 2025, https://en.wikipedia.org/wiki/Susette_La_Flesche.
98. Ibid.
99. "Francis La Flesche," Wikipedia, accessed spring 2025, https://en.wikipedia.org/wiki/Francis_La_Flesche.
100. "Susette La Flesche," Wikipedia.
101. Ibid.
102. Tim Pacl, "Boy Scouts of America Founder: Charles Eastman," Capitol Area Council North Shore District Boy Scouts of America, Mar. 14, 2023, https://nsdbsa.org/boy-scouts-of-america-founder-charles-eastman/.

Charles Eastman. Library of Congress.

As a child I understood how to give; I have forgotten that grace since I became civilized. I lived the natural life, whereas I now live the artificial. Any pretty pebble was valuable to me then; every growing tree an object of reverence. Now I worship with the white man before a painted landscape whose value is estimated in dollars! Thus the Indian is reconstructed, as the natural rocks are ground to powder, and made into artificial blocks which may be built into the walls of modern society.[104]

Having a foot in both cultures, Eastman offered a way to reconcile a version of Christianity with Native religion, though he rejected "Christian Civilization": "There is no such thing as 'Christian civilization'," he concludes. "I believe that Christianity and modern civilization are opposed and irreconcilable, and that the spirit of Christianity and of our ancient religion is essentially the same."[105]

Pratt also argues that Eastman played a role in the larger intellectual movement of the late 19th and early 20th Century:

> [He] became part of the Pan-Indian movement that began in the late 19th century through the work of a number of Native intellectuals, many educated in boarding schools. The signal organization for the movement was the Society of American Indians (SAI), founded in 1911 . . . . The SAI's goals and program were never clearly settled, but the work of several of its leaders adopted views that followed the path set by Eastman.[106]

his time.[103] He posits that Eastman, in *The Soul of the Indian*, offers a philosophical framework used by Indigenous people in their stand against settler colonialism. At the center of the framework is the belief that "every creature possesses a soul in some degree, though not necessarily a soul conscious of itself. The tree, the waterfall, the grizzly bear, each is an embodied Force, and as such an object of reverence." Within the worldview in which every created being has a soul, Eastman argued that people behave differently, with respect. Eastman considers this way of life "religious," and explains, "Every act of [an Indian's] life is, in a very real sense, a religious act. He recognizes the spirit in all creation, and believes that he draws from it spiritual power." Being thankful daily in prayer develops reciprocal relations with all creation. From this "ontological view of relational beings," Eastman provides a critical perspective on settler society. He says,

Further reading for Charles Eastman:

Eastman (Ohiyesa), Charles Alexander. *The Soul of the Indian: An Interpretation*. Boston and New York: Houghton Mifflin Company, 1911. https://hdl.handle.net/2027/uc2.ark:/13960/fk3ws8hs13

Eastman (Ohiyesa), Charles A. *From the Deep Woods to Civilization: Chapters in the Autobiography of an Indian*. Boston: Little, Brown, and Company, 1916. https://hdl.handle.net/2027/mdp.39015063093663

---

103. Scott L. Pratt, "Agency and Sovereignty in American Indian Philosophy," *Pragmatism Today* 10, no. 2 (2019): 16-23, https://www.pragmatismtoday.com/winter2019/Agency-and-Sovereignty-in-American-Indian-Philosophy-Scott-L-Pratt.pdf
104. Charles Eastman, *The Soul of the Indian* (Boston and New York: Houghton Mifflin, 1911), 88, quoted in Pratt, "Agency and Sovereignty…".
105. Interpretation and Eastman's quotations from Pratt, "Agency and Sovereignty," 17.
106. Pratt, "Agency and Sovereignty," 17.

Angel De Cora, c. 1900. Nebraska State Historical Society.

Angel De Cora, *Hinook-Mahiwi-Kalinaka* (1871–1919)

Angel De Cora was a Ho-Chunk artist, educator, and activist. She was born on the Winnebago Indian Reservation in 1871. Her Winnebago name translates to "Fleecy Cloud Floating in Space," and she was a member of the Thunderbird clan. In 1883, she was taken without her parents' consent to the Hampton Normal and Agricultural Institute in Virginia, a school for Black freedmen which began accepting Native children in 1878; she graduated in 1891. De Cora excelled in art and continued her education at Smith College's School of Art , graduating in 1896, to much acclaim. At the Drexel Institute of Art, Science, and Industry in Philadelphia, De Cora undertook the study of illustration under Howard Pyle. Soon after, her work was accepted and published in national magazines like *Harper's New Monthly Magazine.* Her artistic studies continued at the Cowles Art School in Boston, and the Boston Museum of Fine Arts School, where she had received a prestigious scholarship.[107]

De Cora achieved success as an illustrator and designer for several significant publications. In 1906, she took up a position to teach Native American Art at the Carlisle Indian Industrial School, where she developed a program to teach Native students traditional design. Of this innovative program, she wrote:

> The art department of Carlisle has taken a departure from the regular routine work of public schools. We do not study any of the European classics in art. We take the old symbolic figures and forms which we find on beadwork, pottery, and baskets for the basis of our study. We are familiarizing ourselves with the different styles and methods; then we create designs according to these old established methods and apply them to the products of the workshops of the school in such ways as wood-carving, printer's borders, metal work, wall decoration, weaving and needlework.
>
> There is a general revival throughout the country of the old handicrafts and skilled hands are in demand. Let me tell you that the Indian is an apt pupil for any sort of handicraft. The basket and textile weavers, pottery and metal workers are already well established. Each of these industries can be expanded in various directions both for utility and ornament.
>
> The simple dignity of Indian design lends itself well to ways of conventional art and I think the day has come when the American people must pause and give recognition to another phase of the Indian's nature which is his art.[108]

De Cora was recognized nationally and toured the country giving lectures and inspiring students. De Cora passed away from pneumonia and influenza in 1919. Though her time on earth was brief, De Cora left a considerable legacy. Neebinnaukzhik Southall, in her article "AIGA Design Journeys: Angel De Cora," provides a brief overview of De Cora's life and

---

107. Neebinnaukzhik Southall, "AIGA Design Journeys: Angel De Cora," The Native Graphic Design Project, (November 16, 2015): https://www.neebin.com/nativedesign/?p=426.
108. Proceedings of the Twenty-fifth Annual Meeting of the Lake Mohonk Conference of Friends of the Indian and other Dependent Peoples, Lake Mohonk Conference, 1907, 16-18, quoted in Neebinnaukzhik Southall, "AIGA Design Journeys: Angel De Cora."

Frontispiece for *The Middle Five* by Angel De Cora. Courtesy of Nebraska State Historical Society.

legacy.[109] Southall calls attention to speeches that De Cora gave that emphasize three points that were at the core of De Cora's message to a wider, white culture that operated with a constrained view of Native art and artists. According to Anne Gere, these were, "Indians' inherent artistic talent, the value of Indian art, and its place in American art."[110]

De Cora's independence and innovation, especially while as a practicing artist and teacher, ensured the survivance of Native art and culture.[111] The Angel De Cora Museum And Research Center is located on the Winnebago reservation. According to its website, their mission is:

> to identify, preserve, protect, and promote the history, art, culture, accomplishments and sacrifices of the Winnebago Tribe of Nebraska and its people. The museum also provides the community and public an opportunity to explore, learn, and experience the rich and unique history and culture. We are entrusted with the protection and revitalization of our Hōcąk traditions and are tasked with documenting lifeways, the retention of traditional knowledge, and other aspects of our cultural heritage .[112]

Further reading for Angel De Cora:

De Cora, Angel. "Angel De Cora—An Autobiography." *The Red Man* (March 1911): 279-85. https://carlisleindian.dickinson.edu/publications/red-man-vol-3-no-7

Fay, Eileen. "Angel De Cora: Indigenous American and Pyle Student." Brandywine Museum of Art Blog, March 1, 2021. https://www.brandywine.org/museum/blog/angel-de-cora-indigenous-american-and-pyle-student

Henry Roe Cloud, *Wo-Na-Xi-Lay-Hunka* (1884–1950)

Henry Roe Cloud was born on the Winnebago Indian Reservation on December 28, 1884. He was originally called *Wo-Na-Xi-Lay-Hunka*, or Chief of the Place of Fear. At the age of seven he was sent to the Genoa Indian Industrial School for two years, after which he returned home to Winnebago, and attended the Winnebago Indian school. There he converted to Christianity, and the name "Henry Cloud" was given to him by school administrator. In a flu epidemic *Wo-Na-Xi-Lay-Hunka*'s parents, grandparents, and many other relatives died between 1896 and 1897, after which he was again sent off the reservation to boarding school, first to the Santee Mission School, and then to Mount Herman School in Massachusetts. He excelled at Mount Herman and was accepted at Yale University. While attending Yale, he was adopted by Mary and Reverend Walter C. Roe, and subsequently he took Roe as a middle name.[113] In 1910, Roe Cloud became the first Native person to graduate from Yale, and he continued his education at the Auburn Theological

---

109. Neebinnaukzhik Southall, "AIGA Design Journeys: Angel De Cora.
110. Anne Ruggles Gere, "An Art of Survivance: Angel DeCora at Carlisle," *American Indian Quarterly* 28, no. 3/4 (2004): 649. http://www.jstor.org/stable/4138937
111. For a more complete discussion of this see Gere, "An Art of Survivance," 651.
112. "About Us," Angel De Cora Museum & Research Center, accessed April 9, 2025, https://winnebagotribe.com/angel-decora-museum/
113. Judith Ann Schiff, "Wonah'ilayhunka, Class of 1910," *Yale Alumni Magazine* (November/December 2003), https://archives.yalealumnimagazine.com/issues/03_11/old_yale.html

Henry Roe Cloud, c. 1910. Nebraska State Historical Society.

> "Everything Indian was to be destroyed [in the boarding schools]. How well do I remember marching with a dozen other Indian lads half a day round and round in a room in the government school because we were talking our Native language."
>
> Henry Roe Cloud, 1941

Seminary, earning a Bachelor of Divinity in 1913, and a year later he received a master of Divinity degree from Yale.

Roe Cloud's granddaughter, Renya K. Ramirez, a Native feminist and anthropologist, provides this brief assessment of his major achievements:

> Henry Roe Cloud was a pivotal activist, policy-maker, and intellectual in the early twentieth century. A major intellectual contribution was his argument that Native Americans should attend college. As a result, he founded and ran the very first college preparatory school for Indian youth, a revolutionary approach, since during the same time period Indian youth were usually sent to federal boarding schools that were solely vocational in nature. He coauthored the "Meriam Report" of 1928, and, according to available evidence, coauthored the Indian Reorganization Act of 1934—an act with positive and negative attributes. For example, it supported the indirect rule of tribal nations, while it founded contemporary tribal governments that could then organize and fight for tribal sovereignty.[114]

Ramirez's account of her grandfather's life is remarkable in many ways. Her approach is nuanced and culturally sensitive, in the course of which she explains Native protocols for archival materials and control of sensitive data. Furthermore, she is able to contextualize key documents published by Roe Cloud, such as his autobiography, which was written for a white audience in the early 20th century. Ramirez extended the article cited here into a book-length treatment of Roe Cloud and his wife, Elizabeth Bender Cloud. The citation for the book, and Roe Cloud's autobiography are listed below.

Further reading for Henry Roe Cloud:

Ramirez, Renya K. *Standing Up to Colonial Power: The Lives of Henry Roe Cloud and Elizabeth Bender Cloud.* Lincoln: Nebraska University Press, 2018.

Cloud, Henry Roe. "From Wigwam to Pulpit: A Red Man's Own Story of His Progress from Darkness to Light." Accessed April 9, 2025. https://hotcakencyclopedia.com/ho.Cloud-FromWigwamToPulpit.html

---

114. Ramirez, Renya K. "Henry Roe Cloud: A Granddaughter's Native Feminist Biographical Account." *Wicazo Sa Review* 24, no. 2 (2009): 77–103. http://www.jstor.org/stable/40587782

Appendix I: Treaties between Nebraska tribes and the US Government, 1820-1854

*Tribal names and spellings are preserved from titles of treaties on website, and may differ from accepted contemporary names and spellings."

Year	Title*	Signatories*	Type	Link
1820	Treaty with the Mahas, 1820	Omaha	Treaty, not ratified	https://treaties.okstate.edu/treaties/treaty-with-the-omaha-1820-22917
1825	Treaty with the Oto and Missouri Tribe, 1825	Missouri, Ottoe	Treaty, ratified	https://treaties.okstate.edu/treaties/treaty-with-the-oto-and-missouri-tribe-1825-0256
1825	Treaty with the Pawnee Tribe, 1825	Pawnee	Treaty, ratified	https://treaties.okstate.edu/treaties/treaty-with-the-pawnee-tribe-1825-0258
1825	Treaty with the Ponca, 1825	Ponca	Treaty, ratified	https://treaties.okstate.edu/treaties/treaty-with-the-ponca-1825-0225
1830	Treaty with the Sauk and Foxes, etc., 1830	Fox, Iowa, Mdewakanton, Missouri, Omaha, Ottoe, Sac, Sauk and Fox, Sisseton, Wahpekuta	Treaty, ratified	https://treaties.okstate.edu/treaties/treaty-with-the-sauk-and-foxes-etc-1830-0305
1833	Treaty with the Oto and Missouri, 1833	Missouri, Ottoe	Treaty, ratified	https://treaties.okstate.edu/treaties/treaty-with-the-oto-and-missouri-1833-0400
1833	Treaty with the Pawnee, 1833	Grand Pawnee, Pawnee Loups, Pawnee Republicans, Pawnee Tappahs	Treaty, ratified	https://treaties.okstate.edu/treaties/treaty-with-the-pawnee-1833-0416
1833	Treaty with the Kickapoo, Piankeshaw, Kaskaskia, Omaha, Delaware, Ottoe, Pawnee, Iowa, Peoria, Kansa, Pottawatomi, Shawnee, Wea, and Ottawa, 1833	Delaware, Iowa, Kansa, Kaskaskia, Kickapoo, Omaha, Ottawa, Ottoe, Pawnee, Peoria, Piankishaw, Potawatomi	Treaty, not ratified	https://treaties.okstate.edu/treaties/treaty-with-the-kickapoo-piankeshaw-kaskaskia-omaha-delaware-ottoe-pawnee-iowa-peoria-kansa-pottawatomi-shawnee-wea-and-ottawa-1833-22926

Appendix I: Treaties between Nebraska tribes and the US Government, 1820-1854 (continued)

*Tribal names and spellings are preserved from titles of treaties on website, and may differ from accepted contemporary names and spellings."

1836	Treaty with the Iowa, etc., 1836	Iowa, Sac and Fox of Missouri	Treaty, ratified	https://treaties.okstate.edu/treaties/treaty-with-the-iowa-etc-1836-0468
1836	Treaty with the Oto, etc., 1836	Missouri, Omaha, Ottoe, Santee, Sioux, Yankton	Treaty, ratified	https://treaties.okstate.edu/treaties/treaty-with-the-oto-etc-1836-0479
1838	Treaty with the Omaha, Otoe, and Iowa, 1838	Iowa, Omaha, Otoe	Treaty, not ratified	https://treaties.okstate.edu/treaties/treaty-with-the-omaha-otoe-and-iowa-1838-22928
1848	Treaty with the Pawnee - Grand, Loups, Republicans, Etc., 1848	Grand Pawnee, Pawnee Loups, Pawnee Republicans, Pawnee Tappahs	Treaty, ratified	https://treaties.okstate.edu/treaties/treaty-with-the-pawnee-grand-loups-republicans-etc-1848-0571
1854	Treaty with the Omaha, 1854	Omaha	Treaty, ratified	https://treaties.okstate.edu/treaties/treaty-with-the-omaha-1854-0611
1854	Treaty with the Omaha, 1854	Omaha	Treaty, ratified	https://treaties.okstate.edu/treaties/treaty-with-the-omaha-1854-22548
1854	Treaty with the Oto and Missouri, 1854	Missouri, Ottoe	Treaty, ratified	https://treaties.okstate.edu/treaties/treaty-with-the-oto-and-missouri-1854-0608
1854	Treaty with the Otoe and Missouria, 1854	Missouri, Otoe	Treaty, not ratified	https://treaties.okstate.edu/treaties/treaty-with-the-otoe-and-missouria-1854-22550
1854	Treaty with the Confederated Oto and Missouri, 1854	Missouri, Ottoe	Treaty, ratified	https://treaties.okstate.edu/treaties/treaty-with-the-confederated-oto-and-missouri-1854-0660

Appendix II: Treaties between Nebraska tribes and the US Government, 1855 - 1869

Tribal names and spellings are preserved from titles of treaties on website, and may differ from accepted contemporary names and spellings.

Year	Title*	Signatories*	Type	Link
1857	Treaty with the Pawnee, 1857	Grand Pawnee, Pawnee, Pawnee Loups, Pawnee Republicans, Pawnee Tappahs	Treaty, ratified	https://treaties.okstate.edu/treaties/treaty-with-the-pawnee-1857-0764
1865	Treaty with the Omaha, 1865	Omaha	Treaty, ratified	https://treaties.okstate.edu/treaties/treaty-with-the-omaha-1865-0872
1865	Treaty with the Ponca, 1865	Ponca	Treaty, ratified	https://treaties.okstate.edu/treaties/treaty-with-the-ponca-1865-0875
1865	Treaty with the Winnebago, 1865	Winnebago	Treaty, ratified	https://treaties.okstate.edu/treaties/treaty-with-the-winnebago-1865-0874
1868	Treaty with the Sioux-Brule, Oglala, Miniconjou, Yanktonai, Hunkpapa, Blackfeet, Cuthead, Two Kettle, Sans Arcs, and Santee-and Arapaho, 1868	Arapaho, Blackfeet, Brule, Cuthead, Hunkpapa Sioux, Miniconjou, Oglala, Sans Arc, Santee, Sioux, Two Kettle, Yanktonai	Treaty, ratified	https://treaties.okstate.edu/treaties/treaty-with-the-sioux-brule-oglala-miniconjou-yanktonai-hunkpapa-blackfeet-cuthead-two-kettle-sans-arcs-and-santee-and-arapaho-1868-0998
1869	Treaty with the Otoe and Missouria, 1869	Missouria, Ottoe	Treaty, not ratified	https://treaties.okstate.edu/treaties/treaty-with-the-otoe-and-missouria-1869-22861

Native Americans, Part II

By Kevin Abourezk

Introduction

The Civil Rights Movement of the 1950s and 1960s – aimed at abolishing legalized racial segregation and discrimination across the United States – found expression in Nebraska in many ways. From college protests to marches in Lincoln, the movement found a home within the youth and counterculture communities of Lincoln and Omaha.

But less known is the way the movement impacted Native American populations, especially those in remote Nebraska communities.

"Just as young Hispanics, Asians, and Native Americans across the nation were learning the lessons of the black experience of the 1960s and expressing their identity as they sought to claim their own niche in society in the early 1970s, so too Mexican Americans and Indians were becoming more visible in Nebraska," write authors James C. Olson and Ronald C. Naugle.[1]

The most visible push for Native American civil rights could be seen in the efforts of the American Indian Movement, an indigenous rights organization established in 1968 in Minneapolis. The organization emerged on the national scene following its occupation of Alcatraz Island in 1969 before taking over Mount Rushmore and the Mayflower II.

In Nebraska, AIM garnered headlines while protesting the February 1972 death of Raymond Yellow Thunder, a 51-year-old Lakota man whose beaten body was found in a pickup truck in Gordon. But even before Yellow Thunder's death, Native American people in Nebraska towns like Alliance and Scottsbluff fought for their civil rights following the deaths of Native people in jails and at the hands of non-Native perpetrators.

Omaha Nation elder Eleanor Baxter recalls life in Nebraska during the Civil Rights era.

> "Indian people were barely recognized. We had to fight our way. We were called savages, dirty Indians. We were called names. But we were kids so we fought back. … We'd tell the white kids we were fighting, 'You guys should jump on the Mayflower and go back across the ocean.'"[2]

Native advocates succeeded in creating a state organization charged with monitoring Native issues and legislation and coordinating the efforts of state agencies as they responded to Native needs and concerns. The Nebraska Unicameral chartered the Nebraska Commission on Indian Affairs in 1971 under the leadership of Leonard Springer, vice-chair of the Omaha tribe and leader in the Native American Church.

---

1. James C. Olson and Ronald C. Naugle, *History of Nebraska* (University of Nebraska Press, 2015), 381.
2. Wynne L. Summers, *Women Elders' Life Stories of the Omaha Tribe, Macy, Nebraska, 2004-2005* (University of Nebraska Press, 2010), 40.

In *Roots of Justice: A History of Race and Racism in Nebraska*. Edited by Kevin Abourezk, with an Introduction by M. Dewayne Mays and Paul A. Olson (Lincoln, Nebraska: Truth and Reconciliation Nebraska, 2025). Copyright © 2025 by the authors; CC-BY.
DOI: 10.32873/unl.dc.rj3

While many historians mark the first instance of American Indian activism in Nebraska as the 1972 AIM march in Gordon following Yellow Thunder's death, still others point to the efforts of Native people in western Nebraska to call attention to the deaths of Native inmates as among the first examples of indigenous activism in the state.

And still others argue the long road to civil rights for Natives in Nebraska began even earlier.

Author David Christensen argues that the roots of civil rights for Native people in Nebraska developed in the early 20th century in western Nebraska's potato fields.[3]

Kinship in the Potato Fields

During World War I, labor shortages on farms in western Nebraska brought many Lakotas from the Pine Ridge and Rosebud reservation to harvest potatoes in fields surrounding places like Alliance and Scottsbluff. Lakota laborers and farmers maintained amicable relationships built on mutual need during the early war years. Off-reservation, seasonal work was a vital source of income for many Lakota families who could not rely solely on federal aid and did not own lands upon which to grow crops or raise livestock.[4]

The federal policy of allotment – which carved up Indian lands and gave them to individual tribal citizens – had led to many Native families selling their individual allotments to non-Natives.

Thus, many western Nebraska communities welcomed caravans of Lakotas each harvest season. The fact that most Lakota families returned home to their reservations after the harvest greatly reduced any potential racial tensions between Natives and non-Natives. Indeed, many developed kinship relationships with farmers, and Native people never tried to organize for workers' rights.

In 1916, farmers in Gordon, Nebraska asked John Brennan, Pine Ridge superintendent, to send Lakotas to help with the harvest. Brennan promised that "a sufficient number will answer the call to supply the needs around Gordon."[5]

A year later, the United States' entry into World War I increased the need for agricultural production and reduced the number of available farm hands, which led to a greater need for Lakota labor.

One of the few instances of racial strife during the early potato harvest years occurred in 1924 in Alliance, when the Lakota practice of drying meat became a point of contention. Residents living near a Lakota camp began complaining about the smell of drying meat. City officials forced the Lakotas to move to nearby city land, which lacked water and forage for their horses. The local newspaper called on officials to remedy the situation.[6]

The start of the Great Depression in 1929 led to a shift in racial relations between Natives and non-Natives in western Nebraska.

An increase in white migrant labor in the region led to increased competition between Native and non-Native farm workers. Drought further exacerbated this tension by reducing the amount of available agricultural jobs. Once welcoming communities began to complain about Lakotas, who they now considered economic competition.

In 1930, a drought on the Pine Ridge Reservation led to crop failures of 50 percent, forcing more Lakotas to seek work in nearby western Nebraska communities. As they arrived in places like Alliance and Scottsbluff, they were faced with competition for jobs from white transient workers.[7]

That racial tension increased as the Depression wore on and the need for farm labor dwindled. In 1931, Pine Ridge Superintendent James McGregor told the Bureau of Indian Affairs that many of the 100 Lakotas who left for harvest that year returned with empty wagons and no flour, coffee or beef.[8]

But by 1933, the demands of white workers for higher wages created economic opportunity for Lakotas, who didn't mind earning lower wages and who typically left town after harvest, unlike white

---

3. David Christensen, "The Ground You Walk on Belongs to My People: Lakota Community Building, Activism, and Red Power in Western Nebraska, 1917-2000" (PhD dissertation, University of Nevada, Las Vegas, 2016), 22.
4. Christensen, "The Ground You Walk On," 5.
5. Superintendent to Lloyd Jordon, September 25, 1916, Laborers, Box 128, General Records, General Correspondence by Subject, Pine Ridge Agency, Records Group 75, NARAKC. Quoted in Christensen, 49.
6. *Alliance Times-Herald* (Alliance, NE), Sept. 23, 1924, 1, 4; Sept. 26, 1924, 12.
7. E. W. Jermark to Commissioner of Indian Affairs, July 11, 1930, 970, Box 719, Main Decimal Files, General Records Group 75, Pine Ridge Agency, NARAKC; Microfilm Roll 107, 1929 Annual Narrative Report, Superintendents' Annual Narrative and Statistical Reports, BIA 1907-1938, Pine Ridge, NARADC. Quoted in Christensen, 79.
8. 1932 Annual Narrative Report, Microfilm Roll 107, Superintendents' Annual Narrative and Statistical Reports, BIA 1907-1938, Pine Ridge, NARADC. Quoted in Christensen, 81.

transients who often remained after harvest and drained Depression-era relief supplies.

In 1935, Franklin D. Roosevelt's New Deal brought work relief programs to western Nebraska, as well as to reservation communities. Newly created agencies like the Public Works Administration (PWA), Civilian Conservation Corps and Works Progress Administration (WPA) created millions of jobs.

In western Nebraska, those agencies hired workers to build roads, parks and civic buildings. New Deal wages enticed many farm hands to give up the plow and pick up the shovel, creating a labor shortage in the potato fields.

Many Lakota workers, who otherwise might have left their reservations for harvest work, stayed home to complete New Deal projects. Farmers struggled to compete with federal jobs, which guaranteed a wage as compared to wages for farm work, which depended on yields. Lower yields meant less pay.

By 1942, nearly three in four Rosebud men worked for federal relief agencies.[9]

The outbreak of World War II in 1939 ended relief work as the government shifted funds from New Deal programs to defense production, forcing Lakota workers back to the potato fields of western Nebraska. But the rise in Lakota farm laborers didn't last long, as Japan's bombing of Pearl Harbor in December 1941 led to America's entry into the war and a boom in defense employment.

In 1942, the War Department selected 11 sites in Nebraska for army airfields, including Scottsbluff and Alliance. Construction on the airbases required a large labor force, including 5,000 workers needed for Alliance alone. Lakotas rose to the challenge, and nearly 3,000 Lakota went to live in tents in Alliance in order to help build the airbase, which became operational in August 1942.[10]

But the completion of the Alliance airfield didn't mean an end to defense work for Lakotas as work soon began on airfields in Scottsbluff and Ainsworth. Many Lakota men joined the armed services by 1942, further reducing the availability of Native workers.

Defense work offered higher wages than farm work. However, it also led many Lakotas to decide to live in Alliance and Scottsbluff permanently, and that led to increased racial tensions. Those tensions came to a head in 1942 when word reached the reservation that Alliance would not allow Lakotas to stay in town, though the Alliance paper later reported that the town never decided to keep out Lakotas but did ask some "bad actors to leave town."[11]

Many residents of western Nebraska communities believed it was the federal government's responsibility to provide social services to Lakota and denied them much needed services, including medical care.

In Alliance and Scottsbluff, Lakota people remained in the towns' south sides. Segregated Lakota camps in both towns demonstrated deplorable conditions, with Native people forced to live in tents and lacking access to showers or indoor toilets. In Scottsbluff, Lakota had to get water from the river, and they fashioned stoves from old gas tanks or barrels.[12]

Sizeable Lakota communities in these towns created racial strife in 1943, when the Army banned soldiers from visiting the Lakota camp in south Alliance for fear of enlisted men contracting diseases from prostitutes. Military police guarded the viaduct under the railroad tracks that led to the Lakota camp to keep soldiers from entering and Lakota women from leaving. The issue led to local residents and the Army stereotyping Lakota people as filthy and disease-ridden.

Ted Solway, an Oglala Lakota living in Alliance, spoke to a local reporter on behalf of his people, arguing that the city and army should not blame Lakota women but rather should point the finger at white men who were targeting young Lakota girls who didn't understand the consequence of their actions.[13]

His statements were an early example of Native people in western Nebraska defending themselves. But Solway's words mattered little as police began forcing alleged prostitutes to leave town.

---

9. Biolsi, *Organizing the Lakota*, 113-115; Useem et al., "Wartime Employment," 2; See also the 1935 Rosebud Narrative Report, Microfilm Roll 118, Superintendents' Annual Narrative and Statistical Reports, BIA 1907-1938, Rosebud, NARADC. Quoted in Christensen, 86.
10. Monroe, *An Indian in White America*, 17-18; Cedric DeCory, interview by David Christensen, October 26, 2011, Scottsbluff, Nebraska; *Alliance Times-Herald*, 15 September 1942, 1; 22 September 1942, 1; 29 September 1942, 1; *Scottsbluff Star-Herald*, 4 October 1935; 6/16/1942-10/5/1942, Box 3, Rosebud Sioux Tribal Council and Committee Minutes 1936-1965, Series 45, Rosebud Agency, NARAKC. Quoted in Christensen, 88.
11. Useem, et al, "Wartime Employment," 3. Franco, "Beyond Reservation Boundaries," 245-250. Quoted in Christensen 90.
12. Cedric DeCory, interview by David Christensen, Oct. 26, 2011, Scottsbluff, Nebraska. Quoted in Christensen, 92.
13. *Alliance Times-Herald* (Alliance, NE), Nov. 23, 1943, 1.

The tent towns weren't the only form of segregation in western Nebraska towns. Restaurants and other businesses hung signs that read: "No Indians or dogs allowed."[14]

Many stereotyped Lakotas as alcoholics. Each Monday on the front page, the *Alliance Times-Herald* listed Lakotas arrested with headlines such as "Braves Caught Drinking," "In Trouble for Fire Water," "Drunken Indian Freezes to Death" and "Indians Gulped Too Much Liquor."[15]

A committee of "responsible Indians" and city officials decided that Lakotas should move back to the reservation where people trained to work with Indians could help them.

For Lakotas living and working in western Nebraska, two world wars and the Great Depression created a rollercoaster of opportunity and much altered lifestyles over the course of several decades. Communities that had once been hospitable to migrant Lakota laborers turned against them as job opportunities shrunk during the Great Depression, but defense work offered new opportunities for Lakotas during World War II. Permanent Lakota settlements further exacerbated racial tensions, and Lakotas began experiencing segregation and discrimination in western Nebraska.

In his memoir, *An Indian in White America*, Lakota leader Mark Monroe compared his life in Wood, S.D., to his later life in Alliance: "When we lived in Wood, there was some racial tension, but it wasn't as bad as this. In Alliance we were just different, and we couldn't do anything right."[16]

But the racial tensions of the first half of the 20th Century in western Nebraska would seem minor compared to the problems of the post-World War II years.

Following the war, Lakota people continued to find themselves the subject of unjust practices, including those of farmers who refused to pay to transport Lakota families to the reservation. In 1947, the *Alliance Times-Herald* stated examples of such practices, mainly beyond Alliance. In some cases, farmers did not assist Lakota workers who needed hospitalization or even provide first aid in cases of injury.

The newspaper related one case involving a farmer who refused to call a doctor for an ill Lakota worker, who died. The farmer refused to return the man's body to the reservation, forcing the man's family to drive to the farm to get him. The family's pickup truck broke down near Alliance, and they were forced to carry the man's body six miles to town.[17]

Mistreatment of Lakota farm laborers forced the Oglala Sioux Tribal Council to step up. The council decided to establish a system by which it would supply western Nebraska farmers with workers on a contractual basis. The contract would protect both farmers and Lakotas, requiring workers to fulfill their part of the agreement in exchange for being provided transportation to and from the reservation and healthcare in the case of on-the-job injuries. Farmers also were expected to arrange entry into public schools for children of Lakota families working more than three weeks.[18]

The Oglala tribal council's efforts, however, did little to ease the troubles of poor Lakota families living in tent camps on the outskirts of western Nebraska communities. An *Alliance Times-Herald* article in the summer of 1948 was headlined: "Indian Living in Squalor – Need Help." The story reported that Native people lived in "conditions that wouldn't be allowed for cattle."[19]

The newspaper called for purchasing and relocating an Army air barracks to South Alliance where it could be furnished with sanitary facilities for use by Native people. But donations were scarce, as many residents still believed the federal government provided assistance to off-reservation Lakotas.[20]

But some farmers and churches donated to a fund established by the Alliance Council of Churchwomen. Still, some residents objected to the housing plan, complaining that Lakotas stole gardening supplies.

The project went forward, and sponsors bought the building from the city for $300, and had it moved to South Alliance, where it became a community center replete with sanitary facilities, including hot water, washtubs, sinks and toilets. It became the first project of its kind to provide sanitary facilities for Lakota workers in western Nebraska.[21]

The Oglala tribal council didn't stop fighting for the rights of farm workers. In 1948, the council held a meeting in which an editor of a Nebraska newspaper

14. Monroe, *An Indian in White America*, 20. Quoted in Christensen, 95.
15. *Alliance Times-Herald* (Alliance, NE), March 23, 1943, 1; June 29, 1943, 1.
16. Monroe, *An Indian in White America*, 21. Quoted in Christensen, 98.
17. *Alliance Times-Herald* (Alliance, NE), Sept. 14, 1948, 1.
18. *Alliance Times-Herald* (Alliance, NE), Sept. 21, 1948, 1; *Hemingford Ledger* (Hemingford, NE), Sept. 23, 1948, 1.
19. *Alliance Times-Herald* (Alliance, NE), Aug. 3, 1948, 1.
20. Alliance Times-Herald (Alliance, NE), July 30, 1948, 1.
21. Alliance Times-Herald (Alliance, NE), Aug. 13, 1948, 1; Sept. 27, 1948, 1; Oct. 1, 1948, 1.

spoke about the racism that Lakotas were forced to endure in western Nebraska. Joe Leedom Jr., editor for the *Gordon Journal*, described his community as "a front line town in the battle of racial prejudice." He urged the council to ensure Lakotas left the reservation with skills that would make them a competitive labor source.[22]

A natural disaster in January 1949 would further reveal the legal quagmire in which the Lakotas living in western Nebraska found themselves. That month, a massive blizzard left communities in western Nebraska and South Dakota buried in snow and Lakotas living in tent camps cold and hungry.

Local, state and federal officials sparred over which should bear the responsibility of providing relief for off-reservation Lakotas. Nearly 250 Lakotas in Alliance and 300 in Gordon living in tents and shacks endured frigid temperatures and snow. In Alliance, the Red Cross, local residents, the local newspaper and a grocery store donated food, clothing and $180 to the Lakotas.[23]

But in Gordon, town leaders sought to shift responsibility for aiding the Lakotas to the federal government in what would become a reoccurring theme in Nebraska history as federal and local leaders have sought to deprive themselves of the responsibility of aiding off-reservation Native Americans. But Pine Ridge Superintendent C.H. Powers refused aid, leaving Mayor L.E. Morgan to contact Nebraska Gov. Val Peterson. Morgan informed the governor that his city lacked funds to help the Lakotas. Peterson turned to the federal government for help.[24]

Finally, on Jan. 25, William Zimmerman, commissioner of Indian Affairs, allotted $28,000 in federal funds for relief of Lakotas living both on and off the reservation in western Nebraska and South Dakota. In the end, only $2,500 of those funds actually trickled down to the Lakotas living in western Nebraska, and each Lakota family received just $15 to $25.[25]

The Red Cross actually outspent the federal government, providing $3,256 to aid Lakotas in western Nebraska.[26]

Gov. Peterson was outraged and sent a telegram to Secretary of the Interior Julius Krug calling the federal aid to the Lakotas a disgrace. "In my judgment, such allowances in the middle of one of the worst winters in history is hopelessly inadequate and reflects great shame on the Government of the United States," Peterson wrote.[27]

Thirteen days later, on Feb. 16, Krug responded, saying it was not the government's responsibility to aid Indians living off reservations.[28]

The western Nebraska communities and the Lakotas living there would have to make do. For the Lakotas, the blizzard of 1949 served to further illustrate their de facto terminated status and all the challenges their circumstances created, especially in times of need.

Those challenges persisted into February 1952, when a newspaper in Lincoln published an article entitled "Indians Settle Permanently, Raise Problem for Gordon: Uncle Sam's Former Wards Quit Reservation, Lose Dole." The article described the impact of the federal government's decision not to support Lakotas living off their reservations and it took aim at the Lakotas' inability to assimilate.[29]

Omaha Land Claims

In eastern Nebraska in 1951, the Omaha Tribe decided to challenge its historical treatment by the federal government.

Just five years before, Congress passed the Indian Claims Commission Act, which allowed tribes to submit grievances of every conceivable type against the

---

22. Minutes of the Tribal Council, 1948, Box 1207, Records of the Oglala Sioux Tribal Government, RG 75, NARAKC. Quoted in Christensen, 107.
23. Report on Indians, January 17, 1949, Folder 627, Box 60, RG1 SG33, Val Peterson Governor Papers, NSHS cited hereafter as NSHS; Dalstrom, "'I'm Never Going to Be Snowbound Again'," 13. Quoted in Christensen, 108.
24. Telegram, L.E. Morgan to Val Peterson, January 12, 1949, Folder 627, Box 60, RG1 SG33, Val Peterson Governor Papers, NSHS. Quoted in Christensen, 110.
25. Telegram, John Provinse to C.H. Powers, January 25, 1949, 031.3, Box 154, Main Decimal Files, General Record, Pine Ridge Agency, Records Group 75, NARAKC; Telegram Hugh Butler to Val Peterson, January 28, 1949, Folder 627, Box 60, RG1 SG33, Val Peterson Governor Papers, NSHS. Quoted in Christensen, 111.
26. C.H. Powers to Val Peterson, January 29, 1949, 031.3, Box 154, Main Decimal Files, General Record, Pine Ridge Agency, Records Group 75, NARAKC; 627, Box 60, RG1 SG33, Val Peterson Governor Papers, NSHS. Quoted in Christensen, 112.
27. Telegram, Val Peterson to Julius Krug, February 3, 1949, Folder 627, Box 60, RG1 SG33, Val Peterson Governor Papers, NSHS. Quoted in Christensen, 112.
28. Julius Krug to Val Peterson, February 16, 1949, Folder 627, Box 60, RG1 SG33, Val Peterson Governor Papers, NSHS. Quoted in Christensen, 112.
29. *Lincoln Journal and Star*, Feb. 24, 1952, 2-D.

U.S. government, including claims based on land theft and fraudulent treaties. The Claims Commission, however, could only award monetary judgments and could not restore land to claimants, nor could it award interest on amounts owed to claimants.[30]

The Omaha filed their complaint with the Claims Commission on Aug. 8, 1951. The tribe asserted that it had been induced into signing treaties prior to 1854 through fraud and misrepresentation by government agents and that it was paid for its lands only a fraction of what those lands were worth. The 1854 treaty was the tribe's major land cession and included all the tribe's lands west of the Missouri River, except for 300,000 acres that would become its reservation.[31]

The centerpiece of the tribe's claims involved 4.5 million acres that the tribe had ceded to the government, for which it had been paid $881,000 or 19.6 cents an acre. For all the land the tribe lost, including the 4.5 million acres, the tribe was awarded $2,760,833.86 by the Claims Commission. But including its other claims, the tribe was awarded a grand total of $2.9 million. The tribe paid each adult of its almost 3,000 tribal members $750 each and put the rest toward economic and social improvements, including three new family housing units and a new community building.[32]

Public Law 280

Not long after the Omahas filed their claim with the Claims Commission, federal lawmakers created new challenges for the tribe.

In 1953, Congress passed Public Law 280, which allowed the federal government to transfer civil and criminal jurisdiction over reservations to state and local governments in five states – Nebraska, California, Minnesota, Oregon and Wisconsin. The Omaha Tribe opposed the law, which ultimately had unintended consequences for the tribe, including racial tension and jurisdictional chaos.

"Like the allotment experiments seventy years earlier, the transfer of federal criminal jurisdiction over the Omaha reservation to the state of Nebraska produced disastrous results," wrote author Mark R. Scherer.[33]

In a May 16, 1949, report to the commissioner of Indian Affairs, Winnebago Superintendent H.E. Bruce described disparate treatment of Native law breakers. From 1946 to 1948, Thurston County jail records show Indians had been prosecuted for 285 offenses, while whites had been charged with 162. "Indians committed 64 percent of the violations of law in a county in which they constituted only 20 percent of the population."[34]

As a result of the state and Thurston County taking over criminal jurisdiction of the Omaha Reservation, the reservation's lone Bureau of Indian Affairs police officer lost his job. And the county was quickly overwhelmed by the sudden unfunded increase in its law enforcement responsibilities, which included prosecuting Indians for both major crimes and misdemeanors. Criminal cases involving Indians in Thurston County increased from 249 in 1954 to 353 in 1958, and jail costs in the county increased more than 178 percent from 1950 to 1959. The jail lodged 93 Indians in 1949, compared to 334 in 1958. Total criminal cases handled in the county increased from 380 in 1955 to 1,120 in 1970.[35]

In 1961, Nebraska state lawmakers attempted to address the growing law enforcement crisis in Thurston County and in two other counties affected by Public Law 280. At a committee hearing for a bill that would provide additional deputy state sheriffs in the three counties, *Lincoln Star* executive editor W. Earl Dyer Jr. told lawmakers that the state had "the moral and legal responsibility to see to it that law and order is established in Thurston County – and that this blemish is removed from the political face of the state."[36]

The Unicameral passed the bill creating three new deputy state sheriffs positions, but the bill – which would become known as the Indian Bounty Act – would create new problems of its own. The law provided three deputy state sheriffs for each county in which 60 percent or more of the people convicted of state criminal violations were Indians. The law created racial tension as "Indians and their supporters

---

30. Mark R. Scherer, *Imperfect Victories: The Legal Tenacity of the Omaha Tribe, 1945-1995* (University of Nebraska Press, 2009), 49-51.
31. Scherer, *Imperfect Victories*, 51-52.
32. Scherer, *Imperfect Victories*, 64.
33. Scherer, *Imperfect Victories*, XV-XVI.
34. Scherer, *Imperfect Victories*, 21.
35. Scherer, *Imperfect Victories*, 26.
36. Scherer, *Imperfect Victories*, 29.

contended that county officials now believed that the most expedient method to obtain increased funding was to arrest more and more Indians."

In addition, local, state and tribal authorities decried the passage of federal legislation in 1955 that legalized the sale of alcohol to Indians, an act that many say only exacerbated lawlessness on the reservation. An Omaha tribal council member called it the "worst mistake the Government and State ever made."

At the same time, tribal leaders blamed prejudicial policing on the part of Thurston County authorities as the cause of racial strife and escalating crime statistics. "Indians would be placed in jail upon arrest for minor offenses for which non-Indians would merely be told to appear in court," Omaha Tribal Chairman Edward Cline told Congress.[37]

The problems experienced in Thurston County as a result of Public Law 280 were being seen on reservations across the country. As a result, a Senate subcommittee began studying the law's impacts on tribes, states and local governments. After hearing testimony from tribal leaders about the law's disastrous impact, the subcommittee issued a report in 1966 that created provisions for returning criminal jurisdiction back to the federal government. But states would first have to request it, and the federal government would have to approve it.[38]

In April 1969, the Nebraska Legislature officially asked to retrocede jurisdiction over Thurston County's Native population back to the federal government. Soon after, Interior Secretary Walter Hickel accepted Nebraska's request, though it only affected the Omaha Reservation as the Winnebago Tribe had decided not to undergo retrocession. As a result of the federal government's decision to only approve part of the state's request for retrocession, the state of Nebraska attempted to withdraw its request, taking its case to the courts.[39] Initially, the state won a decision from the Nebraska Supreme Court supporting its request, but a later U.S. District Court Decision and federal appellate court decision reversed the state court's decision.[40]

Poverty in Western Nebraska

Meanwhile, Nebraska Gov. Robert Crosby decided it was important to seek to alleviate the harm that racism and discrimination caused.

In 1953, Crosby created the Human Relations Committee, a state agency charged with ensuring the civil rights of all Nebraskans by rooting out prejudice and discrimination. The organization contacted welfare agencies in western Nebraska seeking information on Lakota and Mexican-American populations.[41]

But before those welfare agencies responded, city and county officials in Chadron and Dawes County had decided enough was enough. Upon visiting the Lakota camp in February 1954, Sheriff James Butler ordered the Lakotas to leave town. The *Chadron Record* described the camp as "rat infested' and a "potential disease center." That month, the Human Relations Committee investigated the Lakotas' plight in Chadron, finding the removal of the Lakotas was based on the deplorable condition of their camp rather than the racial bias of town leaders.[42]

By early March, all but one Lakota family had left Chadron and returned to the reservation.

"Like elsewhere in the U.S. West, civic officials and residents used disease to stereotype racial groups. A characterization of uncleanliness and disease helped to justify removal of Lakotas from western Nebraska communities," wrote author David Christensen in his 2016 doctoral thesis.[43]

In his 2016 book *A Doctor Among the Oglala Sioux: The Letters of Robert H. Ruby 1953-1954*, author Robert H. Ruby described the refusal of Nebraska hospitals and social workers to serve Lakota residents. The former Pine Ridge doctor wrote that those providers often would dump Lakotas on the reservation rather than provide them with care.

"The moment one gets ill Nebraska wants to shove them back to the reservation hospital. This is discrimination. The people who have established residency should be entitled to the community services of the place in which they reside," Ruby wrote.[44]

---

37. Scherer, *Imperfect Victories*, 30.
38. Scherer, *Imperfect Victories*, 35-36.
39. Scherer, *Imperfect Victories*, 39.
40. Scherer, *Imperfect Victories*, 40.
41. Robert Crosby to Arthur McCaw, September 4, 1953, Folder 96, Box 3, RG1 SG 34, Governor Papers of Robert B. Crosby, NSHS. Quoted in Christensen, 116.
42. *Chadron Record* (Chadron, NE), Feb. 11, 1954, 4.
43. Christensen, 122.
44. Ruby, *A Doctor Among the Oglala Sioux*, 131. Quoted in Christensen, 123.

In early March 1954, the issue of discrimination against Lakotas living in western Nebraska would come to a head.

On March 7, 1954, on a highway east of Chadron a 15-year-old Lakota girl, Jessie Red Hawk, lay on the pavement bloodied and dead from a fractured skull. Later, authorities would learn from Red Hawk's brother that two non-Native men had forced his sister into the back seat of the car, the door had opened and Red Hawk had fallen from the moving car. The two men then kicked Red Hawk's brother out and sped away.

The two men involved, Robert Walton, 22, and Mickey Shelly, 20, both of Gordon, would later be convicted of assault and battery and each receive six months in jail.

In nearby Gordon, in an unrelated incident on March 17, an officer tried to arrest Vincent Broken Rope for intoxication, but Broken Rope ran and the officer shot him in the lower back. Seven weeks later, Broken Rope died.[45]

The two deaths left many Lakotas enraged. They demanded justice. The Oglala Sioux Tribal Council called on Lakota people to boycott Gordon if a thorough investigation wasn't completed.

The two deaths became a watershed moment in race relations in western Nebraska. No longer would Lakota people stand quietly by as their people were murdered. No longer would they silently endure racism, segregation, and police brutality.

The Bureau of Indian Affairs eventually launched an investigation into allegations that racial prejudice influenced the cases of Red Hawk and Broken Rope. Dawes County Attorney Ernest Johnson certainly seemed to believe discrimination was at work. In June 1954, he wrote a letter to South Dakota Congressman Ellis Yarnal Berry alleging that Walton and Shelly's convictions were an injustice and warranted investigation by the Justice Department or Federal Bureau of Investigation.[46]

In October, Johnson wrote to Gov. Crosby, stating he believed that the jury failed to find Walton and Shelly guilty of manslaughter because of race. "I personally feel that had the deceased been a white girl, the jury would have convicted the defendant," he wrote.[47]

In 1954, off-reservation Lakota people remained in limbo as local, state and federal officials sought to pass responsibility for them to each other. Lakotas turned to their tribal governments and churches for assistance and protection. Their calls for civil rights would continue throughout the 1950s. Their pleas for justice would mirror the pleas of tribes across the country.

But federal assimilation efforts had little effect on Lakotas living in western Nebraska, who were considered de facto terminated people by federal officials as they were living off the reservation and in rural settings.

An April 1954 visit by recently appointed Pine Ridge superintendent Benjamin Reifel would bring the issue of discrimination against Lakotas in western Nebraska into sharper focus. Reifel, a Lakota himself who had been born on the Rosebud Reservation of South Dakota, was appalled by the conditions in which the Lakotas were living in Alliance.

And Reifel called on Alliance businesses to remove their signs prohibiting "Indians or dogs." He warned that more Lakotas would be moving to Alliance as only about 75 Pine Ridge Lakotas were able to earn enough money as farmers to sustain themselves, while the other 1,500 families were forced to seek employment off the reservation.

"You must see that they get work, that they get schooling and leadership — that their personalities do not become shriveled up," Reifel stated.[48]

In July 1954, Esther Goldsmith, director of the Scotts Bluff County public welfare department, responded to Human Relations Committee inquiries, stating Lakotas in Scottsbluff lived in hovels and many made money selling beadwork while others worked construction. She said Mexican-Americans and Lakotas failed to prosper and drained county social and medical resources.[49]

Zeola Barnes, Box Butte County welfare director, told the Human Relations Committee that Lakotas mostly did migrant agricultural work and mostly lived in tents south of the railroad tracks, along with Mexican-Americans and African-Americans.

Barnes reported that housing discrimination did not exist, though she also reported that just 5 of 50 Lakota families (the *Alliance Times-Herald* estimated

---

45. Christensen, 99.
46. Christensen, 128.
47. Ernest Johnson to Robert Crosby, October 6, 1954, Folder 241, Box 6, RG1 SG 34, Governor Papers of Robert B. Crosby, NSHS. Quoted in Christensen, 129.
48. *Alliance Times-Herald* (Alliance, NE), April 1, 1954, 1.
49. Esther Goldsmith to Verne Vance, July 27, 1954, Folder 241, Box 6, RG1 SG 34, Governor Papers of Robert B. Crosby, NSHS. Quoted in Christensen, 117-118.

as many as 300 Lakota families lived in the town) and four of 47 Mexican-American families living in Alliance were given housing in a city housing project, compared to 86 white families that resided in the project.[50]

In western Nebraska, Lakotas also faced educational discrimination.

At Grandview Elementary near South Alliance, educators created the "opportunity room," which served to confine Lakota children of all ages and where teachers taught rudimentary reading, writing and math. Lakota children faced physical abuse from their peers, and complaints to city and school officials failed to remedy the situation. Many Lakota students dropped out.[51]

Zeola Barnes told the Human Relations Committee that only one Lakota boy was in high school and that the Alliance school system employed no minority teachers. And she defended use of the "opportunity room," saying educators used it to get often transient Lakota children caught up.[52]

"Barnes' response was another example of non-Indians in western Nebraska failing to see discrimination in their towns," Christensen wrote.

In interviews with the late Rosebud Lakota Cedric DeCory, Christensen learned that students in Scottsbluff schools also faced discrimination. DeCory told him that teachers called Lakota students "savages" and "cowards."[53]

The social issues plaguing Lakota residents of Nebraska would bleed into May 1958, when 59 local and county officials, tribal leaders, Bureau of Indian Affairs officials and local citizens attended the second Conference on Indian Affairs in Rushville. Attendees learned that 90 percent of arrests of Lakotas in Sheridan County were for alcohol-related crimes. Attendees decided to create an organization that would meet twice a year, starting with a meeting in November in Scottsbluff, home to 1,500 Lakotas.[54]

The Inter-Cultural Association would be charged with improving the lives of Lakota people in western Nebraska. It would become a vital resource for Lakotas moving into the 1960s.[55]

To the east, the Ponca Tribe of Nebraska was fighting for its survival. In 1966, the federal government rescinded federal recognition of the tribe. The federal government had begun a policy of termination of tribes in the 1940s, believing that rescinding federal recognition of tribes would allow their members to better assimilate into American society. In all, 109 tribes were terminated during the 1950s and 1960s and more than 1.3 million acres of tribal land was lost.[56]

It would take 24 years and many years of lobbying Congress and the Nebraska Unicameral for the Ponca Tribe to regain its state and federal recognition and become restored as a tribe. In the intervening years, the tribe's lands and much of its cultural traditions and language were lost.[57]

Blackbird Bend

Even before the American Indian Movement occupied Alcatraz Island and the Bureau of Indian Affairs building in Washington D.C., Omaha tribal activists and leaders began their own fight to regain their ancestral homelands along the Nebraska-Iowa border.

In 1966, the Omahas sought to regain 11,000 acres that had once been part of their Nebraska reservation before the Missouri River channel shifted, and the land became part of the state of Iowa. The tribe's efforts to regain the land through the courts became known as the Blackbird Bend litigation and spanned nearly two decades, eventually reaching as far as the U.S. Supreme Court.[58]

The tribe's efforts weren't relegated only to the courts. In April 1973, during the same time that the Wounded Knee siege was taking place in South

---

50. Zeola Barnes to Mayme Stukel, June 18, 1954, Folder 241, Box 6, RG1 SG 34, Governor Papers of Robert B. Crosby, NSHS. Quoted in Christensen, 118.
51. Mark Monroe, *An Indian in White America*, 18-21; Leslie Durhman, "Nowadays We Call it South Alliance: The Early History of a Lakota Community" (master's thesis, University of Arizona, 1997), 52. Quoted in Christensen, 131.
52. Zeola Barnes to Mayme Stukel, June 18, 1954, Folder 241, Box 6, RG1 SG 34, Governor Papers of Robert B. Crosby, NSHS. Quoted in Christensen, 131.
53. Christensen, 132.
54. Summary of the Second Conference on Indian Affairs, May 14, 1958, 050.1, Box 167, Main Decimal Files, General Records, RG 75, NARAKC. Quoted in Christensen, 134-135.
55. Proposed Indian Commission, Box 99, RG1, SG39, Norbert Tiemann Papers, NSHS. Quoted in Christensen, 135.
56. Scherer, *Imperfect Victories*, 6-7.
57. "Ponca Tribe of Nebraska History." Ponca Tribe of Nebraska. Accessed October 1, 2023. https://www.poncatribe-ne.org/culture/history
58. Scherer, *Imperfect Victories*, 89.

Dakota, a dozen carloads of Omahas set up tipis on the land and brought a framed copy of the 1854 treaty upon which their claim was based. The occupiers ended their occupation, but two years later, tribal members reoccupied the Blackbird lands, this time endorsed by the tribal council and the Bureau of Indian Affairs, which supported the tribe's efforts to regain the land.[59]

On May 19, 1975, the U.S. Department of Justice filed a lawsuit before the Federal District Court for the Northern District of Iowa seeking 2,900 acres within the Blackbird Bend for the Omaha Tribe. Omaha tribal leaders were outraged that the federal government was only seeking 2,900 acres believing they were owed much more than that.[60]

A federal district judge ruled against the Department of Justice, claiming the Omahas had failed to prove the 2,900 acres had been detached from their reservation, but the Eighth Circuit Court of Appeals reversed the ruling in April 1978, holding that the Iowans who occupied the land and the state of Iowa bore the burden of proof to show that the land belonged to them. The appellate court ordered the land be given to the Omaha Tribe. But the state appealed the ruling to the U.S. Supreme Court, which ruled the appellate court was wrong to apply the burden of proof statute to the state of Iowa. The high court ordered the appellate court to reconsider its ruling, which it did. The appellate court and the lower district court eventually decided the Omaha Tribe should be awarded all but 700 acres of the 2,900 acres in question. However, the courts decided another 300 acres of the Blackbird Bend lands should not be awarded to the tribe. In the end, the Omahas were able to recoup 1,900 acres of land.[61]

The tribe has used part of the land they recovered to build a casino, Blackbird Bend Casino.

Reuben Snake

In northeast Nebraska in 1969, a Winnebago activist, Reuben Snake, began what would become a decades-long fight for justice for his people. One of his first acts was to organize a boycott after non-Native citizens of Walthill on the Omaha Reservation circulated a petition condemning all Native people. The petition was a reaction to the rape of a young white woman by some Native men from the Omaha Reservation. Snake organized a boycott of Walthill that led to the townsfolk apologizing for circulating the petition. "Right then I began to see what was possible through organization. I realized what we can accomplish if we set our minds on doing something."[62]

Snake continued his activism in 1970, when the U.S. Army Corps of Engineers tried to condemn 627 acres of Winnebago land on the east bank of the Missouri River in Iowa to build a large water recreation complex. As a publicity stunt, some Winnebagos sailed across the Missouri in two small boats carrying signs that read: "This is Winnebago Indian land by treaty of March 8, 1865. No Trespassing."

"So that was the great launching of the Winnebago Navy as we sailed across the mighty Missouri to enforce our rights to our land."[63]

The Winnebagos took their case to federal court, where they won. Today, the land is home to the tribe's lucrative WinnaVegas Casino.

Indian Commission

Another valuable resource for Natives living in Nebraska would be the Nebraska Indian Commission, a state agency first imagined by Gov. Norbert Tiemann in 1969. The Nebraska Legislature would later cement the commission's authority in state statute in 1971, charging it with doing "all things which it may determine to enhance the cause of Indian rights and to develop solutions to problems common to all Nebraska Indians."[64]

But before the Legislature's actions, Tiemann issued an executive order on April 7, 1970, that established the Governor's Commission on Indian Affairs. He appointed only Nebraska Indians to serve on the commission, believing the organization should become a vehicle for self-determination for his state's Native citizens. Commissioners included 13 members: three each from the Omaha, Winnebago and Santee tribes, as well as two from Omaha, one from Lincoln and one at-large member.

---

59. Scherer, *Imperfect Victories*, 94.
60. Scherer, Imperfect Victories, 99.
61. Scherer, *Imperfect Victories*, 109-110.
62. Reuben Snake, *Reuben Snake, Your Humble Serpent: Indian Visionary and Activist* (Clear Light Pub, 1996), 110-111.
63. Snake, *Reuben Snake*, 149-151.
64. "Who We Are." Nebraska Commission on Indian Affairs, August 7, 2023. Accessed Oct. 2, 2023. https://indianaffairs.state.ne.us/who-we-are-what-we-do

He tasked the commission with addressing the socioeconomic concerns of Nebraska's Native population, as well as advancing their civil rights. And the governor allowed the commission to hire a paid executive director.

The commission's first executive was a Santee Dakota named Robert Mackey, who had served in the Marines during World War II and later had earned a bachelor's degree in business administration. He would become a voice for Nebraska's struggling Native population and champion for their civil rights.

In August 1970, Mackey toured western Nebraska, discovering that Lakotas earned low wages and earned no benefits working for Nebraska ranchers and farmers. Many lived in old chicken shacks and boxcars. Most earned little assistance from county or federal programs.[65]

Later that year, a series of incidents in western Nebraska jails would lead Mackey to seek to hold law enforcement and jail officials accountable.

The first incident occurred on Oct. 30, 1970, when a jailer found 26-year-old Arthur Gene Black Horse dead in his cell. The Lakota man had hung himself with a belt. Deputy Attorney General Gerald S. Vitamvas determined there was a lack of evidence for charging anyone with a crime and claimed that it was the Nebraska Department of Justice's responsibility for examining the alleged incident of police brutality.[66]

Mackey continued calling for an investigation. Even as Nebraska authorities debated who, if anyone, should look into Mackey's allegations, another jail incident would illustrate his concerns.

On Dec. 31, 1970, 34-year-old Joe No Leaf was found dead in an Alliance jail, having hung himself with a sweatshirt. And barely six months later, an 18-year-old Lakota man died in the Box Butte County Jail in Alliance, having hung himself with a bath towel.

Chillo Whirlwind Soldier Swalley's death further enraged western Nebraska Lakotas and led to further calls for investigation by Mackey. A suicide note left by the young man explained his hopelessness about the socioeconomic situation in Alliance.[67]

But it would take a fourth western Nebraska jail death to spur action by state officials.

On July 15, 1971, Irene Blackfeather had been arrested for intoxication and was taken to the Box Butte County Jail. The next morning, the 43-year-old Lakota woman began calling for help and was found in her cell vomiting. Emergency personnel were called, but the woman died before they arrived.[68]

Lakotas criticized police for failing to recognize Blackfeather suffered from liver problems that required medication.

On the pages of the *Alliance Herald*, a debate raged over who was to blame. Some criticized the lack of support for Lakotas, while others called them "lazy tax burdens" and "drunks."[69]

A week after Blackfeather's death, Box Butte County Attorney Paul D. Empson requested $5,000 from the county's Board of Commissioners to pay for an investigator and consultant to look into the Lakota jail deaths. "The reason for this request is that another person of Indian descent has died in a jail within our county."[70]

While the 512 Lakotas living in Box Butte County made up a small percent of the population, they made up all four jail deaths.

An outraged Mackey told a reporter just days after Blackfeather's death: "There are four people buried real deep and forever."[71]

On July 22, 1971, Mackey contacted several federal agencies seeking an investigation into the deaths, and he continued calling for a state investigation. He reached out to the state attorney general's office but was told the state lacked funds or staff to conduct an investigation. However, the governor's office requested reports from Mackey and Box Butte County officials on the jail deaths. Finally, Gov. J.J. Exon launched an investigation.[72]

---

65. Robert Mackey to Vernon Ashley, August 17, 1970, Indian Commission, Box 144, RG1 SG39, Governor Papers of Norbert Tiemann, NSHS. Quoted in Christensen, 145.
66. Gerald Vitamvas to Robert Mackey, November 12, 1970, Alliance, NE, Law and Order Problem 1971, box 1, RG93 SG4, Nebraska Indian Commission, NSHS. Quoted in Christensen, 149.
67. *Alliance Times Herald* (Alliance, NE), October 30, 1970, 1; December 31, 1970, 1; June 28, 1970, 1.
68. *Alliance Times Herald* (Alliance, NE) July 16, 1971, 1.
69. In the collected *Alliance Times Herald* editorials sent to editor Hugh Bunnell in the Indian-White Relations File, Knight Museum and Sandhills Center, Alliance, NE (cited hereafter as IWRF). Quoted in Christensen, 156.
70. Paul Empson to Board of County Commissioners, July 22, 1971, Alliance, Box 13, RG1 SG40, Governor Papers of J.J. Exon, NSHS; also available IWRF. Quoted in Christensen, 156.
71. *Lincoln Journal Star* article, available, Indian-White Relations File, Knight Museum and Sandhills Center, Alliance, NE. Quoted in Christensen, 137.
72. Robert Mackey to J.J. Exon, July 26, 1971, Alliance, Box 13, RG1 SG40, Governor Papers of J.J. Exon, NSHS. Quoted in Christensen, 162.

After nearly a month, the governor's office announced its findings. No one person or group could be held accountable because "if one wishes to commit suicide, even in jail, sooner or later the opportunity will arise," the announcement read.[73] The governor's office found that the living conditions of western Nebraska's Native population was unacceptable, and his office directed the Nebraska Commission on Law Enforcement and Criminal Justice to fund improvements to Alliance city jails and training for law enforcement.

Mackey criticized the governor's findings, calling them a "bland writeoff."[74] And he renewed his efforts to initiate a federal investigation into the jail deaths.

In September 1971, U.S. Attorney Richard Dier forwarded Mackey's concerns about the jail deaths to the Federal Bureau of Investigation and the Civil Rights Division of the U.S. Department of Justice. In October, DOJ investigators arrived in Alliance.

Simultaneously, the Box Butte County District Court launched its own investigation.

Finally, in July 1972, Lakotas received one of their wishes when Alliance City Manager LeRoy Schindler dismissed police officer Donald Montgomery, who had been the subject of several complaints of police brutality against Natives and non-Natives.

Wrote *Alliance Times Herald* editor Hugh Bunnell: "A door has opened a crack in Alliance. ... Let's help that door to open in 1971, not lean against it."[75]

The investigations into the jail deaths and the removal of Montgomery served to acknowledge the voices and concerns of Lakota people, and they served to cement the Nebraska Indian Commission's role as a defender of Indian civil rights in the state.

"The jail deaths rallied Lakotas to protest racism and nefarious law enforcement practices. Yet, the issue was more than just police abuse, their efforts challenged Alliance's non-Indian residents to acknowledge the effects racism placed on the Lakota community," Christensen writes.[76]

But even as local and federal authorities investigated alleged police brutality in western Nebraska, an event occurred that would bring some of the most vocal and aggressive Native activists in America to come to Nebraska.

Helping Indians Help Themselves

Tribal self-determination came to eastern Nebraska starting in 1969, when a group of Native Americans, with the help of the City Mission, established Indian Center Inc., a community center in Lincoln that would provide social services and advocacy to Native Americans. The center's board president, Oliver Saunsoci, said the center was established to help Native Americans help themselves because local social welfare programs had failed to serve their needs. He claimed Native Americans were often offered one-way bus tickets back to their reservations when they sought help. He called on local Native Americans to surrender tribal rivalries to work together to improve their lives. "Before we can get anywhere with our problems in the white man's community, we've got to first forget the old tradition of discrimination among Indian tribes," he said.[77] Saunsoci emphasized the historical context of Native American self-determination movement across the country. "There is a real movement afoot among our people to quietly gather forces — not to riot but to ask for and deserve a better standard of living and morals for the American Indian."

Perhaps emboldened by their Native American neighbors to the west, Native Americans in Omaha opened the Sioux Indian Center on Oct. 4, 1975. At the center's grand opening, many notables attended, including Mayor Edward Zorinsky, Chief Red Cloud — "chief of the Oglala Sioux" — and Nebraska Indian Commission Director Robert Mackey. Two medicine men wearing "ceremonial costumes" prayed for the center's success. Mrs. Alex Lunderman, described as a "center volunteer," said the center would provide food, housing and transportation to Indians and non-Indians who needed help. Volunteers would staff the center, which was financed through donations and a $6,000 grant from the Catholic Campaign for Human Development.[78]

Indian self-determination in Nebraska also came in the form of tribally controlled higher education institutions, today known as tribal colleges. The first of these in Nebraska had its origins in 1973, when Northeast Technical Community College in Norfolk established three satellite campuses on the Santee

---

73. Glen Soukup to John Sullivan, August 26, 1971, Alliance, Box 13, RG1 SG40, Governor Papers of J.J. Exon, NSHS. Quoted in Christensen, 164.
74. *Alliance Times Herald*, Sept. 11, 1971, 1.
75. Draft of Hugh Bunnell's editorial, no title or date provided, IWRF. Quoted in Christensen, 173.
76. Christensen, *The Ground You Walk On,"* 111.
77. Bess Jenkins, "Lincoln's Indians Join Together to Encourage Integration," *Lincoln Journal Star*, June 8, 1969, newspapers.com.
78. "Mass Opens Sioux Center," Omaha *World-Herald*, October 4, 1975, newspapers.com.

Sioux, Omaha and Winnebago reservations, which it collectively called the American Indian Satellite Community College. In 1978, Congress passed the Tribally Controlled Colleges and Universities Assistance Act, which authorized direct federal funding for higher education institutions controlled or chartered by tribes. Two years later, the Santee Sioux, Winnebago and Omaha tribes took control of the American Indian Satellite Community College, renaming it the Nebraska Indian Community College, with the support of Northeast Technical's leaders.

"The desire of the Indian for educational self-determination certainly represents the wishes of Indian officials for full control on each reservation. In that regard, we would be very pleased to see it funded and established," said Northeast Technical President Robert P. Cox. By 1983, the Nebraska Indian Community College boasted 450 full- and part-time students, of which 21 earned diplomas that year made of inscribed buckskins stretched across tree branches.[79]

It would take another 16 years for a second tribal college in Nebraska to be established. The Winnebago Tribe of Nebraska chartered Little Priest Tribal College in May 1996 as a two-year associate degree institution, according to the college website. The college was also meant to offer Ho-Chunk language and culture classes, as well as provide training opportunities for upgrading job skills and improving employment opportunities.

A Cold Night in Gordon

The night was brisk as four young men and a woman in a light blue Ford Custom cruised the streets of Gordon, Nebraska.

Robert Bayliss gripped the wheel as he and his five passengers looked for the old Indian man they had beaten up before. They found him walking near the rodeo grounds.[80]

Les Hare jumped out, called the man names and pushed him. Bayliss sped away, but then the group decided to find the Indian again. They found him in a junk car lot sitting inside a blue pickup with wood side panels. They started hitting him and pulled down his pants. They then shoved him into the trunk and drove to the Legion Hall.

Les Hare and his brother Pat had been banned from the Legion Hall. So, they decided, as a bit of revenge, to take the naked Indian and shove him into the building, where a USO benefit was taking place. The Indian man was in the Legion Hall just a few seconds before a man covered him up and the bartender led him out the front door into the freezing cold, wearing only a shirt and socks.

It was Feb. 12, 1972. The Indian man's name was Raymond Yellow Thunder, and his problems had just begun.

Later that night, the Hares and their friends came upon Yellow Thunder again, walking on the side of the road, still not wearing any pants. They pulled over and tossed him in the trunk again. They drove around for 45 minutes before leaving Yellow Thunder at a laundromat.

The old Indian checked himself into the jail for a voluntary sleepover.

Almost a week later, he would be found dead in a truck behind a Gordon car lot.

His death would ignite a firestorm of criminal proceedings and social justice activism that would reverberate beyond the streets of Gordon.

Just days after Yellow Thunder's death, in early March 1972, Severt Young Bear knocked on Russell Means' hotel room in Omaha, where Means was attending an AIM conference. "Sorry to wake you," he told the imposing Means. "But we need your help."

He informed Means about Yellow Thunder's death. Means decided that seeking justice for Yellow Thunder would give AIM a foothold on a reservation and the credibility they needed to expand across the country.

"The American Indian Movement had few followers on the reservation, and the leadership had been looking for ways to change that. AIM was made up of big-city intellectuals with roots in sixties activism; they had little cachet in the countryside."[81]

The next day, he took the stage at the AIM conference in Omaha and told its members about Yellow Thunder's death.

"This organization ought to go to Gordon where the action is! It should lead us to that racist town!"[82]

The members of AIM agreed and began loading into cars headed first for Pine Ridge, where they planned to hold a rally.

---

79. Tom Allan, "Tribes Seek Community College," Omaha *World-Herald*, February 16, 1980, newspapers.com; Allan, "Indian College Aims at Peaks in Education," Omaha *World-Herald*, May 22, 1983, newspapers.com.
80. Magnuson, *Death of Yellow Thunder,* 111.
81. Magnuson, *Death of Yellow Thunder,* 56.
82. Magnuson, *Death of Yellow Thunder,* 61.

FBI and State Patrol teletypes relayed urgent messages warning of the coming storm.

SEVERAL HUNDRED INDIANS PLAN TO GO TO GORDON, NEBRASKA NIGHT OF MARCH SIX TO BURN BUILDINGS IN REPRISAL FOR DEATH OF RAYMOND YELLOW THUNDER.[83]

Nebraska officials sparred over the events. Sheridan County Attorney Michael Smith told an AP reporter that rumors were being reported as fact, citing an indignant letter sent to him by Nebraska Indian Commission Program Director Ken Bordeaux, who wrote: "Will [these] kinds of atrocities and outrages against our Indian people persist? Must other citizens stand by and let this happen or are they, too, still fighting the Indian wars of the last century?"[84]

Bordeaux called for a grand jury, claiming Yellow Thunder's skull had been crushed. Smith told the AP reporter that Bordeaux didn't know what the autopsy said and that Yellow Thunder hadn't died of a crushed skull. And he told the reporter that Yellow Thunder had been inside the Legion Hall for less than 30 seconds and had never been forced to dance Indian style, as many news reports had suggested, "There really isn't much of a story," Smith said.

At 7:30 p.m. March 7, 1972, nearly 700 AIM supporters gathered for the rally in Pine Ridge.

Smith and state patrol investigator Max Ibach tried to defuse the situation by speaking at the Pine Ridge rally but were shouted down by AIM supporters. AIM leaders called for the manslaughter charges to be refiled as first-degree murder charges and the false imprisonment charges increased to kidnapping.

And they wanted a second autopsy.

"If you're not willing to meet our demands, I suggest you get out of Pine Ridge," AIM leader Dennis Banks said.

Then Means spoke. He described Yellow Thunder as a quiet man who had been brutalized and forced to dance naked in a Legion Hall as white people laughed. He talked about the reservation's history and reminded his audience of the hundreds of women and children murdered at Wounded Knee.

"The Oglalas had never heard an Indian like Means before. He was one part American Horse, one part Malcolm X, and one part his Iowa Technical College speech professor who'd given him a 'C' seven years earlier for moving around too much and not making eye contact with the audience," Magnuson wrote in an account he characterized as narrative nonfiction style.[85]

The next day, AIM rolled into Gordon.

As the organization's supporters walked down tree-lined streets, local residents locked their doors and became scarce.

As they passed the post office, Means paused to pull down the American flag and drape it around his shoulders to the cheers of protestors. Farther down the street, some protestors pulled down the flag at the American Legion Hall.

They made their way to the Neighborhood Center, where they held their rally.

"We came here today to put Gordon on the map. But if our demands aren't met, and met soon, we'll come back and take Gordon off the map!"[86] Means said.

AIM eventually decided to occupy the city auditorium, where they called on Gordon city officials and the governor to hear their demands. Mayor Bruce Moore showed up to defend his town but was yelled at by protestors.

The activists then heard from local Native residents, who talked about police brutality and systemic racism. One resident, Robert Two Crow, 23, told the protestors he had seen local police beating up drunk Natives and later forcing them to rake leaves or pick up trash to work off their fines.

Gov. J.J. Exon's representatives, Clive Short, director of buildings and grounds, and Indian Commission Director Robert Mackey also arrived to speak to the gathered protestors.

Mackey told the crowd he had called for a federal grand jury to investigate Yellow Thunder's death. But some AIM members wondered why Exon had sent such a low-level bureaucrat as Short to speak to them.

Means called Short a "bellboy, and the activists sentenced Exon "to hell" for sending him.[87]

Magnuson describes Reva Evans, editor and publisher of the *Gordon Journal*, and her efforts to set the record straight in regard to Gordon and what she considered slander against it by the militant outsiders. It

---

83. Magnuson, *Death of Yellow Thunder*, 129.
84. Magnuson, *Death of Yellow Thunder*, 129-130.
85. Magnuson, *Death of Yellow Thunder*, 136.
86. Magnuson, *Death of Yellow Thunder*, 140.
87. Magnuson, *Death of Yellow Thunder*, 144.

took two days for Evans to set foot in the auditorium. And despite that, nothing negative about Gordon ever appeared in her newspaper.

"Evans believed Gordon was a perfect town beyond reproach, where whites and Indians lived together side by side in perfect harmony. Means believed the town was inhabited by uncaring white devils, who looked at Indians as subhuman. The truth probably lay somewhere in between."[88]

On the second day of the occupation, AIM leaders met with Sheridan County Attorney Smith, who told them that he wouldn't be able to prove murder, with its burden of proving intent to kill. He told them the best he could do was prove manslaughter and false imprisonment.

But Smith did give in to a few of AIM's demands, including that a second autopsy be conducted and that an investigation into Gordon officer John Paul be carried out.

And he agreed to set up a human relations council made up of clergy and local Lakota people.

"Smith was pleased because, in reality, he'd promised them very little. AIM leaders were pleased because they could proclaim victory."[89]

But the autopsy found the same thing that the first one had, that Yellow Thunder had died of a subdural hematoma, not of a crushed skull, and that he hadn't been tortured. And officer Paul was never investigated, suspended or fired.

Only the human relations council would endure.

But the fight for justice for Yellow Thunder had only just begun. And it would be up to Smith to win it.

The trial of Pat and Les Hare began on May 21, 1972, in Alliance, Nebraska. AIM supporters set up a drum in the center of the rotunda in the Box Butte County courthouse.

Inside the courtroom, Yellow Thunder's family, the Hares' mother and *Gordon Journal* publisher Reva Evans sat in the audience behind Pat and Les Hare, who wore pressed suits and neckties. Everyone could hear and feel the drum.

Smith began the trial with his opening statement, in which he described how the Hares and their friends had found and beaten Yellow Thunder before shoving him into their trunk and driving him into the Legion Hall, where they pushed him inside.

Smith had convinced Bernard Lutter, a passenger in the car, to testify against the Hares. "Even with Lutter's cooperation, Smith felt he had a delicate and difficult case." Lutter hadn't directly witnessed Les jumping on Yellow Thunder. He ended his statement saying he would prove that the brain hemorrhage that took Yellow Thunder's life was directly linked to the beating he endured at the hands of the Hares.

The Hares' attorney, Charles Fisher, then took the floor, arguing that his clients had only been trying to help Yellow Thunder that night and that they never harmed him. And he countered the claims of false imprisonment, saying that Robert Bayliss's car had a latch in the trunk that would have allowed Yellow Thunder to get out anytime he wanted.[90]

For several days, Smith and Fisher sparred over the details of what had actually happened to Yellow Thunder. The jury heard from a pathologist who told them he didn't know when Yellow Thunder had been injured or died, and they heard from the Hares' half-brother, who testified that he hadn't seen any marks on the victim's face or body when he saw him at the laundromat that night. And they heard from the Gordon police chief and Sheridan County sheriff, who both said they had not seen a special latch inside Bayliss's trunk.

And they heard from Bayliss, who said he installed the latch in his trunk because his son had locked himself inside once.

Then Pat Hare took the stand. He related a fanciful story of encountering a drunk Indian gentleman while out driving with his friends. Les got out and visited with the man before driving away. Later, they saw Yellow Thunder walking into a used-car lot.

"Why, it's too cold out tonight," Les said. "That Indian gentleman will pass out and freeze to death if we don't help him."

They found Yellow Thunder passed out in an old truck and decided to put him in the trunk of Bayliss's car. But first they decided to take off his pants as part of a light-hearted attempt to wake the man up. And they then decided to take him to the Legion Hall and push him inside.

Pat Hare then testified that they later found Yellow Thunder walking down the street half-naked and the man agreed to climb into their trunk.

"The story would have been laughable if Yellow Thunder's death weren't so tragic."[91]

Michael Smith tore into the man's story, lampooning Hare for claiming to be a good Samaritan while admitting that he took off Yellow Thunder's pants and forced him into the Legion Hall.

---

88. Magnuson, *Death of Yellow Thunder*, 151.
89. Magnuson, *Death of Yellow Thunder*, 153.
90. Magnuson, *Death of Yellow Thunder*, 199.

In his closing remarks, Smith again attacked Pat's version of events.

"The testimony given to you by the defendant Melvin P. Hare is incredible. In fact, the word was created for this kind of testimony," he said.[92]

Just six hours later, the jury had its verdict. The foreman proclaimed Les and Pat Hare guilty of false imprisonment and manslaughter.

Somewhere below, the drummers pounded a victory song.

AIM celebrated at the city auditorium as the Hares made their way home to their mother's. Later that August, Les was given six years and Pat two years, though Les served just two of the six years and Pat 10 months of the two-year sentence.

The Fight Isn't Over

In November 1972, members of AIM occupied the Bureau of Indian Affairs building in Washington, D.C., following its Trail of Broken Treaties.

Less than a week later, Oglala Lakota activist Bob Yellow Bird, his wife Joann and his brother-in-law Bill Cross and nearly 50 others occupied Fort Robinson near Crawford, Nebraska, which the federal government had rendered surplus land. Yellow Bird believed the Fort Laramie Treaty of 1868 required the government to return surplus land to the Lakota. They occupied the fort for 14 hours.

In February 1973, its supporters then set their sights on Custer, S.D., where a trial involving a Native man who had been stabbed was taking place. The AIM protest during the trial ended in a riot.[93] Later that month, AIM activists gathered in a community building west of Pine Ridge to discuss the police state that had taken over the reservation. Tribal President Dick Wilson was cracking down on AIM and its supporters – mostly traditional Oglala Lakota – and had called in federal authorities to quell AIM. The group's supporters were being forced to endure drive-by shootings and beatings.

Inside the log cabin-style community center, elders called on AIM to fight back.

The militants crammed into dozens of cars and began driving through the dark, meandering past fortified government buildings in Pine Ridge and into the countryside on the road to Wounded Knee.

Bob Yellow Bird joined them there. The Vietnam veteran dug bunkers and patrolled the perimeter along with other veterans.

AIM's demands were sovereignty for Native people, the return of the sacred Black Hills and abolishment of the tribe's government.

Nebraska towns just across the border from the reservation made big money entertaining out-of-towners, including government agents.

After 71 days, the siege ended and AIM and its supporters went home.

But for many of the activists who held as many as 300 FBI agents and U.S. Marshalls at bay for more than two months, their life-and-death struggles would soon become legal problems.

Many of them would face trial on various charges related to the siege. And many of them would see their cases handled by the same judge, U.S. District Court Judge Warren Urbom, and many would go to trial in Lincoln.

Judge Urbom

In late 1973, Judge Gerald Heaney of the Eighth Circuit Court of Appeals asked Urbom to serve as one of several district judges to travel to South Dakota to try cases arising from the Wounded Knee Siege. Those trials, however, didn't include those of the two highest profile leaders of the siege – Russell Means and Dennis Banks – whose trials would take place in St. Paul, Minnesota.

"I accepted the invitation with the expectation that I'd spend a week trying Native Americans. I stayed a year," Urbom said.[94]

Initially, the plan was to have Urbom handle all his cases in Sioux Falls, South Dakota. In the first case he handled, US v. Baker and Decora, Urbom ruled evidence taken from a roadblock couldn't be admitted, leading to the case's dismissal.

Soon, it was decided that all of the non-AIM leader cases would be moved from Sioux Falls to Lincoln. In January and February 1974, Urbom dismissed 25 of 30 of those cases because of lack of evidence.

Urbom quickly earned the respect of many of the defendants who entered his courtroom. Much of that respect came from his willingness to allow Native defendants to say prayers before the start of

---

91. Magnuson, *Death of Yellow Thunder*, 208.
92. Magnuson, *Death of Yellow Thunder*, 209.
93. Magnuson, *Death of Yellow Thunder*, 219.
94. Warren K. Urbom, *Called to Justice: The Life of a Federal Trial Judge* (Bison Books, 2012), 129.

proceedings and to say their oaths on sacred medicine pipes.

"I saw no problem with the request, because the purpose of an oath is to impress the witness, not the judge or jury, with the importance of telling the truth."[95]

Urbom didn't require the installation of security devices in his courtroom. Before his first trial, he allowed the defendants to host a ceremony that lasted two hours and featured the presence of three different tribes.

To accommodate the Native defendants in Lincoln, many people opened their homes to defendants and their friends and families. One local man, Bud Irons, donated the use of a former Air Force barracks. Local nonprofit leader Beatty Brasch and Rev. Bob Jeambey created the Lincoln Committee of Concerned Citizens to help transport Indian defendants from the barracks to the courthouse, as well as to help with medical care and food.

But not everyone was as welcoming toward the Native visitors. Urbom said he heard reports of subtle bigotry toward Indians by white residents, "including poor or no service to Indian customers at eating establishments and taverns."[96]

Urbom adjudicated the cases of 150 defendants, of which he dismissed charges for 101 without a trial and tried 49. Of those 49, he found 43 not guilty or dismissed their charges for lack of evidence. He found six guilty, but of those six, four had their convictions reversed by the Eighth Circuit Court of Appeals and two were sentenced to probation. "Were the appropriate sentences given? Yes, I think so."[97]

Urbom considered his time spent adjudicating the Wounded Knee cases exceptional.

"There is no question that it was one of the richest experiences of my life. Issues were new and hard. The lawyers were amazingly dedicated. The Indians were deeply engaged in a cause."[98]

Yellow Bird's Fight for Justice

In 1974, Yellow Bird led a protest down Gordon's Main Street. He walked into a meeting of the Human Relations Council and submitted a list of grievances. He wanted an end to racism by local doctors and decent jobs for Lakotas, and he demanded that Gordon police stop taking drunks to the Rushville jail and leaving them there to make their way home.[99]

Gordon Journal publisher Reva Evans blasted Yellow Bird, leading her column with a quote from King Lear: "How sharper than a serpent's tooth it is / To have a thankless child."[100]

Yellow Bird and Bill Cross continued their fight, cranking out editions of the *Crazy Horse Advocate*, their own personal social justice journal. And they continued their efforts to have Fort Robinson returned to the Lakota. State Sen. Ernie Chambers even sponsored a bill to give the fort to the Oglala Sioux Tribe, but the bill never made it out of committee.[101]

In May 1974, Yellow Bird hosted a workshop in his backyard seeking an end to racism in western Nebraska. Indian Commissioner Bob Mackey and Reva Evans both attended. "Anytime an Indian tries to do something, he's considered a radical," Yellow Bird said.[102]

AIM kept trying to do something to the north. Its war with the Dick Wilson regime and federal authorities peaked again in June 1975 when two FBI agents followed two fugitives onto an AIM encampment near Oglala and were shot and killed. Among the activists present during the shootout was a Turtle Mountain Ojibwe named Leonard Peltier, who was later convicted of killing the agents.

"To some, Peltier was the Indian Nelson Mandela, a political prisoner, unjustly jailed for a crime he did not commit. To the FBI, he was a cold-blooded murderer," Magnuson wrote.[103]

In western Nebraska, another Lakota leader was continuing his efforts to improve the lives of Lakotas living in Alliance. With Lakota leader Mark Monroe at the helm, the Alliance Indian Center offered

---

95. Urbom, *Called to Justice*, 140.
96. Urbom, *Called to Justice*, 141.
97. Urbom, *Called to Justice*, 179.
98. Urbom, *Called to Justice*, 174.
99. Magnuson, *Death of Yellow Thunder*, 231.
100. Magnuson, *Death of Yellow Thunder*, 232.
101. Magnuson, *Death of Yellow Thunder*, 233.
102. Magnuson, *Death of Yellow Thunder*, 232.
103. Magnuson, *Death of Yellow Thunder*, 237.

counseling to alcoholics, housing and job service, as well as health services, including a nutrition program that served one hot meal a day. By August 1975, the center served 6,663 meals to 499 low-income people.[104]

Not all Natives living in Alliance supported Monroe's efforts, however. In August 1975, Lillian Bordeaux and other Natives formed the Alliance United Lakotas to serve the Lakota community. The organization did not associate with AIM and established programs for youth, medical services, scholarships and legal support.[105]

In late 1975, a major change in leadership within the Nebraska Indian Commission led to the ouster of the organization's executive director, Bob Mackey. After criticizing the work of a Native advocacy organization called the United Indians of Nebraska, Mackey became the subject of criticism by Gov. J.J. Exon and Monroe, who asked Exon to fire Mackey. On Jan. 10, 1976, the commission fired Mackey for telling Exon that tribal governments were unstable. The commission later hired Felix White Jr., Winnebago, to replace Mackey.

Meanwhile, Bob Yellow Bird continued his fight for justice.

In late 1975, Yellow Bird began working with a Nebraska Indian Commission volunteer and an attorney for Panhandle Legal Services to compile statistics related to alleged police brutality. They discovered that most of the arrests in Sheridan County were for intoxication and most of those arrests were of Native Americans.[106]

On the evening of March 11, 1976, the Indian Commission came to Gordon to hold an on-site hearing. A few hours before the meeting, two of Gordon's policemen resigned after clashing with an attorney for the U.S. Civil Rights Commission. Russell Means attended the meeting and gave a fiery speech. "The town of Gordon has regressed rather than progressed. It is as bad if not worse than it was in 1972," he said.[107]

Encouraged by Means' speech, Yellow Bird and 100 supporters left the Indian Commission hearing to attend a city council meeting, where they yelled at city officials. County Attorney Michael Smith decided to hire private investigators to look into the claims of police brutality. Their investigation found that officers "do not seem to feel that they are public servants, but rather overlords whose word is law, and if they give a command it had better be obeyed, and immediately and without question."[108]

Within months, Police Chief Bob Case had resigned.

Meanwhile, Yellow Bird's long struggle for civil rights was about to come to an abrupt end.

Yellow Bird's Fall

On May 4, 1976, he went out barhopping with Bill Cross and Joann. They ended up at the Hacienda Lounge, where they got into a fight with three men. Yellow Bird left and came back with a .22-caliber pistol and shot one of the men in the stomach and another in his rear and arm. He left town and became a fugitive.

That July, he turned himself in. Two months later, while out on bail awaiting trial, he and Joann and several others were drinking in the Sheridan Lounge when they got into a fight with the owner and police were called.

Police arrived, and Joann attacked an officer who was trying to restrain Yellow Bird. The officer kicked the pregnant woman in the stomach while another officer kicked her on the waist. She fell back against a patrol car and slumped to the ground, holding her stomach. After that night, she would never feel her baby kick again.[109]

More police arrived, and Yellow Bird and his compatriots were all arrested and taken to jail.

With AIM's support, the Yellow Birds filed an $8 million lawsuit against local officials and the Sheridan Lounge owner, Don Brown. But first he had to fight his previous charges.

In December, he went to trial for the earlier shootings. He argued he feared for his life in the racially charged atmosphere of Gordon and had shot the two men in self-defense. The jury agreed and acquitted him of both charges.[110]

Emboldened, Yellow Bird next went to war with Mark Monroe, director of the Alliance Indian Center, for control of the center. On April Fools' Day

---

104. Christensen, "The Ground You Walk On," 206.
105. Christensen, "The Ground You Walk On," 212.
106. Magnuson, *Death of Yellow Thunder*, 238.
107. Magnuson, *Death of Yellow Thunder*, 241.
108. Magnuson, *Death of Yellow Thunder*, 242.
109. Magnuson, *Death of Yellow Thunder*, 247.
110. Magnuson, *Death of Yellow Thunder*, 250.

1978, he and Joann and a few others went to Monroe's home in Alliance and attempted to drag Monroe from his home. Monroe broke free and stumbled to his bedroom where he kept a handgun. He chased the intruders from his home, firing his gun at the fleeing car.[111]

Monroe called the sheriff's department and Sheriff Bill Stairs arrived just as Yellow Bird returned with a rifle, resulting in a shootout. Stairs chased the two cars in Yellow Bird's caravan. Yellow Bird and Joann fled to Martin, S.D., but he eventually turned himself in.

A jury believed his version of the events and acquitted him of all felony charges, though he was convicted of misdemeanor assault and given 30 days in jail. Still, he decided to avoid jail time by leaving Gordon.[112]

Yellow Bird returned for the Sheridan County Lounge civil lawsuit in which he convinced the jury that the police involved in the riot were at fault. The jury awarded the Yellow Birds $300,000. But barely a year after they left Nebraska, Joann swallowed a dose of strychnine and died, her death ruled a suicide.[113]

Yellow Bird spent the jury award and in the early 1990s, he lost a game of Russian roulette and became paralyzed on his left side. He died in 1997 at the age of 52 from complications from a lung infection.

A New Approach

Beyond the fiery activism of the American Indian Movement, a more legalistic approach to civil rights action took hold in western Nebraska in the years following the death of Raymond Yellow Thunder.

In 1976, the Nebraska Indian Commission joined Lakota organizations in western Nebraska in seeking to improve conditions for Lakota inmates in the Sheridan County Jail in Rushville. On Aug. 12, Don Bearrunner wrote to AIM lawyer Dale Mason detailing civil rights violations within the Sheridan County legal system, citing excessive bail and alcohol-related fines against Lakotas.[114]

On September 3, 1976, Nebraska Indian Commission member Carl Janis and a Nebraska Health Department official inspected the Sheridan County Jail and requested input from inmates, who claimed deplorable conditions within the jail such as overcrowding and unwillingness by jailers to allow Lakotas to make phone calls. The inmates also claimed the public defender cared little for Lakota clients and often pushed those clients to plead guilty to lesser charges rather than defend them in court.

On November 30, 1976, after two years of Stephen Janis' lobbying for expansion, the Panhandle Legal Services Board of Directors passed a reorganization plan to expand its services beginning January 1, 1977.[115] Lakotas in Dawes, Sheridan, and Box Butte counties would no longer have to rely on public defenders for legal guidance.

In February 1977, the Legal Coalition Conference was held in Lincoln with a goal of increasing awareness of and addressing discrimination issues in western Nebraska. Representatives from the Civil Rights Division of the Department of Justice, the American Civil Liberties Union and the Native American Rights Fund attended.

Around the same time, Stephen Janis convinced the Indian Health Services to reimburse the West Nebraska General Hospital for treatment of Lakotas.[116]

In May 1978, the Law Enforcement Assistance Administration released a report on law enforcement in Gordon, noting that although Lakotas made up less than 10 percent of the town's population, they comprised 92 percent of all arrests. Most of those arrests were for alcohol-related offenses.[117]

In the Dec. 20, 1978, edition of the *Gordon Journal*, Kaye Buckles of the Gordon Human Relations Council described the actions the town had made to improve Native and non-Native relations. Those actions included implementing a screening process to ensure quality officers are hired, using a $389,000 Community Development Grant to improve areas of town

---

111. Magnuson, *Death of Yellow Thunder*, 252.
112. Magnuson, *Death of Yellow Thunder*, 253.
113. Magnuson, *Death of Yellow Thunder*, 254.
114. Don Bearrunner to Dale Mason, August 12, 1976, Correspondence Scottsbluff Office 1976, Box 3, RG 93 SG1, Nebraska Indian Commission Files, NSHS. Quoted in Christensen, 224.
115. Stephen Janis to Bert Schoetgner, December 20, 1976, Correspondence Scottsbluff Office 1976, Box 3, RG 93 SG1, Nebraska Indian Commission Files, NSHS. Quoted in Christensen, 226.
116. Rice Leach to Gary Gunder, April 8, 1977, Correspondence Scottsbluff Office 1977, Box 3, RG 93 SG1, Nebraska Indian Commission Files, NSHS. Quoted in Christensen, 230.
117. In Law Enforcement Assistance Administration Police Technical Assistance Report, March 1978, Correspondence Scottsbluff Office 1978, Box 3, RG 93 SG1, Nebraska Indian Commission Files, NSHS. Quoted in Christensen, 223.

inhabited by Lakotas and providing financial support for two alcohol treatment programs. Buckles praised the town for working to end racial discrimination.[118]

In February 1979, the Nebraska State Advisory Committee to the U.S. Commission on Civil Rights held a subcommittee hearing in Gordon and found the town had improved race relations, particularly within its police department.[119] But in March 1979, Stephen Janis – now an advisory committee member – testified in Washington D.C. before the U.S. Commission on Civil Rights that Lakotas were still suffering disparate treatment by Sheridan County authorities. He cited statistics from April 1971 to November 1978 that showed that of the 26 defendants that could have been charged as habitual criminals, only eight received such charges, and of those eight, seven were Native American.

Janis also testified that a housing survey conducted in Scotts Bluff County showed more than 90 percent of Lakotas described their housing as substandard and less than 5 percent owned homes. Most Lakotas in Gordon lived in a shanty town near the railroad tracks.

As efforts persisted to raise awareness about such disparities, the Nebraska Indian Commission, along with other state advocacy commissions, began to come under budget fire.

In 1979, the Nebraska Legislature considered consolidating the Nebraska Indian Commission, Mexican American Commission, Commission on the Status of Women and Commission on Aging but failed to pass legislation to do so. That November, Executive Assistant and future governor Kay Orr notified Marvin Buzzard, the recently hired Nebraska Indian Commission executive director, that the commission needed to complete a survey. Within a year, the governor's Task Force on Governmental Improvement recommended eliminating the commission and other state-funded advocacy agencies to cut state government costs.

Meanwhile, Lakotas living in western Nebraska continued to suffer deplorable socioeconomic conditions.

A 1981 grant application by the Platte Valley Lakota Association reported the findings of surveys conducted by Creighton University, the Nebraska Indian Commission and the Nebraska State Advisory Committee. The surveys showed that 56 percent of Panhandle Lakotas lacked a high school diploma and 30 percent disliked the Anglo-centric curriculum at local schools. Unemployment ranged from 25 to 30 percent while nearly 58 percent of families interviewed reported annual incomes of $5,000 or less.

In 1982, the Unicameral rejected an amendment to defund the governor's commissions.

A year later, Gov. Bob Kerrey took office, and the Legislature finally decided to defund the governor's commissions. The Indian Commission was forced to close its western office. The commission's new director, Reba White Shirt, led the fight for refunding, though Kerrey urged commissions to find other sources of funding.

The defunding of the Indian Commission meant there was no organization to lobby state lawmakers and the governor on behalf of Native people or investigate civil rights violations. Racism, police brutality and educational neglect only worsened during this period.

By July 1986, the Unicameral approved funding to the Indian Commission but at a much-reduced rate of $70,646 for fiscal year 1986-1987.

The 1986 election of Kay Orr as governor did not improve the commission's prospects. She proposed phasing out state funding for all the commissions.

Commission member Phyllis Stone defended the Indian Commission in a March 1987 legislative hearing. The Rosebud Lakota woman argued that despite Native people being a smaller minority than other minorities, they deserved state support. "We were here first. We are your Native people and it behooves the state of Nebraska to uphold the responsibility it chose to take from the federal government in 1953."[120]

Charles Trimble, president of the American Indian National Republican Federation wrote to the newly elected governor to urge her to increase funding for the Indian Commission. Orr told him she agreed with the commission's importance but opposed spending taxpayer dollars for it.

"This position stems not from tight budgets, but a conservative philosophy about the proper role of government. Advocacy-type entities are most effective when they are financially independent of the government officials who set policy," she told Trimble.[121]

---

118. "Rumblings," *Gordon Journal* (Gordon, NE), Dec. 20, 1978.
119. *Scottsbluff Herald* (Gordon, NE) May 11, 1978.
120. Phyllis Stone, March 8, 1987, Indian Commission Budget, Box.025 RG001, SG43, Kay Orr Papers, Nebraska Indian Commission Files, NSHS. Quoted in Christensen, 243.
121. Kay Orr to Charles Trimble, June 2, 1987, Indian Commission Budget, Box.025 RG001, SG43, Kay Orr Papers, Nebraska Indian Commission Files, NSHS. Quoted in Christensen, 244.

Orr's line-item veto left the commission for $23,549 for fiscal year 1988-1989 for the commission.

Native people continued to call attention to civil rights concerns for Native people in western Nebraska. In late summer 1988, Department of Justice federal mediator Pascual Marquez arrived to conduct meetings in Gordon. He heard from Lakotas who reported that the police entered homes without warrants, unjustly arrested juveniles and taped their interrogations without their legal guardians present. Marquez planned to conduct workshops to improve communications between police and Lakotas.[122]

Despite such efforts, tensions remained high between police and Lakotas in western Nebraska. In 1992, a Gordon police officer shot and killed Dennis Cross, a Lakota, after Cross pointed a rifle at the officer. It was later found that Cross' rifle was empty. On Feb. 21, a jury determined officer Curtis Schipper's actions were justified. That same year, Lakotas submitted complaints to the city of Alliance alleging local police were harassing them and practicing selective enforcement. A city investigation failed to quell Lakotas' concerns, though the city manager decided officers needed cultural sensitivity training.[123]

On April 28 and 29, 1992, the Nebraska State Advisory Committee held hearings to discuss civil rights in western Nebraska, focusing on Scottsbluff, which had a Lakota population of 662; Alliance, with 302 Lakotas; Chadron, with 355 Lakotas; and Gordon, with 524 Lakotas. At the hearing, Stephen Janis described the dual system of justice, housing discrimination and lack of healthcare for Natives. Connie Stairs testified about prejudice by store employees, who followed Lakotas around stores. Susan Esparza, executive director of the Native American Center in Chadron, spoke about Lakotas being called "squaw" and being told "dirty Indian, go back to your tepees."

Police chiefs in the four communities defended their departments, maintaining that their departments had good relations with Lakotas. Alliance Police Chief Robert Jatczak expressed wanting to recruit a Native officer.

In September 1993, the Nebraska Indian Commission held a hearing to discuss western Nebraska Lakotas' needs. Some Lakotas decried the Department of Social Services' unwillingness to abide by federal laws preventing the unjust removal of Native children from their families and tribes. One mother complained that her children had been removed twice and a foster parent had molested her daughter.[124]

It wasn't just police and city officials that exhibited prejudice against Native people. In 1995, a banking regulatory agency found that the First National Bank of Gordon had demonstrated discriminatory loan practices against Lakotas from September 1992 to March 1994, primarily against Lakotas living on the Pine Ridge Reservation. In response to complaints by the Department of Justice, the Gordon bank signed a $275,000 settlement to reimburse affected customers.[125]

Then in May 1998, the death of another Lakota inmate in the Alliance jail reignited claims of police brutality. The inmate, 22-year-old Shane Dawn, was found hanging from a shoelace and a T-shirt in his cell. His family believed jailers beat him to death. "I don't believe my son committed suicide," his mother said.[126]

Despite Alliance officials' claims in the 1970s that they had reformed their jailing practices to prevent suicides, Dawn's death proved otherwise.

The Bones Controversy

In 1775, the Omaha Tribe established a village near Homer, Nebraska, in northeast Nebraska called Tonwantonga, or Big Village. Nearly 165 years later, a federal Works Progress Administration project excavated the village, leading to many skeletal remains and artifacts being transferred to the Nebraska State Historical Society to be studied.

In 1987, the Nebraska Indian Commission and tribal leaders called on the state Legislature to pass legislation to protect unmarked burial sites and return Native American remains and artifacts to tribes.

---

122. PR Gregg, "Gordon Residents Say Bias in City," *Indian Country Today*, Aug. 30, 1988, 1.
123. *Alliance Times-Herald*, (Alliance, NE) July 10, 1992; July 27, 1992; Stephen Janis, "Racism: 'Some Day We Will Have Equal Rights'"; *Indian Country Today*, May 19, 1993, A6.
124. Commission on Indian Affairs, Sept. 30, 1993, 1993 Misc. Correspondence, Box 5, RG93 SG1, Nebraska Indian Commission Files, NSHS. Quoted in Christensen, 252.
125. "DOJ Sues Nebraska Bank For Lending Bias Against Indians," ABA Bank Compliance 17 (May 1996), 5; David Melmer, "Redlining Rates: Nebraska Bank Lands in Court Over Interest Charged American Indian," *Indian Country Today*, April 30, 1996, A1; "Discrimination Case Settled by Nebraska Bank: Agreement Sets Aside $275,000," *Indian Country Today*, May 19, 1997, A1. Quoted in Christensen, 254.
126. Marie Porterfield, "Jail Death of Lakota Man Sparks Community Anger: Shane Dawn Case Reminds Many of Abuse in Alliance," *Indian Country Today*, July 21, 1998, A1.

"Those are our ancestors and we want to show them respect," said Louis LaRose of the Winnebago Tribe during a March 12, 1987, legislative hearing.[127] Later that year, state Sen. Jim Pappas introduced a bill to protect Native American graves and return remains and artifacts. But his bill faced opposition from the State Historical Society and University of Nebraska anthropologists.

A particularly vehement critic of the bill was the Historical Society's Director, James A. Hanson, who lamented that the bill would lead to the society losing more than 10,000 irreplaceable artifacts. But a Historical Society Board member and NU anthropologist, Roger Welsch, criticized the bill's opponents for calling the legislation a "raid on the Historical Society collections."[128]

In 1988, the Pawnee Tribe of Oklahoma approached the Nebraska State Historical Society seeking the return of the remains of nearly 1,500 ancestors. At first, the state agency rejected the request, but in 1989, the Nebraska Legislature considered the legislation to require the return of Native remains and funerary objects. The debate over the bill was contentious and pitted science and museum advocates against champions of human rights and religious freedom. The Legislature eventually passed the Nebraska Unmarked Human Burial Sites and Skeletal Remains Protection Act.[129]

Despite the passage of the state legislation, a University of Nebraska-Lincoln anthropology professor, Karl J. Reinhard, was accused in 1998 of mishandling Native remains and failing to abide by the new state law. A graduate student alleged he had manipulated a child's skull so it appeared to be talking, but Reinhard defended himself, calling the allegations "fantasy." "The bone stuff is essentially hysteria being fed by a few faculty members," he said.[130] However, a State Patrol investigation yielded no criminal charges, and the university signed an agreement with tribes to return the remains.[131]

In 1999, Congress passed the Native American Graves Protection and Repatriation Act or NAGPRA, which requires federally funded institutions across the country to inventory skeletal remains and funerary objects and consult with tribes regarding repatriation. By 1999, nearly 700 sets of skeletal remains and associated mortuary objects in the possession of History Nebraska, (the Nebraska State Historical Society) had been returned to tribes. Most went to the Pawnee Tribe, though some also went to other tribes with historical roots in Nebraska, including the Otoe-Missouria Tribe and the Iowa Tribe.

"Whether it's seeds or an ancestor, their belongings, or even the small children in the boarding schools, missing and murdered tribal members, being returned to their people, they need to put them in place. It's a bringing back of something to its mother," said Stacy Laravie, Ponca tribal preservation officer.[132]

Bringing Back the Buffalo

As the twentieth century wound down, Native Americans in Nebraska began focusing on cultural revitalization and health. Efforts began to reverse the impact of centuries of colonization and its disastrous impacts on Native Americans' health and cultures.

The Winnebago Tribe welcomed home its first bison to its northeast Nebraska reservation in 1994, when the tribe purchased 10 bison from a Seward farmer. But that would be only the start. The tribe began acquiring more animals from federal refuges in North and South Dakota, as well as Fort Niobrara near Valentine. The tribe established its Winnebago Bison Project as a way to provide low-cholesterol, low-fat meat to its members in an effort to reverse soaring rates of diabetes. By November 1996, 52 bison roamed a pasture on a steep hillside on its reservation. The herd was among three kept by Nebraska tribes and among 5,000 bison tended nationwide by

---

127. Associated Press, "Indian leaders support bill protecting graves," *Lincoln Journal Star*, March 13, 1987, newspapers.com.
128. J.L. Schmidt, "Opponents of grave-protection bill labeled hysterical by its Lincoln supporters," *Lincoln Journal Star*, February 15, 1988, newspapers.com.
129. Evolempirecreative. "The Native American Graves Protection and Repatriation Act: History Nebraska's Repatriation Program." History Nebraska, July 27, 2023. Accessed Oct. 2, 2023. https://history.nebraska.gov/the-native-american-graves-protection-and-repatriation-act-history-nebraskas-repatriation-program
130. Joe Duggan, "Indians to call for professor's suspension," *Lincoln Journal Star*, September 12, 1998, newspapers.com.
131. Trudell, Tim. "Nebraska Museums Have Yet to Return over 100 Sets of Native American Remains." Flatwater Free Press, Sept. 15, 2023. Accessed Oct. 2, 2023. https://flatwaterfreepress.org/nebraska-museums-have-to-return-over-100-sets-of-native-american-remains
132. Trudell, Tim. "Nebraska Museums Have yet to Return over 100 Sets of Native American Remains." Flatwater Free Press, Sept. 15, 2023. Accessed Oct. 2, 2023. https://flatwaterfreepress.org/nebraska-museums-have-to-return-over-100-sets-of-native-american-remains

30 tribes through a government-funded program called the InterTribal Buffalo Council.

"The buffalo took care of us for many years. Now, in the cycle we're in, we have to take care of the buffalo until the cycle comes full circle again," said Louis LaRose, former Winnebago tribal chairman and director of the Winnebago Bison Project.[133]

A News and Political Warrior

Few modern Nebraska Native Americans have had more of an impact on policy and Indigenous civil rights than Charles "Chuck" Trimble. Born on March 12, 1935, on South Dakota's Pine Ridge Indian Reservation, Trimble was a journalist and civil rights leader who served as the former executive director of the National Congress of American Indians (NCAI) and founder of the American Indian Press Association, today known as the Indigenous Journalists Association. He founded the press association, which served as a news service for tribal newspapers across the country, citing a lack of coverage of Native American issues. Trimble attended Holy Rosary Mission boarding school and later graduated from the University of South Dakota, served in the U.S. Army and later studied journalism at the University of Colorado.

As the head of NCAI from 1972 to 1978, Trimble worked to protect tribal sovereignty and ensure tribes' concerns were addressed by federal lawmakers. "I was fortunate to have served through the decade most prolific in the enactment of legislation for new policy, programs, and resources, as well as executive actions favorable to Indian tribes and off-reservation Indian communities," Trimble wrote in an address for the organization's 2009 convention. He cited Congressional legislation such as the Indian Self-Determination and Education Assistance Act, the Indian Financing Act, and the Indian Health Care Improvement Act, as well as the "unprecedented return of significant lands to tribes," as issues he was able to address as NCAI executive director.

Among his other accomplishments was starting a newspaper on the Colville Reservation in Washington and writing newspaper columns on topics ranging from tribal politics and languages to aging. He was inducted into the South Dakota Hall of Fame in 2013 and received several honorary degrees and numerous awards, including the 1998 Pioneer Award from the NEBRASKAland Foundation. In Nebraska, Trimble spent many years serving organizations devoted to historic preservation, including the Nebraska State Historical Society, where he served as a board member from 1991 to 1997, the last three years spent as board president. He served on the boards of the Omaha Landmarks Heritage Preservation Commission and the John G. Neihardt Foundation.

Trimble died on March 2, 2020, of natural causes at the age of 84. "His passing has left a big hole in the field of Native American journalism," Oglala Lakota journalist Tim Giago wrote after Trimble's death.[134]

The Fight for Whiteclay

It took nearly two decades of fighting for Indigenous civil rights to bring about the 2017 closing of beer stores in Whiteclay, an unincorporated Nebraska village near the South Dakota border. The deaths of two Lakota men in 1999 near the border town of Whiteclay, Nebraska, inflamed Lakota people. On June 8, 1999, the bodies of two Lakota men – Ronald Hard Heart and Wilson "Wally" Black Elk – were found on the Pine Ridge Reservation, a few hundred yards north of Whiteclay. Authorities determined they had both been murdered.

Whiteclay had once served as a buffer zone to protect Lakotas from bootlegging, but President Theodore Roosevelt had opened up the area to settlement in 1904.[135] Soon after, settlers opened shops, a general store, gas stations and saloons. In 1953, the federal government ended the law making it illegal to sell alcohol to Indians. Whiteclay was also a place of celebration. Each year, a carnival and a rodeo came to town.

By 1962, the town had its own sheriff's deputy after state lawmakers approved funds for the position. Jim Talbot was the first to take the job. "He was by all accounts one of the most evenhanded lawmen to ever wear a badge in Sheridan County."[136] But the Unicameral cut funding for the deputy position in 1974. Sheridan County officials decided to shut down Whiteclay's bars, which had become too rowdy, but allowed stores to sell beer to be taken off the premises.

---

133. Paul Hammel, "Tribes Seek Double Comeback: Return of Bison Seen as a Way to Provide Jobs, Food, Pride," *Omaha World-Herald*, November 1, 1996, newspapers.com..
134. Associated Press, "Native journalist, activist Trimble dies," *Lincoln Journal Star*, March 6, 1920, newspapers.com.
135. Magnuson, *Death of Yellow Thunder*, 260.
136. Magnuson, *Death of Yellow Thunder*, 267.

"Whiteclay soon became the Little Skid Row on the Prairie."[137]

But the town saw more than just brawls.

On Oct. 27, 1978, four masked men wielding three revolvers and an M-1 rifle entered Jaco's Off Sale Bar and held the owner and clerk at gunpoint. The owner and clerk ducked out of the room, as the four men began shooting. One of the intruders, Wade Vitalis, shot his compatriot, Duane Morgan, in the head, killing him.

Rumors began spreading on the reservation that the bar owner had killed Morgan. About 30 of his angry friends and relatives descended on the bar.[138]

Following the deaths of Hard Heart and Black Elk, protestors gathered at Billy Mills Hall for a rally on June 26, 1999. Famed AIM leaders Dennis Banks, Clyde and Vernon Bellecourt, and Russell Means all came. "We're up against people who think it's OK to kill Indian people. They think it's okay because they'll get away with it," Banks said.[139]

AIM accused white supremacists, a beer store owner and a sheriff's deputy for the two mens' murders. But Magnuson offers another theory. Hard Heart, he wrote, was one of Sheriff Terry Robbins's informants in Whiteclay.

"Did someone seek revenge on Ronnie for being an informant? It was a possible motive for the crime and something his family and AIM wouldn't want to hear."[140]

On June 27, nearly 1,000 protesters marched from Pine Ridge to Whiteclay. They stopped at the site where Hard Heart's and Black Elk's bodies had been found and prayed. Then they continued into Whiteclay, shouting and pumping their fists.

"Burn it down," yelled one man.

They stopped in front of Mike Coomes's Pioneer Package Store and AIM leaders began speaking using a PA system on a flatbed truck. They invoked broken treaties and Roosevelt's decision to open the Whiteclay buffer zone to settlement.

At the behest of Means, protestors tore down the "Welcome to Nebraska" sign.[141] Then the protest spun out of control as angry Lakota men threw rocks and bottles at buildings and began approaching beer stores, but Lakota employees at one store and heavy grilling covering windows and steel doors on another held them back. Eventually, they made their way to VJ's Market, which had flimsy doors and no Lakota employees to protect it. They began looting the store and even attempted to light the building on fire.

Protesters even climbed into a fire truck after chasing off its crew and drove it toward the reservation. Eventually, Chief Oliver Red Cloud and councilman Milo Yellow Hair convinced protesters to go home.[142]

But they weren't finished, a week later 1,000 protesters returned to Whiteclay, where they were met by 150 state troopers and tribal police. They pushed up against police shields and shouted at officers. One by one, protest leaders began stepping across the state border in defiance of officers' orders. They included Means, councilman Tom Poor Bear, former tribal president John Yellow Bird Steele and six others. All were handcuffed and taken to jail.

Oliver Red Cloud spoke: "I want you to tell the governor that we want our land back."[143]

The Whiteclay Nine, as they would be known, were released and taken back to the border, as protest leaders urged their followers to return to Pine Ridge. Back on the reservation, they gathered in Billy Mills Hall and listened to a powerful speech by Means.

"The audience filed out of Billy Mills Hall into the late afternoon heat. It was a great speech. But not a damn thing changed."[144]

Just four days later, President Bill Clinton and the Rev. Jesse Jackson came to the reservation. Clinton promised many things, including building a Lakota Sioux Heritage Center and a wind and solar energy farm, and upgrading telecommunications lines.

"The president and his entourage climbed back in their helicopters and flew away. It was an exciting day. A great speech. But not a damn thing changed."[145]

Over the next several years, Nebraska politicians and Native activists continued to descend on Whiteclay. Some made promises. Nearly all decried the deplorable living conditions of the reservation's

---

137. Magnuson, *Death of Yellow Thunder*, 268.
138. Magnuson, *Death of Yellow Thunder*, 271.
139. Magnuson, *Death of Yellow Thunder*, 279.
140. Magnuson, *Death of Yellow Thunder*, 281.
141. Joe Duggan, "Whiteclay protest turns violent," *Lincoln Journal Star*, June 27, 1999.
142. Magnuson, *Death of Yellow Thunder*, 285.
143. Magnuson, *Death of Yellow Thunder*, 289.
144. Magnuson, *Death of Yellow Thunder*, 291.
145. Magnuson, *Death of Yellow Thunder*, 294.

residents. In 2001, Nebraska Gov. Mike Johanns even traveled to Pine Ridge to hold a summit with tribal leaders over Whiteclay. Still, nothing changed in the small unincorporated town, where nearly 4 million cans of beer were sold each year.

On June 6, 2003, Col. Tom Nesbitt of the State Patrol and Nebraska Attorney General Jon Bruning met with activists in Whiteclay. Meanwhile, in Lincoln, Nebraska, Winnebago activist Frank LaMere kept the issue alive. Three separate pieces of legislation were introduced in the Unicameral. On March 1, 2003, Vernon Bellecourt and Nesbitt spoke during a meeting hosted at the University of Nebraska-Lincoln. "We're beginning to get a little bit impatient with how Nebraska authorities are handling this cancer; and that's what this is, a cancer," Bellecourt said. Nesbitt defended his agency, saying he didn't have enough troopers to patrol every liquor store, though they did attempt several undercover operations.[146] LaMere countered, saying, "God forbid that one young white woman or one young white man dies in Whiteclay tonight; we'd shut the damn thing down in the morning!"

The state of Nebraska would eventually shut down the Whiteclay beer stores, but it wouldn't happen until April 19, 2017, when, after nearly two decades of activism, the Nebraska Liquor Control Commission voted not to renew the town's four liquor licenses.

Former Oglala Lakota President Bryan Brewer and LaMere, in tears, embraced after the vote. "We've never come this far," Brewer said. "I'm just so happy for our people."[147]

Welcoming Home Displaced Peoples

In 2007, Roger Welsch – the University of Nebraska anthropologist who championed the rights of the Pawnee to reclaim their ancestral remains and artifacts from the Nebraska State Historical Society – and his wife Linda made a landmark decision to give their 60-acre farm near Dannebrog to the Pawnee Tribe of Oklahoma, whose ancestors once called the region home. The Pawnee, like other tribes forced from Nebraska, ceded its land to the federal government after settlers began crowding their small reservation and stealing timber and livestock from the tribe with impunity. Nearly 500 Pawnees moved to Indian Territory, today Oklahoma, in the fall of 1873 as part of an exodus that would continue for the next several years. At a spring 1874 gathering of tribes in Indian Territory, today Oklahoma, a Pawnee identified as Ese-do-to-des told of the abuses his people suffered in Nebraska. "We are surrounded up there on all sides by the white man. I and my people will come here and surrender our part to him," he said. In October 1874, most Pawnees left for Indian Territory, and removal led to the deaths of nearly a third of the tribe as a result of disease and starvation.[148]

More than 130 years later, the tribe would once again be able to call Nebraska home. In July 2018, Roger Welsch recounted the moment in 2007 when he and his wife decided to give their land back to its original inhabitants. He said a contingent of Pawnee had traveled to Nebraska to rebury some of the ancestral remains that they had reclaimed from state collections on the Welsches' land in Dannebrog. "Here were distinguished celebrities, leading men in the tribe, in suits, good clothes, and I had to stand there and watch them wade into the river, crying and pulling the water over their hair, drinking the water because it was their river. It's the Loup River, the Loup Pawnee River," he said.[149]

Beyond the Welsches' decision to give their land to the Pawnee, farmers and organizations, including the Great Platte River Road Archway Monument in Kearney, have worked to give the Pawnee access to their lands to use for planting their sacred corn, which had nearly been lost in the tribe's relocation to Oklahoma. Today, the Pawnees can boast 20 corn gardens grown by 14 different central Nebraska farmers.

Another former Nebraska tribe forced to relocate to Oklahoma has begun making inroads back to their ancestral homelands in recent years. On Sept. 21, 2022, a delegation of nearly 60 Otoe-Missouria tribal members gathered in Lincoln as part of the first annual Otoe-Missouria Day at the University of Nebraska-Lincoln. History professor Margaret Jacobs and Sicangu Lakota journalist Kevin Abourezk hosted the event as part of an ongoing effort to welcome back the Otoe-Missouria to southeast Nebraska. The tribe ceded the lands that would become Lincoln in 1833 and in 1854 through treaties that the tribe signed

---

146. Magnuson, *Death of Yellow Thunder*, 297.
147. *Lincoln Journal Star*, April 20, 2017, A1.
148. Susan A. Miller and James Riding In, editors. *Native Historians Write Back: Decolonizing American Indian History* (Texas Tech University Press, 2011), 159-160.
149. Director Charles Kennedye, "The Return of the Pawnees," Nebraska Public Media Foundation, 2021.

under duress from settlers. The tribe moved to the Big Blue Reservation near Beatrice until 1881 when Congress sold the reservation, forcing the Otoe-Missouria to leave for Indian Territory.

At the September 2023 Otoe-Missouria Day event, tribal member Cory DeRoin walked a native prairie in Lincoln and shared his thoughts about being able to revisit the lands of his ancestors. ""Our old folks are looking down on us, happy that we're here, that we're able to come back and walk in their footsteps," he said. "In my heart, I feel like I'm at home."[150]

Bibliography

Abourezk, Kevin. "Walking in Their Ancestors' Footsteps." *Indian Country Today*. 30 Sept. 2023. Accessed 9 April 2025. https://ictnews.org/news/walking-in-their-ancestors-footsteps

Allan, Tom. "Indian College Aims at Peaks in Education." *Omaha World-Herald*. 22 May 1983, 42.

Allan, Tom. "Tribes Seek Community College." *Omaha World-Herald*. 16 Feb. 1980, 18.

Associated Press. "Indian Leaders support bill protecting graves." *Lincoln Journal Star*. 13 Mar. 1987, 19.

Associated Press. "Native Journalist, Activist Trimble Dies." *Lincoln Journal Star*. 6 Mar. 2020, A8.

Christensen, David. "The Ground You Walk on Belongs to My People: Lakota Community Building, Activism, and Red Power in Western Nebraska, 1917-2000." PhD thesis, University of Nevada, Las Vegas, 2016. https://digitalscholarship.unlv.edu/cgi/viewcontent.cgi?article=3654&context=thesesdissertations

Duggan, Joe. "Questions Unearthed, Answers Remain." *Lincoln Journal Star*. 19 July 1998, 1, 5.

Hammel, Paul. "Tribes Try Comeback with a Mainstay." *Omaha World-Herald*. 1 Nov. 1996, 1-2.

Junior League of Lincoln History. RG4943.MI. Nebraska State Historical Society. "DVD reference copies available." Videotapes of completed educational documentaries that made use of interviews with tribal elders of Native tribes residing in the Great Plains, including Nebraska. Tribes represented are the Brule Sioux, Oglala Sioux, Omaha, Otoe-Missouria, Pawnee, Santee, and Winnebago. Titles include: Hollow of Echoes: Tales of the Winnebago People; Mr. Fool Bull Reminisces; Pawnee People: Land and Lifestyle; Spirit Lake People: The Santee Sioux; True Story: Oral Traditions of the Omaha Indians; Tunkasila Fool Bull; Upstream People: Traditions of the Omaha Tribe; Where We Raise Our Hands: Pawnee Religion and Oral Tradition. People interviewed: Fool Bull, Richard; Bluebird, Lydia; Turner, John; Turner, Suzette; Blaine, Garland; Robertson, Paul; Smith, Irene; Peniska, Edna; White, Felix.

Junior League of Lincoln History. RG4943.MI. Nebraska State Historical Society. "Location of Originals Original 16mm films are housed at the University of Nebraska-Lincoln's University Archives and Special Collections." History Nebraska Archives Record RG4943. MI: RG 4943.MI also contains the raw, unedited film of interviews with Nebraska/Great Plains elders done by the Junior League of Lincoln cited in the citation above. Videotape copies of filmed interviews with tribal elders of Native tribes residing in the Great Plains, including Nebraska. Tribes represented are the Brule Sioux (Richard Fool Bull), Oglala Sioux (Lydia Bluebird), Omaha (John and Suzette Turner), Otoe-Missouria (Truman Washington Dailey and others of the Otoe-Missouri), Pawnee (Garland Blaine), Santee (Paul Robertson, Irene Smith and Edna Peniska), and Winnebago (Felix White). The project, called both the "Indian Literature Project and the "Indian Culture Project," was sponsored and funded by the Junior League of Lincoln with technical support of Nebraska Educational Telecommunications. The interviewer was usually Paul Olson of the University of Nebraska. Cf. History Nebraska Archives Record, Junior League Indian Literature Project (AV2.091).

"LPTC Mission & Philosophy." Little Priest College. Accessed 8 Apr 2025. http://www.littlepriest.edu/mission-philosophy

Magnuson, Stew. *The Death of Raymond Yellow Thunder: And Other True Stories from the Nebraska-Pine Ridge Border*. Texas Tech University Press, 2008.

---

150. Kevin Abourezk, "Walking in Their Ancestors Footsteps," *Indian Country Today*, September 30, 2023.

"Mass Opens Sioux Center." *Omaha World-Herald*. 4 Oct. 1975, 30.

Native Historians Write Back: Decolonizing American Indian History. Edited by Susan A. Miller and James Riding In. Texas Tech University Press, 2011.

Olson, James C. and Ronald C. Naugle. *History of Nebraska*. University of Nebraska Press, 2015.

Potter, Lori. "Long Thought Extinct, a Native Corn Re-emerges." Flatwater Free Press, 19 Nov. 2021. Accessed 9 April 2025. https://flatwaterfreepress.org/long-thought-extinct-a-native-corn-re-emerges-in-the-heartland/

"The Return of the Pawnees." Directed by Charles Kennedye and co-produced by Kevin Abourezk and Margaret Jacobs. Nebraska Public Media Foundation, 2021. Video. Running time 11:41.

Snake, Reuben. *Reuben Snake, Your Humble Serpent: Indian Visionary and Activist*. Clear Light Pub., 1996.

Scherer, Mark R. *Imperfect Victories: The Legal Tenacity of the Omaha Tribe, 1945-1995*. University of Nebraska Press, 2009.

Schmidt, J.L. "Opponents of Grave-Protection Bill Labeled Hysterical by its Supporters." *Lincoln Journal Star*. 15 Feb. 1988, 6.

Summers, Wynne L. *Women Elders' Life Stories of the Omaha Tribe, Macy, Nebraska, 2004-2005*. University of Nebraska Press, 2010.

Urbom, Warren K. *Called to Justice: The Life of a Federal Trial Judge*. Bison Books, 2012.

A History of African Americans in Nebraska

Author: Preston Love, Jr., M.P.S
Lead writer: Adam Fletcher Sasse, MELPS
Lead Research Assistant: Le Clara Gilreath, M.A, MBA
Research Assistant: Portia Love, MS
Editor: Heather Fryer, Ph.D.

Black people have been present in Nebraska from its earliest days as a U.S. territory. The first U.S. Census of Nebraska, conducted in 1860, counted eighty-one Black people who, together, formed .28 percent of the young territory's 28,841 residents. That number grew to 3,443 Black residents in 1900, representing 3.5 percent of the 102,555 residents of the state of Nebraska. The number and location of Black Nebraskans varied greatly through the twentieth century, comprising 13.7 percent of the state's population in 1940 and 11.8 percent in 2020. Although African Americans have been relatively small in numbers, the historical record reflects the formative role that they have played in Nebraska's history, and in the national movements for political equality and racial justice. The struggles Black Nebraskans endured as they contributed to the political, economic, social, and cultural development of the state prepared them for leadership on the national stage. If one is to know the history of Nebraska, and of Nebraska's influence on U.S. history, they must know the history of Nebraska's Black people and Black communities.

This history begins well before Nebraska became a state in 1867, a U.S. territory in 1854, or even before the U.S. acquired it as part of the Louisiana Purchase in 1803. José Naranjo was a scout for Sir Pedro de Villasur, a Spanish explorer based in present-day New Mexico. Naranjo was the son of a Hopi mother and an African father, who so impressed the Spanish viceroy in Mexico City with his capabilities as a scout, guide, interpreter, and intermediary between the Native and Spanish leaders that he named Naranjo "Captain of War." Naranjo traveled with Villasur's forty-six man expedition into Pawnee country. He helped Villasur's party cross the Platte River at Grand Island, then crossed the Loup River where they were met with some hostility by Oto and Pawnee scouts. Though cognizant of the Native nations' warnings, Villasur led his men to the area near Grand Island where Naranjo and the other men under Villasur's command set up camp. The Pawnee launched a defensive attack killing Villasur and thirty-four of his men, including Naranjo, who had served him most capably. Although the historical record is not completely

In *Roots of Justice: A History of Race and Racism in Nebraska.* Edited by Kevin Abourezk, with an Introduction by M. Dewayne Mays and Paul A. Olson (Lincoln, Nebraska: Truth and Reconciliation Nebraska, 2025). Copyright © 2025 by the authors; CC-BY. DOI: 10.32873/unl.dc.rj4

Moses Speese family near Westerville, Custer County, Nebraska, 1888. Solomon D. Butcher Collection, Nebraska State Historical Society.

clear, Naranjo may be the first Black person to arrive, and to die, in Nebraska.[1]

The Louisiana Purchase brought the colonized Native lands that would become the Nebraska Territory into the United States in 1803. Thomas Jefferson commissioned Meriwether Lewis and William Clark to explore the Great Plains and the Rocky Mountains as a Corps of Discovery from 1804-1806. A Black man known only as "[Clark's] Servent [sic], York" brought invaluable skills to the expedition. Far too little was recorded about York, but Lewis and Clark's daily journals noted how heavily they relied on his superior abilities as a navigator, hunter, and frontiersman. The Corps of Discovery traveled the Missouri River and camped on the Nebraska side, where they regularly encountered Otoe and Omaha peoples. York came back through the area a second time in 1806, as he returned to the East Coast with William Clark.[2]

As more Americans followed the Corps of Discovery, Fort Lisa, where Omaha's Hummel Park stands today, became an unofficial American embassy to Native American nations in the region. There were unnamed Black residents recorded at that fort throughout its existence between 1810 to 1820, many of whom, like York, came to the territory as servants to white diplomats, explorers, and traders. A Black man recorded as "Baptiste" was captured by the Omaha Nation near Bellevue around 1830. Baptiste was thought to be the first Black man in Nebraska for many years and, at 112 years old, was the oldest person in Nebraska in 1894.[3]

---

1. "Villasur Sent to Nebraska," Nebraska Public Media, NebraskaStudies.org, accessed July 9, 2024. See Chapter 1 of this volume for the histories of the Indigenous nations within the borders of what became Nebraska.
2. Meriwether Lewis, William Clark, et al., *The Journals of the Lewis and Clark Expedition*, ed. Gary Moulton (Lincoln: University of Nebraska Press / University of Nebraska-Lincoln Libraries-Electronic Text Center, 2005). http://lewisandclarkjournals.unl.edu
3. Nebraska Writers' Program, *The Negroes of Nebraska*, 8.

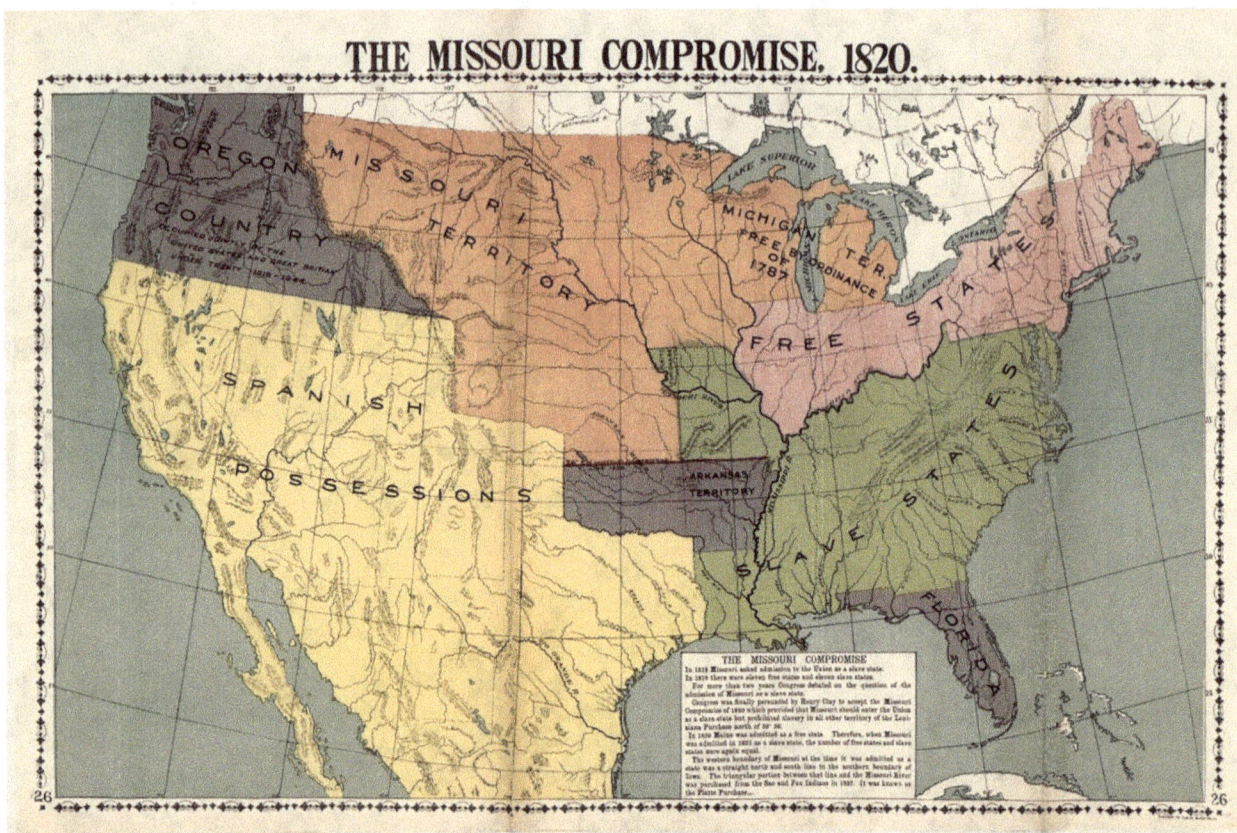

Map of the Missouri Compromise. McConnell Map Co. 1919, Library of Congress,

Pioneers from The Church of Jesus Christ of Latter-Day Saints had African Americans among them when they established Winter Quarters in the present-day Florence neighborhood of Omaha in autumn 1846. They appear separately in the records as "colored servants," in part because people of African descent were barred from membership in the Mormon church. Jacob Bankhead is believed to have been the first Black person buried in Nebraska when he was interred at Winter Quarters cemetery in Florence[4] in 1847. Aside from the fact that Bankhead was one of eleven human beings listed on John Bankhead's property list, very little is known of this Black man who rests in grave #126.[5]

Although the histories of Black Nebraskans are not well documented, one fact is clear: Black Nebraskans were freedom seekers from the start and fought for equality against very long odds. Most white Americans believed the tenets of racism that supported slavery, but those tenets were weak enough that some white allies saw through them and acted in support of Black freedom seekers. While it is true that the ideology of enslavement formed the historical context in which Americans lived, government leaders and everyday Nebraskans made choices about whether, when, and how to honor the inherent human dignity of their Black neighbors. They also made choices about whether, when, and how to exploit popular beliefs about racism for their own political, economic, and social advantages, and to perpetuate the falsehood that as a white person they were inherently superior to others. Their choices determined how high the obstacles to freedom would be, but the real history-making story is how Black people continued to determine their own futures in defiance of white supremacy.

Seeking Freedom in Nebraska Territory

Nebraska's Black freedom seekers stood on the front lines of the United States' struggle over the future of enslavement. Nebraska Territory, acquired by President Thomas Jefferson as part of the Louisiana Purchase in 1803, became the terrain on which American

---

4. Omaha annexed Florence in 1917, making the former Mormon town part of the historically Black district of North Omaha.
5. Winter Quarters Cemetery, BYU Winter Quarters, https://winterquartersbyu.earlylds.com/maps/winter-quarters-pioneer.html, accessed June 2, 2024.

laws defining freedom and governing slavery were to be written. The Missouri Compromise of 1820 prohibited slavery north of a boundary drawn at 36'30" latitude. Slavery would continue unimpeded in the territories to the south of the line.

In theory, the Compromise would settle the "Slavery Question" by balancing the number of new slaveholding states coming into the union with the number of free states, but the conflicts intensified between territories, and within them. Slaveholders claimed an inalienable right to keep and use their property without government interference, including the "slaves" that they purchased at auction or claimed from birth. Americans who recognized the humanity of enslaved people rejected slaveholders' property rights claims as another form of tyranny and called for the protection of Black Americans' inalienable rights to freedom and to the fruits of their labor.[6]

Those who stood for "slaveholders' property rights" had supporters in "free" Nebraska. Weak enforcement of the Missouri Compromise enabled Army officers at Fort Atkinson near present-day Fort Calhoun to enslave Black people at the installation from its opening in 1820 to its closure in 1827. Army officers at the first Fort Kearny (near Nebraska City) held several enslaved people at the fort between 1846 and 1848. This practice continued when the Army relocated to the second Fort Kearny (near Kearney) in 1848, when more enslaved people were recorded there.[7]

Democratic Senator Stephen Douglas of Illinois intensified the "slavery question" in 1854 when he introduced the Kansas-Nebraska Act to repeal the Missouri Compromise. In addition to creating separate "Kansas Territory" and "Nebraska Territory,"[8] the Kansas-Nebraska Act left the question of whether to permit slavery to the will of the white residents of each territory—possibly expanding legalized enslavement beyond the South. Even if white Nebraskans rejected enslavement in the territory, the Kansas-Nebraska Act would extend the Fugitive Slave Act of 1850 to Nebraska, permitting a "slave owner" to pursue and kidnap a freedom seeker in the territory. After months of heated debate, Congress passed the Act in May 1854. Instead of territorial residents determining the status of slavery in their territories, Southern proponents of both slavery and abolition rushed to settle Kansas to tip the scale in their favor.

Tensions erupted in violence as pro- and anti-slavery Southerners clashed in their desperate bid to outnumber each other. "Bleeding Kansas" put the North and the South one step closer to the looming Civil War.[9] Strong opposition gave rise to the Anti-Nebraska Movement, which soon spread across the country. Members of the Anti-Nebraska movement were anti-slavery and pro-democracy activists who faced dangers from enslavers, kidnappers, and others who profited from enslaving Black people. These pro-slavery forces formed a strong resistance in Missouri, lining the route to the new territory to terrorize, ambush, trap, or kill the white abolitionist "Free Staters" who traveled from eastern states to prevent slavery in Nebraska. To keep them safe, abolitionist leader John Brown fought attacks on Free Staters along the Missouri River in 1856 by forging the Jim Lane Trail from Iowa City through Nebraska City, ending in Topeka along roughly the same route as Highway 75. Named after an abolitionist militia leader in Kansas named James H. Lane, the Lane Trail was the westernmost arm of the Underground Railroad, the network of routes used by an estimated 100,000 by formerly enslaved people freedom seekers who fled to the north. John Brown served as a "Conductor" in Nebraska, guiding freedom seekers through Cass, Otoe, Johnson, and Pawnee Counties via the Lane Trail.[10]

Freedom seekers did not merely pass through the segment of the Underground Railroad that moved them across Nebraska Territory. The stops along the way formed points of resistance to slavery in and outside of Nebraska. A barn belonging to David and Ann Dorrington was among the safe harbors in Falls City

---

6. McConnell Map Co, and James McConnell. McConnell's Historical Maps of the United States. [Chicago, Ill.: McConnell Map Co, 1919] Map. https://www.loc.gov/item/2009581130/
7. Annie Pflaum and Will Stoutamire, Fort Kearny State Historical Park: A Brief Historical Overview, University of Nebraska Kearney and Nebraska Game and Parks, June 1, 2021,
8. The map is sourced (without permission) from BlackPast.org {1854) Kansas-Nebraska Act Primary Document.
9. "Kansas Nebraska Act of 1854; 1854; Enrolled Acts and Resolutions of Congress, 1789 - 2011; General Records of the United States Government, Record Group 11; National Archives Building, Washington, DC. https://www.archives.gov/milestone-documents/kansas-nebraska-act
10. Map available for purchase from Mapshop.com (details: https://www.mapshop.com/034-underground-railroad-1860-on-roller-w-backboard/)

for formerly enslaved people traveling along the Lane Trail. The barn was built in the same year, 1857, that the Nebraska House in Brownville was the site of a bloody shootout between formerly enslaved people and kidnappers.

In that year, Nebraska City was another flashpoint for resistance to slavery when a brigade of abolitionists rushed the city to find and free enslaved Black people. The militia converged on the residence of Stephen Friel Nuckolls, a prominent businessman. Finding no sign of Nuckolls, the abolitionists left—but not without helping two enslaved men free themselves. Two men enslaved to the Nuckolls family, Shackford ("Shack") and Shade, were highly valuable and highly visible in Nebraska City. Shade was "owned" by Stephen's father, Ezra, who "loaned" him to his son for household labor. Shackford, "owned" by Stephen Nuckolls, generated income for the businessman, who "rented" his labor to the *Nebraska City Press*. Nuckolls suffered economic loss and a blow to his image as Nebraska City's exemplary slaveholder when Shack and Shade, who may have been brothers, took advantage of the chaos caused by the abolitionists to escape from his household.

One year later, in 1858, Celia and Eliza Grayson—sisters to one another and possibly to Shack and/or Shade—dealt Nuckolls a second blow when they escaped to the free state of Iowa. John Williamson, an abolitionist of Afro-Cherokee descent took the Graysons to a station on the Underground Railroad where they were ferried across the Missouri River to Civil Bend, Iowa.[11] Nuckolls sounded the alarm that abolitionists had "enticed" Celia and Eliza away from his house, mobilized search parties, and took out newspaper ads, and offered a large reward for the return of "his property."[12] After a two-year hunt, Nuckolls and a professional kidnapper found Eliza Grayson in Chicago in November 1860 but her capture would not be easy. A large group of free Blacks rushed to defend Grayson with such fury that the outcome of the skirmish is unclear in the historical record. Some say that U.S. marshals arrested Grayson and Nuckolls for disturbing the peace. Others say that Nuckolls broke away from the crowd, fearing they

> **Great Excitement—Escape of Negroes—$200 reward.**
>
> Quite a sensation was created in town yesterday morning by the fact being known that two female servants had been enticed away from our townsman, Mr. S. F. Nuckolls, by some vile, white-livered Abolitionist. Many of our citizens are out in search of the runaways. They escaped on Thursday evening. Mr. Nuckolls offers a reward of $200.00 for their apprehension and delivery to him in Nebraska City. They will doubtless be found in some Abolition hole.

$200 reward offered for capturing the Grayson sisters, 1858. *Nebraska City News Press*, November 27, 1858, Nebraska State Historical Society.

would kill him.[13] A group of abolitionist activists freed Grayson from the jail and helped her to escape to Canada. Back in Chicago, nine defendants went before a grand jury in Chicago in 1861 on charges of violating the Fugitive Slave Act.[14] The "Eliza Grayson Freedom Case" became part of the national conversation on the legitimacy of slavery and whether the Fugitive Slave Act could possibly be just.[15] The courtroom became a forum for this conversation, especially when one of the defendants made such a strong case for dismissing the indictment that the judge referred the case to the circuit court where it was ultimately dismissed.[16]

All the enslaved people owned by Alexander Majors in Nebraska City became successful freedom seekers by late 1860. Majors co-owned Majors, Russell, and Waddell, Nebraska's largest freighting company that controlled much of the transportation business in the West.[17] While Majors' defenders maintained that his Christian faith approved enslavement as a system of caring for people unable to care for themselves,[18]

---

11. Gail Shaffer Blankenau, "Journey to Freedom from Nebraska Territory," *Nebraska History* (Summer 2022): 79.
12. Blankenau, "Journey to Freedom," 80.
13. Blankenau, *Journey to Freedom*, 134.
14. "The Eliza Grayson Case," *Chicago Tribune*, December 7, 1861, 4.
15. "The Union Again Threatened: The Colored Person Loose," *Chicago Tribune*, November 13, 1860, 1.
16. "The Eliza Grayson Case," *Chicago Tribune*, February 14, 1861, 1.
17. "From Wealth to Poverty, *Nebraska City News*, March 28, 1895, 3.
18. Alexander Majors," *The Conservative*, February 1, 1900, 2.

the truth was that the Black people who labored for him made the freighting company so profitable. The loss of Majors' enslaved labor destabilized the system that had enabled Majors to expand his empire instead of paying people for their work, and precipitated a decline in his fortunes when the railroads made freighting companies obsolete and there was not sufficient enslaved labor to build another equally profitable business.[19] Risking torturous punishments or death to escape, Black freedom seekers opened the possibility of using the knowledge, skills, and labor that their enslavers stole from them to support themselves and their families in lives of their own making.

Otoe County Sheriff William Birchfield auctioned two enslaved people called Hercules and Martha at the county courthouse in Nebraska City on December 5, 1860. Hercules and Martha were included on the list of "goods, chattels, lands, and tenements" owned by Charles F. Holly, who defaulted on his debts. Birchfield advertised in November that "one negro man" and "one negro woman" would go to the "highest and best bidder."[20] Slavery was also concentrated at federal installations like the second Fort Kearny where Mary Cheroot, age forty-five from Missouri; Mary Badeau, age thirty-five from Missouri; Henry Cheroot, age ten from Missouri; Charlotte, age twenty-six from Missouri; James, age fifteen from Missouri; Jane Steele, age thirty-one from Kentucky; Israel, age fourteen from Florida, and Jane, age eighteen from Kentucky were on base as the chattel property of U.S. Army officers.[21]

The growing presence of slavery in Nebraska Territory spurred a local abolitionist movement. The legislature passed a bill in 1859 to prohibit slavery in Nebraska Territory. Governor Samuel W. Black, an ardent pro-slavery Democrat, vetoed the bill in January 1860 on the grounds that the territorial enabling acts that permitted the legislature to draft a state constitution did not empower it to enact a new antislavery law. The slavery question would have to be settled in the state constitution.[22] The *New York Times*

Slave sale in Nebraska City, 1860. *Nebraska City News Press*, December 8, 1860, Nebraska State Historical Society.

called Black's decision "among the greatest farces which even in the history of Representative Government have been enacted"[23] and several members of the Legislature did not buy Black's argument either. In January 1861, weeks before the first shots were fired in the Civil War, the Legislature revived the anti-slavery bill. Governor Black made the same objections. The Legislature nonetheless overrode the Governor's veto with a greater majority than two-thirds required.[24] Soon after, Black put his pro-slavery politics aside, resigned as territorial governor of Nebraska to return to his home state of Pennsylvania to join the 62ndVolunteers. Colonel Black was killed while leading a charge against Confederate soldiers at Gaines Mill, Virginia.[25]

Civil War and Reconstruction in Nebraska

Nebraska was distant from the battlefields of the Civil War, but the conflict made its imprint on the territory in many forms.[26] More than three thousand men, one in three of military-eligible Nebraskans, served in the First Nebraska Regiment while the six thousand not

---

19. "Alexander Majors Dead," *Nebraska City News Press*, January 15, 1900, 3.
20. "Sheriff's Sale," *Nebraska City News*, November 24, 1860; Frederick Luebke, *Nebraska An Illustrated History* (Lincoln: University of Nebraska Press, 2005), 160.
21. Annie Pflaum and Will Stoutamire, Fort Kearny State Historical Park: A Brief Historical Overview, University of Nebraska at Kearney and Nebraska Game and Parks, https://storymaps.arcgis.com/stories/f0461d4de46c453697db-31763fe195bf, accessed June 1, 2021,
22. Biographical Note, Governor Samuel W. Black Records, Nebraska State Archives RG001, SG006, https://history.nebraska.gov/wp-content/uploads/2021/10/doc_RG001_SG006_Samuel_Black.pdf ;
23. "Black v. Popular Sovereignty," *New York Times,* January 21, 1860, 4.
24. "Nebraska General Assembly," *New York Times,* January 3, 1861, 5.
25. James C. Mill, "In Old Nebraska," *The Stapleton Enterprise*, May 6, 1948, 4.
26. History of Nebraska (Lincoln: University of Nebraska Press, 2015),

eligible for the military worked double time on farms and in factories to fill the labor shortages on the home front. Black Nebraskans were in that number, some having been prewar residents of the territory, others moving to Nebraska because of the war, but all forming a new generation of leadership in communities across America's thirty-seventh state. S.J. "July" Miles escaped enslavement, joined the Union Army, and settled in Omaha after the war.[27] Robert Ball Anderson left enslavement in Kentucky by telling his "owner" that he was joining the Union Army. He would write in his autobiography, "now I am a free man, a citizen of the United States, a property owner, and boss of my own ranch" in Box Butte County—built on the first homestead claimed by an African American.[28]

Anderson Bell, born enslaved in Mississippi, joined the 1st Missouri Colored Regiment and moved to Omaha after the war. His daughter's wedding to the son of fellow veteran John Alexander made the front page of the *World-Herald*. The two "grizzled relics of the Old Dominion" were lauded for "patching up their youthful errors" by solemnizing their children's marriage, not accounting for the fact that enslaved people were often denied the right to marriage or to raise their children.[29] Richard "General" Curry opened a successful barbershop in Omaha after the war and was also a regular figure in the news for his leadership in the local Republican Party. Josiah "Professor" Waddle was recognized as one of Omaha's youngest Civil War veterans. He left his home in Springfield, Missouri, to serve as an orderly and a drummer for the 79th Kansas Infantry at age fourteen. He settled in Omaha after two and a half years in the military and became an active member of the veteran's organization the Grand Army of the Republic. "Professor" Waddle was a barber, instrumental music teacher, and bandleader for nearly fifty years.[30]

George W. Mattingly, "pioneer homesteader of Butler County" was emancipated by his white grandfather[31] and left Kentucky to muster into the Army. Mattingly settled in Butler County in 1866,

Homesteader Robert Ball Anderson, 1843-1930. *From Slavery to Affluence: Memoirs of Robert Ball Anderson, Ex-Slave* (Steamboat Springs, Colorado, 2nd ed., 1967).

establishing a homestead south of David City in 1874. Through his hard work as a homesteader, he built an estate valued at approximately $50,000 (or $1,587,000 in 2024 dollars).[32] After establishing himself in Nebraska, Mattingly returned to Kentucky in search of the family he left behind. His wife had been sold to another plantation before the war; their two children had died, as had Mattingly's father, brothers, and sisters, who were killed in the race riot under way when Mattingly arrived.[33] Nebraska Judge L.T. McCaskey, who knew Mattingly had been denied an education

---

27. "Miles Was a Slave," *Hastings Daily Tribune*, June 14, 1941, 5.
28. Federal Writers Project, *The Negro in Nebraska*, 8-9; Robert Ball Anderson,
29. "Two Ex-Slaves Meet to Join Their Children," *Omaha World-Herald*, May 2, 1901, 1.
30. "Civil War Veterans at Reunion Revive Memories of Battlefields and Days in Camp," *Omaha Evening Bee-News*, December 28, 1933, 4; "Young Civil War Veteran," *Omaha World-Herald*, August 12, 1929, 4; "Civil War Vet Makes Trip to Gettysburg," *Omaha Star*, July 16, 1938, 1; G.A.R. Women Giving Program," *Omaha World-Herald*, August 27, 1933, 18.
31. Mattingly was referred to as a "half-breed," indicating his grandmother was Black and enslaved and his grandfather her white enslaver.
32. "Sholes Folks Have Good Claim to Estate of Negro Farmer," *The Randolph Times*, July 17, 1930, 1.
33. "About George Mattingly," *The People's Banner*, June 14, 1923, 1.

during his enslavement, taught him to read. A devout Catholic, Mattingly donated part of the growing profits from his farm to St. Mary's Church in David City, which still has the stained glass his donations helped purchase. Noted in his 1924 obituary as "the only colored civil war veteran in Butler County,"[34] Mattingly had amassed more than four-hundred acres of farmland in Colorado and Nebraska—including several lots in David City—valued at $80,000 in 1928 (approximately $1.6 million in 2024 dollars). There were no heirs; his first wife, identified as "a slave girl," his second wife and their three children all predeceased him, resulting in a twelve-year legal contest. Two men persuaded the court they were "proven heirs" and Judge McCaskey and C.W. Bennison were awarded the greater share as contingent heirs. Both men died before receiving their shares, but the Mattingly case challenged stereotypes of African American inferiority. Having started life enslaved, Mattingly was a phenomenal example of the self-made man equal to the ranks of Nebraska's white business and political leaders.[35]

Black civilians also formed lives and communities in wartime Nebraska. Freedom seekers continued to move away from enslavement toward new opportunities. Congress passed the Railroad Act in 1862, creating new jobs in a new industry that encouraged Black workers to the Nebraska Territory. The Homestead Act of 1862 opened millions of acres for individuals to claim 160 acres if they could pay the $12 fee (about $308 in 2020 dollars) and had never borne arms against the United States. If, after five years, the homesteader could show improvements on the land and present favorable testimony from witnesses that they used it well, the homesteader acquired the title for the land and owned it outright. African Americans were excluded from the Homestead Act until the end of the Civil War when the Fourteenth Amendment was ratified and the Civil Rights Act passed in 1866. The Act encouraged formerly enslaved people to move to the Great Plains where they could put their labor and skills into land that would be theirs to profit from—and to pass on to their children.[36]

While the legal barriers to Black land ownership were lowered, financial hurdles remained in place. Homesteaders needed to invest approximately $1,000 ($17,500 in 2020 dollars) to pay for wagons, provisions, draft animals, farm equipment, fences, housing materials, seeds, and the equipment to dig a well. Annual expenses were unpredictable and Black homesteaders rarely had access to loans. While homesteading did give many African Americans a means to earn their own living—and to develop significant wealth in some cases—fewer Black homesteaders put down deep roots on their homesteads than white homesteaders.[37] These conditions drove many Black freedom seekers from Nebraska, setting the conditions for the state's historically small number of Black landowners.

Despite the challenges, a growing number of Black people were living out the whole of their lives in Nebraska. The first formal burial of a Black person within the Omaha city limits took place in 1863, when an unnamed man was interred at Prospect Hill Cemetery. There were more than eight hundred African American burials at this cemetery dating from that year until 1971, including several soldiers. That same year, on September 9, 1863, Adam Walker and Manda James became one of the first, if not *the* first Black couple to be granted a marriage license in Nebraska.[38]

The earliest known photograph of African Americans in Nebraska was taken in Brownville in 1864. It shows several people on wagons in front of a row of businesses. Brownville became an increasingly important place for Black people in Nebraska during this era as they migrated into the state from the southeast. Benton Aldrich and his wife Martha were white farmers, community leaders, and outspoken abolitionists near Brownville who employed Black migrants and helped them get their footing in Nebraska in the 1860s and 1870s. Their assistance and Black migrants' determination made Brownville a destination for twenty families of newly free Black Tennesseans moved to Brownville as a group in 1877. Harriette Green was just two years old when her parents, two sisters, and four brothers traveled with this group. She lived in Brownville for 90 years, where she raised

---

34. "Aged Colored Man Called," *The Ulysses Dispatch* May 1, 1924, 1.
35. "I.T. McCaskey Was the Last One Claiming Negro Estate," *Lincoln Journal Star,* February 17, 1936, 3.
36. Andrew Muhammad, Christopher Sichko, and Tore C. Olsson, "African Americans and Federal Land Policy: Exploring the Homestead Acts of 1862 and 1866," *Applied Economic Perspectives and Policy* 46: 1 (March 2024): 96-97.
37. Muhammad, Sichko, and Olsson, "African Americans and Federal Land Policy," 101.
38. Douglas County Nebraska, Marriage License Records 1855-1908, September 9, 1863, 111, Nebraska State Historical Society and Archives.

her family, was a respected member of the community, and was laid to rest there—alongside her grandfather, mother, and other family members in 1969.[39] Brownville would not be the only Black settlement in Nebraska and Harriette Green would be just one of many Black pioneers who became part of Nebraska's communities.

The African American community in Hastings took root in 1876 when Horace Newsome opened both a barbershop and *The Western Post*, a newspaper reporting on issues of concern to the Black community. This is roughly the same period when another of Hastings' noteworthy Black citizens, Harry Rogers Smith, settled in town as a teamster and handyman at a local livery. Smith was an able horseman and an impressive shot with a pistol. When "war" broke out between Hastings and Juniata in 1878 over which town would be the county seat, Smith was called into service. Juniata had been the seat of Adams County but as Hastings grew in size and influence, county leaders called for a change of seat. When Juniata refused to cooperate with the move the question was put to voters, who elected Hastings as the county seat. In a last-ditch act of resistance Juniata officials refused to move county records to Hastings. County officials entrusted the delicate matter of obtaining the records to Curt Alexander who brought Smith to help. The scene in Juniata was dicey; protesters were standing outside the county records office when Alexander and Smith arrived. Local people credited Smith with the successful, and peaceful, extraction of the records. The skill he employed that day changed the course of Adams County history and Hastings remains the county seat at the time of this writing.[40]

Nebraska's Black residents became part of the fabric of life in the Territory at an especially contentious moment in its racial politics. White Nebraskans came out in support and opposition to President Abraham Lincoln's Emancipation Proclamation and the opportunities for African American autonomy, citizenship, and military service it created. Anti-emancipation Democrats charged "radical abolitionists" with destroying liberty and progress while Lincoln's Republican supporters blasted Democrats as "secession sympathizers" or, simply, as "traitors ."[41] These arguments were less concerned with the futures of Black people in Nebraska than of the fate of the territory's petition for statehood which had been delayed by the war.

Statehood, Reconstruction, and the Growth of Black Communities

As the first territory to petition the U.S. government for statehood after the Civil War, Nebraska was in the unique position of having to comply with the Fifteenth Amendment of the Constitution, which enshrined Black men's right to vote. The amendment had been passed, but not yet ratified. Congress required the territorial legislature to amend the draft constitution to prohibit "…abridgment or denial of the exercise of the elective franchise or of any other right to any person by reason of race or color…" to be admitted for statehood.[42] Otoe County representative J. Sterling Morton (best remembered today as the founder of National Arbor Day) stood devoutly dedicated to white supremacy and advocated preserving the Union by institutionalizing slavery across the U.S. He wrote in protest, "It will be more manly to accept negro suffrage by legal enforcement than to humiliate ourselves by its voluntary adoption as the price of admission to the Union… We take n—-r only when forced to it by Congress and therefore are for remaining at present a territory."[43]

Territorial Governor Alvin Saunders called a special session of the legislature to approve the deletion of the word "white" from the voting qualifications

---

39. "Mrs. Harriette Green Passes," *Omaha Star*, December 11, 1969, 6; Obituaries: Green, *Lincoln Star*, December 8, 1969, 23; Robyn Murray, "The Exodusters Who Came to Brownville," Nebraska Public Media, August 19, 2016. https://nebraskapublicmedia.org/en/news/news-articles/the-exodusters-who-came-to-brownville/
40. "Prairie to Prominence: Hastings' First 10 Years," Adams County Nebraska Historical Society, https://www.adamshistory.org/index.php?option=com_content&view=article&id=33:prairie-to-prominence&catid=2&Itemid=42 ; Bish, "The Black Experience in Selected Nebraska Counties," 84-85.
41. Office of the Adjutant General, "Roster of Nebraska Volunteers from 1861-1869," comp. E.S. Dudley, (Hastings, Nebraska: Wigton & Evans State Printers); James E. Potter, *Standing Firmly by the Flag: Nebraska Territory and the Civil War* (Lincoln: University of Nebraska Press, 2013), xiii-xiv.
42. Potter, *Civil War in Nebraska*, xvi.
43. David Bristow, "Was J. Sterling Morton a Racist? Here's What the Arbor Day Founder Said and Did," Nebraska History Blog, March 29, 2019, https://history.nebraska.gov/was-j-sterling-morton-a-racist-heres-what-the-arbor-day-founder-said-and-did/#:~:text=Morton%20was%20an%20ardent%20defender,not%20entitled%20to%20equal%20rights, accessed July 2, 2024.

in the draft state constitution. This would allow for Black Nebraskans to vote, own land, hold political office and exercise the privileges of U.S. citizenship and Nebraska state residency. The constitution was amended, and President Andrew Johnson signed a proclamation granting Nebraska statehood on March 1, 1867. Nebraska thus became the first and only state to grant suffrage to Black men under a specific mandate imposed by Congress. Some Nebraskans framed Black suffrage as an injustice to white farmers—"the bone and sinew of Nebraska"—and as federal incursion on state's rights, casting one prominent white lawyer in favor of the amended state constitution as "the Africanized champion of Federal usurpation."[44] The path to statehood led to suffrage for Black Nebraskans but it also made Black Nebraskans scapegoats for all manner of white grievances about states' rights, economic competition, and the preservation of white supremacy.

In the last territorial legislature before statehood, racist policymakers turned their rhetoric toward the schools: "The people of Nebraska are not yet ready to send white boys and white girls to school to sit on the same seats with negroes; they are not yet ready to endorse in this tacit manner the dogma of miscegenation, especially are they yet far from ready to degrade their offspring to a level with so inferior a race."[45] A column in the *Omaha Daily Herald* warned that even if the state passed laws punishing white parents who stopped their children from marrying a Black person, "the instincts of white people" toward segregation and racial inequality "could not be legislated away, any more than one [legislative bill] could change the Ethiopian pigment, alter the craniums, or Romanize the nasal protuberances of the inferior race."[46] Their racism was amplified by a mob of four hundred white supremacists who attacked a group of twenty Black men who came to the polls to vote in Omaha.[47] When a reader named "Republican" asked the editors of the *World Herald* whether they condemned the violence against the Black voters, the response was: "We oppose all forcible resistance to the so-called law forcing negro suffrage upon this people against their known will. Until pronounced not law by the proper tribunals, we are in favor of obeying that and all other so-called laws." [48]

Challenges to Black constitutional rights came in all forms, from subtle forms of discrimination to lawsuits challenging Black Nebraskans' constitutional rights to threats—and acts—of racial violence.

Nebraska was one of many states where "sundown towns" and "sundown counties" displayed signs, signals, and weapons warning Black people that they risked death if they remained within the town borders or the county line after sundown. Black travelers slept in their wagons or by the side of the road to avoid sundown towns, even when there were vacancies at hotels. Some were clustered in southeast Nebraska along the old Lane Trail. They were also spread along the Platte River where wagons of Black settlers started heading west after the Civil War. There are accounts of sundown rules in Lincoln, Havelock,[49] Fremont, Minden, Nebraska City, Plattsmouth, and Tecumseh from the end of the Civil War to the turn of the twentieth century.[50] The city of Fremont was identified as a sundown town as recently as 2010.[51]

Racial violence did not stop at threats or minor altercations. An elderly couple was abducted, and the man ultimately murdered, in a late-night robbery in Nebraska City in 1878. A mob of three hundred

---

44. Ronald C. Naugle, John J. Montag, and James C. Olson, *History of Nebraska* 4th ed (Lincoln: University of Nebraska Press, 2014), 119-22; Potter, *Standing Firmly By the Flag*, 280; "The Herald and the Farmers" and "A Fair Proposition," *Omaha Daily Herald*, April 30, 1867, 2.
45. James A. Lake and Richard Hansen, Negro Segregation in Nebraska Schools," *Nebraska Law Review* 33:1 (1954): 51.
46. "The African in the Public Schools," *Omaha Daily Herald*, February 8, 1867, 2.
47. "Doubtful Honors," *Nebraska Herald*, March 13, 1867, 1.
48. "Question," *Omaha World-Herald*, March 13, 1867, 2.
49. Havelock was an independent municipality established in 1893 and incorporated into the city of Lincoln in 1930 that centered around a Burlington Railroad shop. Known as a sundown town, Havelock maintained racial segregation by retaining its race-restrictive housing until the 1970s. See Douglas Keister and Edward F. Zimmer, Lincoln in Black and White, 1910-1925 (Charleston, SC: Arcadia Publishing, 2008), 26 and James W. Loewen, "Lincoln," History and Social Justice, Tougaloo College, https://justice.tougaloo.edu/sundowntown/lincoln-ne/, accessed May 27, 2024.
50. James W. Loewen, Historical Database of Sundown Towns, History and Social Justice Project, Tougaloo College, https://justice.tougaloo.edu/location/nebraska/ ; Tim Sullivan and Noreen Nasir, "AP Road Trip: Racial Tensions in America's 'Sundown Towns,'" Associated Press, October 13, 2020, https://apnews.com/article/virus-outbreak-race-and-ethnicity-violence-db28a9aaa3b800d91b65dc11a6b12c4c.
51. Afi Odelia-Scruggs, "Nebraska Law is a Return to Racist Past," NPR.org, July 7, 2010, https://www.npr.org/2010/07/07/128354693/the-root-nebraska-law-is-a-return-to-jim-crow-past.

Lynching of Jackson and Martin near Nebraska City, 1878. *Nebraska City News Press*, December 14, 1878, Nebraska State Historical Society.

white men lynched two Black defendants, Henry Jackson and Henry Martin, when an Otoe County judge handed down a second-degree murder conviction in 1878.

Lynching was a form of public violence designed to reinforce white supremacy after the abolition of slavery and that culminated in the public execution of an individual by lawless mobs who claimed to be bringing "criminals" to justice. Before Reconstruction, U.S.-born and immigrant whites, Mexicans, and Chinese Midwesterners were subject to death by lynch mob. As formerly enslaved African Americans moved northward from the former Confederate states, Black people became the near-exclusive targets for this deadly public violence. Black people formed such a great majority of lynching victims that the practice became associated with anti-Black racism.[52]

A typical post-Reconstruction lynching started with an accusation of a Black person of a crime, often without evidence, and kidnapping them from their home, business, jail cell awaiting trial, or wherever they were. Denying these Black citizens due process, the mob would force the victim to a public place where white people often gathered with their families to see the spectacle of a Black person being tortured and killed (usually by hanging).[53] Reflecting the attitudes of the times, a so-called liberal newspaper in Omaha called *The Republican* ran the headline, "A Little Wholesome Lynching" in reference to the Jackson and Martin lynching, characterizing the men as "murderous and raping beasts and monsters."[54] This coverage continued a twenty-year pattern of pernicious media portrayals of African Americans in Nebraska that persisted for another 140 years.[55]

Despite the dangers that racism posed to African Americans in Nebraska, the new state became a destination for migrants determined to live as fully equal U.S. citizens in the heart of the expanding American West. Black migration to Nebraska picked up in 1877 when Congress ended Reconstruction without securing the constitutional rights guaranteed to Black people in the Fourteenth and Fifteenth Amendments to the Constitution. The federal government lost its political will to protect the rights of formerly enslaved Americans, allowing both southern and northern states to enact laws and practice customs that reinforced racial inequality. These systems of laws and customs were called "Jim Crow." They extended from laws allowing the arrest of a Black person for "loitering" in public (often interpreted as doing *anything* in public other than working) to requiring Black people to address white people as "Mr." or "Mrs." and white people to address Black people by their first name, if at all. A Black person offering a handshake to a white person

---

52. James E. Potter "Wearing the Hempen Neck-Tie': Lynching in Nebraska, 1858-1919." *Nebraska History* 93 (2012): 144 https://history.nebraska.gov/wp-content/uploads/2018/05/doc_publications_NH2012Lynching.pdf4.
53. Philip Dray, *At the Hands of Persons Unknown: The Lynching of Black America*, (New York: Modern Library, 2003); https://naacp.org/find-resources/history-explained/history-lynching-america; https://www.pbs.org/wgbh/american-experience/features/emmett-lynching-america/
54. Potter, "Wearing the Hempen Necktie," 145.
55. Jeremy Harris Lipschultz and Michael L. Hilt, "Race and Local Television News Crime Coverage" *Communication Faculty Publications* (2003): 3; Denis G. Paz, "The Black Press and the Issues of Race, Politics and Culture on the Great Plains of Nebraska, 1865-1985" in *The Black Press in the Middle West, 1865-1985* ed. Henry Lewis Suggs (Westport, CT: Greenwood Press, 1996). Today, the men are both buried in Nebraska City's Wyuka Cemetery.

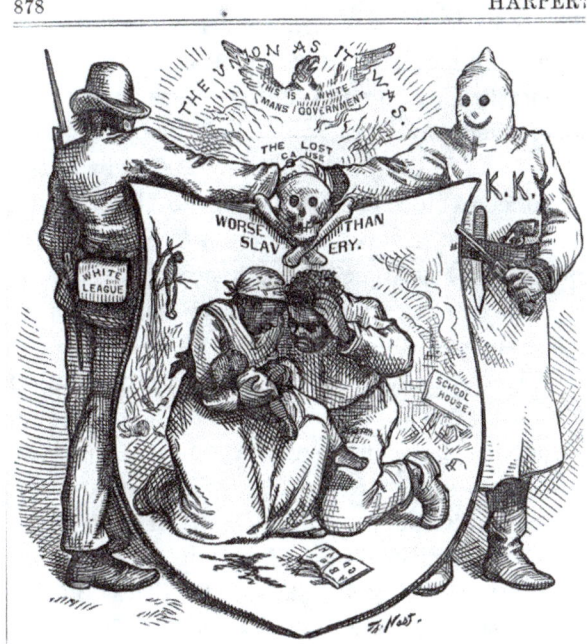

"Worse than Slavery," Thomas Nast cartoon, 1874. Library of Congress.

Under the Jim Crow system, the law served to protect the rights of white Americans only, and to assure that Black Americans remained trapped in a subservient, second-class status resembling enslavement to the greatest degree possible.[58]

Sociologists documented an especially sharp spike in Black migration to Omaha in 1877 when the Union Pacific Railroad brought large numbers of Black workers from the Jim Crow South to break the Railroad Workers Union strike.[59] Bringing Black strikebreakers across state lines to cross white picket lines put these Black workers in grave danger, yet it became commonplace for the railroads, meatpacking plants, and extractive industries to leverage class and race to keep their labor costs low, and to undercut the power of growing labor unions. For some of these Black workers Omaha became as dangerous as any southern city.[60]

was strictly forbidden. A Black person faced punishment for crossing into "white only" spaces on train cars or other public accommodations. If a Black man offered his arm to assist a woman, he risked being jailed for rape.[56] White communities strictly enforced Jim Crow laws. In larger cities, arrests of Black people for small crimes were punished with long sentences as prison laborers. Smaller towns kept Black people "in their place" through the ever-present threat of lynching. When violent mobs demanded the expulsion of a "Black menace," 150 African Americans were driven away from Lincoln in 1879, and from Tecumseh in 1880; most left permanently to spare their lives.[57] Although the murder of American citizens was arguably unconstitutional, white police officers and public officials sworn to defend the rights of all Americans often participated in or watched the lynching of Black citizens as a form of retribution or entertainment.

Industry's temporary Black migrations were outpaced and outlived by the number of Black soldiers posted in Nebraska and, in several cases, settling there. After the Civil War, Black soldiers from the Ninth Cavalry called the "Buffalo Soldiers" were sent to the West in segregated regiments. Historians are not certain of the origin of the name, but most attribute it to Native Americans who named them after the buffalo because the Black soldiers' hair reminded them of fur of the bison and their soldiering of the bison's fierceness. Starting from a small number stationed in Nebraska, the Buffalo Soldiers grew to become a significant presence in one decade. While they were paid a pittance, military pay for a Buffalo Soldier was better than any civilian wage paid to a Black worker.[61] Over the next thirty years, many of the Buffalo Soldiers made western Nebraska their lifelong home.

General George Crook, commander of Fort Omaha, selected a site near Valentine for what became Fort Niobrara, the southernmost fort to fight the Indian Wars in 1879. Soldiers from the Ninth Cavalry and

---

56. The Jim Crow Museum, https://jimcrowmuseum.ferris.edu/what.htm.
57. Nebraska Writers' Program 1940, *The Negroes of Nebraska*, 11; Bish, "The Black Experience in Selected Nebraska Counties," 83; James Patrick Morgans, *John Todd and the Underground Railroad: Biography of an Iowa Abolitionist*. (United Kingdom: McFarland Incorporated, 2006), 75, 86, 92.
58. Douglas A. Blackmon, *Slavery by Another Name: The Re-Enslavement of Black Americans from the Civil War to World War II* (New York: Penguin, 2008), 7-10.
59. David J Peavler Trowbridge, "'A Double Mixture: Equality and Economy in the Integration of Nebraska Schools, 1858-1883," *Nebraska History* 91 (2010): 138; Quintard Taylor, *In Search of the Racial Frontier: African Americans in the American West* (New York: W.W. Norton, 1999), 193, 205.
60. Gary Johansen 1970, "Black Homesteaders." *Sunday World-Herald Magazine of the Midlands* (March 5, 1970): 19.
61. U.S. National Park Service, "Buffalo Soldiers: Guardians of California's National Parks," https://www.nps.gov/subjects/buffalosoldiers/index.htm, accessed July 6, 2024.

some white-only units were stationed at Fort Niobrara to monitor the Yankton, Rosebud, Standing Rock, and Lower Brule. Black settlements emerged around the fort to serve the Buffalo Soldiers, their families, and veterans through the 1880s and 1890s. There were several Black-owned saloons, brothels, and gambling houses where, according to various accounts, the Buffalo soldiers were welcomed to patronize along with white customers. When the Ninth Cavalry left the fort in 1895 the groundwork for Black migration and permanent Black settlement was laid.[62]

Reconstruction brought the first great wave of migration of formerly enslaved Black people from the South who were newly free to move to Nebraska, or to any part of the U.S. that they wished. Thousands of settlers referred to as Exodusters traveled to Kansas and into Nebraska. Exodusters sought land in Nebraska and justice for Black southerners. Benjamin "Pap" Singleton, recognized as the father of the Exodusters, explained in his testimony before Congress,

> I love the South, and I want every one of my people to come out, to teach the South a lesson, that she may know if she thinks more of bulldozing than she does of the colored man's muscle; the colored man's muscle is her interest; and these dare devils that ride around in the night and abuse the people, when the country ought to be harmonized, then I say to them go, whenever they change from that, I want them to go back.[63]

Robert Ball Anderson, who had spent his earlier life enslaved, was the first African American to homestead in Nebraska. Hundreds of the formerly enslaved followed the trail Anderson blazed, despite many Nebraskans' objections to their presence. Together, Nebraska's Exodusters formed three Black towns: Overton in Dawson County in 1885, Brownlee in 1905, and DeWitty (later renamed Audacious) in 1907.[64]

The Exodusters also increased the Black populations of Nebraska City, Omaha, and Lincoln.[65] White residents of Plattsmouth are said to have helped increase the number of Exodusters in Nebraska City by taking up a collection to send 163 in Plattsmouth to "where they were needed and could be used" in 1871.[66] A group of 450 Black people had just come to settle in Nebraska, causing white residents a "terrible scare." Despite attempts at intimidation, Black people moved to Nebraska City in great enough numbers to found Mt. Zion African Methodist Episcopal Church in 1879. A committee of supportive white people welcomed forty-two Black settlers to Lincoln, though later reports said that white people stopped 150 African Americans who had traveled from Mississippi from building homes in Lincoln. No one stopped the Black community from starting Black churches, and by 1880 Lincoln had two, Quinn Chapel AME Church, founded in 1871, and Mt. Zion Baptist Church in 1879.[67]

Black children became subject to Jim Crow when Nebraska schools became early sites for Reconstruction-era conflict. Tensions rose in 1867 when the governor asked the legislature to consider a "revision or amendment of the school law" to allow Black children to attend public schools. The Fourteenth Amendment to the U.S. Constitution guaranteed equal protection under the law to African Americans, but the term "equal protection" did not specify whether the state had to guarantee Black children access to the same education as white children. Segregationist education leaders in Omaha and Nebraska City took advantage of this ambiguity to open segregated schools for Black children—over the protests of some Black parents.[68] In Omaha, the so-called "colored school" served at least twenty-seven students from 1865 to 1872.[69] Segregation

---

62. Thomas R. Buecker, "Prelude to Brownsville: The Twenty-Fifth Infantry at Fort Niobrara, Nebraska, 1902-06." *Great Plains Quarterly* 16 no. 2 (Spring 1996): 95-106.
63. 40th Congress, 2nd Session, Senate, Testimony of Benjamin Singleton, Select Committee to Investigate the Removal of the Negroes from the Southern States to the Northern States, Part III (Washington: USGPO, 1880), 384.
64. Ronald C. Naugle, John J. Montag, and James C. Olson, *History of Nebraska*, 4th ed., (Lincoln: University of Nebraska Press, 2014), 203.
65. Richard Edwards, "African Americans and the Southern Homestead Act," *Great Plains Quarterly* 39 no. 2 (2019): 225, doi:10.1353/gpq.2019.0018.
66. Bish, "The Black Experience in Selected Nebraska Counties," 2.
67. John Douglas Keister Johnson and Edward F. Zimmer, *Lincoln in Black and White: 1910-1925* (Charleston, SC: Arcadia Press, 2008), 91; Erin Andersen, "Lincoln's Quinn Chapel celebrates 140 years, " Lincoln Journal Star, updated July 28, 2011 Cindy Lange Kubick, *Lincoln Journal Star*, updated May 15, 2021.
68. "State Brevities," *Benkelman Republican*, June 6, 1890, 6; "Colored Men Protest," Grant *County Tribune*, June 5, 1890, 2.
69. Adam Fletcher Sasse, "A History of Segregated Schools in Omaha, Nebraska," North Omaha History, February 5, 2024, https://northomahahistory.com/2018/02/06/a-history-of-segregated-schools-in-omaha-nebraska/#:~:text=There%20were%20at%20least%20two,School%20from%201928%20to%201968, accessed May 8, 2024.

Quinn AME Church congregation, circa 1910-15, 1026 F Street, Lincoln. Courtesy of Ruth Patrick Thomas and Jimmy Thomas through Ed Zimmer.

was carved into Nebraska's social landscape as Black churches, Black businesses, and Black towns and neighborhoods developed at a distance from the mainstream.

Lynching grew in frequency in the late 1880s with little response from law enforcement and the courts. Amanda Hoffman, a white woman in Valentine, reported being assaulted by an African American man in 1887. Jerry White was accused of the crime in a preliminary hearing at the Cherry County Courthouse. The Valentine sheriff traveled sixty miles to Long Pine to arrest White and another officer would bring White back to Cherry County to stand trial. Before that could happen, a "large body of masked men" came to the jail at night, forced White from his cell and lynched him from a telegraph pole. The sheriff arrived with a posse, but claiming it was too small to intervene, allowed Jerry White to die without intervention. Nobody was arrested for the crime.[70]

George Smith, an African American hotel waiter also known as Joe Coe, was lynched by a mob in downtown Omaha in 1891. Smith was arrested and charged with the sexual assault of a young girl.[71]

The newspapers were already stoking rageful calls for revenge and made things worse by reporting a falsehood: that the girl had died. A mob estimated between five and ten thousand people stood in front of the jail, ignoring orders to disperse from the sheriff and the governor-elect. Police were outnumbered; the mob broke into the jail easily and spent two hours removing Smith from his cell without interruption. His captors severely beat him before placing a rope around his neck, using it first to drag his broken body through the street, then to hang him from telephone wires on Harney Street for all to see.[72]

Although it was unconstitutional, and likely rare, the *Omaha Bee* reported in 1890 that a Black man was enslaved by a white farmer near Tobias, Nebraska. The farmer, Milton Williford, apparently purchased the man as an eight-year-old child in Kentucky. For at least ten years the man was held captive, denied education, and received no pay for his labor. A newspaper report said, "He doesn't know A from B and can't count more than a dozen. He doesn't

---

70. Potter, "Wearing the Hempen Necktie," 145.
71. Potter, "Wearing the Hempen Necktie," 145.
72. Potter, "Wearing the Hempen Necktie," 143-44.

even know his own name and goes by the nickname 'Till.' His clothes are rags and insufficient to keep him protected from the cold, and yet he toils from early morning until late at night... receiving uncomplainingly all the abuses heaped upon him." When an *Omaha Bee* reporter visited the farm, he interviewed neighbors to learn the man's conditions were terrible, filled with beatings, canings, and other physical abuse, as well as neglect and many other deprivations.[73]

Within a day, the *Omaha World-Herald* sent a reporter to investigate and rebuked all of the *Bee*'s claims, saying the story was a "rank fake" and that the paper "will probably have a libel suit on their hands."[74] They claimed it was a political gambit to manipulate Black voters, and when reports came of Black activists in Omaha organizing to free the man, they said those leaders "have been deluded by the shrewd republican managers..."[75] The paper went so far as to refer to these activist leaders as "pretended believers among the [African American] people of Omaha."[76] The *Omaha World-Herald* continued to demean attempts by Omaha's Black community to free the man, who was supposedly reluctant to leave the Williford farm. A month later Silas Robbins and Matthew Ricketts, among others, went to court charging Williford with violating the Fourteenth Amendment. According to the *Bee*, the case was "backed by the wealthiest citizens of this city and state." Williford claimed he could not afford the trip and neither he nor the enslaved man appeared for the initial trial date.[77]

The case went to trial two weeks later. Each charge against Williford was argued and "proven," and an examination of the man's back found it "literally covered with scars." The case was settled by granting the man freedom, dropping all charges, and each side paying half the costs. The *World-Herald* treated the incident as an aberration, writing that his treatment was "simply the kindly protection of a generous hearted farmer" and claiming that was why the trial was dismissed.[78] There is no report on what happened to the formerly enslaved man afterward.

Buffalo Soldier, 9th Cavalry, Co. D., wearing sharpshooter collar insignia. C.C. McBride photograph, Crawford, Nebraska, 1880-1890, Library of Congress.

A white Army officer at Fort Robinson, notorious for his refusal to treat African American officers and Buffalo Soldiers as his equals, was court-martialed in 1881 for verbally abusing, pistol-whipping, and beating a Black soldier. The assailant was promoted to the rank of captain in 1899, having shown little to no change in his racist stance. When Lieutenant Charles Young, an African American officer from West Point, arrived at Fort Robinson in 1889, this captain refused to serve with him. The isolation and violence leveled against Lieutenant Young resulted in his transfer from Fort Robinson in less than one year. Young's excellence earned him promotion to the rank of colonel and

---

73. "Emancipation All a Myth?" *Omaha Daily Bee*, September 11, 1890.
74. "A Rank Fake," *Omaha World-Herald*, September 17, 1890.
75. "They Bit Readily," *Omaha World-Herald*, September 19, 1890.
76. "Like a Campaign Snap," *Omaha World-Herald*, September 20, 1890.
77. "Till Not Produced," *Omaha World-Herald*, November 12, 1890; "The Slave Liberated," *Omaha Daily Bee*, November 21, 1890.
78. ["Untitled."] *Omaha World-Herald*. November 21, 1890.

afforded him a distinguished military career.[79] After more than a century of invisibility, Charles Young was promoted "honorably and posthumously" to the rank of brigadier general in 2021.

Continued harassment and violence against Black soldiers moved Henry V. Plummer, the Army's first Black chaplain, to start a newspaper called the *Fort Robinson Weekly Bulletin*. A popular preacher and temperance advocate who organized an unpopular activist campaign to ban the sale of alcohol at the fort, Plummer was no stranger to opposition. After seeing Black soldiers routinely face abuse when they went to nearby Crawford, Plummer called for Black soldiers to physically defend themselves. Shortly after, in 1894, another Black soldier testified against trumped up charges that Plummer was constantly intoxicated, supplied liquor to other soldiers, and behaved inappropriately while drinking. Even though the testimony was not corroborated by others, Plummer was found guilty and court-martialed. His career in the military behind him, Plummer moved to Omaha. He eventually left Nebraska to become a religious leader in Washington, D.C., and Kansas City.[80]

The segregation and discrimination at Fort Robinson were replicated across many professions, making the attainment of professional training, licensure, and a practice a tremendous feat for African Americans. As Nebraska's African American communities grew, so did the number of Black professionals who provided essential services to Black clients. As members of white professional circles, they also provided leadership at the local, state, and national levels. Matthew O. Ricketts graduated from the Omaha Medical College (now the University of Nebraska College of Medicine) in 1884, becoming the first African American graduate from an institution of higher education in Nebraska. Born enslaved in Missouri, Ricketts' importance to African Americans in Nebraska expanded from leadership in medicine to advocacy for racial justice, to serving in the Nebraska Legislature.[81] His

Studio portrait of Matthew O. Ricketts, circa 1893. Nebraska State Historical Society

professional circle grew to include Dr. Jesse H. Hutton, Dr. August C. Edwards, and dentists Dr. W. W. Peebles and Dr. Craig Morris, who were political and community leaders in their own right.

Black churches formed a foundation for African American communities. Ella Jean Seay Rogers, a lifelong member of Mount Nebo Missionary Baptist Church from age three, explained: "After slavery it was the thing that kept [formerly enslaved people] together. It helped people survive. It was their hope. It was how and where they shared information. It was where they prayed. That's our survival mode. It still is."[82] A sizable Black neighborhood formed in Omaha around 15th and Douglas streets

---

79. Brian G. Shellum, *Black Officer in a Buffalo Soldier Regiment: The Military Career of Charles Young*, (Lincoln: University of Nebraska Press. 2010), 11; Brian G. Shellum, "Charles Young and the Buffalo Soldiers After the Indian Wars," *Nebraska History* 95 (2014): 33-34; Dontavian Harrison, "Colonel Charles Young Posthumously Promoted to Brigadier General at West Point," May 2, 2022, U.S. Army, https://www.army.mil/article/256278/col_charles_young_posthumously_promoted_to_brigadier_general_at_west_point#:~:text=Undersecretary%20of%20the%20Army%20Gabe,the%20honorary%20promotion%20on%20Oct, accessed June 30, 2024.

80 Stover, Earl F. "Chaplain Henry V. Plummer, His Ministry and His Court Martial." *Nebraska History 56*, no. 1. (March 1975): 20-50; Frank N. Schubert, *Outpost of the Sioux Wars: A History of Fort Robinson* (Lincoln: University of Nebraska Press, 1995), 126-137.

81. Alonzo Smith, "Matthew O. Ricketts (1853-1917), The Black Past, https://www.blackpast.org/african-american-history/ricketts-matthew-oliver-1853-1917/, accessed June 18, 2024.

82. Leo Adam Biga, "The Black Church in Omaha," NOISE, August 20, 2021, https://www.noiseomaha.com/profiles/the-black-church-in-omaha-mt-nebo, accessed June 18, 2024.

Rev. O.J. Burckhardt. Nebraska State Historical Society

Artist Anna Burckhardt. Nebraska State Historical Society

where St. John's African Methodist Episcopal Church, Nebraska's first African American house of worship, was founded in 1865.[83] Zion Baptist Church, established in Omaha in 1884, was the largest Black church in Nebraska by 1900. Destroyed by the Easter Sunday tornado of 1913, Zion was rebuilt and has continued since. From 1900 through 1940, it was a frequent venue for national Civil Rights leaders to speak and during the Civil Rights Movement of the 1950s and 1960s it was home to many rallies, planning sessions and other events. St. Phillip the Deacon Episcopal Church was a Black-only congregation established in Omaha's Near North Side neighborhood in 1887.[84] The Reverend John Albert Williams started ministering at St. Philip in 1891. He became the foremost leader of Omaha's Civil Rights Movement for the next two generations, starting a newspaper, leading the struggle in several pivotal battles, and launching the Omaha chapter of the NAACP.[85]

Lincoln was also a center for Black religious leadership. Reverend Oliver Burckhardt moved to Lincoln after completing his studies at the Lincoln Institute in Jefferson City, Missouri. He married Lincoln artist Anna Jones in 1898 and the two were deeply involved in community affairs. Responding to the needs of African Americans in Cherry County, Reverend Burckhardt founded the African Methodist Church in 1908. He extended his pastoral outreach to inmates in the Nebraska State Penitentiary in his twenty-year role as associate pastor. In Lincoln, he was an active member of the Urban League and organizer of the Interdenominational Christian Alliance of Lincoln. All services and gatherings were interdenominational and interracial, rejecting denominational divides and Jim Crow segregation to gather as Christians. Such meetings exposed the illogic and moral bankruptcy of religious and racial divides, weakening the foundation of white supremacy little

---

83. Monica Joe, "St. John African Methodist Episcopal Church, Omaha, Nebraska (1865-), BlackPast, March 23, 2014, https://www.blackpast.org/african-american-history/st-john-african-methodist-episcopal-church-omaha-nebraska-1865/, accessed July 8, 2024.
84. The church operating under that name until 1986. That year, it merged with a historically white congregation to create an intentionally integrated church, and its successor congregation, Episcopal Church of the Resurrection, continues today.
85. Adam Fletcher Sasse, "A History of St. Philip the Deacon Episcopal Church," North Omaha History, May 11, 2019, https://northomahahistory.com/2019/05/11/a-history-of-st-philip-the-deacon-episcopal-church/.

by little as more people joined the Alliance in fellowship. Spearheading interracial fellowship was yet another way that Black religious leaders built broader-based support for the Civil Rights movement of the 1950s and 1960s.[86]

Small-town churches were points of connection to employment opportunities and safe spaces to figure out how to navigate the racism parishioners faced outside the doors. RaDaneil Arvie, daughter of Mount Nebo pastor Reverend Terry Arvie, described Black churches as "the only institution we had that was really for us and had our interests at heart…It was the only place where we could self-determine our own destinies."[87] Leslie Daughtery established the Hamilton Methodist Church in the early 1880s, where Black Methodists gathered for worship and a broader swath of the community heard presentations like "A Knight of the Twentieth Century."[88] Providing a religious, social, recreational, and cultural center, this first African American church was the nexus for Black people in Hastings.

Clubs and associations connected Black Nebraskans to national networks. The first organization of Prince Hall Masons in Nebraska formed in Omaha in 1866 with business owner Richard D. Curry as the leader. The Prince Hall Masons are the first-ever and longest continuing Black fraternal organization in the U.S. Prince Hall Freemasonry was founded in 1775 by civil rights leader and abolitionist Prince Hall along with fourteen other free Black men who, like Hall, had been inducted into the Freemasons. Free Black men were drawn to Freemasonry's self-presentation as a "universal brotherhood", but it did not extend to opening membership in white lodges to African Americans. Prince Hall's petitions to the leadership in England established African Lodge No. 1 in 1775. Dedicated to the Masonic mission of cultivating a morality-centered upwardly mobile middle class, Prince Hall Masonry sought to lay the foundation for African American citizenship and improvement of the conditions of life for Black people.[89] The Prince Hall Masons were forced to organize separately from white Masons to conduct social, educational, cultural, and other uplifting activities throughout the community. The organization expanded statewide and remains active in Nebraska today.[90]

The Omaha branch of the Young Men's Colored Independent Political Club held its first meeting in 1886. Their longstanding discontent with Republicans and Democrats led to the formation of these independent groups, intended to educate and advocate for political action to reflect African American interests irrespective of any one party. The apex of their influence might have been in the 1910s, when they kept an establishment at North 14th and Douglas streets. However, organizations for politically active, non-party-loyal African Americans remain a part of Nebraska's political landscape.[91]

The first Black-owned, Black-focused newspaper in Nebraska, the *Western Post*, was published in Hastings between 1876 and 1877. Four more Black newspapers went into circulation before 1900: the *Afro-American Sentinel* started by Cyrus Bell (Omaha, 1893-1899); *The Enterprise* (Omaha, 1893-1911) and the *Leader* (Lincoln, 1899).[92] *The Progress*, founded by Ferdinand L. Barnett in 1889, focused on the pro-South, anti-Black policies that perpetuated lynching and other forms of racial violence. White officials did not condone lynching but did not condemn it strenuously enough either. *The Progress* would remedy this by calling attention to the number and brutality of lynchings, and by encouraging "indignation meetings" to put the heat on law enforcement to respond, on politicians to enact rigorous anti-lynching laws, and to call on the public

---

86. Oliver J. Burckhardt Papers RG3248.AM, Nebraska State Archives, https://history.nebraska.gov/collection_section/oliver-j-burckhardt-1868-1949-rg3248-am/ ; Nebraska State Historical Society, Burckhardt House, National Register of Historic Places, May 24, 1999, https://npgallery.nps.gov/GetAsset/eb7d936f-a4c1-41c2-971a-b338645a4a2d/, "Church Services," Shopping Guide October 3, 19
87. Leo Adam Biga, "The Black Church in Omaha," NOISE, August 20, 2021, https://www.noiseomaha.com/profiles/the-black-church-in-omaha-mt-nebo, accessed June 18, 2024; Henry Louis Gates, Jr., *The Black Church: This Is Our Story, This Is Our Song* (New York: Penguin Books, 2020), 109-118
88. "Methodist Church," *The Hamilton County Register*, December 4, 1908, 5.
89. Price Hall Freemasonry: A Resource Guide, Library of Congress, https://guides.loc.gov/prince-hall-freemasonry, accessed June 22, 2024; William Alan Muraskin, *Middle Class Blacks in a White Society* (Berkeley: University of California Press, 2021), 22-24.
90. Most Worshipful Prince Hall Grand Lodge: Free and Accepted Masons of Nebraska Inc., https://www.mwphglnebraska.org, accessed 7/1/2024/.
91. "Colored Men in Convention," *The Phonograph*, April 4, 1884, 6.
92. Paz, ""The Black Press," 5.

The Dixie Ramblers, circa 1940. UNL History Harvest

to prevent future incidents.⁹³ Longtime editor Walter J. Singleton published contributions from such notable writers as Henry V. Plummer, Alfred Barnett, and James Bryant. While often at odds with the other newspapers, *The Progress* enjoyed statewide distribution through the end of its run in 1906. *The Enterprise*, a statewide pro-Republican paper, was founded in Omaha in 1893 by George F. Franklin as the "official journal of the Nebraska State Afro-American. As challenging as it was to run a Black newspaper, African Americans journalists and publishers persisted, knowing the importance of the news coverage and opinions they provided.

Black art, literature, and music formed another pillar of Nebraska's burgeoning African American communities in the 1880s. The first African American women's musical group in Nebraska was started in 1880 by Josiah Waddle, a Civil War veteran who moved to Omaha from Nebraska City. His fifteen-piece band and orchestra performed statewide for several years.⁹⁴ A popular traveling group of African American performers called the Slayton Jubilee Singers became a mainstay at the new Crete Chautauqua in 1883. A summertime phenomenon until 1898, the Chautauqua was massively successful at drawing crowds of five thousand and more for the weeks-long music festival.⁹⁵

Ragtime was as popular in Nebraska as it was across the U.S. at the turn of the twentieth century. It was introduced to the state by African Americans in the 1890s and early 1900s. John William "Blind" Boone from Missouri—one of the most famous ragtime players—performed over fifty times in Nebraska between 1885 and 1920. An enormously popular performer,

---

93. Amanda Frisken, *Graphic News: How Sensational Images Transformed Nineteenth-Century Journalism*, (Champaign, IL: University of Illinois Press, 2020), 135-36.
94. Adam Fletcher Sasse, "A Biography of Josiah Waddle," North Omaha History, October 17, 2022, https://northomahahistory.com/2022/10/17/a-biography-of-josiah-waddle/, accessed August 7, 2024.
95. "Nebraska Chautauquas," Explore Nebraska History, accessed August 7, 2024, https://mynehistory.com/items/show/,439.

Boone was "no stranger to Kearney" by 1897, nor to any other Nebraska town with a concert hall.[96] The Original Creole Ragtime Band filled the seats at the Orpheum and Empress Theaters, among others. Dan Desdunes' "Happy Feeling Rag" was a standard at Nebraska gatherings upon its publication in 1912.[97] Ragtime bands in Nebraska that morphed into jazz included the Jungle Rhythm Boys and Basie Givens Orchestra, paving the way for Omaha to become one of the hubs for American jazz musicians.[98]

Organizing for Reform – 1890s

Omaha's economic growth transformed it from a river town to an engine of the Midwest's railroad, agricultural, and meatpacking industries. Chicago companies Armour, Cudahy, and Swift made South Omaha the third largest meatpacking center in America. Ten railroads had routes through Omaha and grain markets netted the city over $180 million per year. The population tripled in ten years. The boom was spectacular in many ways but did bring stresses and excesses that led some to call Omaha "the wickedest city in America." The reputation came from the Third Ward, where the commercial retail center met the transience of the Missouri River. It became a hub for saloons, gambling houses, brothels, and various illegal activities. Iowa native Tom Dennison, a denim-and-diamonds frontiersman who made his fortune from his chain of gambling houses in mining towns across Colorado, became a major player in Omaha's vice scene. Though he had been in Omaha only a short time, Dennison had seen several public officials in his establishments. Protecting these secrets won him fast allies in City Hall and on the police force.[99]

Dennison was no racial liberal, but he recognized the power of consolidating support from minority communities. Vic Walker and Jack Bloomfield—both African American men—served as go-betweens between Dennison and Black power brokers. He engaged Omaha's Republican political machine and influenced political outcomes by engineering election fraud, often in the forms of registration fraud and repeat voting. Movements for temperance, election reform, and Black civil and political rights were anathema to Dennison's machine politics, making Black politicians, organizations, and media important players in the larger fight against corruption and social disorder.[100]

Black participation in electoral politics became a norm in Nebraska by the end of the decade. Millard F. Singleton was elected vice president of the Omaha Colored Republican Club in 1889. In the years afterwards, he was constantly leading political organizing across the state. In 1890, he helped re-establish the Nebraska branch of the Afro-American League and served as Nebraska representative to its national convention. Claus Hubbard made an unsuccessful run for a seat in the Nebraska legislature in 1889 but remained influential in state politics, starting as manager for Matthew Ricketts' 1891-92 campaign for state legislature.

In 1893 Ricketts became the third African American to run for the Nebraska Legislature and the first to serve. He served two terms in the Nebraska House of Representatives until 1897 before the body became unicameral. There would a be nineteen-year gap between the first Black legislator and the second one, with a total of fifteen Black legislators elected to the Nebraska Unicameral as of 2024.[101] Edwin Overall

---

96. "A Large Audience," *Semi-Weekly Kearney Hub and Central Nebraska Press*, December 16, 1897, 3.
97. Jesse J. Otto, "Dan Desdunes: New Orleans Civil Rights Activist and 'The Father of Negro Musicians of Omaha,'" *Nebraska History* 92 (2011): 106-117.
98. Preston Love, "Junior Raglin, the Omaha Kid," *Omaha World-Herald*, November 9, 1975, 144.
99. Orville D. Menard, *River City Empire: Tom Dennison's Omaha* (Lincoln: University of Nebraska Press, 2013).
100. See Menard, *River City Empire*, Chapter 2.
101. Adam Fletcher Sasse,"A Biography of North Omaha's Dr. Matthew O. Ricketts," North Omaha History, September 23, 2015, https://northomahahistory.com/2015/09/23/omahas-matthew-o-ricketts/ ; "Republicans Elect Two Race Candidates to the Legislature," *The Monitor*. November 05, 1926, *Chronicling America: Historic American Newspapers*. Lib. of Congress. < https://chroniclingamerica.loc.gov/lccn/00225879/1926-11-05/ed-1/seq-1 /.. The fifteen legislators are Dr. John A. Singleton (1926–1928), Ferdinand L. Barnett (1927-1928) were the first Black senators to hold office simultaneously. They were followed by Dr. Aaron M. McMillan (1929-1930), Johnny Owen (1932-1935), John Adams, Jr. (1935-1941), Rev. John Adams, Sr. (1949-1962), Edward Danner (1963-1970), and George W. Althouse (1970). JoAnn Maxey (1977-1979), was the first African American woman appointed to the Unicameral. Ernie Chambers (1971–2009 & 2013–2020), representing North Omaha for forty-six years, is the longest-serving state senator in Nebraska history. Brenda J. Council (2009-2013), Tanya Cook (2009-2016), were the first African American women elected to the Unicameral. At the time of this writing, Senators Justin Wayne (2017-) and Terrell McKinney (2020-) are serving legislative terms at the time of this writing; Adam Fletcher Sasse, "A History of North Omaha's African American Legislators" North Omaha History, March 18, 2023, https://northomahahistory.com/2019/03/18/a-history-of-north-omahas-african-american-legislators/.

was the second African American candidate for the Nebraska Legislature. Although he lost his race, he did have the support of the Republican Party and the endorsement of organized labor, forming a strong political coalition. The local Black newspaper, *The Progress*, blamed his loss on white Republicans not voting for him because he was Black. He went on to be the first Black candidate for the Omaha City Council when he ran as a Populist candidate on a pro-labor platform in 1893.[102]

Although he lost this election, too, Overall's campaign contributed to the increasing Black participation in shaping and advancing political platforms that addressed African Americans' concerns.

The Afro-American Democratic Association met for the first time in Omaha that same year. J.W. Alexander succeeded in starting the association despite facing threats of violence.[103] Among one hundred members attending were Lewis Washington, Ferdinand Barnett, and Alfred Barnett. Speakers voiced their disappointment, frustration and anger with the Republican Party and talked about running their own candidates, holding their own events, and raising their profile.[104]

A statewide conference to re-establish the Nebraska Afro-American League took place in 1890 with representatives from Columbus, Blair, Plattsmouth, Aurora, Chadron, Overton, Schuyler, and Ansley. While there, the organization of statewide representatives made statements against Southern oppression and the Northern caste system, as well as discussing segregated restaurants, segregated barbers and segregated public houses (bars) across the state. Many important Black leaders from Lincoln and Omaha were present too, including Cyrus Bell, Matthew Ricketts, and Alfred Barnett. Bell caused a debate among the group by encouraging Nebraska Black voters to vote their conscience instead of voting strictly Republican. Bell's suggestion met resistance, especially from delegates who lived outside of Omaha.[105]

Reverend George Woodbey (1854-1937) became a national voice for social reform. Born enslaved in Tennessee in 1854, Woodbey became a Baptist

Rev. George Woodbey. Wikimedia Commons.

minister and moved to Omaha in the 1880s. When the Nebraska Prohibition Party made him their candidate in the 1890 lieutenant governor's race, he became the first African American to run for the office. Woodbey lost his race for lieutenant governor but his gifts as an orator kept him on the political stage. He became the first African American in Nebraska to run for U.S. Congress in 1894, running again as a member of the Nebraska Prohibition Party. After losing his congressional race, Woodbey joined the Populist People's Party to support William Jennings Bryan in his 1896 presidential campaign.[106] Woodbey joined the Nebraska Socialist Party in 1901 and became a nationally prominent party leader after moving to California the next year.

---

102. "Voice of Colored Voters." *Omaha World-Herald*. October 31, 1893.
103. "Whitecapped a Black Man." *Omaha World-Herald*. October 26, 1893.
104. "Tired of the G.O.P." *Omaha World-Herald*. November 2, 1893.
105. "Colored Men's Convention" *Omaha Bee,* May 1, 1890, 5.
106. Philip S. Foner, "Reverend George Washington Woodbey: Early Twentieth Century California Black Socialist." *The Journal of Negro History,* 61 no. 2 (April 1976):138; Charles Robert Holm, "'To Be Free from The Slavery of Capitalism': David Walker, Peter H. Clark and George Washington Woodbey's Black Socialist Thought," Master's thesis. The University of Texas at Austin, 2021; Robert Fikes, "George Washington Woodbey," *The Black Past,* https://www.blackpast.org/african-american-history/woodbey-george-washington-1854/.

Many Black activists, including Woodbey, saw socialism as the avenue for continued empowerment after Emancipation. Uniting all workers across racial lines to ensure they reap the full value of their labor and that they are full and equal participants in the democratic process was a promising, if imperfect platform. As Woodbey explained, "In the days of chattel slavery the masters had a patrol force to keep the negroes in their place and protect the interests of the masters. Today the capitalists use the police for the same purpose." Slaveholders no longer enslaved Black labor, he argued, because capitalists made workers of all races into wage slaves.[107] When Eugene V. Debs ran as the Socialist candidate for President in 1901, he chose Woodbey as his Vice-Presidential running mate. The campaign was extremely difficult; both Woodbey and Debs were beaten and jailed multiple times for promoting their political platform. Woodbey's claims that Socialism was a political expression of Christian ideals—which included racial equality—drew especially strong responses. Woodbey remained pastor at Mt. Zion Church in San Diego and a leading voice for the Socialist Movement well into the 1920s.[108]

Black women made essential contributions to the success of civil rights and reform movements and did so without access to the vote. Omaha was the home to the first chapter of the National Federation of Colored Women when it was founded in 1895.[109] After moving to Omaha in 1891, Ella Mahammitt helped found the National Federation of Afro-American Women and represented Nebraska at the first National Conference of the Colored Women of America in 1895.[110] The National Federation of Afro-American Women and the National League of Colored Women merged to form a new organization in 1896, the National Association of Colored Women (NACW). The NACW fought for rights for women and for African Americans by focusing on women's suffrage, overturning Jim Crow laws, and bringing an end to lynching.[111]

Anna Woodbey on Prohibitional National Ticket. *The New Patriot*, July 27, 1895, Nebraska State Historical Society.

Mahammitt drew criticism within the Black community for being politically active, though she was hardly the only woman on the African American political scene in Omaha.[112] Ophelia Clenlans, an outspoken activist focused on women's rights and interracial marriage, was appointed to the executive board of the National Federation of Afro-American Women, a leader of the Omaha Colored Women's Club, and an officer in the Order of the Eastern Star. Politically engaged Black women had such respect for Clenlans that they considered her their statewide leader during these critical years of political reform.[113]

Anna Woodbey, secretary of the Nebraska Prohibition Party, was named the party's candidate for the Douglas County seat on the University of Nebraska Board of Regents in 1895. The party made

---

107. Paul Heideman, "Socialism and Black Oppression," *Jacobin*, April 4, 2018, https://jacobin.com/2018/04/socialism-marx-race-class-struggle-color-line.
108. Robert Fikes, "George Washington Woodbey," *The Black Past*, https://www.blackpast.org/african-american-history/woodbey-george-washington-1854/.
109. LaVonne Leslie, *The History of the National Association of Colored Women's Clubs, Inc.: A Legacy of Service.* (United Kingdom: Xlibris, 2012), 8.
110. Shelley, "Ella Mahammitt," www.douglascohistory.org/ella-mahammitt-an-american-story/.
111. Rita Shelley, "Ella Mahammitt: An American Story." Douglas County Historical Society, 2023, www.douglascohistory.org/ella-mahammitt-an-american-story/.
112. Shelley, "Ella Mahammitt," www.douglascohistory.org/ella-mahammitt-an-american-story/.
113. Adam Fletcher Sasse, "Notable African American Women in Omaha History," North Omaha History, 2020, https://northomahahistory.com/2020/08/27/notable-african-american-women/.

its nomination as a show of confidence in Woodbey's leadership and in the belief that Woodbey was the first Black woman to appear on a state ticket.[114] Although Woodbey lost this race, she remained a high-profile speaker, minister, and political leader, who was a support to her husband, George Woodbey, in his campaigns for state and national office.[115] Her candidacy also formed part of the nationwide wave of women running for political office with the support of their parties that included U.S. presidential candidates Victoria Woodhull and Belva Ann Lockwood and Toledo City School Board member Pauline Steinem, grandmother of Gloria Steinem, who may have been the first Jewish woman elected to public office.[116]

In 1895, Lucinda "Lucy" Gamble became the first African American teacher in Omaha Public Schools. Her teaching career ended in 1901, when she married newspaper publisher and civil rights leader Reverend John Albert Williams because at that time, married women were prohibited from teaching in the Omaha Public Schools. Married life did not bring an end to Gamble's political and community work: she was chair of the board for the Negro Old People's Home for ten years, a delegate to the Council of the Episcopal Diocese of Nebraska, and a member of the local board of directors of the NAACP.[117] Gamble was a longtime community leader in North Omaha who drew respect for the breadth and impact of her work.[118]

Sowing the Seeds of Civil Rights

June 1891 brought the first celebrations of Juneteenth recorded in Nebraska history. Amidst Nebraska's rising barriers to racial equality, Black Nebraskans gathered at Omaha's Exposition Hall to celebrate the day in 1866 when word of their emancipation reached enslaved people in Texas with live musical performances, speeches, dancing, and lots of good food.[119] Although this is the first Juneteenth on record, Black Nebraskans were likely marking this day of freedom for decades. African Americans in Nebraska strengthened their economic, social, and political powers in the state during the Gilded Age, which lasted from 1877 to 1910.[120]

For Black people the forces of overt white supremacy doubled down on the challenges of the Gilded Age, defined by the disparity between the wealthy and the poor. African Americans statewide struck back with determination, developing increasingly effective methods of community organizing, voter turnout, and collective empowerment in Omaha and Lincoln. Their persistence often paid off; for the first time Black workers experienced more secure employment, their children had access to public schools, and leaders exercised political power in the democratic process. All of this increased the social capital, educational opportunities, and economic capital that every person needed to survive in Nebraska. Despite constant setbacks, through fighting and resistance Nebraska's Black community grew in its numbers, participation in political and economic life, and its contributions to making Nebraska one of the nation's agricultural and transportation powerhouses. The vital role of African Americans was reflected every Juneteenth, especially when Falls City first held its own celebration in 1892, Norfolk in 1899, Nebraska City in 1902, Chadron in 1912, and as celebrations continued across the state into the 1940s.[121]

In the late nineteenth century, the future for racial equality looked promising in some respects. The Nebraska Legislature adopted the state's first civil rights law in 1893. Nebraska Statutes Section 4000, Chapter 10, established that a civil right is "accorded

---

114. "Woodbey for Regent!" History Nebraska, https://history.nebraska.gov/publications_section/woodbey-for-regent/ ; "A Great Convention," *The New Republic*, July 20, 1895, 1.
115. Katherine Clarke, "Anna R. Woodbey (1855-1901)," The Black Past, June 12, 2021, https://www.blackpast.org/african-american-history/people-african-american-history/anna-r-woodbey-1855-1901/.
116. Wendy E. Chimielewski, "Her Hat Was in the Ring: How Thousands of Women Were Elected to Political Office before 1920," Gilder Lehrman Institute, https://www.gilderlehrman.org/history-resources/essays/her-hat-was-ring-how-thousands-women-were-elected-political-office-1920, accessed June 27, 2024.
117. Stu Popisil, "Omaha Civil Rights Leader Williams Remembered as an "Ideal Citizen"," *Omaha World-Herald*, February 22, 2023 (updated March 27, 2023), https://omaha.com/news/local/history/stu-pospisil-omaha-civil-rights-leader-williams-remembered-as-an-ideal-citizen/article_ae696262-9013-11ec-b8b8-279f96d7a882.html.
118. Fletcher Sasse, "A History of St. Philip the Deacon Episcopal Church," https://northomahahistory.com/2019/05/11/a-history-of-st-philip-the-deacon-episcopal-church/
119. "Nebraska Notes," *The Columbus Journal*, September 30, 1891.
120. Thomas Adams Upchurch, *Historical Dictionary of the Gilded Age*. (New York: Scarecrow Press, 2009), 82.
121. Ads and notices are numerous in Nebraska papers, including an ad from *The Voice*, August 4, 1949.

to every member of a district, community, or nation" and that "[all] persons within the state shall be entitled to a full and equal enjoyment of the accommodations, advantages, facilities and privileges of inns, restaurants, public conveyances, barber shops, theaters and other places of amusement, subject only to the conditions and limitations established by law and applicable alike to every person."[122] Omaha's Black newspapers heralded the law for three decades: *The Monitor* printed the introductory section of the law almost weekly for more than a decade, often on the front page of the paper.

The Civil Rights Law seemed to point toward ever greater racial equality and inclusion in Nebraska. From the beginning of statehood, hotels across Nebraska did not allow Black people to stay in them, especially in Omaha and Lincoln. John Lewis opened the Lewis Hotel in downtown Omaha in 1890, providing the first accommodations for African Americans in Nebraska until it closed in 1896. At least fifteen other Black hotels opened across of the state at various times, along with several "rest homes" that acted like a bed and breakfasts.[123] The Black hotel was the only option available to African American travelers, whereas white travelers were free to choose from any number of hotels based on their preferred location, the offerings in the restaurants, or other factors.

Although they were a long way from achieving full civil rights and economic justice, African Americans celebrated their communities' accomplishments and, in doing so, generated the necessary support to continue with hope. In 1894, the first Black-run, Black-focused fair in the United States for African Americans was held in July. Called the Nebraska Afro-American Fair, the event was advertised as allowing only Black people to exhibit, own horses in the races and lead the event. Displays included paintings and needlework, as well as cooking and woodworking. Attendees took trains from west and central Nebraska, as well as Iowa and Kansas.[124] Although there was never a follow-up event, the Afro-American Fair Association that organized the event sponsored the 1895 Emancipation Day celebration in Omaha.[125]

Matthew Ricketts, with the aid of politically engaged Black women, scored a brief legislative victory for civil rights in 1895. Armed with five hundred petition signatures from African American women in Omaha and the language in the Civil Rights Law Ricketts introduced a bill to repeal Nebraska's miscegenation law prohibiting marriage between a white person and a person of African descent. Governor Silas A. Holcomb vetoed the repeal,[126] but Ricketts and the petitioners consolidated opposition to the miscegenation law and brought their objections into Nebraska's public conversation.[127]

Civil rights were curtailed in 1896 when the U.S. Supreme Court ruled in *Plessy v. Ferguson* that racial segregation was constitutional. The decision upheld a Louisiana law that required passenger trains to maintain separate "white" and "colored" sections on trains; only Black nurses tending to white children could ride in the "white" section. Passengers who sat in the wrong section were subject to hefty fines and jail time. Homer Plessy, whose ancestry was 7/8 Caucasian, was part of an organization that sought to test the constitutionality of the law as it applied to interstate train travel. After being arrested for sitting in a white car, Plessy's attorney, Albion W. Tourgée, argued that segregation reinforced white supremacists' false claims about Black "inferiority," that segregation limited Black citizens' free engagement in all aspects of American life, and that a Louisiana law could not be applied across state lines.

The majority opinion held that the fact that seats were available to Black passengers meant that they had equal access to rail transportation. "Separate but equal" became the constitutional standard. "Equal" did not mean "of equal quality." African American citizens were entitled to travel, but they were not entitled to the same assurances of safety and reliability as white people. Perhaps most importantly, the majority opinion supported the white supremacist belief that Black people were less deserving of respect than white people. Justice John Marshall Harlan, the sole dissenting justice, described the law as a means to "interfere with the blessings of freedom; to regulate

---

122. Nebraska State Legislature, 23rd Session, An Act to Provide That All Persons Shall Be Entitled to the Same Civil Rights, to Punish All Persons for Violations of Its Provisions, Laws, Joint Resolutions, and Memorials, Passed by the Legislative Assembly of the State of Nebraska (Lincoln: State Printing Authority,1893), 141-42.

123. Adam Fletcher Sasse, "A History of Black Hotels in Omaha," North Omaha History, November 6, 2015, https://northomahahistory.com/2015/11/06/a-history-of-black-hotels-in-omaha/.

124. "Afro-Americans," *Omaha World-Herald*, May 26, 1894.

125. "Where the Goat Stalketh," *Omaha World-Herald*, July 28, 1895.

126. "Vetoed by Holcomb," *Fremont Daily Herald*, April 12, 1895, 1.

127. Fletcher Sasse, "Notable African American Women in Omaha History," 116.

the civil rights common to all citizens, upon the basis of race; and to place in a condition of legal inferiority a large body of American citizens, now constituting a part of the political community, called the people of the United States...".[128]

Segregation was not new in Lincoln and Omaha, but the *Plessy* decision made racial lines acceptable and fully enforceable.[129] Inequality in education was pronounced in Nebraska. A survey published in *Survey Graphic* found that "California...gives twice as much schooling as Nebraska and six times as much as Kentucky." White schools across the U.S. received substantially more funding, making separate Black schools "a symbol of the inferior social, economic, and political status of colored people in American life in general."[130]

The *Plessy* decision came into force as the entire city of Omaha was abuzz with preparations for the 1898 Trans-Mississippi and International Exposition. The Trans-Mississippi Expo was one of several across the West celebrating the progress America in the hundred years since its founding. Designed to promote Omaha and the surrounding region as part of America's continuing success story, the Expo took place in more than one hundred splendid temporary buildings constructed on 184 acres in present-day North Omaha.[131] More than 2.6 million people came to view more than ten thousand exhibits between June 1 and October 31, 1898.[132]

African Americans took part in the Expo from its inception. They invested their money in the event by buying stock. They submitted exhibits and managed receptions throughout the year. They hosted national conventions, formed a national and bi-racial civil rights organization, and protested segregation before, during and after the event. African Americans worked on construction crews and served as security guards. The Expo's white organizers and investors restricted Black participation to the realms of investor, exhibitor, event sponsor, labor, and attendee. Calls to seat one African American on the Expo's fifty-one-member board of directors were dismissed, assuring that it and the executive leadership would remain all-white.

Expos like the Trans-Mississippi featured displays of "other" cultures in the form of living dioramas.[133] The only presentation of Black people at the supposedly international event was a living history display called "The Old Plantation" that employed the only Black presenters throughout the entire exposition. Designing to reinforce negative stereotypes and promote white supremacy, the display claimed to be the most educational activity in the expo by featuring authentic slave cabins, a "slave church" from Alabama and with performances promoting racist tropes about Black people. This staging of "African American life" featuring "voodooism" and "superstitions" did not resemble the historical experiences of Black people in America and it in no way reflected the lives of Black Nebraskans in 1898.[134]

Amidst the Expo's racist overtones were celebrations of African Americans' achievements. An essay by George Wells Parker, a recent graduate of Omaha High School who entered Howard University, won the Expo's national competition for high school and college writers. Parker returned to Omaha, where he became a prominent journalist and columnist in the Black press, building a readership at the local, state, and national levels. Fifteen-year-old artist Clarence "Cap" Wigington was awarded three first prizes and a medal for the works he submitted to the Expos' juried art competition. Wigington went on to become an apprentice to Omaha's master architect Thomas R. Kimball and to distinguish himself as the first Black architect in Nebraska. He designed several buildings in Omaha before moving to Saint Paul, Minnesota, in 1914.[135]

---

128. U.S. Supreme Court, PLESSY v. FERGUSON, 163 U.S. 537 (1896); "Plessy v. Ferguson," National Archives and Records Administration, https://www.archives.gov/milestone-documents/plessy-v-ferguson.
129. Strand, "Mirror, Mirror...,"190.
130. "Editorial of the Month: Why Separate Schools are Undesirable," *The Crisis* 46:11 (November 1939): 339.
131. James B. Haynes, *Trans-Mississippi and International Exposition of 1898*, (Omaha: Board of Directors Committee on History, 1910), 29-55.
132. "The World's Fair of the Midwest," History Nebraska, https://history.nebraska.gov/the-worlds-fair-of-themidwest/#:~:text=The%20Trans%2DMississippi%20and%20International,from%20June%20to%20November%201898, accessed June 22, 2024.
133. Haynes, *Trans-Mississippi and International Exposition*, 22-23.
134. James B. Haynes, "The Great Event of 1898," *Leslie's Illustrated Weekly*, February 3, 1898, 72-74.
135. David Vassar Taylor with Paul Clifford Larson, *Cap Wigington: An Architectural Legacy in Ice and Stone* (St. Paul, MN: Minnesota Historical Society Press, 2001), 28, 31.

"The Old Plantation," living history exhibit at 1898 Trans-Mississippi Expo in Omaha. Omaha Public Library.

The Expo presented opportunities for African Americans from in and outside of Omaha to convene. Edwin Overall organized the Congress of White and Colored Americans, drawing hundreds from across the region specifically for the three-day event. A conference for the National Colored Personal Liberty League, a meeting of the National Colored Press Association, a gathering for the Western Negro Press Association, and a "Colored People's Day" represented a wide range of Black interests, perspectives, and areas of expertise. The contrast between these real, present-day organizations and the actors in "The Old Plantation" could not have been starker.[136a]

Cyrus Bell tested the effectiveness of the Civil Rights Law in 1897. Under the guise of preparing a guide for Black visitors coming to attend the Trans-Mississippi and International Exposition of 1898, Bell surveyed Omaha businesses on incidents and practices of racial discrimination in their establishments. He published his findings in several editions of his newspaper, *The Afro-American Sentinel*, and expressed his surprise at the respondents' ambiguous answers. While Bell uncovered some instances of overt racism, many businesses—including hotels, restaurants, barbers, and stores—claimed each instance was merely situational. Regardless of the reasons, African Americans were not enjoying the equal right of access to public accommodations that they shared with whites. The text of the law, while hopeful, could not fulfill its promise without effort on the part of all Nebraskans.[136b]

This was the Nebraska that gave rise to John Grant Pegg, the Pullman porter-turned-Cherry County homesteader who stormed onto the African American political scene in Omaha in 1899. Known as "the councilman for the Black community," Pegg was elected president of the Colored Men's Roosevelt Club. Republican Mayor Frank E. Moore hired Pegg as a messenger in 1901. Pegg was respected throughout Omaha as the Sealer of Weights and Measures and within his profession, whose members unanimously elected him sergeant at arms for the National

---

136a David J. Peavler, "African Americans in Omaha and the 1898 Trans-Mississippi and International Exposition," *Journal of African American History* 93:3 (Summer 2008): 337-361: Haynes, *Trans-Mississippi and International Exposition of 1898*, 214, 234-36.
136b Peavler, 343-345.

Conference of Weights and Measures of the United States in 1912.[137] A 1911 feature on Pegg and the material he confiscated from businessmen trying to game the system described him as an "adroit political worker" and "a representative of the colored race in the city administration." The *Lincoln State Journal* featured a poem about Pegg that began: "A lobbyist comes here to leg / For better laws—his name is Pegg / J. Grant Pegg pegs for honest weights / All over these United States / For weights and measures fair and right / J. Grant Pegg labors day and night / Which Any statesman must declare/ Is generous and just and fair."[138] By 1908 he was serving as a page and a doorkeeper at the 1908 Republican National Convention. Pegg's interests extended well beyond politics. In addition to sponsoring African Americans settling in Cherry County, Pegg became a "race man"—the term at the time for a leader dedicated to solving the problems that bore heaviest on African Americans.[139] Pegg was president of the Omaha People's Mutual Interest Club in 1907, president of the Interstate Literary Association of the West in 1908 and the Omaha delegate to the National Negro Business League.[140] As firmly embedded as Pegg was within a major political party and city government –as much as an African American could be during the Jim Crow era—he never let his positions deter him from fighting against racial discrimination. In 1911, Pegg led the successful opposition to a Jim Crow bill in the Nebraska Legislature and stood with Vic Walker and Reverend John Williams in protesting the demotion of Black patrol captains in the Omaha Fire Department.[141]

1880: The Turning Point

Despite the obstacles, African American communities in Nebraska grew in both size and political impact in 1880. Nebraska's 2,385 Black residents represented .05 percent of the state population of 452,402.[142] Growth of the Black populations in Lincoln and Omaha remained steady, with significant increases in Scottsbluff, North Platte, Alliance, and South Sioux City. Black workers in the cities continued be a presence in the skilled labor force and in the trades, with one-third of Black workers in Lincoln employed as cooks, barbers, or carpenters. The 1880 Census charted the start of a forty-year period of African Americans earning their income from agriculture, whether as landowners, renters, or hired farm labor. Homesteaders like William P. and Charlotta Hatter Riley Walker are just one Black farming family who created the conditions for economic mobility for the next generation. The Walkers moved to Brownlee in 1880 and claimed over 1,900 acres in homesteads in Richardson, Dawson, Cherry, and Johnson counties. The Walker children went on to careers in elementary education, higher education, engineering, and nursing. When he passed away 1931, William P. Walker was one of just three African Americans buried in the Brownlee Cemetery.[143]

Several African American families rose to prominence in rural Nebraska through their work to expand Black rural life and to support Black farmers as they made their own claims. They included Joe Speese and John Speese and John Shores and Jerry Shores near Westerville and Robert Conrad and Arnold Richardson in Broken Bow. Several Black families, including the Taylors, the Days and the Woodsons, prospered in the Seward area. After enslavement in Virginia and being run out of Indiana by violence from white supremacists, Moses and Susan Speese moved to the Seward area in 1880, and to Westerville in 1882, where they homesteaded and started their family on 158 acres of land. Moses claimed another 160 acres around 1885, built a sod house, sod hen house, frame stable, a granary and corn crib, and a well and windmill.[144]

Susan, a midwife, delivered many babies in the growing community. The Speese children became ministers, lawyers, and professional musicians, with several of their children performing as a professional touring musical group. Moses Speese died in 1896. He wrote in his later years, "[a]s the years went by my

---

137. "Social Uplift," *The Crisis* 3:6 (April 1912): 229.
138. "John Grant Pegg, Who Exposes 'Tricks of the Trade,'" *Omaha World-Herald,* March 26, 1911, 26.
139. Kadijah Matin, "John Grant Pegg (1869-1916), The Black Past, January 21, 2007, https://www.blackpast.org/african-american-history/pegg-john-grant-1869-1916/, accessed July 2, 2024.
140. "Pegg Back from Negro Convention," *Omaha World-Herald,* September 3, 908, 10.
141. "Omaha Negroes Will Protest Jim Crow," *Omaha Daily News,* February 11, 1911, 1.
142. United States Census, Nebraska Race and Hispanic Origin 1860-1990, Table 42, pdf, https://www2.census.gov › demo › pop-twps0056,
143. Todd Guenther, "The Empire Builders, An African American Odyssey in Nebraska and Wyoming," *Nebraska History* 89 (2008): 176-200.
144. Bish, "The Black Experience in Selected Nebraska Counties," 143.

experience was varied, but I stuck with it and today, after eighteen years, I am out of debt, and it is with pride that I point to 230 acres under cultivation and my whole farm is under fence."[145]

The distribution of Black agricultural workers in farming communities across six Nebraska counties, along with the established Black communities in cities like Lincoln and Omaha, meant that African Americans had the same range of economic and political interests as white Nebraskans by 1880. They, like their white counterparts, engaged in the political process to ensure they were represented in the government. Black candidates and political campaigns saw the first successes in the pivotal year of 1880, starting with the election of Daniel F.S. Rogers for a term as Constable for Omaha's Third Ward, making him the first Black elected official in the state of Nebraska.[146] Rogers' electoral success opened the doors of elected office and law enforcement to yet more Black Omahans. After being elected Omaha's first Black constable in 1887, Millard Singleton was named Nebraska's first African American Justice of the Peace in Nebraska in 1885, serving Omaha's Eighth Ward in both roles.[147]

Labor, too, played a key role in African American politics. A deadlock between the Omaha Smelting Works and its striking workers escalated toward violence in 1880. Management attempted to bring in local workers to replace the strikers. The strikers chased their would-be replacements away at gunpoint. At the end of two weeks, management arranged for the transportation of more than one hundred Black workers from other cities. The *Sidney Telegraph* reported "After getting their complement, fire-arms of all description were distributed to the darkies, and the train pulled out for Omaha." The strikers were stunned by the "invasion" of armed Black outsiders. They retreated briefly and returned with hundreds of outraged, and fearful, supporters. Governor Nance rushed to the scene after mobilizing several units of the state militia to restore order. Strike leaders met with a group of the Black newcomers to explain how they were being used and called for peace by offering to pay their return train fare. The African American workers accepted the offer and joined the white workers on the picket line until transportation arrived.[148] Reports circulated later that the Omaha police chief met the strikebreakers at the train station and threatened them with arrest if they did not leave immediately.[149] Although the strikers and the strikebreakers averted a dangerous armed standoff, the incident reinforced segregationist rhetoric about African Americans posing a threat to white people's livelihoods, their communities, and their lives.

The 1880 strike also demonstrated the power of worker solidarity. African American barbers in Omaha organized Nebraska's first labor union in 1887.[150] From the turn of the twentieth century until the 1930s, Pullman car porters, musicians and a small number of laborers were the only unionized Black workers in Nebraska. Black-only labor unions would continue to grow in Nebraska from that point into the 1960s when organized labor was formally integrated.

The City of South Omaha, established in 1886 to be a home base for the Omaha Stockyards, was Nebraska's most racially, ethnically, and nationally diverse community of unionized and nonunionized workers. A massive operation involving cattle, ranchers, farmers, and salesmen, it was served by the meatpacking industry and the railroad industry. Working in segregated jobs at the Stockyards and in surrounding businesses, African Americans also attended segregated churches and schools and were segregated in public accommodations.[151] William Mitchell crossed South Omaha's racial lines in 1893 when the Cudahy Packing Plant hired him to its firefighting brigade, making him the first recorded African American firefighter in Nebraska.[152]

---

145. Bish, "The Black Experience in Selected Nebraska Counties," 205; John Speese, "A Colored Man's Experience on a Nebraska Homestead," *Omaha World-Herald* 1899.
146. Omaha's Third Ward in 1880 was located between the Missouri River and 15th Street from Cass to Jackson Streets.
147. Nebraska Writers' Program, *The Negroes of Nebraska*, 28.
148. The Strike at Omaha," *New York Times*, May 22, 1880, https://timesmachine.nytimes.com/timesmachine/1880/05/22/issue.html.
149. Richard Evans Keyes, "This Great Fraternity: Nebraska's Grand Army of the Republic, 1867-1920," University of Nebraska Omaha Student Work 476 (1997), 79-80; "Satisfied Strikers," *The Sidney Telegraph*, May 29, 1880, 2. https://digitalcommons.unomaha.edu/cgi/viewcontent.cgi?article=1481&context=studentwork.
150. Taylor, *In Search of the Racial Frontier*, 205.
151. Palma Joy Strand, "'Mirror, Mirror, on the Wall…': Reflections on Fairness and Housing in the Omaha-Council Bluffs." *Creighton Law Review* 183 (2017): 216.
152. "Magic City Gossip," *Omaha Daily Bee*, June 22, 1893,

When workers in the South Omaha meatpacking plants staged a massive strike in 1894 the packinghouses recruited African Americans from the South to break it. White workers showed hostility toward the strikebreakers, first because they crossed the picket line and escalating toward racial violence. The Nebraska National Guard was called in to protect the Black workers and a month later the strike was broken. The meatpacking companies brought Black strike breakers to South Omaha in every major labor action between 1894 to 1948—as did the packinghouses, the railroads, and the smelter in downtown Omaha. Twenty years after the first large scale migration of Black workers during the 1894 meatpacking strike, the same industry was credited with doubling Omaha's African American population when it hired nearly exclusively from the South.[153]

The Black community's greater exercise of power threatened white Nebraskans' exclusive control over political decision making. Their defensive responses heightened racial tensions in communities of all sizes across the state. African Americans in Nebraska City were among those in many communities that resisted segregation in every area of life, in ways that could seem contradictory. Newspapers reported in 1880 that the Black community in Nebraska City called for separate schools for their children. In 1885, rural migration picked up statewide, with about fourteen Black families—totaling at least sixty people—settled along the Wheeler/Holt County line in north-central Nebraska. Charles and Hester Freeman Meehan, an interracial couple, migrated with several families from their native Ontario to settle near Overton in 1884, even though marriages between white and Black people were prohibited by Nebraska law.[154]

The 1880s saw a growing leadership at the grassroots, transition to new leaders, and the acceleration of statewide organizing among African Americans.

Two of these leaders were brothers who moved to Omaha around 1881: Ferdinand L. Barnett, a journalist and government official, and his brother, journalist and civil rights activist Alfred S. Barnett. After starting a Black newspaper called *The Progress*, Ferdinand Barnett went on to serve as a member of the state legislature.[155]

Black Republicans in Nebraska held their first convention in Omaha in 1880. Reverend C.M. Brown of Lincoln, J. Gordon of Otoe County, J. Smith of Washington County, John Lewis from Omaha, Lewis Washington of Central City, and Edwin Overall of Omaha led the gathering. The convention focused on the Black vote and ensuring that Black men do not vote Republican "because they feel bound to, but because they regard it as the party of progress." Other issues included recognizing white politicians who supported Black political involvement and encouraging Southern Black people to move to Nebraska.[156] Criticizing media coverage of the event afterwards, an anonymous writer sent a letter to the editor of the *Omaha Daily Herald* declaring, "The [Republican] party would do nothing for us, so we are compelled to meet together and devise some means for securing our own interests." [157]

Lewis Washington was a noted abolitionist, lecturer, and minister who moved to Omaha in 1880. He was a formerly enslaved man who lectured against slavery and white supremacy in New York, Ohio, Indiana, Illinois, and Wisconsin. In Omaha, Washington was involved in politics and community leadership. He was also the subject of many stories; Washington claimed he was 130 years old in 1898, the year that he died, though records suggest that he lived to age 97 or 98. His claim to have known President George Washington led many to believe that he had been enslaved to the Founding Father, though there is no clear evidence to substantiate this.[158]

---

153. William C. Pratt, "Workers, Unions, and Historians on the Northern Plains." University of Nebraska History Faculty Publications 4 (1996): 240.
154. Calloway and Smith, *Visions of Freedom on the Great Plains*, 30-31.
155. "F. L. Barnett Dies at 70," *Omaha Bee*, July 15, 1932, 3.
156. ""Nebraska's Colored Men." *Omaha Daily Herald*. September 2, 1880, 8.
157. "The Colored Men's Convention," *Nebraska Advertiser*, September 9, 1880, 2.
158. Adam Fletcher Sasse, "A Biography of Lewis Washington," North Omaha History, January 8, 2023, https://northomahahistory.com/2023/01/08/a-biography-of-lewis-washington/ A 1799 inventory shows a four-year-old named Lewis on the list of the dower slaves brought into the marriage by Martha Washington but Lewis Washington of Omaha was born in Maryland and Lewis in the record lived on River Farm in Maryland where he likely was born. This Lewis would have been 103 in 1898, the year Lewis Washington died in Omaha. See Transcript of George Washington's List of Enslaved People, https://www.mountvernon.org/education/primary-source-collections/primary-source-collections/article/george-washington-s-list-of-enslaved-people-1799/.

Victor Walker arrived in Omaha in 1887. A complex figure, Walker was a Buffalo Soldier in western Nebraska before becoming a police officer in Omaha. He quickly became a political operative in the city and then earned his living as a lawyer. Walker soon became involved in the city's criminal machine and was awarded ownership of the Midway Saloon, a notorious and popular bar in downtown Omaha. After upsetting the city's criminal leader, he was kicked out of his bar, beaten by police, and struggled to regain his footing in Omaha before leaving in 1910. During this time, he was noted for advancing African American civil rights and for being a leader of Nebraska's Black community.[159]

The 1890s to 1910s

Obtaining pensions for ex-slaves to compensate them for unpaid labor became a political hot topic in 1890 when Congressman W.J. Connell of Nebraska introduced the Freedmen's Pension Bill, a bill proposed by white Omaha newspaper editor Walter R. Vaughan that was inspired by the system for military veterans' pensions. Vaughan made the case for paying pensions to former slaves to increase wealth in the South in his pamphlet, "Freedmen's Pension Bill: A Plea for American Freedmen." Nebraska Congressman W.J. Connell introduced the H.R. 11119 to the House of Representatives in 1890, bringing "Vaughan's Pleas for the Old Slaves" before Congress.[160] The proposed pensions, ranging from $4 to $15 per month depending on a person's age, drew great support from the formerly enslaved, their families, and their supporters. Opponents dismissed the bill as nothing more than "soothing syrup for negroes."[161] Congressman Connell's bill did not pass, but the principle of compensating the enslaved for their unpaid labor remains an enduring political question of reparations for generations of stolen productivity.[162]

Although they worked hard and fought mightily when needed, much of Nebraska's African American population, both rural and urban, was poor. The wealth gap between all rich and poor grew dramatically during the Gilded Age, making the inequalities between Black people and white people more extreme. African Americans were limited to the work white people gave them.[163] Upwardly mobile middle- and upper-class white Nebraskans worked short days, sent their children to quality public schools, and built fine Victorian-era homes, elaborate churches and public buildings like ancient Greek temples, while African Americans in Nebraska's cities worked as many as sixteen hours per day, six days a week, to pay rent on substandard housing and struggled to put food on the table. Defying white stereotypes as weak, unskilled, and even "uncivilized," African Americans were skilled tradespeople, hospitality professionals, barbers, dentists, attorneys, domestic workers, and business owners.[164]

They, like their white counterparts, founded Baptist and Methodist churches, started local chapters of fraternal organizations including the Prince Hall Masons, the Knights of Pythias, and the Odd Fellows, and ran political campaigns for elected office. Despite the many barriers to political, economic, and social equality during the Gilded Age, Black excellence emerged in Nebraska's African American communities.[165] Far from being passive recipients of white leadership, Black Nebraskans were recognized for their economic and political participation in a variety of settings statewide. Josiah Waddle, who later started bands in Omaha, became the first Black barber in Nebraska City in 1877.[166]

---

159. Orville Menard, *River City Empire: Tom Dennison's Omaha* (Lincoln: Bison Books, 2013), 168-72; "Protests Midway License," *Omaha Daily News*, December 10, 1905, 1; "Holds Shields for Trial," *Omaha Daily Bee*, 5; "Money Paid to Dennison for Protection: Expose of His Methods by Victor Walker, a Former Lieutenant," *Omaha Daily News*, April 24, 1907, 1.
160. Walter Raleigh Vaughan, "Freedman's Pension Bill: Being an Appeal in Behalf of the Men Released from Slavery," (Omaha: W.R. Vaughan), 9.
161. "A Miserable Trick," *The Clarion-Ledger*, July 3, 1890, 4.
162. Miranda Booker Perry, "No Pensions for Ex-Slaves: How Federal Agencies Suppressed Movement to Aid Freedpeople." National Archives, Summer, Vol. 42, No. 2. (2010): https://www.archives.gov/publications/prologue/2010/summer/slave-pension.html.
163. Nebraska Writers' Program, *The Negroes of Nebraska*, 6, 11.
164. Nebraska Writers' Program, *The Negroes of Nebraska*, 15.
165. Nebraska Writers Program, *The Negroes of Nebraska*, 29, 32.
166. Adam Fletcher Sasse, *#OmahaBlackHistory: African American People, Places and Events from the History of Omaha, Nebraska* (CommonAction Publishing, 2022), 49.

Masons on the steps of an unknown location. Nebraska State Historical Society. Nathaniel Hunter (far right) was a longtime leader of the Prince Hall Masons.

Silas Robbins, the first African American admitted to the Nebraska Bar, joined Edwin Overall, Cyrus Bell, and Alphonso Wilson in the leadership of the Nebraska chapter of the Afro-American League. Wilson, an Omaha real estate agent, was a political activist and community organizer who was a delegate to the Nebraska Republican Convention in 1896 and 1901. This expanding circle of Black professionals and business leaders opened new legal and political avenues for civil rights. Although the League disbanded in 1895, it laid the foundation for the formation of Nebraska chapters of the National Association for the Advancement of Colored People, the NAACP.[167]

Black Nebraskans' impact extended well beyond the cities. James "Jim" Kelly was among Custer County's respected cowboys between 1877 and 1879. Kelly got his start working for a notorious Texas cattle baron with fifteen thousand head and became a noted horse trainer in his own right.[168] Amos Harris, also from Texas, came to Franklin in 1890.[169] Becoming an expert cattleman, Harris moved to Greeley County where he lived "an exemplary life" as a rancher, and who was well liked by his white neighbors.[170] He drove cattle from Valley, Garfield, Loup and Greeley Counties. He was also said to read and speak five languages.

As the only Black man in the county, Harris was the subject of stories that say more about racial attitudes in Greeley County at the turn of the twentieth century than they do about Amos Harris.[171] This legendary figure was both phenomenally productive and potentially dangerous, "so powerful that he could pick an ordinary sized man up and carry him under his arm." Amos married Eliza Young of Boelus, Nebraska, in

---

167. "Afro-American League." 1890.
168. Nebraska Writers' Program, *The Negroes of Nebraska*, 8.
169. James E. Potter, "A Peculiar Set of Men: Nebraska Cowboys of the Open Range," *Nebraska History* 94 (2013):130-31.
170. "Mr. and Mrs. Amos Harris of Early Days," *The Scotia Register*, May 30, 1963, 4; Amos Harris Obituary, *Franklin Free Press*, January 29, 1904.
171. Michelle Nielsen Setlik, "The Legend of Amos Harris in Grand Island," *The Grand Island Independent*, April 24, 2024 explores the various versions of the Amos Harris story.

Tombstone of cowboy Amos Harris in Grand Island Cemetery. Nebraska State Historical Society.

1897. The new couple started a new ranch on the Calamus River, about eighteen miles north of Brewster. After losing the ranch "to a homesteader" the Harrises, now with two young children, moved to Ord.[172] After Eliza died of cancer in 1903, Harris remarried and he and his second wife, Lizzie, lived on their farm in Wheeler County. He settled early enough to amass large cattle holdings and was a respected rancher in Aurora for many years.[173]

A new generation of Black leaders prepared to take on systemic racism on every front graduated from Nebraska's colleges and universities at the end of the nineteenth century. W.E.B. DuBois and August Granville Dill would argue that this was not by happenstance, and that on the national level, "The work of educated Negroes is largely the work of leadership."[174] In a national survey of Black college students and graduates, nearly 54 percent were pursuing careers in education to answer the great need since emancipation: "It can be truly said that the progress of the American Negro during the forty-seven years since emancipation has been due largely to the wholesome and helpful influence of these Negro college graduates who have labored as teachers of their people." Twenty percent were going into ministry, because "during and since the slave regime the church has been the chief social center of the Negro people. The church and the people alike have suffered from an ignorant ministry and the end of the suffering is not yet. It is encouraging, however, to find that many educated negroes have entered and are entering this sphere of activity."[175] The growing number of trained Black clergy was a source of hope for many Black communities: "The Negro ministry is rapidly changing from an uneducated to an educated factor in Negro life in America."[176]

Physicians made up seven percent of Black college graduates. Black patients sought out Black physicians, creating a growing demand for their services. Doctors also "have done much to raise the physical and moral tone of the communities in which they have worked and their influence upon the cultural standards of their people has been marked."[177] Roughly four percent went into law, where the barriers against Black professions were high, especially in the South: "the very laws under which he must practice and upon which he must build his methods of procedure are in many instances aimed directly against the people from whom he must draw his clientele… [and] the injustice which the Negro meets all too frequently. In the courts of the South has made the success of the Negro lawyer all the more uncertain." Further, "With judge and jury afflicted with racial prejudice he cannot always be sure of receiving justice at their hands, even though the evidence in the case and the accepted forms of judicial procedure seem to assure success to his efforts." Another problem came from within the Black community: "The Negro lawyer must meet the prejudice, the antipathy and the lack of confidence on the part of his own people" due to the obstacles they face.[178] Unlike teachers, ministers, and doctors, lawyers were not always able to surmount the barriers to practicing law that Jim Crow imposed upon them.

The University of Nebraska recruited its first prominent Black athlete in 1891 and lost him to racism in 1894. George Albert Flippin excelled in baseball, track and field, trap shooting, and football. He also excelled

---

172. Marilee Malicky, "Remembering Amos Harris, Beloved Cowboy and Huge Man," *The Grand Island Independent*, January 16, 2003, 38.
173. Lillian Anthony-Welch "Black People: The Nation-Building Vision" in *Broken Hoops and Plains People* ed. Paul A. Olson (Curriculum Development Center, 1976), 142.
174. *The College-Bred Negro American*, ed. W.E.B. DuBois and August Granville Dill (Atlanta: Atlanta University Press, 1910), 67.
175. "The College-Bred Negro American," ed. DuBois and Dill, 67.
176. *The College-Bred Negro American*, 68.
177. *The American Negro*, 68.
178. *The American Negro*, 69.

University of Nebraska athlete George Albert Flippin. Nebraska State Historical Society.

in academics and leadership; Flippin was president of the Palladian Literary Society and winner of one of its oratorical competitions.[179] His immense talents did not stop white supremacists from making constant racist attacks on and off the field. His teammates, all white, showed solidarity with him more than once against the racism he experienced while traveling for sports, yet racism drove Flippin from football. He left shortly after the University of Missouri refused to play NU because they would not share the field with a Black athlete.[180]

Flippin followed in his father's footsteps in pursuing the study of medicine. Charles Flippin, who was born enslaved, was a veteran of the Civil War. His wife, George's mother, was White. George was born in Ohio in 1868, and the family moved to York County, Nebraska.

George attended the University of Nebraska and the Medical Department of the State University of Illinois at Chicago, graduating in 1900. After completing his internship at Cook County Hospital and practicing at a hospital in Pine Bluff, Arkansas, Flippin returned to Nebraska and opened the first hospital in the town of Stromsburg in 1907. Opening a hospital was a tremendous accomplishment, especially as an African American in the Jim Crow era—but it was also a norm among Black physicians in the Midwest who were restricted to practicing on Black hospital wards, if they could obtain hospital privileges at all. General practitioners were received in white communities with welcome or scorn—even targets of malicious lawsuits or threats of violence—depending upon racial attitudes and the demand for trained medical professionals. White physicians hesitated to

---

179. "Flippin, George A, 1868-1929," University of Nebraska Archives, https://archives.nebraska.edu/agents/people/2133.
180. Jamie Q. Tallman, *The Notorious Dr. Flippin: Abortion and Consequence in the Early Twentieth Century*, (Lubbock, TX: Texas Tech University Press, 2011), 89.

Children from Brownlee settlement in Cherry County, including Howard, Lena and Ava Speese, Herbert Hamos, Mildred and Maire Meehan, Ellen, Anna, Florence, Olivia and Esthyr Ford, and teacher Fern Walker Woodson. Nebraska State Historical Society.

refer patients to Black specialists. Opening a hospital gave African American doctors their best opportunity to practice medicine with minimal interference from Jim Crow.[181]

Inequality in education was pronounced in Nebraska. A survey published in *Survey Graphic* found that "California…gives twice as much schooling as Nebraska and six times as much as Kentucky." White schools across the U.S. received substantially more funding, making separate Black schools "a symbol of the inferior social, economic, and political status of colored people in American life in general."[182]

In 1907, white commentators pointed to a decrease in Lincoln's Black population and declared "the race question seems to be solving itself, the colored population decreasing each year until finally there will be nothing left of it."[183] African Americans noted the 1-2 percent annual decrease in Black birth rates and the nearly 1 percent annual increase in white birth rates and redoubled their efforts to make twentieth century Nebraska the hospitable place for African American citizens that it had not been in the nineteenth. Black Nebraskans may have been fewer in number in Lincoln, but they were not the "vanishing race" that some white Nebraskans envisioned.[184]

The Kinkaid Act of 1904 opened 640-acre tracts of less-desirable land in Western Nebraska to Black and white homesteaders alike, who were called Kinkaiders. The Kinkaiders were optimists with great determination to start very large farms on dry, rocky land without ready irrigation. In starting their farms, African Americans started communities in Dawson,

---

181. Peter J. Kernahan, "Medical Practice and Jim Crow," in *Black Surgeons and Surgery in America* ed. Don K Nakayama (Chicago: American College of Surgeons, 2021), 69-71.
182. "Editorial of the Month: Why Separate Schools are Undesirable," *The Crisis* 46:11 (November 1939): 339.
183. "Race Suicide in Negroes," *Nebraska State Journal,* January 9, 1907, 10.
184. "Race Suicide in Negroes," *Nebraska State Journal,* January 9, 1907, 10.

Harlan, and Cherry counties. Crawford, Stromsburg, and Seward came to have substantial Black populations and the towns of Overton, Brownlee, and DeWitty were founded as Black towns by Black settlers.[185]

DeWitty was established by forty Black families who migrated south from Canada to make land claims in Cherry County, along the North Loup, just outside of Brownlee. Starting literally from the ground up, building sod houses, figuring out which fruits and vegetables they could grow, founding schools, businesses, sports teams, and St. James Episcopal Church. Within a few years DeWitty had three schools, a general store, and an African Methodist Episcopal Church. Today, the town of DeWitty, named for its first postmaster, Charles DeWitty, until he left in 1916 and the town was renamed Audacious, is recognized as the Nebraska's longest-standing Black town.[186]

Black people continued to organize and demand respect for their civil rights. In Lincoln in 1911, more than fifty Black people met at the "colored Masonic hall on South Eleventh street" to protest a segregation bill introduced by state Representative John W. McKissick of Beatrice. Arthur Williams, "one of the leading colored men of the city" called Jim Crow laws to control Nebraska's very small Black population an insult to the intelligence of white and Black Nebraskans. While acknowledging the absurdity of the law, Williams called upon Black voters to "do our duty as men and meet it resolutely. The colored people of this state are above that law, but they must assert themselves and go to the legislature as men to ask that it be defeated. While we believe it will hardly be treated as more than a joke, we can not afford to be caught napping, and must be on the alert to see that we are not made the subjects of discrimination." J.T. Wright declared, "The colored man—and especially the colored man of this state—wants only to be left alone and be given the opportunity and right to make his way."[187] The McKissick bill was killed.

These political successes garnered John Grant Pegg, who had spoken against the bill, the chairmanship of the Western States Negro Republican Convention in 1916. They also amplified Black Nebraskans' demands for full civil rights, which they issued in public gatherings, at the ballot box, and in their daily lives throughout the twentieth century.

Pegg was not alone in his multi-pronged fight for civil rights. The Nebraska Legislature interfered in Dr. George Flippin's personal life in 1913 when it changed the legal definition of a "non-Caucasian" from a person with one-quarter "nonwhite" ancestry (one grandparent) to a person with one-eighth "nonwhite" ancestry (one great-grandparent).[188] Flippin met his first wife, Dr. Georgia Smith Flippin, at medical school. The couple married outside the state of Nebraska and returned in 1907 to start a medical practice in Henderson and later open the first hospital in Stromsburg, where they raised two children.[189] The law may not have changed the Flippins' legal status, but it signaled to the family that their legitimacy, rights, and belonging could be reduced by a vote in the legislature. The Flippins had divorced in 1910, and George married Mertina E. Larson, a member of Stromburg's white Swedish majority, clearly not swayed by the state's racial laws and their implicit judgments about interracial marriages.[190]

Flippin brought the first case under Nebraska's new civil rights law in 1913. Leonard Guttenfelder stood trial for refusing to serve George Flippin at his Reo Café in York. A waitress testified that she offered to serve Flippin in the kitchen, but not the dining room, which Flippin would not accept. After conflicting testimony about whether Flippin drank coffee or ordered a ham sandwich,[191] the jury took less than two minutes to find Guttenfelder guilty. He was fined $100 (approximately $3,170 in 2024 dollars) for denying Flippin service.[192]

Flippin's action was said to inspire others to use the civil rights law to fight discrimination at a time

---

185. Bish, "The Black Experience in Selected Nebraska Counties," 1989.
186. Mikal Brotnov Eckstrom and Richard Edwards. "Staking Their Claim: DeWitty and Black Homesteaders in Nebraska." *Great Plains Quarterly* 38, no.3 (2018): 295-317, doi:10.1353/gpq.2018.0043; Jacob K. Friefeld, Mikal Brotnoy Eckstrom, and Richard Edwards, "African American Homesteader "Colonies" in the Settling of the Great Plains," *Great Plains Quarterly* 39 (Winter 2019):12; Carla Garner, "DeWitty/Audacious, Nebraska (1908-), *The Black Past,* https://www.blackpast.org/african-american-history/dewitty-audacious-nebraska-1908/.
187. "Against "Jim Crow" Bill," *Lincoln Nebraska State Journal,* February 27, 1911, 2.
188. Hildebrand 2010, 168.
189. "Flippin, George A, 1868-1929," University of Nebraska Archives, https://archives.nebraska.edu/agents/people/2133.
190. "Local News," *The Headlight,* April 28, 1910, 5.
191. "The Civil Rights Case," *The York Democrat,* January 2, 1913, 8.
192. "Appeal Civil Rights Case," *Mason City Transcript,* January 9, 1913, 2.

when Nebraska's racial lines seemed to be hardening. When the U.S. Supreme Court handed down its ruling in 1915 that poll taxes disenfranchised Black voters because a great majority were unable to pay, Nebraska kept its state laws permitting poll taxes on the books. Housing developer Samuel Rathbone introduced the first race restrictions in Lincoln property deeds in 1916, reinforcing existing segregation and assuring that Black people would be barred from living in desirable new neighborhoods.[193] Jim Crow laws could not obscure the exemplars of Black excellence in the arts, humanities, and professions burgeoning statewide and it could not convince Black soldiers who served in the Great War that they were any less American than their white counterparts on the front lines of democracy.

The Renaissance Era (1910-1930)

The African American Renaissance was as inspiring in Nebraska as it was in Harlem. "The Harlem Renaissance encompassed poetry and prose, painting and sculpture, jazz and swing, opera and dance. What united these diverse art forms was their realistic presentation of what it meant to be black in America, what writer Langston Hughes called an 'expression of our individual dark-skinned selves,' as well as a new militancy in asserting their civil and political rights."[194] As in Harlem, Black intellectual and artistic expression in Nebraska became a primary source of inspiration and activity statewide. Black musicians, writers, artists, and others emerged during what is referred to as the New Negro Movement—echoing the vibrant intellectual, cultural, and political Harlem Renaissance, also called the New Negro Renaissance.[195] Focusing on the realities of Black Nebraskans' lived experiences, this movement countered longstanding stereotypes across the state through photography, theater, film, music, and multiple genres of writing. During this era, Black athletes, community leaders, laborers, ministers, soldiers, and others broke through Nebraska's Jim Crow color line to make their voices heard as never before—for many, the very lives of Black people depended upon the community making a strong, clear stand for the rights, contributions, and humanity of themselves and their communities. The concentration of creative energy in North Omaha made it the center of an African American Renaissance whose legacy persists in the twenty-first century.

The growth of the state's Black population also helped to amplify African Americans. Their numbers doubled in the decades between 1910 and 1930, bringing new opportunities into being that made the statewide community soar. The Great Migration of Africans from the South to northern industrial cities brought more than two thousand Black newcomers to Nebraska between 1910 and 1920.[196] Seventy-nine percent of African Americans in Nebraska lived in Lincoln and Omaha.[197] Omaha's 4,426 Black residents were the third largest population of African Americans in the West after Los Angeles and Denver and it was on its way to doubling in the next ten years.[198] The city of South Omaha was the third largest city in Nebraska with 26,269 residents, of whom 717 were African American, representing 2.7 percent of that city's population. The two communities would become one in 1917 when Omaha annexed South Omaha.

Religious and secular community leaders created the conditions for the Renaissance to flourish and to stem white supremacist backlash as African Americans resisted racist stereotypes and claimed their place in civic, intellectual, and cultural life. In response to African American discontent with the longstanding political parties, African Americans in Nebraska rallied in 1910 to create Independent Colored Clubs, which were part of a national movement from 1885 to 1922. Rev. Dr. John Albert Williams started laying the groundwork in 1912 to renew the efforts from 1887 to organize an NAACP chapter in Nebraska. Chapter activities began in earnest in 1914 after Reverend

---

193. City of Lincoln, ""LCHR's Redlining: Designed Inequity, A Local Perspective Display and Accompanying Presentation," prod. LNKTV City, YouTube 37:32, April 23, 2021, https://www.youtube.com/watch?v=czE1x2-9hlQ.
194. https://nmaahc.si.edu/explore/stories/new-african-american-identity-harlem-renaissance
195. Richard M. Breaux, "The New Negro Arts and Letters Movement Among Black University Students in the Midwest, 1914-1940." *Great Plains Quarterly*. 265 (Summer 2004): 123; "The Power of Poetry: The New Negro Renaissance to the Black Arts Movement," Smithsonian Institution National Museum of African American History and Culture, 2012, https://nmaahc.si.edu/explore/stories/power-poetry-new-negro-renaissance-black-arts-movement.
196. James Gregory, "Mapping the Great Migration," America's Great Migrations Project, University of Washington, 2022, https://depts.washington.edu/moving1/map_black_migration.shtml.
197. Federal Writers Project, *The Negro in Nebraska*, 14-15.
198. Taylor, *In Search of the Racial Frontier*, 204.

Leola Bullock and Lela Knox Shanks at NAACP Lincoln banquet. Marcella Foster photo collection.

Williams brought national leaders to speak in Omaha.[199] It took more than three years for the emerging local branch to reach the 50 percent white participation that the national organization required of its local chapters, and in July 1918 the NAACP officially registered the Omaha chapter.

The Lincoln chapter of the NAACP formed a few months earlier in April 1918 under the leadership of Oliver Burckhardt, who organized a group of involved citizens including Nebraska's lieutenant governor and the governor-elect. Within a year there were more than one-thousand dues paying members of the NAACP in Nebraska. In 1934, contributions to the national NAACP's twenty-fifth anniversary Penny-a-Head fundraiser came from Omaha and Valentine.[200] Lincoln leaders of the Civil Rights movement of the 1950s and 1960s include Dr. Patrick Wells, Reverend G.L. Collins, Lt. Colonel Paul Adams, Mrs. Leonora Letcher, Mrs. Leola Bullock, Rev. Dr. Everett Reynolds, Mr. Hughes Shanks, and Mrs. Lela Knox Shanks. While membership and activities have wavered throughout the century since it was founded, the Nebraska NAACP thrives today and is widely acknowledged for its important role in state history.[201]

Black organizational life expanded in Lincoln when Prince Hall Masons consolidated across Nebraska in 1919 to form the Most Worshipful Grand Lodge of Nebraska A.F. and A.M. This was the beginning of the second era of Prince Hall Masonry and was led by Nathaniel Hunter, who served as the first Most Worshipful Grand Master of the Nebraska Grand Lodge. There were several Prince Hall Mason lodges across the state, including Lincoln, Hastings, Grand Island, Alliance, Scottsbluff and Omaha. Reverend Trago McWilliams Sr. established *The Review* as the official newspaper of the Prince Hall Masons in 1919 and sold it a year later to *The Monitor*, which continued to publish news of the "Lincoln Department" for two years.[202]

It was an important time to organize on the political, economic, and cultural fronts. The 1915 release of D.W. Griffiths's film *Birth of a Nation*, which glorified the rise of the Ku Klux Klan to "save" white Southerners from emancipated African Americans, drew protest from Black leaders when it opened in theaters across Nebraska. The film was objectionable and so was press coverage. The *Omaha Daily News* misquoted prominent attorney Harrison J. Pinkett as saying that the film was "not seriously objectionable, save in two very minor and unimportant parts" and that he was "urging all to see it." Pinkett responded with a lengthy editorial that gave a corrective to Griffith's version of history, noting that Black freedom struggles before and after Reconstruction were led by "such men as Douglass, Langston, Bruce, Eliott

---

199. "Independent Colored Clubs Movement," n.d. Notable Kentucky African Americans Database https://nkaa.uky.edu/nkaa/items/show/3033.
200. "Along the Color Line: N.A.A.C.P.," *The Crisis* 41:8 (August 1934): 247.
201. Adam Fletcher Sasse, "A History of Omaha's NAACP," North Omaha History, May 15, 2019, https://northomahahistory.com/2019/05/15/a-history-of-the-omaha-naacp/ ; Zachary J. Wimmer, "Triumphs and Troubles: The Early History of the NAACP in Nebraska, 1918-1940," *Nebraska History* 101: 4 (Winter 2020): 152-75.
202. Dennis N. Mihelich, "Boom Bust: Prince Hall Masonry in Nebraska During the 1920s," *Nebraska History* 79 (Summer 1998), 74.

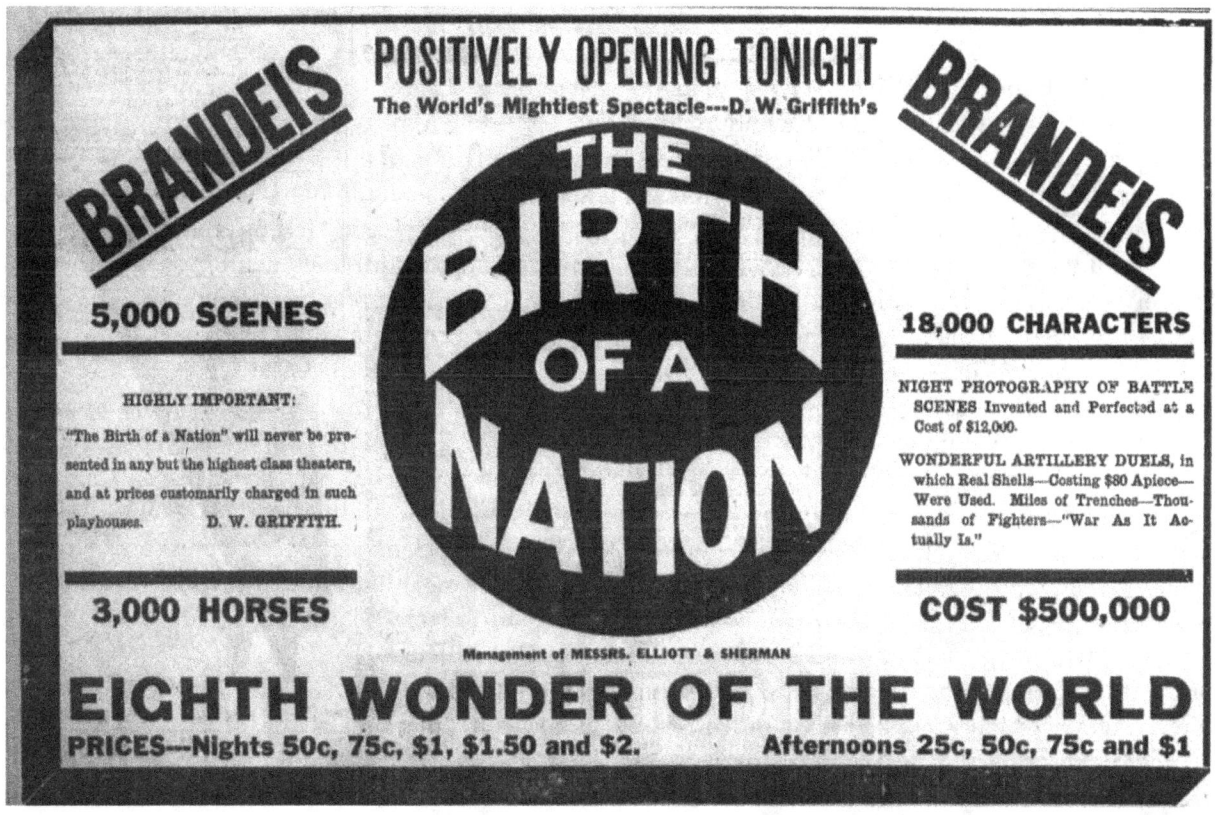

Brandeis Theater ad for *Birth of a Nation*, *Omaha Daily News*, November 15, 1921, Nebraska State Historical Society.

and Pinchback, who have been an inspiration to colored youth throughout the years…" Through education and uplift, African Americans were reestablishing their families, contributing to society, and made demonstrable progress in less than two generations. Pinkett concluded,

> "May we not fairly ask of the English-speaking race, which has done so much to spread the spirit of liberty in the world, if they would not make a better case for their claims to greatness by refusing to further handicap the already unfortunate Negro by exploiting his weakness through a highly-developed photographic art? Are you not strong enough to be just?
>
> "It is a small thing to cripple a man and then chide him for his failure to win the race, as some scenes in this play would do. At best, the lot of the Negro in America today is hard enough, and such plays as "The Birth of a Nation" and "The N——r" should be suppressed, that it may not be made more difficult."[203]

Prejudice Provoking Photo-Play Prohibited

Dixon's Riot-Inciting "Birth of a Nation" Will Not Be Booked Among Auditorium Attractions.

AUTHORITIES ACT PROMPTLY

Acting Mayor Butler Wires Manager Franke Not to Book Photoplay When the Monitor Objects.

"The Birth of a Nation," the Negro-defaming, riot-inciting photoplay of Thomas Dixon's "The Clansman," will not be presented in Omaha's Auditorium and it is a safe conjecture that it will not be presented in any of the moving picture theaters of the city, although that is another story.

Article opposing the showing of *Birth of a Nation*, *The Monitor*, August 28, 1915. Nebraska State Historical Society.

---

203. "Attorney H.J. Pinkett Misquoted by the Omaha Daily News," *The Monitor*, November 27, 1915, 4.

A separate editorial asserted "It was the whites, not the Negroes, who were mostly responsible for the conditions depicted in [*Birth of a Nation*]. It was the whites who were guilty first of the inhumanity and impiety of enslaving and brutalizing the blacks, and guilty next of dealing with the problems following the emancipation with a degree of ignorance and stupidity, unfair to the Negros as it was harmful to themselves, that was a disgrace to civilization."[204] The *Monitor* provided the platform for Pinkett to correct his statement and to correct the historical record that *Birth of a Nation* distorted.

The Black press was powerful and would remain a vital political, social, and cultural organ for African Americans in Nebraska.

Black Nebraskans brought vision and vibrancy to the state's cultural scene. John Johnson started working in Lincoln as a part-time professional photographer, which was an extremely rare career field for African American men during this era. Johnson's images are highly valued today for their candid nature, including parades, family portraits, train wrecks and building sites, in Lincoln, Omaha and Kansas City.[205] George P. Johnson and his brother, actor Noble Johnson, co-founded the Motion Picture Company in Omaha in 1916, bringing Black filmmaking to Nebraska. In 1923 he moved from Nebraska to Los Angeles.[206] Oscar Micheaux was a noted African American novelist and major filmmaker whose first two novels were published in Lincoln. He came to Omaha many times and traveled through the state while homesteading on the Rosebud Reservation in South Dakota. His 1919 feature film *The Homesteader*, the first produced by an African American filmmaker and featuring an all-Black cast, is evidence of the significance of Black creators from the Midwest and the impact of Black artists on Midwestern culture. [207]

During this era, African American bands in Nebraska got business by playing the most popular music—jazz—at high school auditoriums, dance halls, farm buildings and occasionally at amusement parks and county fairs in the smallest towns, sleepiest cities, and most hopping neighborhoods across the state. For several years starting around 1914, a young musician named Maceo Pinkard was working from North Omaha, leading bands and writing music.[208] He was part of Nebraska's rising jazz scene, which picked up momentum in 1917 when Zip's Jazz Band and the Adams Saxophone Jazz Band appeared across the state, and the "Largest and Only Real 'Jazz Orchestra' in Omaha" played at Henshaw Cafe. Black jazz bands drew audiences across Nebraska. More and more Black musicians in Nebraska formed popular bands including Simon Harrold's Melody Boys, the Sam Turner Orchestra, the Ted Adams Orchestra, the Omaha Night Owls, Red Perkins and His Original Dixie Ramblers, and Nat Towles Orchestra. Pinkard advanced Black music in Nebraska by forming his own publishing firm, Maceo Pinkard Music, in Omaha in 1917. He was the first African American in the U.S. to own his own music publishing firm, focused on sharing jazz and promoting his compositions. He sold music nationally and became famous for several hits including *Sweet Georgia Brown*.[209]

Nebraska musicians, singers, and dancers helped bring the United States to its official start of the Jazz Age in 1919. Maceo Pinkard was still working from Omaha when his medley called "Jazz" was picked up nationally and played in Chicago.[210] In 1925, Professor Waddle started Waddle's Ladies Concert Band, the second of his women's-only bands and they played jazz.[211] Jazz musicians were beloved in dancehalls statewide, but within the middle-class African American community, being a jazz musician

---

204. "Whites, Not Negroes, Are Responsible," *The Monitor*, November 27, 1915, 4.
205. Edward F. Zimmer and Abigail B. Davis. 2003. "Recovered Views: African American Portraits, 1912-1925," *Nebraska History* 84 (2003): 59-114.
206. "A Biography of George P. Johnson," North Omaha History, March 1, 2020, https://northomahahistory.com, accessed June 18, 2024.
207. Chester J. Fontenot Jr., "Oscar Micheaux: Black Novelist and Filmmaker" in *Vision and Refuge: Ethnic Writers on the Great Plains*, ed. Frederick Luebke (Lincoln: University of Nebraska Press, 1980),109; City of Lincoln Libraries and Univeristy of Nebraska Lincoln, "Oscar Micheaux," *Nebraska Authors*, https://nebraskaauthors.org/authors/oscar-micheaux, accessed May 22, 2024.
208. Natalie Fitzgerald, "Maceo Pinkard (1897-1962)," The Black Past, October 27, 2018, https://www.blackpast.org/african-american-history/pinkard-maceo-1897-1962/.
209. Richard M. Breaux, "The New Negro Renaissance in Omaha and Lincoln, 1910-1940" in *The Harlem Renaissance in the American West: The New Negro's Western Experience* ed. Cary D. Wintz and Bruce A. Glasrud, (London: Taylor & Francis, 2012),124.
210. Fitzgerald 2018.
211. Fletcher Sasse 2022a.

Wynonie "Mr. Blues" Harris playing at the Dreamland Ballroom. UNL History Harvest.

was not seen as an honorable profession. Although the music continued, the dominance of the style ended around 1930.[212]

The Renaissance in the arts remained unstoppable. Wynonie Harris, known today as a founding father of rock and roll, dropped out of high school to sing and dance professionally in 1931. Born in North Omaha and raised in the theaters and clubs along North 24th Street, Harris became a nationally famous R&B and dirty blues singer whose talents would take him to Los Angeles, where he died at age fifty-one.[213] Lloyd Hunter's Serenaders, one of Nebraska's most popular traveling orchestras since its first shows in 1927, became the first African American band in the state to record a long play record in 1931. Over four decades, Lloyd Hunter's Serenaders played at dances across the Midwest, including fairs, barn dances, community halls and more in Nebraska, Iowa and beyond. It was in this band that two influential figures in American jazz music met in 1941, Omaha's young Preston Love Sr. and Johnny Otis, a white musician who became prominent in Black rhythm and blues.[214]

Wayland Rudd was a popular African American actor born in Lincoln. In 1932, striving to escape Jim Crow in the U.S. he moved to the Soviet Union and became one of its best-known actors of the era. Rudd was noted as the first actor in the U.S.S.R. to perform on stage with white actors.[215] The arts provided entertainment to all Nebraskans struggling through the Depression and, perhaps more significantly, was a place where African American ideas and expression were seen and heard.

212. Breaux, "The New Negro Renaissance," 124.
213. Stuart A. Kallen, *The History of Rock and Roll*, (San Diego, CA: Lucent Books, 2012), 14.
214. Larry Kemp, *Early Jazz Trumpet Legends* (Pittsburgh: RoseDog Books, 2018), 41.
215. Will Mack, "Wayland Rudd (1900-1952)," The Black Past, 2018, https://www.blackpast.org/global-african-history/rudd-wayland-1900-1952/.

"The Window Cleaner" by Aaron Douglas. Sheldon Museum of Art collection.

Kansas native Aaron Douglas studied art at the University of Nebraska, where in 1922 he became the first African American to graduate from NU with a Bachelor of Fine Arts degree. He taught high school in Kansas City, Missouri, for a time before moving to New York City to join the Harlem Renaissance. Later in his life he took a position at Fisk University in Nashville, where he became chair of the art department. Douglas was recognized by contemporaries and historians as "one of the most accomplished and influential visual artists of the Harlem Renaissance." As a successful painter and illustrator, he greatly influenced Black culture and a Black aesthetic and is credited with being a force during the Harlem Renaissance.[216]

A wave of newly founded African American churches supported the Nebraska Renaissance by providing venues for artists and speakers from across the state to reach wider audiences. New congregations formed across Nebraska during the 1910s including St. Benedict Catholic (est. 1918), Pilgrim Baptist (est. 1917), and Clair Memorial United Methodist (est. 1913) in Omaha.[217] Reverend Burckhardt went from Lincoln to DeWitty in 1910 as a missionary to the young Black town. St. James African Methodist Episcopal Church was a fixture in DeWitty from its opening in 1910 to 1925, due in part to Reverend Burckhardt's recruitment of new members over several years. These connections ensured that DeWitty was tied together with the urban population centers in Lincoln and Omaha to form a robust community statewide.

Black leaders and Black newspapers challenged the many forms of Jim Crow from an expanding array of angles. George Wells Parker, working in Omaha as an insurance salesman and leading the Omaha Philosophical Society in 1910, founded the Hamitic League of the World in Nebraska to advocate for Afrocentricity among Black people. His 1925 book *Children of the Sun* presented Africa as the cradle of civilization and suggested that all European culture derived from African culture.[218] Parker was a contributor to Reverend John Albert Williams' newspaper *The Monitor* from 1917 to 1920 and from 1920 to 1921. He went on to become editor of Harrison Pinkett's *The New Era* newspaper before starting his own newspaper, the *Omaha Whip*, in 1921.[219]

The *Monitor* covered local news in Omaha, Sioux City and Lincoln and national events of concern to African Americans and was described in the NAACP journal *The Crisis* as an advance toward social uplift.[220] It published the fourteen points of the Ku Klux Klan on the front page of the newspaper to emphasize the ambitions of the organization statewide, including making the Bible mandatory teaching in schools, instituting Jim Crow rules in public places statewide, abolishing Black secret societies and "forbidding the employment of Negroes for any purpose," among others.[221] In the wake of national scandals within the Klan in 1926, the organization virtually disappeared from all Nebraska media in 1927.[222] Reverend Williams gave the paper away towards the end of his life and *The Monitor* published its last issue one year later.[223]

Nebraska's institutions of higher education saw more and more exemplars of Black excellence among their students. Starting in 1911, Clinton Ross became the third Black football player at the University of Nebraska at Lincoln, playing until 1913. During his last season, Ross became the target of racist protests by Kansas State College (now Kansas State University) and Kansas University, which refused to play against Nebraska while there was an African American player. Kansas barred Black athletes from its team rosters and expected Nebraska to observe the Kansas rule. *The Crisis* quoted this from a Lincoln *Journal* report: "To its credit Nebraska stood out and Ross played. The Negro students at Lawrence were forced to choose between loyalty to their school and loyalty to themselves—their own self-respect. They took the effective way to give expression to their feelings of outraged justice."[224] Once the Kansas-Nebraska standoff captured its attention, the national NAACP put it in the national spotlight.[225] *The Crisis* reported "[r]ather than observe the color line in football the University of Nebraska has withdrawn

---

216. Audrey Thompson, "Great Plains Pragmatist Aaron Douglas and the Art of Social Protest." *Great Plains Quarterly* 20 no.4 (Fall 2000): 311-22.
217. Adam Fletcher Sasse, "A History of Black Churches in Omaha," North Omaha History, January 22, 2017, https://northomahahistory.com/2017/01/22/historic-black-churches/.
218. Adam Fletcher Sasse, "A biography of George Wells Parker," North Omaha History, June 27, 2019, https://northomahahistory.com/2019/06/27/a-biography-of-george-wells-parker/.
219. "Omaha Branch N.A.A.C.P Holds Enthusiastic Meet," *The Monitor*, February 24, 1921, 3.
220. "Along the Color Line: Social Uplift," *The Crisis* 10:5 (September 1915): 217.
221. "'14 Points' of Klan Exposed," *The Monitor*, June 9, 1922.
222. Michael W. Schuyler, "The Ku Klux Klan in Nebraska, 1920-1930." *Nebraska History* 66 (1985): 253.
223. Paz, "The Black Press," 223.
224. "The Crux of the Problem: *The Crisis* 7:3 (1914): 131.
225. "The Ghetto," *The Crisis* 7:2 (1913): 63.

from the Missouri Valley association."[226] Upon Ross's graduation from law school, the magazine observed, "When Kansas University drew the color line on Ross, Nebraska forced them to yield by threatening to break athletic relations."[227]

The *Nebraska State Journal*, arguing that the controversy was more interesting than football and "far more significant," reported that the fifty Black students at KU wore Nebraska colors to the game and cheered loudly for Clinton Ross. A massive parade before the Nebraska-Michigan game in October 1914 made only two stops: one to hear Ross, "the husky negro guard on last year's team" –and now a recent graduate—give "a few words of encouragement to the rooters."[228] Ross earned his law degree from the University of Nebraska in 1915 and moved to Los Angeles a few years later, where he practiced law until his death in 1954.[229]

Black students were subject to discrimination in various forms at the University of Nebraska. *The Crisis* reported in 1929 that Black men had been disqualified from entering a basketball tournament and six Black students had been denied admission to an all-university dance. This was nothing new, nor was it benign: "The University of Nebraska, although supported by the state, has always discriminated in various ways against its colored students."[230] It was compounded by the ways in which white administrators framed racial discrimination. Nebraska colleges reported on the climate for African American students in 1910. At Union College, "We have had several Negro students in the past and accept them in our school at the present time. As far as we are able to judge there has not been much distinction made among our students between the Negro students and the others. It depends very largely upon the student himself how he is received by the student body."[231]

At the University of Nebraska "so far as I know the general student body feels very kindly toward [Black graduates] and towards our Negro undergraduates. On commencement days a negro usually receives as little more applause than a white boy when he walks over the stage. I presume some things happen in his personal relations with his fellow students that are

Clinton Ross, Cornhusker left guard. UNL Libraries, Archives and Special Collections.

---

226. "The Ghetto," *The Crisis* 7:3 (1914): 117.
227. "Our Future Leaders," *The Crisis* 10:3 (1915) 151.
228. "Clash of Gridiron Giants," *Nebraska State Journal* (October 24, 1914), 3.
229. Jason Han, "Clinton Ross and Nebraska's Near 40-Year Ban of Black Athletes," *The Daily Nebraskan*. 2021, https://www.dailynebraskan.com/diversity_inclusion/clinton-ross-and-nebraska-s-near-40-year-ban-of-black-athletes/article_74eaaac6-6cda-11eb-9008-d75cc5043068.html ; "Our Future Leaders," *The Crisis* 10:3 (1915) 151.
230. "Along the Color Line: Trans-Mississippi West," *The Crisis* 36:3 (March 1929): 90.
231. DuBois and Dill, *The College-Bred Negro American*, 25.

Stone marking 100th anniversary of Eta Chapter of Kappa Alpha Psi, the first African American fraternity at the University of Nebraska-Lincoln. Courtesy of Eta Chapter of Kappa Alpha Psi.

not entirely pleasant, but they never come to the surface. I doubt if there is a school in the country which is freer from race prejudice than the University of Nebraska."[232] Black student life in Omaha improved in 1916 when the first Greek fraternity for African American university students in that city was organized. Today, the Alpha Eta Chapter of Kappa Alpha Psi fraternity continues serving both the University of Nebraska at Omaha and Creighton University. The same year, the Eta Chapter of Kappa Alpha Psi was established at the University of Nebraska in Lincoln. It continues to be active as well.[233] Academic access and achievement continued into the 1920s. Elizabeth Williams (née Dorothy Isaac) became the first Black graduate of the University of Omaha in 1924. That same year, T.R.M. Howard became the first and only Black student at Union College in Lincoln. He went to medical school after graduation and became a highly respected physician.[234]

When the United States entered World War I in April 1917, Nebraskans from all walks of life answered the call to serve, including hundreds of Black soldiers from across the state in the Army and Navy. (African Americans were ineligible to join the Marine Corps until 1941). Almost 240 Black men from twelve western Nebraska counties registered for the draft.[235] Closer to home, Black students at the University of Nebraska were confronted with racism when they answered the call to prepare for war. The students who were called for drills were told they would have to go to a "colored college" to train. The Lincoln Branch of the NAACP intervened so that the Black students could train on their home campus, complete their studies, and report for duty on Europe's front lines.[236]

The presence of Jim Crow was not enough to stop more than eight hundred African American soldiers from Omaha who served in the all-Black U.S. Army

---

232. DuBois and Dill, *The College-Bred Negro American* 26.
233. "History," Kappa Alpha Psi Fraternity, Inc., Omaha Alumni Chapter, n.d. https://www.onealumnikapsi.com/about-kappa.html ; Walter Kimbrough, *Black Greek 101: The Culture, Customs and Challenges of Black Fraternities and Sororities*, (Lanham, MD: Rowman & Littlefield, 2012), 105.
234. David T. Beito and Linda Royster Beito, Black Maverick: *T.R.M. Howard's Fight for Civil Rights and Economic Power* (Chicago: University of Illinois Press, 2009), 16-18.
235. Ruby Coleman and Cheri L. Hopkins, *Legacy of African Americans in Western Nebraska: Pioneers, Entrepreneurs and Buffalo Soldiers, vol. 1 & 2* (Independently Published, 2022), 218.
236. "The Army—Social Service," *The Crisis* 17:6 (April 1919): 283.

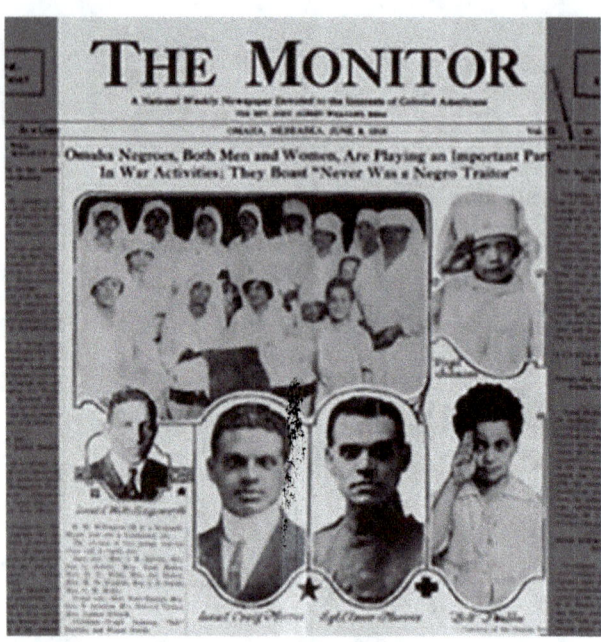

The Monitor touts Omaha Black people's war service, June 8, 1918. Nebraska State Historical Society

92nd Infantry Division while others served in the 93rd Infantry Division. Their ranks included Nebraskan Black community leaders Dr. W.W. Peebles, Harrison Pinkett, Dr. Aaron M. McMillan, Joseph Carr, and Dr. Craig Morris.[237] The refusal of the American Expeditionary Force to have Black men serve under them in combat resulted in soldiers and officers of the 92nd Infantry serving under the command of the French Army. These Black soldiers experienced life among white Frenchmen who did not have the same prejudices as their fellow U.S. citizens. They saw firsthand that it was possible for Black and white people to live as equals, and that Jim Crow was based on biological or social myths.[238]

Wartime mobilization loosened some racial lines and hardened others. After the end of the war in November 1918, former Black soldiers and officers in North Omaha organized a local chapter of the American Legion. The Legion was chartered by Congress as a veterans' organization that promoted Americanism and served soldiers and fellow veterans. Each local post could decide whether to open membership to African American veterans and could encourage, or discourage, the formation of Black auxiliaries.[239] Lieutenant Harrison Pinkett, identified as "the Argonne hero" in the Nebraska press,[240] led the effort to establish North Omaha's Theodore Roosevelt Post #30 for African Americans when the Omaha Post established itself as white-only. Pinkett, an attorney, was in high demand as a public speaker for the way he combined his study of the economic phases of postwar readjustment with "thrilling stories" of "the campaigns which brought down the downfall of the Huns."[241] Fifteen fellow North Omaha veterans successfully petitioned the American Legion to establish Post #30. The organization became a pillar of the North Omaha community by hosting public events, providing scholarships for young people, and bringing new veterans into the organization throughout its ninety-year history.[242]

The soldiers' wartime experiences prepared them for leadership in Nebraska's Black communities. Aaron McMillan, whose parents had been enslaved, worked as a dining car waiter in Texas to put himself through medical school. He opened a successful medical practice in Omaha, where he treated Black and white patients. At the urging of his patients, McMillan ran for state legislature and won against a white candidate in 1929. His tenure would be short; the American Board of Commissioners for Foreign Missions sought his expertise as supervisor of a hospital in Angola newly founded by the American Negro Congregational Churches. He spent more than a decade treating about 10,000 Angolans each year in exchange for family housing in Omaha, a modest salary, and a small stipend for his two sons' education.[243] Dr. McMillan became a voice on the world stage when the *New York Times* published his observation in 1935 that "the natives of South and Central Africa are becoming more conscious of their rights and the safeguarding of those

---

237. Fletcher Sasse, "A History of Black Military Service in North Omaha, Nebraska, North Omaha History, https://northomahahistory.com/2024/05/31/a-history-of-black-military-service-members-in-north-omaha/, accessed July 2, 2024.
238. Tyler Stovall, *Paris Noir: African Americans in the City of Light* (New York: Houghton Mifflin, 1996).
239. Richard Seelye Jones, *A History of the American Legion* (New York: The Bobbs-Merrill Co., 1946), 349.
240. "Membership Campaign," *The Beatrice. Sun*, April 20, 1919, 1.
241. "Lieutenant Pinkett Talks at Club Luncheon," *Beatrice Daily Sun*, April 22, 1919, 1.
242. Robert Houston, "A Medical Plant Built on a Shoestring," *Omaha World-Herald*, March 7, 1940, 5C; "Former Omaha Doctor Dies," Lincoln Journal Star, June 4, 1980, 31.
243. "The Wheel Makes a Complete Turn," *Opportunity: A Journal of Negro Life* 20:3 (March 1942): 68.

rights." The Quana people he served in Angola, he noted, "are highly intelligent, distinguish between right and wrong and show great resentment at being subject to foreign rule."[244]

All African Americans, no matter where in Nebraska they lived, would face waves of racial violence at the close of the 1910s that would test the resilience of their communities and of themselves. It would also test the humanity of white Nebraskans whose system of white supremacy appeared less logical and became more deadly in the years after Black men had sacrificed their lives on the battlefields of Europe in the fight against autocracy and brutality.

Nebraska's Red Summer

Racial tensions escalated during the period author George Leighton termed Omaha's "hot summer of 1919" when "[i]n the town were soldiers, just home from the war, looking for jobs and finding none. The world, had been saved for democracy—hadn't the local papers said so? But earning a living was something else." In the previous decade the city's African American population had doubled. Wartime demand for defense industry laborers generally and to fill in for white workers called to the front lines opened unprecedented areas of employment opportunity for African Americans. Frustrated white workers, returning veterans especially, were encouraged to blame their hardships on the Black people among them who were rising in both numbers and status.[245]

Soldiers coming home to Omaha had to navigate multiple social tensions, all of which fed into racial anxiety toward African Americans. Returning veterans of all races struggled to find jobs, postwar inflation was high, and threats of strikes were met with rumors in the press that Black strikebreakers were on their way to cross the picket lines—even when the strikes were called off. Media sensationalism stoked racial anxiety, which won votes for Mayor Dahlman,

favors for Tom Dennison, and sold copies of the *Omaha Bee*, whose editor, Edward Rosewater, was part of the Dennison political machine.[246] For instance, during the first week of August 1919, the *Omaha Bee* published articles on as many as "500 Negro workers" coming to Omaha looking for work in the packing houses.[247]

When Black community members alerted the mayor to rumors that whites were planning to attack Black workers taking positions as strike breakers, Mayor Dahlman issued a proclaimation that the police were prepared to stop any rioting and appealed to gun and ammunition dealers to be especially careful about who they sell to."[248]

Throughout the summer of 1919, the Omaha media steadily published hyped up reports of Black men preying upon white women, but these cases "collapsed under investigation." In one case, a Black man's employer had to bring the employees' time book to Omaha from Chicago to prove that he was hundreds of miles away from the place where he was alleged to have sexually assaulted a white woman.[249]

In a "morals raid" on September 11, 1919, Omaha police went after an African American bellhop named Eugene Scott who was only doing his job. The World War I veteran ran for his life as officers chased Scott through the streets, yelling racial slurs until they shot and killed him in an alleyway.[250]

Reverend John Albert Williams led Black leaders in a mass meeting the next day and decided not to take specific action until a trial was held for the responsible officers. Three officers stood trial and were found innocent of the shooting. The City Council considered suspending them but did not. The *Omaha Bee* described the shooting as reckless and indiscriminate, noting it as the "crowning achievement" of a "disgraceful and incompetent" police department. A suit was brought against the officers, and five years later, in 1924, a district court jury declared the men innocent and awarded them $20,000.[251]

---

244. "Says African Natives Resent Foreign Rule," *New York Times*, July 17, 1935, 7.
245. George R. Leighton, "Omaha, Nebraska: The Glory Has Departed," in *Five Cities: The Story of Their Youth and Old Age* (New York: Harper & Brothers, 1939).
246. "Dennison's Political Machine," Nebraska Studies, https://www.nebraskastudies.org/en/1900-1924/racial-tensions/dennisons-political-machine/, accessed June 29, 2024.
247. "More Than 500 Negroes Come to City in a Week," *Omaha Daily Bee*, August 13, 1919.
248. "Dahlman Fears Race Riot," *Lincoln Journal Star* (July 19, 1917), 12.
249. George R. Leighton, "Omaha, Nebraska: The Glory Has Departed," in *Five Cities: The Story of Their Youth and Old Age* (New York: Harper & Brothers, 1939),
250. George R. Leighton, "Omaha, Nebraska: The Glory Has Departed," in *Five Cities: The Story of Their Youth and Old Age* (New York: Harper & Brothers, 1939),
251. Adam Fletcher Sasse, "A History of Police Brutality in Omaha," North Omaha History, March 14, 2022, https://northomahahistory.com/2022/03/14/a-history-of-police-brutality-in-omaha/.

Lynch mob at the Douglas County Courthouse, Red Summer 1919. University of Washington.

The Omaha papers ran headlines all summer that both reflected and heightened racial tensions. Stories suggesting that African Americans recruited to northern industries for war work "go home" to the Jim Crow South ran alongside headlines about "Negroes" and "Bloodshed" in Chicago that gave the impression that African Americans were murdering white people indiscriminately, while the story revealed that Black people were being killed in the course of defending themselves from racial violence.[252] This was the atmosphere in which a white woman reported on September 25 that a Black man assaulted her as she walked down the street with her boyfriend. Dozens of Black men were arrested by Omaha police over the next several days before the alleged victim identified 41-year-old Will Brown, a meat packer in South Omaha, as her alleged assailant.

Brown, whose rheumatic condition severely limited the strength and mobility of his hands, appeared to attorney Harrison Pinkett as an unlikely assailant when he visited Brown in jail.[253] This fact would never be considered by a jury, because Brown would never have a trial. A mob arrived at the Douglas County Courthouse downtown, convinced the police that they intended no harm, and within hours did immense harm by breaking into the building and demanding Will Brown.

The white mayor of Omaha, Edward Parsons Smith, was nearly lynched himself when he attempted to calm the mob and was rescued with little time to spare his life. Brown did not get the same reprieve. The mob broke into the jail and forced Brown into the streets before a crowd whose cheering had begun as a member of the mob tied a rope to an electric light post in anticipation of lynching Will Brown.[254] An ultra-violent photo from that night showing a grinning white mob surrounding Brown's burning corpse appeared in newspapers across North America. An editorial in the *Winnipeg Telegram* condemned the image as "loathesome" and the "gloating" mob "lend[ing] connivance to such inhumanities by decreeing that God, man and the law shall be so defied" were "not fit for entry into a League of Nations." The photo is widely viewed today.[255] Although the news media exposed the brutality, recent studies of media narratives in the months preceding the lynching of Will Brown confirms the longstanding criticism from within the Black community that news editors' use of sensationalism to sell papers created the conditions that made the mass participation in the brutality possible.[256]

---

252. As an example, see "Friendless Negroes Are Invited 'Home'" and "Race War Subsiding in Chicago," *Omaha Daily Bee*, August 1, 1919, 1.
253. Fred D. Dixon and Mr. H. J Pinkett, "Mr. H. J. Pinkett, *Nebraska, 1938*," U.S. Works Projects Administration, Federal Writers Project, Folklore Project 1936-39, Library of Congress, pdf https://www.loc.gov/item/wpalh000827/, accessed June 27, 2024.
254. "Lynching from Start to Finish," *Omaha World-Herald*, September 29, 1919, 2.
255. Orville D. Menard, "Tom Dennison, *The Omaha Bee*, and the 1919 Omaha Race Riot," *Nebraska History* 68: (1987):152-16 1987; Orville D. Menard, "Lest We Forget: The Lynching of Will Brown, Omaha's 1919 Race Riot," *Nebraska History* 91 (2010): 152-165.
256. "Omaha Bows in Shame." *The Monitor*. October 2, 1919.; Emily Cameron Shattil and Dan Shattil, "The Will Brown Lynching." *Omaha World-Herald*. December 18, 2022.

Historians have yet to agree upon the role Dennison or his organization played in instigating or escalating the violence. The evidence shows very clearly, however, that Dennison benefited from the appearance that his reformist opponents were unable to govern. Smith could not recover from the image cast by his public hanging and was succeeded by James Dahlman, returning to office as "the perpetual mayor" in 1921. Dennison delivered electoral victories to his chosen candidates in exchange for favors that kept his vice operations thriving and his position as Omaha kingpin assured for over a decade.[257]

This brutal expression of white supremacy had multiple and profound consequences, particularly for North Omaha. The rioters set themselves upon the Near North Side neighborhood in attempts to burn, loot and riot. Although North Omaha was integrated before 1919, the few segregated blocks where Black people were permitted to live were in the neighborhood. Unwilling to take murderous white mobsters' threats idly, many African Americans in North Omaha armed themselves and kept watch on the roofs of their homes.[258] The Army was called in from Fort Omaha and Kansas City, ostensibly to quell the rioters, but with the effect of making Omaha's Black neighborhood into a militarized zone. An armed hot air balloon hovered above the neighborhood while fifteen hundred soldiers armed with machine guns stood on the perimeter of the Near North Side and in the center of African American commercial life for one week.[259]

This military boundary formalized housing segregation from 1919 onward. On October 1, an Army colonel announced that Black people had to stay within Omaha's "Black Belt" (the Army's term for the African American housing area in North Omaha) for the Army to protect them. This is the first—but not the last—formal US government decree of housing segregation in Omaha. Black workers stayed home from jobs, Black-owned businesses closed for a week and the Army stopped all Black social activities.[260] Immediately after the lynching and riot, Reverend John Albert Williams published an editorial in *The Monitor* saying that the city's crime boss drove the entire event from behind the scenes. Williams wrote that the event was caused by a "hidden, but not wholly concealed hand, of those who would go to any extreme to place themselves in power."[261]

The Red Summer of 1919 proved to be part of a nationwide campaign of terroristic white supremacy unleashed in rioting in more than thirty cities and a rural county in Arkansas, killing more than three hundred Black people across the country. Historians cite numerous causes, including economic interests of major industrialists and social manipulation from criminal elements, as in Omaha.[262] African Americans fought back in Nebraska, as they did across the United States. Community organizing, political activism and economic development did not stop because of the Will Brown riot. There were many injustices on many fronts, and Black Nebraskans would not let them stand.

Stopping Jim Crow

The 1920s saw a shift in Nebraska's African American population from a diffusion across the state to concentrations in North Omaha and Lincoln. Decades of housing consolidation gave North Omaha the housing stock, services, jobs, and a distinct Black neighborhood that drew 70 percent all Black Nebraskans in 1920.[263] Lincoln's Black community was also on the rise with a more than 58 percent increase between 1904 and 1920.[264] The population of DeWitty, by contrast, decreased from 185 in 1918 to just 90 in 1920. While Cherry, Blaine, Sioux, and Wheeler counties each had five or more Black farmers in 1910, there were no Black farmers in Blaine and Wheeler counties in 1920, and Sioux and Cherry counties showed rapid decline in their African American populations.[265] The terrible quality of the land, over-mortgaging of assets, and poor cultivation methods led to Black farmers losing their farms through foreclosure, sales to larger ranchers, or by simply leaving the area. The unspoken

---

257. John Kyle Davis, "The Gray Wolf: Tom Dennison of Omaha," *Nebraska History* 58 (1977): 26-44.
258. "Mob Threatened to Visit Residential Section," *The Monitor*, October 2, 1919.
259. "Balloon Men Pitch Camp in 'Black Belt,'" *Omaha World-Herald*, October 1, 1919, 4.
260. "U.S. Soldiers Guarding the City." *Omaha World-Herald*, September 29, 1919.
261. "Omaha Bows in Shame," *The Monitor*, October 2, 1919.
262. Menard, "Tom Dennison, The Omaha Bee, and the 1919 Omaha Race Riot," 164; Cameron McWhirter, *Red Summer: The Summer of 1919 and the Awakening of Black America*, (New York: Henry Holt, 2011), 11.
263. Bish, *The Black Experience in Selected Nebraska Counties*, v.
264. Jennifer Hildebrand, "The New Negro Movement in Lincoln, Nebraska." *Nebraska History* 91 (2010): 166-189.
265. Bish, *The Black Experience in Selected Nebraska Counties*, 214.

realities of systematic racism and *de facto* segregation gave Black farmers fewer financial avenues and legal protections than white landowners. The small number of Black farmers remaining in Nebraska faced yet another hardship: isolation from the rest of the Black community.

Black churches played a central role in that community. As during previous surges in growth, several historic Black congregations in Nebraska were founded in the 1920s, many in Omaha, including Salem Baptist (est. 1922), Cleaves Temple CME (est. 1920), Mt. Nebo Baptist (est. 1921) and Morning Star Baptist (est. 1921). Educated at Bellevue College, Rev. Russel Taylor was a leader in the Black town of Empire, Wyoming, on the Nebraska border. After leaving Empire in 1920, he moved back to Omaha and led a Presbyterian congregation in the Near North Side. Reverend Taylor was very involved in Civil Rights advocacy in the city, frequently allying with Reverend John Albert Williams and other established leaders. He was a prolific writer, frequent public speaker and often preached in his own church about Civil Rights. After his church was burned down in mysterious circumstances, his congregation fired him, ostensibly for his Civil Rights-oriented activities.[266]

St. Paul AME Church in Beatrice was a social and cultural center for African Americans in Beatrice and surrounding areas, hosting performances of the Lincoln Great Gospel Choir, and speeches from leaders like Dr. John Adams, presiding elder of the Omaha district and state senator from Omaha.[267]

Solomon's AME Church in Grand Island provided another hub for community building. The church and a committee of Black leaders headed by Henry Washington sponsored an annual National Negro History program in February, the month that Carter G. Woodson proclaimed to be Negro History Week, and which evolved into Black History Month. Aaron McMillan was the featured speaker in 1949, with Omaha singer Rosa Buckner and pianist Camille Dunham Lewis giving a performance.[268]

The Red Summer of 1919 exposed Omaha's systemic racism but it did not alter it. Redlining became an increasingly overt practice in Omaha's real estate industry after the lynching of Will Brown and the militarization of North Omaha in the wake of the riots. The term "redlining" refers to formal segregation against the people residing in so-called "hazardous" areas, indicated on maps by red lines. "Hazardous" was a code for "Black," making redlining resulting in racial discrimination in housing, education, access to public amenities, and putting distance between African Americans and economic opportunities.[269]

Focused on selling homes in western suburbs beyond North 40th Street, real estate agents, landowners, home insurers and bank lenders colluded to ensure wealthy white people moved from the North Omaha community into new developments, while African Americans were shuttled into residential areas that, by design, became increasingly dilapidated and undervalued. This was enforced by the presence of the U.S. Army in the Near North Side after the September 1919 race riot and by a map drawn by their commanding officer, a colonel who designated the city's "Black Belt" around the neighborhood where most African Americans in Omaha lived during this era, from Cuming to Lake streets and from North 24th to North 26th streets.[270]

Analysis of real estate advertisements after the lynching of Will Brown registers the first identifiable instance of white flight in Nebraska, precipitated by rioters' focus on the Near North Side neighborhood. Despite the Army restrictions ending within a week, white homeowners of upper-middle houses moved away in large numbers from the Near North Side immediately afterwards. Middle- and upper-class whites who owned homes, attended schools and kept churches in the area flooded to new neighborhoods away from African American people. White property owners continued to own most of the businesses and the commercial real estate. This had consequences for the next fifty years afterward, including benign neglect by the City of Omaha resulting in derelict civic infrastructure like sidewalks, streets, and sewers; lack of commercial upgrades including updated stores and retail styles; elimination of safe and healthy recreational opportunities for residents; de-emphasis on residential in-fill and historical preservation.[271]

---

266. Todd Guenther "'The Kingdom of Heaven at Hand': Rev. Russel Taylor and the Struggle for Civil Rights in 1920s Omaha," *Nebraska History* 92 (Winter 2011): 184-193.
267. "Lincoln Choir Will Sing at AME Church," *Beatrice Daily Sun*, September 18, 1949, 1.
268. "Omahan to Speak on Negro History Program Feb. 9," *The Grand Island Independent*, February 2, 1949, 4.
269. Strand, "'Mirror, Mirror, on the Wall...', 186.
270. "A Street of Dreams," Nebraska Public Media, video, 58 min., 1994.
271. Sarah Sedivy, "Systematic Barriers to Success: The Impact of Redlining on Modern Educational Outcomes in Omaha Public Schools," Student Thesis, University of Nebraska at Omaha, 2023, 6.

Lincoln was also a site of struggle and growth as Black leaders resisted constraints on their self-determination and success. Horace Colley began an apprenticeship in the fur department at Miller & Paine department store at age fifteen and, after working in Detroit for twenty years, opened Colley Fur Studio on South Eleventh Street in 1940. He calculated that he could sustain his business on the patronage of the one-thousand-person Black community alone and competed with white furriers by offering top-notch workmanship and value. Colley's mother, a respected Lincoln seamstress, introduced him to her customers and the Urban League supported his successful petition to the city council to operate his studio outside of a designated business zone. White furriers were not so supportive of Colley at first, but his skill and business acumen brought him into their professional circle: "When I first opened my business in Lincoln, many of the fur merchants were hostile toward me, but they have overcome their hostility. I even do contract work for some of them now, and they go out of their way to assist me in many ways," Colley wrote.[272]

While business relationships could forge ties between white and Black Nebraskans, racism was deeply embedded in most everyday aspects of political, economic, and social life. Like most states, Nebraska levied poll taxes, which presented a significant obstacle for African American voters whose lower rates of pay made it harder to come up with the tax. Voters in Nebraska City, for instance, were advised by the City Council in 1857 that the poll tax for that year would be $1.50, or roughly $31.73 in the 2020s.[273][274] In 1926, the U.S. Supreme Court upheld housing segregation in the landmark case of *Corrigan v. Buckley*. The court ruling that the Constitution allowed race restrictive covenants underpinned housing segregation across the country, including in Omaha, Lincoln and across Nebraska.[275] Segregation was not limited to Nebraska's housing markets. African American physician Dr. David Wendell Gooden reported in 1927 that, "It is almost impossible to get a Negro into a hospital even in the charity wards in

Ku Klux Klan in Scottsbluff. Downey Family photo, Nebraska State Historical Society.

Omaha... In the few cases where a Negro is admitted, the Negro physician must turn over the case to a staff [white] physician. The patient loses the advantage of being attended by the man who has followed his case from the beginning and the doctor loses his fees."[276]

African Americans challenged Jim Crow on every front, from an expanding array of strategies and viewpoints. In 1921, the Omaha chapter of Marcus Garvey's United Negro Improvement Association (UNIA) was started in Omaha with Baptist minister Reverend Earl Little and his wife, Louisa Little, as head organizers. Their launch coincided with the "explosive arrival" of the Ku Klux Klan, or KKK, in Nebraska.[277] The first KKK group in Nebraska started in Omaha in 1921 after the visit from the Klan's national leader. The Klan targeted the Littles with threats that were so severe, they left Omaha with their year-old son Malcolm in 1925. Although Malcolm's life in Omaha was short, he became the city's most famous native son through his national and international leadership for civil rights. He opened his memoir, *The Autobiography of Malcolm X*, with the story his mother told him of the hooded Klansmen surrounding their house with rifles,

---

272. Horace E. Colley, "I Give Complete Fur Service," *Opportunity: Journal of Negro Life* 35:4 (October-December 1947): 197-98.
273. "City Taxes," *Nebraska News*, September 12, 1857, 4.
274. Harvey Walker, "The Poll Tax in the United States," *The Bulletin of the National Tax Association*, 9 no.2 (November 1923): 47.
275. Michael Jones-Correa, "The Origins and Diffusion of Racial Restrictive Covenants," *Political Science Quarterly* 115 no. 4, 556.
276. "Tell Negro Needs," *Omaha World-Herald*, February 1, 1927.
277. Manning Marable, *Malcolm X: A Life of Reinvention*, (New York: Viking, 2011), 21.

Klan rally in Neligh. Photographer Emanuel Wolfe, Nebraska State Historical Society.

shouting for Reverend Little to come out, Louisa visibly pregnant and alone with three small children. The Klansmen warned her to leave town "because 'the good Christian white people' were not going to stand for my father's 'spreading trouble' among the 'good' Negroes of Omaha with the 'back to Africa' preachings of Marcus Garvey." They left, torches burning, but not before shattering the windows first, shouting threats into the night. Both his uncle Oscar and his father would die at the hands of white men and Malcolm Little, even as a small boy, lived with a belief that he, too, would die by racial violence—a belief that proved correct. El Hajj Malik el Shabazz, born Malcolm Little just forty years before, died of an assassin's bullet on February 21, 1965, while delivering a speech in New York. Though born amidst Klan violence Shabazz grew into a force against this and all other deep-rooted forms of white supremacy.[278]

Although the KKK was concentrated in Omaha and Lincoln, it had members across the state, repeating scenes like that at the Little house time and time again. Within one month, the *Omaha Bee* featured official reports from the KKK that its organizers had launched groups in Omaha, Lincoln, Hastings, Sutton, Neligh, McCook, North Platte, Fremont, Grand Island, Minden, Holdrege, South Sioux City and Nebraska City.[279] There were 36 local units of the KKK in Nebraska in towns with Black communities of any size,[280] with active chapters in several towns with no Black population at all.[281] Even when a local KKK aimed their violence toward Catholics, Jews, other non-Evangelical Protestants, and other non-white people, their chapters' literature made a point of targeting African Americans.

The governor of Nebraska, Samuel McKelvie, came out against the organization to *The New York Times* in

---

278. Malcolm X and Alex Haley, *The Autobiography of Malcolm X As Told to Alex Haley*, (New York: Ballentine Books, 2015), 1-2. Numerous Omaha residents have struggled to memorialize and honor the force of the Black man who became Malcolm X, yet, there has never been a building, street, park, library or museum officially named for Omaha's most powerful and famous native son. It took until 2022 for the State of Nebraska to add Shabazz to its Hall of Fame—and, in doing so, naming its first Black honoree. Villegas 2022, 1.
279. Schuyler, "The Ku Klux Klan in Nebraska," 256.
280. Coleman and Hopkins, *Legacy of African Americans in Western Nebraska*, 127.
281. John Kneebone, et al., "Mapping the Second Ku Klux Klan, 1915-1940," Virginia Commonwealth University Libraries, 2015, https://labs.library.vcu.edu/klan/learn.

1921 and a congressional representative led a federal probe into the KKK that year.[282] Yet the Klan grew in its numbers and vehemence across Nebraska starting from 1,100 statewide members in 1922 to 45,000 members in 1923. The Lincoln chapter had an estimated five-thousand members and was the "largest and most vocal in the state," with openly active members on the University of Nebraska campus.[283]

The Klan became a visible part of life in Nebraska by 1923 with cross-burnings and demonstrations becoming commonplace.[284] More than one thousand members paraded in the streets at the statewide convention held in Lincoln in 1924. That year, a rash of cross burnings was reported in the month of April. The towns of Doniphan, Oak, Beaver City and Fremont all reported terroristic activity. Four crosses burned simultaneously in Oak. Beaver City was encircled by crosses made from telephone poles, raised on the four hills surrounding the city. A dozen public buildings in Fremont, including schools, were also the sites for blazing crosses.[285] Two months later, on June 26, 1924, a Klan rally at the Seward Fairgrounds drew one thousand participants.[286] Even without overt political support, the organization was, and remained, culturally influential for years.

Carter G. Woodson pushed back against racism by pushing for the dissemination and celebration of Black history during the African American Renaissance, asserting "If a race has no history, if it has no worthwhile tradition, it becomes a negligible factor in the thought of the world and it stands in danger of being exterminated."[287] Woodson launched the first celebration of Negro History Week, which led to African American History Month, in 1925. Widely honored with the honorific "the father of Black history," Woodson is credited with establishing the study of Black history and promoting it extensively.[288] The next year in 1926, *The Monitor* started promoting the week annually and published a long collection of

Charles B. Washington at Governor Griswold's signing of proclamation for Negro History Week in Nebraska, 1946. MacDonald Studio Collection, Nebraska State Historical Society.

Black history facts every year to celebrate, with the *Omaha World-Herald* recognizing the week for the first time in 1928. Woodson came to Omaha to speak in 1932 to launch celebrations in the city.[289] At the University of Nebraska in Lincoln, student Charles Washington received a proclamation from the Nebraska governor celebrating the National Negro History Week,[290] which took place in 1947, with leadership from the YWCA.[291]

Harry Haywood, born in South Omaha in 1898, recounted white supremacists terrorizing his family in their home, in much the same way as KKK threatened the Earl and Louisa Little. Haywood went on to become a noted author, publishing several books with financial backing from internationally renowned Black singer Paul Robeson. Robeson and Haywood shared a commitment to radical politics that for Haywood, had its roots in his young life in Omaha. In his autobiography, Haywood cited the lynching of Will Brown in 1919 as seeding his beliefs about the

---

282. Schuyler, "The Ku Klux Klan in Nebraska," 248.
283. "Kampus Klan: The University of Nebraska-Lincoln and the Ku Klux Klan, in the Early 1920s," ed. Ryan Treick," Digital History Project, University of Nebraska at Omaha, 2008.
284. Schuyler, "The Ku Klux Klan in Nebraska," 235.
285. "Fiery Cross Observed in Four Nebraska Towns," *The Plattsmouth Journal*, April 10, 1924; "Klan Fires Four Crosses in Town," *Omaha Morning Bee*, April 07, 1924.
286. "Ku Klux Klan Hold Meeting," *Blue Valley Blade*, July 2, 1924, 1.
287. Diane Osman and Erin McGraw, "Father of Black History," University Libraries Blog Archive. 478, January 31, 2023.
288. Lerone Bennett Jr., "Carter G. Woodson, Father of Black History". United States Department of State, 2005, https://web.archive.org/web/20110401191535/http://www.america.gov/st/diversity-english/2005/June/20080207153802liameruoy0.1187708.html.
289. "Urges Chance for Negro," *Omaha World-Herald*, February 13, 1932.
290. "Society Chatter," *Omaha Star*, February 21, 1947.
291. "In Recognition of Negro History Week Mayor Marti Has This to Say," *The Voice*, February 14, 1947.

relationship between capitalism and anti-Black sentiment in America. The lynching did not intimidate Haywood. It radicalized him.[292]

Haywood came to view anti-Black racism as a global problem and, like fellow Omahan Malcolm X, became a global voice for change. After serving in the Army's 8th Regiment in World War I, Haywood joined the African Blood Brotherhood, a secret society based in New York City, in 1922. His service in the antifascist International Brigades during the Spanish Civil War and the Merchant Marine in World War II reinforced what he was learning about communist and anticolonial politics in the Brotherhood. Drawn to communism's rejection of colonialism and the racism that underpinned it, Haywood became a committed communist himself. He, like his benefactor Paul Robeson, left the United States for the Soviet Union, where he lived for four years and contributed to the Comintern Resolutions on the African American Question. He met many anticolonial leaders during this period, including Ho Chi Minh. Seeing commonalities between imperialism in Asia and Africa and white supremacy in the United States, Haywood became a leading voice for racial equality for African Americans and economic justice for workers of all races. As head of the Negro Department of the Communist Party of the United States in the 1930s, Haywood brought the struggles against white supremacy and worker exploitation to the national and international stage.[293]

African Americans in Omaha started a local chapter of the Urban League in 1927. The national organization was established in 1910 in New York City to aid African Americans who migrated from rural areas in the South to adjust to living in urban industrial centers. The Urban League advocated for African Americans and against discrimination while organizing self-help programs such as employment, education and scholarship funds, health and recreation, and outreach to improve race relations across the city. The Omaha chapter was the first founded west of the Mississippi River and continues to promote social equality through economic independence by forming partnerships that promote opportunity for African Americans and improved dialogue among Nebraskans of all races.[294]

Attorney Ray L. Williams moved to Omaha in 1927 to direct the Colored Free Employment Bureau and the Colored Chamber of Commerce. Omaha dentist John A. Singleton, was elected to the Nebraska Legislature in 1927, making him the second African American to serve, —nineteen years after Matthew Ricketts completed his term of office. In a historic first, two African Americans served in the Legislature concurrently. Ferdinand Barnett was elected to serve coterminously with Singleton, making the legislature more representative of Nebraska's population than at perhaps any point in history. The number of Nebraska's Black attorneys was also increasing, most notably when John Grant Pegg was admitted to the Nebraska Bar in 1928. In 1929, Zanzye Hill made history as the first African American woman to graduate from the University of Nebraska Law School and the first African American woman to practice law in Nebraska.

African Americans' part in writing, implementing, and enforcing the laws was the culmination of years of commitment to reversing Jim Crow. It did not bring an end to systemic racism and, as previously, made some white supremacists feel justified in doubling down on discrimination, harassment, intimidation, or racial violence to keep Black Nebraskans "in their place." The expulsion of African Americans from North Platte in 1929 demonstrated African Americans' continued vulnerability to white supremacist excesses. Louis Seeman, a Black business owner, shot a North Platte police officer, reportedly while resisting arrest (though this remains a matter of debate), killing the officer. White police, firemen and the Nebraska Army National Guard surrounded Seeman's house. When he refused to come out, they threw flaming rags into the house to smoke him out of the attic—and to terrify Black observers. Storming into the house, they found Seeman hiding in a crawlspace. Before Seeman could be arrested, charged, and put on trial he was fatally shot in the ambush. Police and newspaper reports indicated that Seeman shot himself to avoid arrest, but the absence of witnesses

---

292. Harry Haywood, *Black Bolshevik: Autobiography of an Afro-American Communist*, (Chicago: Liberator Press,1978), 83-86.
293. Daren Salter, "Harry Haywood (1898-1985)", *The Black Past,* January 19, 2007, https://www.blackpast.org/african-american-history/haywood-harry-1898-1978 ; Harry Haywood Archive, The Marxist-Leninist, https://marxistleninist.wordpress.com/harry-haywood-archive/.
294. "History of the Urban League of Nebraska," Urban League of Nebraska, https://urbanleagueneb.org/about-us/history-of-the-urban-league-of-nebraska ; Adam Fletcher Sasse, "A History of the Omaha Urban League," January 28, 2019, https://northomahahistory.com/2019/01/28/a-history-of-omahas-urban-league/.

Scene of the double killing that led to the expulsion of Black people from North Platte in 1929. *Omaha World-Herald*, July 16, 1929, Nebraska State Historical Society.

cast doubt on whether Seeman truly died by suicide or if he was lynched by the police.[295]

As Seeman's body was retrieved from his house, a mob of more than one hundred white men led by KKK members went to every African American house in North Platte, threatening them with the same fate as Seeman if they did not leave town by 3:00 that afternoon. The seventy-five Black people in the town fled with only the clothes they were wearing.[296] A spokesperson for the Klan explained that the operation was a reasonable means of bringing order to the town, ascribing Seeman's actions to all Black people in North Platte. The Klan presented this act of mass terror as "just a little scare that will make African Americans better citizens." This was a "scare" that drove them from their homes and businesses and reminded them that their personal safety as a Black person could never be assured. Afterwards, the Nebraska governor and state attorney general met with delegations of Black leaders from Omaha and Lincoln to assure them that the state would make a full investigation. However, no arrests were ever made.[297]

Seeman's death is among the last recorded lynchings of an African American in Nebraska history. The lynchings of Henry Martin and Harry Jackson in Nebraska City in 1878, the lynching of Jerry White in Valentine in 1887, the lynching of George Smith in Omaha in 1891, the lynching of Will Brown in Omaha in 1919, and the lynching of Louis Seeman in North Platte in 1929 all form a legacy for which Nebraska has yet to take full accountability, and which continues to bear on African Americans in the present.[298] These six African Americans represented about eight percent of the roughly fifty-eight people targeted by lynch mobs between 1859 and 1919, when African Americans formed less than one percent of the population of Nebraska. Being Black was, on its own, a risk factor for disabling or deadly racial violence.[299]

These conditions forged an African American identity in Nebraska that survived another fifty years afterward. Community-oriented, determined family-building workers and leaders made the negative media portrayals seem like caricatures and increasingly, white people were forced to reconcile the racist myths with practical realities. This was the result of the renaissance of this era. During the next period, Black people would face the forces of white supremacy repeatedly and frequently overcome them. However, racism would not go away without a fight.

The 1930s

The Black population of Nebraska in 1930 was 13,752, forming .99 percent of the state's 1,377,963 residents. By that year, 90 percent of Nebraska's African American residents lived in Lincoln or Omaha, with the 11,125 African Americans in Omaha comprising approximately 5 percent of the city's population.[300] After increasing from eight Black residents in 1880 to fifty-two by 1890, York County had dropped to twenty-two African American residents in 1930. Many

---

295. David Bristow, "No Mob? No Riot? What Really Happened When North Platte Force Black Residents to Flee, "History Nebraska blog, : https://history.nebraska.gov/no-mob-no-riot-what-really-happened-when-north-platte-forced-black-residents-to-flee/, accessed July 17, 2024.

296. David G. Dales, "North Platte Racial Incident: Black-White Confrontation, 1929," *Nebraska History* 60 (1979): 424-446.

297. David Bristow, "No Mob? No Riot? What Really Happened When North Platte Force Black Residents to Flee, "History Nebraska blog, : https://history.nebraska.gov/no-mob-no-riot-what-really-happened-when-north-platte-forced-black-residents-to-flee/, accessed July 17, 2024.

298. Potter, "Wearing the Hempen Neck-Tie," 152.

299. Natalie Bielenberg, "Racial Bias and the Death Penalty in Nebraska (2005-2019)," Honors Thesis, University of Nebraska at Omaha, 2020, 2.

300. Lillian Anthony-Welch, "Black People: The Nation-Building Vision," 115.

Black families outside of Omaha relied on income from the railroad industry or from low paying jobs, including laundry, construction, or shining shoes.[301] Some of the 102 African Americans in Adams County, like Ted E. Smith, started successful businesses in the most punishing economic times. Smith Disposal Service began its fifty years of operation in 1930 in Hastings—making Smith the founder of the area's longest running Black-owned business.[302]

The Great Depression tightened its grip on Nebraska between 1930 and 1936. The compounding effects of white supremacy and systematic racism made the Great Depression disproportionately hard-hitting for African Americans statewide. The great gains made by Black packinghouse workers in the 1920s were not entirely wiped out during the Great Depression but it dealt a blow to progress. The 20 percent increase in Black employment in the 1920s dropped sharply, especially among Black industrial workers who were the "last hired" and, thus "first fired." The impact upon their purchasing power, savings, investments, and progress toward building generational wealth was profound for Black people in Nebraska and across the United States.[303] Survival became the modality for Nebraska's entire Black community. The lowered morale during this grim period was visible at every turn in the Black community, from economic life to entertainment and recreation.[304] No one in the Black community escaped the devastating effects of the nation's economic disaster.

To make matters worse, parts of Nebraska were covered by the Dust Bowl. Suffocating heat, terrible windstorms and extended droughts during these years destroyed farmers' crops.[305] Crop failures and low prices raised fear, frustration, and, in many white farmers, racial animosity. Black farmers who rented the land and farmhouses could not pay rent and farmers who owned their land could not make payments. These factors combined to drive almost all of Nebraska's Black farmers off the land

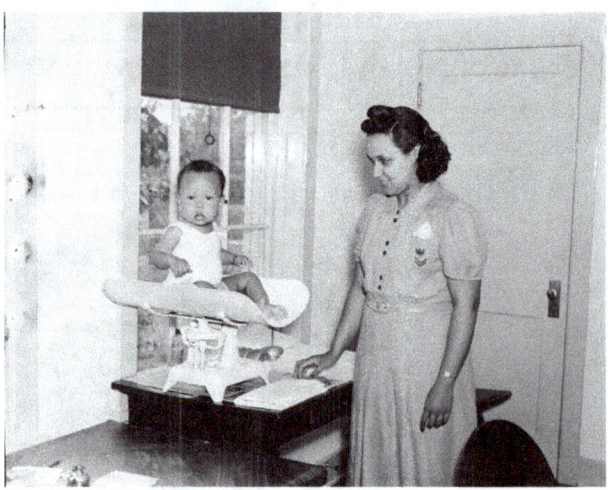

Baby being weighed at the Urban League in Lincoln, 20th and T streets, 1942. MacDonald Studio, Nebraska State Historical Society.

and into Omaha, Lincoln, or out of state.[306] Rarely did they find the relief that they needed. The strong social safety net that the Omaha community created after the devastating Easter Sunday tornado of 1913 had been stretched to its limits as newcomers of all races moved into the city.

By this point, Black Nebraskans had a long history of organizing to expand opportunities and defend civil rights in times of political, social, or economic distress. In 1931, Omaha played host to the City Interracial Committee. Originally a group of African American and white youth facilitating youth forums about race, the group eventually expanded and held an annual conference and other activities. They were active for approximately five years.[307] Black organizations like the Unemployed Married Men's Council, established with a separate branch serving African Americans in 1932, were especially important to relief efforts during the Depression. Cited by several contemporary reports as a successful "self-help" project the Council provided moral support, legal advice, food, and temporary housing for African American families. Infighting brought the work of the Council to

---

301. Bish, "The Black Experience in Selected Nebraska Counties," 30.
302. Mrs. R. Starr, "The Hastings Negro Year Book: a Progressive Age for a Progressive People," (Hastings, NE: Mrs. R. Starr), 1961
303. James Harvey Kerns, "Industrial and Business Life of Negroes in Omaha." M.A. thesis, Municipal University of Omaha, 1932, 37-38.
304. Nebraska Writers' Program, *The Negroes of Nebraska*, 23; Murphy 2020.
305. Friefeld et.al., "African American Homesteader "Colonies," 11-34.
306. Marilyn Irvin Holt, *Nebraska During the New Deal: The Federal Writers' Project in the Cornhusker State* (Lincoln: Bison Books. 2019), 70.
307. Adam Fletcher Sasse,"A History of Police Brutality in Omaha," March 14, 2022, https://northomahahistory.com/2022/03/14/a-history-of-police-brutality-in-omaha/.

Clyde T. Malone, executive director of the Lincoln Urban League after founder Millard Wood. Courtesy of Jeannie Malone Freels through Ed Zimmer.

an end after just one year.[308] While the Council surely helped some Black families survive the Depression, it also reinforced segregation as a norm—even amidst a national emergency.

The Urban League of Lincoln opened in 1932 with a report on housing for the city's African American population, which was overwhelmingly "ill-kept" and "congested" within segregated districts. Sixty-two percent of Lincoln's Black population lived in just three of the city's twelve wards, with almost 30 percent of Lincoln's African American population living in a single ward. One ward did not have any Black residents. The same 1932 survey found that out of one hundred wage earners, there were twenty-nine different vocations, mostly unskilled, semi-skilled and personal service jobs. A great majority of men worked as laborers, porters, waiters, or janitors and women as domestic workers, charwomen, or laundry workers.[309] The State of Nebraska employed eighteen African Americans, of whom six were janitors and four were charwomen. One of Lincoln's largest employers, the University of Nebraska, had no African Americans on its payroll.[310]

The election of Democratic President Franklin D. Roosevelt to his second term in office in 1936 reflected a massive shift in African American politics. The Republican Party put little energy into issues of concern for African Americans in the decades after abolition and Reconstruction. Black voters were wary of Roosevelt during his first presidential campaign in 1932, but the clear signs of economic recovery from his New Deal programs and his greater (though far from complete) support for equal opportunity and racial integration garnered the support of most of the nation's Black voters. The New Deal forced each of these parties to clarify their stances on these issues and while change had been underway since the 1860s, in 1933 it was clear that the parties had switched platforms, and the Democrats became the party of big government while Republicans called for limiting federal power. By 1936 nearly all Black voters, including those in Nebraska, switched from voting for Republican candidates to voting for Democratic ones.[311]

The New Deal started laying the groundwork for African Americans' economic recovery and their political realignment in 1933. A variety of federal programs were set up nationwide to fund public works projects, finance reforms, and enact new regulations. The programs were created to ensure that workers had wages, which also ensured that businesses would have paying customers, which started the economy moving again. Nebraskans participated in a variety of New Deal programs including the Civilian Conservation Corps (CCC), the Works Progress Administration (WPA), the Civil Works Administration (CWA), the Farm Security Administration (FSA), the Social Security Administration, the Federal Emergency Relief Administration (FERA), the National

---

308. Wayne Weishaar and Wayne William Parrish, *Men Without Money: The Challenge of Barter and Scrip*, (New York: G. P. Putnam's Sons, 1933), 70; Nebraska Emergency Relief Administration, *Report of the Nebraska Emergency Relief Administration: June 1, 1933-January 1, 1938, to R.L. Cochran, Governor* (Lincoln: Burr Publishing Company, 1938), 60.
309. Dennis Mihelich, "The Lincoln Urban League: The Travail of Depression and War," *Nebraska History* 70: 4 (Winter 1989): 303-16.
310. Jennifer Hildebrand, "The New Negro Movement in Lincoln, Nebraska," *Nebraska History* 91:4 (Winter 2010): 166-189.
311. Russell Brooker, "Political Parties in Black and White," America's Black Holocaust Museum, https://www.abhmuseum.org/political-parties-in-black-and-white/.

Youth Administration (NYA), the National Industrial Recovery Act of 1933 (NIRA), and the Public Works Administration (PWA). The Urban League of Lincoln partnered with the federal government to ensure that African Americans would not be overlooked in the recovery effort. Governor Dwight Griswold and NYA state administrator Gladys Sharp attended the dedication of a $30,000 community center built on city-owned land by NYA laborers and with funds raised by the Urban League. The center provided space for African American community, social, and public service projects with permission granted to New Deal programs to run programs from this Black community space.[312]

Archie Alexander, an African American architect, was hired by the PWA to design its Loup River Power Plant in Columbus, Nebraska. Renowned as a bridge and road builder across the country, Alexander is thought to be the first Black architect to design a civic structure in the state.[313] Alexander's work for the PWA was a singular milestone that was nonetheless representative of expanded opportunity for Black people generally.

While the New Deal expanded opportunities for African Americans' economic recovery it did not bring an end to racism. In some cases, in fact, New Deal programs reinforced longstanding forms of segregation and discrimination. President Roosevelt and his New Deal administration made token gestures towards African Americans, but their programs routinely discriminated against Black people in Omaha, across Nebraska, and nationwide.[314] Skeptical about whether African Americans would benefit, Black workers pressed for employment opportunities and joined new labor unions.

That same year, in 1933, Congress passed the Home Owners' Loan Corporation Act as part of the New Deal. The Act provided billions of dollars in long-term, low-interest mortgage loans to protect American homeowners from losing their homes to foreclosure. While it was a lifeline for many white homeowners, for Black Americans, this government agency set the conditions for financial disadvantages that would last generations.[315] Under HOLC, the banking and insurance industries used redlining to depress housing values in Black neighborhoods to promote white supremacy.

Architect Archie Alexander. Library of Congress.

Lincoln and Omaha became part of the program in 1936. That year, each city developed a mapping process in which red lines were drawn around areas where federal funds should not be dispersed. In Lincoln and Omaha, the areas occupied by African Americans were red-lined as "dangerous" and denied all funding opportunities. The maps were developed by local real estate agents, insurance dealers, property owners and government officials and became the official federal policy for funding—and a biased one, at that. The Federal Writers' Project, active in Nebraska from 1935 until 1942, completed a report on Omaha stating, "At the prosperity peak in 1929, the Negro group of Omaha have the highest ratio of homeowners and home buyers of any city in the United States." Standing in contrast to the findings of HOLC, this report offers a glimmer of unbiased perspective missing from policy discourses that commonly portrayed historic African American communities in Nebraska as constantly unattractive and derelict.[316]

---

312. "Lincoln Urban League Dedicates New Community Center," *Opportunity: a Journal of Negro Life* 20:7 (July 1942): 216.
313. *African American Architects: A Biographical Dictionary, 1865-1945*, ed. Dreck Spurlock Wilson 2004. (United Kingdom, Taylor & Francis, 2004, 11.
314. Holt, *Nebraska During the New Deal*, 90.
315. Strand, "'Mirror, Mirror, on the Wall...," 185-86.
316. Lincoln Libraries n.d.

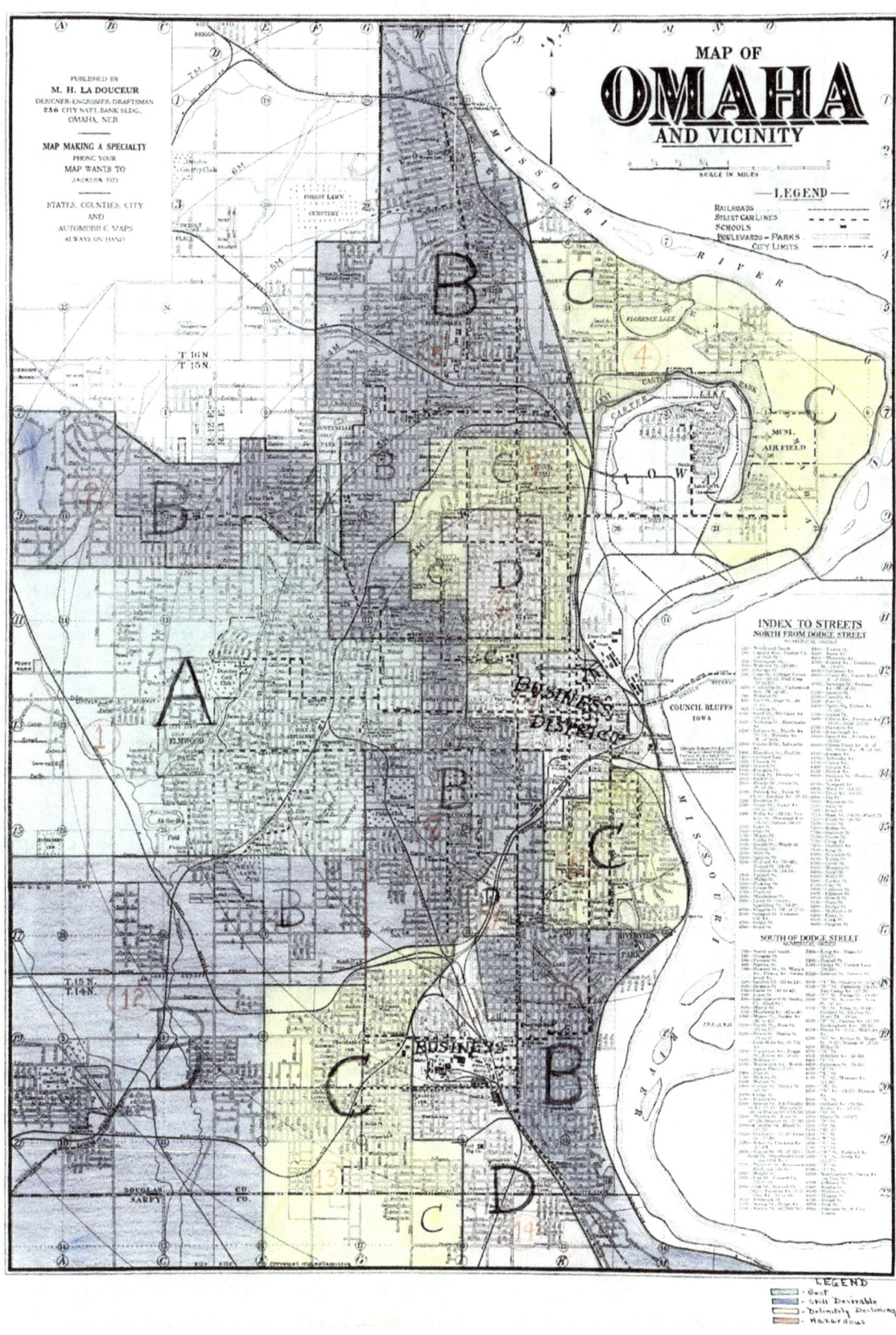

Redlining map of Omaha, Home Owners' Loan Corporation. "Mapping Inequality: Redlining in New Deal America," dsl.richmond.edu.

Logan Fontenelle housing project in North Omaha. Farm Security Administration/War Information Office, Library of Congress.

This was not the first instance of redlining in either city and it would it not be the last.[317] The PWA and the federal United States Housing Authority (USHA) were responsible for the construction of the Logan Fontenelle Housing Projects, the first public housing in Nebraska, which opened in 1938 in the Near North Side neighborhood of Omaha. The units were not originally intended for Black residents, but demand was so urgent and high that the projects were doubled in size in 1941. For several years, the 500-plus units were segregated. They were integrated after 1963 and permanently demolished in 1996.[318]

The Federal Writers' Project (FWP) captured the stories and experiences of Black people in a very different way, by hiring unemployed writers to conduct research and record oral histories. In 1941, the Woodruff Printing Company published the FWP project The *Negroes of Nebraska*, the first comprehensive guide to Nebraska's Black history, written by Fred D. Dixon and Albert J. Burks, both of Omaha, and illustrated by Paul Gibson, an African American artist in Omaha.[319]

The first *Negro Directory of Omaha* was published in 1936. It was created by Ruth M. Doss, whose

---

317. Adam Fletcher Sasse, "A History of Black Hotels in Omaha," November 6, 2015, https://northomahahistory.com/2015/11/06/a-history-of-black-hotels-in-omaha/ ; Odochi Akwani, "'Racial Redlining' Panel Educates Community on Lincoln's History," Nebraska News Service, November 1, 2020.; "Mapping Inequality: Redlining in New Deal America 1935-1940," ed. Robert K. Nelson and Edward L. Ayers, in *American Panorama: An Atlas of United States History*, https://dsl.richmond.edu/panorama/redlining/.
318. Adam Fletcher Sasse, "A History of the Logan Fontenelle Housing Projects," August 8, 2015, https://northomahahistory.com/2015/08/20/a-history-of-the-logan-fontenelle-housing-projects/.
319. Richard C. Witt, "The WPA Federal Writers' Project in Nebraska," MA Thesis, University of Nebraska Lincoln, 1980, 13-17 and 21-23; Holt, *Nebraska During the New Deal*, 56, 89-91.

"Cateress" Mrs. T.P. Mahammitt endorses Omar Cake Mixes, *Omaha World-Herald* ad, October 13, 1948. Nebraska State Historical Society.

husband Peter was the publisher through his corporation, P.C. Doss and Company. Perhaps the most educated chef in Omaha's history to this point, Sarah Helen Tolliver Mahammitt, independently published her *pièce de résistance* in 1939. Entitled *Recipes and Domestic Service*, it was the guide she created to embody her lifetime of teaching through her business, The Mahammitt School of Cookery.[320] In addition to studying at Le Cordon Bleu in Paris later in life, Mrs. Mahammitt was also credited with teaching hundreds of African American women in North Omaha about fine cooking and successful kitchen management.[321] Two years earlier Thomas P. Mahammitt was the first Black person in the country to be awarded the Boy Scouts' highest honor for adult volunteers in 1934—the same year the local media named him "Omaha's most distinguished Negro citizen."[322] A lifelong entrepreneur, Mahammitt was a restaurateur and caterer who also ran a Black newspaper and was heavily involved throughout the civic life and politics of African Americans in Nebraska. He was widely regarded as one of the most important community leaders in North Omaha when he died at age 88.[323]

Mildred Brown and her husband Edward Gilbert brought one of Nebraska's most significant newspapers into being in 1938 with the publication of the *Omaha Star*. This was no easy feat during the Depression, but Brown saw the *Star* as fulfilling many needs for the Black community. In addition to providing news and commentary on issues of concern to African Americans, Brown insisted that the *Star* foreground positive news that celebrated individual achievements, honored families and organizations that made a positive impact, put a spotlight on positive role models, and connected readers to opportunities. The *Star* gave African Americans hopeful and uplifting news during the hardships of the Depression that could leave people feeling hopeless. Brown's main objective was to create a publication free of negative Black stereotypes that permeated most papers. The *Star* spread the news to its six thousand readers and, in doing so, spread "joy and happiness" by giving Black readers a positive image of themselves, their communities, and their futures.[324]

The *Omaha Star* was also a vehicle for social and political change. Its motto read "dedicated to the service of the people that no good cause shall lack a champion and that evil shall not thrive unopposed." Brown published the names of businesses and institutions that did and did not discriminate against Black workers, and local people—especially young people—could find fair and respectful employment at the *Star*. Their experiences at the Star prepared them to demand fair and respectful treatment in the workforce more broadly. Brown, who had been a teacher, invested a great deal of time supporting and nurturing her youngest employees to work to their highest potential and to know their inherent value and worth. She also provided scholarships for local African American students to honor and support their pursuit of education.[325]

---

320. Sarah Helen Tolliver Mahammitt, *Recipes and domestic service: The Mahammitt School of Cookery*, Omaha: Mahammitt School of Cookery, 1938.
321. Adam Fletcher Sasse, "A Biography of Helen Mahammitt," North Omaha History, September 9, 2019, https://northomahahistory.com/2019/09/04/a-biography-of-helen-mahammitt/.
322. "Scout Honors Are Awarded," *Omaha World-Herald*, January 31, 1934.
323. "Thomas Mahammitt Veteran Caterer, Dies," *Omaha World-Herald*, March 29, 1950, 30. co
324. Mildred Brown, Oral History Interview with Mildred Brown, 1971, Columbia Center for Oral History, Columbia University; "Mildred Brown: Omaha Star Founder," *Nebraska Studies*, http://netwagtaildev.unl.edu/nebstudies/en/1925-1949/mildred-brown-omaha-star-founder/.
325. Amy Helene Forss, *Black Print with a White Carnation: Mildred Brown and the Omaha Star Newspaper,* 1938-1989 (Lincoln: University of Nebraska Press, 2014).

Mildred Brown and children outside *Omaha Star* Building, circa 1958. Nebraska State Historical Society.

Brown became a prominent figure in the realms of business, publishing, and human rights. She is among the few women—and is the only African American—to be inducted into the Omaha Business Hall of Fame. Later in her life, President Lyndon Johnson appointed her goodwill Ambassador to East Germany. Brown always remained focused on the *Star's* original mission and, as a result, kept the paper going through her life and after, into the present day.

Four years later, *The Negro Motorist Green Book* would tell another part of the story [326] of Nebraska business. Racist practices kept Black travelers from staying in white-owned hotels for decades in every state across the country. The *Green Book* was originally published to share safe places for Black people to sleep, generally establishments owned by other African Americans. Travel accommodations for Black people in Nebraska were noted for the first time in 1940. There were six hotels and tourist homes in Nebraska featured in the first edition located in Fremont, Hastings, Lincoln, and Omaha. Near the end of the publication's run in 1960, there were almost twenty locations in Ainsworth, Chadron, Fremont, Lincoln, Omaha, Scottsbluff, Sidney and Valentine.[327]

The 1940s

African Americans in Omaha alone numbered 14,171 or 1.07 percent of the state's total of 1,315,834 residents in the runup to U.S. entry into World War II in 1941.[328] The growing number of Black citizens in the state left the white population visibly shaken,

---

326. "Mildred Brown: Omaha Star Founder," *Nebraska Studies*, http://netwagtaildev.unl.edu/nebstudies/en/1925-1949/mildred-brown-omaha-star-founder/, accessed 7/20/2024.
327. Victor H. Green, *The Negro Motorist Green Book Compendium*, New York: About Comics, 2019.
328. Anthony-Welch, "Black People: The Nation-Building Vision," 143.

with white politicians increasingly foregrounding their anti-Black sentiments and the white-dominated media openly discriminatory toward Black people. Black political representation remained ineffectual against this white majority and educational opportunities necessary to develop the next generation of Black leaders were still separate from, and unequal to, those of Nebraska's white students.[329] After a long gap and lots of advocacy, in 1940 the Omaha School District hired its first African American teachers in decades. As young people, Dorothy Eure and Jack West Sr. formed a Civil Rights youth activism project in Omaha called the Tomorrow's World Club in 1940. The Club formed at a moment life in the United States—and around the globe—would enter a period of rapid change; the young people who would inherit the world to come after World War II would face immense challenges and unprecedented possibilities, many of which presented themselves right where they were, in Nebraska.

World War II affected African Americans in Nebraska in nearly countless ways. The nation entered World War II slowly, producing war matériel to support the Allied fight against Nazi Germany and fascist Italy while hoping to somehow maintain neutrality. President Franklin Roosevelt issued Executive Order 8802 that banned racial discrimination in the defense industry but did not integrate the military.

Signing up for the military in large numbers, young Black men from Nebraska became soldiers, sailors and for the first time since the Revolutionary War, Marines.[330] More than one thousand African American men served as pilots in the Army Air Corps pilots in World War II. Approximately sixteen hundred Black pilots and support staff would train at the Army Airfield in Tuskegee, Alabama, between 1941-1945. The Tuskegee Airmen escorted Allied bombers through hostile European airspace with some of the lowest loss rates in the war. Six Nebraskans flew these wartime missions as Tuskegee Airmen: Paul Adams, Alfonza W. Davis, John L. Harrison Jr., Woodrow F. "Woody" Morgan, Ralph Orduna, and Edward W. Watkins.[331a] Those men were later honored with the Congressional Gold Medal and inducted into the Nebraska Aviation Hall of Fame as the Tuskegee Airmen of Nebraska. Adams, a graduate of South Carolina State College, became one of the first Black teachers in Lincoln Public Schools after he retired from the military in 1963. Paul Adams Elementary School in Lincoln was named for him in 2008.[331b] Davis, listed as missing in action in 1944, received his award posthumously. The 1937 Tech High School valedictorian and member of the Creighton University Class of 1941 became the first African American from Nebraska to graduate from flight training at Tuskegee Institute. A recipient of the Purple Heart, Distinguished Flying Cross and the Distinguished Unit Citation, Alfonza Davis Middle School in Omaha is named in honor of his patriotic service. The Nebraska Chapter of the Tuskegee Airmen—one of fifty-six across the United States—was the Alfonza Davis Chapter.[332]

Tuskegee Airman Paul Adams, U.S. Army 332nd "Red Tail" Fighter Group. Courtesy of Gloria Middlebrooks and Michael L. Adams.

---

329. Melissa Amateis, *World War II Nebraska*, (Charleston, SC: Arcadia Publishing 2020),12, 32, 51, 126.

330. Dennis Mihelich, "The Lincoln Urban League: The Travail of Depression and War," *Nebraska History* 70 (1989): 313.

331a Lynn Homan and Thomas Reilly *Black Knights: The Story of the Tuskegee Airmen*, (United States: Arcadia Publishing, 2018), 272.

331b Lt. Col. Paul Adams Obituary. https://www.legacy.com/us/obituaries/name/paul-adams-obituary?pid=179065751, accessed July 24, 2025.

332. Jack Williams, "Last Member of Famed Tuskegee Airmen From Nebraska Dies at 96," Nebraska Public Media, February 16, 2021, https://nebraskapublicmedia.org/es/news/news-articles/last-member-of-famed-tuskegee-airmen-from-nebraska-dies-at-96/, accessed June 21, 2024.

Tuskegee Airman Robert Holts. Courtesy photo.

Robert Holts was eighteen years old when he and five of his close friends at Omaha Central High School enlisted in the Army Air Corps in 1942. Two of those Central students— Holts and Joe Carter—served with the Tuskegee Airmen during the war. Holts was sworn in at Fort Crook (now Offutt Air Force Base) before being shipped to Fort Leavenworth, Kansas, where recruits were issued uniforms and sat for Army General Classification Testing. New recruits who scored 110 or higher were eligible to take the tests for Aviation Cadet Training or Officer Candidate School. Holts and other Black recruits did not know that this opportunity was available to them "and we were not told about them."[333] He did not think much about the fact that there were no white soldiers among them until he arrived for basic training at Jefferson Barracks, Missouri: "I was astounded at what I was observing; I had never seen so many Negroes concentrated in one place before! And that's not all. These people were all recruits, Buck Privates, and not an officer or Black Non-Commissioned Officer on the post that was visible to me!" It was thirteen weeks later before he saw a Black officer—a warrant officer who was a chaplain.[334]

Holts served as draftsman for the 332nd Fighter Group and the 477th Bombardment Group, drawing maps that guided his commanders' battle plans. "My specific duties were with the Base Statistical Control section under the leadership of Lieutenant William T. Coleman Jr. and Lt. Emmet J. Rice. Our responsibilities included amassing all detailed recurring reports vital to the Operations and Training and Logistics of the activities at the Airbase and transmitting required information to proper sources on a timely basis," Holts said in his account.[335] He rose to the rank of corporal, feeling through his service "like I was part of America." He was honorably discharged in 1946.[336] After many years in Detroit, where he worked as a mail carrier, Holts returned to Omaha, was inducted into the Nebraska Aviation Hall of Fame in 2007 and was the last surviving Tuskegee Airman in Nebraska until his death in 2021.[337]

Navy Mess Specialist 1st Class Petty Officer Charles Jackson French became "Omaha's Fighting Son" and "Hero of the Solomons" during the Battle of Guadalcanal when Japanese destroyers fired on his ship, the USS *Gregory*, on September 4, 1942. The ship went down into shark-infested waters in just three minutes. Until that fateful moment, French had hardly interacted with his fellow sailors. Segregation restricted Black sailors to mess hall assignments. Even swim calls were segregated; white and Black sailors were not to swim together. The color line dissolved that night as French tied a rope around his waist, jumped into the dangerous waters, and spent

---

333. Jack Williams, "Last Member of Famed Tuskegee Airmen From Nebraska Dies at 96," Nebraska Public Media, February 16, 2021, https://nebraskapublicmedia.org/es/news/news-articles/last-member-of-famed-tuskegee-airmen-from-nebraska-dies-at-96/, accessed June 21, 2024.
334. "Robert D. Holts," CAF Rise Above, February 18, 2021, https://cafriseabove.org/robert-d-holts/, accessed June 20, 2023.
335. Elle Love, "Remembering Nebraska's Last Tuskegee Airmen," NOISE, February 22, 2021, https://www.noiseomaha.com/profiles/2021/2/22/remembering-nebraskas-last-tuskegee-airmen-robert-holt, accessed June 20, 2024.
336. Seritha Jones, "Back in the Day, Nov. 11, 2017: Nebraska's last living Tuskegee Airman is Grand Marshal of Parade," *Omaha World-Herald*. November 11, 2023.
337. Eugene Curtin, "Lone Survivor Robert Holts the Last of Nebraska's Tuskegee Airmen," *Omaha World-Herald*, February 18, 2015, https://omaha.com/community/bellevue/lone-survivor-robert-holts-the-last-of-nebraska-s-tuskegee-airmen/article_67f591c5-7df3-5124-b369-95729edd4cc5.html, accessed June 20, 2024.

the next eight hours as "the human tugboat" pulling rafts of injured soldiers to safety. All but eleven members of the *Gregory*'s crew survived the devastating enemy attack.[338]

French was a national mystery for a few days, known only as "the negro mess attendant" until an NBC reporter identified him by name, and a national hero ever since. The Theodore Roosevelt Lodge of the American Legion organized a well-attended hero's welcome.[339] He was greeted by a biracial welcoming committee and a parade on North 24th Street and he spoke to a football crowd at Creighton University.[340] The *Omaha Star* paid tribute to French's selflessness, love, loyalty, and devotion to mankind, by calling on readers to petition the Secretary of the Navy to award French the Distinguished Service Medal.[341]

Nebraskans showed respect and even affection for many of its African American soldiers, but with Jim Crow still firmly in place, this was far from universal. Before the war, Reece "Goose" Tatum was a world-famous Harlem Globetrotter. After joining the Army Air Forces in 1942, Tatum was stationed at the Lincoln Army Airfield where he was an entertainer to the troops for most of the war.[342] Harrison "Harry" Tull, by contrast, became a Tuskegee Airman in 1943 and rose to the rank of lieutenant colonel. Yet he was arrested and released from active duty in 1945 for entering a white-only officers club in Alabama with a group of other Black officers. Reinstated to active duty during the Korean War, he retired in 1970 while at Offutt Air Force Base and lived in Omaha until he died.[343]

Lieutenant Charline Jane May, who was born in Falls City, Nebraska, encouraged more Black women to serve in the Women's Army Auxiliary Corps when it was having a recruiting problem in the Midwest: of the six thousand WAACs at Fort Des Moines, Iowa, only 184 were African American. At the urging of the Omaha and Kansas City Urban Leagues, the Army assigned Lieutenant May the new position of Negro Recruitment Officer in 1943. She had served as recreation director for the Urban League of Lincoln while completing degrees in sociology and psychology from

Charline Jane May, *The Voice*, April 15, 1948. Nebraska State Historical Society.

---

338. Xander Gamble, "Charles Jackson French: The Human Tugboat," America's Navy News Stories, February 24, 2022, https://www.navy.mil/Press-Office/News-Stories/Article/2946177/charles-jackson-french-the-human-tugboat/, accessed July 1, 2024.
339. "Solomons Hero Welcomed Back," *The Columbus Telegram,* October 31, 1942.
340. "Omaha Hero of Solomons Guest Tonight," *Omaha World-Herald,* October 31, 1942; "Omahans Honor Swimming Hero of the Solomons," Omaha Star, November 6, 1942, 1; Adam Fletcher-Sasse, "A History of Black Military Service in Omaha History," North Omaha History, May, 31, 2024, accessed July 30, 2024.
341. "Hero of Solomons Deserves Distinguished Service Medal," *Omaha Star,* November 6, 1942, 1.
342. Samuel Momodu, "Reece 'Goose' Tatum (1921-1967)," BlackPast.org, 2020, https://www.blackpast.org/african-american-history/reece-goose-tatum-1921-1967/.
343. Danielle Grannan, "Offutt Community Honors Fallen Airman with Road Dedication," United States Air Force, April 13, 2010, https://www.af.mil/News/Article-Display/Article/117011/offutt-community-honors-fallen-airman-with-road-dedication/.

South Omaha stockyards, 1938, U.S. Farm Security Administration/Office of War Information. Library of Congress.

Nebraska Wesleyan. Her address before the Nebraska Conference on Interracial Social Action on "Negro Youth's Viewpoint on the War" made her a popular speaker in Nebraska and a great spokesperson for the WAAC. By emphasizing that "this war is a women's war as well as a man's war" and that Black women had a place in the WAAC she opened the door for more Black women to serve.[344]

Black civilians in Nebraska fully mobilized for the war effort. Rowena Moore noticed that Black women who entered the workforce during World War II received lower pay, were given more arduous jobs, and were subject to discrimination in hiring and promotions on the basis of being both women and Black people. She organized workers at the South Omaha meatpacking plant where she was employed and in 1941 co-founded a union of Black women called the Defense Women's Club to secure jobs for Black women and push for fair and equitable treatment in the workplace. Moore kept challenging racist practices in the industry until she was fired. After that, Moore spent a decade promoting traveling performances by Omaha gospel quartets, holding musical fiestas that brought the music of as many as sixteen quartets to meatpacking workers and others who gathered in celebration of Black music and human rights.[345]

African Americans were a significant part of the workforce at the Naval Ammunition Depot in Hastings, which the Navy built in 1942. The $71 million depot, occupying two thousand buildings on forty-nine thousand acres, employed more than nine thousand military and civilian personnel, including 1,458 African American enlisted men along with another 383 Black civilians. The 1940 U.S. Census showed seventy Black residents in the city, a number that had ballooned to one thousand by 1943. *De facto*

---

344. "Omaha and Kansas City Urban Leagues Assist in WAAC Recruiting," *Opportunity* 31:1 (January 1943): 19.
345. Alonzo Smith, "Nebraska Black Oral History Project: Interview with Rowena Moore." University of Nebraska–Lincoln Department of Black Studies, Great Plains Black History Museum, Nebraska Association for the Study of African American Life and History, History Nebraska, University of Nebraska at Omaha, 1982.

Jim Crow segregation gripped the city and within a few years Hastings had a segregated downtown with separate shopping streets for whites and African Americans. The federal public housing projects and Navy housing were strictly segregated, too. The facility operated in some form into the Vietnam War and closed by 1966.[346]

Several other plants devoted to war production sprang up in Nebraska during World War II and employed African Americans. The Glenn L. Martin Bomber Plant opened in Bellevue in 1942 to produce medium bomber airplanes and two years later started producing the largest bomber in World War II, the B-29 Superfortress. Malcolm Chambers, the father of Sen. Ernie Chambers, was among 765 African Americans were employed there during the war. The plant operated into 1945.[347] The Cornhusker Army Ammunition Plant, built in 1942 on twelve thousand acres in Grand Island, operated during World War II through the Vietnam War. The Nebraska Ordnance Plant near Mead covered 17,250 acres. The Sioux Army Depot consisted of more than a thousand buildings on 22,000 acres near Sidney. It operated from 1942 through the Vietnam War. Each of these plants employed an indeterminate number of African Americans.[348]

To house the workers at the Ammunition Depot in Hastings, the Navy constructed a public housing project for six thousand residents with a segregated area of 260 units for African Americans. There was a separate community council for Black families. When the war ended in 1945 many African American families immediately moved away. Those who stayed left either in 1954, when the Navy turned over Spencer Park to the Hastings Housing Authority, or in 1957 when the buildings became a senior retirement center. This large population of Black workers brought to Hastings specifically for the war faced overt discrimination that was supposedly uncommon with the smaller number of African American residents in the city before the war.[349]

Work at the Hastings Ammunition Depot was nonstop and often dangerous. Corrine Smith, Bessie Lee, and Juanita Stith narrowly escaped serious injury when a primer accidentally exploded in the factory. Lee and Smith already shared the distinction of being

"World's Fastest Women" Corinne Smith, Mrs. Bessie Lee and Juanita Stith. UNL Libraries, Archives and Special Collections.

the first two Black women hired at the depot; with Stith, the three were named the "first ladies of the area" for the speed with which they fled to safety and their concern for the safety of others. A second explosion in April 1944 killed eight workers, wounded 35,

---

346. Hurt, R. Douglas Hurt, *The Great Plains during World War II*, (Lincoln, Nebraska: University of Nebraska Press, 2008), 258.
347. Ali Johnson 2016, 8; Hurt, *The Great Plains in World War II*, 71, 78.
348. United States National Park Service, Sioux Ordnance Depot Fire & Guard Headquarters Registration Form, 1994, npgallery.nps.gov/GetAsset/e6e93892-4003-4e2a-b222-cebb94bf8db4.
349. United States National Park Service, Sioux Ordnance Depot Fire & Guard Headquarters Registration Form, 1994, npgallery.nps.gov/GetAsset/e6e93892-4003-4e2a-b222-cebb94bf8db4.

and left at least five missing.[350] Five months later, in September 1944, three African American soldiers from the segregated Ordnance Battalion were assigned to build, maintain, and load rockets, shells, mines, and other dangerous explosives. Adolph Johnson of Indianapolis, Indiana, Jesse C. Wilson of Rayville, Louisiana and J. C. Miles of Start, Louisiana died instantly when the massive artillery shell they were working on exploded unexpectedly and seventy other people were injured. In keeping with the Depot's practice of naming streets after workers who died on the job, street signs memorializing Johnson, Rayville, and Miles were raised in their honor.[351] Waging war posed dangers to Americans of all races, but African Americans were almost always assigned to the most dangerous positions where, despite the visible burdens of racial discrimination, they gave their all to the fight for global democracy. After her near-death experience on the job Bessie Lee said, "I'm glad to be able to help on the line toward the war effort…and I'm hoping all the time Hitler and Hirohito will be done away with as soon as possible."[352] African Americans were fighting for a double victory in World War II.

The rhythms of everyday life continued for long-established Nebraskans during the war. Although the war effort brought Nebraskans together as "Americans, All!" discrimination remained in force. Three years into the war experience in Omaha, in 1944, the Tomorrow's World Club's informal survey of local businesses' hiring practices yielded numerous replies of, "We don't hire Negroes." Tomorrow's World had a column in the *Omaha Guide* where it published news of the club, incidents of racial prejudice, and words of encouragement for readers like the poem "Drive On, Black Boy," written by a club member. The final stanza read, "Drive on Black Boy / Against Injustice, Prejudices, and Strife / Against Obstacles and disappointments / You're driving toward a better life." Access to health care was no better. The Nebraska Negro Medical Society was a professional organization that was active from 1941 to 1945. Dr. Craig Morris was the president of the organization and actively led their advocacy, public education, and professional development efforts. They were involved in statewide "drives against tuberculosis and social diseases," held public meetings on venereal diseases and sponsored a "Fresh Air Camp" for African American children. The organization included many notable doctors such as Dr. Price Terrell, Dr. D.W. Gooden, Dr. W.W. Solomon, Dr. Wesley Jones, Dr. Herbert Wiggins, and Dr. G.B. Lennox.[353]

Anticipating African Americans returning to sub-par segregated healthcare services, in 1945 Black community leaders in Omaha began planning a Black-owned, and -operated hospital for the African American community called the Provident Hospital. Since the 1890s, almost a dozen other such institutions were planned or even opened for a short time in North Omaha but never worked in the long-term. Provident was to be a fifty-room hospital in a newly constructed Black neighborhood, but it, too, was never built. Their work culminated in 1945 with the proposed opening of a new hospital in North Omaha for African Americans.[354] The project floundered and the organization dissipated after Dr. Morris suddenly moved to California that year.[355]

In 1945, John R. Butler launched the Near North Side YMCA in a rented building to serve the African American community, particularly Black servicemen from Offutt, which did not have integrated recreation facilities. Butler headed up a building campaign, fundraising and programming for a new recreation center that he led through the early 1960s. Today, the Butler-Gast YMCA in North Omaha is partly named in his memory.[356]

African Americans were rarely served by banks in Omaha. They did not open branches in North Omaha and engaged in savings, checking, and lending

---

350. "Eight Streets in Bomb and Mine Area Named in Memory of Victims of Recent Accident There," *The Powder Keg* vol. 1 no. 34 (April 28, 1944): 1.
351. Walter L. Miller, "U.S. Naval Ammunition Depot, Hastings, Nebraska, 1942–1966: A History Sketch." [DVD]. Lincoln: Nebraska State Historical Society.
352. "They're the First Out of the Building When Minor Explosion Occurs," *The Powder Keg*, (U.S. Naval Ammunition Depot, Hastings, Nebraska), vol. 1 no. 4 (October 8, 1943): 1.
353. "Negro Medic Society Re-elects Dr. Morris," *Omaha World-Herald*, June 14, 1941, 7.
354. "Provident Hospital Plans Are Drawn," *Omaha World-Herald*, July 17, 1945, 4.
355. Adam Fletcher Sasse, "A History of North Omaha's Provident Hospital," North Omaha History, May 10, 2018, https://northomahahistory.com/2018/05/10/a-history-of-north-omahas-provident-hospital/ ; "Closes Dental Offices Here," *The Omaha Guide*, December 1, 1945, 1.
356. Adam Fletcher Sasse, "A History of the Near North Side YMCA," North Omaha History, February 6, 2018, https://northomahahistory.com/2018/02/06/near-north-side-ymca/.

practices that stonewalled Black families' attempts to build wealth into the 1960s. Men returning from the service in World War II and women who were employed in wartime manufacturing had money to invest. Attorney Charles F. Davis worked with Dr. Craig Morris and others to create an answer. In 1944, a group of Black community leaders opened the Carver Savings and Loan Association in North Omaha. From the time it opened in 1946, Carver offered checking, savings, and loans to its members. Davis and his daughter Elizabeth Davis Pittman, who became the first Black woman judge in Nebraska, used part of the facility for their law offices, and for more than a decade Carver S&L was a lauded and popular place. It operated until 1965.[357]

Omaha's music scene never missed a beat during the war. The International Sweethearts of Rhythm, the first integrated all-women's band in the United States, took root in Omaha in 1941. Local swing band singer Anna Mae Winburn became the band leader that year in North Omaha. In the 1940s the band featured some of the best female musicians in the country, playing swing and jazz on a national circuit. A newspaper announced the band was "one of the hottest stage shows that ever raised the roof of the theater!" Omahan Helen Jones Woods was the premier trombonist with the band and went on to become the matriarch of her North Omaha family, including her daughter, business mogul Cathy Hughes. The band disbanded in 1946.[358]

A gospel quartet founded in Omaha during the war, The Loving Four, became nationally famous, traveling the country and influencing the popularity of gospel music nationwide. Researchers have heaped praise on the group, calling them "one of the earliest full-time independent professional traveling gospel quartets" and "one of the first gospel groups to use guitar accompaniment."[359]

Luigi Waites was an internationally known jazz drummer from Omaha. Around 1940, he started his career playing in nightclubs around Omaha. After graduating from Central High and serving in the Army during World War II, he recorded several albums. Toward the end of his life, Waites received several awards in Nebraska for his influence. And it was 1943 when Preston Love Sr., then a young saxophonist in North Omaha, got his big break with the Count Basie Orchestra. Recording with the band through 1947, Love became a nationally renowned professional sideman before becoming a band leader for the Preston Love Orchestra. He continued working nationally, wrote his autobiography, led bands, and worked for the *Omaha Star*.[360]

North Omaha impresario Jimmy Jewell Jr. left behind his wife and business to join the US Army during World War II. The Army seized his business, the Dreamland Ballroom on North 24th Street, for use as a USO Club to entertain African American soldiers stationed in the Omaha area. Other USO facilities in Omaha were segregated, making the Dreamland an essential outlet. In 1945, after he left the Army and returned to North Omaha, Jewell joined the volunteer management team for the USO Club. However, he was forced to sue the government to regain ownership. When the building was returned to Jewell without compensation, he sued the government for their lack of reimbursement. In a landmark case, he was granted $3,000 for damages and compensation. He returned the business to its iconic status immediately afterwards.[361]

African Americans coming home to Nebraska from their service in the fight to save global democracy encountered racism, segregation, and discrimination at the national and local levels, often in covert forms. As an example, in 1948 President Truman signed Executive Order 9981 stating "there shall be equality of treatment and opportunity for all persons in the armed forces without regard to race, color, religion, or national origin" in all branches of the armed forces. The language of the President's

---

357. "Lots of Only: Mrs. Pittman Is Sole Negro Woman Lawyer." *Omaha World-Herald*, February 27, 1949, 20C; Toni Heinzl, "Pittman Mourned as Pioneer, Inspiration," *Omaha World-Herald*, 1998; Adam Fletcher Sasse, "History of the Carver Savings and Loan Association," North Omaha History, September 21, 2020, https://northomahahistory.com/2020/09/21/a-history-of-the-carver-savings-and-loan-association/.
358. Liz Sher, "The International Sweethearts of Rhythm," *Sage: A Scholarly Journal on Black Women*, 4 no.1: 59–60, 59; Antoinette Handy, *The International Sweethearts of Rhythm: The Ladies' Jazz Band from Piney Woods Country Life School*. Lanham, MD: Scarecrow Press. 1998.
359. Tom Jack, "The Omaha Gospel Complex in Historical Perspective." *Great Plains Quarterly* 20 (Summer 2000): 229.
360. Preston Love, *A Thousand Honey Creeks Later: My Life in Music from Basie to Motown and Beyond*, (Wesleyan University Press, 1997), 126.
361. Dreamland Ballroom, North Omaha History Harvest, University of Nebraska Lincoln, 2011, https://historyharvest.unl.edu/items/browse?tag=Dreamland+Ballroom.

Count Basie Band at the Dreamland Ballroom. UNL History Harvest.

order was clear, but its implementation met resistance from soldiers and officers. It took a presidential commission to investigate effective methods of desegregation and the battlefield realities of the Korean War to make integration of the military a lived reality.[362]

Closer to home, racial discrimination remained visible everywhere. Swimming pools were one of the first and most frequent sites of struggle for desegregation in Nebraska from the end of World War II through the 1960s. The first incident took place in Lincoln in 1946 when Joe Ishikawa, director of playgrounds, was instructed to distribute tickets for a free swim day to any children he saw, except for Black children. Ishikawa was a fierce advocate for civil rights. He had recently been relocated to Lincoln from a Japanese American incarceration camp and joined the local Urban League on his arrival. Ishikawa wrote a letter of protest to his employer and worked with the Urban League, the NAACP, and the American Veterans Committee to pressure the City Council to desegregate city pools. Their combined outreach brought a multi-racial coalition of two hundred people to the City Council meeting where Ishikawa made the case for desegregation. Together, Black civil rights organizations and their supporters of all races shamed the City Council to officially desegregate the swimming pools in Lincoln.[363]

Race-restrictive covenants reinforced existing patterns of housing segregation and more overtly endorsed white socioeconomic dominance. As an example, the 1947 covenant for the Underwood Hills

---

362. Executive Order 9981: Desegregation of the Armed Forces (1948), National Archives and Records Administration, https://www.archives.gov/milestone-documents/executive-order-9981, accessed June 20, 2024.
363. Joe Ishikawa interviewed by Tom Ikeda, January 10, 2008, segment 25, Densho Digital Archives, https://ddr.densho.org/media/ddr-densho-1000/ddr-densho-1000-205-transcript-92aee799fa.htm, Jesse S. Ishikawa, "The Desegregation of the Lincoln Municipal Swimming Pool, *Nebraska History* (Fall 2018): 159-166.

Lincoln protest march, 1966. Nebraska State Historical Society.

subdivision in Omaha, read "no person other than that of the Caucasian race shall be or become the grantee or lessee of said premises, nor except as a servant of the family living thereon be granted the privilege of occupying the same." Enforcing race-restrictive roles, this institutional racism clearly posits white people as superior over African Americans and ensures Black people are allowed in the neighborhood only because of their value to white people. Although the U.S. Supreme Court ruled in *Shelley v. Kraemer* in 1948 that race-restrictive covenants in government and private housing violated the Fourteenth Amendment, such covenants were evident in Omaha subdevelopments from the 1920s through the 1960s.[364] Segregation was deepening, keeping structures of inequality in place.

The Civil Rights Struggle in Nebraska, 1950s-1960s

George Robinson, leader of the Urban League of Omaha, reported in 1950: "Negroes have far more difficulty getting mortgage money. Lending institutions have their rules, some of which are subject to interpretation. In the case of the Negro, the rules are always rigid. For example, when both husband and wife work, the lending institution will only consider the husband's income, even though the wife is past child-bearing years. The experience of the Negro is that they must put up higher down payments and pay a larger total sum."[365] This practice remained in Omaha and Lincoln through at least 1964 and was one of many foci of the growing Civil Rights Movement.

---

364. Jeanette Gabriel, Christina Dando, and Jennifer Harbour, "Uncovering Racially Restrictive Covenants: Omaha's Spatial Justice Project," Center for Great Plains Studies, University of Nebraska Omaha, 2022, https://mediahub.unl.edu/media/19093.

365. Gabriel, Dando, and Harbour, "Uncovering Racially Restrictive Covenants," https://mediahub.unl.edu/media/19093.

Nebraska's growing number of African American religious leaders laid the foundation for civil rights activism in the post-World War II era. The Reverend Belva Spicer of Lincoln was ordained a minister of the African Methodist Episcopal Church in 1948. The presiding bishop noted that as one of three women ordained that day, Reverend Spicer helped forge a path for more Black women to enter the ministry.[366] She served AME churches in Grand Island and Hastings, and in 1950 founded an AME Church in North Platte.[367] Returning to her earlier vocation as a teacher, Reverend Spicer taught Native American children in South Dakota schools from 1956 to 1970. The Bureau of Indian Affairs awarded her a Medal of Honor for her excellence in the classroom.[368]

Reverend Rockefeller "R.F." Jenkins also advanced civil rights in and outside the church. He became the first African American minister in the Missouri Synod in Nebraska in 1954, as the new minister of New Hope Lutheran Church in Omaha. He would later co-found 4CL, the leading civil rights organization in Nebraska during the early 1960s. Father Joseph Warren Anderson, an alumnus of Father Flanagan's Boys Town, in 1951 became the first African American Catholic priest ordained in Nebraska.[369] Three years later, Monsignor Patrick Flanagan protested the local Father Flanagan Council of the Knights of Columbus's denial of membership to three Black candidates "despite what was reported as overwhelming sentiment in favor of admittance." The local council renamed itself after Monsignor Flanagan's brother, Father Edward Flanagan, in honor of his founding of Boys Town and his work with neglected children. In a letter to the Council, Monsignor Flanagan asserted that his brother "pioneered in Christian social advancement of the Negro people" and that he founded Boys Town as one of the few places in the United States where boys of "every race, creed, and color" – including many African American boys – were welcomed as family

The Rev. Sirilda Belva Spicer. Donna Mays Polk, *Black Men and Women of Nebraska* (Nebraska Black History Preservation Society, 1981).

and considered equals. In light of this "unpleasant publicity" Monsignor Flanagan asked the Knights of Columbus to cease calling themselves the Father Flanagan Chapter. Archbishop Gerald T. Bergan followed with a statement expressing his confidence that the chapter would put an end to the cause of the "sorry spectacle." The Grand Knights issued an apology.[370] The Omaha Archdiocese hired its first African American teacher, Tessie O. Edwards, in 1958.[371]

The Civil Rights era entered a new phase as the elders who fought against enslavement and Jim Crow passed away. When S.J. "July" Miles died in 1941, he was the last surviving African American Civil War veteran in Nebraska.[372] Lucinda Woods, who was born enslaved in Tennessee, was one of the oldest residents of Scottsbluff at the time of her death in 1951. Woods moved to Nebraska with her husband in 1917. In a newspaper article from the time, she recalled slaves being tied to trees and beaten with "blacksnake whips." Once sold for $1,000, Mrs. Woods was taken from her mother at age five and given by her owner to

---

366. "AMEs Close 28th Annual Nebraska Conference in Omaha; Inspired Meeting," *The Voice* vol 2 no. 4 (October 21, 1948) 1; Annie Russell, "Spicer, Sirilda Belva," *The Westminster Handbook to Women in American Religious History* ed. Susan Hill Lindley and Eleanor J. Stebner (Louisville, KY: Westminster John Knox Press, 2008), 210.
367. "New AME Church is Organized in North Platte," *The Voice* vol. 4 no. 11 (January 5, 1950): 1.
368. Johnson, Marilyn, "Sirilda Belva Spicer: Educator and Minister," *Perspectives: Women in Nebraska History*, June 1984, Nebraska Department of Education and the Nebraska State Council for the Social Studies, 77-78.
369. "Boys Town Receives Its First Negro Priest," *Omaha World-Herald*, June 5, 1951.
370. "Looking and Listening," *The Crisis*, 61:10 (December 1954): 605.
371. Jack Angus, *Black and Catholic in Omaha: A Case of Double Jeopardy: The First Fifty Years of St. Benedict the Moor Parish*, (iUniverse Self-Publishing Platform, 2001), 153.
372. Holt, *Nebraska During the New Deal*, 69.
373. "Scottsbluff Woman to Be 100 Friday," *Omaha World-Herald*, March 9, 1950.

his daughter as a wedding gift.[373] William Thornton Patrick, a noted Black resident of Grand Island, was the son of a formerly enslaved man who had moved to Nebraska as a Pony Express Rider. Patrick moved from Hamilton County to Grand Island where he was a farmer and railroad worker before becoming a hotel doorman at Grand Island's finest hotel. For two decades he was an unofficial ambassador for the city's guests and was noted for his presence and skills when he died in 1952.[374]

Two years after Patrick's death, in 1954, the U.S. Supreme Court ruled in *Brown v. Board of Education* that school segregation is unconstitutional. The justices found that *Plessy v. Ferguson* was wrong; "separate" education for Black students was by no means "equal." Even though the ruling gave legal basis for school desegregation, in Nebraska the actual process of implementation was slow and contentious. In Omaha and Lincoln, the media reported large scale white resistance to school integration. This resistance had recent roots in 1945, when the Tomorrow's World Club started a campaign, under the guidance of Arthur McCaw and Leota Jones, to pressure the school board to hire Black high school teachers.[375]

Their efforts laid the groundwork for later success, but that success came slowly. More than twenty years later, Omaha Public Schools was found out of compliance with the order and was forced to integrate by the federal government. Several all-white suburban school districts in enclaves around the city grew exponentially in the intervening years, creating a two-tiered education system for which "urban vs. suburban" was code for "Black vs. white." School officials in Lincoln were slow to integrate the schools but did take measures to avoid pressure from the federal government to implement school busing—the program of assigning and transporting students to schools to create more racially balanced student bodies that would become explosive in cities like Boston in the 1970s.[376] Even when the policy ended the plague of "separate but (un)equal" education its imprints remain in what Thurgood Marshall called "intangible factors" that come from the appearance that Black schools and their students were somehow inherently "inferior" to whites.[377]

The desegregationist spirit of *Brown v. Board of Education* did not reach the popular Peony Park, an amusement center in Omaha where the 1955 Amateur Athletic Union swim meet was being held. Officials barred two African American swimmers from competing because the park refused them entrance to the pool, even though such discrimination violated Nebraska law. A group of NAACP youth activists successfully filed suit against Peony Park. After paying their $50 fine, the owners resumed their usual discriminatory practices. Mildred Brown called for a more robust response from Peony Park patrons by drawing the contrast between Omaha's fragmented African Americans and the cohesion that made the Montgomery Bus Boycott a success in Alabama.[378] It would be eight years before the collective action Brown advocated put economic pressure on the owners of Peony Park to end its racial exclusion. Civil rights work continued in earnest in those intervening years. The Lincoln Action Coordinating Team (ACT) was an informal group of Black and white Civil Rights advocates focused on direct action. ACT made news for the first time in 1959, and Omaha's 4CL interfaced with ACT on several occasions.[379] Nebraska's Civil Rights Movement grew stronger and more widespread, forging connections with the national movement for Civil Rights. Reverend Dr. Martin Luther King, Jr. made his first trip to Omaha in 1958 to speak at the Civic Auditorium and to preach at Salem Baptist Church.[380]

Reverend Melvin L. Shakespeare, pastor of the African Methodist Church in Hastings, and his wife, Rubie Shakespeare, launched a Black newspaper in Lincoln called *The Voice* in 1946. "Dedicated to the promotion of the culture, social and spiritual life of a great people," the paper advocated greater employment opportunities, tolerance, and advanced

---

374. David Bristow, "Who Is This Man? The Black Doorman at the Hotel Yancey, Part 2." History Nebraska [blog]. https://history.nebraska.gov/who-is-this-man-the-black-doorman-at-the-hotel-yancey-part-2/2021.
375. Eileen Wirth, *The Women Who Built Omaha: A Bold and Remarkable History*. Lincoln, NE: Bison Books, 2022), 161.
376. Melissa Matczak, "Omaha Schools to Revisit Integration Omaha School Integration History." *Omaha World-Herald*. September 29, 1997.
377. Earl Warren and Supreme Court of The United States, U.S. Reports: Brown v. Board of Education, 349 U.S. 294. 1954, Periodical, https://www.loc.gov/item/usrep349294/.
378. Davis, "Fighting Jim Crow in post-World War II Omaha 1945-1956," 215.
379. Nebraska Advisory Committee to the United States Commission on Civil Rights 1975, 66.
380. "Segregation Fighter Sees Success Ahead," *Omaha World-Herald*, June 19, 1958.

THE VOICE

Volume 1, Number 1 — Lincoln 3, Nebraska — October 11, 1946

Clyde Malone Attends National Urban League Conference

Voice to Award Scholarship

In keeping with the purpose for which this publication is intended, a Scholarship will be awarded on the basis of merit to a High School graduate each year, beginning in 1947. It may be used in any university or technical school the winner may select. The student's scholastic standard will receive customary consideration, but added to this will be adaptability and willingness to accept responsibilities.

Dramatic Club And Community Chorus

Mr. George Randol will direct a dramatic club and community chorus at the Urban League.

His experience and training, as a Broadway actor, motion picture director and concert singer make for interesting and professional instruction. Plans are already under way and included in it will be Serious Drama, Choral Singing, plays, comedies and pantomines. The classes will meet each evening at 8 p.m. and everybody is invited to join.

The Voice

The Voice, yes the Lincoln Voice today makes it's debut.

Not a plaint nor altogether is it a voice of hilarity. But rather a determined, indomitable voice making an appeal for a united effort on the part of the Negro citizenry of this great educational and cultural center to raise sights to higher goals.

A voice crying out to Lincoln citizens at large for greater opportunities in fields of employment that we might live more abundantly. A voice asking for tolerance and fair play. A voice that will not be stilled so long as any group is denied inalienable rights guaranteed under the constitution.

A voice urging our youth to complete college educations.

Voice stressing the dire need of trained, enlightened, Christian leadership, cautioning against loose living.

A voice denouncing unscrupulous politicians who would sell us down the river.

A voice asking fuller cooperation among our churches. Pleading with Negro business to assist in making greater opportunities for Negro youth who have prepared themeselves to assume increased responsibilites.

A voice constantly championing the cause of the underprivileged. Finally a voice that shall ever listen to that "Still Small Voice" that has guided men on the upward trail since the beginning of time.

Rev. T. T. McWilliams, Sr.

Minister Returns

Rev. R. E. Handy was re-appointed to Quinn Chapel A.M.E. Church at the close of the Annual Conference which convened in Atchison, Kansas, Oct. second.

Rev. Handy came here a year ago from the Colorado Conference and has enjoyed a successful pastorate.

First Polio Case

Little Sandra Kaye Springs, daughter of Mr. and Mrs. Wm. Springs Jr., was stricken with polio. She is now at the Orthopedic Hospital. She is reported to have a very mild case and getting along very well.

Housing and Employment Major Interest

Executive Secretary, Clyde Malone was among the 300 persons attending the four-day session of the National Urban League Annual Conference, which closed its sessions at Kiel auditorium Saturday September 28, in St. Louis, Mo.

With speakers ranging from a Navy admiral and millionire's son to labor leaders and ordinary laymen, the conference was filled with discussions and reports on the year's work in the 96 cities where there are Urban League affiliates.

Endorsement and support of the "crucial efforts of democratic unions to organize the South" was pledged.

Noting that "only through increased industrialization of that region with equal frieght rates and the organization of southern white and Negro workers can permanent be made in the deplorable conditions of both;" and the forces that oppose and terrorize any close fraternity of white and Negro people" the resolution stated the League would urge full support of the "democratic unions" by the Negro community and urge "non-democratic "unions" by the Negro community and urge "non-democratic" unions to discontinue their practices.

A resolution on World Peace declared this country's first "obligation to the welfare of nations is the job of implementing our bill of rights and making America a place where the guarantees of its Constitution are without prejudice or favor in the protection of every citizen." Coupled with this achievement, the resolution continued, "there must, of course, be a wise and generous foreign policy consistent with democratic ideals."

Sec. 562, P. L. & R.

PEOPLE YOU SHOULD KNOW

Reverend and Mrs. John Favors

Rev. John Favors, pastor of Mt. Zion Baptist Church for two and a half years, is a teacher in the Omaha School System. After having attended Arizona State Teacher's College in Tempe, Arizona, he was graduated from Bishop College in Marshall, Texas. At present, the Rev. Mr. Favors is writing his Master's thesis in the department of School Administration at the University of Nebraska, and is enrolled in the University of Omaha. He plans to get his Ph. D. at the University of Nebraska. He is the son of Rev. Charles Favors, pastor of Pilgrim Baptist Church of Omaha, formerly of Phoenix, Arizona. He possesses a rich singing voice.

Mrs. Kathryne Favors, formerly of Omaha, Nebraska attended Omaha Public Schools throughout the high schools, and is a graduate of Fisk University in Nashville, Tennessee. She attended the Creighton University in Omaha two summers and at present is writing her Master's Thesis in the Department of Secondary Education at the University of Nebraska. Mrs. Favors is a teacher in the Omaha School System and plans to start work on her Ph. D. in January at the University of Nebraska. She has given many excellent dramatic concerts. Both Rev. and Mrs. Favors like music and are especially fond of hymns and classical music. They like to spend quiet evenings at home, they enjoy football games, and are interested in anything for the advancement of their race.

The debut of *The Voice* in Lincoln, *The Voice*, October 11, 1946. Nebraska State Historical Society.

educational goals for African Americans. *The Voice* also reported on the Black community in Lincoln, Hastings, and other Nebraska towns and, until it closed in the early 1950s, supported the work of the *Omaha Star* in emphasizing the strengths of Black people and Black communities.[381] The *Star* was under the editorship of African American journalist Charles B. Washington beginning in 1946. The youngest editor of any Black newspaper nationwide, he worked for the paper for almost forty years. He was also a television host and a leader in state politics, advancing the mission started by Mildred Brown.[382]

Young people were well acquainted with racism. In 1950, for instance, Black students were not permitted to perform in an opera at Central High.[383] School segregation remained legal until 1954, so young people were at the forefront of the struggle for equal rights under the Constitution. Their experiences in the 1940s and 1950s prepared many in this generation to lead the Civil Rights movement of the 1960s.

Campus activism for civil rights in Omaha started in 1947 when Father John Markoe and a multiracial core of students founded The Omaha DePorres Club.

Students and community members of all backgrounds met at Creighton University to address racial discrimination.[384] The original members of the club included Max Brownell, Bertha Calloway, Tessie Edwards, Oscar and Alma Hodges, Denny and Jean Holland, Ola McCraney, Wilbur Phillips, Irvine Poindexter, Louis Ries, Darrel and Agnes Stark, Harold Tibbs, Tom and Virginia Walsh, Margarita Washington, and Helen Woods. The club conducted nonviolent civil disobedience in the Omaha community. Some of the first sit-ins in the United States took place at Omaha lunch counters and businesses that refused to serve African Americans. The club sponsored Nebraska's first-ever "Inter-racial Youth Rally" in 1949 with speeches from the leader of the Urban League and the youth activities writer for the *Omaha World-Herald*. *The Omaha Star* reported, "The future of Omaha and of America is in the hands of youth. They can wipe out race prejudice and Jim Crow. This

Mildred Brown with Father Markoe and the DePorres Club. Nebraska State Historical Society.

Youth Rally can be the beginning of a transformation of Omaha..."[385] Creighton eventually removed the DePorres Club from campus, but Father Markoe and the growing circle of activists continued to insist upon desegregation in Omaha, which had become—and remains—one of America's most segregated cities.[386]

The University of Nebraska enrolled the second largest number of African American students among the mixed-race state schools (enrollment in historically Black colleges and universities was significantly higher) in 1949. The numbers were both encouraging and sobering: The Ohio State University enrolled 937, the University of Nebraska 56, and the University of Colorado came in third with 50 students.[387] The Municipal University of Omaha (now the University of Nebraska Omaha) enrolled 62 undergraduates in the same year.[388] The growing numbers of Black students were a relatively small part of student bodies of several thousand. These conditions made Nebraska universities fertile ground for local and national civil rights leadership to grow. Before

---

381. Cindy Lange-Kubick, "From the Shakespeares, a Voice for and by the Black Community in Lincoln," *Lincoln Journal Star*, February 4, 2021.
382. "Washington Worked for Rights," *Omaha World-Herald*, May 1, 1986.
383. Heinzl, "Pittman Mourned as Pioneer, Inspiration."
384. Matt Holland, *Ahead of Their Time: The Story of the Omaha DePorres Club*, (Createspace Independent Publishing Platform, 2014), 31.
385. "Interracial Student Rally," *Omaha Star*, April 8, 1949.
386. Holland, *Ahead of Their Time*, 45.
387. "The American Negro in College," *The Crisis* 57:8 (August-September 1950): 499.
388. "The American Negro in College," 500.

Reception Held Honoring Mr. Arthur McCaw

—Photo by William White

Saturday evening, January 10, 1953, a reception was held honoring Mr. Arthur McCaw, newly appointed State Budget Director at the Near Northside YWCA.

Many of Mr. McCaw's friends were present to congratulate him on his new position.

Pictured left to right are members of the McCaw famiy:

Bernice McCaw, chicago, Illinosi; Melba McCaw, New York City, New York; Joan McCaw, Nebraska University student; Mrs. Valeria McCaw, public

school art teacher; Mr. Arthur McCaw; Janice McCaw, University of Nebraska student; Melvin McCaw, Central High school student; and Gertrude Williams, Maywood, Illinois.

Reception for newly appointed State Budget Director Arthur McCaw. *The Omaha Star*, January 16, 1953. Nebraska State Historical Society,

taking his prominent role on the national civil rights scene, Whitney Young Jr. taught at the University of Nebraska and Creighton University while serving as the leader of the Urban League in Omaha from 1950 to 1955. In the first year, Young felt that he had the support of the whole community. Within a year, he partnered with the City of Omaha and the Nebraska Legislature to work with several Nebraska employers to improve hiring, promotion, and termination procedures to promote fairness and equality in the job market. Young made his mark on the national stage as executive director of the National Urban League, which put him at the forefront of civil rights leadership starting in 1961.[389]

The early 1950s drew many young Nebraskans directly toward civil rights activism at home and others into the newly desegregated armed forces as the United States entered the Korean War in 1950. During the next three years, 600,000 African American soldiers would fight with 9.3 percent of them killed in the war.[390]

This was the first American war to have integrated troops because of a presidential order. In October 1951, the U.S. Army 24th Infantry Regiment, established in 1869 and referred to as the Buffalo Soldiers, was formally disbanded. The unit had served during the Spanish-American War, World War I, World War II and the beginning of the Korean War. When it was

---

389. Davis, "Fighting Jim Crow in Post-World War II Omaha," 110, 118, 135.

390. Morris J. McGregor, Jr., Integration of the Armed Forces, 1940-1965 (Washington, DC: United States Army Center of Military History, 2001), 291-314; "African-Americans in the Korean War," Korean War Legacy Foundation, koreanwearlegacy.org; National Park Service, Charles Young Buffalo Soldiers National Monument, www.nps.gov/chyo/learn/historyculture/busokoreanwar.htm.

disbanded, *de jure* segregation in the U.S. Army ended. State Budget Director Arthur B. McCaw, the first Black person appointed to a governor's cabinet position in 1952, played a part in stabilizing the Korean peninsula in 1956 when he had a position in the International Cooperation Administration in South Korea.[391] McCaw's global view of human rights also drove his commitment to the work of the NAACP. After serving as president of the Omaha NAACP McCaw was appointed to President Lyndon B. Johnson's Committee on Civil Rights in the 1960s.[392]

Rodney S. Wead made an enormous impact on the civil rights movement at the local level. His leadership in developing social services, promoting economic development, and advancing African American studies and alternative education started in 1958 and made a difference in the lives of untold numbers of Nebraskans over many years. Born during the New Deal, Wead believed "it was embedded in me to appreciate and advance housing programs for the poor, seek financial reforms for the disenfranchised, employment, and education attainment."[393] Seeing the relationship between access to banking services and meeting housing and educational needs, Wead opened the state's first Black-owned bank and the credit union to serve low-income people.

His most far-reaching enterprise, however, was Wead's launch of KOWH, Nebraska's first Black-owned radio station, in 1970. The station played jazz, R&B and soul music to more than 70,000 African American listeners in Nebraska, Iowa and Missouri in its nine-year history.[394] One of the most influential players in the U.S. media landscape, Urban One founder Cathy Hughes, got her start in radio at KOWH. Hughes came to KOWH after working at *The Omaha Star*. A position as administrative assistant in the School of Communications at Howard University took her to Washington D.C. Howard promoted Hughes to general sales and, eventually, general manager of the university radio station WHUR-FM, making her the first woman station manager in Washington. While at Howard she developed the "Quiet Storm," a format that became a signature in urban radio airing on nearly five hundred stations across the U.S.[395] Hughes went on to establish her media empire and to continue making media history as the first woman to own a radio station ranked number one in a major market, first African American woman to head a publicly traded corporation traded on the U.S. Stock Exchange, and the first Black woman inducted into the National Association of Broadcasters' Broadcasting Hall of Fame.[396]

Nebraska was also the training ground for nationally prominent athletes. The year 1961 saw Gayle E. Sayers graduate from Omaha Central High School as a star athlete. He went on to become a highly successful professional football player. A member of the Pro Football Hall of Fame, he is consistently cited as one of the greatest Nebraska football players of all time.[397] The 1971 film *Brian's Song*, based on Sayers' autobiographical account of his friendship with a teammate who struggled with cancer, made Sayers a household name among millions of Americans who never once saw a football game.[398] Bob Boozer was a star professional basketball player from Nebraska. After graduating from Technical High School in Omaha in 1954, he was a star athlete in college. He went on to win a gold medal in the 1960 Summer Olympics and won an NBA Championship as a member of the Milwaukee Bucks in 1971.[399] Bob Gibson, a gifted athlete in several sports, played for the Harlem Globetrotters in 1957 before signing with the St. Louis Cardinals professional baseball team. An all-star nine years in a row, he won two world

---

391. "Former Budget Director Program Officer in Korea," *Lincoln Journal Star*, June 26, 1959, 6.
392. Dennis Dickerson, *Militant Mediator: Whitney M. Young Jr.* (Lexington: University Press of Kentucky, 1998), 130-131.
393. Ann Wead Kimbrough, *Above and Beyond: How a Tall, Lanky Kid from the Omaha Housing Projects spent a Lifetime Helping Others Top Their Dreams* (Awvb Publishing, 2021), 12.
394. Adam Fletcher Sasse, "A History of KOWH, North Omaha's Radio Station," North Omaha History, September 15, 2016, https://northomahahistory.com/2016/09/15/kowh-was-north-omahas-radio-station/.
395. "About Cathy Hughes," Cathy Hughes School of Communication, Howard University, https://communications.howard.edu/about-cathy-hughes, accessed July 13, 2024.
396. "Cathy Hughes," History Makers, September 21, 2004 and March 2, 2005,
397. Dirk Chatelain, *24th & Glory: the Intersection of Civil Rights and Omaha's Greatest Generation of Athletes* (Omaha: Omaha World-Herald, 2019), 8.
398. Mary McNamara, "Gale Sayers and 'Brian's Song' changed sports movies, and male friendship, forever," *Los Angeles Times*, September 24, 2020, https://www.latimes.com/entertainment-arts/story/2020-09-24/gale-sayers-dead-brians-song-sports-movies-male-friendship.
399. Steve Marantz, *Rhythm Boys of Omaha Central* (University of Nebraska Press, 2011), 47.

series and was a National League MVP in 1968. The Baseball Hall of Fame inducted him in 1981.[400]

Preston Love Jr. became the first Black athlete from Omaha to be drafted by a NFL team, the Detroit Lions, in 1964. After earning advanced degrees he became an educator in Black Studies, a community organizer in North Omaha, and entered national politics as campaign manager for Jesse Jackson's 1984 presidential bid and as a two-time candidate for the United States Senate.[401] Nebraskan Marlin Briscoe a star athlete in multiple sports at Omaha South High School, became the first Black quarterback in professional football when he signed with the Denver Broncos in 1968 and played professionally for nine years.[402] Johnny Rogers, after playing in the National Football League, winning a Heisman Trophy and being named Cornhusker Player of the Century, came back to Omaha and became a community leader and successful entrepreneur.[403]

Nebraska's Black athletes' excellence in their sports was a gift to the community in itself, but their willingness to dedicate their platforms and resources for civil rights and opportunity for all made an especially powerful contribution to the movement for true equality. Their ability to command the attention and respect from Black and white audiences enabled them to tell the truth about race in America, and in Nebraska, and, most significantly, to be heard.

The combined efforts of Nebraska's civil rights activists made several early significant gains in Omaha in 1963. There were several organizations and individuals at the forefront including the Citizens Coordinating Committee for Civil Liberties, or 4CL. Founded by Rev. Dr. Kelsey A. Jones and Reverend Rudolph McNair, its leaders included Dorothy Eure, Mildred Brown, and Raymond Metoyer Sr. Focused on direct action and nonviolent civil disobedience, 4CL held protests around Omaha to end Jim Crow segregation using picketing, stand-ins during City Council meetings, teach-ins, and other efforts to foster positive structural changes throughout the city. Saying, "Omaha is the Mississippi of the North," the organization diagnosed the city saying it "perpetuated... the familiar pattern of economic and social discrimination, segregation and calculated degradation." An *Omaha Star* article continued saying, "As for what we want—First, we do not want any measure of compromise. We do not want any revenge. We want justice. We want full citizenship, and we want it now!"[404]

4CL campaigns focused on housing, jobs and education and targeted a variety of organizations and businesses including Omaha City Council, Omaha Human Rights Commission, Reed's Ice Cream, the *Omaha World-Herald*, Coca Cola Bottling Company, and the S.S. Kresge Company store, among many others.[405] One former 4CL member described the group's work saying, "We integrated different places and we petitioned for jobs and open housing. We marched on city hall. We did things like this that brought about some changes. We were considered troublemakers and that's what it takes to get the changes."[406] Continuing throughout the 1960s, the organization faced continuous controversy as the City of Omaha insulted their efforts and denied their authority. Mayor James Dworak referred to Jones and McNair as "yahoos" in the media. The 4CL's sponsoring organization, the Ministerial Alliance, publicly lambasted their activism and they broke off just six weeks after they started. In early 1963, the City of Omaha Human Rights Commission was

---

400. Gibson and Pepe 1968; Moffi and Kronstadt 1994, 111.Many years later, in 2015, the *Omaha World-Herald* ranked seven of the top hundred Nebraskan athletes of all-time from the neighborhood. They included the number one athlete, baseball player Bob Gibson (1935-2020), as well as football player Gale Sayers (1943-2020), basketball player Bob Boozer (1937-2012), football player Johnny Rodgers (1951), football player Marlin Briscoe (1945-2022), basketball player Ron Boone (1946) and football player Roger Sayers (1942). See Chatelain 2019, 8.
401. Aaron Sanderford, "Democrat Preston Love, a North Omaha Advocate, to Run for U.S. Sen. Pete Ricketts' Seat," *Nebraska Examiner*, January 11, 2024, https://nebraskaexaminer.com/2024/01/11/democrat-preston-love-a-north-omaha-advocate-to-run-for-u-s-sen-pete-ricketts-seat/, accessed July 7, 2024.
402. "Marlin Briscoe," National Football Foundation Hall of Fame. https://footballfoundation.org/hof_search.aspx?hof=2389; "Briscoe Statue Unveiled at Baxter Arena." Omaha Mavericks. September 23, 2016. https://omavs.com/news/2016/9/23/211185768 .
403. Chatelain, *24th and Glory*.
404. "An Ugly Story Told: Omaha Called 'Mississippi of North,'" *Omaha Star*, June 28, 1963.
405. Sam Castan, "The Negro Faces North. Omaha, Nebraska: The New Mood Shocks the City," *LOOK*, (December 17, 1963): 36-40.
406. Leo Adam Biga, "Goodwin's Spencer Street Barber Shop: We Cut Heads and Broaden Minds, Too," Leo Adam Biga's My Inside Stories, April 29, 2010, https://leoadambiga.com/2010/04/29/2010a.

Peony Park in Omaha locks its gates to resist integration, *Evening World-Herald*, July 17, 1963. Nebraska State Historical Society.

formed in response to the protests of 4CL. Immediately after, 4CL denounced the Commission as a puppet of the white leadership in the city.[407]

African American Airman Fred Winthrop and Captain Michael King also pushed back by pressing charges against the Malec family, owners of Peony Park, after being refused entry to the swimming pool in 1963. This renewed wave of racial discrimination crested just eight years after the Peony Park owners lost in the NAACP lawsuit. When city officials were reluctant to enforce the law, the NAACP Youth Council organized demonstrations outside the gates on Cass Street that lasted for months, significantly damaging the park's profits. Because of the force of the picketing and boycotting, Peony Park changed its means of discrimination. Peony Park became a private club that required swimmers to fill out an application to use the pool. White swimmers were admitted upon handing over their application and Black swimmers were told they needed sponsors, or that their applications were otherwise inadequate for admission.[408] News reports suggested that the Black youth asking to swim were attempting to instigate violence, but a young employee of Peony Park told his mother that he and his coworkers had been instructed to start a physical altercation with the Black protestors. The employee's mother, fearing an outbreak of violence, took the matter to a Catholic priest, who in turn reported the plan to the local news media. Under the force of public pressure and the moral censure of the Catholic Church Peony Park allowed all visitors to swim in the pool without regard to race and without an application. Omahans of all races swam at Peony Park until the park closed in 1993.[409]

The Civil Rights Movement had an impact on Nebraska communities well beyond Omaha. African American community leaders and activists and white allies organized to challenge discriminatory practices and push racial equality. Throughout the 1960s, there were protests, demonstrations, and initiatives to promote racial equality and combat racism in Lincoln and beyond. Less visible, though no less significant gains toward lasting change were also made. In 1961, a book called *The Hastings Negro Year Book: A Progressive Age for a Progressive People* was written by Mrs. Robert Starr and published by J. Edwin Ruffin. Its listings of names and addresses for Hastings' African American population in that year was just one community organizing tool developed in this decade.[410]

---

407. Adam Fletcher Sasse, "A History of the Citizens Coordinating Committee for Civil Liberties, or 4CL, in Omaha," North Omaha History, August 24, 2015, https://northomahahistory.com/2015/08/24/a-history-of-omahas-citizens-civic-committee-for-civil-liberties-or-4c.

408. David Bristow, "'We Just Wanted to Swim, Sir,'" *The Reader*, February 5, 2009.

409. David Bristow, "NAACP Youth Council's Peaceful Swimming Pool Protest Deemed "Hysteria" in 1963 Omaha," History Nebraska Blog, https://history.nebraska.gov/flashback-friday-naacp-youth-councils-peaceful-swimming-pool-protest-deemed-hysteria-in-1963-omaha/, accessed July 2, 2024.

410. "The Hastings Negro Year Book: a Progressive Age for a Progressive People/ [compiled by] Mrs. Robert Starr, an accomplished floral designer," (Hastings, NE: Mrs. R. Starr, 1961).

Mildred Brown, publisher of *The Omaha Star*, greets Lyndon B. President Johnson, 1965. Nebraska State Historical Society.

Malcolm X speaks in Omaha, June 30, 1964. Elmer Kral Collection, Nebraska State Historical Society.

Congress passed the Civil Rights Act of 1964 to extend civil, political, and legal rights and protections to all African Americans and to end segregation in public and private facilities. Seen as the pinnacle of the nonviolent civil disobedience movement led by Reverend Dr. Martin Luther King, Jr. and others, this act changed the course of daily life for every person in America. The Act prohibited racial discrimination in hotels, restaurants, theaters, and other public service providers, which were segregated for the century beforehand. It made workplace discrimination illegal and promoted equal employment opportunities for all people. Public schools other federally funded educational programs also had to stop discrimination, adding heft to the prior *Brown vs. Board of Education* ruling from the U.S. Supreme Court.

4CL brought Malcolm X back to his birthplace in 1964 to speak at the Civic Auditorium and make an appearance at Elks Hall on Lake Street in Omaha.[411]

Ernie Chambers, at that time in his formation as one of Nebraska's longest-serving legislators, wrote that hearing Malcolm X speak in person, in Omaha, had "profound significance" for the community.[412] The same year, Rev. Dr. Martin Luther King, Jr. returned to Nebraska to deliver "Christian Responsibility in the Racial Revolution" to five thousand attendees at the Methodist Student Movement Conference in Lincoln.[413] In it, he called upon the audience to recognize "the essential immorality of racial segregation" declaring, "We as Christians must see not only the unconstitutionality of segregation, we must reaffirm over and over again that racial segregation is sinful and immoral, whether it's in the public schools, whether it is in housing, whether it is in Christian church or any other area of life, segregation is morally wrong and sinful [because] it is based on human laws that are out of harmony with the moral, natural, and eternal laws of the universe."[414]

---

411. Duane Snodgrass, "Anything Whites Can Do Blacks Can Do Better," *Omaha World-Herald*, July 1, 1964.
412. Ernie Chambers, "Book Review: *Bertha W. Calloway and Alonzo M. Smith 'Visions of Freedom on the Great Plains: An Illustrated History of African Americans in Nebraska*," *Great Plains Quarterly* 20;2. (Spring 2020):168.
413. "King labels..." 1964. Audio of Dr. King's speech is available at History Nebraska: https://history.nebraska.gov/martin-luther-king-jr-visit-to-lincoln/#:~:text=On%20December%2030th%2C%201964%2C%20Martin,Responsibility%20in%20the%20Racial%20Revolution.
414. Martin Luther King, Jr., "Christian Responsibility in the Racial Revolution," Methodist Student Movement Conference, Lincoln, Nebraska, December 30, 1964, History Nebraska Digital Archives: https://history.nebraska.gov/martin-luther-king-jr-visit-to-lincoln/#:~:text=On%20December%2030th%2C%201964%2C%20Martin,Responsibility%20in%20the%20Racial%20Revolution

By the 1960s, nearly all the 29,262 African American residents forming 2.07 percent of the state's population of 1,411,000 people were concentrated in Omaha. However, a significant Black community existed in Lincoln, with small numbers of African Americans in other cities throughout the state. Limited job opportunities, lower wages, and occupational segregation were common in Lincoln, and despite college educated African Americans graduating from the University of Nebraska, the city relegated many Black workers to lower-paying and menial jobs despite their qualifications.[415]

African American students in Omaha did not fare much better. By 1961, there were fifty-seven African American teachers in the Omaha Public Schools represented a significant increase in number, but not a move toward desegregation. Omaha's Black teachers worked in the same seven schools, with eighty majority white schools without a single Black teacher. Not until 1959 was the first African American teacher hired to work at the secondary level. That school, Horace Mann Junior High, was the first majority Black secondary school in Omaha with a seventy-one percent African American student body. Black teachers were not hired to high schools in Omaha until 1963. Even after an affirmative action program hired more Black teachers in the 1960s, more than half of the district's ninety-eight schools had no African American faculty members in 1972.[416] In Lincoln, Forrest M. Stith became the first African American teacher in Lincoln Public Schools in 1955. Reverend Stith had been a traveling minister and an Army chaplain in World War II and returned to Lincoln after the war to earn bachelor's and master's degrees at the University of Nebraska. His son, Forrest C. Stith, was elected United Methodist bishop in 1984, the denomination's youngest bishop.[417]

Frustration built up over a century of racial injustice rose to the surface within Omaha's African American community with young people expressing it most visibly. The quality of schools, redlining in the housing market, police brutality and many other factors were readily talked about with little substantive response from government officials. Young people were acutely aware of the constant disadvantages they faced compared to their white counterparts. In the spring of 1966, accusations of vandalism increased exponentially in the North Omaha community while spontaneous gatherings of hundreds of youth and young adults happened in major intersections throughout the community. Police responded with arrests and citations, but the events continued happening with greater frequency and impact.[418]

Gathering in 103-degree heat, the first in a series of riots began in North Omaha when African American youth had an altercation with members of the Omaha Police Department. Demolishing police cars and smashing storefront windows up and down North 24th Street, the riots continued unchecked for three days. After the Nebraska National Guard was assigned to the neighborhood and city and state government officials started meeting with rioting youth, the state government and national organizations made promises for changes focused on afterschool activities and youth activities, the riots stopped.

However, this was a pause and not a cessation in the violent protests. Before the end of the month, the Nebraska National Guard was called in to stop more rioting in North Omaha.[419] According to one observer, "As money was flowing to meet the demands of the rioters, it was also moving to arm the police department in the event of another riot." The Omaha Police Department stocked up on anti-riot gear and weaponry and dispersed them liberally to all police expected to engage in the struggles they anticipated returning—and return they did.[420]

A second riot started one month later when an off-duty policeman shot and killed an African American youth named Eugene Nesbitt. Following his funeral, crowds on North 24th Street threw Molotov cocktails and broke windows. Buildings throughout North Omaha were firebombed and destruction was widespread over the next several days. The Omaha mayor claimed that the riots were orchestrated by the Black

---

415. Hildebrand, "The New Negro Movement in Lincoln, Nebraska,", 169; Lincoln Commission on Human Rights "LCHR's Redlining: Designed Inequity, A Local Perspective Display and Accompanying Presentation," April 23, 2021, YouTube video, 37:32.
416. Gary Bennett, "A Study of Court-Ordered Desegregation in The School District of Omaha, Nebraska, 1972-1977," PhD diss. University of Nebraska – Lincoln, 1979, 34-37; Wilbert H. Bledsoe, *The Status and Perceptions of Black School Administrators in Omaha*, PhD diss, Oklahoma State University. 1984, 4, 9.
417. Cindy Lange-Kubick, "Trailblazing Teacher," *Lincoln Journal Star*, February 6, 2018, A3.
418. "Police Beef Up after North Side Vandalism," *Omaha World-Herald*, April 2, 1967.
419. Howard, "Then the Burning Began," 33-39; Steve Marantz, *The Rhythm Boys of Omaha Central: High School Basketball at the '68 Racial Divide* (Lincoln: Bison Original, 2011), 25.
420. Howard, "Then the Burning Began," 47.

Civil rights march at 24th and Ohio streets, Omaha, 1968. © Rudy Smith/*Omaha World-Herald*

Panther Party, placing the blame on the Black community. The Nebraska governor told the media it happened because the rioters lived in "an environment unfit for human habitation."[421] Since his concessions to Black youth after the July riots in July did not produce the results that he wanted, the governor said, "there will be no deals with hoodlums again in connection with racial violence." The white media in Omaha concentrated on Nesbitt's race and criminal record without questioning the actions of the policeman who shot him in the back.[422]

More than one thousand protesters showed up to Omaha City Council meetings in 1966 to oppose plans to "rehabilitate" the Near North Side neighborhood, including the construction of the North Freeway. Demolishing more than one thousand homes, churches, businesses, and other public places, the construction of the North Freeway bisected Omaha's historic African American neighborhood. Creating massive earthen berms, moving commuters through the community without connecting to the people and services, and obliterating the physical and metaphysical fabric of the neighborhoods therein have lasting effects that are still being felt today.[423]

Charging the city with the erasure of Black history and the promotion of white supremacy, Black protests apparently went unheard. Several noted Nebraska African American community leaders were openly vocal against the project, including Ernie Chambers

---

421. Marantz, *The Rhythm Boys of Omaha Central*, 25.
422. Ali Johnson 2012, 47; The riots were captured in a documentary film called *A Time for Burning* was released in 1966. It is the story of a white Lutheran congregation in Omaha that tried reaching out to the Black community in North Omaha and featured a young Ernie Chambers. It also featured footage of the riots that summer. Nominated for Best Documentary Feature in the 1967 Academy Awards, the film was included in the Library of Congress National Film Registry in 2015. Carter n.d.
423. Center for Public Affairs Research. 1992. *The State of Black Omaha: Housing Conditions*. University of Nebraska at Omaha, 5.

and Brenda Council, among others.[424] Related protest arose over the construction of the Sorensen Parkway in the 1990s, again protested by Chambers along with Fred Conley. This construction led to a two-and-one-half mile long trunk jutting through the city's historic African American neighborhood that ends abruptly where white neighborhoods effectively stopped its construction.[425]

March 1968 brought a new wave of protests when Alabama governor George Wallace announced a campaign stop in Omaha to promote his white supremacist campaign for president. A crowd of young Black and white activists protested at the Civic Auditorium. After counter-protesters began acting violently toward the youth activists, police beat dozens of protesters. An African American youth was shot and killed by a police officer during the melee and fleeing protesters supposedly caused thousands of dollars of damage to businesses and cars. Soon after, an African American 16-year-old named Howard L. Stevenson was shot dead by an off-duty policeman during a riot on March 5, 1968. Despite using a riot gun while off-duty, the policeman was never charged with a crime.[426] Young Ernie Chambers stopped a potential riot by students at Horace Mann Junior High School by talking to them about the issues they faced—and listening to what they had to say.[427]

The Omaha chapter of the Black Panther Party opened its office in North Omaha in 1968. Their mission was fully in practice by the next year, defending African Americans from the effects of racism by leading several free breakfast programs, summer Freedom Schools, and clothing drives. The Black Panthers' defense of African Americans from white supremacy included carrying firearms to protect them from racial violence and police brutality. The organization became a lightning rod for the media and politicians, who turned white Nebraskans against the organization. That summer, Nebraska media and politicians repeatedly blamed the BPP for riots, sniping incidents, firebombings, and break-ins throughout North Omaha.

A wave of rioting began in June 1969 after a fourteen-year-old African American girl named Vivian Strong was shot and killed by a white Omaha police officer as she ran from him. A judge found the officer innocent of manslaughter and released him on a $500 bond. After several days of unrest, the Nebraska governor again called in the Nebraska National Guard and the riot was quelled on June 24. This last major riot in Nebraska was seen by most people as the final nail in the coffin for the commercial sector along North 24th Street, North 16th Street and other areas in the Near North Side.[428] In July 1969, there was a late-night shooting, and several items were stolen from the Omaha Black Panthers (BPP) headquarters. After a disagreement with the national BPP, Omaha's chapter was closed.

The end of the Omaha BPP did not bring an end to Black activism. Within days, a group of former Omaha Black Panthers led by Edward Poindexter, a Vietnam veteran who became a delegate to the 1968 Democratic National Convention. formed the National Committee to Combat Fascism.[429] That year, student activists at UNO called Black Liberators for Action on Campus started to address issues related to African Americans in higher education, including the creation of a Black Studies program at the university. More than fifty African American students led a sit-in at the UNO president's office and some of their demands were met.[430]

Regardless of what anyone might have believed about African Americans' "place" in the state of Nebraska, their influence, contributions, and centrality to life in the state was undeniable. So too were their multiple gains in the Civil Rights struggle.

---

424. Sharra Lynne Montag, *A Game of Roads: the North Omaha Freeway and Historic Near North Side*, MLS Thesis, Creighton University, 2015, 9.
425. "The Bulldozers Are Coming...," *Omaha Star*, October 14, 1966.
426. Charlotte Reilly, "'Nothing Wrong with Prejudice and Discrimination:' Omaha Newspaper Coverage of the Civil Rights Movement in 1968," Thesis. University of Nebraska at Omaha, 2019.
427. United States Congress, House, 91st Congress 2nd Session, *Hearings Before the Committee on Internal Security: Black Panther Operations and Investigation Activities in Des Moines, Iowa, and Omaha, Nebr.*(Washington: USGPO, October-November 1970); Joshua Bloom and Waldo E. Martin, Black Against Empire: The History and Politics of the Black Panther Party (Berkeley: University of California Press, 2016), 2, 192.
428. Howard, Ashley M., "Then the burning began: Omaha, riots, and the growth of black radicalism, 1966-1969" (2006). Student Work. 552. https://digitalcommons.unomaha.edu/studentwork/552.
429. Yohuru Williams, "Introduction," *Liberated Territory: Untold Local Perspectives on the Black Panther Party*, ed. Yohuru Williams and Jama Lazerow (Durham, NC: Duke University Press 2009), 1-23.
430. Leo Adam Biga, "Coloring History: A Long, Hard Road for UNO Black Studies," Leo Adam Biga's My Inside Stories, 2010, https://leoadambiga.com/2010/08/25/coloring-history-a-long-hard-road-for-uno-black-studies/

People at Omaha house displaying a banner for the Black Panthers Party-led National Committee to Combat Fascism. *Omaha World-Herald*/John Savage Photography Collection at The Durham Museum.

State statutes reflected this fact with the passage of the Nebraska Civil Rights Act of 1969. This new civil rights law focused on housing and prohibited discrimination based on race, color, religion, or national origin, but explicitly excluded gender. Blockbusting, race-restrictive covenants, and other typical racist tactics were made explicitly illegal. Yet throughout the 1970s, Nebraska remained stubbornly racially segregated in public spaces like restaurants, bars, hotels, theaters, and other establishments. Due to "sundown town" practices statewide, African Americans were often denied service in towns across the state. In Lincoln and other cities, when Black customers were served, they were restricted to specific areas of restaurants and theaters and given unequal treatment. As with Omaha, the specific experiences of individual African Americans varied throughout the state.[431]

Firefighters battle blaze on June 24, 1969, after North Omaha riot. © Rudy Smith/*Omaha World-Herald*.

Nebraska's post-civil rights era is marked by the ongoing physical depletion of the state's Black

---

431. James W. Loewen, *Sundown Towns: A Hidden Dimension of American Racism* (New York: New Press, 2005), 96, 218, 187, 265.

community in the 1970s with fewer dwellings within Black neighborhoods, longer commutes to get to education and work, physical barriers dividing the largest Black neighborhood, and the widening gulf between white Omaha and Black Omaha. The national trend of white flight from cities to suburbs was reflected in the simultaneous loss of 56 percent of North Omaha's white residents and twenty-seven percent gain in Black residents.[432]

Nebraska's Black business community, most of which was in North Omaha, was decimated by the disinvestment that came with white flight, along with benign neglect on the part of city and county authorities.[433] An analysis of 1970 U.S. Census data concluded, "If a ghetto is described as a quarter of a city where minority group members are forced to live because of social, legal, and economic pressures, then the Omaha ghetto has not changed significantly in the past decade,"[434] noting that less than .5 percent of the population of Omaha west of North 48th Street was Black, with just one in thirty-five Black people living west of that street.[435]

Many of the Black-owned restaurants and nightspots, hardware and furniture stores, clothing stores, beauty shops and barbers, auto parts shops and more that lined the North Omaha throughfares around North 24th Street all but disappeared. The Black professional offices, including doctors, dentists, lawyers, accountants, and funeral homes all left the community. The issue of school busing also brought Nebraska into the national spotlight. Busing, a program for desegregating schools adopted by many U.S. cities in the 1970s, ended for the Omaha Public School district in 1999. The voter-approved measure to end busing was affirmed by the U.S. Supreme Court in *United States of America v. The School District of Omaha, State of Nebraska* 1974.

Ed Poindexter and David Rice at Omaha Courthouse after 1971 conviction. © Rudy Smith/*Omaha World-Herald*.

A 1996 analysis by the *Omaha World-Herald* found that the initial goal of the Omaha Public Schools desegregation plan—that no Black students attend mostly Black schools—was never met.[436] The same report found that in 1995, for the first time since 1976, most African American elementary students attended schools that were mostly Black. Resegregation almost immediately set in and white flight to suburban school districts around Omaha continued.[437] In 2019, a study of 242 cities nationwide by the UNO Center for Public Affairs Research found Omaha Public Schools are more segregated than most others.[438] A pattern initially identified by the U.S. Supreme Court's 1976 ruling against Omaha's school system, these findings were reinforced by independent data in 2022.[439]

The racial divide grew greater in 1970 when a bombing in North Omaha killed a patrolman with the Omaha Police Department. Within hours, the department arrested twenty-five African Americans in North Omaha. Twenty were charged with minor

---

432. John P. Zipay, "1970 First Count Census Data: Population and Housing Characteristics for Douglas County, Nebraska," 1971, University of Nebraska at Omaha, 4.
433. Marantz, 95; Calloway and Smith 1998, *Visions of Freedom on the Great Plains*, 37.
434. John P. Zipay, "1970 First Count Census Data: Population and Housing Characteristics for Douglas County, Nebraska," 1971, University of Nebraska at Omaha, 4.
435. Zipay 1971, "1970 First Count Census Data," 5.
436. Nygren, Judith, "Busing for Integration: A 20-Year Perspective - Integration Facts Norbert Schuerman," February 12, 1996, Omaha World-Herald, accessed August 9, 2024 from newsbank.com.
437. Buttry, S., James-Johnson, A., "Busing Debate Revives Fears of Past Opponents Proponents How Omaha's Busing Program Works," July 15, 1996, Omaha World-Herald, accessed August 9, 2024 from newsbank.com.
438. Center for Public Affairs Research, 2019, "Metro Area School Segregation." University of Nebraska Omaha, accessed August 9, 2024 from https://www.unomaha.edu/college-of-public-affairs-and-community-service/governing/archive/metro-area-school-segreation.php.
439. Bridget Fogarty, "In One Heavily Segregated City, the Pandemic Accelerated a Wave of White Flight," *The Hechinger Report*, March 15, 2022, https://hechingerreport.org/in-one-heavily-segregated-city-the-pandemic-accelerated-a-wave-of-white-flight/.

infractions, while five were held for the bombing. Two were eventually charged, Wopashitwe Mondo Eyen we Langa, born David Rice, and Edward Poindexter. The court sentenced both men to life in prison in 1971, where we Langa died in 2016 and Poindexter in late 2023. Even in the face of numerous appeals, retrials, presentations of new evidence, recent research indicating a law enforcement coverup and conspiracy to indict these Black community leaders, and the designation of we Langa and Poindexter as political prisoners, their sentences remained in place.[440]

While he was in prison, from 1971 until his death in 2016, Mondo we Langa continued his activism as editor of the *Harambee Flame*, the official newsletter of Harambee Afrikan Cultural Organization (HACO). The *Flame* was published by African American men of HACO imprisoned in Tecumseh and Lincoln. HACO continues today as a "self-betterment club" that "provides an opportunity to explore the root of the African American culture and heritage, including the past, present and future."[441] We Langa published articles, opinion pieces, short stories, memoir, and poetry from unpublished writers who foregrounded the power they drew from their African heritages. The journal was, above all, a repudiation of white supremacist stereotypes of Black men, a disproportionate number of whom were incarcerated.

Ernie Chambers began his service in the Nebraska Legislature amidst these tensions in 1971. He campaigned for a seat on the Omaha School Board in 1969 while still a student at Creighton Law School. Although he lost both elections, Chambers would emerge as a steadfast advocate for civil rights and, on this basis, started his first of what would be a record number of terms in the state legislature. The "Defender of the Downtrodden" fought to overturn the death penalty, end corporal punishment in Nebraska's public schools, mandate a grand jury investigation when a person dies in police custody, eliminate sales tax on groceries, adopt district-based voting to give nonwhite citizens a fair shot at election to public office, bar the execution of juveniles and those with intellectual disabilities, ensure equal state pensions to women, and establish government liability for bystanders injured in police chases. Senator Chambers put Nebraska at the forefront of national

Ernie Chambers at the Spencer Street Barbershop, October 1970. © Rudy Smith/*Omaha World-Herald*.

and international leadership by moving Nebraska to divest its assets from South Africa in 1980, as an act of resistance to its racist system of apartheid. Nebraska voters' approval of an amendment to the state constitution imposing term limits on state legislators put Chambers' service in the Unicameral on pause in 2009. The voters elected him back to the Unicameral from 2013 to 2020. Now in his post-legislative career, Chambers remains one of Nebraska's most effective leaders in his post-legislative career as a voice for civil rights and religious freedom, a community and political organizer, and a mentor and role model for a new generation of leaders.[442]

The turn of the millennium brought a mixed picture of great success and work to be done to fulfill Nebraska's motto of "equality before the law" and the first freedom seekers' vision of a prosperous, self-determined life for the 68,541 Black members of Nebraska's 1,711,263 population.[443] African Americans held leadership positions in lawmaking, law enforcement,

---

440 Richardson 2018; Robert Bartle, "Rice-Poindexter: A 50-Year Legal Odyssey," *Nebraska Lawyer*, May/June 2021.

441. Harambee Afrikan Cultural Association, *Harambee Flame*, collection http://lunacollections.lunaimaging.com/luna/servlet/detail/lunacol~1~1~1063~223?qvq=w4s:/who%2FHarambee%2BFlame%2F&mi=0&trs=1.

442. Tekla Agbala Ali Johnson, *Free Radical: Ernest Chambers, Black Power and the Politics of Race*, (Lubbock: Texas Tech University Press, 2016).

and in adjudicating the laws. In 2003, the first Black police chief of the Omaha Police Department was hired by the City of Omaha. Thomas Warren served twenty-eight years with the department, including four years as chief. After retiring from government, he became president and CEO of the Urban League of Nebraska. Starting in 2021 he became the Omaha mayor's chief of staff.[444] In 2005, Marlon Polk became the first African American appointed to serve as a district court judge in Nebraska. He was appointed to the seat after graduating from University of Nebraska-Lincoln and Creighton and working as a private attorney for almost a decade. He continues serving as a district court judge today.

Nebraska's African American leaders became increasingly competitive candidates for national office in the post-Civil Rights era. Ernie Chambers ran for a U.S. Senate seat in 1988. Although he lost the Senate race, Chambers made history as the first African American in Nebraska to run for the seat. Preston Love Jr. entered the national political scene in 1984 as the campaign organizer and national manager for Jesse Jackson's bid for the presidency. Love, like Chambers, campaigned for the U.S. Senate in a history-making write-in campaign in 2020.[445] At the time of this writing, in 2024, Nebraska had yet to elect a Black person to Congress.[446]

Conclusion

This historical account of African Americans in Nebraska ends in 2008, the year when community organizer, constitutional scholar, and Illinois Senator Barack Obama was elected the first Black president of the United States of America. From this point onward, scholars, researchers, writers, students, and the public have been examining the roles of African Americans in Nebraska as never before, bringing to light the bold, powerful effects of Black people in the state. This contribution underscores the many ways in which African Americans have enacted American values of freedom, equality, and democracy in Nebraska. It also reveals the persistence of systemic racism, decades and generations after Abraham Lincoln put his Emancipation Proclamation into effect. It was 2006 when a Nebraska state trooper was found to be a Ku Klux Klan member who was active in Klan chatrooms. At first, he evaded termination from the force by invoking the arbitration clause state's collective bargaining agreement. The Nebraska Supreme Court called for the trooper's dismissal, finding that the decision reached in arbitration to retain him on the force violated "the explicit, well-defined, and dominant public policy that laws should be enforced without racial or religious discrimination, and the public should reasonably perceive this to be so." The trooper was fired permanently—though not automatically.[447]

The hesitation to fire the Klan-affiliated law enforcement officer took place in a state whose largest city, Omaha, had a 30 percent Black poverty rate with Black child poverty at 59.4 percent. Omaha ranked 25th among the one hundred U.S. metropolitan areas with the highest Black poverty rates, putting it ahead of New Orleans, Detroit, Chicago, New York, and Los Angeles. With the exception of Minneapolis, Omaha had the highest Black poverty rate of any Midwestern city.[448] While African American poverty in Omaha had been referred to as "irretractable" and "stubborn" in the past, this statistical evidence shows the city has failed to make significant progress in rectifying income inequality perpetuated by white supremacy since Omaha's founding.

Throughout the state's history, systemic racism in Nebraska has been strengthened by Jim Crow segregation, racial discrimination, and numerous forms of social and economic forces—some subtle, others extreme. After experiencing enslavement, Black people faced white supremacy *en masse* throughout the state during the Civil War, while Reconstruction was underway, and afterward. Forced to migrate from the

---

443. U.S. Census Bureau, Summary Population and Housing Characteristics PHC-1-29, Nebraska, (Washington: USGPO, 2002) 60.
444. Reece Ristau, "Stothert Picks Ex-Police Chief for Post - Stothert Names Thomas Warren Sr., former Omaha Police Chief, as Next Chief of Staff," *Omaha World-Herald*, June 4, 2021.
445. Preston Love, Jr., "The Jackson Papers: Post 1965 Voting Rights Act, Pre-Obama Era: The Jesse Jackson Run for President," (Omaha: Preston Publishing. 2018), 4.
446. Ali Johnson, *Free Radical*, 175.
447. Michael German, "Hidden in Plain Sight: Racism, White Supremacy, and Far-Right Militancy in Law Enforcement" Brennan Center for Justice, August 27, 2020, https://www.brennancenter.org/our-work/research-reports/hidden-plain-sight-racism-white-supremacy-and-far-right-militancy-law.
448. Henry J. Cordes, Cindy Gonzalez & Erin Grace, "Omaha in Black and White: Poverty amid Prosperity," *Omaha World-Herald*, April 15, 2007.

South because of racism, new Nebraskans faced Jim Crow segregation in their new state. While the forces of the Dust Bowl were merciless on everyone in the state, Black people were disproportionately impacted. The world wars drove men to join the military and women to support their families and communities, ironically instilling a commitment to democracy never seen before known and hard fought to exist in the future. Following those phenomena, a trend continued of Black people moving away from Nebraska or gravitating to Omaha and Lincoln. With that said, the African American presence in Nebraska is now completely urban-centered among the city's largest population centers.

To understand the post-civil rights era in Nebraska, and for the benefit of future researchers and readers, it is important to acknowledge the Black population centers in Nebraska today, and the Black people in Nebraska who are now making history.

In Lincoln, Sändra Washington and Bennie Shobe serve on the City Council, which welcomed its first Black member in 1969 when Harry W. "Pete" Peterson was elected. Lincoln was also home to Sen. JoAnn Maxey, who became the first Black member of the Lincoln Board of Education in 1975, and in 1977, the first Black woman to serve in the Nebraska Legislature. No African Americans were serving on Lincoln's school board and or in its legislative delegation in 2024.

Several leaders in Omaha should be noted, such as Willie Barney and the Empowerment Network, Preston Love Jr. with his activism and a record-breaking 2020 campaign for U.S. Senate, Carmen Tapio for her business success and others. Sens. Terrell McKinney (2020-) and Justin Wayne (2017-2025) represent North Omaha in the Legislature. In the media sector Black leaders today include Terri D. Sanders of *The Omaha Star* and Paul B. Allen IV of 1st Sky Omaha, who are creating a powerful space for "practicing journalism as activism." Culxr House, a nonprofit founded in 2019, was started by Marcy Yates to be a safe and empowering place for artistic expression.

Many other Black leaders abound in Nebraska into the 2020s. There are particular trailblazing Black people in Nebraska today including Dr. Cheryl Logan, who became the first African American superintendent of the Omaha Public Schools (2018-2023); Veta Jeffery who was the first Black president of the Omaha Chamber of Commerce (2022-2023); Ben Gray, who became the first African American City Council member elected for four terms (2009-2021); Chris Rodgers, who became the first Black chair of both the Douglas County Commission (on the Commission 2005 to present) and Douglas County Health Board; Precious McKesson, became the first African American presidential elector representing Nebraska in 2020; and Terence "Bud" Crawford, who became a World Boxing Champion.

Beyond individuals and organizations, other efforts are emerging as well, including popular history awareness campaigns and increasing academic awareness in Omaha's higher education institutions focused on white supremacy through redlining and other institutional racism. For a decade, the Omaha Public Schools have hosted a summer history program for high school students called Making Invisible History Visible to learn about Omaha's past through the lenses of low-income people and people of color. Each of these is a start to something greater.

This review of more than four hundred years of history has made apparent the holes in Nebraska's African American historical canon. Areas including Black politics, the Black church, self-sufficiency and the Black economy, the arts and community organizing require greater depth of exploration. The experience of enslaved Blacks in Nebraska was written off by white supremacist historians; this area demands critical examination. Monolithic representations of Black excellence, particularly in the areas of athletics and entertainment, require more nuance and context. We still know too little about the cross-state pioneer Black experience, the ongoing presence of Black entrepreneurship, the emergence of *de facto* and *de jure* segregation statewide, and the federal government's incursions into Nebraskan Black autonomy.

This study intends to be the catalyst for the study and dissemination of the history of African Americans in Nebraska—not its end.

Voices of Latinidad: A Truth and Reconciliation Movement to Preserve Latino and Latina History

By J.S. Onésimo (Ness) Sándoval

Abstract

This chapter began as a quest to tell the story of Latinidad in Nebraska. It is not meant to be a historical account of Latinos or Latinidad, nor a socioeconomic analysis. Instead, it has evolved into an accessible narrative highlighting the accomplishments of Latinos in Nebraska. The accounts and data presented serve as a public testimony and starting point for discussions that acknowledge Latinos' presence. These accounts were not designed as an academic treatment for scholarly work but aim to inspire future scholars to research the lives and accomplishments of Latinos in Nebraska. Latinos have long been an integral part of Nebraska's social fabric, contributing significantly to its cultural diversity. As the largest minority group in Nebraska, Latinos play a vital role in shaping the state's demographics. According to the latest census, Latinos are in every county, showcasing their widespread presence. Several counties are experiencing growth in Latino populations, leading to vibrant Latino communities in cities like Schuyler and Lexington, known as "Latino Pueblos." Additionally, several census tracts now have a Latino majority, reflecting their increasing influence. This demographic shift underscores the growing importance of Latino contributions to the state's social, economic, and political landscape. Their continued presence and influence will undoubtedly shape Nebraska's future for generations to come.[1]

---

1. I would like to express my sincere gratitude to the ROJ leadership for their invaluable guidance and support throughout this project. Special thanks to Annabell Hazelton and Ellie Heinrichs, the research assistants, for their dedication and effort. I also appreciate Vanessa de Becze, a Ph.D. student at St. Louis University, for her insightful feedback and constructive comments on the penultimate draft of this chapter. Lastly, I extend my heartfelt thanks to all the participants in the Nebraska listening session, whose voices and contributions were greatly valued.

  Figures and Tables can be enlarged for greater readability in the online version of the chapter.

In *Roots of Justice: A History of Race and Racism in Nebraska*. Edited by Kevin Abourezk, with an Introduction by M. Dewayne Mays and Paul A. Olson (Lincoln, Nebraska: Truth and Reconciliation Nebraska, 2025). Copyright © 2025 by the authors; CC-BY. DOI: 10.32873/unl.dc.rj5

La Historia Latina

The Roots of Justice (ROJ) project serves as a platform for capturing and amplifying the diverse voices and perspectives that have shaped Nebraska's history. ROJ provides an opportunity to uncover and share stories that challenge the dominant historical narrative and shed light on the experiences of marginalized communities, including Latinos. By giving voice to these narratives, ROJ aims to disrupt the prevailing notion that discrimination and marginalization were minimal towards minority groups in Nebraska's history (Marzen 2013).[2] Through the personal accounts and lived experiences shared within the project, ROJ seeks to illuminate the realities of discrimination, resilience, and resistance faced by Latinos and other marginalized communities. By presenting a more inclusive and comprehensive historical view, ROJ contributes to a deeper understanding of the diverse fabric of Nebraska's history and fosters a more inclusive and just society.

By embracing the power of storytelling and providing a platform for previously unheard voices, ROJ invites individuals from different generations and backgrounds to contribute their perspectives, ensuring that Nebraska's history is told from multiple vantage points. This collaborative and participatory approach encourages dialogue, empathy, and a deeper appreciation for the experiences and contributions of all Nebraskans.

In fact, when Latinos are given the opportunity to tell their story, you will hear stories of contested struggle to find a space of identity, to find justice, and to find equity (Winston 2019). If we listen carefully, we can hear the voices of our children, parents, and grandparents. This chapter of ROJ provides an analytical lens to understand the history of Latinos living in Nebraska. Too often, when we read the history of Nebraska, some voices are missing, excluded, or ignored. The goal of this chapter is to begin a conversation that includes the experiences and contributions of Latinos in Nebraska, as told by those once-excluded voices. We, as a people, need to know our history as we build new businesses, communities, and friendships. There are many different paths for Latino voices. There is value in listening to the previous generation of Latinos. This chapter is not a comprehensive history of Latinos in Nebraska. To write that history would require several volumes. Rather, the goal of this chapter is to write a public history about the major milestones, events, and people who made and continue to make Nebraska their home.

Latinidad

In this chapter, the term "Latinidad" is used to encompass the shared cultural, historical, and social experiences of individuals typically classified as Hispanic or Latino (Aparicio 2003). While different terms such as Hispanic, Latino, Chicano, and Latinx [3] are used by individuals in Nebraska to describe their identities (Chávez-Moreno 2021), Latinidad remains a powerful and dynamic concept that captures the lived experiences of Latinos. It challenges mainstream narratives about race relationships and represents resilience and resistance against discrimination and marginalization (Chavez 2009).

Latinidad in Nebraska has shaped identities and influenced the cultural and political landscapes, with a distinct history that is reflected in rural and urban migration patterns (Bacon 2016; Rochín 2000). The term goes beyond the ethnic categories created by the census and provides a more inclusive understanding of identity. It recognizes the complexities and nuances within the Latino community, acknowledging the diversity of backgrounds, histories, and perspectives that contribute to a collective sense of belonging.

While Latinidad is not officially recognized by the census, it serves as a valuable lens to comprehend the multidimensional aspects of Latino identities. It highlights the richness of the Latino socioeconomic identity and embraces cultural heritage and collective experiences. However, for the purpose of analyzing demographic patterns, data using the categories of "Hispanic" or "Latino" is relied upon.

It is important to acknowledge that the categories used to describe lived experiences of Hispanics/Latinos are fluid and subject to change. The U.S. Census Bureau is anticipated to modify its definition of "Hispanic/Latino" (Mora 2014; Dávila 2012; Rodríguez

---

2. One of the examples of the discrimination was the Fremont Immigrant Ordinance. https://fremontne.gov/DocumentCenter/View/770/Ordinance-5165-Immigration-PDF?bidId=.

3. A publication by Pew Research Center found that 3 percent of Hispanics use Latinx. (Noe-Bustamante, Mora, and Lopez 2020).

2000).[4] Additionally, considering an individual's immigration status is crucial in understanding the complexities of Latino identification and its impact on experiences and access to resources.

Approaching discussions about Latino identity with sensitivity is essential, recognizing that it is a multifaceted concept influenced by cultural and legal aspects. This chapter primarily focuses on the current understanding of Latino identity as defined by the U.S. Census, while acknowledging the additional layer of complexity brought by immigration status.[5] By appreciating the intersectionality and nuances within the Latino community, a comprehensive understanding of Latino identity can be achieved.

Latino Geographies

In this chapter, the evidence gathered over eighteen months was examined within a socioeconomic framework to shed light on agriculture's role in attracting the first wave of Mexican immigrants to settle in Nebraska. Figure 1 illustrates the significance of agriculture in creating job opportunities that attracted immigrants. This figure offers an analytical lens through which to systematically study the impacts of agriculture in both urban and rural Nebraska. This framework serves as a heuristic tool to understand the central role of agriculture in shaping both urban and rural regions of Nebraska. It also provides a map for exploring the influence of *Latinidad* in these areas, whether rural or urban.

Additionally, using this heuristic, the research reveals the emergence of different types of Latino destinations, with some new destinations evolving into Latino-majority towns, or "Latino-majority Pueblos." These towns, which did not exist in the early twentieth century, offer valuable insights into the intersection of race, immigration, ethnicity, and the political economy in these areas, as depicted in Figure 2.

These figures serve as a catalyst for future research agendas aimed at comprehensively understanding the historical demographic transitions of Latinos that occurred in the early twentieth century, as well as the ongoing demographic shifts taking place across Nebraska. The transitions in Nebraska's Latino population are influenced by different waves of immigration and internal migration within the Latino

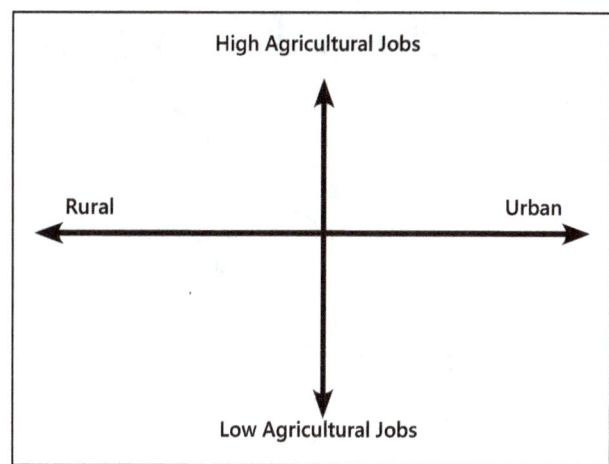

Figure 1. A conceptual framework to understand historical and contemporary migration.

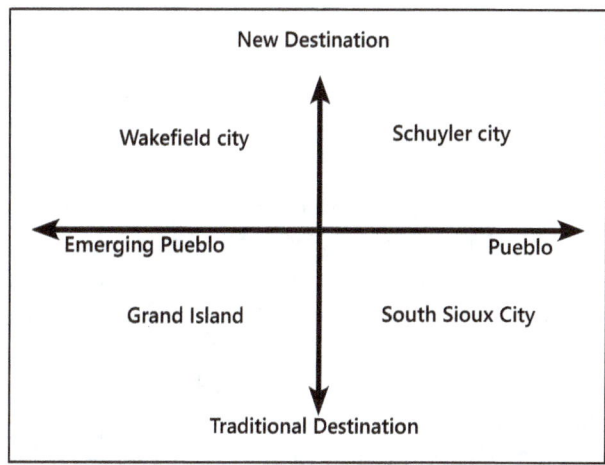

Figure 2. A conceptual framework to contemporary settlement patterns.

community. Exploring the dynamics of these transitions allows researchers to uncover the complex factors that have shaped the state's social, economic, and cultural landscapes. By studying the push-and-pull factors, settlement patterns, and socioeconomic outcomes of different waves of Latino immigration and migration, researchers can gain insights into the historical forces at play and their impact on Nebraska's Latino community. This deeper understanding contributes to a more nuanced and comprehensive understanding of Latino history in Nebraska, as well as its broader implications for the diverse communities within the state.

---

4. NPR has a good discussion on this topic. https://www.npr.org/2023/01/26/1151608403/mena-race-categories-us-census-middle-eastern-latino-hispanic.
5. This page lists the official ethnic and racial classifications. https://orwh.od.nih.gov/toolkit/other-relevant-federal-policies/OMB-standards.

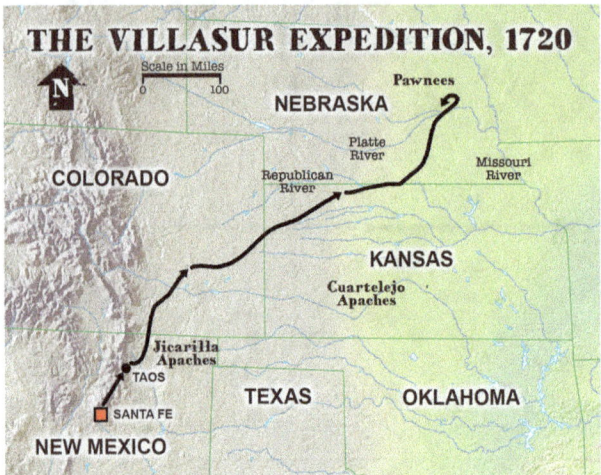

Figure 3. A conceptual map of the Villasur Expedition, 1720. Source of picture: https://www.nebraskastudies.org/en/1500-1799/villasur-sent-to-nebraska/#lg=1&slide=1 .

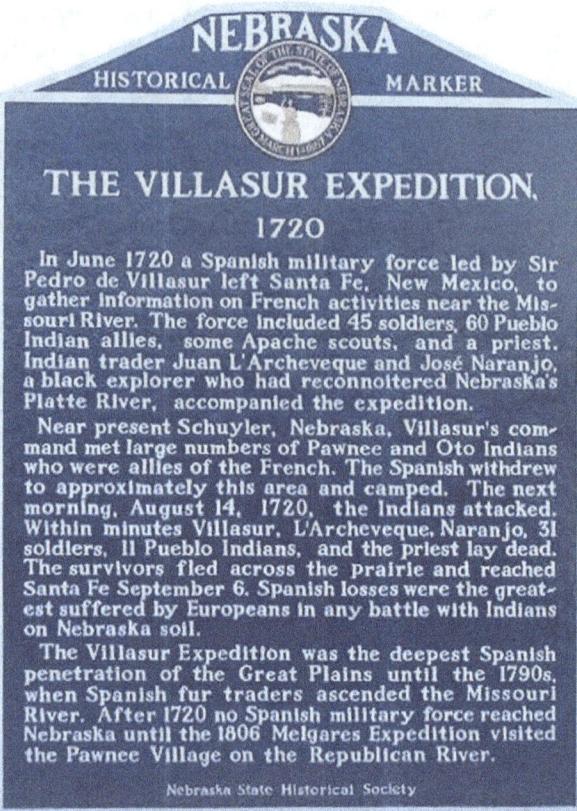

Figure 4. Historical Marker of Villasur Expedition, 1720. Source of picture: http://nebraskastudies.org/en/1500-1799/villasur-sent-to-nebraska/recording-the-massacre/#lg=1&slide=1 .

I. Latinidad in the Great Plains

The history of Latinos in Nebraska has a long and complex narrative. Many Latinos originally arrived in Nebraska as migrant workers and were recruited to work in the state's agricultural industry. Academic research (Bristow 2022; Davis 2002; Gouveia and Stull 1997; Lissette 2014) has shown that the history of Latinidad can be traced back before Nebraska became a state in 1867 to around 1720 during the Villasur Expedition.[6, 7] Historians have documented that the Villasur Expedition is an important footnote in Nebraska's history (see Figures 3 and 4). Documents reveal that the Spanish military expedition took place in what is now the central United States, near present-day Columbus, Nebraska. The Villasur Expedition holds significance not only for Latinos but also for Native Americans. It represents a pivotal event marked by contested space, complex relationships, and tensions among different groups. Symbolically, the Villasur Expedition can be remembered as a historical moment of conflict and tension between various cultural and political forces that emerged in Nebraska, including places like Scottsbluff, Omaha, and South Sioux City. The struggle for contested space continues to be present in many cities in Nebraska, as demographic forces shape the evolving meaning of justice, equality, and equity.

II. Latinidad along El Río

The academic literature describes the history of settlement patterns in Nebraska (Hernández 2017). Some scholars have argued that we know very little about the migration patterns of Nebraska and have argued that most of the stories are anecdotal (Rochín and Siles 1996). However, it is clear that the Platte River shaped the migration patterns of the early Latino settlers. The Platte River provided labor market opportunities that existed in the early twentieth century – such as jobs in agriculture and railroads. In Scottsbluff, for example, the sugar beet industry provided job opportunities to the migrant population, mainly Mexican immigrants. Research has shown that railroads were critical in shaping the migration patterns in Nebraska. The meat packing plants also shaped and continue to shape these patterns. It is interesting to note that Schuyler was the

---

6. For more information about the Villasur Expedition you can visit https://mynehistory.com/items/show/412.
7. For more information about the Villasur Expedition you can visit http://nebraskastudies.org/en/1500-1799/villasur-sent-to-nebraska/recording-the-massacre/.

"first cattle boomtown".[8] This historical distinction is important given the demographic profile of Schuyler today. The weighted influence of the "first cattle boomtown," has made Schuyler a hyper pueblo, where 72 percent of the residents are Latino.

One of the best socio-historical analyses of the Platte River is by Roger Davis (2002). His paper shows that by the turn of the twentieth century, Nebraska had developed core economies such as railroads, meat packing, and sugar beet fields that were emerging with plentiful job opportunities. These jobs served as significant pull factors for both Americans and immigrants who were seeking a place to pursue the American Dream and establish a new home. Concurrently, the push factor for the Mexican population coincided with the Mexican Revolution in 1910. In search of safety, employment, and a peaceful environment, many families fled Mexico and sought refuge in the United States. Davis adroitly argues, "Over the 20th century the history of the Hispanic presence along the Platte, and across Nebraska generally, would change dramatically. Similar to the rise and fall of the Platte itself, the dynamics of Mexican emigration and immigration present a pattern of growth, decline, restoration, and dramatic expansion" (2002, 30).

The presence of the Mexican immigrant population would start to show up in the U.S. Census. These documents would show how the weighted history of the settlement patterns would shape these first Latino destinations.

Railroad Industry

Studying labor patterns provides valuable insights into the development of infrastructure in the United States, including Nebraska. Research indicates that the rail lines in Nebraska, as in other regions, required ongoing maintenance, upgrades, expansion, and replacement to meet the growing demands of transportation (Olson 1966). Omaha played a central role as the primary destination for railroad workers in Nebraska. However, as the rail lines expanded and extended their reach, other locations began to emerge along these routes, eventually becoming destinations for the first Mexican settlements in the state. One such example is Hershey, situated just north of I-70 and approximately 14 miles east of North Platte. Nielsen (1993) provides an extraordinary account of the settlement of Mexican immigrants in Hershey. In her book, she presents narratives that highlight a general pattern of demographic transitions. Typically, it was the male head of the household who would initially make the move, seeking employment opportunities, while the rest of the family would follow once the head of the household found stable work. Mexican labor played a crucial role in the development and maintenance of the railroads. In fact, one scholar has argued that Mexicans had a significant presence in "over the track maintenance operations" (Smith 1981, 243)

Sugar Beet Industry

After settling in the towns along the Platte River, Mexican immigrants often found employment in the sugar beet fields. This sector of agriculture offers an insightful perspective on the study of exploitation and living conditions on the margins (Gaber and Cantarero 1997). In the early twentieth century, the sugar beet industry faced a significant challenge in securing a stable labor force. Consequently, Mexicans came to have a dominant presence in the sugar beet fields of western Nebraska. According to Davis, by 1926 "the Great Western company transported 14,500 workers to its fields and employed 55 labor agents along the Rio Grande. By 1929, the number of Mexicans and their families working in the sugar beet fields had reached nearly 30,000" (Davis 2002, 35).

The literature for this period highlights the significant presence and contribution of Mexican labor in the sugar beet industry. The demographic evidence clearly demonstrates that permanent Latino settlements were concentrated in western and eastern Nebraska, as well as along the Platte River.

Cattle Industry

While the railroads and sugar beet fields would change Scottsbluff, Grand Island, and other towns along the Platte River, Omaha would experience a similar pattern of change with railroads, but the cattle industry would play an important role shaping the spatial morphology of South Omaha. Omaha played and continues to play a pivotal role in Nebraska's agricultural and economic landscape.[9] Serving as a central hub for livestock trading and processing, the

---

8. See Roger P. Davis, "Latinos Along the Platte: The Hispanic Experience In Central Nebraska," *Great Plains Research* 12: (2002), pp. 27-50. http://www.jstor.org/stable/23780007.

9. This video provides a short introduction to the Stockyards in South Omaha. https://www.ketv.com/article/forgotten-omaha-the-stockyards/8963868.

stockyard became a bustling and vibrant marketplace. Thousands of cattle were brought to Omaha by rail, making it a crucial point for the transportation and distribution of livestock.[10] Research has shown that from the conclusion of World War II until 1973, Omaha emerged as a prominent center for cattle processing, dominating 80 percent of the state's meat packing operations. This significant industry employed more than 13,000 individuals, contributing to the region's economic vitality. The meat packing plants in Omaha played a vital role in the local and regional economy, attracting a diverse workforce, including Mexican immigrants. The industry's growth and success during this period marked Omaha as a major player in the meat packing revolution, solidifying its position as a key hub in the nation's agricultural landscape (Davis 2002; Valdés 2000).

As Nebraska's economy evolved, meat packing plants opened in other cities such as Lexington, Columbus, Grand Island, Schuyler, and Scottsbluff (Bristow 2022). Mexican immigrants and Mexican Americans developed an ethnic niche in these occupations, meaning they were overrepresented in the meat packing industry in Nebraska (Davis 2002; Gouveia and Powell 2007; Gouveia and Saenz 2000; Valdés 2000; Bristow 2022).[11] However, new census data showed some interesting changes taking place in some of the new Latino destinations in Nebraska (Dalla et al. 2004). I will discuss these emerging patterns in the latter part of this paper.

In this section, I have focused on three core industries that were pivotal in providing employment opportunities for new residents in Nebraska. However, it is important to recognize that other agricultural sectors, such as pinto beans, corn, and alfalfa, also played significant roles in the state's economic development. While these industries contributed substantially to Nebraska's growth, they also brought with them considerable challenges and hardships for workers.

Additionally, reports and investigations have highlighted ongoing issues of exploitation, particularly in the meat packing industry. A recent *60 Minutes*[12] segment brought attention to these concerns, underscoring the urgent need for improved working conditions and fair treatment for employees in these critical sectors.

III. El Primer Censo

As the agriculture economy developed in Nebraska, Latino workers, with Mexicans being the first among them, migrated to the state and played a crucial role in various industries. They made significant contributions to the construction of the railroad system, worked in the sugar beet and corn fields, and found employment in the meat and poultry plants. The emerging job opportunities in railroads, meat packing houses, and farm labor acted as attractive factors for many families, drawing them to many towns along the Platte River (Gouveia and Powell 2007; Davis 2002; Rochin, Siles, and Gomez 1996).

These opportunities not only provided a means of livelihood but also offered a pathway for pursuing the American Dream. They played a pivotal role in opening up the towns for settlement and development as both Americans and immigrants sought a place to establish their homes and pursue their aspirations. As a result, the Latino population in Nebraska experienced growth over the past 120 years.

Nebraska Statehood

The formal history of Nebraska dates to March 1, 1867, when it officially became a state. The initial census conducted in 1870 showcased the diversity of its population. Notably, the 1870 census showed that Nebraska was a significant destination for immigrants (See Table 1). It is worth noting that a higher percentage of immigrants resided in Nebraska (25 percent) at that time compared to the current immigration rate in the United States (14 percent). Among the immigrant groups, the largest settlements were found in Douglas County (7,737), Otoe County (2,736), and Lancaster County (1,737) (Census Bureau 1870).

The 1870 census provides insights into the presence of various ethnic groups that are now included in the broader Latino pan-ethnic categories, including Cubans, Spaniards, and Mexicans, who were already residing in Nebraska during that period. As Nebraska experienced continued growth and attracted new residents, immigrants from diverse backgrounds continued to establish their homes in the state. To gain a nuanced understanding of Latino history in Nebraska,

---

10. There is a dedicated Wiki page for the Union Stockyards. https://en.wikipedia.org/wiki/Union_Stockyards_(Omaha).
11. The meat packing plants in Scottsbluff closed in the late 20th and early 21st century.
12. https://www.cbsnews.com/video/slaughterhouse-cleaning-company-employed-children-how-hiring-went-wrong-60-minutes-video-2023-05-07/.

Table 1. Nativity – 1870 Census. U.S. Census 1870, Digitally transcribed by Inter-university Consortium for Political and Social Research..

County	Total	Native Born	Foreign-Born	Percent Foreign-Born
Douglas County	19,982	12,445	7,537	38%
Otoe County	12,345	9,609	2,736	22%
Lancaster County	7,074	5,337	1,737	25%
Dodge County	4,212	2,556	1,656	39%
Richardson County	9,780	8,253	1,527	16%
Saunders County	4,547	3,214	1,333	29%
Cuming County	2,964	1,641	1,323	45%
Cass County	8,151	6,843	1,308	16%
Washington County	4,452	3,442	1,010	23%
Platte County	1,899	988	911	48%

one can examine either Omaha in the eastern part of the state or Scottsbluff in the western part. While there may be similarities in the push-pull factors that influenced migration to these areas, there are also subtle differences that shape their unique experiences (Muñoz and Ortega 1997).

Immigration to the region that eventually became Scottsbluff began before its official founding in 1899. Among these early immigrants were families from Germany and Russia, each with their own unique stories and aspirations. Additionally, Mexican immigrants were part of this early wave of settlers, although a specific source is needed to provide further evidence.[13] Research indicates that Mexican immigrants during this time were typically young and unmarried (Davis 2002; Sanchez 2010a; Valdés 2000; Sanchez 2010b). Due to the significant influx of this demographic group, scholars commonly referred to them as "Solteros" (Davis 2002), meaning unmarried individuals in Spanish. Initially, many Solteros did not view Nebraska as a permanent home. However, due to the availability of local job opportunities in sectors such as railroads and agriculture, the Mexican population gradually established roots in various towns across the area.

Despite their differences, immigrants in Scottsbluff shared a common goal: to make a better life for themselves and their families. They faced many challenges and obstacles along the way, but they were determined to succeed.

Over time, these immigrants became an integral part of the fabric of communities like Scottsbluff, contributing to their culture, economy, and community. Today, the descendants of Mexican immigrants in Nebraska continue to honor their ancestors' rich and complicated history. They take pride in their Latinidad and celebrate it as a vital part of their identity. Through the passage of oral histories from one generation to another, they preserve the stories, experiences, and traditions of those who paved the way before them. These narratives serve as a powerful connection to their roots and provide a sense of cultural

---

13. See Gamio, 1931.

Table 2. Spanish Origin or Descent – 1970 Census . 1970 U.S. Census.

County	Total Population	Spanish Origin or Descent	% Spanish	Foreign-Born	From Mexico	From Cuba	% Latino
Nebraska	*1,482,412*	*21,067*	*1.4%*	*204,352*	*5552*	*608*	*3%*
Douglas County	389,455	7,055	1.8%	58,153	1,691	325	3%
Scotts Bluff County	36,432	3,295	9.0%	6,559	1,186	10	18%
Lancaster County	167,972	2,113	1.3%	19,914	633	160	4%
Sarpy County	63,696	1,592	2.5%	7,875	164	59	3%
Lincoln County	29,538	1,373	4.6%	2,944	370	0	13%
Hall County	42,851	972	2.3%	4,909	362	0	7%
Dawson County	19,467	731	3.8%	2,351	134	0	6%
Buffalo County	31,222	615	2.0%	3,078	149	0	5%
Keith County	8,487	369	4.3%	979	110	0	11%
Box Butte County	10,094	366	3.6%	1,373	158	0	12%

continuity, ensuring that the legacy of their ancestors remains alive and cherished. Several counties became gateway destinations for Latino residents. Scottsbluff was not the only town shaped by the early Mexican immigrants. Many of the towns along the Union Pacific Railroad lines in Nebraska would soon experience an influx of Mexican immigrants.

With the increasing presence of Latinidad in these communities, conflicts emerged. The history of this conflict in Nebraska remains untold in academic literature (Ceballos and Yakushko 2014). There is a large body of knowledge that documents the different types of Mexican removal programs during the 1930s, '40s, and '50s. Removal from relief rolls, discrimination in hiring practices, and forced repatriations were the main factors that contributed to the sudden decline of the Mexican-origin and immigrant populations in the Midwest (García, 2004).

The growing body of scholarship on Mexicans in Nebraska has brought attention to the impact of oppressive programs and policies on the community. Notably, Professor Ralph F. Grajeda's work has shed light on the injustices faced by Mexican-born parents, many of whom had U.S.-born children serving in World War II (Garza 2006, 2019).[14] His research reveals that these parents were frequently targeted by immigration authorities, highlighting the discriminatory practices and challenges they encountered (Grajeda 1976, 68).

The U.S. government did not collect data using the category of "Spanish origin" until 1970. However, empirical evidence clearly demonstrates the impact of Latinos on many towns throughout Nebraska. While our data is limited, we can trace the presence of Latinidad before 1970. By 1960, Scottsbluff County had the largest number of Mexican immigrants, with 1,601 individuals, followed by Douglas County with 1,547 individuals, and Lincoln County with 547 individuals. By the 1970s, we begin to find data that distinguishes between native-born and foreign-born residents. (See Table 2).

By 1970, it is evident that Scottsbluff County had a population consisting of 9 percent "Spanish origin" residents, making it home to the second-largest Latino population in Nebraska. However, in terms of overall percentage, Douglas County reported the largest Latino population, with Latinos representing only 2 percent of the total population. These statistics highlight the presence of Latinos in both counties and their growing influence in shaping the demographic landscape of Nebraska.

Figure 5 depicts the overall trend for the Latino population in Nebraska since 1970.[15] It is worth noting that the census demographic projections made in the 1990s regarding the number of Latinos living in Nebraska by 2025 turned out to be inaccurate (Davis 2002). The Latino population growth was faster than the projection. As per the 2020 census, the Latino population in Nebraska stands at approximately 235,000 individuals, solidifying their position as the largest minority group in the state. This significant growth in the Latino population underscores the importance of

---

14. See the important work of Bryan Winston. https://mappingthemexicanmidwest.bryanwinston.org/.
15. A small research brief, by Daniela Mattos (2017) showed the trend up to 2016.

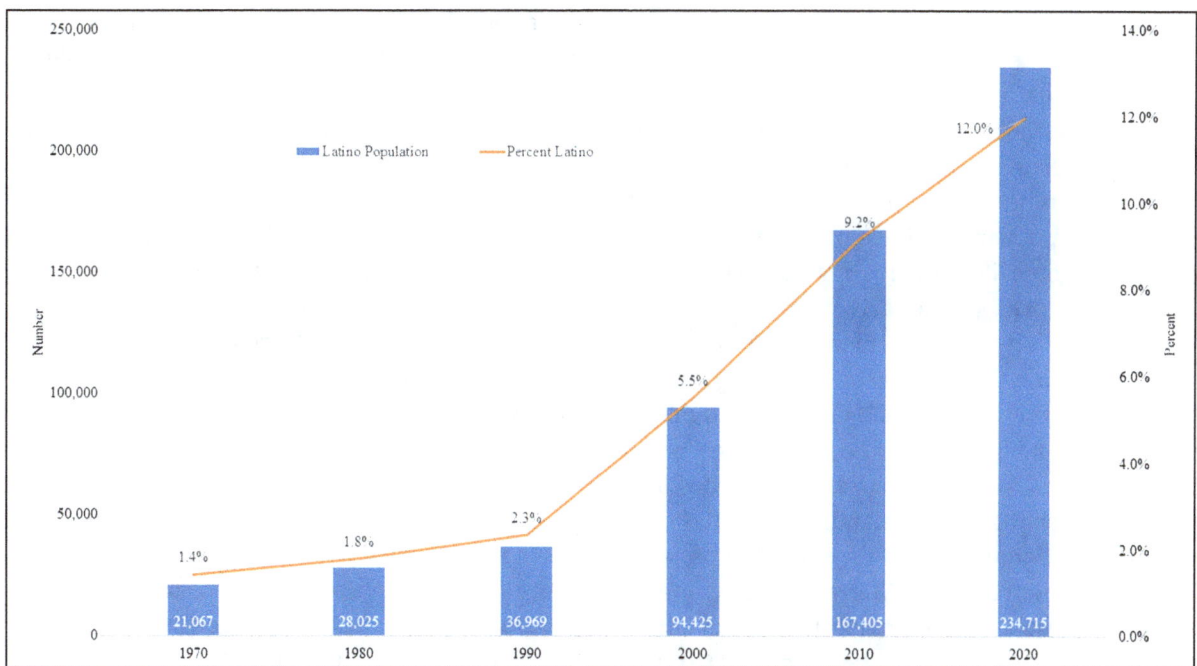

Figure 5. Nebraska Latino Population Trends. U.S. Census Decennial Survey.

understanding and addressing the unique needs and experiences of this community in Nebraska. In the latter part of this chapter, additional demographic data from the American Community Survey will be presented, offering further insights into the Latino population in Nebraska. This data will provide a more comprehensive understanding of key demographic characteristics, such as age, education, income, and employment, among others. By examining these demographic indicators, we can gain a deeper understanding of the socioeconomic landscape and the lived experiences of Latinos in the state.

The next part of this chapter will shift focus to highlighting Latinidad voices. It will provide a platform for individuals within the Latino community to share their personal stories, perspectives, and experiences. By centering these voices, we aim to shed light on the diverse narratives and lived realities that contribute to the rich tapestry of Latinidad in Nebraska. These personal accounts will provide a nuanced and humanizing portrayal of the Latino community, capturing the challenges, triumphs, and aspirations of its members.

IV. Los Voces

The ROJ team organized listening sessions across Nebraska, providing a platform for community leaders, residents, and the youth to come together and share their perspectives on Latinidad. These sessions aimed to amplify the voices and stories of the Latino community, which often have been overlooked or marginalized in historical narratives.

During these sessions, it became evident that the residents strongly believed that telling their history would elevate Nebraska as a significant focal point in Latino history. They recognized the importance of shedding light on the experiences and contributions of Latinos who have been part of the state for many generations. As family stories were shared, a sense of pride in being part of the Husker community emerged, but so did the pain associated with the difficulties their grandparents endured.

Participants emphasized the challenges faced by their grandparents, including discrimination, poverty, and exploitation. They highlighted the sacrifices made by their families, who endured these hardships with the hope of creating a better life for their children. The stories shared during these sessions served as a testament to the resilience and determination of the Latino community in Nebraska, who have persevered through adversity in pursuit of a brighter future.

By acknowledging and sharing these stories, the residents and participants of the listening sessions aimed to bring attention to the struggles, triumphs, and aspirations of their community. They sought to ensure that the history of Latinos in Nebraska is not forgotten or disregarded but rather is celebrated and integrated into the broader narrative of the state. Through their collective efforts, they hope to create a path towards a more inclusive and equitable future for all residents of Nebraska.

Omaha

Omaha, the metropolitan region with the largest Latino population in Nebraska, has historically been a significant destination for Latinos. The reasons for Latinos migrating to Omaha are multifaceted, but employment opportunities have played a significant role. The academic literature highlights the influence of the cattle industry on the early migration patterns of Latinos, shaping their movement to various destinations, including Omaha (Bacon 2016; Davis 2002, 2008; Gouveia and Powell 2007; Gouveia and Saenz 2000; Gouveia and Stull 1997; Rochín and Siles 1996).

However, Omaha stands apart from other destinations like Scottsbluff, Grand Island, and North Platte due to an additional factor in its migration pattern: military job opportunities. Many Latinos came to Omaha to serve in the Air Force, particularly at Offutt Air Force Base. The military, including its installations, played a significant role in the development and integration of Latinidad in the region.

The impact of the military on Latinidad in Omaha will be explored further in subsequent sections of this chapter, delving into its influence on the social, economic, and cultural dynamics of the Latino community. The military's presence and the opportunities it provided for Latinos contributed to the unique experiences and contributions of the community in Omaha, shaping the broader narrative of Latinidad in the region.

One of the most interesting stories told in this meeting was about the Mutualista Society. According to Charles M. Tatum, "Mutualistas provided most immigrants with a connection to their mother country and served to bring them together to meet their survival needs in a new and alien country. Cultural activities, education, healthcare, insurance coverage, legal protection, and advocacy before police and immigration authorities, and anti-defamation activities were the main functions of these associations." (Tatum 2001, 12)

As Latinos faced discrimination, mutualista societies were important because they provided social support when many families experienced an unwelcoming and exclusionary community (Ruiz 2010). Even though growing up in Omaha had turbulent moments, the rich history of Latino families will always be as or more important than the historical forces that worked to oppress them. Many of the participants expressed that the hurt never goes away but the great history of their people will inspire future generations. One person said, "We as people have paid our dues. … We are not inferior to anyone." The quote is a reminder that Latinidad has always been present in Nebraska. Perhaps the early generation may have been silent, but the next generation of Latinos would have access to education, power, and leadership opportunities that would give them a platform to talk about their stories.

The stories shared with the ROJ team highlight the significance of diversity and the contributions made by Latinos in various fields. One particular narrative emphasizes the pride felt by parents whose children broke racial barriers and achieved notable milestones, such as becoming the first Latino police officer and the first Latino deputy chief U.S. Marshal for Nebraska. These achievements symbolize the perseverance and determination of the younger generation in fighting for their rights and pursuing the American Dream.

Being the first in any endeavor is often challenging, requiring individuals to overcome obstacles and navigate uncharted territory. These stories underscore the resilience and tenacity demonstrated by Latino individuals who have strived to make a positive impact and create opportunities for themselves and future generations.

These individuals' experiences and accomplishments reflect the broader narrative of Latinos in Nebraska, who have faced and continue to confront barriers, discrimination, and systemic challenges. Their stories contribute to the collective history of Latino communities in the state and serve as a testament to their resilience, aspirations, and pursuit of equal rights and opportunities.

The diversity we see today was a result of conflict because in order to live the American Dream in Nebraska, you had to fight for it, and it was very challenging. The Latinos who tried to enter law enforcement had to fight. Many people argue that the fight continues today. One example mentioned was the contested race for the Douglas County Sheriff in 2022. Greg Gonzalez ran against Aaron Hanson and lost by 1,093 votes.[16] However, the Latino community has a different interpretation of the event. Some residents reported that "History repeated itself. … What they did to Greg … was a modern-day lynching. … Those who could have stood up … did not." It was clear that the election loss was a bittersweet moment for the Latino community in Omaha.

---

16. Please contact Dr. Sándoval for this information.

When researching this case, I was shocked by some of the online quotes that question the character of Greg Gonzalez. Tim Dunning, the retiring Douglas County Sheriff, issued this statement: "I don't think this guy should be sheriff. ... I was the sheriff for 26 years. I consider the people there my family, and I just feel that the person who runs that office needs to be accountable and needs to be honest."[17] Many people found this statement to be offensive and tasteless given the important role of the family in the Latino community. The participants were clear about their contributions, "Mejicanos, we've done our part. ... We earned our way."

Despite the anger about the pejorative politics around the Greg Gonzalez election, one thing that was present in the stories was the concept of "comunidad."[18] Time and time again, you would hear the beautiful stories of family memories ... tios and tias ... abuelitas and abuelitos. Everyone "served everybody in town." "We are a generous community ... where much is given, much is expected." Our grandparents sacrificed for us, and now we make the sacrifice for our children, and they will make the sacrifice for their children. Many of the respondents said the younger generations get emotional when thinking of the sacrifices of the older generations.

The spirit of Latinidad is present in our children today. It's present in schools, and in the universities. Latinos have always dreamed that their children would be successful. People were generous with their time, effort, and academic parenting (e.g., James Ramirez [19]). The role of the University of Nebraska at Omaha (UNO), University of Nebraska-Lincoln (UNL), and Creighton, was apparent at this meeting. Parents wanted their children to get a higher education, but they wanted their children to stay close to home. Access to these educational institutions was part of the American Dream. Education was power. Education was a way to defend the community. Education was a path to upward mobility. Education was the ultimate expression of pride in culture, pride of belonging. Education in all its manifestations encompassed the spirit of the meeting. Their voices were being heard and documented for future generations of Latinidad.

UNO would be an important intellectual home for many of these students. Today, UNO is home to the Office of Latino/Latin American Studies.[20] The office is home to the *Journal of Latino/Latin American Studies* (*JOLLAS*), an academic journal that became an outlet for academic research about life in Nebraska.

Scottsbluff

During a listening session in Scottsbluff, Nebraska, the stories shared by community members highlighted the distinct migration patterns and experiences of Latinidad in this rural, western part of the state. Unlike Omaha, Scottsbluff lacks military bases and prominent educational institutions like UNO or Creighton. Instead, the stories emerged from families residing in small towns surrounding the Scottsbluff region. Despite these differences, the narratives shared at the Scottsbluff meeting echoed the stories told in Omaha, shedding light on the challenges and overt discrimination experienced in small towns across Nebraska.

The stories from Scottsbluff were particularly vivid and graphic, emphasizing the harsh realities of overt discrimination faced by Latino individuals and families in small-town settings. These narratives provide a deeper understanding of the unique struggles encountered by Latinos in rural communities, where access to resources, opportunities, and support systems were limited. By amplifying these stories, the ROJ project aims to bring attention to the often-overlooked experiences of Latinos living outside major urban centers and foster a more inclusive understanding of Latinidad in Nebraska.

The parallel experiences shared in both Omaha and Scottsbluff demonstrate the pervasiveness of discrimination and the resilience of Latino communities across different geographical contexts in Nebraska. These stories serve as a powerful reminder of the need to address systemic inequities, promote cultural understanding, and work toward creating inclusive communities where everyone can thrive, regardless of their background or location.

For example, one person shared the following short story growing up in the 1950s: "They [teachers] were

---

17. For more information see: https://omaha.com/news/local/govt-and-politics/former-douglas-county-sheriff-calls-for-candidate-of-opposing-party-to-drop-out/article_0edc69ee-457e-11ed-88c7-9b6ef46b38d9.html.
18. "Comunidad" is translated to "community."
19. There is a blog about Jim Ramirez and his contributions. https://leoadambiga.com/2010/08/01/jim-ramirez-a-man-of-the-people/.
20. https://www.unomaha.edu/college-of-arts-and-sciences/ollas/index.php.

the ones that made us feel we weren't on the same level as the white kids. It was the teachers that kept us down. ... They would line us up in the hallway to put lice powder on our hair." Stories like this are common throughout the Southwest. The act itself reflects power relationships, and even though it is in the past, the memory lives on. Memories of injustice, discrimination, and cruelty are the fuel for the new generation of Latinos to understand Latinidad in Nebraska.

What these listening sessions showed is that the history of Latinos and Latinas has yet to be fully told and discussed by others. The "Los Pueblos" section of the chapter describes segregation patterns in many cities in Nebraska (Wahl, Gunkel, and Shobe 2005). However, it was in this listening session that concepts and experiences of living in segregated neighborhoods emerged. Participants wanted to share what life was like growing up in segregated barrios or neighborhoods in western Nebraska. There was segregation in the schools, churches, and neighborhoods (Spadt 2016).[21] One participant explained that in Scottsbluff, the dividing line became Overland, saying, "We [Mexican Americans] could not live on the other side of Overland Drive."

In Scottsbluff, participants referred to the practice of what sociologists called symbolic violence. Symbolic violence is a subtle form of violence used to exert power over groups of individuals (Bourdieu 1984). People recalled speaking Spanish in public and being scolded by schoolteachers and their parents. This sentiment was highlighted when participants shared stories of parents who wanted their children to speak English because they believed that the racism they faced was the result of their poor English. Many bilingual participants continue to face discrimination today. The participants shared stories of people complaining when they speak Spanish in public spaces such as stores or airports. However, it can be argued that the U.S. is changing, and speaking two or more languages is now viewed as an asset. It is another form of cultural capital that has monetary value. The discrimination that exists around speaking Spanish in public is related to the belief that "the people around us get uneasy because they think we're speaking about them," according to one participant.

It was clear from the stories in this listening session that the tension concerning bilingualism was something that many participants were dealing with today.

Another interesting theme related to English as the preferred language was its relationship with religion. There is a general feeling that the first Latino settlers preferred English because it was viewed as the Christian language (Lampe 1977).

A final theme that emerged and has real value in the contemporary discourse about Latinos is the diversity within the Latino community. Latino is a pan-ethnic group. One of the hallmark debates in social science research and even in the telling of the history of Latino people is the assumption that Latinos are a homogeneous group, but they are actually a group with diverse political views, diverse expressions of culture, and diverse norms and social expectations.

Like Omaha, where Our Lady of Guadalupe (OLG) played an important role in the history of Latinos in Nebraska, these churches exist "as a place of refuge for people who are seeking a home, who are seeking freedom from persecution and discrimination." The symbolic importance of OLG is important. The church records show that it became a parish in 1943. The parish church's ministry began in the 1900s, making it one of the oldest Latino ministries in Nebraska (Spadt 2016). Time and time again, participants shared how important faith was in their lives. They turned to faith when facing discrimination. They turned to faith when facing segregation. They turned to faith when facing exploitation.

Grand Island

Grand Island, situated in central Nebraska, shares similarities with Scottsbluff in terms of the push-pull factors that shaped Latinidad migration patterns. However, the economic development driven by the meat packing industry sets Grand Island apart from Scottsbluff. The listening session in Grand Island revealed narratives that resonated with the themes shared in Scottsbluff and Omaha. Participants recounted family autobiographies encompassing experiences of discrimination, exclusion, celebration, and other significant themes.

These stories, though often viewed as sources of shame by participants, are precisely what the ROJ project aims to embrace and elevate. By providing a platform for sharing these narratives, the project seeks to debunk any sense of shame and instead foster a sense of pride in the diverse family histories that form an integral part of Nebraska's overall history.

---

21. "The other Catholic church in town didn't allow people of Hispanic descent, and eventually, Our Lady of Guadalupe was established, and is still a cultural hub today." See Spadt 2016.

The stories shared during the listening session underscore the struggles and sacrifices endured by families, ultimately highlighting their resilience as survivors.

One participant captured the essence of these stories by emphasizing the foundational values instilled by their parents, which centered on religion and education. These values, passed down through generations, serve as a testament to the enduring strength and determination of Latino families in Nebraska. The ROJ project aims to celebrate and honor these stories, recognizing them as an integral part of the state's collective history and heritage.

During the listening session, a new theme emerged, shedding light on the complex dynamics of language and identity among Latinos in Nebraska: reverse racism. Participants highlighted the pressure they experience to navigate multiple worlds with different sets of expectations, particularly when it comes to language. In public spaces, there exists an expectation to be proficient in both English and Spanish.

One participant shared a personal story that exemplified this theme. He recounted an encounter in which he chose to speak English to a group of Hispanic women. To his surprise, one of the women expressed disappointment that he did not address them in Spanish. In response, he explained that he grew up hearing Spanish only in his grandparents' home. However, he was advised that to succeed in the United States, he needed to prioritize English and assimilate into the dominant culture. As a result, he lost his family's language.

This narrative highlights the internal struggle faced by many Latinos, torn between maintaining their heritage language and assimilating to the cultural expectations of their new environment. The pressure to speak English and Spanish fluently can create challenges for individuals who feel the weight of cultural expectations and the need to navigate multiple linguistic and cultural identities.

The participant's story underscores the complexities of language assimilation and the loss that can accompany it. It serves as a reminder that the Latino experience in Nebraska encompasses various layers of negotiation and adaptation, and that individuals may face internal conflicts as they strive to reconcile their cultural heritage with society's demands.

Another participant shared a story about being discriminated against by Latinos because they thought she was "a double agent, working for the white community or white interests." Participants shared stories about rumors of how people got jobs. Other participants described people saying things like, "She got the job because she's Mexican." Someone else told her, "You're OK. You're not like them because you were born here." The complex identity issues within the Latino community have never been fully resolved. Quotes from these listening sessions should be a reminder that Latinos are negotiating their identities every day. The demographic transitions of the Latino population are unique. Each day, every hour, new Latinos arrive in the United States. How do these new Americans develop bonds with Mexican Americans who have been in Nebraska since the 1920s?

During the listening sessions, the topic of interethnic and interracial marriage emerged as a significant theme, raising questions about the acceptability and implications of marrying outside one's ethnic or racial group, as well as considerations of social class. The discussions around these topics revealed the complexity and range of opinions within the community.

Participants shared their perspectives on whether it is acceptable for Latinas or Latinos to marry individuals from different ethnic or racial backgrounds. There was a sentiment expressed that marrying outside the community's expectations could potentially lead to a dilution or loss of Latino identity. Some individuals expressed concerns about the perceived erosion of cultural heritage when marrying someone from a different background.

These discussions shed light on the concerns and conflicts experienced by some parents in relation to the younger generation's attitudes toward their Latino heritage. There was a shared sentiment that some young individuals may not fully embrace or acknowledge their Latino identity, which can lead to a sense of disappointment or frustration among older generations. Participants emphasized the importance of embracing one's background and heritage, expressing a desire for their children and grandchildren to be proud of their Latino roots.

One participant highlighted the significance of language as a means of fostering pride and connection to Latino heritage. She made a deliberate effort to speak Spanish to her grandchildren, aiming to instill a sense of pride and appreciation for their cultural background.

These discussions underscore the ongoing dialogue within the community about the preservation of Latino identity and the challenges posed by interethnic and interracial marriage. They reflect the complexities of navigating cultural dynamics, generational differences, and the pursuit of individual happiness within the context of cultural heritage.

The listening sessions provided a profound realization that identity is often shaped by personal experiences, family struggles, faith, and local communities rather than the broader social constructs and demographic categories like "Latino" or "Latinidad." Many participants shared that they did not become aware of their Mexican identity or the societal categorization of being Mexican until they reached the age of 10 or 11. Prior to that, they primarily identified themselves as Americans, feeling a deep connection to the country they called home.

The participants expressed a sense of longing for acceptance and embrace from the larger society, particularly for their children who were born and raised in Nebraska. They described a feeling of being caught between their American identity and the perception that the state did not fully embrace them or recognize their children as fellow Americans or authentic Huskers. This sentiment highlights the complex experience of individuals who navigate multiple layers of identity and struggle with the tension between their cultural heritage and their sense of belonging in the broader American context.

These stories underscore the importance of personal narratives and lived experiences in shaping individual and collective identities. They reveal the limitations of relying solely on social constructs and demographic categories to understand the diverse and nuanced experiences of a community. The participants' emphasis on family, faith, and local neighborhood as defining factors of their identity speaks to the significance of intimate connections and community bonds in shaping one's sense of self and belonging.

Listening to these stories and acknowledging the struggles faced by individuals and communities offer an opportunity to foster greater understanding, acceptance, and inclusivity. Recognizing and embracing the multifaceted nature of identity can contribute to a more comprehensive and authentic portrayal of the experiences and contributions of diverse communities within the broader social fabric.

V. El Movimiento Chicano

Lincoln's Latino community has made a profound impact on the city, significantly shaping its social and cultural landscape. As the capital of Nebraska and home to the University of Nebraska-Lincoln, Lincoln holds a unique place in the state's identity. The university's presence has drawn a diverse range of students and professionals, including many Latinos, who enrich the city with their cultural traditions and intellectual contributions. The academic and research opportunities provided by the university have likely played a key role in attracting Latinos to the city, establishing Lincoln as a sought-after destination for higher education and academic growth.

Lincoln offers a unique perspective in the history of Latinidad, serving as a significant focal point in the Chicano/a Movement. It can be studied not only as a hub of student activism but also as a strategic location where the movement influenced state policymakers. The city's role in shaping both grassroots efforts and legislative change highlights its importance in the broader context of the Chicano/a struggle for rights and recognition.

Regardless of the starting point for the analysis, the census data sheds light on Latinos in Lincoln, which may differ from those Latinos in Omaha, Scottsbluff, Grand Island, etc. The demographic patterns among Latinos residents reflect the unique opportunities and resources available in the city, such as employment, educational institutions, and community support systems. The influence of Latinos on Lincoln extends beyond demographics and settlement patterns (Garza 2006, Winston 2019). The Latino community has contributed to the city's cultural, economic, and social spheres through entrepreneurship, arts and entertainment, activism, and community engagement. Their presence has enriched the city's diversity, fostering intercultural exchange and promoting a broader understanding of different perspectives and experiences.

By recognizing the impact of Latinos in Lincoln, we can gain a deeper appreciation for the contributions they have made and continue to make to the city's growth and development.

The Chicano Movement

The Chicano Movement began in the American Southwest. However, the movement would soon find its way to Nebraska.[22] One of the first institutions devoted to advocating for Latino interests was the Chicano Awareness Center (CAC), established in 1971 in Omaha.[23] The history of these institutions

---

22. Omaha Public Schools has a webpage dedicated to the Chicano Movement. https://www.ops.org/Page/1849.
23. https://www.latinocenter.org/who-we-are/history/.

shows how Chicano consciousness played an important role in creating institutional pathways to advocate for Latinos. A series of meetings that began in the basement of the local Latino church flourished into a plan to create the CAC. One of the key leaders instrumental in the foundation of the CAC was Reverend Robert Navarro. With the leadership of Navarro, CAC would be an anchor and a voice nimble and flexible enough to adapt to the emerging pan-Latino population's growing needs. CAC's name eventually would change to Latino Center of the Midlands in 2016.[24]

The Chicano Movement also found a home in other institutions with different leaders. Several participants from the Omaha listening sessions remembered the dedication of Dr. Jim Ramírez in helping young Latinos get an education at the University of Nebraska at Omaha. His roots were established in South Omaha. He had firsthand experience of the hard-working conditions in the meat packing facilities. Through hard work and resilience, he earned his doctorate degree and advocated for the next generation of Latinos. Ramirez's service and dedication paralleled the aspirations and goals of the young Chicano Movement that was emerging in all corners of Nebraska.

The rise of student organizations such as United Mexican American Students at Chadron State College, Aztlán at Nebraska Western College, the Chicano Association of United Students for Action at the University of Nebraska at Omaha, and the Mexican American Student Association at the University of Nebraska-Lincoln provide evidence of the increasing political awareness and activism among Chicanos and Latinos during the Chicano Movement era. These organizations played a key role in fostering a sense of identity, solidarity, and empowerment within the Latino community, while also advocating for social, political, and educational reforms. Their efforts contributed significantly to the broader Chicano Movement in Nebraska, influencing both campus culture and state policies.

These student organizations played a pivotal role in advocating for the rights and interests of Chicano and Latino students, as well as raising awareness about broader social and political issues affecting their communities. They provided a platform for students to come together, voice their concerns, and take collective action to bring about change.

For example, Figure 6 shows a letter that established the President's Advisory Committee on Mexican-American Affairs at UNL in 1970. The Chicano

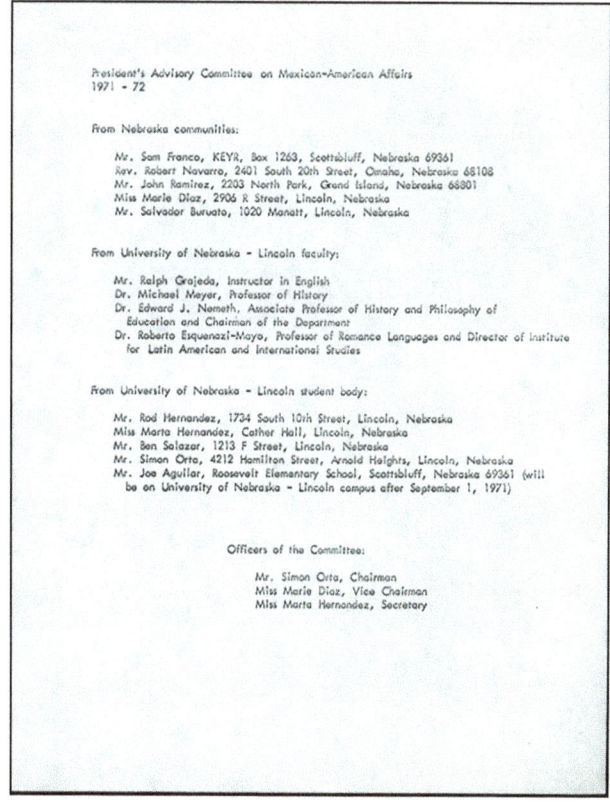

Figure 6. "Member list, Presidents Advisory Committee on Mexican-American Affairs," *Nebraska U*, accessed August 13, 2025, https://archives-spec.unl.edu/projects/item/2726.

Movement was key to the committee's creation. UNL needed to recognize and address the needs of, and challenges faced by Chicanos throughout the state. The student organizations were strong and vocal. Figure 7 shows a letter from MASA demanding the resignation of certain committee members. The letter indicates that there were disagreements and frustrations within the student body regarding the committee's effectiveness in addressing the needs and concerns of Chicano students regarding UNL and communities throughout Nebraska.

MASA's action underscored the importance of student activism and the demand for meaningful representation and support from university administration. Student movements like this highlight the power of student voices in shaping institutional policies and practices, as well as the ongoing struggle for authentic representation and inclusion. The experiences and activism of student organizations like MASA provide valuable insights into the broader social and political climate of the time, as well as the efforts of Chicanos and Latinos to assert their identities, promote social justice, and advocate for equitable treatment within

---

24. https://www.latinocenter.org/who-we-are/history/.

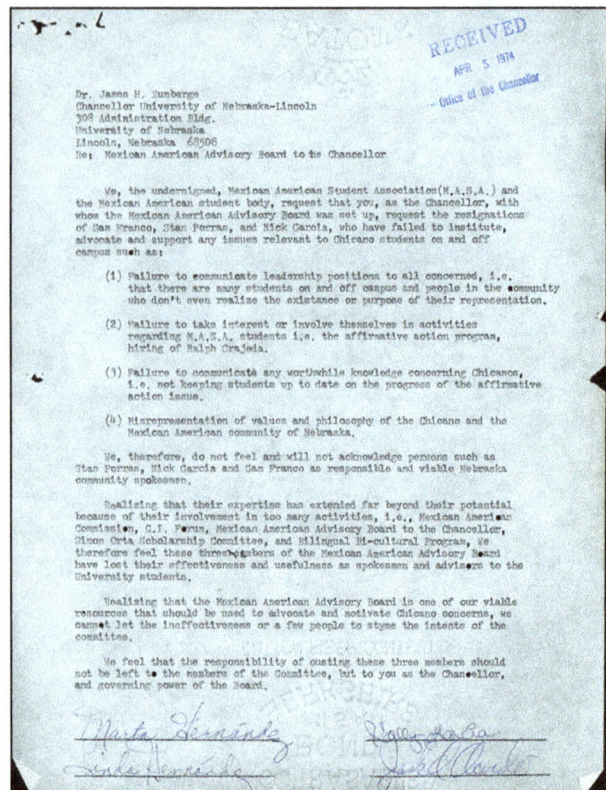
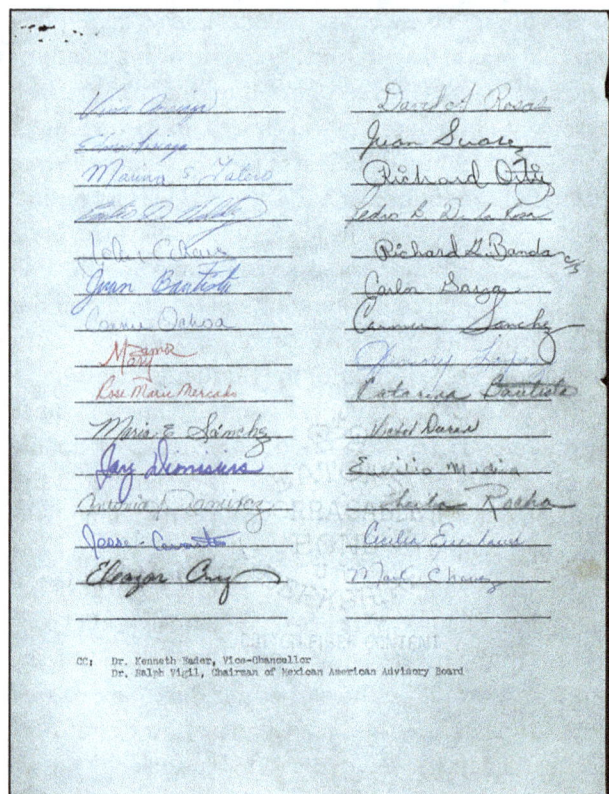

Figure 7. "Request for the resignation of committee members by MASA," *Nebraska U*, accessed August 13, 2025, https://archives-spec.unl.edu/projects/item/2754.

educational institutions. Their contributions have helped pave the way for future generations of Latino students and continue to inspire ongoing efforts for inclusivity and social change.

The establishment of the Simón Orta Scholarship in 1974 was a significant milestone in recognizing and supporting the academic achievements and aspirations of Mexican American students at UNL.[25] Orta becoming the first Mexican American to graduate with a doctorate from UNL in 1973 served as an inspiration for future generations.

The scholarship in his name not only honored his academic achievements but also aimed to provide financial assistance to Mexican American students pursuing higher education at UNL. Scholarships like the Simón Orta Scholarship play a vital role in removing barriers to education and empowering underrepresented students to pursue their academic goals.

By providing financial support and recognition to Mexican American students, the scholarship serves as a catalyst for increasing access and representation in higher education. It helps create a more inclusive and equitable learning environment where students from diverse backgrounds can thrive and contribute to their communities.

The Simón Orta Scholarship stands as a testament to the power of representation, the value of educational attainment, and the commitment to supporting the academic journeys of Mexican American students. It serves as a reminder of the importance of recognizing and celebrating the achievements of individuals who have paved the way for others, while also fostering opportunities for future generations to succeed.[26]

MASA's commitment to advocating for the best interests of Latino students is exemplified through their annual Chicano Awareness Week (See Figure 8). This weeklong event serves as a platform to raise awareness, promote cultural pride, and celebrate the contributions of the Chicano/Latino community.

Chicano Awareness Week provides a range of activities and events that engage students, faculty, and the broader community in meaningful discussions, cultural displays, artistic performances, educational workshops, and more. Through these initiatives,

25. One of the founding members of the ROJ team, Dr. Paul A. Olson, served on the dissertation committee for Simón Orta.
26. For more information see: https://www.dailynebraskan.com/three-honored-with-masa-scholarships/article_7500cc30-1939-51cd-bf1d-4a6826038054.html.

MASA aims to foster a deeper understanding of Latinidad, while also creating a supportive and inclusive environment for Latino students on campus.

By organizing Chicano Awareness Week, MASA plays a crucial role in promoting cultural appreciation and empowerment within the university community. This annual event serves as an opportunity to highlight the achievements and experiences of Latino students.

Moreover, Chicano Awareness Week offers a platform for networking, community-building, and leadership development among Latino students. It provides them with opportunities to engage with other students, connect with influential speakers and mentors, and develop a sense of pride and belonging at UNL. Chicano Awareness Week reflects MASA's ongoing dedication to advocating for the needs, interests, and cultural identity of Latino students. It serves as a vital platform for raising awareness, fostering inclusivity, and empowering a new movement of leadership in the spirit of the Chicano Movement.

Nebraska Commission on Mexican Americans

The establishment of the Nebraska Commission on Mexican Americans in 1972 marked a significant moment in Nebraska's history, as it became the first state to create an institutional voice to represent the interests and concerns of Mexican Americans. This development was closely tied to the broader Chicano Movement, which sought to address the social, political, and economic inequalities faced by Mexican Americans and promote cultural pride and empowerment. However, despite the shared goal of advocating for the rights and well-being of Latinos in Nebraska, there were tensions and conflicts within the movement. These tensions arose from differing visions and strategies for achieving change and addressing the challenges faced by the Latino community. One source of tension was the geographical divide between Omaha and Lincoln, and Scottsbluff, which represented two distinct populations with different needs and priorities (Davis 2008).

The Chicano Movement, La Raza Unida Party, and the GI Forum all played significant roles in shaping the history of the Nebraska Commission on Mexican Americans. Each organization had its own leadership and strategies, leading to differences in approach and priorities. These conflicts and disagreements

Figure 8. A conceptual framework to understand historical and contemporary migration. The picture is from an email sent to MASA Alumni.[27]

highlighted the complexity of uniting diverse voices and perspectives within the Latino community and working toward common goals.

Despite these tensions, the Nebraska Commission on Mexican Americans served as an important platform for advocating for policy changes that would improve the quality of life for Latinos across the state. It provided a space for dialogue, collaboration, and the articulation of the community's concerns. While challenges and tensions persist today, the establishment of the commission represented a crucial step toward achieving greater representation, recognition, and equality for Latinos in Nebraska.

The concept of social capital, as described in sociology literature, refers to the resources, connections, and relationships that individuals and communities possess that can be mobilized to achieve certain goals or bring about social change (Portes 1998). Social capital can include trust, shared values, reciprocity, and access to networks and information. In the case of the Nebraska Commission on Mexican Americans,

---

27. A similar picture can be found on Twitter. https://twitter.com/unlmasa/status/1644413066409385990.

social capital played a crucial role in its establishment (Ramos et al. 2017). The historical records indicate the creation of the commission would get its start from a friendship in Scottsbluff, Nebraska. The interactions and relationships between state Senator Terry Carpenter and Severian "Sam" Franco were instrumental in shaping the decision to create the commission. These individuals, through their personal connections and influence, were able to mobilize support and convince others of the need to address the concerns of the Mexican and Chicano population in Nebraska. Through their relationship, Franco was able to build trust, share insights, and effectively communicate the needs and aspirations of the community he represented. By utilizing his connection with Terry Carpenter, Franco effectively advocated for the establishment of the Nebraska Commission on Mexican Americans, that would be an institutional voice that would represent and address the concerns of Latinos in the state.

Stan Porras was the first executive director of the Nebraska Commission on Mexican Americans. He played a crucial role in establishing the commission's norms and structure. He envisioned the commission as a service agency rather than an agency that created conflict, emphasizing its role as a bridge between the people and the state government. Being the first commission in the United States dedicated to Latino advocacy, Porras recognized the importance of fostering collaboration and providing services to the community.

Said Porras: "We are a liaison between the people and the state government. This is a service agency, not a force of power, and our concern is service, not power." His statement reflects his commitment to creating a space where the needs and interests of the Latino community could be effectively addressed. By positioning the commission as a service-oriented entity, Porras aimed to establish a cooperative relationship with the state government and facilitate positive change through dialogue and assistance.

His emphasis on service over power highlights the commission's mission to serve the community and advocate for their interests rather than pursuing a confrontational approach. This approach sought to build trust, promote understanding, and work collaboratively toward improving the quality of life for Latinos in Nebraska. By adopting a service-oriented perspective, Porras aimed to provide a platform for Latino voices and ensure the state government heard and addressed their concerns (Davis 2008).

The Nebraska Commission on Mexican Americans experienced controversies throughout its existence, and one of the most significant was the decision to change its name to the Nebraska Commission on Latino-Americans. This name change reflected a shift in how the commission aimed to represent and serve Nebraska's diverse communities.[28] Given that this is a government body, it is unclear how the history of the Nebraska Commission on Mexican-Americans should or will be preserved for the public. Unlike other organizations that preserve the history of their institution (e.g., CAC), there is only one small reference to its history.[29] The commission's website states:

"The Mexican American Commission was first established with the passage of LB1081 during the 1972 Legislature. On July 15, 2010, LB139 officially changed our name to the Nebraska Commission on Latino-Americans."

Institutions are subject to change, and the Nebraska Commission on Latino-Americans is not immune to these types of changes. Its future trajectory and the terminology used to represent Latino communities in Nebraska remain uncertain. It is possible that new terminologies may emerge in the coming decades to reflect evolving understandings of identity and community. Furthermore, the commission's future could be influenced by legislative actions. It is conceivable that legislation may be introduced to modify or even eliminate the commission altogether given contemporary animus toward immigrants at the state level.

Despite these potential changes, the commission continues to evolve and adapt to the shifting demographics and needs of Nebraska's Latino population. New voices and leaders from different parts of Nebraska, such as Shelby, Madison, Columbus, and Hastings, now serve on the commission. Their inclusion represents the growing presence of Latinos in these regions and the recognition of their unique perspectives and experiences.

By including representatives from diverse communities, the commission aims to ensure that a broader range of voices are heard and that the needs of Latinos in different parts of Nebraska are effectively addressed. As Nebraska's Latino population continues to grow and change, it is essential for institutions like the commission to adapt, engage with

---

28. For more information see https://nebraskalegislature.gov/FloorDocs/101/PDF/Final/LB139.pdf.
29. For more information see https://latinoac.nebraska.gov/about.htm.

new voices, and remain responsive to the evolving needs and aspirations of the community they serve. This ongoing evolution ensures that the commission remains relevant and effective in advocating for the rights, well-being, and empowerment of Latinos in Nebraska.

VI. Los Veteranos

Boys of the Barrios (BOB)

"We are Americans first, of Mexican descent." This was a common theme in all the listening sessions. Latino veterans from across the state who served in World War II, the Korean War, and Vietnam returned home and made demands for justice, equality, and equity.

Nebraska Educational Television produced a short documentary in 2020 on Latino veterans in Nebraska titled "The Boys from the Barrio."[30] It is important to note that the Pentagon has no official count of Latinos in the Vietnam War. Latinos were counted as white.[31] This changed as the term Hispanic or Latino became an official category in the 1980 census. Many veterans said they were viewed as second-class citizens. The Barrio Boys, as they call themselves, organized the effort to create a memorial for future generations to remember the great sacrifices that were made by Latino families (See Figure 9). Dr. Marty Ramirez organized the construction of the monument with his classmates.[32] The first monument was unveiled in 2019 (Ramirez and Cantú 2018). The memorial consists of three new monuments with approximately 600 names of individuals that served the U.S. Latinos historically and currently have served proudly in the U.S. armed forces to protect the United States

Ramirez recalls moments of his life "when people come up, and say, 'Thank you for your service.' It's like hitting me with a stun gun," he said. "I don't know how to react, seriously. I just kind of say, 'Thank you.'"[33]

In 2022, UNL held a webinar with some of the Boys from the Barrio (BFB) who shared in great

Figure 9. Veteran's Memorial in Scottsbluff, Nebraska.

detail the project's history.[34] This is a remarkable webinar filled with rich stories about how the memorial was built. The BFB all agreed that the memorial was an important reminder to their generation and future generations that the sons and daughters of immigrants accomplished something for their country. When they were called to serve their country, they said, "Yes." They left the small towns in the valley, their family and friends, and postponed marriage and educational opportunities. The BFB and the memorial are reminders that Latinos are proud of their shared sacrifice. They accomplished something for themselves, their family, their communities, their state, and their country. They served their country with courage and pride. The memorial will be a lasting monument that reminds not only Latinos but all Americans that Latinos in Nebraska are Americans, and their journey to tell their history has just begun.

---

30. For more information see https://www.youtube.com/watch?time_continue=49&v=mVqBCscCEKA&source_ve_path=MTM5MTE3LDI4NjY2&feature=emb_logo.
31. Denkmann, Libby. "This play is keeping alive the 'hidden history' and memories of Chicanos who served in Vietnam." September 25, 2018. https://laist.com/news/kpcc-archive/the-pentagon-doesn-t-know-how-many-chicanos-served
32. The other leaders were Greg Rodriguez, Joe Perez, and Gavino Saldivar.
33. For more information see https://nebraskapublicmedia.org/en/news/news-articles/your-story-wont-be-forgotten-600-names-added-to-scottsbluff-war-memorial/.
34. "Chicano Mexican American Veterans," (webinar) Reckoning and Reconciliation on the Great Plains: Confronting Our Past, Reimagining Our Future, 2022 Summit, Great Plains Studies Center, University of Nebraska-Lincoln, https://mediahub.unl.edu/media/19131.

The children and grandchildren of the immigrants have found their voice, have found a platform to begin a dialogue about the true meaning of truth and reconciliation. The sentiment from BFB is that it is time for Nebraska to honor the contributions and accomplishments made by Latino families, individuals, and organizations. Through this research project, it has become clear that the history of Latinos in Nebraska is an important topic to understand. Latinos have contributed to local economies, to the educational and political institutions of Nebraska. With the projected demographic changes for Nebraska, this project provides an important voice for future generations to get a brief understanding of Latinidad and reminds them that it is appropriate to stop, pause, and ask critical questions about the history of Nebraska.

American G.I. Forum

Another important voice that deserves recognition is the American GI Forum, which represents Latinos who served in the military. Founded in 1948 as a congressionally chartered Hispanic veterans and civil rights organization, the American GI Forum played a pivotal role in advocating for the rights and recognition of Latino veterans.[35] The voices of Nebraska's GI Forum chapters were crucial in the 1970s. American veterans of Latino descent fought for their country and upon returning to their homes in Nebraska they were confronted with the reality of inequality and injustice. The GI Forum chapters in Scottsbluff, Grand Island, and Omaha played an important role and provided a formal voice in solidarity with the Chicano Movement. For example, GI Forum members played an important role in shaping the Nebraska Commission on Mexican Americans. Prior to the official Nebraska legislation, a Mexican American Commission was created and chaired by B.N. "Nick" Garcia, who at the time was the head of the GI Forum (Davis 2008).

The discussions in the 1970s revealed important themes and tensions, such as the Latino community being a diverse and heterogeneous community, even differentiating among the Mexican, Chicano, and Mexican immigrant populations. The problems faced by Chicano and Mexican Americans were different from the problems facing the migrant workers in western Nebraska (Davis 2008). Voices from members of the GI Forum pointed out that the commission created too many programs for the migrant workers (who may have been seen as transient) while ignoring the problems and challenges of the "Mexican-American citizens" (Davis 2008).

This tension is still present today. Statistics about the diversity of the Latino population, layered with different waves of historical and contemporary immigration patterns, will be discussed later in this chapter.

VII. Los Pueblos

1980 Census

Latino Pueblos has emerged as an important concept, and it has gained attention within the literature dedicated to Latino cities and communities,[36] although it is important to note that there is no universally agreed-upon definition for a Latino Pueblo. In the narrative that follows, we will focus on the demographic shifts and transformations that have shaped these communities in Nebraska, as well as explore their ongoing evolution. The story of Latino Pueblos in Nebraska is one of transformation. These communities have experienced shifts in population composition, cultural expressions, and socioeconomic patterns. By understanding these changes, we can gain insights into the vibrant nature of Latinidad in the state. Looking ahead, it is clear that Latino Pueblos will continue to be present in Nebraska, like Lexington and Schuyler (Hartford Courant 2002; Potter, et al. 2004; Potter, Cantarero, and Pischel 2008). These cities will be shaped by future waves of immigrants recruited to work in meat packing houses. A new generation of Latinos will become citizens of Nebraska (Ruta 2021). The emerging wave of Latinidad will continue to challenge and reshape the integration of Latinos within the broader fabric of Nebraska society.

Latino communities existed before the 1970 and 1980 census. It is possible to quantify and geographically visualize these cities and communities using the historical census data that has been released. However, the scope of the research is beyond the goals of the ROJ project. These stories have yet to be told.

---

35. See, "American G.I. Forum of Texas," *Handbook of Texas*, Texas State Historical Association, https://www.tshaonline.org/handbook/entries/american-gi-forum-of-texas.
36. One of the best analyses of the demographic pattern of Latinos is by Aliaga Lissette (2014).

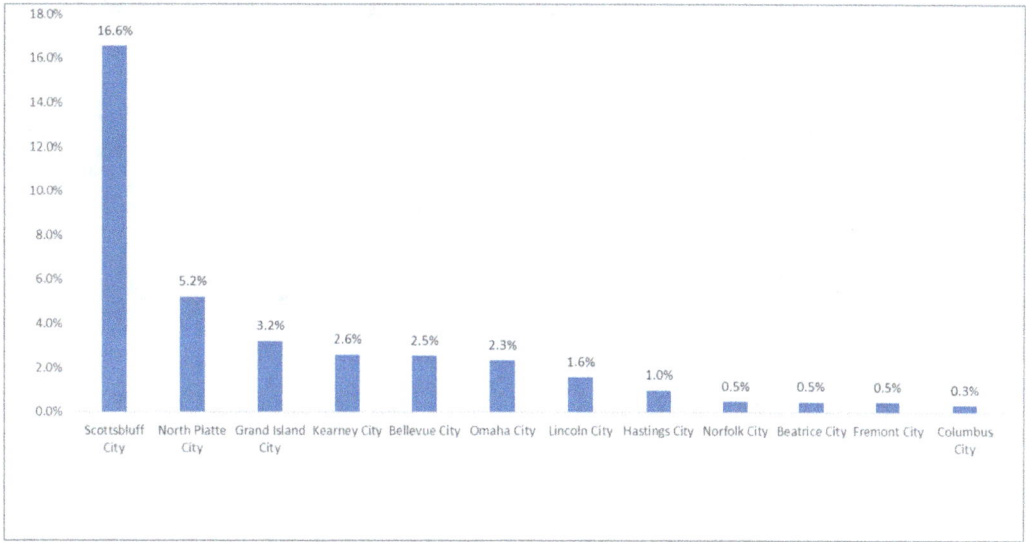

Figure 10. The Percent of the Population was classified as Spanish Origin in 1980. U.S. Census Bureau, 1980 Decennial Census.

As more Latina and Latino historians enter the discourse, we will start to hear a burgeoning narrative that reflects the themes raised in Los Voces. However, beginning in 1980, a new dataset was released that captures U.S. residents who were classified as Hispanic or Latino. The term used in the 1980 census was "Persons of Spanish Origin." I presented Figure 5 earlier in this chapter, which showed that 2 percent of the population in Nebraska was classified as Hispanic. Demographers typically use the state percentage as a baseline to determine if geographic regions can be classified as destinations or gateway cities for minority populations (Vasquez, Seales, and Marquardt 2008). The 1980 census yielded expected results, with Scottsbluff leading the way in terms of the largest percentage of Latino population, followed by North Platte and Grand Island. These cities have long been recognized in historical literature as having substantial Latino communities. Furthermore, Omaha boasted the largest Latino population, followed by Lincoln and Scottsbluff. (See Figure 10)

The 1980 census does show that the two cities with higher educational institutions – UNL, UNO, and Creighton – started to attract Latinos with higher educational attainment levels than in other cities. For example, in Lincoln, about 1 in 3 Latinos aged 25 and older had some college, and one third (33 percent) of those with some college education had a college degree or higher. In Omaha, about 1 in 5 (19 percent) had some college education, and nearly half (45 percent) of these residents had a college degree or higher. In cities along the Platte River, the data show a different story. In Scottsbluff, 16 percent of the population had some college, and only 13 percent of these residents had a college degree or higher. In Grand Island, only 6 percent of the population had some college, and about one third had a college degree or higher.

Another theme that supported the general narrative from Los Voces was that the first major wave of Latinos were of Mexican origin. Scottsbluff reported the highest percentage of those with Mexican descent at 93 percent, followed by Grand Island (90 percent) and Omaha (82 percent). Lincoln represented the emerging idea of a pan-Latino population. (See Table 3.)

Another feature that stands out in the 1980 census is how young the Latino population was in many cities. For example, 70 percent of the children aged 3 and older enrolled in school in Scottsbluff were in kindergarten and elementary school. A similar percentage was found in North Platte (72 percent). In Omaha and Lincoln, due to the universities, we see lower numbers of younger Latinos at 56 percent and 43 percent, respectively. However, the Latinos living in Lincoln in 1980 had the highest percentage of students enrolled in college (33 percent).

Missed in this analysis of Latino Pueblos from 1980 are the small rural communities that had significant Latino populations. We are able to capture this presence using 1980 census data at the county level. The largest Latino population lived in Douglas County (8,236 residents). The second-largest Latino population was in Scottsbluff County (4,714), followed by

Table 3. Key Demographic for Cities with more than 1,000 Latinos in 1980. U.S. Census Bureau, 1980 Decennial Census.

	Persons Not of Spanish origin	Mexican Origin	Percent Mexican	Persons 25 Years Old and Over Of Spanish Origin	Percent Over 25	Percent Some College	Percent College or More
Omaha City	7,319	5,970	82%	3126	43%	19%	45%
Lincoln City	2,745	1,925	70%	1004	37%	30%	33%
Scottsbluff City	2,347	2,193	93%	913	39%	16%	13%
North Platte City	1,279	1,125	88%	494	39%	12%	38%
Grand Island City	1,066	961	90%	376	35%	6%	33%

Lancaster County (2,879). This is incredible for Scottsbluff County because half of the Latinos (2,367 out of 4,714) lived outside of the City of Scottsbluff. By 1980, every county except Arthur, Hayes, McPherson, and Thomas had Latino residents.

2000 Census

The 2000 census marked a pivotal moment in American history, revealing the transformative changes occurring in cities across the United States. Notably, the growth of the Latino population was remarkable, and Nebraska was no exception to this trend. In fact, a significant demographic shift had taken place since the 1980 census, where the Latino population surpassed the African American population at the state level (Ravuri 2003).

In 1990, Nebraska had 56,711 African American residents compared to 36,936 Latino residents. However, over the following decade, the Latino population surged to 94,425 residents, while the African American population grew to 67,537. This growth set the stage for the emergence of the first Latino-majority Pueblo in Lexington, Nebraska, where 51 percent of the population identified as Latino (Bodvarsson and Van den Berg 2003). Similarly, Schuyler experienced significant change, with 47 percent of its population classified as Latino, while South Sioux City reported a Latino population comprising 25 percent of its residents (Palacios and Khrais 2017).

Although Scottsbluff also saw an increase in the percentage of Latinos from 17 percent to 23 percent, it was no longer the city with the highest proportion of Latinos. This shift in dynamics underscored the evolving landscape of Latino demographics in Nebraska.

The 2000 census not only highlighted the phenomenal growth of the Latino population but also showcased the emergence of Latino-majority Pueblos in Nebraska, signifying a substantial transformation in the state's demographic composition.

The demographic history of Latinos in new destinations like Lexington, Schuyler, and South Sioux City highlights the importance of push-and-pull factors of agriculture-related industries (Palacios and Khrais 2017; Pitt 2021). Latino Pueblos also have symbolic value, just like the Veteran's memorial in Scottsbluff. The new gente (people) in these cities is a testament to not only their contributions to these cities through their work, but also the resilience of Latino communities.

Research shows how the people in these growing Latino communities were met with the harsh reality of racism. The local newspapers documented the arrival of Latinos, mainly Mexican immigrants. New job opportunities were opening in the meat packing industries, mostly located along Interstate 80. Many Latinos migrated to these cities to find stable employment and a new home to live out the American dream. They soon found out that part of the American experience would involve facing language barriers, discrimination, exploitation, and socioeconomic disparities. Similar to the stories told in Los Voces, these new Latino residents would establish strong and cohesive communities that relied on mutual support and the solidarity of family and friends. The 2000

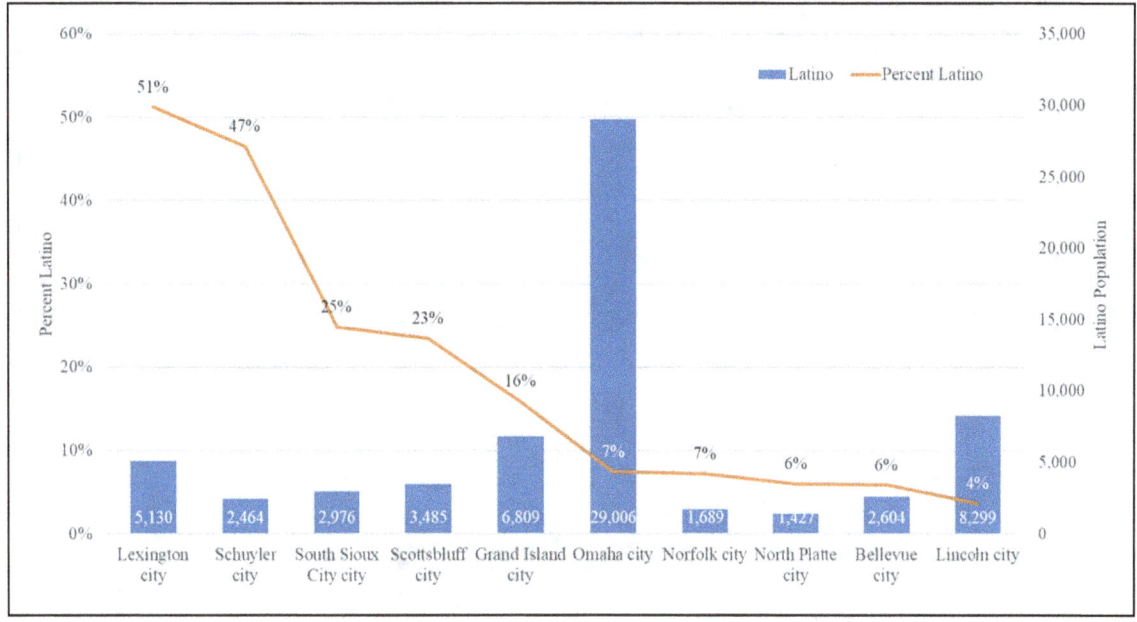

Figure 11. The Percent of the Population was classified as Hispanic in 2000. U.S. Census Bureau, 2000 Decennial Census.

census revealed that these new destinations, similar to the past development in Scottsbluff, North Platte, and Omaha, continued to attract Latinos. These new communities preserved their rich cultural traditions and planted demographic seeds that will continue to change Nebraska. (See Figure 11)

The 2000 census also provided new insights about the age of Nebraska's Latino population. One of the most amazing demographic trends was the increase in young Latinos throughout Nebraska. Among the top ten cities with the highest percentage of Latinos, Latinas were younger than Latinos, except for Scottsbluff. Among these cities, the oldest Latino population was 24 years old (as measured by median age), and the median age for Norfolk was 21 years old.

2020 Census

The 2020 census will be remembered as a controversial one, marked by the challenges posed by the COVID-19 pandemic and concerns about manipulation of the census count. Despite these circumstances, the census data revealed a significant demographic change for Latinos in Nebraska when compared to the 1980 census. The Latino population, which constituted only about 2 percent of the state's population in 1980, had grown to 12 percent.

The 2020 census reported a total Latino population of 235,715 people, with over 67,000 Latinos choosing Nebraska as their home. This remarkable demographic growth has had a profound impact on many cities in the state. Notably, four cities have now become majority Latino "Pueblos." Schuyler stands out with 72.5 percent of its residents being Latino, followed by Lexington with 65.2 percent Latino residents. Additionally, more than half of the residents in Madison (51.6 percent) and South Sioux City (50.7 percent) identify as Latino. Other cities, such as Crete and Wakefield, are on the verge of reaching majority-Latino status (Potter, Cantarero, and Pischel 2008).

While there has been significant growth among the Latino population in Scottsbluff (31.7 percent), where approximately one out of three residents are now Latino, it no longer ranks among the top 15 cities in Nebraska in terms of the highest percentage of Latino residents.

These census findings highlight the increasing presence and influence of the Latino community in Nebraska. The growth of Latino "Pueblos" and the expanding Latino populations in various cities signify a shift in demographics that will undoubtedly have far-reaching implications for the social, cultural, and economic landscape of Nebraska. It is essential for communities and policymakers to recognize and respond to these demographic changes, ensuring equitable representation, access to resources, and opportunities for all residents, regardless of their background or ethnicity.

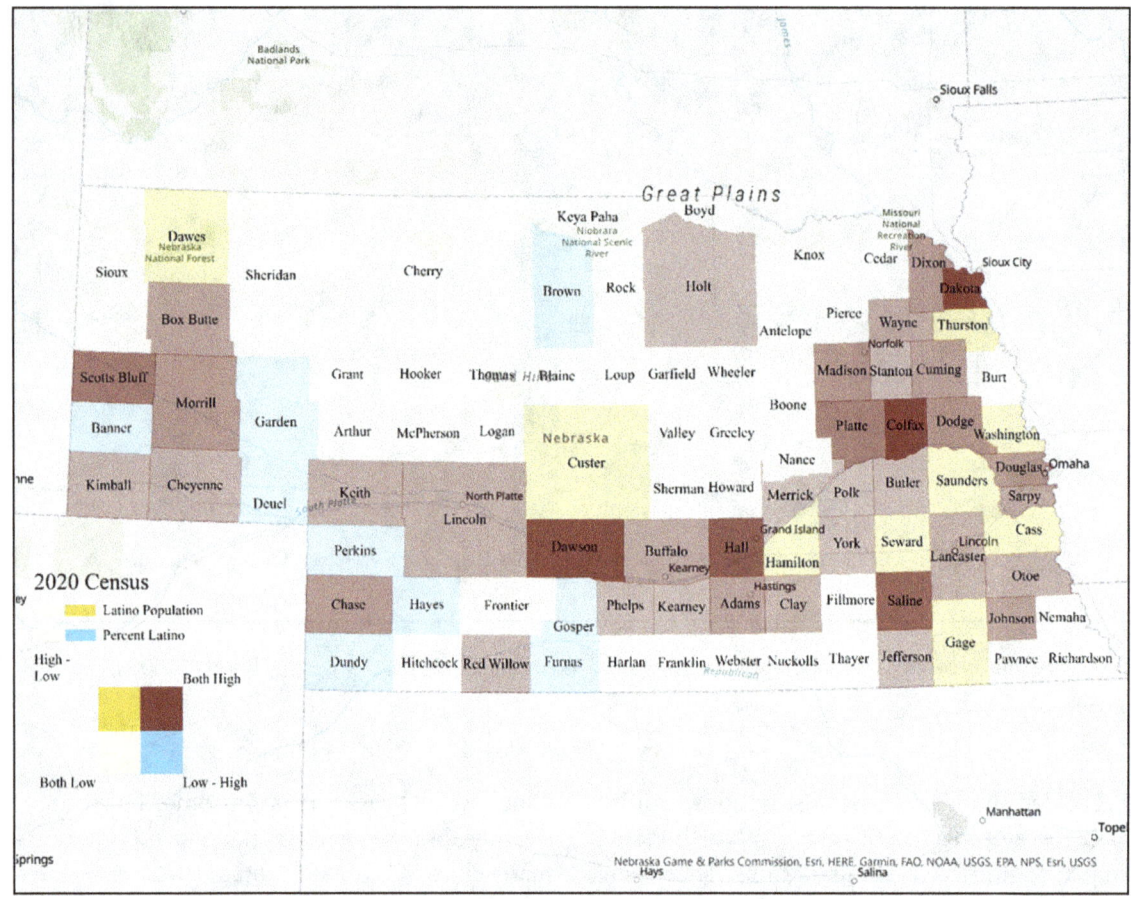

Figure 12. Percent Latino and Latino Population- 2020 Census. U.S. Census Bureau, 2020 Decennial Census..

The largest Latino populations in Nebraska are found in Omaha, Lincoln, Grand Island, Bellevue, and South Sioux City. According to recent data, two counties are approaching a majority Latino population: Colfax County, with 47 percent Latino residents and home to Schuyler, and Dakota County, with 41 percent Latino residents and home to South Sioux City. Other notable counties include Hall County, with 30 percent Latino residents and home to Grand Island, Saline County at 28 percent Latino with Crete as its hub, and Scottsbluff County at 23 percent. In terms of total Latino population size, Douglas County has the largest number, followed by Lancaster and Sarpy counties. (See Figure 12.)

American Community Survey

The U.S. Census has provided additional data from the American Community Survey that help illustrate the demographic transitions within the Latino population. Tables 4-9 provide key demographic characteristics for selected cities.

Ethnic Origin

Overall, in the state, about 3 in 4 Latinos are of Mexican heritage. However, the data shows that this pattern deviates in Fremont (55 percent Mexican), Lexington (51 percent Mexican), and Schuyler (46 percent). While Mexicans constitute the largest ethnic group in these cities, the Central American population is the second largest, comprising 36 percent in Fremont, 41 percent in Lexington, and 36 percent in Schuyler. Self-identified Guatemalans were the largest ethnic group, followed by Salvadorans.[37]

It is interesting to note that Madison and South Sioux City did not experience these demographic changes. In Madison, 87 percent of the Latino population is of Mexican descent, while 4 percent are from Central America. In South Sioux City, 86 percent are of Mexican descent, and 10 percent are from Central America. Additionally, Grand Island has the largest Cuban population among these selected cities and is also home to the largest Central American population in terms of absolute numbers, primarily from

---

37. For a brief overview of the Maya Pixan in Omaha see, "About Us," *Comunidad Maya Pixan Ixim,* https://www.pixanixim.org/about.html.

Table 4. Hispanic or Latino by Specific Origin. ACS 2021 (5-Year Estimates) U.S. Census Bureau.

	Nebraska		Columbus		Fremont		Grand Island		Lexington		Lincoln		Madison		Omaha		Schuyler		Scottsbluff		South Sioux City	
	n	%	n	%	n	%	n	%	n	%	n	%	n	%	n	%	n	%	n	%	n	%
Not Hispanic or Latino	1,726,787	88.5%	18,244	76.2%	23,004	84.4%	35,332	67.0%	3,787	36.7%	265,771	91.9%	986	50.4%	417,328	85.5%	1,845	28.3%	10,419	71.8%	7,195	52.2%
Hispanic or Latino:	224,693	11.5%	5,710	23.8%	4,241	15.6%	17,423	33.0%	6,538	63.3%	23,365	8.1%	969	49.6%	70,731	14.5%	4,681	71.7%	4,092	28.2%	6,601	47.9%
Mexican	161,377	8.3%	3,793	15.8%	2,334	8.6%	9,964	18.9%	3,305	32.0%	15,843	5.5%	841	43.0%	53,131	10.9%	2,165	33.2%	3,542	24.4%	5,682	41.2%
Puerto Rican	7,009	0.4%	43	0.2%	53	0.2%	156	0.3%	0	0.0%	1,038	0.4%	0	0.0%	2,535	0.5%	0	0.0%	93	0.6%	226	1.6%
Cuban	5,395	0.3%	458	1.9%	91	0.3%	1,259	2.4%	228	2.2%	719	0.3%	77	3.9%	830	0.2%	110	1.7%	22	0.2%	0	0.0%
Dominican Republic	957	0.1%	0	0.0%	0	0.0%	0	0.0%	0	0.0%	219	0.1%	0	0.0%	231	0.1%	0	0.0%	0	0.0%	0	0.0%
Central American:	30,327	1.6%	1,257	5.3%	1,511	5.6%	4,358	8.3%	2,709	26.2%	2,358	0.8%	41	2.1%	8,428	1.7%	1,696	26.0%	41	0.3%	686	5.0%
Costa Rican	284	0.0%	0	0.0%	0	0.0%	0	0.0%	40	0.0%	0	0.0%	0	0.0%	96	0.0%	0	0.0%	0	0.0%	0	0.0%
Guatemalan	17,281	0.9%	647	2.7%	989	3.6%	3,042	5.8%	1,830	17.7%	1,078	0.4%	6	0.3%	3,425	0.7%	1,606	24.6%	41	0.3%	622	4.5%
Honduran	3,601	0.2%	436	1.8%	104	0.4%	232	0.5%	537	5.2%	83	0.0%	0	0.0%	1,195	0.2%	28	0.4%	0	0.0%	0	0.0%
Nicaraguan	448	0.0%	0	0.0%	0	0.0%	57	0.1%	0	0.0%	3	0.0%	6	0.3%	301	0.1%	0	0.0%	0	0.0%	0	0.0%
Panamanian	338	0.0%	0	0.0%	12	0.0%	0	0.0%	0	0.0%	64	0.0%	0	0.0%	103	0.0%	0	0.0%	0	0.0%	0	0.0%
Salvadoran	8,161	0.4%	174	0.7%	406	1.5%	1,007	1.9%	342	3.3%	1,017	0.4%	29	1.5%	3,257	0.7%	62	1.0%	0	0.0%	64	0.5%
Other Central American	214	0.0%	0	0.0%	0	0.0%	0	0.0%	0	0.0%	73	0.0%	0	0.0%	51	0.0%	0	0.0%	0	0.0%	0	0.0%
South American:	5,660	0.3%	153	0.6%	13	0.1%	562	1.1%	128	1.2%	682	0.2%	3	0.2%	2,550	0.5%	0	0.0%	117	0.8%	0	0.0%
Argentinean	481	0.0%	0	0.0%	0	0.0%	0	0.0%	97	0.9%	71	0.0%	0	0.0%	129	0.0%	0	0.0%	0	0.0%	0	0.0%
Bolivian	134	0.0%	0	0.0%	0	0.0%	0	0.0%	0	0.0%	8	0.0%	0	0.0%	27	0.0%	0	0.0%	0	0.0%	0	0.0%
Chilean	1,122	0.1%	18	0.1%	0	0.0%	209	0.4%	0	0.0%	74	0.0%	3	0.2%	685	0.1%	0	0.0%	0	0.0%	0	0.0%
Colombian	1,579	0.1%	27	0.1%	13	0.1%	7	0.0%	31	0.3%	106	0.0%	0	0.0%	775	0.2%	0	0.0%	43	0.3%	0	0.0%
Ecuadorian	284	0.0%	0	0.0%	0	0.0%	14	0.0%	0	0.0%	44	0.0%	0	0.0%	176	0.0%	0	0.0%	0	0.0%	0	0.0%
Paraguayan	3	0.0%	0	0.0%	0	0.0%	0	0.0%	0	0.0%	0	0.0%	0	0.0%	0	0.0%	0	0.0%	0	0.0%	0	0.0%
Peruvian	855	0.0%	87	0.4%	0	0.0%	10	0.0%	0	0.0%	213	0.1%	0	0.0%	306	0.1%	0	0.0%	74	0.5%	0	0.0%
Uruguayan	137	0.0%	21	0.1%	0	0.0%	0	0.0%	0	0.0%	0	0.0%	0	0.0%	0	0.0%	0	0.0%	0	0.0%	0	0.0%
Venezuelan	976	0.1%	0	0.0%	0	0.0%	295	0.6%	0	0.0%	152	0.1%	0	0.0%	411	0.1%	0	0.0%	0	0.0%	0	0.0%
Other South American	89	0.0%	0	0.0%	0	0.0%	27	0.1%	0	0.0%	14	0.0%	0	0.0%	41	0.0%	0	0.0%	0	0.0%	0	0.0%
Other Hispanic or Latino:	13,968	0.7%	6	0.0%	239	0.9%	1,124	2.1%	168	1.6%	2,506	0.9%	7	0.4%	3,026	0.6%	710	10.9%	277	1.9%	7	0.1%
Spaniard	2,701	0.1%	0	0.0%	29	0.1%	109	0.2%	17	0.2%	188	0.1%	0	0.0%	619	0.1%	20	0.3%	69	0.5%	0	0.0%
Spanish	3,043	0.2%	0	0.0%	0	0.0%	683	1.3%	0	0.0%	598	0.2%	7	0.4%	402	0.1%	151	2.3%	81	0.6%	0	0.0%
Spanish American	410	0.0%	0	0.0%	0	0.0%	0	0.0%	0	0.0%	9	0.0%	0	0.0%	0	0.0%	284	4.4%	0	0.0%	0	0.0%
All Other Hispanic or Latino	7,814	0.4%	6	0.0%	210	0.8%	332	0.6%	151	1.5%	1,711	0.6%	0	0.0%	2,005	0.4%	255	3.9%	127	0.9%	7	0.1%
Total Population	1,951,480		23,954		27,245		52,755		10,325		289,136		1,955		488,059		6,526		14,511		13,796	

Guatemala and El Salvador. (See Table 4.) These findings align with research conducted by John F. Thomas (1967), who noted that many Cubans migrated to Grand Island over the past 30 years due to recruitment efforts by meat packing companies in Florida. Additionally, some Cubans relocated to Nebraska because the state was designated as a refugee resettlement area. Cuban refugees began arriving in Nebraska as early as the 1960s, seeking refuge and employment opportunities.

Place of Birth

As discussed earlier in this chapter, one of the key tensions within the Latino population revolves around negotiating identities between U.S.-born Latinos and those born in another country. Examining the statistics on place of birth provides fascinating insights when considering the historical context of migration patterns along the Platte River.

In Nebraska, 43 percent of Latinos are born in the state, highlighting the presence of a significant native-born Latino population. Approximately 22 percent of Latinos were born in another U.S. state and migrated to Nebraska, while one-third of residents are classified as immigrants. However, discerning a clear pattern that distinguishes between Latino citizens and immigrants within specific cities proves challenging. Table 5 illustrates the complexity of negotiated identities across Nebraska's cities.

For instance, Schuyler, the city with the highest percentage of Latinos in the state, also has the highest proportion of foreign-born Latinos among the selected cities. Similarly, Lexington, another majority-Latino Pueblo, boasts a significant population of foreign-born Latinos. Columbus, known as the site of the first historical encounter with Latinos, reports that 49 percent of its Latino population is foreign-born, with South Sioux City reporting a similar figure. These cities, along with the traditional destination cities along the Platte River, are experiencing change driven by immigration from Mexico and Central America (Massey, Rugh, and Pren 2010).

Scottsbluff stands out as a city undergoing different dynamics, as only 12 percent of its Latino population is classified as foreign-born. Furthermore, when considering the number of Latinos who moved to these cities from other states, Scottsbluff reports the lowest percentage of newcomers. In fact, except for Scottsbluff, more than half of the selected population was either born in another state or foreign-born. In Scottsbluff, 70 percent of Latinos were born in Nebraska, while the second-largest population of state-born Latinos is in Lincoln, accounting for 50 percent. This

Table 5. Place Of Birth (Hispanic or Latino) In the United States. ACS 2021 (5-Year Estimates) U.S. Census Bureau.

	Nebraska		Columbus		Fremont		Grand Island		Lexington		Lincoln		Madison		Omaha		Schuyler		Scottsbluff		South Sioux City	
	n	%	n	%	n	%	n	%	n	%	n	%	n	%	n	%	n	%	n	%	n	%
Born In State Of Residence	96,650	43.0%	1,869	32.7%	1,554	36.6%	6,959	39.9%	2,019	30.9%	11,620	49.7%	285	29.4%	31,831	45.0%	1,169	25.0%	2,886	70.5%	739	11.2%
Born In Other State In The United States	48,929	21.8%	972	17.0%	902	21.3%	2,976	17.1%	1,160	17.7%	5,249	22.5%	261	26.9%	12,761	18.0%	111	2.4%	683	16.7%	2,507	38.0%
Native; Born Outside The United States	4,667	2.1%	72	1.3%	105	2.5%	249	1.4%	21	0.3%	513	2.2%	0	0.0%	1,331	1.9%	116	2.5%	34	0.8%	225	3.4%
Foreign Born	74,447	33.1%	2,797	49.0%	1,680	39.6%	7,239	41.6%	3,338	51.1%	5,983	25.6%	423	43.7%	24,808	35.1%	3,285	70.2%	489	12.0%	3,130	47.4%
Total:	224,693		5,710		4,241		17,423		6,538		23,365		969		70,731		4,681		4,092		6,601	

suggests that many Latinos born in Nebraska may have migrated from other parts of the state to Lincoln, while those living in Scottsbluff were likely born in Scottsbluff or nearby towns in western Nebraska.

These findings highlight the intricate dynamics of birthplace and migration within Nebraska's Latino population, underscoring the diverse trajectories and experiences that shape Latinidad across different cities in the state.

Nativity and Foreign-born Status

Table 6 provides valuable statistics on Nebraska Latino residents categorized by age, nativity, and foreign-born status. The data reveal interesting insights when analyzed through various analytical lenses. For instance, Scottsbluff has the highest percentage of native-born Latinos at 88 percent, followed by Lincoln at 74 percent and Omaha at 65 percent.

One interpretation of the table is that Schuyler has a significant population of Latino immigrants, accounting for 70 percent of its total population. Furthermore, within this immigrant group, 72 percent do not possess U.S. citizenship. Another perspective is that half of Schuyler's overall population consists of Latino immigrants who lack U.S. citizenship. Whichever way one chooses to interpret the data, it is clear that the Latino population in Nebraska is vulnerable. Even in Scottsbluff, which has a sizable population of 489 Latino immigrants, a striking 73 percent of them do not possess U.S. citizenship. This trend persists across all cities, where the majority or a significant proportion of immigrants lack U.S. citizenship.

These findings emphasize the vulnerability of the Latino population, highlighting the challenges and potential barriers they face, particularly in relation to immigration status and access to certain rights and privileges. It underscores the importance of

Table 6. Nativity And Citizenship Status (Hispanic or Latino). ACS 2021 (5-Year Estimates) U.S. Census Bureau.

	Nebraska		Columbus		Fremont		Grand Island		Lexington		Lincoln		Madison		Omaha		Schuyler		Scottsbluff		South Sioux City	
	n	%	n	%	n	%	n	%	n	%	n	%	n	%	n	%	n	%	n	%	n	%
Under 18 Years	89,095	39.7%	2,230	39.1%	1,860	43.9%	6,849	39.3%	2,480	37.9%	8,865	37.9%	350	36.1%	28,655	40.5%	2,007	42.9%	1,745	42.6%	2,504	37.9%
Native	82,580	36.8%	2,014	35.3%	1,791	42.2%	6,277	36.0%	2,080	31.8%	8,554	36.6%	318	32.8%	26,553	37.5%	1,127	24.1%	1,650	40.3%	2,308	35.0%
Foreign Born	6,515	2.9%	216	3.8%	69	1.6%	572	3.3%	400	6.1%	311	1.3%	32	3.3%	2,102	3.0%	880	18.8%	95	2.3%	196	3.0%
Naturalized U.S. Citizen	1,093	0.5%	92	1.6%	51	1.2%	8	0.0%	94	1.4%	10	0.0%	7	0.7%	223	0.3%	210	4.5%	0	0.0%	18	0.3%
Not A U.S. Citizen	5,422	2.4%	124	2.2%	18	0.4%	564	3.2%	306	4.7%	301	1.3%	25	2.6%	1,879	2.7%	670	14.3%	95	2.3%	178	2.7%
18 Years And Over	135,598	60.3%	3,480	60.9%	2,381	56.1%	10,574	60.7%	4,058	62.1%	14,500	62.1%	619	63.9%	42,076	59.5%	2,674	57.1%	2,347	57.4%	4,097	62.1%
Native	67,666	30.1%	899	15.7%	770	18.2%	3,907	22.4%	1,120	17.1%	8,828	37.8%	228	23.5%	19,370	27.4%	269	5.7%	1,953	47.7%	1,163	17.6%
Foreign Born	67,932	30.2%	2,581	45.2%	1,611	38.0%	6,667	38.3%	2,938	44.9%	5,672	24.3%	391	40.4%	22,706	32.1%	2,405	51.4%	394	9.6%	2,934	44.4%
Naturalized U.S. Citizen	23,757	10.6%	1,011	17.7%	530	12.5%	1,963	11.3%	1,435	21.9%	2,186	9.4%	104	10.7%	6,669	9.4%	701	15.0%	131	3.2%	1,572	23.8%
Not A U.S. Citizen	44,175	19.7%	1,570	27.5%	1,081	25.5%	4,704	27.0%	1,503	23.0%	3,486	14.9%	287	29.6%	16,037	22.7%	1,704	36.4%	263	6.4%	1,362	20.6%
Total Latino Population	224,693	100.0%	5,710	100.0%	4,241	100.0%	17,423	100.0%	6,538	100.0%	23,365	100.0%	969	100.0%	70,731	100.0%	4,681	100.0%	4,092	100.0%	6,601	100.0%
Native	150,246	66.9%	2,913	51.0%	2,561	60.4%	10,184	58.5%	3,200	48.9%	17,382	74.4%	546	56.3%	45,923	64.9%	1,396	29.8%	3,603	88.0%	3,471	52.6%
Foreign Born	74,447	33.1%	2,797	49.0%	1,680	39.6%	7,239	41.5%	3,338	51.1%	5,983	25.6%	423	43.7%	24,808	35.1%	3,285	70.2%	489	12.0%	3,130	47.4%
Naturalized U.S. Citizen	24,850	11.1%	1,103	19.3%	581	13.7%	1,971	11.3%	1,529	23.4%	2,196	9.4%	111	11.5%	6,892	9.7%	911	19.5%	131	3.2%	1,590	24.1%
Not A U.S. Citizen	49,597	22.1%	1,694	29.7%	1,099	25.9%	5,268	30.2%	1,809	27.7%	3,787	16.2%	312	32.2%	17,916	25.3%	2,374	50.7%	358	8.7%	1,540	23.3%

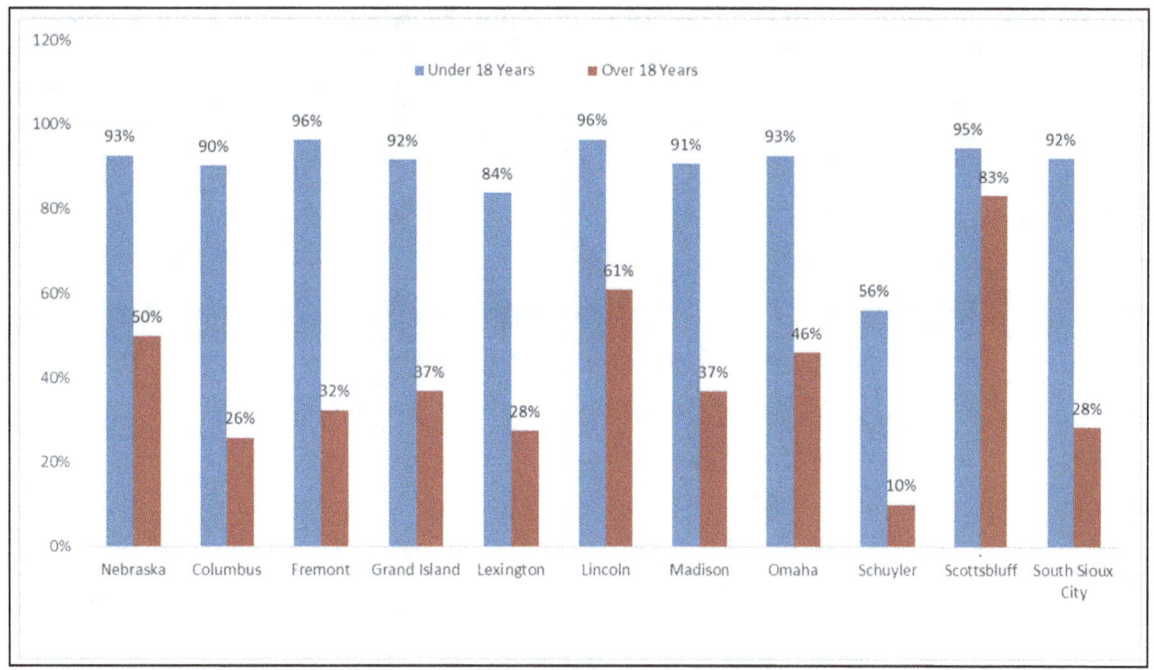

Figure 13. Nativity Status by Age (Hispanic Or Latino). ACS 2021 (5-Year Estimates) U.S. Census Bureau.

addressing the needs and concerns of this population to ensure equitable opportunities and support within the communities they reside in Nebraska.

Age

When examining the statistics by age, intriguing patterns emerge. Except for Lexington and Schuyler, all cities reported that at least 90 percent of Latinos under 18 years old were born in the United States. Lexington stands out with 84 percent of its Latino youth being born in the U.S., while Schuyler deviates from the trend, with only 56 percent of its youth being U.S.-born. In terms of the 18 and over population, Lincoln and Scottsbluff are the only cities where the majority are native-born citizens. Scottsbluff, in particular, has a notable 22-percentage-point higher proportion of the 18 and over population compared to Lincoln.

These findings shed light on the varying dynamics of nativity and age within the Latino population across different cities in Nebraska. The higher percentage of U.S.-born youth suggests a trend toward generational shifts and the development of a second generation that is increasingly rooted in the United States. On the other hand, the majority of the 18 and over population being native-born citizens in Lincoln and Scottsbluff highlights the presence of established Latino communities where generations have been born and raised in Nebraska. (See Figure 13.)

Language

Language plays a significant role in the context of immigration, and examining the data on Latinos provides an intriguing perspective on the relationship between language and Latino communities. Notably, among native-born Latinos, there is a division between English-only speakers and those who speak another language. Only in Lincoln and Scottsbluff do the majority of native-born Latino citizens speak English only. Schuyler, once again, stands out as an exception, with just 1 percent of the native-born population identifying as English-only speakers. South Sioux City and Madison have slightly higher percentages compared to Schuyler.

In previous generations, one of the defining characteristics was the motivation and desire of immigrants to ensure their children learned and spoke English, viewing it as a key to success and achieving the American dream. However, learning a new language, including English, is a challenging and time-consuming process for immigrants across the United States.

Interestingly, Schuyler has the lowest percentage of Latino immigrants who reported speaking English "very well" at 16 percent. Conversely, Columbus has the highest percentage of Latino immigrants who speak English "very well" at 35 percent.

These findings highlight the diverse linguistic profiles within the Latino population in Nebraska and underscore the complexities immigrants face in

Table 7. Nativity By Language Spoken At Home By Ability To Speak English For The Population 5 Years And Over (Hispanic Or Latino). ACS 2021 (5-Year Estimates) U.S. Census Bureau.

	Nebraska		Columbus		Fremont		Grand Island		Lexington		Lincoln		Madison		Omaha		Schuyler		Scottsbluff		South Sioux City	
	n	%	n	%	n	%	n	%	n	%	n	%	n	%	n	%	n	%	n	%	n	%
Native:	124,800	62.9%	2,148	43.4%	1,867	52.6%	8,028	52.7%	2,517	43.0%	14,769	71.3%	471	53.2%	37,937	60.8%	814	19.9%	3,172	86.6%	2,892	48.6%
Speak Only English	63,468	32.0%	731	14.8%	487	13.7%	3,382	22.2%	680	11.6%	8,961	43.2%	65	7.3%	16,347	26.2%	5	0.1%	1,884	51.5%	380	6.4%
Speak Another Language:	61,332	30.9%	1,417	28.7%	1,380	38.9%	4,646	30.5%	1,837	31.4%	5,808	28.0%	406	45.8%	21,590	34.6%	809	19.7%	1,288	35.2%	2,512	42.2%
Speak English "Very Well"	50,074	25.2%	1,050	21.2%	1,216	34.3%	3,941	25.9%	1,422	24.3%	4,538	21.9%	346	39.1%	17,337	27.8%	494	12.1%	1,116	30.5%	1,977	33.2%
Speak English Less Than "Very Well"	11,258	5.7%	367	7.4%	164	4.6%	705	4.6%	415	7.1%	1,270	6.1%	60	6.8%	4,253	6.8%	315	7.7%	172	4.7%	535	9.0%
Foreign Born:	73,717	37.1%	2,797	56.6%	1,680	47.4%	7,217	47.3%	3,338	57.0%	5,960	28.8%	415	46.8%	24,435	39.2%	3,285	80.1%	489	13.4%	3,058	51.4%
Speak Only English	4,285	2.2%	104	2.1%	21	0.6%	492	3.2%	316	5.4%	517	2.5%	0	0.0%	1,254	2.0%	31	0.8%	23	0.6%	235	4.0%
Speak Another Language:	69,432	35.0%	2,693	54.5%	1,659	46.8%	6,725	44.1%	3,022	51.6%	5,443	26.3%	415	46.8%	23,181	37.2%	3,254	79.4%	466	12.7%	2,823	47.5%
Speak English "Very Well"	21,040	10.6%	948	19.2%	370	10.4%	2,086	13.7%	919	15.7%	1,756	8.5%	100	11.3%	6,842	11.0%	521	12.7%	91	2.5%	629	10.6%
Speak English Less Than "Very Well"	48,392	24.4%	1,745	35.3%	1,289	36.3%	4,639	30.4%	2,103	35.9%	3,687	17.8%	315	35.6%	16,339	26.2%	2,733	66.7%	375	10.2%	2,194	36.9%
Total:	198,517	100.0%	4,945	100.0%	3,547	100.0%	15,245	100.0%	5,855	100.0%	20,729	100.1%	886	100.0%	62,372	100.0%	4,099	100.0%	3,661	100.0%	5,950	100.0%

language acquisition. The lower English proficiency among Latino immigrants in Schuyler suggests potential barriers to communication and integration, while the higher proficiency in Columbus indicates greater linguistic adaptation and potential opportunities for successful integration. This is an interesting finding given the proximity of Columbus and Schuyler. (See Table 7.)

Education

Educational attainment has long been considered a cornerstone of achieving the American Dream, and this theme has resonated strongly in the listening sessions. While the demographic portrait of Latinos in Nebraska presented thus far has been interesting and, in some ways, positive, the statistics on Latino educational achievement should serve as a wake-up call for leaders across the state (Hamann and Harklau 2010). These statistics reveal underlying inequalities among Latinos that must be addressed. (See Table 8)

Nationally and at the state level, approximately 1 in 3 adults holds a "bachelor's degree or better" (33.7 percent nationally and 33 percent in Nebraska). Among the white non-Hispanic population, these numbers are even higher (37.4 percent nationally and 35.3 percent in Nebraska). However, at the state level, only 14 percent of Latinos have acquired a "bachelor's degree or better." While Lincoln reported the highest percentage at 20 percent, several cities had distressingly low single-digit percentages, such as Columbus (7 percent), Fremont (5 percent), Madison (9 percent), Schuyler (6 percent), and South Sioux City (5 percent). Considering the significant number of native-born Latinos in Nebraska, one would expect the percentage to be higher than 10 percent.

On the other end of the educational spectrum, around 8 percent of Nebraska residents report having

Table 8. Educational Attainment for the Population 25 Years and Over (Hispanic or Latino). ACS 2021 (5-Year Estimates) U.S. Census Bureau.

	Nebraska		Columbus		Fremont		Grand Island		Lexington		Lincoln		Madison		Omaha		Schuyler		Scottsbluff		South Sioux City	
	n	%	n	%	n	%	n	%	n	%	n	%	n	%	n	%	n	%	n	%	n	%
Less Than High School Diploma	39,123	36%	1,277	43%	880	47%	3,381	39%	1,550	48%	3,388	31%	220	43%	13,292	40%	1,373	63%	421	22%	1,488	46%
High School Graduate (Includes Equivalency)	29,148	27%	899	30%	520	28%	2,499	29%	727	23%	2,686	25%	99	19%	8,929	27%	496	23%	682	36%	737	23%
Some College Or Associate's Degree	24,597	23%	586	20%	391	21%	1,879	22%	519	16%	2,673	24%	142	28%	6,679	20%	159	7%	624	33%	853	26%
Bachelor's Degree Or Higher	15,193	14%	220	7%	88	5%	892	10%	417	13%	2,175	20%	47	9%	4,622	14%	140	6%	188	10%	158	5%
Total	108,061	100%	2,982	100%	1,879	100%	8,651	100%	3,213	100%	10,922	100%	508	100%	33,522	100%	2,168	100%	1,915	100%	3,236	100%

earned "less than [a] high school diploma." However, for the Latino population at the state level, the percentage is alarmingly high at 36 percent who report having "less than [a] high school diploma." With the exceptions of Lincoln and Scottsbluff, all other cities report percentages of 40 or above in this category. (See Table 7.)

Regarding the population with less than a high school degree, Lincoln shows a percentage of 31 percent, while Scottsbluff reports 22 percent. Once again, Schuyler stands out as an outlier with a significantly higher percentage of 63 percent driven by the high rate of immigration.

These statistics highlight the urgent need to address educational disparities among Latinos in Nebraska. The low percentage of Latinos with bachelor's degrees or higher suggests barriers to higher education and limited access to opportunities that can impede greater economic and social mobility. The high percentage of Latinos without a high school diploma indicates a significant educational deficit that can impede their ability to thrive in an increasingly competitive job market.

Poverty

The poverty rate is widely recognized as a significant measure of inequality in contemporary social science (Enchautegui 1997; De La Rosa 2008). In the United States, the overall poverty rate stands at 12.6 percent, while in Nebraska, it is slightly lower at 10.3 percent. For white residents, the poverty rates are 9.2 percent for the U.S. and 8.1 percent for Nebraska, indicating relatively lower levels of economic hardship compared to the overall population.

However, it is crucial to acknowledge the disproportionately high levels of poverty experienced by Latinos, regardless of the cities we examine. At the state level, the Latino poverty rate in Nebraska reaches 18 percent, highlighting the significant economic challenges faced by this specific population. It is notable that Scottsbluff, despite having the highest number of native-born Latinos, also has the highest poverty rate at 23.5 percent. This finding challenges the assumption that native-born populations would experience better economic outcomes. It suggests that other factors, such as the availability of employment opportunities and the overall economic landscape of a particular area, play a significant role in shaping poverty rates.

On the other hand, cities with a higher proportion of Latino foreign-born populations, such as Schuyler, Madison, and South Sioux City, seem to have lower Latino poverty rates compared to other cities. This observation implies that these rural towns may offer different employment opportunities or have specific factors that contribute to better economic outcomes for Latino immigrants.

Understanding the nuances and variations in poverty rates among different cities and regions is crucial for developing targeted interventions and policies. It highlights the importance of tailoring approaches to address the specific needs and circumstances of each community. By recognizing the diversity within the Latino population and considering the unique economic dynamics of different areas, we can strive toward more effective strategies to reduce poverty and promote equitable opportunities for all residents (Sandoval and Ruiz 2011).

The disparity in youth poverty rates between Schuyler and Scottsbluff highlights the varying economic conditions and challenges faced by young Latinos in these communities. Scottsbluff's higher youth poverty rate of 13 percent indicates a greater prevalence of economic hardship among young individuals, while Schuyler's lower rate of 4 percent suggests relatively better economic circumstances for young people in that area. Similarly, Madison and South Sioux City, both Latino-majority communities, also demonstrate lower youth poverty rates of 4.9 percent and 4.8 percent, respectively.

One aspect of the 1970s Chicano Movement in Nebraska was to challenge the systemic social and economic inequalities faced by many Latino communities, including unequal access to quality education. The Chicano leaders and activists of that time fought tirelessly for equality and justice, aiming to address these disparities and create a more inclusive society. While Nebraska has experienced demographic changes and increased diversity over the past five decades, the persistence of economic inequality is a sobering reality. When comparing the Latino population to the white non-Hispanic population, significant disparities in economic well-being persist. This disparity underscores the ongoing need to address economic inequities and create pathways for upward mobility within the Latino community.

Efforts to tackle economic inequality and promote opportunities for Latino individuals and families are crucial in ensuring a more just and equitable society. This includes targeted initiatives to address disparities in education, employment, access to resources, and wealth accumulation for both native-born and foreign-born Latino residents in Nebraska. By recognizing

Table 9. Poverty Status in the Past 12 Months by Age (Hispanic or Latino). ACS 2021 (5-Year Estimates) U.S. Census Bureau.

	Nebraska		Columbus		Fremont		Grand Island		Lexington		Lincoln		Madison		Omaha		Schuyler		Scottsbluff		South Sioux City	
	n	%	n	%	n	%	n	%	n	%	n	%	n	%	n	%	n	%	n	%	n	%
Income In The Past 12 Months Below Poverty Level	39,414	18.0%	916	16.1%	607	14.6%	3,453	20.1%	1,160	17.8%	4,998	22.5%	112	11.8%	13,121	19.0%	569	12.6%	958	23.5%	593	9.0%
Under 6 Years	7,174	3.3%	161	2.8%	150	3.6%	806	4.7%	195	3.0%	985	4.4%	11	1.2%	2,022	2.9%	3	0.1%	95	2.3%	78	1.2%
6 To 11 Years	6,505	3.0%	201	3.5%	104	2.5%	549	3.2%	358	5.5%	650	2.9%	21	2.2%	2,318	3.4%	101	2.2%	300	7.4%	89	1.4%
12 To 17 Years	5,562	2.5%	90	1.8%	77	1.9%	583	3.4%	96	1.5%	708	3.2%	14	1.5%	2,156	3.1%	53	1.2%	116	2.9%	145	2.2%
18 To 59 Years	18,120	8.3%	464	8.2%	276	6.6%	1,346	7.9%	470	7.2%	2,427	10.9%	66	6.9%	6,140	8.9%	412	9.1%	334	8.2%	223	3.4%
60 To 74 Years	1,400	0.6%	0	0.0%	0	0.0%	118	0.7%	41	0.6%	167	0.8%	0	0.0%	308	0.5%	0	0.0%	37	0.9%	58	0.9%
75 To 84 Years	266	0.1%	0	0.0%	0	0.0%	0	0.0%	0	0.0%	61	0.3%	0	0.0%	107	0.2%	0	0.0%	15	0.4%	0	0.0%
85 Years And Over	387	0.2%	0	0.0%	0	0.0%	51	0.3%	0	0.0%	0	0.0%	0	0.0%	70	0.1%	0	0.0%	61	1.5%	0	0.0%
Income In The Past 12 Months At Or Above Poverty Level	179,283	82.0%	4,762	83.9%	3,553	85.4%	13,698	79.9%	5,355	82.2%	17,268	77.6%	841	88.3%	55,774	81.0%	3,947	87.4%	3,112	76.5%	6,000	91.0%
Under 6 Years	23,781	10.9%	658	11.6%	634	15.2%	1,831	10.7%	566	8.7%	2,139	9.6%	88	9.2%	7,655	11.1%	594	13.2%	460	11.3%	612	9.3%
6 To 11 Years	21,967	10.0%	668	11.8%	480	11.5%	1,567	9.1%	598	9.2%	2,148	9.7%	57	6.0%	6,840	9.9%	474	10.5%	407	10.0%	654	9.9%
12 To 17 Years	22,307	10.2%	450	7.9%	415	10.0%	1,369	8.0%	667	10.2%	2,163	9.7%	159	16.7%	6,889	10.0%	617	13.7%	367	9.0%	925	14.0%
18 To 59 Years	98,671	45.1%	2,657	46.8%	1,871	45.0%	7,780	45.4%	3,065	47.1%	9,822	43.2%	422	44.3%	30,886	44.8%	2,111	46.7%	1,547	38.0%	3,403	51.6%
60 To 74 Years	10,327	4.7%	302	5.3%	153	3.7%	1,050	6.1%	400	6.1%	921	4.1%	88	9.2%	2,780	4.0%	151	3.3%	268	6.6%	302	4.6%
75 To 84 Years	1,848	0.9%	27	0.5%	0	0.0%	94	0.6%	42	0.6%	232	1.0%	27	2.8%	559	0.8%	0	0.0%	31	0.8%	104	1.6%
85 Years And Over	482	0.2%	0	0.0%	0	0.0%	7	0.0%	17	0.3%	43	0.2%	0	0.0%	165	0.2%	0	0.0%	32	0.8%	0	0.0%
Total	218,697	100.0%	5,678	100.0%	4,160	100.0%	17,151	100.0%	6,515	100.0%	22,266	100.1%	953	100.1%	68,895	100.0%	4,516	100.0%	4,070	100.0%	6,593	100.0%

and actively addressing these disparities, Nebraska policymakers can work toward creating a more inclusive and equitable future for all its residents.

In the next section of this chapter, I will delve into these issues further, examining the spatial patterns and dynamics within selected cities. This analytical approach will provide insights into the specific factors influencing economic inequality and help identify potential strategies for addressing these disparities. By understanding the spatial patterns of economic inequality, policymakers and stakeholders can develop targeted interventions and initiatives to promote economic equity and improve the well-being of Latino communities in Nebraska. (See Table 9.)

VIII. Los Barrios

Neighborhoods play a crucial role in the social sciences as they provide valuable insights into how immigrants and diverse communities form and interact (Sandoval 2011; Sandoval and Ruiz 2011). The study of neighborhoods allows researchers to examine various aspects of community dynamics, social networks, and economic activities, shedding light on the experiences and challenges faced by immigrant populations (South, Crowder, and Chavez 2005). Immigrant, ethnic, and racial groups may cluster in certain neighborhoods due to discrimination in the housing market. However, research has shown that these communities tend to develop businesses and enterprises that cater to the specific needs and preferences of their own community members, as well as contribute to the local economy (Ventura 2021). These businesses not only provide economic opportunities for immigrants but also contribute to the cultural vibrancy and diversity of the neighborhood (Sandoval and Jennings 2012).

Throughout cities in Nebraska with larger Latino populations, we can observe the significant impact of the Latino population on the spatial morphology of these urban and rural areas. The presence of a sizable Latino community influences the physical layout, development patterns, and cultural landscapes of these cities. It can result in the creation of distinct ethnic enclaves or neighborhoods where Latino residents cluster together, shaping the overall socioeconomic fabric of the neighborhoods and communities.

The spatial morphology of cities with significant Latino populations reflects the dynamic interplay between the Latino residents and how they use space and the broader urban environment (Wahl, Breckenridge, and Gunkel 2007). It highlights the ways in which diverse populations shape and transform the physical and cultural landscape of a town, creating a mosaic of identities and experiences.

Figures 14-20 exhibit the spatial distribution of the Latino population and the percentage of Latinos in different census tracts. The utilization of dark red shades to depict Latino Barrios allows for a clear visual representation of these neighborhoods. The figures unveil intriguing spatial patterns within cities, with one particularly striking example being the pronounced clustering of Latino neighborhoods in South Omaha (Reed 2023; Wright, et al. 2014).

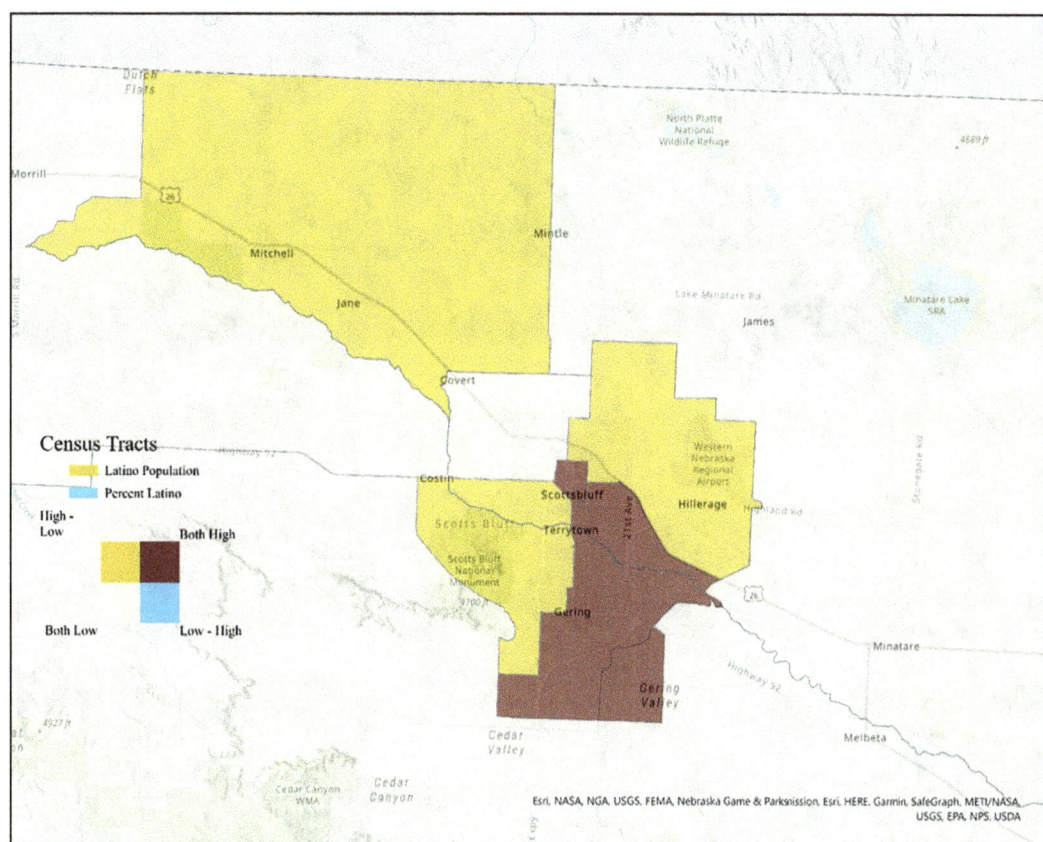

Figure 14. Percent Latino and Latino Population — Scottsbluff. U.S. Census Bureau, 2021 Five-Year American Community Survey.

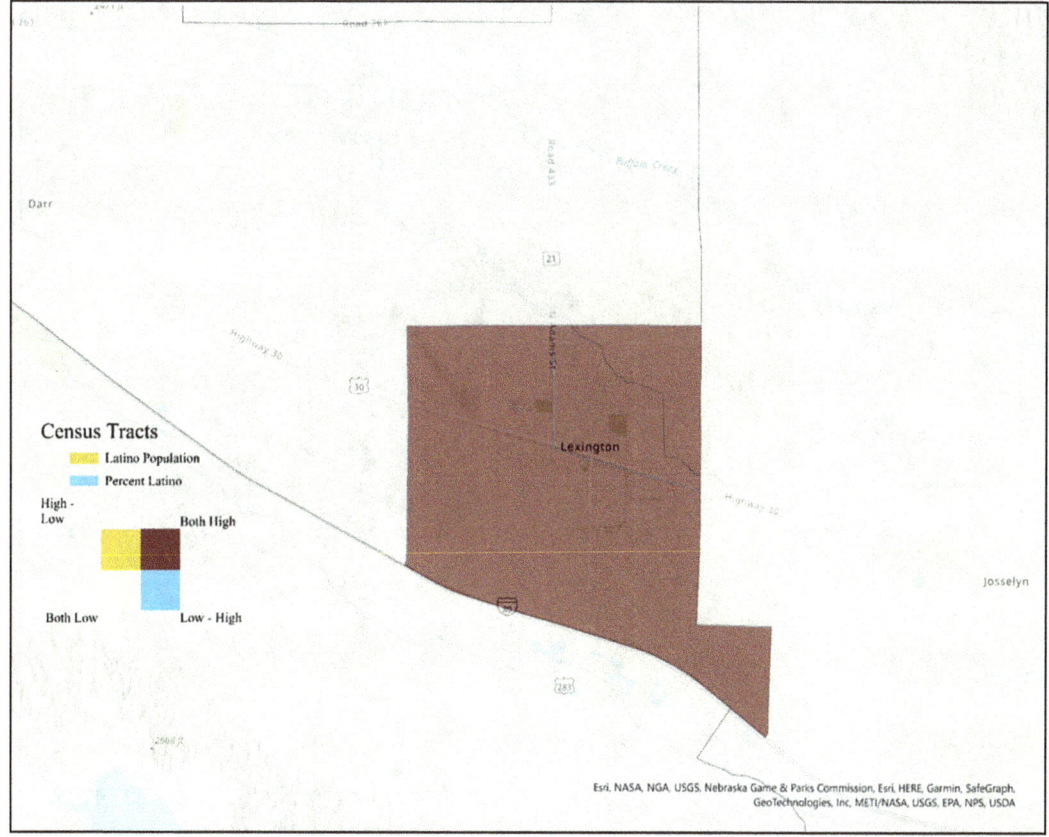

Figure 15. Percent Latino and Latino Population — Lexington. U.S. Census Bureau, 2021 Five-Year American Community Survey.

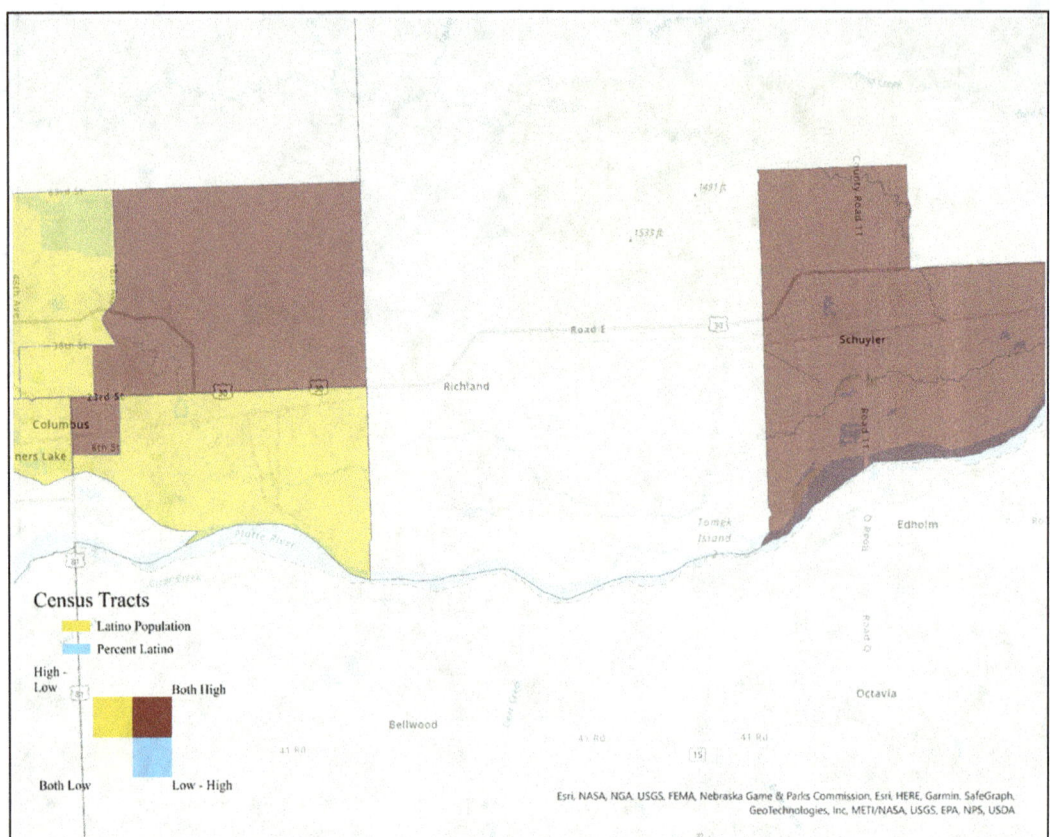

Figure 16. Percent Latino and Latino Population — Columbus and Schuyler. U.S. Census Bureau, 2021 Five-Year American Community Survey.

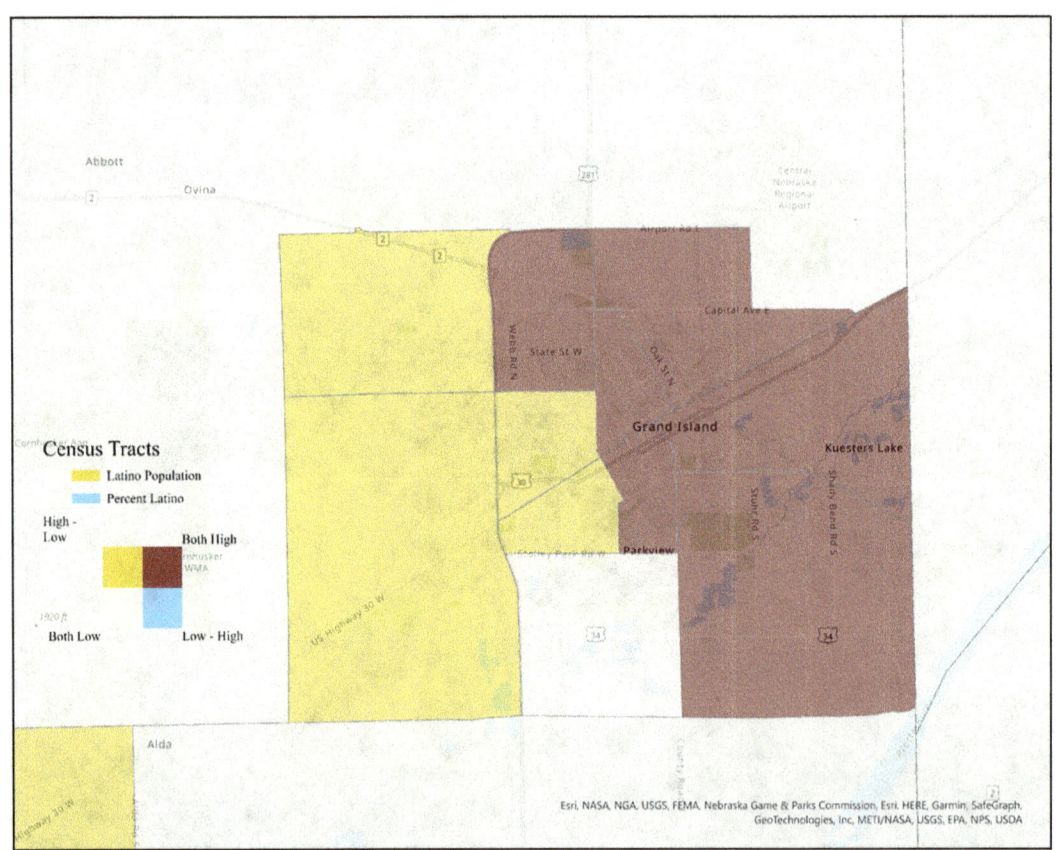

Figure 17. Percent Latino and Latino Population — Grand Island. U.S. Census Bureau, 2021 Five-Year American Community Survey.

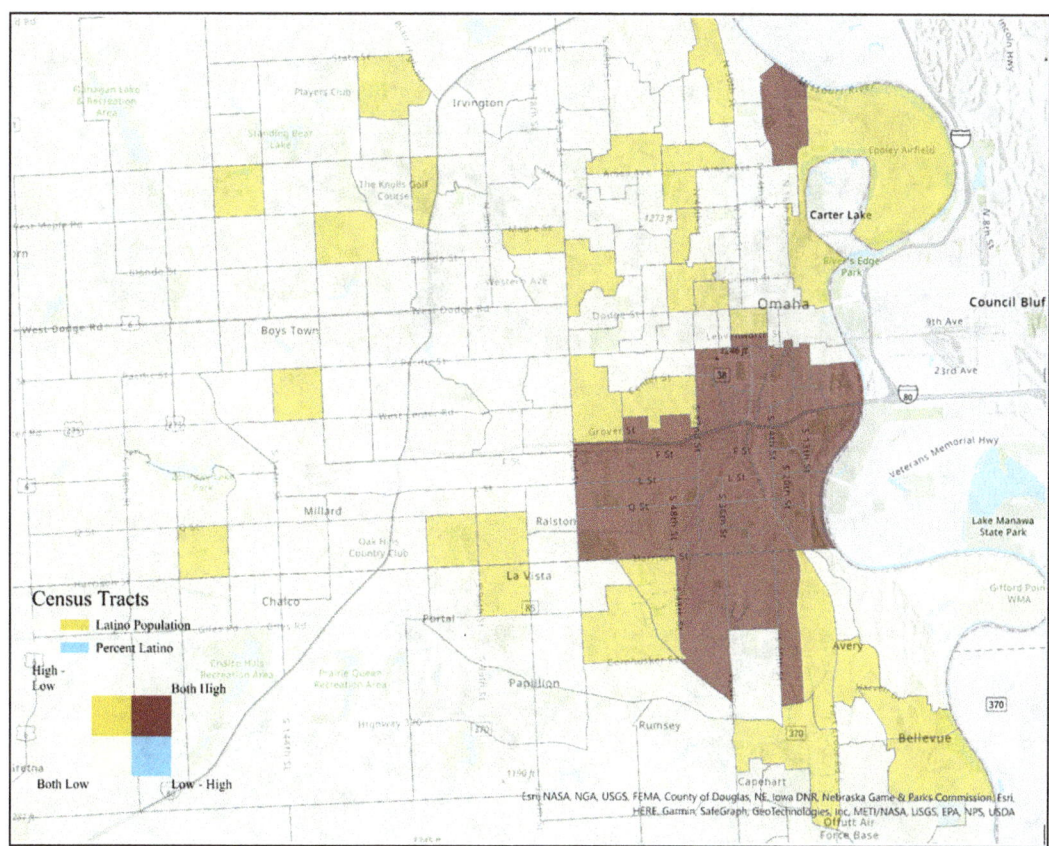

Figure 18. Percent Latino and Latino Population — Omaha. U.S. Census Bureau, 2021 Five-Year American Community Survey.

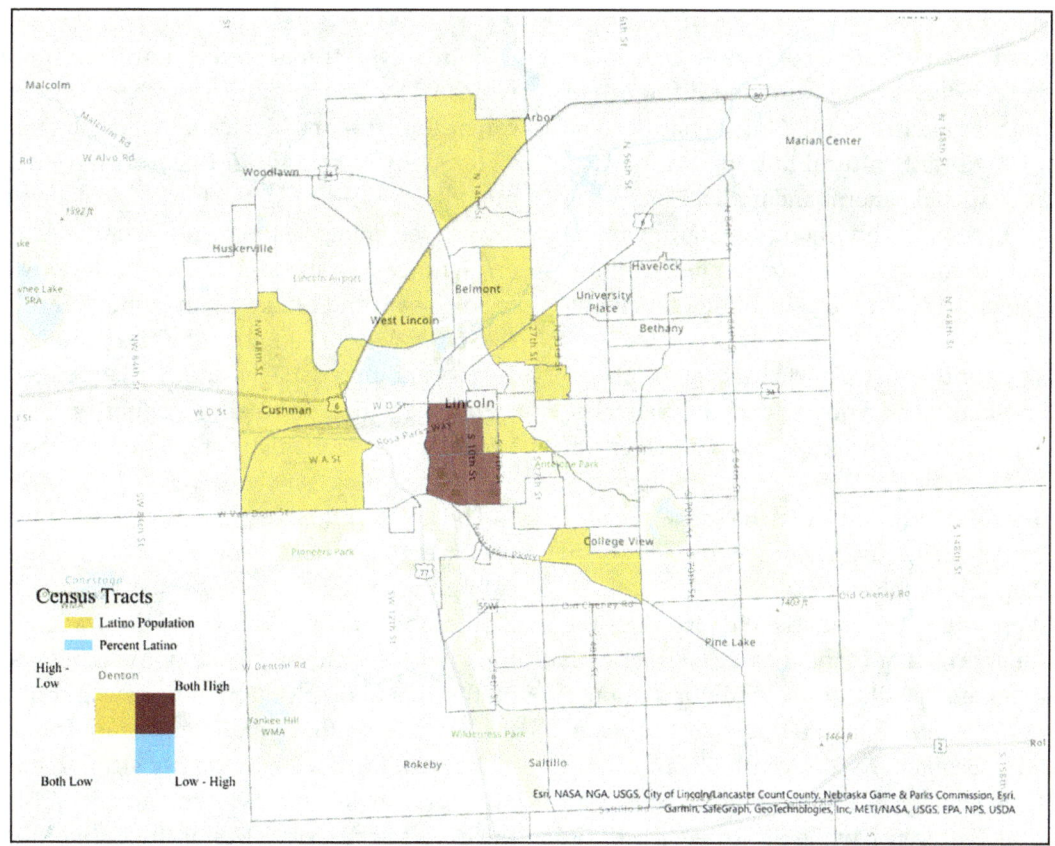

Figure 19. Percent Latino and Latino Population — Lincoln. U.S. Census Bureau, 2021 Five-Year American Community Survey.

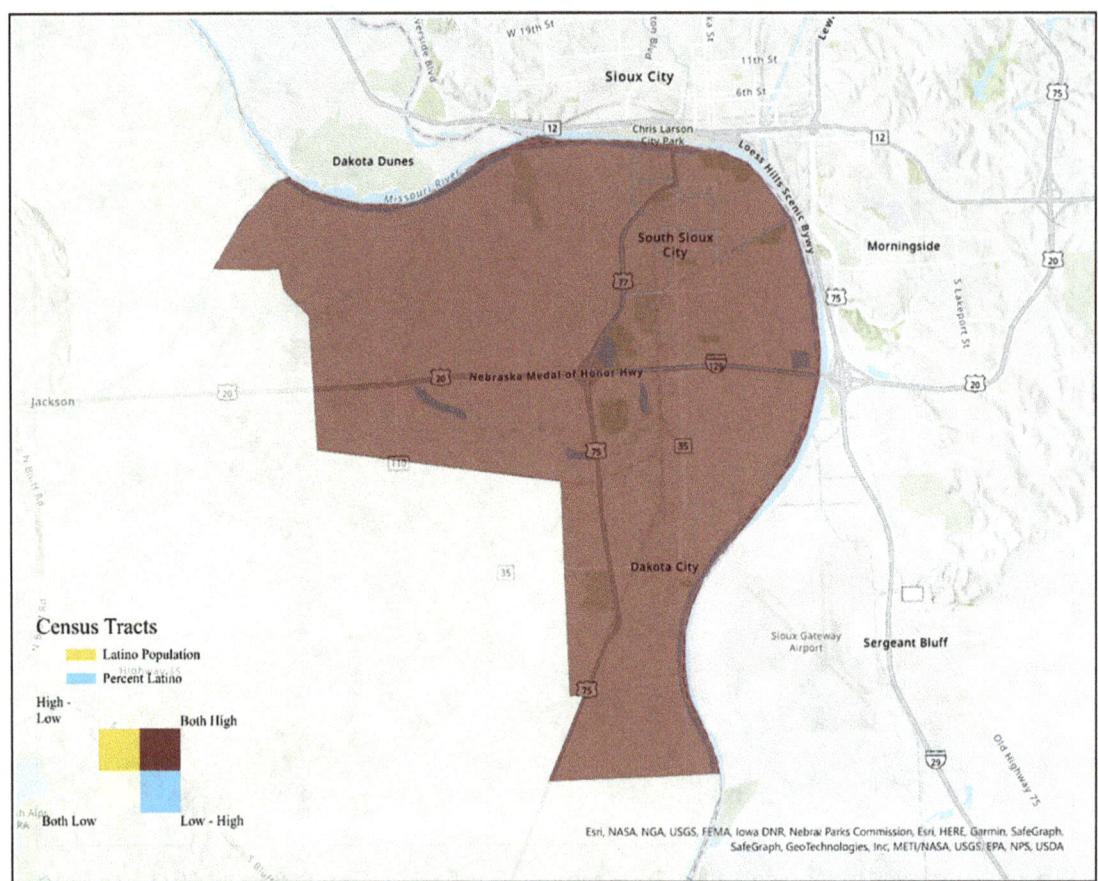

Figure 20. Percent Latino and Latino Population — South Sioux City. U.S. Census Bureau, 2021 Five-Year American Community Survey.

The concentration of Latino communities in South Omaha can be traced to the weighted influence of early settlement patterns. South Omaha has become a distinct and vibrant cultural hub within the city. Studying these spatial patterns and understanding the dynamics of Latino neighborhoods in South Omaha can contribute to informed urban planning, community-building efforts, and the promotion of inclusivity and diversity.

There are twenty census tracts that can be classified as Latino-majority barrios, with six of them classified as hyper-Latino barrios where 70 percent of the residents are Latino. These tracts are primarily located in the following cities: Omaha (n=14), Schuyler (n=1), Grand Island (n=2), South Sioux City (n=1), Crete (n=1), and Scottsbluff (n=1).

Table 10 provides key data that characterizes the Latino population living in the tracts. The tract with the highest percentage of foreign-born population is in Schuyler (53 percent), while the lowest percentage is found in Scottsbluff (5 percent). The tract with the highest percentage of Latinos born in Nebraska is Scottsbluff (78 percent), while the lowest tract is in South Sioux City (18 percent).

Four of the tracts have a Latino population in which 90 percent or more are either Mexican American or foreign-born Mexican. In fact, all tracts except two (Schuyler and Grand Island) have a Mexican majority. Additionally, the tract in Scottsbluff has the lowest percentage (44 percent) of native-born speakers who speak another language among Latinos aged 5 years and older. On the other hand, there are five tracts where 90 percent of the population aged 5 years and older speaks another language. The foreign-born Latino population primarily speaks Spanish and many of them are still in the process of learning to speak English "very well."

The maps and table provide compelling evidence of concentrated clusters of Latino census tracts, indicating the presence of Latino Barrios in several cities throughout Nebraska. The identification of twenty tracts with significant Latino populations sheds light on the spatial distribution of these communities and their impact on the overall demographic landscape.

The findings not only demonstrate the existence of Latino Barrios but also offer valuable insights into the diverse characteristics of the Latino population across different tracts and cities. The variations in

Table 10. Key Demographic Characteristics for Latino Barrios in Nebraska. U.S. Census Bureau, 2021 Five-Year American Community Survey.

Geo_FIPS	County ID	County	Principal City	Total Population	Latino Population	Percent Latino	Percent Foreign-Born	Latinos Born In Nebraska	Percent Mexican	Percent Central American	Native-born Latino - Speak Another Language*	Speak English "Very Well"*	Foreign-born Latino - Speak Another Language*	Speak English "Very Well"*
31055003200	55	Douglas County	Omaha	2528	1906	75%	44%	34%	77%	20%	93%	66%	98%	25%
31055002700	55	Douglas County	Omaha	2618	1921	73%	38%	43%	89%	5%	82%	79%	94%	18%
31047968400	47	Dawson County	Omaha	5196	3773	73%	43%	28%	52%	37%	88%	71%	93%	26%
31055002600	55	Douglas County	Omaha	2115	1512	71%	29%	47%	66%	34%	78%	62%	99%	5%
31055002000	55	Douglas County	Omaha	3285	2315	70%	31%	45%	77%	18%	77%	88%	95%	26%
31037964800	37	Colfax County	Schuyler	6661	4681	70%	53%	25%	46%	36%	99%	61%	99%	16%
31055002800	55	Douglas County	Omaha	3465	2217	64%	31%	44%	75%	18%	90%	74%	96%	17%
31079000200	79	Hall	Grand Island	4604	2899	63%	27%	37%	63%	31%	48%	80%	96%	22%
31055003000	55	Douglas County	Omaha	7118	4478	63%	27%	42%	91%	5%	77%	85%	97%	22%
31055002500	55	Douglas County	Omaha	2791	1740	62%	19%	46%	91%	9%	68%	78%	57%	37%
31055003300	55	Douglas County	Omaha	1885	1172	62%	27%	49%	84%	14%	58%	72%	90%	18%
31055002900	55	Douglas County	Omaha	5780	3251	56%	32%	40%	84%	5%	61%	78%	92%	12%
31055002400	55	Douglas County	Omaha	3969	2207	56%	25%	49%	89%	10%	72%	56%	95%	23%
31047968500	47	Dawson County	Omaha	5534	3069	55%	39%	37%	51%	45%	60%	92%	89%	39%
31043010200	43	Dakota	South Sioux City	6495	3504	54%	31%	18%	99%	1%	85%	64%	87%	23%
31079000300	79	Hall	Grand Island	6049	3178	53%	28%	34%	26%	46%	66%	87%	83%	27%
31151960602	151	Saline	Crete	3482	1825	52%	34%	20%	65%	29%	89%	89%	100%	31%
31055003900	55	Douglas County	Omaha	2498	1280	51%	37%	22%	57%	16%	90%	81%	98%	29%
31055003100	55	Douglas County	Omaha	3808	1951	51%	32%	24%	72%	27%	98%	76%	98%	34%
31157953700	157	Scottsbluff	Scottsbluff	3509	1728	49%	5%	78%	95%	0%	44%	78%	86%	28%

Note: * = Hispanic or Latino population 5 years and over

language usage, country of origin, and proportion of foreign-born residents among the identified tracts highlight the complexity and diversity within these communities.

By understanding the spatial morphology and demographic makeup of Latino Barrios, policymakers, researchers, and community organizations can gain a deeper understanding and appreciation of the unique experiences and cultural dynamics within these neighborhoods. This knowledge can inform targeted initiatives, programs, and services that cater to the specific needs and aspirations of the Latino population, promoting social integration, economic opportunities, and cultural preservation.

IX. El Futuro

The primary objective of this chapter was to provide an overview of the history of Latinidad and explore the current trends and experiences of Latinos in Nebraska. While the chapter only scratches the surface of the significant events and experiences of Latinos in the state, it contributes to the growing body of literature that is shaping the canon of Latinidad scholarship. By delving into the history and current trends, this chapter aims to provide a foundation for further exploration and research into the diverse experiences and contributions of Latinos in Nebraska.

Figure 18 illustrates the potential demographic change for Latinos in Nebraska. These projections are consistent with early reports that predicted significant Latino population growth (Tobia 2016). As the largest minority population in the state, Latinos have a significant presence. In fact, in the 100 largest cities in Nebraska, Latinos outnumber the Black population in 99 cities [38], the Asian population in 97 cities [39], and the Native American[40] population in 97 cities. Latinidad will continue to grow and become more influential in Nebraska. The increasing Latino population in the state, as demonstrated by the demographic trends, suggests that Latinos will play an increasingly significant role in shaping the social, economic, and cultural landscape of Nebraska. It is important for residents, policymakers, and educators in Nebraska to recognize and embrace the growing Latinidad. Nebraska has a choice. The state can harness the potential of Latinidad to foster social cohesion, economic prosperity, and cultural diversity. Nebraska can be viewed as a

---

38. The Black population (n=386) in Chadron is larger than the Latino population (n=202).
39. The Asian population in Auburn (n=48), Tekamah (n=38), and Superior (n=31) is larger than the Latino population (n=36, n=33, and n=27), respectively.
40. The Native American population in Falls city (n=140), Gordon City (n=294), Louisville (n=40) is larger than the Latino population (n=15, n=71, and n=25) respectively.

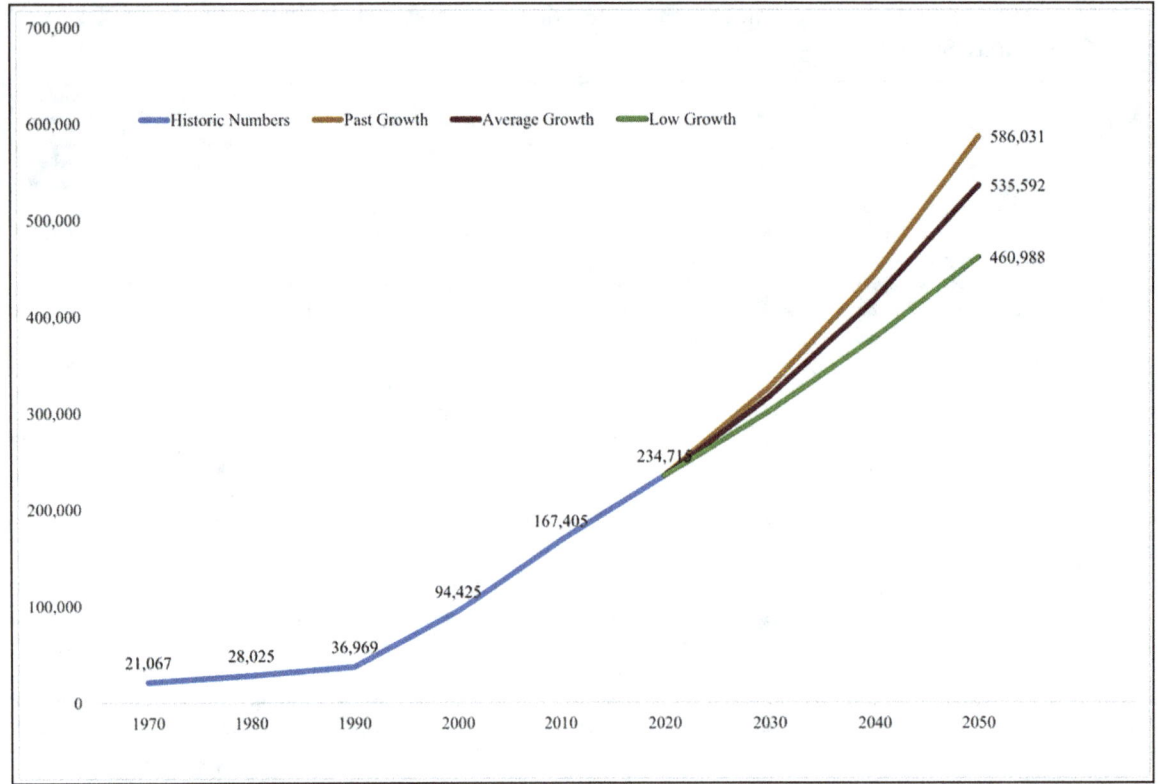

Figure 21. Population Projection for Nebraska. Projections are calculated by the author of this chapter..

model where all racial groups are invited to the table for collaboration that fosters a vibrant and inclusive society for generations to come.

Nebraska has a choice. It can become a leader in the nation that embraces Latinidad as an integral part of its future or it can continue with its pattern of animus and hatred for those who are different (Benjamin-Alvarado, DeSipio, and Montoya 2009).

I have high hopes that this chapter will serve as a valuable resource for a new generation of public intellectuals who are eager to embark on an intellectual journey and contribute to the growing body of scholarship on Latinidad in Nebraska. The lived experience of Latinos in Nebraska is multifaceted, encompassing both rural and urban settings and spanning various industries, including agriculture, education, railroads, meat packing, and the military. Latinos have played a pivotal role in shaping every facet of Nebraska's culture, and their influence will continue to shape Nebraska's future.

This chapter finds inspiration in the broader movement of the Truth and Reconciliation project, which strives to acknowledge and rectify the frequently neglected aspects of history in textbooks, political speeches, and the institutional leadership in Nebraska. The project recognizes the importance of uncovering and sharing stories of Latinos in Nebraska that may have been overlooked or marginalized or intentionally excluded.

A new generation of Latinos is actively reimagining political and educational spaces, driven by their aspirations for greater opportunities and representation. They are aspiring to professions in fields such as medicine, law, engineering, and various other diverse careers. As the United States undergoes increasing diversification and experiences of a growing Latino population, Nebraska is no exception. The evolving demographics and contributions of Latinos are shaping the state's social, cultural, and economic landscape, fostering a more inclusive and vibrant future (Cusido 2017).

Cesar Chavez once said:

"It is my deepest belief that only by giving our lives do we find life. I am convinced that the truest act of courage, the strongest act of manliness is to sacrifice ourselves for others in a totally non-violent struggle for justice."[41] The ROJ project exemplifies the profound belief that self-sacrifice can have transformative

---

41. "Education of the Heart: Cesar Chavez in his own words," United Farm Workers, https://ufw.org/research/history/education-heart-cesar-chavez-words/.

power in changing the narrative of Latinos living in Nebraska. By recognizing the underrepresentation and often overlooked stories of Latino communities, the ROJ leadership team has dedicated itself to amplifying these voices and narratives. The project seeks to empower and give agency to all minority communities, enabling them to reclaim their own narratives and shape not only the historical discourse but also the discourse of Nebraska's future.

Bibliography

"About Us." *Comunidad Maya Pixan Ixim*. https://www.pixanixim.org/about.html.

"American G.I. Forum of Texas." *Handbook of Texas*. Texas State Historical Association. https://www.tshaonline.org/handbook/entries/american-gi-forum-of-texas.

Aparicio, Frances R. 2003. "Jennifer as Selena: Rethinking Latinidad in Media and Popular Culture." *Latino Studies* 1 (1).

Bacon, David. 2016. "Latino Immigrants Are Changing the Politics of Nebraska." *The American Prospect*. https://prospect.org/power/latino-immigrants-changing-politics-...-nebraska/.

Benjamin-Alvarado Jonathan, Louis DeSipio, Celeste Montoya. 2009. "Latino Mobilization in New Immigrant Destinations: The Anti-HR 4437 Protest in Nebraska's Cities." *Urban Affairs Review* 44 (5): 718-735. https://doi.org/10.1177/1078087408323380.

Bodvarsson, Örn, and Hendrik Van den Berg. 2003. "The Impact of Immigration on a Local Economy: The Case of Dawson County, Nebraska." *Great Plains Research* 13 (2): 291-309. http://www.jstor.org/stable/23779602.

Bourdieu, Pierre. 1984. *Distinction: A Social Critique of the Judgement of Taste*. Cambridge, MA: Harvard University Press.

Bristow, David L. 2022. "How a Lexington meatpacking plant changed Nebraska." History Nebraska. https://history.nebraska.gov/how-a-lexington-meatpacking-plant-changed-nebraska/.

Ceballos, Miguel, and Oksana Yakushko. 2014. "Attitudes toward Immigrants in Nebraska." *Great Plains Research* 24 (2): 181-195. http://www.jstor.org/stable/44685181.

Census Bureau, U.S. 1870. *1870 Decennial Census*.

Chávez, Karma R. 2009. "Remapping *Latinidad*: A Performance Cartography of Latina/o Identity in Rural Nebraska." *Text and Performance Quarterly* 29 (2): 165-182. https://doi.org/10.1080/10462930902774866.

Chávez-Moreno, Laura C. 2021. "The Problem with Latinx as a Racial Construct vis-à-vis Language and Bilingualism: Toward Recognizing Multiple Colonialisms in the Racialization of Latinidad." In *Handbook of Latinos and Education*, edited by Enrique G. Jr Murillo, Dolores Delgado Bernal, Socorro Morales, Luis Jr Urrieta, Eric Ruiz Bybee, Juan Sánchez Muñoz, Victor B. Saenz, Daniel Villanueva, Margarita Machado-Casas and Katherine Espinoza. New York, NY: Routledge.

Cusido, Carmen. 2017. "'A Hidden Gem': Nebraska Latinos Tout Its Rich History and Diversity." April 10, 2017. https://www.nbcnews.com/news/latino/hidden-gem-nebraska-latinos-tout-its-rich-history-diversity-n744611.

Dalla, Rochelle L., Francisco Villarruel, Sheran C. Cramer, and Gloria Gonzalez-Kruger. 2004. "Examining Strengths and Challenges of Rapid Rural Immigration" *Great Plains Research* 14 (2): 231-251. http://www.jstor.org/stable/23779480.

Dávila, Arlene. 2012. *Latinos, Inc.* Berkeley, CA: University of California Press.

Davis, Roger P. 2002. "Latinos Along the Platte: The Hispanic Experience In Central Nebraska." *Great Plains Research* 12 (1): 27-50. http://www.jstor.org/stable/23780007.

———. 2008. "Service Not Power: The Early Years of the Nebraska Commission on Mexican Americans, 1971 - 1975." *Nebraska History* 89: 67-83. http://www.nebraskahistory.org/publish/publicat/history/full-text/NH2008Service.pdf.

De La Rosa, Mario R. 2008. "An Analysis of Latino Poverty and a Plan of Action." *Journal of Poverty* 4 (1-2): 27-62.

Enchautegui, Maria E. 1997. "Latino Neighborhoods and Latino Neighborhood Poverty." *Journal of Urban Affairs* 19 (4): 445-467.

Gaber, Sharon Lord, and Rodrigo Cantarero. 1997. "Hispanic Migrant Laborer Homelessness in Nebraska: Examining Agricultural Restructuring as One Path to Homelessness." *Social Thought & Research* 20 (1/2): 55-72. http://www.jstor.org/stable/23252135.

Gamio, Manuel, ed. 1931. *The Mexican Immigrant, His Life-story: Autobiographic Documents*. American Immigration Collection. Library of American Civilization. Chicago: University of Chicago Press.

García 2004. Please contact Dr. Sándoval for this information.

Garcilazo, Jeffrey. 2016. *Traqueros: Mexican Railroad Workers in the United States, 1870-1930*.

Garza, James A. "The Long History of Mexican Immigration to the Rural Midwest." *Journal of the West* 45, no. 4 (Fall 2006): 57-64.

Garza 2019. Please contact Dr. Sándoval for this information.

Gouveia, Lourdes, and Mary Ann Powell. 2007. "Second-Generation Latinos in Nebraska: A First Look." Migration Policy Institute. https://www.migrationpolicy.org/article/second-generation-latinos-nebraska-first-look.

Gouveia, Lourdes, and Rogelio Saenz. 2000. "Global Forces and Latino Population Growth in the Midwest: A Global Forces and Latino Population Growth in the Midwest: A Regional and Subregional Analysis Regional and Subregional Analysis" *Great Plains Research* 10 (2): 305-328. http://www.jstor.org/stable/23778286.

Gouveia, Lourdes, and Donald Stull. 1997. "Latino Immigrants, Meatpacking, and Rural Communities: A Case Study of Lexington, Nebraska." *JSRI Research Report* 26.

Grajeda, Ralph F. 1976. "Chicano: The Mestizo Heritage." In *Broken Hoops and Plains People: A Catalogue of Ethnic Resources in the Humanities: Nebraska and Thereabouts*, 47-98. Lincoln, NE: University of Nebraska Press.

Hamann, Edmund T., and Linda Harklau. 2010. "Education in the New Latino Diaspora." *Faculty Publications: Department of Teaching, Learning and Teacher Education* 104. https://digitalcommons.unl.edu/teachlearnfacpub/104.

Hartford Courant. 2002. "One City, Two Worlds." *Hartford Courant*. Last Modified January 30, 2019. https://www.courant.com/2002/11/26/one-city-two-worlds/.

Hernández Chávez, Eduardo (Compiler & Translator), and Elvira C. Hernández (Narrator). 2017. *Elvira: A Mexican Immigrant Woman*. Ediciones Lengua y Cultura.

Lampe, Philip E. 1977. "Religion and The Assimilation of Mexican Americans." *Review of Religious Research* 18 (3): 243-253.

Lissette, Aliaga Linares. 2014. "A Demographic Portrait of the Mexican-Origin Population in Nebraska." Office of Latino/Latin American Studies University of Nebraska at Omaha. https://digitalcommons.unomaha.edu/cgi/viewcontent.cgi?article=1002&context=latinamstudies_ollas_reports.

Marzen, Chad G. 2013. "Hispanic In the Heartland: The Fremont, Nebraska Immigrant Ordinance and The Future of Latino Civil Rights." *Harvard Journal on Racial and Ethnic Justice* 29: 69-93.

Massey, Douglas S., Jacob S. Rugh, and Karen A. Pren. 2010. "The Geography of Undocumented Mexican Migration." *Mexican Studies/Estudios Mexicanos* 26 (1): 129-152. https://doi.org/10.1525/msem.2010.26.1.129. http://www.jstor.org/stable/10.1525/msem.2010.26.1.129.

Mattos, Daniela. 2017. "Latino Immigration and Community Development in Rural Nebraska." University of Nebraska-Lincoln. https://digitalcommons.unl.edu/agecon_cornhusker/924/.

Mora, Cristina G. 2014. *Making Hispanic: How Activists, Bureaucrats, and Media Constructed a New American*. Chicago: The University of Chicago Press.

Muñoz, Ed A., and Suzanne T. Ortega. 1997. "Regional Socioeconomic and Sociocultural Differences Among U.S. Latinos: The Effects of Historical and Contemporary Latino Immigration/Migration Streams." *Great Plains Research* 7 (2): 289-314. http://www.jstor.org/stable/23777815.

Nielsen, Elaine. 1993. *Hershey, Nebraska: 1892-1992*. Hershey, NE: Hershey Centennial Committee.

Noe-Bustamante, Luis, Lauren Mora, and Mark Hugo Lopez. 2020. *About One-in-Four U.S. Hispanics Have Heard of Latinx, but Just 3% Use It*. Pew Research Center. https://www.pewresearch.org/hispanic/wp-content/uploads/sites/5/2020/08/PHGMD_2020.08.11_Latinx_FINAL.pdf.

Olson, James C. 1966. *History of Nebraska*. Lincoln, NE: University of Nebraska Press.

Palacios, Daisy, and Reema Khrais. "How Latinos are Transforming the Economy of a Small

Rural Town." *Marketplace.* September 8, 2017. https://www.marketplace.org/2017/09/08/how-latinos-transforming-economy-small-rural-town/.

Pitt, David. 2021. "Census: Metro populations grew, rural areas lost in Nebraska, Iowa." *AP News*, 2021. https://www.wowt.com/2021/08/12/census-metro-populations-grew-rural-areas-lost-nebraska-iowa/.

Portes, Alejandro. 1998. "Social Capital: Its Origins and Applications in Modern Sociology." *Annual Review of Sociology* 24: 1-24.

Potter, James, Rodrigo Cantarero, X. Winson Yan, Steve Larrick, and Blanca Ramirez-Salazar. 2004. "A Case Study of the Impact of Population Influx on a Small Community In Nebraska." *Great Plains Research* 14 (2): 219-230. http://www.jstor.org/stable/23779479.

Potter, James J., Rodrigo Cantarero, and Nicholas Pischel. 2008. "Demographic Characteristics and Concerns of New Arrivals to Rural Nebraska." *Journal of Architectural and Planning Research* 25 (1): 42-53. http://www.jstor.org/stable/43030819.

Ramirez, Marty, and Norma E. Cantú. 2018. "Nebraska Memories: The Barrio Boys of Scottsbluff." *Diálogo* 21 (1): 101-105.

Ramos, Athena K., Marcela S. Suarez, Melissa Leon, and Natalia Trinidad. 2017. "Sense of community, participation, and life satisfaction among Hispanic immigrants in rural Nebraska." *Social Science in Health* 19 (4): 308-320. http://dx.doi.org/10.1016/j.kontakt.2017.09.005.

Ravuri, Evelyn. 2003. "Changes in Asian and Hispanic Population in the Cities of the Great Plains, 1990-2000." *Great Plains Research* 13 (1): 75-96. http://www.jstor.org/stable/23804536.

Reed, Charley. 2023. "New UNO Report on Omaha's Latino Population." University of Nebraska Omaha. https://www.unomaha.edu/news/2015/12/new-uno-report-on-omahas-latino-population.php.

Rochín, Refugio I. 2000. "Introduction: Latinos on the Great Plains: An Overview." *Great Plains Research* 10 (2): 243-252. http://www.jstor.org/stable/23778282.

Rochin, Refugio, Marcelo Siles, and Jose Gomez. 1996. "Latinos in Nebraska: A Socio-Historical Profile." *JSRI Statistical Brief* 9.

Rodríguez, Clara E. 2000. *Changing Race: Latinos, The Census and The History of Ethnicity*. New York, NY: New York University Press.

Ruiz, Vicki L. 2010. *From Out of the Shadows: Mexican Women in Twentieth-Century America*. 10th ed. Albuquerque: University of New Mexico Press.

Ruta, Ulicinaite. 2021. "Nebraska immigrant and refugee population on the rise." 2021. https://www.3newsnow.com/news/local-news/nebraska-immigrant-and-refugee-population-on-the-rise.

Sanchez, Thomas. 2010a. "The Diversity and Commonalities of Latinos in the United States." *Journal of Latino and Latin American Studies (Jollas)* 3 (4): 115-157.

———. 2010b. "Negotiating Latino Immigrant Identity in Rural Nebraska." *The Journal of Latino-Latin American Studies* 3 (4): 115-117.

Sandoval, J.S. Onésimo. 2011. "Neighborhood Diversity and Segregation in the Chicago Metropolitan Region, 1980-2000." *Urban Geography* 32 (5): 609-640.

Sandoval, J.S. Onésimo and Joel Jennings. 2012. "Barrios and Hyper Barrios: How Latino Neighborhoods Changed the Urban Built Environment." *Journal of Urbanism* 5 (2-3): 111-138.

Sandoval, J.S. Onésimo and Bienvenido Ruiz. 2011. "Pan-Latino Neighborhoods: Contemporary Myth or Reality?" *Sociological Focus*: 295-313.

Smith, Michael. 1981. "Beyond the Borderlands: Mexican Labor in the Central Plains, 1900-1930." *Great Plains Research* 1 (4): 239-251.

South, Scott J., Kyle Crowder, and Erick Chavez. 2005. "Migration and Spatial Assimilation Among U.S. Latinos: Classical Versus Segmented Trajectories." *Demography* 42 (3): 497-521. http://www.jstor.org/stable/4147359.

Spadt, Zach. 2016. "Our Lady of Guadalupe Celebrating 90 Years." *Scottsbluff Star-Herald*, 2016. https://starherald.com/our-lady-of-guadalupe-celebrating-90-years/article_9cce0dfc-4bfb-5caf-a6ae-a3778fdda0e7.html.

Tatum, Charles M. 2001. *Chicano Popular Culture: Que hable el pueblo*. Tucson, Arizona: Tucson: University Press.

Tobia, Mike. 2016. "Nebraska's Latino Population Expected to Triple by 2050, Study Says."

December 20, 2016. https://www.foxnews.com/politics/nebraskas-latino-population-expected-to-triple-by-2050-study-says.

Thomas, John F. "Cuban Refugees in the United States." *The International Migration Review* 1, no. 2 (Spring 1967): 46-57. Sage Publications, Inc.

Valdés, Dionicio Nodín. 2000. *Barrios Norteños: St. Paul and Midwestern Mexican Communities in the Twentieth Century*. Austin, TX: University of Texas Press.

Vasquez, Manuel, Chad Seales, and Marie Marquardt. 2008. "New Latino Destinations." *Latinas/os in the United States: Changing the Face of América*. https://doi.org/10.1007/978-0-387-71943-6_2.

Ventura, Risell. 2021. "As time passes by, the growth of Hispanic businesses in Nebraska increases." June 25, 2021. https://nebraska.tv/newsletter-daily/as-time-passes-by-the-growth-of-hispanic-businesses-in-nebraska-increases.

Wahl, Ana-María Gonzalez, R. Saylor Breckenridge, and Steven E. Gunkel. 2007. "Latinos, Residential Segregation and Spatial Assimilation in Micropolitan Areas: Exploring the American Dilemma on a New Frontier." *Social Science Research* 36 (3): 995-1020. https://doi.org/10.1016/j.ssresearch.2006.07.004.

Wahl, Ana-María Gonzalez, Steven E. Gunkel, and Bennie Shobe. 2005. "Becoming Neighbors or Remaining Strangers? Latinos and Residential Segregation in the Heartland." *Great Plains Research* 15 (2): 297-327. http://www.jstor.org/stable/23779540.

Winston, Bryan. 2019. "Nebraska's Mexican Communities, 1910 - 1950." History Nebraska. https://history.nebraska.gov/nebraskas-mexican-communities-1910-1950/#:~:text=Ten%20percent%20of%20Nebraskans%20are,story%20of%20the%20early%20decades.

Winston, Bryan. 2025. *Mapping the Mexican Midwest*. https://mappingthemexicanmidwest.bryanwinston.org/.

Wright, Richard, Mark Ellis, Steve R. Holloway, and Sandy Wong. 2014. "Patterns of Racial Diversity and Segregation in the United States: 1990–2010." *The Professional Geographer* 66 (2).

Family photo courtesy of Dr. Ishii-Jordan.

Exclusion from the Good Life: The Impact of Anti-Asian Racism on Asian Nebraskans

Heather Fryer and Sharon R. Ishii-Jordan[1]

In 1875, a Chinese immigrant named Sin Goon moved to North Platte on the plains of western Nebraska. Like so many aspiring businessmen there, he sought to earn a living serving railroad workers. But some residents of the fledgling community didn't appreciate his decision to move there and expressed their disdain by smashing his Front Street laundry windows and threatening him with an anonymous letter that warned of the Ku Klux Klan being "on his track." While he initially fought to stay in North Platte, even hiring a lawyer and having his windows repaired, he decided days later to leave.

1. The authors gratefully acknowledge the contributions of research assistant Emily Binder, who worked alongside us from the start of this project.

In *Roots of Justice: A History of Race and Racism in Nebraska.* Edited by Kevin Abourezk, with an Introduction by M. Dewayne Mays and Paul A. Olson (Lincoln, Nebraska: Truth and Reconciliation Nebraska, 2025). Copyright © 2025 by the authors; CC-BY. DOI: 10.32873/unl.dc.rj6

His story, while noted by historians for its brutality (the local newspaper reported he had been "beaten, kicked, stoned, and insulted), his exclusionary treatment is a familiar one to so many Asian immigrants to Nebraska. They have suffered the dehumanizing effects of racism, laws designed to limit their numbers or prevent them from becoming citizens, and the implicit and explicit expectations from their neighbors to stay quiet about their treatment, to be the invisible, model minority.

To understand how Americans of Asian descent experienced, adjusted, and overcame negative experiences in Nebraska, recognizing the external forces on their lives is paramount. The experiences of Asians in their diaspora across the U.S. and Nebraska during a 150-year span have been shaped by both external (global and domestic) and internal (personality and resilience) factors. The presence of stereotypes specifically targeted toward Asian Americans due to exotic imaginings, pseudoscience, and economic fears, in addition to the images created by national media, gave rise to society's acceptance of stereotypes. These external factors contributed to a belief that continues to this day by non-Asians that Asian-looking people do not fit the image of who an American is. Government policies enacted over the past couple centuries seemed to cement the impression that careful diligence must be directed toward this group of people – based solely on their genetic inheritance and society's preconceived notions. This chapter provides the background to realizing the impact of anti-Asian racism on Asian Nebraskans.

Nearly half of all people of Asian descent in the United States, 45 percent, live in the West. Of these, one third live in California,[2] where their histories are visible because of their greater numbers, their distinctive neighborhoods, and their recognized impact on social movements. On the Great Plains, where their numbers have been smaller, Asians have been largely invisible. In this chapter, "Asian" is defined by the major immigrant groups represented in the U.S. Census for Nebraska between 1870 and 1980, when the U.S. Congress passed the Refugee Act (a history that is covered in another chapter in this volume).[3] This category includes immigrants from China, Japan, Korea, the Philippines, and South Asia, as well as their descendants. In 2023, just 3.5 percent of Nebraska residents were of Asian descent,[4] but they surpassed Nebraska's

---

2. Abby Budiman and Neil Ruiz, "Key Facts about Asian Americans, a Diverse and Growing Population," Pew Research Center, April 29, 2021, https://www.pewresearch.org/short-reads/2021/04/29/key-facts-about-asian-americans/#

3. "Asian" can appear to be a straightforward category because, unlike "white" and "Black," it seemed to refer to a region and not a race. But The US Census Bureau currently defines "Asian" as "A person having origins in any of the original peoples of the Far East, Southeast Asia, or the Indian subcontinent including, for example, Cambodia, China, India, Japan, Korea, Malaysia, Pakistan, the Philippine Islands, Thailand, and Vietnam." Stop AAPI Hate includes Pacific Islanders, who the Census Bureau identifies separately as "a person having origins in any of the original peoples of Hawaii, Guam, Samoa, or other Pacific Islands." These categories of "Asian origin" have been shifting since 1860, when census takers in California (and only in California) were first instructed to count the number of "Chinese" in their communities. The growing demand for labor spurred immigration from across East Asia, and especially China. As these numbers increased, so too did the government's interest in tracking the number of these newcomers who were not "white," "Black," or "Indians not taxed." Census categories expanded in 1870 to include national origin categories, race, and ethnicity. In 1880 the census tracked "White," "Black," "Mulatto," and "Chinese." Enumerators were instructed to count all Asians as "Chinese" regardless of whether they or their relatives came from China. This, and the category "Chinese" appeared on the national census. "Japanese" was added in 1890.

In 1910 the Census Bureau added the category "other races" to designate everyone who was neither white, Black, mulatto (an antiquated word for person with Black and white ancestry), Chinese, Japanese, or American Indian. South Asians from Indian and neighboring nations were tucked into this category. Japan's annexation of Korea in 1910 made Koreans subjects of the Empire of Japan and, in a legal sense "Japanese," but few if any Koreans identified themselves with their "oppressor nation." The 1930 Census expanded Asian categories to count "Ch" for Chinese, "Jp" for Japanese, "Fil" for Filipino, "Hin" for Hindu (regardless of their religion), and "Kor" for Korean. Instead of an "other" category, enumerators were instructed to write out the individual's "color" or "race." Nebraska enumerators seemed to take some license with their classifications of "color" and "race." The 1910 census taker for Box Butte County recorded Hom Suey Wo as "Chinese (white)" while the census taker for Douglas County classified Ling Hom as "Chinese (colored)." This raises questions about what, exactly, it meant to be "Asian" in Nebraska at various points in US history. For a detailed account of how the government created racial and ethnic categories for the census see Margo J. Anderson, *The American Census: A Social History* 2nd ed. (New Haven: Yale University Press, 2015).

4. Cindy Gonzalez, "Nebraskans Offer Personal Insights on Bill to Create State-Funded Asian American Commission," *Nebraska Examiner*, January 27, 2023, https://nebraskaexaminer.com/2023/01/27/nebraskans-offer-personal-insights-on-bill-to-create-state-funded-asian-american-commission/.

Latino community as the fastest growing population in 2015, increasing 70 percent between 2000 and 2015.[5] This growth is due to the expansion of long-established Asian-Nebraskan families, the arrival of new immigrants pursuing opportunities in education, the professions, and business, and the growing number of Asian people being resettled in Nebraska after entering the U.S. as refugees. Across the Midwest, people of Asian descent are becoming an ever-greater part of life in the American Heartland. Yet for all of their contributions they remain largely invisible.[6]

It is tempting to read invisibility as an indication that people of Asian descent moved to Nebraska and settled right into the Good Life with their Caucasian counterparts without difficulty. But population totals and historical silences are not evidence of racial equality. The laws, policies, economic records, migration maps, and the words printed in newspapers, delivered in speeches and testimonies, conveyed in letters, preserved in journals, and passed down through family and community stories tell a different story. Amidst American lives marked by many successes runs a current of anti-Asian exclusion, discrimination and racial violence that became naturalized as part of the United States' diverse social landscape. Like any natural feature considered unremarkable, it is a part of the environment that goes unseen.

In her book on the invisibility of Asian Americans in the Midwest, Monica Mong Trieu quotes author Cathy Park Hong's explanation of the dangers posed by letting injustice become naturalized to the point that it disappears from history: "The problem with silence is that it can't speak up and say why it's silent. And so silence collects, becomes amplified, takes on a life outside our intentions, in that silence can get misread as indifference or avoidance, or even shame, and eventually this silence passes over into forgetting."[7]

There is a dual injustice in each act of forgetting. First, the pain, loss, and damage to the people who were harmed is treated as being of no account. Second, society fails to see the patterns and recurring practices that continue to cause harm and perpetuate injustice. Anti-Asian racism cannot resolve itself. As prominent white Nebraskans from William Jennings Bryan, T.C. Osborne, Episcopal Bishop George Allen Beecher, and Father Edward J. Flanagan would later demonstrate, resisting anti-Asian racism requires a clear view of the beliefs, structures, and practices that have flowed into this historical current since the first Asian workers joined their European counterparts in Nebraska in the 1870s. Reversing this current took effort, and even posed risks. For each of them, stemming the historical current was important because they knew Asian people as people, not as anthropological specimens, media creations, or threatening stereotypes. Then, as now, dehumanization and racial injustice went hand in hand.

Nebraskans of Asian descent have had similar historical experiences as Indigenous, African American, and Latino Nebraskans. These commonalities stemmed from the practice of excluding Nebraskans classified as "non-white" from decision-making, prosperity, social belonging, and protections of their constitutional and human rights. Exclusion and discrimination depend on racial stereotyping for justifications for treating certain groups of people in ways that would otherwise be considered illegal, unethical, and even immoral. Stereotyping attributes a set of characteristics to an entire group of people, most of which are exaggerated or wholly untrue. A stereotype cannot provide accurate information about people or groups, but it can provide a rationale for inflicting harm on all people of that racial, ethnic, national, or religious "type" (usually cast as a form of justice or self-defense). Historically, white Americans viewed their non-white neighbors in terms of their racial stereotypes, instead of as individuals with dreams, fears, talents, and complex circumstances shaping their lives. From its first days as a U.S. territory in 1854 and continuing after statehood in 1867, Nebraskans used the same system of stereotypic social categories as the rest of the nation, which made it all but impossible to engage with Asian newcomers as people.[8]

Sin Goon's story of emigrating from China to open a laundry in North Platte in 1875 only to be threatened and attacked by his neighbors illustrates the impacts of harmful stereotypes. Vandals smashed the windows of his Front Street laundry on a Saturday night. Two days later, Sin Goon received an

---

5. "How Asian Immigration is Changing America's Heartland," NBC News, June 12, 2014.
6. Huping Ling, *Chinese Americans in the Heartland: Migration, Work, and Community* (New Brunswick: Rutgers University Press, 2022), 2.
7. Monica Mong Trieu, *Fighting Invisibility: Asian Americans in the Midwest* (New Brunswick: Rutgers University Press, 2023), 11-14.
8. Sarah Deutsch, *Making a Modern U.S. West: The Contested Terrain of a Region and Its Borders, 1898-1940* (Lincoln: University of Nebraska Press, 2022).

anonymous letter warning that the Ku Klux Klan were "on his track." Sin Goon consulted a lawyer and, after giving some thought to his situation, had the windows repaired and announced he was staying in town and his laundry was open for business.[9] Two weeks later, he left. According to the *North Platte Nebraskian*, Sin had been "beaten, kicked, stoned, and insulted" by everyone from a representative of a North Platte business association to young boys who threw rocks at him without consequence. The constant pounding of brick-bats, sticks, and stones against his windows and doors made life and laundry impossible. Oddly, despite the harassment and violence leveled against him, much of North Platte thought highly of Sin Goon. He was recognized as a "tip-top washer and ironer" who was "very quiet and well-behaved." Yet no matter how good a neighbor and launderer Sin Goon might have been, to those who threatened and harassed him he was an eternal foreigner who had no place in America, and certainly not in North Platte.[10]

Sin Goon's story has been repeated across time and place by other Asian immigrants in Nebraska, with variations continuing into the twenty-first century. Racially exclusionary state laws prevented Asian immigrants from owning land, marrying Caucasians, and working toward "the Good Life" that the popular, unofficial state motto promises. Asian victims of violent crimes received little to no response from law enforcement, especially when the perpetrator was white. As with Sin Goon's arrival in North Platte, most of these historical developments have their origins in white Nebraskans' anxieties about being "invaded" by Asians, and their misconceptions about Asian people were reinforced by anti-Asian stereotypes. These stereotypes, in turn, became a basis for law, policy, and everyday interactions.

Where Did the Stereotypes Come From?

Racial Pseudoscience

When the United States established the Territory of Nebraska the people in power were "white," which meant that they were descendants of Northern European immigrants. In 1854, when white settlers claimed Nebraska as their own, most Americans believed that race was not just about skin color or cultural differences. Instead, they envisioned a hierarchy of races in which Northern Europeans were the most evolved and non-white peoples lagged behind in evolutionary development. Samuel Morton, the physician, anatomy professor, and a pioneer in the field of physical anthropology, advanced this idea in *Crania Americana* in 1839. The book was based on Morton's system of craniology, which involved measuring the size and comparing the shapes of human skulls. Morton theorized that human qualities like intelligence, reason, social organization, and morality were racial characteristics, and that each racial group had more or less of these capabilities depending upon the average size of its skull.

According to Morton's measurements, Europeans (who he referred to as "Caucasians") had the largest, most evenly proportioned skull size. This, he concluded, made Europeans the race of "the highest intellectual endowments" who had "peopled the finest portions of the earth" and that Europeans were the "fairest" – meaning "whitest" and "most beautiful" – of the world's people. Morton found Asians (who he referred to as "Mongolians") had somewhat smaller average skulls and "sallow or olive colored skin." He noted that although Mongolian skulls were measurably smaller than Caucasian, they were larger than Native Americans and people of African descent, giving them a greater capacity for learning than other non-whites.[11]

Morton qualified Mongolians' intellectual abilities as limited and treacherous. "In their intellectual character the Mongolians are ingenious, imitative, and highly susceptible of cultivation [i.e. learning]," he concluded, adding, "[s]o versatile are their feelings and actions, that they have been compared to the monkey race, whose attention is perpetually changing from one object to another."[12] Morton's questionable "scientific method" of melding his skull measurements with his own subjective views led him to conclude that Caucasians had a higher intellect from

---

9. *The North Platte Nebraskian*, September 4, 1875, 3.
10. *The North Platte Nebraskian*, September 18, 1875, 3; Mark R. Ellis, "Chinese," *Encyclopedia of the Great Plains*, University of Nebraska digital publication, http://plainshumanities.unl.edu/encyclopedia/doc/egp.asam.007 .
11. Samuel Morton, *Crania Americana; or, a comparative view of the skulls of various aboriginal nations of North and South America. To which is prefixed an essay on the varieties of the human species* (Philadelphia, J. Dobson, 1839). For more about the development and effects of racial pseudoscience see Karen E. Fields and Barbara J. Fields, *Racecraft: The Soul of Inequality in American Life* (New York: Verso, 2014); Angela Saini, *Superior: The Return of Race Science* (Boston: Beacon Press, 2019); and Lee D. Baker, *Anthropology and the Racial Politics of Culture* (Durham: Duke University Press, 2010).
12. Morton, 69.

RACES.	No. of skulls.	Mean internal capacity in cubic inches.	Largest in the series.	Smallest in the series.
Caucasian.	52	87.	109.	75.
Mongolian.	10	83.	93.	69.
Malay.	18	81.	89.	64.
American.	147	82.	100.	60.
Ethiopian.	29	78.	94.	65.

Source: *Crania Americana* 1839, 260. https://hdl.handle.net/2027/uiuc.5188360?urlappend=%3Bseq=274

which they built civilizations based on innovation, order, reason, and beauty. Asians, Morton claimed, created civilizations based on primitive ideas and clever inventions copied from Europeans.

Scientists have since shown that craniology led to false conclusions. Geneticists have established that the DNA of any two people from any two racial backgrounds is approximately 99.9 percent identical, making all human beings far more similar than different. Social scientists and psychologists have shown that beliefs, behaviors, and ways of living are the result of individual temperament and culture – not of skull size or innate racial characteristics. Yet Morton's theory had greater influence upon American law, policy, society, culture, and the way that white Americans viewed Asian people.[13] The president of the American Sociological Association said plainly in 1901 what Morton's science had implied to most white observers: that Asian immigration would end in "race suicide" for white Americans.[14] The American Federation of Labor and the Asiatic Exclusion League put this question to white workers in 1905: "Meat vs. Rice: American Manhood against Asiatic Coolieism: WHICH SHALL SURVIVE?"[15]

Americans, including those in Nebraska Territory, had encounters with Native Americans, African Americans, and Latino people. Most of these encounters occurred in the context of dispossession, war, slavery, and other forms of violence, all rooted in racial stereotypes of people who had been part of the American story, but they did have contact with real people. Asians first began to immigrate to the United States in significant numbers in the mid-nineteenth century – long after the Europeans seized Indigenous land, moved enslaved African people to work on it, and began colonial incursions into Spanish America. Asian immigrants arrived in an America built on racial inequality and were received as people who Americans might have read or heard about but did not encounter in person until at least the 1850s. Like Sin Goon, Asians were strangers who lived within Nebraskans' imaginations long before they lived in their communities. *Crania Americana* was part of the American imagination for more than a decade before the first Asians arrived in Nebraska, giving it and publications like it time to deeply imprint stereotypes in people's thinking.

Economic fears

In 1878 readers of the *Wahoo Independent* were following hearings in the California Senate on "the social, moral, and political effect" of the immigration of Chinese laborers to the state. The Nebraska paper published every word of Californians' testimony, including that of San Francisco shoe manufacturer Abraham Altmeyer, who was eliminating the 350-person Chinese immigrant workforce that made his factory profitable in the previous five years. Altmeyer said that he first sought Chinese immigrant labor when experienced white shoemakers demanded "extravagant" wages. His Chinese employees worked 10 hours per day for less than half the wages of white workers. There was no need to pay Chinese immigrants the full value of their labor, Altmeyer said, because they lived in cheap boarding houses, ate only rice, wore the clothes they brought from China, and needed little else to survive, survival, it seemed, being the whole of a Chinese person's life ambition. Altmeyer did invest in efforts to closely supervise his employees from China. When asked if the Chinese were "dishonest, as a rule," Altmeyer replied, "They will bear close watching. I think they will take things whenever they can." He did not give any examples to support this belief.

---

13. For detailed data debunking scientific racism see Chapter 3, "The Demise of Scientific Racism," in Ali Rattansi *Racism: A Very Short Introduction* (New York: Oxford University Press, 2020), 34-49.
14. Sanjoy Chakravorty, Devesh Kapur, and Nirvikar Singh, *The Other One Percent: Indians in America* (New York: Oxford University Press, 2016), 7.
15. Samuel Gompers and Herman Gutstadt, *Meat vs. Rice: American Manhood against Asiaitic Coolieism: Which Shall Survive?* Reprinted with Introduction and Appendices by the Asiatic Exclusion League, (San Francisco: American Federation of Labor, 1901), frontispiece.

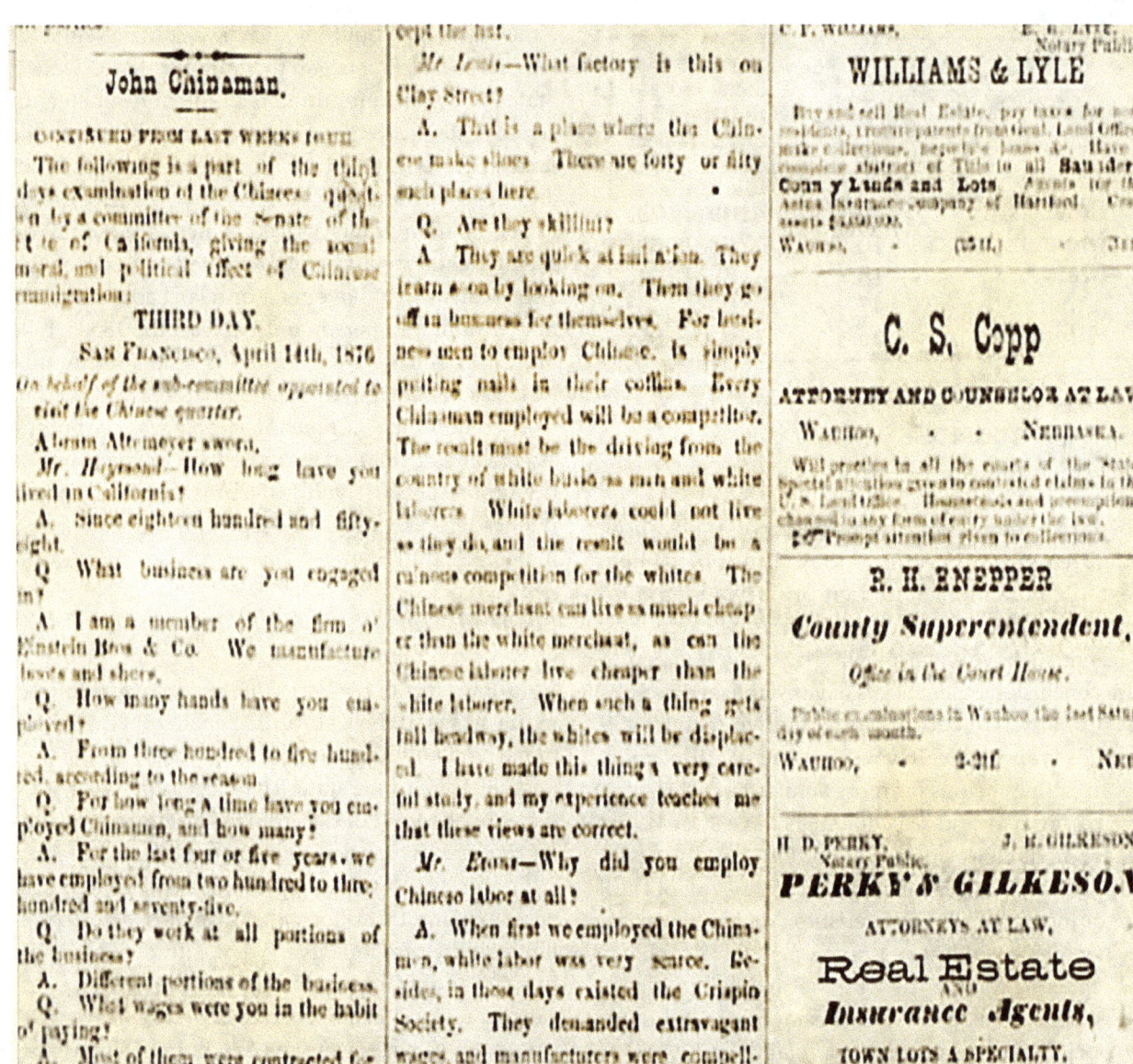

"John Chinaman," *Wahoo Independent*, October 26, 1876.

Examples of theft were perhaps unnecessary for the senators because the real problem, in Altmeyer's view, was not that Chinese immigrant workers might steal tools or shoe leather. Altmeyer testified that the Chinese were "quick at imitation" – as described by Samuel Morton – and that they would "go off in business themselves." He warned the California Senate, "[e]very Chinaman employed will be a competitor. The result must be the driving from the country of white business men [sic] and white laborers. White laborers could not live as they do, and the result would be a ruinous competition for the whites. The Chinese merchants can live much cheaper than the white merchant, as can the Chinese laborer live cheaper than the white laborer. When such a thing gets full headway, the whites will be displaced." The testimony from California warned readers in Wahoo that Chinese immigrants did not intend to build lives for themselves in America, but to steal everything that white Americans like themselves had built in California – or Nebraska.[16]

National media

The *Wahoo Independent* published the California testimony on "the Chinese Question" under the title "John Chinaman" over the course of several days. "John Chinaman" was a generic name that became

---

16. "John Chinaman," *The Independent* (Wahoo, Nebraska), October 26, 1876, 2.

"What Shall We Do With John Chinaman?" *Frank Leslie's Illustrated Newspaper*, 1869. https://www.loc.gov/pictures/item/2001696535/

a racial slur against Chinese immigrants, both in the United Kingdom and in the United States. Everyone recognized "John Chinaman" by his long queue, the darker-than-sallow complexion that Morton described, and the exaggerated facial features that did not look quite human. Many illustrators drew John Chinaman to look like a rat, drawing from popular rhetoric about Chinese immigrants being vermin to be kept out, run out, or done away with. This 1876 political cartoon from the popular *Frank Leslie's Illustrated Magazine* shows an Irish immigrant preparing to throw John Chinaman back into the Pacific Ocean by his "tail," and an Anglo-American man directing John Chinaman toward the cotton fields in the South to replace the enslaved Black labor force white plantation owners lost to Emancipation.

Nebraskans were already familiar with "John Chinaman" when Sin Goon left North Platte in September 1875. The *North Platte Nebraskian* wrote of Sin's departure, "While we could wish for more humane treatment for John Chinaman wherever his lot might be cast, yet we have very little room for hope that his future will be characterized by a greater freedom from cruel stoning than has been his past …" even though "… the Chinaman has the same rights as any man in this country of ours."[17] It was common for journalists to engage in the dehumanizing practice of referring to Chinese immigrants as simply as "Chinamen" or, if talking about an individual, "the Chinaman" – a news story might mention the person's name and individual circumstances once but call that person "the Chinaman" from then on. This reinforced the perception that Asians were problems, not people.

---

17. *The North Platte Nebraskian,* September 18, 1875, 3.

Although Nebraska newspapers regularly ran syndicated stories from larger cities, it is curious that a small-town Nebraska newspaper would publish the proceedings from a California hearing over many consecutive issues when the states' demographics were dramatically different. The news of Sin Goon's short venture in North Platte drew attention, in part, because he was one of a very few Asian immigrants in Nebraska in 1875. The U.S. Census Bureau recorded no people of Asian descent in 1870 and only seventeen people of Chinese or Japanese descent in 1880 – fourteen in Omaha and three in Lincoln.[18] Given these numbers, it is hard to imagine that Nebraskans would have felt the presence of Asian immigration to be a pressing issue, were it not for the frequency of alarming accounts from California. National media stories that were syndicated to Nebraska newspapers put California's "Chinese Question" – along with Oregon's "Japanese Problem" and Washington's "Hindoo Invasion" – alongside Nebraska's local breaking headlines. The inside sections also featured Asians as strange people with "queer and curious habits," creators of objects of exotic beauty, and, alternately, as allies or enemies of the United States, depending upon U.S. foreign policy interests in the Pacific. Accounts from Christian missionaries cast Asian peoples as "heathens" whose societies and cultures were backward and impossible to understand.[19]

The information they gleaned included positive characteristics such as the politeness of the Japanese that was praised effusively, only to be reduced to a shocking negative caution. "At the same time we can see how possible it may be that the very 'prince of darkness' is a gentleman," the *Omaha Daily Herald* exclaimed 1879.[20] Such a racist manipulation of manners was not evident in a 1913 article in the *Omaha Bee* wherein a letter to a child exhorts, "A boy well bred is an ornament to the world."[21]

Popular culture filled this void of understanding of real Asian people with fictional Asian characters that reflected racial anxieties, fascination with the "exotic," and unquestioned stereotypes about what they referred to as "the Celestial race." Before radio and television, Americans followed serialized fiction in the newspaper. Readers then, like now, loved stories of romance, adventure, and conflict in exotic locales with colorful characters. Cliffhangers left readers in suspense, heightening the thrill and ensuring that readers will buy the paper the next day. Asian locations and characters were very popular among Nebraska readers, though Asian Nebraskans would not have recognized themselves or their ancestors in these stories.[22]

Author Sax Rohmer's tales of the murderous master criminal Dr. Fu Manchu ran in newspapers across the U.S. and Nebraska from the 1910s to the 1950s. The leader of the Si-Fan tong held four doctorates from four European universities, all of which he used to advance the glory of China. His team of assassins targeted Westerners, all paid through Dr. Fu-Manchu's profitable drug smuggling, human trafficking, and other morally abhorrent enterprises.

Endlessly stroking his extraordinarily long moustache, Rohmer's tong leader combined Western science and "Oriental magic" to transform organisms from the natural world like venomous snakes, deadly pathogens, and poisonous plants into deadly weapons that left no trace of his crimes. Fu Manchu sullied young Chinese women by sending them to examine the corpses to confirm that his victims were dead. Nebraska readers got this chilling description of the Chinese mastermind in 1916:

> "[Dr. Fu-Manchu] came forward with an indescribable gait, catlike, yet awkward ... never turning away the reptilian gaze of those eyes, which must haunt my dreams forever. I had never supposed prior to meeting Dr. Fu Manchu that so intense a force of malignancy could radiate – for it seemed to radiate – from any human being."[23]

His daughter, Fah Lo Suee, was her father's equal in deception and manipulation, suggesting that "Chinese characteristics" were biological traits inherited through one's parents – a suggestion Samuel Morton would likely endorse.

---

18. United States Bureau of the Census, *Population by Race, Cities, and Towns, Etc., 1880 and 1870* (Washington, D.C.: USGPO, 1881).
19. John Kuo Wei Tchen and Dylan Yeats, *Yellow Peril! An Archive of Anti-Asian Fear* (New York: Verso, 2014).
20. *The Omaha Daily Herald*, Nov 16, 1879, 7.
21. Ella Wheeler Wilcox, "Letter to a Lad of 10 in Praise of His Manners – A Boy Well Bred is an Ornament to the World," *The Omaha Bee*, June 9, 1913, 7.
22. Christopher Frayling, *The Yellow Peril: Dr. Fu Manchu and the Rise of Chinaphobia* (London: Thames & Hudson), 2014.
23. "The Fifth Fu-Manchu Story: The Call of Siva," *Omaha Daily News*, May 7, 1916, 39.

The Insidious Dr. Fu-Manchu. Courtesy of the Rohmer Estate.

The perilous image of the Chinese immigrant was also supported by members of the medical community who attached Orientalism to a morally and degrading opium addiction that was not viewed as a medical condition to be treated but as a characteristic of the Chinese determined to draw white Americans into the insidious dens that would imperil "American national integrity."[24] Moreover, the melodramas performed in Nebraska from national stages, such as "Midnight in Chinatown" performed in Lincoln in 1900 and "Chinatown Charlie, The Opium Fiend" performed in Omaha in 1906, made acceptable the racist caricatures and stereotypes in the form of humor generated on stage, as African Americans had also experienced.[25]

Fu Manchu, Chinatown Charlie, and characters like them provided embodiments of what anti-Asian groups called "the Yellow Peril." Nebraskans took many different defensive measures against this "peril," which they perceived as rising in times of political or economic distress and receding in times of peace and prosperity. Asian Nebraskans had no control over when and how their neighbors or elected officials saw themselves as "imperiled," which made it difficult to ever feel completely safe in their sense of belonging.

Asians as eternal foreigners

Samuel Morton, Abraham Altmeyer, and Sax Rohmer talked in different ways about Asians as thieves who coveted what white people had. The more deeply the stereotype of the predatory Asians took hold, the stronger white Americans' impulse to keep Asians away from centers of power and prosperity in American life. Many white Californians came to believe that immigrants wanted much more than their wealth: Asian immigrants, they warned, had come to conquer the Golden State for China or Japan. Others rejected the conquest theory, positing instead that Asian laborers were stealthily building an Asian-majority state within the United States where they would "steal" every bit of power, wealth, and freedom from white Californians. Nebraska media continued to spread news from California newspapers about the invasion of "Japanese coolies" ("coolie" was a derogatory term for a low-wage unskilled Asian worker) into their state taking over land and creating communities against which no white man could compete because "absentee landlords" allowed Japanese laborers to farm and manage the fields with their efficiencies but also with a lifestyle of long hours, no family life, and lack of comforts that white men require.[26]

Organizations like the Asiatic Exclusion League and the Native Sons of the Golden West formed to "defend California" from Asians who, in their view, were less intelligent than whites, but were clever enough to imitate white success and leave them displaced, destitute, and subject to unscrupulous overlords like John Chinaman and Fu Manchu. Anti-Asian organizations pressed the California legislature to

---

24. Timothy A. Hickman, "Drugs and Race in American Culture: Orientalism in the Turn-of-the-Century Discourse of Narcotic Addiction," *American Studies* 42:1 (Winter 2000): 71-91.
25. Funke Opera House advertisement. *The Lincoln Courier*, April 14, 1900; Krug Theater advertisement "Chinatown Charlie, the Opium Fiend" *The Omaha Sunday Bee*, September 23, 1906, 3.
26. "The Japanese 'Invasion,'" *The Nebraska Independent*, January 17, 1907, 7.

pass laws that restricted the rights of the Asian immigrant workers whose labor brought high profit margins. A series of race-based California laws were passed that barred immigrants from Asia from owning land, marrying Caucasians, living in certain parts of cities, and using public accommodations available to white Californians.[27]

As immigrants from Asia moved from their first ports of entry on the West Coast to find new opportunities in the Great Plains, many white Nebraskans looked to California as the map to their future. The Ku Klux Klan ran Sin Goon out of North Platte, but more immigrants would come to fill labor shortages in Nebraska's growing industries. Many Nebraskans accepted the small numbers of immigrants from China, Japan, the Philippines, Korea, and South Asia who came to work, study, or join families in the late nineteenth and early twentieth centuries. Many others, including Nebraska legislators, put up the same legal barriers to moving beyond wage labor that California did. California, Nebraska, and all states that wanted to pass anti-Asian legislation were aided by federal law and policy that made Asians ineligible for U.S. citizenship – and for the protections that come with it – from 1870 to 1952.

How stereotypes became Nebraska laws

Territorial, state, and federal laws built upon one another to create barriers to opportunity. Many of them reflected white lawmakers' belief in the John Chinaman stereotype and extended this belief to all people of Asian descent. Most, if not all, had their foundation in the Naturalization Acts of 1790 and 1870. The Naturalization Acts determined who could become a U.S. citizen and under what circumstances. The Naturalization Act of 1790 established that "free white persons" were eligible to become U.S. citizens. Congress had to amend the Act in 1870 to reflect the fact that formerly enslaved African Americans were now free persons born in the United States, and as such were fully legal citizens. American citizenship was now expanded to include "free white persons," "aliens of African nativity," and "persons of African descent," and nobody else. Asian immigrants were neither "white" nor "African," so they occupied a third category: "aliens ineligible for citizenship."[28]

Ah Yup sued in the Ninth Circuit Court for the right to become a naturalized U.S. citizen in 1878. The court ruled against Ah, stating that people of "the Mongolian race" were not white and certainly not African. The Supreme Court upheld this position two more times in its rulings against longtime Japanese Californian, Takao Ozawa, in 1922 and Punjab-born U.S. Army veteran Bhagat Singh Thind in 1923. As far as the federal courts were concerned, an immigrant from Asia could not move beyond the constraints of their racial classifications.[29] Many would live their lives as outsiders in the nation they considered home. This was as true for Asian immigrants in the Midwest as for those on the West Coast.

Asian immigrants started to migrate to Nebraska in the early 1880s, just as the U.S Congress was debating the Chinese Exclusion Act in 1882. It was the first in a series of restrictive immigration laws and the first to target one specific ethnic group. The Chinese Exclusion Act put a ten-year halt to all immigration, except for Chinese government envoys, diplomatic officials, and a small number of similar elites. Workers, however, would be barred from entry for the ten years of the Chinese Exclusion Act, and then for another ten years under the Geary Act. In addition to prohibiting most emigration from China, the Geary Act required Chinese immigrants already in the U.S. to carry a certificate of residence at all times or risk deportation. This was only required of Chinese immigrants, no one else.[30]

The Chinese Exclusion Act reduced the number of Chinese immigrants in Nebraska, which increased the demand for immigrant workers from other Asian countries. Japanese, Korean, Filipino,

---

27. Roger Daniels, *The Politics of Prejudice: The Anti-Japanese Movement in California and the Struggle for Japanese Exclusion* (Berkeley: University of California Press, 1999); Erika Lee, *The Making of Asian America: a History* (New York: Simon and Schuster, 2015), 89-173; Patricia Nelson Limerick, *Legacy of Conquest: The Unbroken Past of the American West* (New York: W.W. Norton, 1987), 271-275.
28. Marian L. Smith, "Race, Nationality, and Reality," *Prologue Magazine* (U.S. National Archives) 34:2 (Summer 2002), www.archives.gov/publications/prologue/2002/summer/immigration-law-1.
29. U.S. Reports: *Ozawa v. United States*, 260 U.S. 178 (1922), https://www.loc.gov/item/usrep260178/, U.S. Reports: *United States vs. Thind*, 261 U.S. 204 (1923) https://www.loc.gov/item/usrep261204/.
30. An act to execute certain treaty stipulations relating to the Chinese, May 6, 1882; Enrolled Acts and Resolutions of Congress, 1789-1996; General Records of the United States Government; Record Group 11; National Archives; An act to execute certain treaty stipulations relating to Chinese, U.S. Statutes at Large, Volume 22 (1881-1883), 47th Congress. 85-88.

"The Golden Gate of Liberty—The Only One Barred Out," *Frank Leslie's Illustrated Newspaper*, [1882]. https://lccn.loc.gov/2001696530

and other newcomers found that white Nebraskans did not recognize the difference between them and the Chinese. The stereotypes they applied to the Chinese, who were now considered so undesirable as to be completely excluded from the United States and so untrustworthy as to warrant surveillance within the U.S., was often extended to all members of the "Mongolian," "Oriental," or "Celestial" race. This perception of all Asians as eternal foreigners meant that even Nebraskans who were born in the United States and had U.S. citizenship by birthright were treated as foreigners from their ancestral countries.

Despite the dangers of invisibility, many Asian Nebraskans were reluctant to push back against these legalized forms of inequality, wisely heeding the Japanese proverb that "the nail that sticks up will get pounded down." Most sought refuge in their invisibility from anti-Asian groups like the Ku Klux Klan and legislators who might otherwise pass more laws against politically outspoken Asian communities. Asian Nebraskans, particularly newer immigrants and refugees, still live within a vicious cycle of being harmed as a result of their invisibility but having only invisibility to protect themselves.[31]

The fact that their history is not well known within the larger history of Nebraska contributes to the invisibility of Asian Nebraskans and the ways in which the inequalities that limited their opportunities emerged from a particular confluence of historical circumstances. The history that follows is not a complete record of every person, every event, or even every Asian nationality represented among Nebraska's peoples from the 1890s to the present. It is a big-picture history that shows the roots of injustice against Nebraskans of Asian descent, the many ways in which anti-Asian racism took hold in Nebraska, how some individuals and groups confronted anti-Asian racism, and what Nebraskans can do today to stem the historical current of anti-Asian prejudice.

Laws against interracial marriage

For most people, regardless of race, the foundation of a "good life," as promised in Nebraska's popular slogan, is made up of some combination of a good job, a welcoming community, ownership of land, a home, or a business, and/or having a family of one's own. Federal and Nebraska state laws made all these difficult for Asians to obtain. "Miscegenation" is a word for intermarriage between a white person and a non-white person. The word is not in common use today, but in the nineteenth and early twentieth centuries miscegenation was a matter of great concern. Proponents of "racial science" like *Crania Americana* believed Caucasians would lose their "finer" qualities if their children had a non-white parent. Many whites worried that children of interracial marriages would change the population from a white to a "brown" majority. This worry was bolstered by the voluminous literature on the importance of white children being "well-born" if the nation was to survive. Michael Guyer's 1916 book *Being Well-Born* said of interracial marriage,

> Some of the dangers of racial deterioration which threaten us because of our laxity regarding immigration have already been indicated. ... From the rate at which immigrants are increasing it is obvious that our very life-blood is at stake. For our own protection we must face the question of what types or races should be ruled out. Aside from the dangers which lie in the defective

31. Trieu, *Fighting Invisibility*, 8-9.

or unsuccessful types ... there is great hazard in the mongrelizing of distinctly unrelated races no matter how superior the original strains may be

— a conclusion, Guyer admitted, lacking reliable data but to be heeded nonetheless.[32] Thirty-eight states, including Nebraska, passed anti-miscegenation laws that made it a crime for white and non-white people to marry.

Different states had different laws about who white people could and could not marry. Nebraska's first anti-miscegenation law made marriage between white and Black partners illegal. In 1911 the law expanded to forbid marriage between a white person and a person with one or more Black grandparents. In 1929, the statute was amended to "forbid marriages between persons of the Caucasian race and those persons with one eighth or more Asian blood." This means that a Nebraskan with one great-grandparent of Asian descent was legally "too Asian" to marry a white Nebraskan.[33]

Miscegenation laws posed real problems for Asian men, in particular, because the 1917 Immigration Act barred all immigration from the Asiatic Zone. Most of the first immigrants had been single men like Sin Goon, who traveled and settled alone. Perhaps Sin planned to return to China to marry and to bring his wife to Nebraska. Or maybe he thought he would marry another Chinese immigrant. Immigration laws made either case unlikely, and anti-miscegenation laws made marrying a white woman impossible. Asians could marry people from other Asian communities, but Japanese, Korean, and Filipino immigrants were also mostly men. Anti-immigration and anti-miscegenation laws worked together to reduce the Chinese population in the United States by approximately 40 percent between 1890 and 1920.[34]

Laws against owning land

Asians in Nebraska (except Filipinos) were also prohibited from owning land. In 1913, California passed the Webb Alien Land-Holding bill barring Asians from purchasing land without stating so directly. It prevented "all aliens ineligible for citizenship" from owning land in California, and the only persons that fit that description were all Asians except Filipinos. Persons emigrating from all other countries in the world could still purchase land in California. This language of lawful acts was soon used in other Western states and arrived in Nebraska's legislature for debate by 1921. With strong opposition from Japanese Americans in Nebraska and members of the clergy who spoke highly of Japanese residents, such as Reverend George Beecher, Bishop of the Episcopal Missionary District of Western Nebraska and Reverend Thomas C. Osborne of Bayard, the words "aliens ineligible for citizenship" was dropped from the Alien Land Law in favor of language that would apply to all aliens. The Nebraska law prevented – and continues to prevent – any alien from owning property in Nebraska for more than five years. While the law appears to be non-discriminatory, it was designed to restrict Japanese immigrants, in particular, from owning land.[35]

When consideration was given to amending Nebraska's law in 1921 to follow the path of California and other western states in specifically denying Japanese the ability to own real estate through incorporation of the legal descriptor "aliens ineligible for citizenship," Japanese immigrants such as North Platte residents Richi Ugai, Charles Shinn, and Hugh Wada and many Nebraska supporters who were not of Asian descent spoke in defense of the Japanese immigrants as hard-working, generous, and respectable community members who would become citizens if they could. These 1921 comments countered those of other Nebraskans who parroted what they heard from California and national media describing all Japanese as vile or despicable individuals not inherently able to assimilate into the United States. In a compromise, the Nebraska legislature voted to deny all non-citizens the right to own land, rather than use wording that aimed specifically against the Japanese aliens. However, a

---

32. Michael F. Guyer, *Being Well-Born: An Introduction to Eugenics* (Indianapolis: The Bobbs-Merrill Company, 1916), 296-297.
33. James Browning, "Anti Miscegenation Laws in the United States," *Duke Bar Journal* 26:41 (1951), 28.
34. Data drawn from tables in Campbell Gibson and Kay Jung, Historical Census Statistics on Population Totals by Race, 1790 to 1990, and by Hispanic origin, 1970 to 1990, for the United States, Regions, Divisions, and States, (Washington, D.C.: United States Census Bureau, 2002), https://www.census.gov/library/working-papers/2002/demo/POP-twps0056.html
35. Stephen W. Kay, "Japanese Immigration and Nebraska's 1921 Alien Land Law" *Nebraska History* Winter 2022.

disparate impact remained in veiled discrimination because while other aliens could choose to become citizens to own land, Japanese immigrants were unable to become American citizens until 1952. This law remains on the books at the time of this writing (2023), raising the possibility that Asians could experience this disparate impact at any point in the immediate future.[36]

Changing the Alien Land Law from a restriction against Asian immigrants to a restriction against all non-U.S. citizens showed that some Nebraska leaders saw Japanese immigrants as being foreign because they were born in another country, not because they were of Samuel Morton's "Asian" type. The benefits of this change only extended so far. European immigrants were eligible for citizenship, so those who became naturalized citizens became eligible to purchase land in Nebraska. This avenue was not open to Asians. The long-term effect of the revised law was to make Nebraska a society of mostly white landowners with a population of landless Asian immigrants. Their options were to form businesses or to work for whites. Without the civil liberties protections that came with citizenship, Asian immigrants had to rely on the white majority to allow them to live and work freely, without exploitation or threats of violence.

Asian Nebraskans worked within the limits of the Immigration Acts, their ineligibility for citizenship, miscegenation laws, and the alien land law to build their lives, contribute to the growth of the state, and, for many, to achieve great things. Their success, and in some cases their survival, depended upon staying within the limits set by Nebraska's white majority. Staying within the limits meant different things to different people at different times, yet it was a common thread across Asian Nebraskans' life experiences.

Coming to Nebraska

The Nebraska of the late 1800s and early 1900s was a place in transition as Asian immigrants slowly migrated from Pacific coastal entry points in Canada, the U.S., and Mexico.[37] In this place only a generation prior, Indigenous populations were forced away from the lands of their ancestors by wagon loads of European Americans from the eastern reaches of the United States bent on their own destiny, by former Black slaves and Civil War soldiers from the east and south seeking space and freedom, and by Spanish-speaking immigrants from the southern and southwestern lands expanding into the fading rural Wild West. It was within this setting that the first Chinese and Japanese immigrants had to quietly endure or battle the images and expectations imposed on them from those in powerful positions and non-Asian backgrounds whose ignorance of the roots of their cultures often created distress.

The Chinese appeared to be the first to immigrate in the 1870s with twelve men and one woman living in Omaha at the time of the first Chinese burial at Prospect Hill Cemetery in 1874. The Omaha City Directory listed two Chinese laundries for the first time on Tenth Street downtown.[38] After the 1882 Chinese Exclusion Act (and the 1902 Chinese Exclusion Act that made the provisions of 1882 permanent), the Chinese population in the U.S. began to decline as its composition was mostly men without families. By 1890, there were 224 Chinese in Nebraska arriving in second migrations from California and other western states where their main occupations were in railroads, mining, and laundry work.

The Chin family came from the Canton region of China where the great-grandfather served as a houseboy for the San Francisco mayor in the early 1800s. Because he had no official immigration paperwork, he was due to be expatriated back to China, but the mayor was able to secure documentation so he could stay in the U.S. He later returned to China, married, and returned to the U.S. The family's story is shared by Dennis Chin, former teacher and administrator in Bellevue. Grandfather Chin Ah Gin (note: the surname is placed first) was born in California and worked there until he went to China to marry.

---

36. Stephen W. Kay, "Japanese Immigration and Nebraska's 1921 Alien Land Law," *Nebraska History* Winter 2022. Nebraska, Iowa, Minnesota, Missouri, North Dakota, Oklahoma, South Dakota, and Wisconsin do have restrictions on non-citizen ownership of agricultural lands, but these restrictions are not based on race. Foreign citizens and corporations not incorporated in Nebraska are prohibited from owning land outside of or three miles beyond a city or village or leasing it for more than five years. See J. David Aiken, "Nebraska Restrictions on Foreign Land Ownership," *Cornhusker Economics* 572 (February 2021): https://digitalcommons.unl.edu/agecon_cornhusker/572

37. For more on immigration from Asia see Ronald Takaki, *Strangers from a Different Shore: A History of Asian Americans* (Boston: Back Bay Books, 1998).

38. Bing Chen, "Brief History of Chinese in Omaha," May 10, 2018, 7, unpublished manuscript in possession of the author.

He returned to the U.S. with his family of five daughters and an adopted nephew to work as potato farmers in the Stockton, California, area. Eventually Chin Ah Gin moved to Duluth, Minnesota, to open a couple restaurants, and then came to Omaha for the Trans-Mississippi Exposition of 1898. By 1900, more Chinese immigrants who stayed in Nebraska operated restaurants, mercantile enterprises, laundries, and other businesses in Omaha. In 1916, a hall for the Omaha Chinese Merchants Association was opened on the site of the On Leong Tong (originally a Chinese-American brotherhood with criminal ties) in downtown Omaha. Upon deciding to stay in Omaha, Chin Ah Gin opened the Mandarin Restaurant in 1912, which he ran until he established King Fong restaurant downtown at 315 South Sixteenth Street in 1920 as part of a corporation with stock shares for the purpose of providing opportunities for immigrants from China to work. He became embedded in the Omaha community through networks with the mayor, chief of police, and other business owners. As a patriarch of the Chinese in Omaha, he settled disputes in Chinatown, met with immigrants seeking employment, and regulated the activities in Chinatown. The police did not need to respond to concerns because Chin Ah Gin and the On Leong Tong, a Chinese merchants association, maintained control in that community. Many of the conflicts were between the different groups of Chinese (from mainland China, Taiwan, Singapore and Hong Kong, and the American-born Chinese) and between groups with different global political interests.

The grandson Dennis Chin recalls his family living with his grandfather in a large house in Omaha that had formerly belonged to the mayor outside of the Chinatown boundaries. Chin Ah Gin forbade his grandchildren from visiting Omaha's Chinatown for their own safety because of the nefarious activities such as gambling that occurred, and he wanted the family to maintain their integrated status in the larger Omaha community and focus on attending higher education. Dennis' father Carl Chin completed a chemical engineering degree in California and became the chief chemist for the Omaha Public Works, while his wife from the Canton region of China worked in the Omaha Public Schools. He was asked by Chin Ah Gin to continue the work with Chinatown and provide resources for Chinese immigrants while the elder left Omaha for California in 1954. Eventually another family, the Hueys, took over management of King Fong restaurant, re-incorporated it into their name, and kept it in business for several decades. Dennis completed a college degree, worked for Union Pacific, and later returned to college for a teaching certificate in math and computers to teach and become an administrator for a school in Bellevue.

Dennis Chin. Courtesy of Dennis Chin.

In reflecting on the history of Chinatown, Dennis felt his grandfather and others played a major role in creating a place for Chinese immigrants to begin a life in Nebraska as laborers. As the immigrants changed from laborers to professionals, the community changed. The immigrants moved out of the Chinatown boundaries between Capitol Avenue and Cass Street, and "Chinatown" ceased to exist for the purpose that originally sustained the geographic community.[39] The second Tong House continues to stand at 1518 Cass Street in Omaha and is on the National Register of Historic Places in Omaha.

The increased strength and prosperity of Chinatown did not always protect its business owners from harassment and violence. In some cases, it made Chinese business owners more conspicuous targets. An Omaha man of Chinese descent, Ham Pak, was brutally murdered in 1907 by three young white men in what they said was an attempt to rob his chop suey restaurant. The newspapers gave the details of Pak's assault which went on for several minutes as he fought back, and which ended with a fatal stab with an icepick. The three assailants – Basil Mullen, George Pumphrey, and Willis Allmack, one of Pak's employees – testified that they tried to obtain chloroform to knock Pak unconscious. Unable to find it, they stabbed and bludgeoned Pak, even as he pleaded and fought for his life. Pumphrey, who dealt the fatal blow, testified that he struck Pak repeatedly while trying to take his watch. Pak, for his part, tried to defend himself with a meat cleaver without success.

Mullen later testified, and the newspaper reported, "The Chinaman got on his knees and got a meat cleaver. He struck at Pumphrey. Pumphrey got his

---

39. Dennis Chin interviewed by Sharon Ishii-Jordan, March 1, 2023.

club and rained more blows on him. The Chinaman rolled over and rubbed his foot against Harry. He said something in Chinese. [Mullen] said 'I think he's about all in.'" Allmack believed that Pak had $3,000 in the restaurant; he didn't. Ham Pak, an Omaha businessman, lost his life for $40, a revolver, and a ring that his three killers pawned to split the proceeds. It was, by any measure, a senseless loss of life brought on by an act of torture.[40]

Basil Mullen, George Pumphrey, and Willis Allmack stood trial for their crimes and were incarcerated, but not for the full terms of their sentences. Both the court and the public looked at the totality of these young men's lives and believed that extended imprisonment for crimes committed at the ages of 17-20 were unwarranted. These were people with families and dreams and potential. Mullen was a charmer; the newspaper reported that he was "affectionately greeted by a number of women" at Pumphrey's trial.[41]

Governor Ashton C. Shallenberger reduced Pumphrey's life sentence in 1911 to seven years on the grounds that Pumphrey was a model prisoner and was young when he murdered Pak, who the newspapers most often referred to as a "Chinaman" or a "Chinese restaurant keeper." The Nebraska courts, governor, media, and public saw what was lost when a young man spent life in prison and viewed Mullen, Allmack, and Pumphrey in the fullness of their humanity. Pak remained a "Chinaman" – more of a thing than a person whose age, family members, and hopes for his future received no mention. It was a clear indication that the persistent stereotyping and exclusion of Asian Nebraskans as "aliens ineligible for citizenship" had convinced white Nebraskans that Asians were also ineligible for just and humane treatment in society and the legal system.[42]

Chinese immigrants moved from the West Coast and settled across Nebraska, working mostly as cooks, laundrymen, and railroad workers in Douglas, Lancaster, Cherry, and Dawes counties,[43] with a notable number working at the cotton mill in Kearney.[44] However, by 1890, the census recorded 224 Chinese in Nebraska, which was the peak of this immigrant group after which their numbers declined due to the immigration limitations brought on by the Chinese Exclusion Act. Japanese immigrants took up the jobs left unfilled by declining Chinese numbers between 1880 and 1900 on the Plains, in railroad, mining, and agriculture. In 1904-1905, the Russo-Japanese War was waged with the economic challenges brought on by any military conflict, and Japanese immigrants left their homeland in larger numbers coming to the coast and then to the interior of the country. By 1910, many Japanese immigrants settled in western Nebraska to work in the sugar beet industry and on the Burlington Northern Railroad. Communities of Japanese immigrants across the high plains of eastern Colorado, southeastern Wyoming, and western Nebraska came together in social and Christian gatherings. Rich soils across the Platte Valley enticed others to keep moving eastward across Nebraska to farm with large numbers settling in North Platte and Lincoln County.

John Miyoshi recalls his family's stories of their migration to Nebraska. Takehiko Miyoshi arrived in Seattle from the Fukuoka area of Japan in 1909 on a ship that ended in Seattle, and he decided to stay there to work. He met and married Tekeyo and returned to Japan for the wedding ceremony in 1916. Takehiko eventually began working for Union Pacific Railroad where his job ended in North Platte, Nebraska. He and his wife stayed and began farming between Hershey and North Platte, living in a sod house which still stands in its original location. They raised corn, cows, and engaged in truck farming with vegetables. There may have been about twenty Japanese farmers in the area at the time.[45] National acts of discrimination and exaggerated accounts of immigration numbers inflated their numbers in Nebraska. Although Nebraska newspapers published West Coast accounts of the necessity of anti-Japanese sentiments in supporting anti-alien land laws, occasional printing of protests against racially discriminatory land laws were issued. Fact-finding discounted the "hordes of Japanese who are pouring into the state" of California with the release of figures from the commissioner of immigration showing that in the three years prior to 1911, the number of Japanese immigrants actually decreased by almost 5,000.[46]

---

40. "Allmack Charged with the Murder of Chinaman Pak," *Omaha Daily News*, July 24, 1907, 1.
41. "Mullen Tells How Chinaman Was Slain," *Morning World-Herald*, December 7, 1907, 6.
42. "Mullen Tells How Chinaman Was Slain," *Morning World-Herald*, December 7, 1907, 6.
43. United States Department of Commerce, Bureau of the Census, Report on the 13th Census Taken in the Year 1910, vol. 3 (Washington: USGPO, 1913).
44. Archives Department, Buffalo County Historical Society.
45. John Miyoshi interviewed by Sharon Ishii-Jordan, March 1, 2023.
46. California, Japan, and the Administration," *The Commoner* (Lincoln, Nebraska), 13:17 (May 2, 1913): 3-5.

Since they were not allowed to become U.S. citizens, the Alien Land Law excluded the Miyoshi immigrants from land ownership. However, their hard work enabled Tekeyo to save silver coins in cans at home, and when she had enough, they bought land in the name of their oldest daughter, who was an American-born teenager and was not restricted by the alien land law in place. The Miyoshi family had eight children, and two sons and one daughter stayed in the North Platte area as farmers. One son completed a degree in horticulture at the University of Nebraska and engaged in potato research with a professor. With his connections among Japanese farmers in central and western Nebraska, he engaged the farmers with test plots in Hershey, North Platte, and Alliance. In 1959, he acquired an orchard in Nebraska City, so he moved his family to farm there. John, a sansei (third-generation Japanese American) in the family, reflected on the impact of WWII on his family's Japanese culture. He said the war changed everything for them. His grandfather wanted the children to speak English, so they became bilingual; the family also changed from Buddhists to Christians so as not to draw attention to themselves.

During the 1910s, Japanese immigrants settled in eastern Nebraska to work in the meat-packing plants and start their own businesses. The men lived in boarding houses in South Omaha, close to the plants. A sociological study of race relations in 1917 made specific mention of the cleanliness and organizational internal structure of the Japanese in maintaining efficient self-management of the South Omaha boarding house.[47] Sometimes, Japanese workers were brought to work at plants to replace white laborers who had gone on strike to demand better wages and safer working conditions. Immigrant workers were often connected to jobs through labor contractors, who helped white employers by recruiting, training, and serving as translators for Japanese workers. In 1907, South Omaha students and their parents protested the presence of Japanese students who enrolled in their schools when their parents came to work as strikebreakers. Eight hundred school children blocked the teachers and the Japanese students from the school building, yelling "down with the Japs!"[48] Two years later, Omaha mayor James Dahlman reinforced anti-Japanese sentiment by throwing a rope around two Japanese diplomats who asked him about the local practice of cow-punching. This public gesture was humiliating to the Japanese community and frightening to the diplomats who had to wonder if they might be lynched.[49]

Japanese entrepreneurs also bore the burdens of racial discrimination, being called derogatory names as their numbers increased across Nebraska. Ihachi (James) Ishii departed the Hiroshima area of Japan in 1906 and arrived in the U.S. after traveling through Hawaii and working in silver mines in Mexico for several months. He arrived in El Paso via train and continued to Colorado, then Kansas City, and finally Omaha to work in the packing plants at each stop. Ihachi was seeking his elder brother Seitaro Ishii who had arrived in the U.S. a couple years earlier and was working in Omaha. They lived in a men's boarding house in South Omaha. In about 1913, Seitaro moved to the Japanese community in Scottsbluff, opening the Royal Café and Billiards where he ran a successful business until his untimely death from appendicitis in 1920. Meanwhile, his younger brother saved enough money to attend driving school and became a chauffeur and butler to Minnie Storz Higgins for several years.

When Ihachi married a Bohemian-American woman, Anna Zadina, in 1919, they had to have their ceremony in Red Oak, Iowa, due to Nebraska's anti-miscegenation law. This law impacted those of Asian descent in their ability to marry whites, especially in a state like Nebraska with a predominantly Caucasian demographic. In another example, John Miyoshi married a Caucasian woman that he met at the University of Nebraska, and they had to be married in Council Bluffs due to the law. Nebraska's law specifically stated that "persons with 1/8 or more negro, Japanese or Chinese blood" could not marry a white person.[50] Some Japanese men found wives through the picture bride phenomenon in which their families in Japan arranged for marriage with a woman through long-distance photos. Other Japanese and Chinese men chose to marry white women, but were forced to wed in Colorado, Iowa, Kansas, or South Dakota where anti-miscegenation laws had been repealed; however, Nebraska recognized the legal marriage when the couple returned to their homes across Nebraska.

47. Jesse Frederick Steiner, *The Japanese Invasion: A Study of the Psychology of Inter-Racial Contacts* (Chicago: A.C. McClurg, 1917), 133.
48. "Revolt Over Japanese: South Omaha School Children Want Them Expelled," *New York Times,* April 18, 1905.
49. "Dahlman Lassoes Japanese," *New York Times,* May 12, 1907.
50. Nebraska State Legislature, Seventy-Third Session Introducer's Statement of Purpose for LB 179, February 1, 1963.

Another challenge for Anna Ishii was the 1907 Expatriation Act, which also removed the US citizenship of American-born women who married any non-citizens. It made the decision to marry a heavy-hearted choice for women. In 1922 the Married Women's Independent Nationality Act (also called the Cable Act) revised the Expatriation Act of 1907, reversed the loss of citizenship from women who married noncitizens, unless they married aliens ineligible for citizenship, in other words, Asian immigrants. Those American women still were denied the ability to reinstate their citizenship. Ihachi eventually apprenticed to a photographer and established his own successful photography business Ishii Studio and Gifts in South Omaha at Twenty-fourth and L streets. Ihachi James and Anna had four sons, but the young boys grew up with parents who could not become or had lost their U.S. citizenship based on racial discrimination.

A more acceptable Asian migration

The divide between "Asianness" and "Americanness" was blurred in the Immigration Act by the categorization of Filipinos as U.S. nationals who, as residents of the U.S. insular territory of the Philippines, were eligible to immigrate to the United States. Filipinos' inclusion as colonial subjects of the United States created a complicated dynamic of belonging and foreignness for all who came to the U.S.,[51] especially to Nebraska. The First and Second Nebraska Regiments were mobilized in Lincoln in April 1898, supported the capture of Manila in July 1898, and were assigned to garrison duty for the rest of the year. Sixty-four Nebraskans were killed and several hundred wounded in their fight to suppress the Filipino resistance led by Emilio Aguinaldo. When regular Army units replaced the volunteer units in 1899, Nebraska's fighters were received in Lincoln with a "royal welcome."[52] Mission activity continued in earnest throughout the U.S. occupation, and as a result at least 15 percent of Nebraskans born in the Philippines were born to white missionaries.[53]

Family photo courtesy of Dr. Ishii-Jordan.

While Filipinos did not immigrate to the U.S. in the same numbers as the Chinese and Japanese in the early part of the twentieth century, many of the dozens who worked in private homes as drivers or servants fostered interpersonal relationships between Filipino workers and their white employers. These relationships remained unequal, but they were more humanizing than the distanced relationships with other Asians. As Christians and U.S. colonial subjects who often bore Spanish heritage and names, Filipinos were more likely to be considered "white" than other Asians, especially in the case of the wealthier pensionados. Census enumerators in Lancaster County classified some as "white" and others as "Filipino," and some as "alien" and others not, absent any clear markers of dual heritage or transnational citizenship.[54]

---

51. Yen Le Espiritu, *Home Bound: Filipino American Lives across Cultures, Communities, and Countries* (Berkeley: University of California Press, 2003), 1-4.
52. "First Nebraska Regiment," *History Nebraska Blog*, https://history.nebraska.gov/publications_section/first-nebraska-regiment/
53. United States Department of Commerce, Thirteenth Census of the United States, 1890 and 1910, Records of the Bureau of the Census, Record Group 29. National Archives, Washington, D.C.
54. United States Department of Commerce, Thirteenth Census of the United States, 1910, Records of the Bureau of the Census, Record Group 29, National Archives, Washington, D.C.

Filipino students found opportunities to immigrate for higher education when the 1903 Pensionado Act provided sponsorships to Filipino students from wealthy families to study in American universities. The U.S. had five years earlier gained control of the Philippine islands from Spain after the Spanish-American War ended, and the goal of the legislation was to help young Filipinos learn about American culture, educate them, and return them to the Philippines to help assimilate the colony. Six pensionados attended the University of Nebraska as part of the approximately 500 Filipino students who studied in the U.S. in exchange for 18 months of government service back in their homeland. Sometime between 1903 and 1905, Vincente Villanueva and his older brother Bonifacio left the rural area of Batangas on the island of Luzon to attend the University of Nebraska and graduated in 1910 with engineering degrees. As per the program, they returned to the Philippines to become leaders in the colony. Although the Villanueva brothers never returned to Nebraska, Vincente's youngest daughter immigrated in the 1960s to earn a graduate degree from Michigan and teach at an elementary school in Des Moines. Alita eventually became a guidance counselor in Council Bluffs, while her granddaughter played basketball for Creighton University in the 1990s and later coached basketball for UNL, completing the circle.[55]

From the Korean Peninsula to Nebraska

Korean immigration was also relatively small. Those who sought work beyond the cane fields of Hawaii came to industrial centers like South Omaha, where jobs in and around the stockyards were plentiful. Korean immigrants were hard-working and used their wages to care for their families and for other Koreans in need. The first Korean to die in Douglas County was a man named Y.S. Cho. Like many immigrants, Cho was without family to arrange or pay for a funeral. The Korean community in South Omaha pooled their money for a funeral. According to the *Omaha Daily Bee*, the Koreans "provided handsomely for their countryman." Cho was the first Korean to be buried in South Omaha, at Laurel Hill Cemetery. He would not be the last, and each time Korean neighbors would fill the role of family.[56]

Young-Man Park arrived in the U.S. in 1905 to study at the University of Nebraska and while there, he started the Korean Youth Military Academy. A number of young Korean students were brought to Kearney in 1906 to attend the Kearney Military Academy and a Cadet Company at Kearney High School. The purpose of the school was to provide Korean youth with the military skills to defend Korea's independence if the Japanese military pursued Korea after defeating Russia. When Japan seized Korea in 1910, Park opened a second academy at Hastings College, where 80 students trained to regain Korea's independence between 1910-1914.[57] The young boys stayed with Kearney families while they pursued their studies. They spent their days in Bible study and military studies courses, taught in Korean at the academy. In the evening, the students assisted their host families with household work and agricultural chores. Over the next decade, some of the boys eventually completed their secondary education in Kearney or Hastings, and pursued further studies at the University of Nebraska, Yale, and the Michigan School of Law or joined the U.S. Army. One entrepreneur established La Choy Foods with a college classmate after wanting to make his own bean sprouts at home.[58]

Koreans in Nebraska had shown themselves to be hard-working, generous, and fiercely committed to the same values of freedom and independence as the American revolutionaries who fought for independence from Great Britain. The city of Lincoln declared itself with pride to be the "largest Korean student center in America."[59] Yet support for Korea's freedom fighters, who came from wealthier Christian families, came at the expense of workers like Y.S. Cho in South Omaha. A newspaper feature on the all-Nebraska Korean drills taking place at Hastings College said this of working-class immigrants: "The Korean student is proud of his vocation. He takes little account of the Korean in America who is not a student. The man who is here merely to perform menial labor and who has no 'aim' in his migration from the shores of [Korea] commands very little consideration from the student."[60]

Using some of Morton's typologies, the article separates Korean students who were preparing to

---

55. Mekita Rivas, "A Legacy of Education" *Nebraska Quarterly* (Summer 2023): https://www.huskeralum.org/s/1620/magazine/interior.aspx?sid=1620&gid=1&pgid=3095
56. "First Correan Funeral," *Omaha Daily Bee*, December 18, 1908, 7.
57. "Hastings College Honors Koreans," *Omaha World-Herald*, July 13, 2002, 8.
58. Margaret Stines Nielsen, "The Korean Connection, *Buffalo Tales*, vol 20, No. 3 (August 2010) *The Korean American Story*, https://koreanamericanstory.org/written/the-korean-connection/.
59. "Lincoln Leads All Other Cities in Number of Korean Students," *The Lincoln Star*, March 25, 1911, 10.
60. "Lincoln Leads All Other Cities in Number of Korean Students," *The Lincoln Star*, March 25, 1911, 10.

return to Korea from the Korean immigrants who were forming communities and contributing to the economic development of Nebraska: "By some marvelous method of caretaking, the young Korean student in Lincoln manages to wear one suit much longer than an American boy and manages to keep it in presentable condition at all times. Most of them are well set up and are sound, husky physical specimens, although below the American average in height." Most importantly, in light of Nebraska's miscegenation law, which applied to Koreans, "Koreans told reporters that they had 'no aspiration to associate familiarly with the American girl, his time in America being much too precious to be spent on mere girls.'"[61]

By 1915, Asian immigrants were part of life in cities, towns, and farming communities across Nebraska. Their numbers were still relatively small, so forming networks of support through social gatherings, clubs, churches, and newspapers in English and immigrants' native language was important. Immigrants gave each other information to help them adjust to their new lives in Nebraska. They helped each other observe important holidays and religious practices. Immigrant communities shared favorite foods and stories from the homeland in their native language. In their communities, Asian immigrants had a break from feeling like outsiders and received the support they needed to become more fully part of American life.

Omaha's Chinatown and South Omaha's Korean community are just two examples. Japanese communities formed in farming communities. Community life centered around social halls, churches, and the many hotels, restaurants, import shops, and other businesses that became favorites among the Japanese and non-Japanese alike. Two halls that served their communities for decades were in Scottsbluff and Mitchell. Filipinos were part of student life and the Nebraska workforce, living as both "Americans" by virtue of their territorial status and as "Asians" where racial boundaries were concerned. These communities became increasingly important as the number of Asian immigrants grew more numerous. As white Westerners, including Nebraskans, came to fear an "invasion," their leaders passed laws written to restrict Asians' civil liberties and their participation in the state's economy, politics, and society. The period between the 1920s and 1950s brought some of the most dramatic shifts in thinking – and in law and policy – about Asians' "foreignness" and "belonging" in America.

The Dangerous Climate of White Supremacy

Nebraska was well known for its corn and cattle, but its literacy rates were the state's point of pride in 1896. For the second year in a row, Nebraska ranked first in the nation in literacy. This spoke well of Nebraska's education system and the standard of living in the relatively new state. The Immigration League attributed Nebraska's success to its white Northern European majority. Most Nebraskans came from "better" stock, they said, and from countries whose languages were similar to English. The Atlantic states were "disadvantaged" by the presence of more "foreign" immigrants from Southern and Eastern Europe, and the southern states were "disadvantaged" by the number of Black Americans who had long been denied education altogether. By this logic, if Nebraska was to retain this distinction it would have to jealously guard its white majority. The Immigration Restriction League did not have to do much to persuade Nebraskans to restrict the most "foreign" among them.[62] This involved stoking Nebraskans' fears that their Asian neighbors could only ever be hostile foreigners no matter how hardworking, honest, kind, or devoted to the United States they showed themselves to be.

In 1921, reporter Ross L. Hammond sat with a delegation from the Japanese Diet (the rough equivalent of the U.S. Congress) that he suspected of being "on a quest for knowledge concerning [Americans'] mode of living, our industrial attainments, our political and social problems, and everything else that may be of advantage to a Nippon to know." Drawing from Morton, he framed these Asian delegates as imitators to be feared because, having defeated Russia in the Russo-Japanese War in 1905, they had "quickly learned the ways and the wiles of the civilized world." At issue were the alien land laws and other laws that discriminated against Japanese nationals. Hammond was not concerned about easing these tensions between the U.S. and Japan. In an article in the *Fremont Tribune* syndicated across Nebraska, he warned that giving the Japanese access to even the smallest parcels of land would open the door to invasion. The Japanese, "inured to hardships" and "accustomed to self-denial," he said, would seek to take possession of U.S. food supplies and starve white Nebraskans out. White Nebraskans, he noted, were too civilized to "work our women and children in the fields, by day and by night" as

---

61. "Lincoln Leads All Other Cities in Number of Korean Students," *The Lincoln Star*, March 25, 1911, 10.
62. "An Unrestricted Evil," *The Lincoln News*, January 27, 1896, 6.

Asians would do, in something of a diabolical Fu Manchu fashion.

Hammond's warnings did not stop there: "Beyond the danger of the threatened and disputed oriental invasion is a larger danger of the mixture of the races." Asians were "ethnologically different" people with "low levels of English literacy" who could not be assimilated into Nebraska's European majority. It was another way of restating that people of Asian descent could never be Americans.[63] Many Nebraskans believed that their state was at risk and that Asians were the clear and visible threat, despite their small numbers. Keeping their numbers small and maintaining their distance from Nebraska land, decision-making, and even family life was a concern that many, but not all, white Nebraskans acted upon.

Some prominent white Nebraska leaders rejected Hammond's views of Asian people and their right to live in Nebraska. Episcopal Bishop George Beecher and Reverend Thomas Osborne both denounced anti-Asian discrimination in the language of the Alien Land Law. William Jennings Bryan thought highly of the Japanese, sponsoring Japanese leader Hiram Hisanori Kano to come to the United States to study agriculture and, under Bishop Beecher's guidance, achieve ordination as an Episcopal minister. Bryan also argued that Asians in the U.S. must be treated according to the dictates of the Constitution, just as U.S. citizens were.[64] While Bryan was an advocate for Asians in the U.S. and for individual Asians he knew personally, he also campaigned to extend the Chinese Exclusion Act, stating overtly that immigration from China threatened the livelihoods of U.S. citizens. His opposition to U.S. annexation of the Philippines was based on his larger opposition to Asian immigration. Indeed, he argued before Congress:

> "It is not strange that the laboring men should look with undisguised alarm upon the prospect of oriental competition upon the farms and in the factories of the United States. Our people have legislated against Chinese emigration, but to exclude a few Chinese and admit many Filipinos is like straining at a gnat and swallowing a camel."[65]

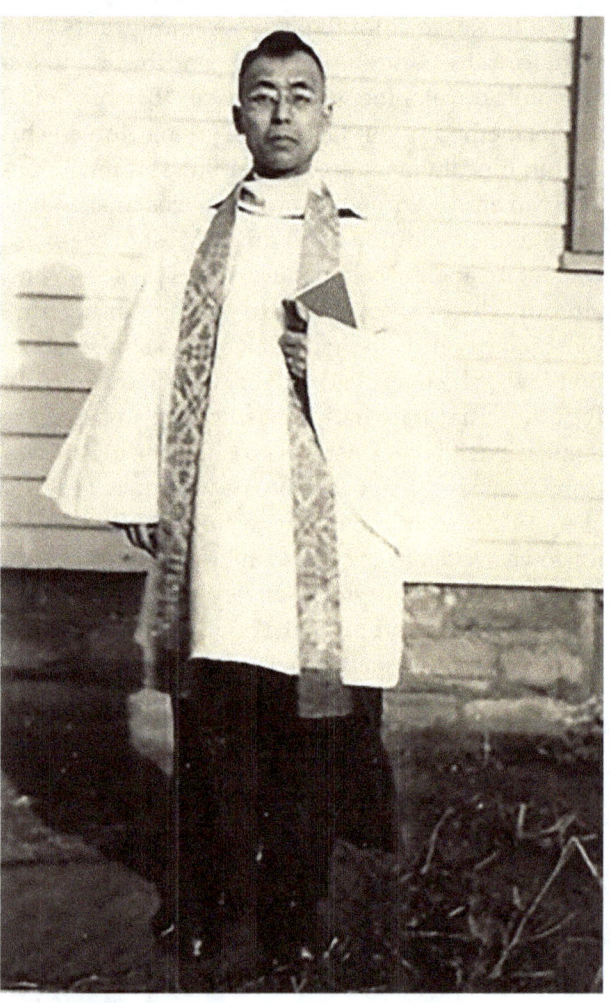

Father Kano. Courtesy of Church of Our Savior, North Platte.

On balance, the tide of public opinion flowed against Asian Nebraskans in the 1920s and 1930s, despite people like the Miyoshis, the Villanuevas, the Chins, and many others having been good neighbors, employees, business owners, and customers for many years. The divide between white Nebraskans' ideas about Asian people and the real Asian people who settled in Nebraska remained very wide as a second generation of Asian Nebraskans came of age. Red lining – refusing housing to people of color in "white" neighborhoods – reinforced stereotyping and segregation in Nebraska's cities. Omaha realtor C.L. Nethaway pledged to his white clientele that he would never sell or rent property to Black, Japanese, or Chinese buyers – stated in offensive racial slurs, which, apparently, did not detract from his business.[66]

---

63. Ross L. Hammond, "Mixing the Races," *The Kearney Daily Hub*, July 1, 1921, 2.
64. William Jennings Bryan, "Asiatic Immigration," n.d., History Nebraska RG3198.AM Series 6, 1.
65. William Jennings Bryan, "Will It Pay?" *New York Journal*, January 15, 1899, excerpted and reprinted by the National Humanities Center, http://nationalhumanitiescenter.org/pds/gilded/empire/text5/bryan.pdf.
66. Palma Strand, "A History of Redlining in Omaha," *North Omaha History*, https://northomahahistory.com/2015/08/02/a-history-of-red-lining-in-north-omaha/.

American-born Japanese and "Chinamen" were not aliens ineligible for citizenship. They were citizens ineligible to live in the neighborhoods of their choice.

Anti-Asian organizations

The Ku Klux Klan remained committed to keeping Asians out of Nebraska since it ran Sin Goon out of North Platte in 1878. The Klan established a headquarters in Omaha in 1921 and ran statewide advertisements for "reputable citizens" to apply for membership. Prominent white citizens received personal invitations to join the Klan, contingent on giving the "correct" answer to the question, "Do you believe in white supremacy?"[67] The Klan boasted twenty-four Nebraska chapters by the end of the year, with 800 Nebraskans joining weekly. The number reached 45,000 in 1923, with active groups in Omaha, Lincoln, Grand Island, Fremont, York, North Platte, Scottsbluff, and Hastings, and individual members across the state. Cross-burnings and Klan conventions became commonplace in Nebraska. Crosses burned in Beatrice, Milford, Seward, Beaver Creek, Barneston, and Hebron on April 24, 1924. Weeks later, on July 25, about 10,000 Nebraskans watched 200 Klansmen on parade in McCook, where they held a rally promoting white Americanism.[68]

Scottsbluff, where Japanese and Mexican immigrants were vital to the agricultural economy, became a hotbed of Klan activity. The Women of the Ku Klux Klan recruited members to their auxiliary,[69] while an offshoot of the organization, called the Minute Men, started a chapter in Scottsbluff. According to Dr. Minor, pastor of the American Christian Church in Denver who addressed potential recruits in Scottsbluff, the southern-based Klan exerted too much control over the locals. The Minute Men would pursue the same agenda, but with local concerns in mind – quite possibly referring to racial anxieties about Asians and Mexicans, and not exclusively about Blacks and Jews. Scottsbluff residents also founded an anti-Klan opposition group called the Guardians of Liberty, which suggests that some white Nebraskans rejected the racism being leveled against their neighbors.[70] It also means that white Nebraskans who joined the Klan or the Minute Men knew that they were making choices about their political beliefs. It cannot be said that white Nebraskans did not hear alternative viewpoints on race and racism in the 1920s. They did and yet were either unable or unwilling to change their thinking.

In 1923 the Woodman Building in Omaha became the headquarters of the American fascist movement. Its leader, James Dahlman, traded the title "Mayor of Omaha'" for "Grand Lictor of the Fascisti" and the Woodman Building was to be renamed "the Imperial Tower."[71] Dahlman pledged to rebuild a "strong ... pure America" by venerating white citizens and eliminating "race hatred" through exclusion and force, promoting the belief that Blacks, Asians, and members of other racial and ethnic groups targeted for violence were themselves the perpetrators of racism. The Fascisti distinguished themselves from the Ku Klux Klan by expanding the definition of "white citizens" to include Catholics and Jews.[72] Fascists in the United States were attracted to Mussolini's muscular nationalism rooted in the recovery of a "glorious national past" through the pursuit of militarism and racial purity. All other races and nations, in Mussolini's doctrine, were to be treated as inferior outsiders. Dahlman's belief in these principles helps to explain why he "lassoed" the two Japanese diplomats who asked him about raising cattle. There was so much crossover in Minute Men and Fascisti membership that investigative reporters at the *Omaha Bee* questioned whether the two organizations and the Ku Klux Klan itself were one and the same.[73] No matter their affiliation, the depth and extent of white supremacist extremism in Nebraska posed dangers to Asian Nebraskans that they could neither predict nor see. The Klan, Minute Men, and Fascisti were all secret societies; only a few prominent leaders made their involvement public.

---

67. "Organize the Ku Klux Klan: Nebraskans Solicited as Members in State Organization," *The Kearney Daily Hub*, July 1, 1921, 2.
68. Michael W Schuyler, "The Ku Klux Klan in Nebraska, 1920-1930," *Nebraska History* 66 (1985): 234-256.
69. Advertisement, "There will be a State Organizer of the Women of the Ku Klux Klan in Scottsbluff, Nebraska, on Thursday, October 14...," *Scottsbluff Daily Star-Herald*, October 12, 1926, 4.
70. "Over Nebraska: Scottsbluff," *Omaha World-Herald*, August 16, 1925, 8.
71. "Mayor Accepts Office as Grand Lictor of Fascisti: Will Become National Head of "Black Shirts:" Thousand Members of "Local Tower" Claimed," *Omaha World-Herald*, May 2, 1923, 1.
72. United States Congress. House. May 21, 1924. *Congressional Record* (Washington DC: USGPO, 1924), 9131; Jorge Dagino, "The Myth of the New Man in Italian Fascist Ideology," *Fascism*, 5(2), 130-148. doi: https://doi.org/10.1163/22116257-00502003
73. "Fascisti of America Cannot Be Located in Omaha; Where Is It?" *Omaha Daily Bee*, October 5, 1923, 14.

The American Legion was especially focused on curbing the population of Japanese Nebraskans. The Lincoln legion warned in 1921 that Japanese immigrants would gain a toehold in Nebraska if the Legislature did not act quickly to pass the Alien Land Law – and to push for further restrictions against the Japanese. California waited too long, the Legion warned, and now the trend in all western states was an "alarming increase of these unassimilable people." At its national meeting, the American Legion leadership called for a law that "forever barred" Japanese from becoming citizens and a constitutional amendment denying birthright citizenship to all children of aliens ineligible for citizenship who were born in the U.S. In other words, if the American Legion had its way, children born in the U.S. to Asian parents would forever be aliens ineligible for citizenship.[74]

Anti-Asian rhetoric aimed at white Nebraskans informed them of the dangers posed to them by Asians. In fact, the pervasiveness of anti-Asian rhetoric created a dangerous environment for individuals of Asian descent. Y.P. Bhosale attended the 1925 meeting of the Nebraska Writers' Guild at the Fontenelle Hotel in Omaha. The University of Nebraska student thought nothing of accompanying some friends to the event until he went to the restroom to adjust his turban. Six white men made derogatory comments about the turban. When Bhosale replied that he did not wish to talk to these men, they lunged at him and began beating and kicking him as they repeated, "Who are you, you foreigner?" Bhosale took a painful blow to the chest but was able to report the incident to hotel security. When questioned about the assault, one of the men denied having hit Bhosale, and the matter was dropped. Bhosale told reporters that he was not badly injured and that the assailants were likely intoxicated, possibly to avoid retribution from the six men. Nebraskans' readiness to accept Bhosale's assault as a misfortune to be expected recalled the readiness with which Nebraskans excused Mullen, Pumphrey, and Allmack for killing Ham Pak on account of their youth and good behavior during their short time in prison. It became an established fact in practice, if not the law, that the penalty was higher for being Asian in Omaha than it was for committing violent crimes against Asian people in Omaha.[75]

Asian lives in Nebraska

Nebraska's anti-Asian laws and practices did not stop Asian Nebraskans from living well and standing for their own rights and freedoms, even at the risk of being the nail that sticks up and is pounded down. Reverend Hiram Hisanori Kano recalled, "We had been enjoying a peaceful and pleasant life in Nebraska. But every day [in the 1920s] newspapers published in the coastal states reported the unhappy news, which made us very sad. And we thought that because of such propaganda, we might someday have to face the same situation."[76] Kano understood their sense of peace could be shattered at any time, in ways that were hard to predict. White Nebraskans also worried about their lives, but the presence and unpredictability of anti-Asian sentiment added an immeasurably greater burden to the people who could be targeted. Japanese Nebraskans proceeded with their lives as Americans who continued Japanese traditions and lifeways to various degrees. Kano joined with local Japanese business leaders to found the Japanese Americanization Society. The purpose of the society was to aid Japanese Nebraskans in adjusting to American life so they could participate without drawing negative attention from white supremacists.[77]

The Filipino Club at the University of Nebraska took its civic roles to both the U.S. and the Philippines seriously. Its members formed relationships with white organizations like the Kiwanis Club by offering musical performances and presentations about the Philippines at events.[78] These personal connections gave white Nebraskans more opportunities to view Filipinos as real people instead of as abstract problems to be addressed through policy changes. The club took part in the public debate over the U.S. occupation of the Philippines by correcting misconceptions of Filipinos as "unfit for self-rule" and "incapable of comprehending liberty." As Filipinos themselves, they attested to their understanding of liberty and their ability to defend it. The University of Nebraska Law Student denounced the propagation of racist images of Filipinos in 1919. Americans who "spent money, time, and energy to scatter thruout [sic] the United States Ugly-looking postcards and other articles labeled 'Filipino house,' or 'Filipino

---

74. "Legion Strongly Favors Nebraska Alien Land Bill," *The Alliance Herald,* February 11, 1921, 2.
75. "Claims Was Mistreated: Y.P. Bhosale, Hindu Student here, Says Was Struck and Kicked in Omaha Hotel," *Lincoln Journal Star,* November 3, 1925, 10.
76. Kano, *A History of Japanese in Nebraska,* 12.
77. Kano, *A History of Japanese in Nebraska,* 8-10.
78. "Filipino Club Gave Fine Entertainment," *Johnson County Journal,* May 28, 1925, 1.

ladies comb.'" World's fairs like the Trans-Mississippi and International Exposition of 1898 put Igorot people in the "native displays" designed to reinforce racial stereotypes about Filipinos as unable to cope with the modern world.[79] A 1924 letter to the editor in the *Nebraska State Journal* admonished the club's adopted nation with phrasing from the American Declaration of Independence, stating, "It is tyranny to continue ruling a nation without the consent of the governed."[80] These eloquent statements on freedom and tyranny should have raised questions about the Asian stereotypes that formed both law and opinion, but most Nebraskans' beliefs remained firm.

The Great Depression was the one period in U.S. history when more people emigrated from the United States than immigrated to it. The Immigration Restriction League warned readers in Scottsbluff that immigrants would flood Nebraska when jobs became available. They saw the Depression as an indication that America could no longer be the world's melting pot: "The welfare of the majority of our people is more important than a gesture of magnanimity."[81] When University of Nebraska sociologist Dr. James Reinhart studied the demographic data from the 1930 census, he found no sign of magnanimity toward Asians. White Nebraskans retained their runaway majority, even before the out-migration began. Of the state's 1,377,963 residents, only 24,361 were classified as "non-white." Japanese Nebraskans formed the largest Asian population by far, with 674 residing mostly in Scotts Bluff and Lincoln counties. Chinese Nebraskans numbered 194; of these, 147 lived in Douglas County. Filipinos were the third-largest Asian community, with fifty-five members. Koreans, South Asians, and Hawaiians combined amounted to a total of nine individuals.[82]

By contrast, nearly 70 percent of Nebraska's population was descended from Northern or Central Europe. Over 10 percent of Nebraskans had roots in Bohemia and fully 35 percent from Germany. It is hard to know every reason why the Asian Nebraskan community remained so small, but the effects of restrictive immigration and citizenship laws, the alien land law, and Nebraska's positive image as a state with few immigrants likely contributed. Very few Asians found a place for themselves in the state.

Allies, enemies, and citizens in World War II

Japan's attack on Pearl Harbor on December 7, 1941, changed the lives of all Americans of Japanese ancestry. Over 120,000 people were forcibly removed from their homes on the West Coast and incarcerated in 10 camps across the Intermountain West and in Arkansas. Nebraska's small Japanese population was not incarcerated, but Reverend Hiram Kano was arrested on the steps of the St. George's Church in North Platte on the same day of the attack, just after concluding morning services. News of the bombing had not reached the congregation, so it was shocking to see the man who led the Japanese Americanization Society, and who served multiple Japanese congregations, taken by FBI agents to the Douglas County jail in Omaha. Nobody knew what the charges were, and Kano was not allowed to contact his family to tell them where he was. Like hundreds of leaders of Japanese-American communities across the U.S., Kano was imprisoned as a dangerous enemy alien because he was a person of influence. He was released on parole in 1944 after three years' incarceration without charges or evidence.[83]

There would be no mass arrests of Japanese in Nebraska, yet Kano's incarceration sent a chill across the community. He wrote in 1986:

> Most Japanese in Nebraska were not placed in internment camps or arrested at the outbreak of World War II, but most experienced hardship and prejudice. Children and young adults who were U.S. citizens by birth were not immune. In the Nebraska Panhandle, mothers recalled clerks who would not sell candy for their children, remembered harassment on the streets, and other incidents. For example, permission from the Wyoming state offices needed to be obtained each time those living on the border of western Nebraska needed to cross the state line, just a few miles away, to visit family, shop, or attend church. Fear of reprisal in the midst of anti-Japanese sentiment took its toll on Japanese traditions. Children no longer learned to speak Japanese. Communication with families still in Japan

---

79. Juan Velasco, "Filipinos Misunderstood," *Nebraska State Journal*, May 4, 1918, 6.
80. L. O. Franco, "The Public Mind: Case of the Filipinos," *Nebraska State Journal*, January 5, 1924, 6.
81. "Editorial Comments from Our Exchanges: Alien Gun Toter Not Deportable," *Northwest Nebraska News*, May 2, 1935.
82. "Germans Constitute Most of Foreign Stock in State," *Scottsbluff Farm Journal*, November 12, 1936, 3.
83. Sheryll Patterson-Black, Introduction to Hiram Hisanori Kano, *A History of the Japanese in Nebraska*, (Scottsbluff, Nebraska: Scottsbluff Public Library, 1984), n.p.

was severed. Some families burned old letters, photographs, and the few precious family treasures they'd brought to America, such as old silk obis, in the fear that these items would be used as evidence against them.[84]

There is evidence that the FBI requested at least one Nebraska bank call in loans and close out the bank accounts of their Japanese-American customers. The bank's manager refused, sparing his Japanese-American neighbors the economic disaster that the FBI knew its actions would cause.[85] Japanese Nebraskans were not held behind barbed wire in camps, but they knew that their rights could be taken from them in other ways at any time, with or without warning.

Creating "good" and "bad" Asians

China, like the United States, had been ruthlessly attacked by the Empire of Japan. The U.S. War Department was especially invested in moving public opinion away from the anti-Chinese stereotypes of John Chinaman and Fu Manchu toward humanizing the Chinese abroad as victims at the hands of the "savage" Japanese. This distinction between "good" and "bad" Asians was demonstrated to Americans through the treatment of Chinese and Japanese people in the United States. The separation of "bad" Japanese from "good" Chinese did not reverse old stereotypes of either. Samuel Morton's "Crania Americana" came back into America's living rooms with *Life* magazine[86] and other publications giving primers in craniology so the public could tell the difference between their Chinese and Japanese neighbors so they knew which to treat sympathetically and which to treat with hostility. The construction of allied and enemy races reinforced the idea that Asian people, whether "good" or "bad," were still eternal foreigners who belonged to their ancestral nations and not to America.[87]

The effect of targeting Asian Nebraskans, whether Japanese or not, hit children especially hard. Alfred Miyagishima never felt different from his non-Japanese friends when he was growing up in Scottsbluff, except when he was around white adults who were open about their anti-Asian prejudice: "They'd make a comment about 'a little Jap boy' or something like that, and I wasn't allowed to do something because 'we don't want that little Jap boy hanging around' or something like that. And I remember that little kid crying, wondering why was I born Japanese? And I didn't understand because you're younger, immature, and you really don't have anyone to ask." His sisters would tell him to pay no attention, saying, "You were put on this earth as Japanese and you should be proud of that." But Alfred remained hurt and confused. He wondered why he was Japanese when it seemed "hundreds and hundreds and hundreds of others" were white. He couldn't understand why his Japanese ancestry made such a difference to his friends' parents, when it made no difference to his friends.[88]

Alfred Miyagishima, like most of his Asian American peers, gained a better understanding of racism as an adult and eventually did not take it so personally. A 2019 policy statement from the American Academy of Pediatrics found that children subjected to racism like Miyagishima suffered long-term harm. Racism is a trigger for chronic stress in children, and stress can create the hormonal changes that lead to inflammation, which is a marker for chronic disease.[89] Studies also show that children treated as racially different from others are often treated as problematic by teachers and other important adults. Young Alfred's exclusion from friend groups and activities for being a "Jap" is one example of this. Harvard also notes that children of color are subject to harsher penalties for small misbehaviors while their capabilities are underestimated. When teachers do not believe in a student, that student is unlikely to believe in themselves. Learning in childhood that one is less capable, less valuable, and less worthy of belonging can have an impact on their education, career, financial security, and home lives. Claire McCarthy, a professor of pediatrics at

---

84. Patterson-Black, np.
85. Richard McDonough, "A Nebraska Banker Who Said 'No' to Seizing Japanese Americans' Assets in World War II," *Scottsbluff Star-Herald*, May 29, 2021.
86. "How to Tell Japs from the Chinese: Angry Citizens Victimize Allies with Emotional Outburst at Enemy," *Life*, December 22, 1941, 81-82.
87. John Dower, *War Without Mercy: Race and Power in the Pacific War* (New York: Pantheon Books, 1986), 15-33.
88. Alfred "Al" Miyagishima interviewed by Tom Ikeda, May 13, 2008, segment 10, Densho Digital Archive, https://ddr.densho.org/interviews/ddr-manz-1-27-10/?tableft=segments.
89. Maria Trent, et.al., "The Impact of Racism on Children," *Pediatrics* 144:2 (August 2019). https://doi.org/10.1542/peds.2019-1765

Harvard Medical School, concluded, "Children are being hurt every day by racism and discrimination, and the effects can be not only permanent but continue through generations."[90]

Nebraska Gov. Dwight Griswold (1941-1947), who served as Commander of the American Legion in 1928,[91] allowed the federal government to incarcerate German or Italian enemy aliens in Nebraska if they remained under guard and available to provide farm or construction labor. Building a Japanese-American incarceration camp, however, was out of the question. Letters from Nebraskans implored the governor to spare them the "problem that has plagued California for years" by keeping the Japanese out of Nebraska. Among the standard warnings were that Japanese workers would commit sabotage, take jobs from white Nebraskans, and overwhelm New Deal public assistance programs, as well as the alarming possibility that they could "be left alone with our Women Folks [sic]." The chairman of the Scotts Bluff County Defense Committee reported that a Chadron man whose son "had been at Pearl Harbor" told the governor that "armed with a bottle of whisky and a gun," he almost shot a Japanese person who was "causing no trouble whatsoever."[92]

Not all Nebraskans were of the same mind. Labor shortages in Lincoln and Scotts Bluff counties moved farmers and industries to urge the governor to recruit Japanese-American workers from the camps. W.T. Trumbull made a plea on behalf of the sugar beet growers in western Nebraska to bring in Japanese workers before the crops were lost, as a matter of patriotic duty: "if such labor is available it [becomes] our duty as American citizens to use that labor, to overlook the question of whether or not we prefer it or like it AND TO ASSUME AND DISCHARGE whatever responsibilities such a course would entail." Those demanding Japanese labor were not always demanding just treatment of Japanese people. For one grower in David City, using Japanese incarcerees would prevent having to rely upon braceros, who were laborers transported to the U.S. as guest workers to fill the wartime labor shortage. This grower concluded, rather dramatically, "I would be willing to stand hostage for the Japanese that would be brought in to save the crops even after the treatment now accorded them but I wouldn't allow my dog to associate with the rank and file of that stuff from the south."[93] Inviting incarcerees from the camps to work in Nebraska did not necessarily signal an end of racial stereotyping; it was, to many whites, a matter of balancing the lesser of two evils – which they meant quite literally.

Griswold refused to allow Japanese workers to enter Nebraska until July 1942. While noting that the labor shortage would worsen in the year ahead, he could not risk the racial unrest he envisioned if "the civilian population" encountered new Japanese people.[94] The governor reversed his decision on September 5, 1943, by approving 1,000 Japanese Americans to work in Nebraska, with guarantees that the new arrivals would be "adequately protected."[95] The governor's positive view of this plan was reinforced by a full year of good results in other states and a well-developed system of surveillance.

Nebraskans who met and interacted with Japanese Americans spoke very differently of the mass incarceration and the benefits of work release. Father Flanagan, who was a vocal opponent of the mass incarceration of Japanese from the beginning, sponsored the release of hundreds of Japanese Americans from the camps to live and work at Boys Town, despite objections from the public. He vouched for the loyalty of Patrick Okura, who was investigated by the House Un-American Activities Committee after Los Angeles Mayor Fletcher Bowron falsely accused Okura of espionage in retaliation for Okura protesting his dismissal from his civil service position and his pending

---

90. Claire McCarthy, "How Racism Harms Children," *Harvard Health Letter* (Cambridge, MA: Harvard Health Publishing): January 8, 2020, https://www.health.harvard.edu/blog/how-racism-harms-children-2019091417788.
91. American Legion, Nebraska State Historical Society Collection Record, RG2959, Nebraska State Archives, Lincoln, Nebraska; "Good Roads Men Gather," *Nebraska Daily News-Press*, October 10, 1929, 2; "Vote for Griswold: The American Legion elected Dwight Griswold its state commander in 1928!," *The Unionist*, November 2, 1934, 7.
92. Governor Dwight Griswold to W.S. Trumbull, Chair Scotts Bluff County Defense Committee, July 7, 1942, Dwight Palmer Griswold Papers, RG 1 SG 32 F217, Series 1: 1942 Correspondence, Nebraska State Archives, Lincoln, Nebraska.
93. Forrest Lear, Hughes Abstract and Loan Co., David City, to Governor Griswold, June 9, 1942, Dwight Palmer Griswold Papers, RG 1 SG 32 F217, Series 1: 1942 Correspondence, Nebraska State Archives, Lincoln, Nebraska.
94. Dwight Griswold to W.S. Trumbull of Scottsbluff, July 13, 1942, Dwight Palmer Griswold Papers, RG 1 SG 32 F217, Series 1: 1942 Correspondence, Nebraska State Archives, Lincoln, Nebraska.
95. Dwight Griswold, Memorandum September 5, 1943, Governor Dwight Griswold Papers, RG 1 SG 32, Nebraska State Historical Society.

incarceration.[96] As one of America's most ardent opponents of the mass incarceration of the West Coast Japanese, Flanagan received complaints from the Omaha community. He responded to a woman whose racism was especially vehement, saying, "I don't think ... that we should be a party to condemning people until they are proven guilty, and I am sure this is your attitude also."[97] To another he wrote, "We must not permit ourselves to be smeared with the same moral filth we are criticizing our enemies."[98]

Flanagan continued to speak highly of Japanese Americans generally, and of those at Boys Town in particular. When asked to write a testimonial for the War Relocation Authority, he emphasized that the thirteen Japanese Americans at Boys Town were valuable employees who got along well with others. In summary, he said, "They make very good citizens."[99] C.E. Metzger, president of the Omaha Livestock Exchange, followed Flanagan's example. He hired two Japanese Americans from camp to work on his farm and spoke highly of their work ethic, the speed with which they adapted to their new conditions, and their value to his business. The Gland-O-Lac Company in Omaha liked the first Japanese-American worker they hired from camp so much that they arranged for his brother to work for them, too. "Everybody likes these boys," the company proclaimed.[100] Evidence was mounting that Japanese-American people were nothing like fearsome Japanese stereotypes presented in *Life* magazine and numerous other wartime publications.

Wartime incarcerees Jack and Alice Kaya had been forced from their home in Los Angeles to the Santa Anita Assembly Center (which had been, and is today, a racetrack), sent to the Tule Lake incarceration site in northern California for less than a year, and were moved to the camp in Jerome, Arkansas. It is from Jerome that they were given $25 each and bus tickets to Omaha, where Jack was hired by the Blackstone Hotel as a cook training other younger camp incarcerees.

When Alice attempted to gain employment at a well-known downtown department store as a seamstress, an occupation she had in Los Angeles, she was told at the interview that "we don't hire Japs here," according to her daughters Carol Mudra, Marilyn Hespen, and Jackie Shindo. However, she was eventually hired by Natelson's as a costume designer. By 1947, the Kayas were able to open their first business near Creighton University named the Grass Shack Café serving Hawaiian and Japanese foods. It became a popular venue for the Hawaiian students at Creighton.[101] While walking to work one day, the police detained him because someone complained that a short Oriental guy had robbed him. Jack took the police to his restaurant to demonstrate that he was a businessman, and they released him. Their success in business and a following of loyal customers led the Kayas to open their next business in 1965, Mt. Fuji Inn, which they maintained for over fifty years.

By 1944, white Nebraskans' requests for Japanese workers like the Kayas exceeded the number of incarcerees who could fill them. The Omaha office that coordinated Nebraska placements reported that the greatest number of requests were for domestic laborers. Many white Nebraskans, who had not wanted Japanese Americans in their state, now wanted them in their homes, having seen beyond the stereotypes. Although 40 percent of the Japanese Americans leaving camp chose agricultural work, the remaining 60 percent were experienced in a wide variety of fields, including the building trades, engineering, law, secretarial, medicine, accounting, social work, the culinary arts, teaching, and many others.[102] White Nebraskans were sometimes surprised to see their Japanese counterparts put their all into the American war effort.

---

96. Seventy-Fifth Congress, House. Investigation of Un-American Propaganda Activities in the United States v. 15 (Washington: USGPO), 8997-9001
97. Heather Fryer, "Border Work: The Migration of Los Angeles Japanese Americans from the Manzanar Relocation Center to Father Flanagan's Boys Town during World War II" in *Permeable Borders: History, Theory, Policy, and Practice in the United States* ed. Paul Otto and Susanne Berthier-Foglar (New York: Berghahn Books, 2020), 77-95.
98. Dwight Griswold to Forrest Lear, June 17, 1942, Dwight Palmer Griswold Papers, RG 1 SG 32 F217, Series 1: 1942 Correspondence, Nebraska State Archives, Lincoln, Nebraska.
99. W. N. Parmenter, Memorandum to Those Interested in Obtaining Evacuee Labor, Dwight Palmer Griswold Papers, Box 25, RG 1 SG 32 F217, Series 1:1942 Correspondence, Nebraska State Archives, Lincoln, Nebraska.
100. W. N. Parmenter, Memorandum to Those Interested in Obtaining Evacuee Labor, Dwight Palmer Griswold Papers, Box 25, RG 1 SG 32 F217, Series 1: 1942 Correspondence, Nebraska State Archives, Lincoln, Nebraska.
101. Sue Story Truax, "Restaurateur Enjoyed Giving Back–Alice Kaya," Omaha *World-Herald*, April 15, 2009, 13.
102. United States War Relocation Authority, "W.R.A News and Highlights; News Letter from Omaha, Nebraska no. 1-11" 1944-45, BANC MSS 67/14c, folder F2.99, The Bancroft Library, University of California Berkeley.

Jack Kaya, Blackstone Hotel cook training young Mr. Okasaki. Soda Fountain. Mr. Amile Okasaki (left), age 19, formerly from the Topaz Relocation Center, a graduate of high school, is shown being served by the hostess of the Coffee Shop at the Blackstone Hotel, where Mr. Okasaki is employed in the stockroom department. The Bancroft Library, University of California, Berkeley, https://oac.cdlib.org/ark:/13030/ft8k4007z4/?brand=oac4

Many had family members who enlisted in the segregated, all-Japanese American 442nd Regimental Combat Team, primarily composed of the young incarcerees from all 10 of the camps.

Ross Harano of Chicago shared his family's story of how his Uncle Earl migrated to Nebraska from an incarceration camp after his brothers had enlisted in the 442nd. Earl Harano and the extended family were sent to the Tanforan Assembly Center in San Bruno, California (another racetrack whose hastily painted horse stalls became housing for incarcerated Japanese) and later were moved to the Topaz, Utah camp where his mother died from a health condition that could not be treated. His two younger brothers Johnny and Roy served in the 442nd Regimental Combat Teams. Johnny was killed in action assisting in the rescue of the Lost Texas Battalion in the Vosges Mountains of France. When they were given permission to depart camp, Earl re-settled in North Platte where he purchased a business and conducted it as the Brown-Harano Photo Studio that had clientele across Nebraska's rural areas, South Dakota, and Kansas. His brother Johnny was laid to rest in North Platte, and Roy joined him in the business after being discharged from the Army.[103]

John Harano, uncle of Ross Harano. Courtesy of Ross Harano.

The onset of war affected Chinese Nebraskans very differently. Congress repealed the Chinese Exclusion Act in 1943. In addition to allowing 105 Chinese citizens to immigrate to the U.S. each year, those immigrants became aliens eligible for U.S. citizenship. This new status only applied to Chinese immigrants because it was enacted to further the U.S. war effort. The Chinese Exclusion Act

---

103. Ross Harano interviewed by Sharon Ishii-Jordan, 2023.

became a vulnerability to the U.S. and had long been a source of tension in U.S.-China relations because Chinese nationals were the only group to have such targeted, specific anti-immigration laws enacted against them. China was a vital ally in the Pacific Theatre of war, so U.S. officials readily made this gesture of good will toward the Chinese people.[104]

An equally important reason for repealing the Chinese Exclusion Act was that Japan's propaganda organs broadcast numerous features about it to China and other Allied nations of color. Racism not only has been a danger to people of color in the U.S., or to American values, it also has endangered national security.[105] White supremacy did contradict the values of democracy, freedom, and human rights for which the United States was fighting. Asian and other allies had to wonder whether it was safe to partner with a powerful nation that believed it was a superior race. Japanese propaganda broadcasts also reached Asian-American soldiers in the field and prisoners of war, many of whom joined the armed forces in the hope that this proof of loyalty would bring acceptance and equality in peacetime.[106]

World War II brought a gradual end to categorizing Asian people as "aliens" ineligible for citizenship, or "undesirables" permanently barred from immigration to the U.S. At the beginning of World War II, the United States viewed Asian people as a race of "others" as described by Samuel Morton. During the war, the U.S. government increasingly identified Asians by their national origin, rather than their race. President Franklin D. Roosevelt drew this distinction in 1943 when he signed the Act to Repeal the Chinese Exclusion Act. He explained to Congress:

> The extension of the privileges of citizenship to the relatively few Chinese residents in our country would ... be additional proof that we regard China not only as a partner in waging war but that we shall regard her as a partner in days of peace. While it would give the Chinese a preferred status over certain other [Asian] people, their great contribution to the cause of decency and freedom entitles them to such preference.[107]

By making this goodwill gesture toward China, Roosevelt reinforced the perception that there is no distinction between Chinese Americans and the citizens of China. Giving China a preferred status based on their contributions to "decency and freedom" suggested that Japanese, Korean, Filipino, Indian, and other Asians had made no such contributions. People of Japanese descent were held in the most sharp contrast to Chinese Americans with the Japanese being dangerous and the Chinese being helpful. This differentiation made Morton less relevant and U.S. foreign policy objectives more determinative of how "American" a Chinese, Japanese, Korean, or Filipino person could be.

One month and one day later, Edward Bing Kan of Chicago became the first Chinese immigrant to become a U.S. citizen since the Chinese Exclusion Act in 1888. After thirty-five years of working as an interpreter for the Immigration and Naturalization Service, Kan's own wish for citizenship was granted.[108] Back in Nebraska, Kay Fong and Jew Yuen Fook applied for citizenship in Lincoln in 1943, North Platte residents Henry Chinn applied for citizenship in 1944, and Harry Sang and Chin Wing Sew in 1945. Tong Chun applied in Grand Island in 1947. Lam Beck You was the first Chinese Nebraskan to apply for citizenship in Omaha in 1944, with dozens to follow through the decade.[109]

---

104. Xiaohua Ma, "The Sino-American Alliance During World War II and the Lifting of the Chinese Exclusion Acts," *American Studies International* 38:2 (June 2000): 39-61.
105. U.S. Department of State, Office of the Historian, "Repeal of the Chinese Exclusion Act, 1943," https://history.state.gov/milestones/1937-1945/chinese-exclusion-act-repeal.
106. Saul K. Padover, "Japanese Race Propaganda," *Public Opinion Quarterly* 7:2 (Summer 1943): 191-204 https://doi.org/10.1086/265613 ; John Dower, *War Without Mercy: Race and Power in the Pacific War* (New York: Pantheon Books, 1986) 5-7.
107. Franklin D. Roosevelt, Message to Congress on Repeal of the Chinese Exclusion Laws. Online by Gerhard Peters and John T. Woolley, The American Presidency Project https://www.presidency.ucsb.edu/node/209602
108. United States Citizenship and Immigration Services, "Edward Bing Kan: The First Chinese-American Naturalized after Repeal of Chinese Exclusion," https://www.uscis.gov/about-us/our-history/history-office-and-library/edward-bing-kan-the-first-chinese-american-naturalized-after-repeal-of-chinese-exclusion.
109. Naturalization Index, Lincoln, Nebraska, RG 21 National Archives at Kansas City, https://www.archives.gov/kansas-city/finding-aids/lincoln-naturalization.html ; Naturalization Index, North Platte, Nebraska, National Archives at Kansas City, https://www.archives.gov/kansas-city/finding-aids/north-platte-naturalization.html ; Naturaliza-

Citizenship did not immediately make all Chinese Americans feel like full U.S. citizens. A letter to an *Omaha World-Herald* columnist from a Chinese Nebraskan explained, "Since the war I have never felt at ease anyplace. Because I have oriental looks, why must I be accused of being a Jap? I'm an American 100 percent. ... People used to smile at me on [sic] the car. Now they whisper, 'There goes a Jap.'" Nebraskans seem to have taken the message from *Life* magazine to scrutinize Asian people, though they did not differentiate between Japanese and non-Japanese as the article intended.

Americans' hostility toward its fellow citizens of Japanese descent did have the effect of dividing Asian Americans against each other. The letter-writer continued, "I have every reason to hate the Japs because they have killed so many of my close relatives. ... I have two brothers in the armed forces and those of us at home try to do our part as well. I have no enemies in America except those who accuse me of being a Jap." Their final plea – "Please, fellow citizens, won't you smile at me again?" – may have rested upon separating from the enemy nation but came across as demonizing the so-called enemy race in concluding, "I'm no Jap."[110]

Japanese Nebraskans continued to be singled out for exclusion and harassment, though mostly from strangers. Roger Sato was a high school student in the North Platte Valley when news of Pearl Harbor reached Nebraska. He could hardly sleep that night because he was afraid of how he might be treated at school the next day. A Caucasian friend came to his house to walk him to school and most of the teachers went out of their way to show their care and concern for all the Japanese students in their school. They put a stop to the few incidents of teasing or hostility toward the Japanese students. Although he knew that some white businesses refused to serve Japanese Americans, Roger still felt he was part of his North Platte community and that his family was safe.[111]

His brother and a friend were treated differently when they tried to get a drink in Scottsbluff while on leave from the U.S. Navy. The bartender ignored the sailors until one of them asked why they had not been asked for their order. He looked at the two servicemen and said, "We don't serve Japs." This refusal of service was part of a larger pattern that Roger Sato had heard about, but rarely experienced firsthand. The Satos were well-respected farmers who contributed greatly to the economy and, since Pearl Harbor, to the war effort by producing consistently high yields. It seemed that when some Nebraskans knew their Japanese neighbors personally, they were inclined to respect them as people. But when a Japanese Nebraskan was a stranger, even a stranger in a U.S. military uniform, Nebraskans saw only a member of the "enemy race" – just as Nebraskans saw only "John Chinaman" in Sin Goon when they ran him out of North Platte in 1875.[112]

Incidents like this made Japanese families protective of their children. Protection, for some, required making their identities invisible. Hope Omachi Kawashima's family moved to Gibbon after being released from the incarceration camp in Topaz, Utah. Her father began truck farming and raising vegetables and chickens to supply a restaurant in exchange for rent and a share of the food. Hope remembered Gibbon as a friendly community. She attributed this, in part, to her father's instructions for answering the question, "What are you?" Instead of saying they were Japanese American, they were to say they were Americans – without using the word "Japanese." Hope believed that most people thought that the Omachis were Native Americans and accepted them on that basis.[113] Although her interactions with others were pleasant, Hope learned at an early age that she was not safe in Nebraska because of something about her that she could not change.

There were promising signs of greater acceptance in the later stages of the war, though some were met with white supremacist backlash. The Nebraska Department of Education expressed an interest in recruiting Japanese-American teachers out of the

---

tion Index, Grand Island, Nebraska, RG 21 National Archives at Kansas City https://www.archives.gov/kansas-city/finding-aids/grand-island-naturalization.html ; Naturalization Index, Omaha, Nebraska, RG 21 National Archives at Kansas City, https://www.archives.gov/kansas-city/finding-aids/omaha-naturalization.html. There are no applications for naturalization from Chinese citizens in the Chadron district records.

110. "I'm No Jap, He Reminds," *Omaha World-Herald*, January 2, 1944, 44.
111. Roger Sato interviewed by Sandra Reddish, Nebraska State Historical Society Archives.
112. Roger Sato interviewed by Sandra Reddish, Nebraska State Historical Society Archives.
113. Hope Omachi Kawashima interviewed by Kristen Luktemeyer, September 10, 2014, segment 24, Densho Digital Archives, https://ddr.densho.org/interviews/ddr-manz-1-154-24/?tableft=segments.

incarceration camps to alleviate a teacher shortage.[114] Yet in Shelton, ninety-one people signed a petition opposing the relocation of any Japanese Americans in the Platte River Valley. The War Relocation Authority attributed this to "petty jealousy and economic rivalry."[115] The movement toward recognition as Americans was a welcome change for Asian Nebraskans, but the discrimination that often followed meant that the ground beneath them was always shifting and rocking. Even eligibility for citizenship, they discovered, did not guarantee that they would experience the safety and stability of being seen as full Americans.

The Chinese Nebraskan letter writer declaring they were not Japanese had reason to question whether they were truly perceived as full Americans. As late as 1948, China was presented as a reasonably trustworthy ally to the U.S. A column in the *Lincoln State Journal* explained, "Altho [sic] of different blood … the fact remains that Uncle Sam sees John Chinaman as a good neighbor and dependable friend."[116] John Chinaman, who had never left the American imagination, fell out of favor with the United States when China became a communist nation in 1949. Chinese Americans came under a second layer of scrutiny when China entered the Korean War on the side of communist North Korea and once again, Chinese Americans felt pressure to prove their full loyalty to the United States, which, for most of them, was the only country they ever knew.

Raising objections to their discriminatory treatment was ill-advised after 1955, when the U.S. Army pamphlet "How to Spot a Communist" was reprinted in national magazines of all kinds. Loyal Americans were to be on the lookout for people who talked "much more than other people" about "civil rights, racial or religious discrimination, [or] immigration laws." The pamphlet advised that such people were, without a doubt, subversive agencies of the international communist conspiracy whose activities were best reported to the FBI.[117] The Army rescinded publication of the pamphlet in response to American Civil Liberties Union[118] protests but the word was already out, suspicions already raised, and Chinese Americans already under public scrutiny.

Losing "alien ineligible for citizenship" status clearly did not reverse a century of anti-Asian prejudice. Yet it was an important development for each community made eligible for citizenship. The Luce-Celler Act reclassified Filipino and Indian immigrants in the U.S. as eligible for naturalization in 1946, just two days before the Philippines gained its independence from the United States and a year before India gained its independence from the British Empire. President Harry Truman supported the change as a means of bringing the world's decolonizing democracies into the U.S. sphere of influence at the start of the Cold War.[119] Ultimately, the Luce-Celler Act was less about anti-racism in the U.S. than anti-communism abroad. The quotas for Filipino and Indian immigrants would be 100 per country, roughly the same number of visas allotted to China. This modest uptick in immigration would be enough to show the world that the U.S. held Filipinos and Indians in high regard, but not enough to create large Asian-American communities.

Japanese and Koreans remained ineligible for citizenship until 1952, when the United States ended its occupation of Japan and entered its second year of the Korean War. The Immigration and Nationality Act (also called the McCarran-Walter Act) of 1952 removed all barriers to Asian immigration and to Asian immigrants becoming naturalized citizens. However, the U.S. State Department historian notes that immigration policy remained discriminatory. The act set the quota for immigrants from the "Asian Pacific Triangle" at 100 individuals based on race, not on nationality.[120] The annual national quota of 100 immigrants per nation meant even with the addition of Japanese and Korean immigrants there would be no significant increase in the Asian-American populations, especially in Nebraska where the number of Asian Americans remained historically low.

---

114. "Nebraska State Asks for Nisei School Teachers," *Utah Nippo,* August 18, 1944, 4.
115. "Petty Jealousy, Economic Rivalry Cause Circulation of Petition, *Utah Nippo,* April 18, 1945.
116. J.E. Lawrence, "Personal Views on the News," *Nebraska State Journal,* November 15, 1948, 20.
117. For example, see Leo Cherne, "How to Spot a Communist: Don't Be a Sucker for a Left Hook," *Look Magazine,* March 4, 1947, 21.
118. "Army Rescinds Book on Reds," *Omaha World-Herald,* June 15, 1955, 35.
119. United States Congress, 60 Stat. 416 No. 79-483, July 1946.
120. United States Department of State, Office of the Historian, "The Immigration and Nationality Act of 1952 (The McCarran Walter Act), https://history.state.gov/milestones/1945-1952/immigration-act .

The McCarran-Walter Act was not treated as especially newsworthy by the *Omaha World-Herald*. A tiny item from the Associated Press that appeared at the bottom of the front page simply said that an immigration reform law had passed and that "a major effect would be to make all Asiatics eligible for naturalization. Present law excludes Japanese, Indonesians, Burmese, [Thai] and some Pacific Islanders from citizenship."[121] For Japanese-American newspapers like the *Yuta (Utah) Nippo* and the *Pacific Citizen*, the news was huge. The 1952 Act ended the blatant discriminatory denial of citizenship for Japanese immigrants, effectively making null any alien land laws based on citizenship eligibility.[122] It was the end of a fifty-year wait for the earliest Japanese immigrants, who took advantage of the Americanization classes that the Japanese American communities across Nebraska initiated to enable their parents and grandparents to finally obtain U.S. citizenship.

The McCarran-Walter Act was also life-changing for first-generation Issei like Ihachi Ishii, who after decades as a successful photographer in Omaha applied for his citizenship in 1955. His wife, Anna Zadina, had her U.S. citizenship restored in 1939, having lost it as a result of immigration laws that penalized white women for marrying Asian men.[123] After decades of uncertainty, the Ishiis could live their lives in Nebraska as a family of citizens instead of a household of "aliens."

Eligibility for citizenship represented a political success for the second- and third-generation Japanese Americans who were birthright citizens of the United States. It was the activism of groups like the Japanese American Citizens League that moved Congress to change the law. This meant that in 1952 Asian Nebraskans were both legally eligible to obtain citizenship and were effective participants in the democratic process. More and more, Asian-American community members formed civic, cultural, and political organizations to make this Cold War political symbolism of their equal status into their lived realities in Nebraska.

Asian immigrants across Nebraska studied for the citizenship test and took their first opportunities to be sworn in as American citizens. Yet remnants of old stereotypes remained, as did the idea that Asian Americans would always harbor more loyalty for their immigrant ancestors' homelands than they would to their own country. The American Legion and the Ku Klux Klan had lost some credibility and support during the war but never let go of their anti-immigration and white supremacist agendas. The Nebraska Legislature unanimously passed LB 164 in 1947 to put subversive organizations like the Klan under greater scrutiny. Three years later, the Klan launched a drive to reorganize its chapters (called klaverns) in Nebraska. The American Legion also enforced racial lines; it lost a white member of the Lincoln Legionnaires Club in 1958 when it prohibited his two Filipino guests from entering. A columnist for the *Columbus Telegram* noted that Governor Val Peterson was the only Nebraska leader to speak "in plain talk" about the resurgence of white supremacist movements in the 1950s.[124] Silence about the threats to Asian Nebraskans' rights and safety made them more invisible, which made them more vulnerable to injustices.

Asian Nebraskans nonetheless found safe ways to voice their grievances and claim their rights as citizens. Japanese Americans were reviled in public rhetoric but also found allies among Nebraskans who opposed wartime incarceration. The University of Nebraska accepted Japanese-American students from the incarceration camps and laid the foundation for non-Japanese students to make them feel part of campus and community life.[125] Reverend Charles Drew rallied fellow Nebraskans to offer jobs and hospitality to Japanese-American newcomers from the camps. Churches and civic organizations in Western Nebraska helped newcomers there to get on their feet after being uprooted from their homes on the West Coast and being released from camp in a matter of just a few years. Father Flanagan continued to denounce racism in every form and support the

---

121. "Racial Bars Ousted in House Measure," (Omaha) *Evening World Herald*, April 25, 1952, 1.
122. https://history.state.gov/milestones/1945-1952/immigration-act
123. Naturalization Index, Omaha, Nebraska, RG 21 National Archives at Kansas City, https://www.archives.gov/kansas-city/finding-aids/omaha-naturalization.html.
124. Nebraska State Legislature, Session Laws, Chapter 58 "Requiring the Filing of Constitutions and Membership of Associations with Secretary of State" (Lincoln: State of Nebraska, March 21, 1947): 190-193; "Subversive Organization Bill 164 is Passed," *Omaha Evening World-Herald*, March 10, 1947, 6; "Refuse to Entertain Filipino Guests," *Beatrice Daily Sun*, October 9, 1958, 6; Edgar Howard, "The Truth and Other Things," *The Columbus Telegram*, March 3, 1950, 4.
125. Andrew B. Wertheimer, "Admitting Nebraska's Nisei: Japanese American Students at the University of Nebraska, 1942-1945," *Nebraska History* 83 (2002): 66-67, 69.

Japanese-American community at Boys Town. Patrick Okura, who Father Flanagan promoted to head of the counseling department at Boys Town, became a national leader in promoting mental health care that addressed the needs and experiences of Asian Americans. In October 1947, Okura was named the founding president of the Omaha Chapter of the Japanese American Citizens League (JACL). The JACL was founded in 1929 and had fifty chapters nationwide when Omaha members organized their chapter in 1947.[126] Nebraskans were not completely new to JACL: several Japanese Americans in Western Nebraska belonged to the chapter in Denver. Having an Omaha chapter made Japanese Nebraskans more visible. They became still more visible when Okura was elected the national president of the JACL in 1963, representing Asian Americans within the broader civil rights movement.

Chinese Nebraskans also supported one another in attaining their rights as American citizens. They came together to support Omaha restaurant owner Wah Huey in his lawsuit against Secretary of State John Foster Dulles in 1955. Huey's suit would compel the U.S. State Department to issue U.S. passports to his two sons, Tong and Yuen Huey, who had been living with their mother in China. Wah Huey immigrated to the U.S. and became a U.S. citizen. He would visit his family in China and return to Omaha, where he earned his living as a waiter at King Fong restaurant. The "small Chinese colony" in Omaha supported the Hueys' reunification and looked forward to "pitching one darn good party" when the boys arrived. In addition to reviewing evidence that Wah Huey was Tong and Yuen's father, his attorney, John Cleary, noted that the State Department "necessarily must be very careful about issuing passports to the Chinese at this time," indicating that during the Cold War, Chinese immigrants could not be so easily trusted. Nevertheless, Omaha's Chinese community openly supported Huey in his right as a U.S. citizen to challenge government policy.[127]

Asian Nebraskans spoke out about their historic invisibility and the injustices to which it subjected them as the landscape changed in the 1960s. The

The first Board of the Omaha Chapter of the Japanese American Citizens League, 1947. The author's mother is seated at the far right. Courtesy of Dr. Ishii-Jordan.

repeal of national quotas with the Immigration Act of 1965 brought an increased number of new Nebraskans from South and Southeast Asia. Asian-American veterans of World War II had long demanded the full and equal rights in the United States that they fought for abroad. This demand for equality aligned with those of other civil rights movements, including the Black civil rights movement led by Dr. Martin Luther King, Jr., and Omaha native Malcolm X (whose family was harassed at gunpoint by the same Ku Klux Klan that threatened Asian Nebraskans in the 1930s).[128] There was no longer a legal question of Asians' Americanness. Whether Nebraskans like Alfred Miyagishima's friends, who were raised to reject their Asian neighbors as outsiders, would also change remained an open question.

From citizenship toward equality in the civil rights era

The New Immigration

In the past, only wealthier Americans had the means to vacation and work abroad, but during the war years, Americans of all economic levels were sent overseas for military service and returned home with firsthand knowledge of diverse cultures – peoples, foods, and

---

126. Robert B. Kugel, *Victory Without Swords: The Story of Pat and Lily Okura, Japanese American Citizens in 1941 America* (Westminster, Maryland: Heritage Books, 2004); Patrick and Lily Okura interviewed by Terry T. Shima, *Kiyoshi Patrick Okura Collection*, Library of Congress, https://www.loc.gov/item/afc2001001.27108/ ; Bill Hosokawa, *JACL in Quest of Justice* (Ann Arbor: University of Michigan Press/W. Morrow Publishers, 1982), 135-36; Elaine Woo, "Patrick Okura, 93; Internment Stirred Activism," *Los Angeles Times*, February 13, 2005, https://www.latimes.com/archives/la-xpm-2005-feb-13-me-okura13-story.html.

127. "Omahan Sues Dulles, Hoping to Bring Sons from China," *Omaha World-Herald*, June 19, 1955, 17.

128. Malcolm X, *The Autobiography of Malcolm X as Told to Alex Haley*, (New York: Ballantine Books, 1984), 1-2.

ways of thinking and living. Although an enlightened acceptance of people and cultural practices that were not considered part of the European-based fabric of America materialized among some of the service members, discrimination still occurred. Besides the slow recognition of Americans of Asian ancestry as part of the multicultural landscape of the U.S., non-Asian Americans had to accommodate the influx of thousands of immigrants beyond the limited numbers allowed in standard immigration quotas at the time.

Census data from 1950 show the increase of Asian Americans in Nebraska that occurred after World War II as a result of the McCarran-Walter Act, the arrival of war brides from Japan and Korea, and transnational adoptions of Asian children to Nebraska homes. Long before the Immigration Act of 1965, family reunification of a sort took place under the War Brides Act of 1945 ("Admission of Alien Spouses and Alien Minor Children of Citizen Members of the United States Armed Forces"). Congress passed the act to enable U.S. soldiers to bring back foreign brides and their children from those unions in the European war theater and China as a distinct category of immigrants not subject to the immigration quotas set forth for their home countries. In 1946 and subsequent extensions, the act was amended to include wives from other countries. As a result, U.S. servicemen brought home "war brides," the women they met and married while living abroad, and immigration numbers increased with these new spousal diasporas. The greatest number of applications for naturalization came from women from Japan, Korea, and China who were eligible for non-quota visas. This meant that U.S. soldiers who married women who might be ineligible for citizenship would receive a spousal visa in the interest of family unification. At least half of the applicants for naturalization in Nebraska district courts had Japanese, Korean, or Vietnamese given names and an unambiguously European surname.[129] As transnational marriages became more commonplace between U.S. servicemen and women from abroad, the restrictions against marriage came into question.

To prepare for an American life, the Red Cross held classes in Japan to teach war brides how to be a good wife, cook American meals, and "walk in high heels." Many took on English names to make it easier for Americans to pronounce, adding another form of invisibility of Asian people within Nebraska's history. "They vanished from public awareness – Japanese women who were barely a blip in immigration history, who married into families of North Dakota farmers, Wisconsin loggers, Rhode Island general store owners."[130] They were entering a country that was rife with racism and segregation, not the dream land that they imagined from the other side of the world. An estimated 300,000 war brides came to the U.S. under this act, and approximately 66,681 were Japanese, especially in the late 1940s-1950s while the U.S. occupied Japan, and 51,747 were Filipinos. Michael Lim Ubac states, "On the whole, the intersection of gender, class and race led to the phenomenon called war brides."[131]

In the fifteen years during and after the Korean War, over 6,000 Korean women immigrated to the U.S. as war brides and at times with the children that the U.S. servicemen fathered. As with the Japanese war brides, the women encountered discrimination and struggles to fit into a society in which they were not only considered foreign but sometimes viewed as the enemy. Their lack of acceptance came not just from white Americans, but from Americans of their own ancestry who viewed them as lower class and from their relatives back in Korea who did not approve of marriage to American soldiers. Once in the U.S., it was difficult for them to be accepted back into their own society. Even more hostile racial comments and treatment were directed at war brides and their children if they married Black GIs.[132]

So, while the post-World War II immigration laws opened the door to newcomers from Asia and the

---

129. Naturalization Index, Lincoln, Nebraska, RG 21 National Archives at Kansas City, https://www.archives.gov/kansas-city/finding-aids/lincoln-naturalization.html; Naturalization Index, North Platte, Nebraska, National Archives at Kansas City, https://www.archives.gov/kansas-city/finding-aids/north-platte-naturalization.html ; Naturalization Index, Grand Island, Nebraska, RG 21 National Archives at Kansas City https://www.archives.gov/kansas-city/finding-aids/grand-island-naturalization.html; Naturalization Index, Omaha, Nebraska, RG 21 National Archives at Kansas City, https://www.archives.gov/kansas-city/finding-aids/omaha-naturalization.html.
130. https://www.warbrideproject.com/wp-content/uploads/2022/03/From-Hiroko-to-Susie_-The-untold-stories-of-Japanese-war-brides-_-The-Washington-Post.html.
131. https://globalnation.inquirer.net/43451/whatever-happened-to-filipino-war-brides-in-us.
132. (https://openspaces.unk.edu/cgi/viewcontent.cgi?article=1071&context=undergraduate-research-journal#:~:text=Following percent20the percent20Korean percent20War percent2C percent20many,struggled percent20to percent-20share percent20their percent20stories.) (Moore, T. 2020-8-1. The Pattern of American Society: Treatment of Korean War Brides in the United States following the Korean War, *Undergraduate Research Journal*, 24 (7): 62-70

McCarran-Walter Act gave them the right to apply for citizenship, these significant changes in the law did not bring racial equality. The act's strict immigration quotas kept Asian immigration lower than European immigration and it did nothing to reverse the racist laws affecting those who were already settled in Nebraska. Many Japanese Nebraskans continued to cross the borders into Iowa, Colorado, and Kansas to marry white Nebraskans into the 1960s because the state did not repeal its anti-miscegenation law until 1963, long after all the states with contiguous borders to Nebraska had repealed their laws. The Alien Land Law, whose language was written to apply to "all aliens" but whose effects had fallen almost entirely on Asian Nebraskans, was still on the books and applicable to those whose applications for citizenship were denied for any reason – all Asian immigrants were eligible to apply for citizenship, but approval of applications was guaranteed to no one. The residue of anti-Asian discrimination remained hidden in this Nebraska law and in other areas of daily life as more and more people of Asian descent made Nebraska their home.[133] It was hard to spot, often hard to describe, but as Asian Nebraskans would discover time and again, it was there.

Nebraska still had fewer than 25,000 persons of Asian ancestry in 1960.[134] The Census Bureau can only provide aggregated data on Asian Nebraskans with that for the North-Central Region. While efficient and, in some cases, respectful of the privacy of people who could be readily identified if they were the only Asian person in their town, this reporting practice does have the effect of exacerbating Asian Nebraskans' invisibility. The published data for the North Central Region does show, however, that persons of Japanese ancestry were the most populous at 29,054, with 87 percent living in urban areas, and had the highest proportion of American-born at 70 percent. Their average income was also the highest of the Asian ancestries at $3,452, with men earning $4,936. The Chinese population was 17,952 with a much higher percentage (94.7 percent) living in urban areas and an average income of $2,682. Less than half (49 percent) were American-born. Filipinos in the North-Central Region had a population of 9,803 with 87.9 percent in urban areas and just over half (51 percent) were American-born. Their average income was $2,776. The disparities in income among these three Asian descendants may reflect the length of family habitation in one place after immigration and the types of jobs that were available to them.[135]

By 1965, Japanese and Chinese continued to form the largest segment of the Asian-American Pacific-Islander population of the U.S. with approximately two-thirds of the share.[136] This steady ratio was set to change when the Immigration Act of 1965 eliminated the national origins quota system that had long disadvantaged Asians. The law reserved 120,000 visas for immigrants from the Western hemisphere and 170,000 for immigrants from the Eastern hemisphere, with priority granted to refugees, highly skilled workers, and family members of people already in the U.S. Members of Congress and the general public who had been wary about welcoming immigrants from Asia took comfort in their assumption that the family reunification preference would keep the number of Asians in the U.S. relatively low. They did not anticipate that the war in Vietnam, the preference for bringing in dissidents and refugees from communist nations, and the number of highly educated Asians granted visas to fill critical shortages would create a large enough immigrant community to make family reunification a significant accelerant of immigration from across Asia.[137]

Nebraska did not suddenly draw new waves of immigrants from every country in Asia, as some might have anticipated. The 1970 Census showed that Nebraska had less than 1 percent Japanese, Chinese, and Filipinos in its population, with 66 out of 93 counties having 5 or fewer of these nationalities. The counties with the largest number of Japanese, Chinese and Filipino residents in 1970 were Douglas with 630 (0.2 percent of the total population), Sarpy with 238 (0.4 percent of the total population), and Scotts Bluff whose 214 Asian residents constituted 0.6 percent of the smaller county's population. Nebraskans of Japanese ancestry formed the majority of Asian residents of Douglas, Sarpy, and Scotts Bluff counties, while the greater number of Lancaster County's Asian residents were of Chinese descent.[138]

---

133. Stephen W. Kay, "Japanese Immigration and Nebraska's 1921 Alien Land Law," *Nebraska History* (Winter 2022):202–213.

134. United States Department of Commerce, Bureau of the Census, 1960 Census of the Population, Supplemental Reports, PC(81)-10, September 7, 1961.

135. https://www2.census.gov/library/publications/decennial/1960/population-volume-2/41927938v2p1a-1ech07.pdf.

136. https://aapidata.com/blog/1965-two-graphs/

137. Robert Tucker, Charles Keeley, and Linda Wrigley, *Immigration and U.S. Foreign Policy*, (Boulder, CO: Westview Press, 1990), 9.

138. https://usa.ipums.org/usa/resources/voliii/pubdocs/1970/Population/31679801n104-107.pdf

South Asian fears

South Asian immigration had long been a concern for anti-Asian organizations, but until the 1970s their numbers had been very small. The first notable jump in the number of people of Indian descent in the United States was from 586 in 1870 to 2,031 in 1900. Many of these young immigrants were Sikhs from Punjab who were misidentified as "Hindus" (Hinduism is just one among many religions practiced in India) by government officials and the media. "Hindu" became both the official government classification for South Asian immigrants and a derogatory term, especially when paired with the word "coolie." First recruited to work on the Western Pacific Railroad, the immigrants from Punjab who settled permanently took jobs in agriculture, construction, and the timber industry. Hindus, along with some Muslims and Sikhs, studied in universities across the U.S., though before 1965 most returned to India after completing their education.[139]

These two South Asian migration streams remained small through most of the twentieth century. The Indian American population grew by fewer than 300 people between 1910 and 1920 but the U.S. government and the national media overwhelmingly framed them as a threat. An article in the popular publication *Overland* claimed that the Hindu Vedas commanded all immigrants from India to "cover the earth," and that these small numbers of railroad workers and college students were launching a holy invasion of the United States.[140] The invasion did not come to pass, yet Congress held hearings in 1914 on the immigration of "Hindu" labor that established that more South Asians were emigrating from the United States than were immigrating to it. Testimony then shifted from the recorded number of immigrants from India to speculation that "Hindus" were entering illegally through the Philippines, Canada, and Central America. A second line of speculation – that "Hindus" might unleash epidemics of hookworm and plague – ran through several hours of testimony, all of which was reported in the Nebraska press.[141]

Nebraskans received Secretary of Labor William B. Wilson's unfounded warning that the "urgent and imperative problem [of] the Hindu immigration" threatened white workers' jobs."[142] This urgency was echoed in an opinion piece in the *Kearney Daily Hub* that was reprinted in the *Lincoln Star*: "California has abundant reason for bucking against a heavy influx of Hindu immigration, promoted by immigrant syndicates in the orient. What with the Chinaman, then the Japanese and now the Hindu, California has been inflicted with the oriental out of proportion."[143] As with Chinese and Japanese immigration, the California scenarios that Nebraskans worried about did not come to pass. The newspapers reported that of the 1,296,372 individuals enumerated in the state of Nebraska for the 1920 U.S. census, a combined total of 30 were South Asian, Filipino, and Korean.[144]

Immigration patterns did not change immediately but for Asians in Nebraska, the U.S. government's renunciation of the racial quota system was significant. After the passage of the Immigration and Nationality Act of 1965 renounced the discriminatory quota restrictions on Asian countries that had been in effect since 1924, a significant number of Asian immigrants were able to exercise the freedoms that other immigrants had enjoyed for decades. The end of race-based immigration seemed to herald a new era of inclusion and equality, encouraging the steady increase of Asian immigrants in Nebraska who have contributed to its growth in various economic fields and quality of life.

Social change and civil rights

More widespread involvement in civil rights action by Asian immigrants and their American-born children and grandchildren came on the heels of African-American civil rights movements and were strengthened by the courage of Asian Issei (first-generation immigrants) and Japanese Americans after passage of the McCarran-Walter Act. Prominent members of the Omaha chapter board of the Japanese American Citizens League (JACL), K. Patrick

---

139. Sanjoy Chakravorty, Devesh Kapur, and Nirvikar Singh, *The Other One Percent: Indians in America* (New York: Oxford University Press, 2016), 6.
140. Chakravorty, Kapur, and Singh, *The Other One Percent*, 8.
141. Sixty-Third Congress. House. Hearings Before the Committee on Immigration Relative to Restriction of Immigrant Hindu Laborers, February 19, 1914, (Washington: USGPO, 1914).
142. "Secretary Wilson Endorses Asiatic Exclusion Measure," *Lincoln Daily News* (now *Lincoln Journal Star*), January 24, 1914, 3.
143. "Nebraska Opinions," *The Lincoln Star*, December 8, 1913, 8.
144. "Nebraska in Brief," *The Friend Sentinel*, June 16, 1921, 2.

and Lily Okura, and Robert and Masako (Em) Nakadoi, along with others in the organization worked tirelessly with their congressional delegates to help pass the bill to erase this racist discriminatory barrier to citizenship. Japanese-American organizations and communities across Nebraska from Scottsbluff to North Platte to Omaha helped to prepare their Issei to become U.S. citizens after fifty years of waiting.

The Reverend M. Manick Samuel was a pathbreaker of a different sort. He made history in 1971 when the United Methodist Church selected him to be the minister of the church in Trumbull. When Reverend Samuel assumed this role, he became the first minister of South Asian descent in Nebraska's history. Methodist ministers played a vital role in communities like Trumbull, where church members numbered 155 in a town of 220 total residents (keeping in mind that some church members likely came from other nearby towns and farming villages). The son of a Methodist minister, Reverend Samuel had already served for more than ten years as a minister in India before immigrating from Marjapur to Atlanta in 1968. His destination was Gammon Theological Seminary, a historically African-American theological institution, where he completed advanced degrees in divinity and sacred theology.[145] Atlanta, with over one million people, and Gammon, where white people were in the minority, were dramatically different communities than Trumbull, Nebraska. In his first five years in the United States, Reverend Samuel experienced American life in markedly different regions, where he interacted with Americans from different racial groups in both urban and rural settings.

Racial inclusion was at the center of the national conversation in 1968 after the assassination of another Christian leader, Baptist minister Dr. Martin Luther King, Jr., whose dream of full equality seemed to have been dashed that April 4th. Trumbull's Methodist community had its own version of this national conversation when the Pastor-Parish Relations Committee was asked how a minister from South Asia would be received. The committee answered, "[A]ll we care about is that he is a Christian." This sentiment held true as Reverend Samuel, his wife Sarojini, and his four children settled into life in Trumbull, where his new congregation was always at the ready to assist the church or a neighbor at any time, in any way. Sarojini Samuel, who had been a teacher in India, played an active role in the United Methodist Women's group. She also traveled across the state, drawing upon her gifts as a teacher to give presentations on women in India and Indian culture. An *Omaha World-Herald* reporter noted that Mrs. Samuel "turned heads in public" as she walked the Nebraska sidewalks wearing her sari, implying that her manner of dress was very noticeably different from that of other women in Trumbull. While likely true, the reporter declared that her six yards of embroidered silk "brighten[ed] the Central Nebraska scene." The Samuels' four children started school in Trumbull, the younger two learning English "by absorption"[146] The Samuels' youngest child, Sylvia, put down roots in eastern Nebraska, and her children are third-generation Nebraskans.

Reverend Samuel described feeling "completely accepted" in Trumbull's rural church and community. "Perhaps in a larger place," he speculated, "there would be (race) distinction, but not here."[147] Small-town central Nebraskans' evident respect for Reverend Samuel – and the Samuel family's embrace of their new community – showed Nebraskans who might never have met an immigrant before that the Samuels were *people like them*, not the fearsome stereotypes South Asian immigrants that had been nurtured in their imaginations by political rhetoric and popular culture. Civic groups regularly invited Reverend Samuel to give talks on India because Nebraskans from all walks of life wanted to learn from this man of great education and stature within the Christian community. He presided over the most sacred days in church members' lives, including weddings and funerals. Any notion that the Samuel family should be separated or excluded from the community of Trumbull, Holdrege, Minden, or any of the other small Nebraska towns where Reverend Samuel served as a leader in the Christian community would have seemed absurd to these rural community residents by the 1970s.[148]

The statewide number of South Asian Nebraskans grew steadily in overall number and in the religious and ethnic diversity of new arrivals in the 1970s. With this expansion came increased civic engagement and

---

145. "The 1969 Gammon Graduates and Their Appointments," *The Foundation* 64:2 (Summer 1969):16.
146. Harold Cowan, "From Marjapur, India to Trumbull, Nebraska," *Omaha World-Herald*, August 6, 1972, 170.
147. Cowan, "From Marjapur, India to Trumbull, Nebraska," 170.
148. "1st United Methodist Church, Holdrege," *Kearney Hub*, May 13, 1989, 24; Carolyn Andersen, "From India to Minden: Manick Samuel Bridges Culture Gap to Preach in USA," *Kearney Hub*, August 2, 1997, 21.

greater visibility. Community leaders established the India Association of Nebraska in 1978. This organization united South Asian Nebraskans in promoting the region's cultural heritage, building a statewide community, calling attention to South Asians' contributions to American life, and representing the South Asian community in humanitarian and other efforts in the state of Nebraska. By serving the South Asian community and the state of Nebraska generally, the Indian Association helped create multiple routes for immigrants and their families to avoid some of the tensions of the past.[149] This support came as South Asian immigration to the U.S. began its climb from 206,000 in 1980 to 2,688,000 in 2019.[150] Douglas County, Nebraska was home to approximately 4,200 immigrants from India, while Lancaster County was home to 1,300.[151] A great number came to Nebraska to advance their careers in health care, information technology, and education, often bringing training and expertise to their professions that were in short supply in the U.S. labor market.[152]

South Asian entrepreneurs were especially successful in the hospitality industry. Hotel owner Ravi Patel attributed this to the importance of hospitality in Indian culture. Paul Ramachadran, a founding member of the India Association of Nebraska who ran hotels in the 1970s before entering the insurance industry, countered that Indian hotel owners, like most immigrants to the United States, wanted to make a good living. Devendra Agrawal, president of the India Association in 1992, explained that South Asian immigrants were encouraged to enter the hospitality industry because they saw their friends successfully build financial foundations in the U.S. in hotel ownership. Extended families often pooled their money to purchase a motel, pitched in their labor to run it, and lived in the rooms so that they could channel their earnings toward the mortgage on the hotel. Naress Bhakta immigrated from Gujarat to help his brother run his hotel in Bakersfield, California. He purchased a hotel of his own in Kansas in 1981 and sold it ten years later to purchase the Excel Hotel in Omaha. Bhakta's purchase came at a point when Caucasian hotel owners began posting signs in their windows identifying their establishments as "American-owned." The Greater Omaha Lodging Association denounced this practice but had limited power to stop it.[153] Old stereotypes of Asians as "eternal foreigners" who, like Bhagat Singh Thind, would never be considered "truly American" remained embedded in Nebraskans' thinking, even as a growing number of Asian and non-Asian Nebraskans rejected white supremacy by calling for an end to Asian exclusion.

Nebraskans' increased rejection of anti-Asian policies and practices came just as Asian immigration to the state was growing in size and diversity. In 1980, the total number of persons of Asian ancestry in America – including 3,259,519 Japanese, Chinese, Filipino, Korean, Asian Indian, and Vietnamese people plus 240,920 people of Pacific Island ancestry (Hawaiian, Guamanian, and Samoan) – was 3,500,439, or approximately 1.5 percent of the total population, a sizeable increase from 0.3 percent in 1900. That same year, Nebraska had a population of 1,569,825 with 8,190 people of Asian ancestry, or 0.5 percent of the population. This included the following specific heritages: 1,378 Japanese, 1,106 Chinese, 867 Filipino, 993 Korean, 928 Asian Indian, 1,438 Vietnamese, 160 Hawaiian, 105 Guamanian, and 27 Samoan. The most significant change from 1970 was the number of Vietnamese, who solidly became the most populous Asian nationality in Nebraska and representing the 56 percent of Asians who were foreign born.[154]

These demographic changes combined with anxieties about U.S.-Asian relations on the political and economic fronts to initiate new waves of anti-Asian hostility. At this point in history, Asians in Nebraska and across the U.S. began to stand together in pan-Asian movements to put a stop to racial hatred. The

---

149. Mission Statement, Indian Association of Nebraska, https://www.indiaassociationofnebraska.org/Aboutus.aspx.
150. Data from U.S. Census Bureau 2010 and 2019 American Community Surveys (ACS) published in Mary Hanna and Jeanne Batalova, "Indian Immigrants in the United States," Migration Information Source.
151. U.S. Immigrant Population by State and County, 2017-2021" Migration Policy Institute, Data from U.S. Census Bureau 2010 and 2019 American Community Surveys (ACS)
152. "Asian-Indian Immigrants Find Success as Innkeepers in U.S., *Omaha World-Herald*, October 4, 1992, 5-E; Madeleine Greene and Jeanne Bataloa, "Indian Immigrants in the United States," Migration Policy Institute, November 8, 2024, https://www.migrationpolicy.org/article/indian-immigrants-united-states#:~:text=In%202023%2C%2074%20percent%20of,occupations%20(see%20Figure%206
153. "Asian -Indian Immigrants Find Success as Innkeepers in U.S., *Omaha World-Herald*, October 4, 1992, 5-E.
154. https://www2.census.gov/prod2/decennial/documents/1980/1980censusofpopu8011u_bw.pdf and https://www2.census.gov/library/publications/decennial/1980/volume-1/nebraska/1980censusofpopu80129unse_bw.pdf

Asian-American Pacific-Islander community gathered for a banquet in Omaha in 1990 to recognize Asian-Pacific Heritage month, bringing together the Filipino-American Association, the Nebraska India Association, the Japanese American Citizens League, the Metro Omaha Chinese Association (a Taiwanese organization), the Korean Association of Nebraska, the Vietnamese Association of Nebraska, and the Lao-Hmong Association of Nebraska. This diverse community of long-established Nebraskans and newer arrivals from Asia made Asian Americans a visible and significant part of life in Nebraska.[155]

Pan-Asian activism

The first generations of Asians in the U.S. had to use their invisibility to prevent being the nail that got pounded down. The generation of Asian Americans who came of age in the 1960s had fewer vulnerabilities. They were unquestionably U.S. citizens, and the Civil Rights Movement created a new language of equal rights for all Americans regardless of their ancestry or the color of their skin. Asian-American organizations had been in place for decades, including in Nebraska, but their focus was largely to address the concerns of their particular immigrant community. While fully assimilated, Asian Americans still faced dangerous forms of invisibility. The murder of Vincent Chin in 1982 laid bare the fact that white supremacists did not target Chinese, Japanese, Filipino, or Korean Americans. They targeted anyone with an "Asian face." From that point forward, Asian-American activists stood together to resist racial violence, both in its overt forms that cause bodily injury and in the more covert forms that assail Asian Americans' emotional well-being and that also prove lethal in all too many cases.

As in decades past, the rise in global economic competition impacts the livelihoods of Americans, regardless of national origin. However, the distinctive physical features of Asian Americans continue to contribute to the notion that they are not real Americans, but foreigners upon whom blame is placed when people's lives are upended with economic downturns. On June 23, 1982, during the height of the auto industry trade wars with Japan, Vincent Chin, a Chinese American who was celebrating his impending marriage the next day in Detroit, was brutally attacked and killed by white Americans who blamed him for losing their jobs in the declining American auto industry. Chin was not of Japanese descent and was not employed in the auto industry. However, he lost his life over racial hatred and discrimination. The attackers were not even given jail time – just probation. Pan-Asian activism became a monolith after the murder of Vincent Chin and the light sentence accorded his racially motivated murderers. The American Citizens for Justice was formed in Detroit to push for justice for the Chin family. Other national groups such as the Organization for Chinese Americans (OCA), founded in 1973, and the JACL joined in their efforts to seek justice and to more broadly break the invisibility cloak and perception of Asian Americans as perpetual foreigners, by advocating for the inclusion of Asians as a protected class in civil rights cases.[156]

Overt racist actions are not the only detriment to persons of Asian descent. The continual promotion of Asian-American stereotypes by non-Asians has moved advocacy groups to speak more forthrightly about microaggressions that impact the development and advancement of Asian Americans. Choi, Park, Noh, Lee, and Takeuchi examined the mental health of young Filipino and Korean Americans as they transitioned to adulthood, and they found that both depressive symptoms and suicidal ideations increased in the four-year tracking of the youth. One of the factors that emerged was societal stereotypes and discrimination. "Racial discrimination had a noticeably large and adverse effect on suicidal ideation."[157] This is equally true of the seemingly positive "model minority" stereotype as of the "eternal foreigner."

The model minority stereotype emerged within the white imagination in response to the notable educational achievement and economic success of many second- and third-generation Asian Americans. They were praised as being universally quiet, accommodating, and even docile – perhaps an exaggeration of their parents' fear of being "nails that stick up." Non-Asian observers declared that Asians had achieved full racial equality and, in fact, surpassed many Caucasians – especially in the realms of mathematics, computer technology, and violin playing. Non-Asians also expected Asians to work hard,

---

155. "Banquet Recognizes Asian Pacific Heritage," *Omaha World-Herald*, May 15, 1990, 17.
156. "Vincent Chin," National Park Service, https://www.nps.gov/people/vincent-chin.htm.
157. T. Choi, M. Park, S. Noh, J. Park Lee, & D. Takeuchi, "Asian American mental health: Longitudinal trend and explanatory factors among young Filipino- and Korean Americans," *SSM Population Health* 10 (April 2020): 7.

be naturally exceptional, and to deny the presence of anti-Asian racism.[158] The more insidious effect was to pit Asians against other subordinated racial groups like Black Americans who, like them, made significant civil rights gains by standing together. Joe Ishikawa, director of playgrounds for the City of Lincoln, worked with the Urban League, the National Association for the Advancement of Colored People (NAACP), and the American Veterans Committee (the racially progressive counterpart to the American Legion) and several members of the clergy to pressure the City Council to desegregate the public swimming pool. Although he nearly lost his job for organizing protests, Ishikawa had come to Lincoln from a wartime incarceration camp and was determined to prevent the harms of racism wherever he could.[159] It was unlikely that a small group of Japanese Americans or African Americans outside of the city government would have desegregated the pools so quickly. Working together, they pressed the City Council to ensure equal access to public accommodations.

Author Gary Duong described the experience of being labeled the "model minority" as

> ... privilege-adjacent. Invisible at times. As an Asian American, that's how I typically used to think of my minority status. Society labels us the 'model minority' when it is convenient. Sometimes we're models to be emulated – when we're not on the receiving end of people's fear, anger and suspicion. ... I had gotten used to not always thinking about what it means to have my ethnicity in the spotlight, or even front of mind. Now, I can't avoid it. It's become clearer to me that the whole idea of the 'model minority' is based on a myth – one that is less a celebration of our accomplishments and more of a convenient tool to mask ongoing discrimination and systemic inequality.[160]

For Duong, the model minority stereotype threatened to pit him against other Asians, other racial minorities, and, in some ways, against himself.

As young Asian Americans attempt to find their identities across bicultural lives (i.e., native heritage and modern American social expectations), the racist stereotypes that they encounter, such as being a model minority or being a perpetual foreigner, become an impairment to navigating positive identities and racial acceptance. This is reflected in a 2023 survey in which Americans were asked to respond to the statement, "Personally, I feel that I belong and am accepted in the U.S." Fifty-seven percent of white Americans agreed with the statement. Only 25 percent of Hispanic Americans and 24 percent of Black Americans agreed. A mere 22 percent of Asian Americans could agree with the statement. Among the Asian-American respondents who did not feel they belonged and were accepted in the U.S., 39 percent said they experienced exclusion in their workplace, 33 percent in their neighborhoods, and 32 percent in schools.[161]

Asian hate in the 21st Century: Why history matters

Terror after 9/11

In early 2001, members of the Hindu Temple in Omaha launched a two-year renovation of a restaurant shaped like an old English castle into their house of worship. Craftsmen from India were working night and day to build a space where approximately 600 families who immigrated from all parts of South Asia could properly practice the faith in which they were raised.[162] Only ten years prior, Hindu families worshipped privately in their homes or with other families in rented halls. As the congregation grew from 400 to about 900 members in the 1990s, the community's

---

158. Rosalind S. Chou and Joe R. Feagin, *The Myth of the Model Minority: Asian Americans Facing Racism* (New York: Routledge, 2015).
159. Joe Ishikawa interviewed by Tom Ikeda, January 10, 2008, segment 25, Densho Digital Archives, https://ddr.densho.org/media/ddr-densho-1000/ddr-densho-1000-205-transcript-92aee799fa.htm, Jesse S. Ishikawa, "The Desegregation of the Lincoln Municipal Swimming Pool, *Nebraska History* (Fall 2018): 159-166.
160. Gary Duong, "You're called a 'model minority' as an Asian American—until they decide you aren't," NPR, May 30, 2022. https://www.npr.org/2022/05/30/1101790205/as-an-asian-american-youre-called-a-model-minority-until-they-decide-you-arent
161. "Attitudes towards Asian Americans and Pacific Islanders," The Asian American Foundation, https://staatus-index.laaunch.org.
162. "Hinduism: a Tapestry of Faith," *Lincoln Journal Star*, September 7, 2001, 37; "Temple Renovation Excites Growing Metro-Area Congregation," *Omaha World-Herald*, June 29, 2002, E2.

need for a temple grew greater.[163] Doubling the size of the temple had represented a greater risk than the temple leadership could have known.

The terrorist attacks of September 11, 2001, brought fear, grief, and enduring loss to all in the U.S. There was a clear danger of violent attacks from terrorist organizations, though at first it was unclear who those organizations were. The immediate calls to control the threat from terrorists emerged from a sense of fear that was familiar to people of Asian ancestry. Across the U.S., Asian Americans perceived as foreigners akin to the al Qaeda terrorists – especially South Asians misread as Arab or Muslim supporters of terror – were assaulted. Some were killed. Nebraskans received unfounded warnings that their Muslim neighbors "who seem like perfectly ordinary, law-abiding citizens until called to jihad – holy war – comes." The more "American" these "eternal foreigners" seemed, the less they were to be trusted. Nebraskans of Arab descent were harassed on the street and received threatening phone calls at home. Anonymous callers threatened a mosque in Lincoln with deadly violence.[164]

A group of white supremacists assaulted an Omaha business owner of Pakistani descent in 2002, yelling racial slurs while beating him. The Omaha community held a rally to denounce hate crimes, which increased fourfold since 2000. The state of Nebraska outlawed hate crimes in 1997,[165] but the law could only do so much to deter people from harming South Asians, Muslims, or other Nebraskans perceived as part of a so-called "enemy race."[166] Omaha seemed to have returned to 1925, when six white men beat Y.P. Bhosale while calling him a foreigner for wearing his turban. This time, however, the public protested the disconnect between classifying racially motivated violence as a crime and not having the will or the means to punish the crime.

Dr. Keay Hachiya and Kaz Tada reminded Nebraskans of the importance of upholding civil rights protections. They drew parallels between their incarceration in the weeks after Pearl Harbor and the rising fear and suspicion of Arab and Muslim Nebraskans after 9/11. The government uprooted them from their homes and stripped them of their constitutional rights in response to public outcry about Japan's attack on Hawaii, though there was no military or security benefit to the mass incarceration.[167] National polling showed that 29 percent of Americans supported a similar mass internment of all immigrants from nations tied to the 9/11 hijackers.[168] Sergeant Ben Kuroki of Hershey – the war hero memorialized in *The Boy from Nebraska* – urged his fellow Japanese Americans to remember the needless suffering of their parents and great grandparents during incarceration. The Kuroki family did not fly a U.S. flag outside of their home. Kuroki said of this, "One thing I've never been is the flag-waving type. … I did it the other way – I fought for it."[169]

George Hachiya drew Nebraskans' attention to the kindness shown to him when he was released from Heart Mountain incarceration camp to continue his studies at the University of Nebraska. The train conductor referred to him as a "Jap boy" during the journey but was greeted warmly by Reverend Robert Drew. Students, faculty, and administrative staff welcomed Hachiya, making him feel as though he was finally "back in the good old U.S. of A."[170] Reverend Drew and others in Lincoln helped Japanese-American students find jobs, activities, and social outlets so they could live like other college students. Nebraskans' kindness to those treated by much of the nation as dangerous outsiders during World War II meant that Nebraskans knew that they could choose how they would respond to the so-called "dangerous foreigners" around them in this new security crisis. Father Flanagan stood up for Patrick Okura and the other Japanese Americans he welcomed to Boys Town. The United Methodist Church chose Reverend Samuel as its minister. Nebraska had a long history of racial exclusion but it also had a history of rejecting

---

163. "A Day of Hindu Prayer," *Omaha World-Herald*, June 9, 2003, 7.
164. Martha Stoddard and JoAnne Young, "Backlash Parallels Americans' Wartime Ordeals," *Lincoln Journal-Star*, September 16, 2001.
165. "Increase in Crimes Reported," *The Schuyler Sun*, July 18, 2002, 16.
166. "Loud Crowd Intolerant of Hate," *Omaha World-Herald*, October 4, 2002, 14.
167. Martha Stoddard and JoAnne Young, "Backlash Parallels Americans' Wartime Ordeals," *Lincoln Journal-Star*, September 16, 2001.
168. Pew Research Center, "Twenty Years Later, the Enduring Legacy of 9/11," September 2, 2021, https://www.pewresearch.org/politics/2021/09/02/two-decades-later-the-enduring-legacy-of-9-11/; Heather Fryer, *Perimeters of Democracy: Inverse Utopias and the Wartime Social Landscape in the American West* (Lincoln: University of Nebraska Press, 2010), 288.
169. "The '59th Mission' Hero Offers Caution," *Lincoln Journal Star*, September 23, 2001, 35.
170. Peg Sheldrick, "Interned Students Found Warm Welcome at UNL," *Lincoln Journal Star*, December 2, 2001, 119 (13M).

anti-Asian stereotypes to form human connections with people who in short order became valued community leaders. The question was, and continues to be, which tradition Nebraskans choose to draw from in times of national distress.

The Omaha Japanese American Citizens League revised its mission statement to address this pattern of racial targeting in Nebraska's history to read, "[O]ur mission is to secure and maintain the civil rights of Japanese Americans *and all others* who are victimized by injustice and bigotry."[171] JACL members organized to stop racial profiling and to stand in solidarity with Arab, Muslim, and South Asian Nebraskans. The Hindu Temple courageously moved forward with its temple renovation. The celebration of its completion in May 2003 represented a triumph of both design and of the South Asian community to establish their roots in Nebraska even in a climate of anti-Asian violence.[172]

Pandemic illness and epidemic violence

Exclusion and invisibility are stubborn forms of injustice to uproot. Exclusion of people allowed myths and stereotypes to flourish, and perceptions of difference to take root. For many Americans, racial stereotypes were all they knew of Asian people, because none were present as neighbors with whom they could interact personally. By the time Asian communities were visible in Nebraska, the gulf was wide and the fear was immense. To complicate matters, people from some Asian countries were considered more "foreign" and "dangerous" than others. These stereotypes and habits of exclusion tend to lie dormant in times of relative peace and prosperity. In time of war, economic instability, and social upheaval, Asian people became the targets of suspicion, blame, and punishment as if all had suddenly turned to "John Chinaman." Exclusionary forces have remained part of Nebraska's recent history. This visualization of population data (see page 256) shows how few people of Asian descent live in each of Nebraska's counties.

The 2020 Census showed that approximately 2.8 percent of Nebraskans identified as being of Asian descent only. Another 2.5 percent identified as being of two or more races, and while it is likely that at least some of that number are partially of Asian descent it is hard to know how many. What is clear is that Asian and Pacific Islanders are the fastest growing ethnic group in Nebraska and with their greater numbers has come greater diversity. Figures from 2019 show that 13 percent of Asians in Nebraska were Chinese, 14 percent were South Asian and another 14 percent Vietnamese. Pacific Islander, Thai, Cambodian, and Karen Nebraskans also play vital roles in Nebraska communities. In addition to being more numerous and more diverse, Asian Nebraskans are leaders in government, business, education, the arts, science, healthcare, and civic organizations. Omaha artist Jun Kaneko is world renowned for his outdoor sculptures. Congressman Don Bacon of Nebraska honored six state leaders of Asian descent on behalf of the United States Congress in 2023. One honoree, University of Nebraska Omaha Chancellor Dr. Joanne Li said in her remarks that "[r]epresentation regardless of your race ensures that every voice gets to be part of the conversation … [n]o matter where we have come from, though, we share one common path forward: we are here to build a brighter future for Nebraska. And a brighter future for all."[173]

While much has changed over a century and a quarter, resilient patterns of anti-Asian stereotyping and scapegoating endanger the lives of Asian Nebraskans and a bright future for all. Only three years prior to Dr. Li's speech, in March 2021, a longtime resident of Omaha's Joslyn Castle district, also of Chinese descent, had long enjoyed walking his dogs in this friendly neighborhood. His routine with the dogs was always the same and never caused problems. One dog stayed on a leash for the entire walk; the other dog would only do his "business" off-leash, and his owner was right there to clean up after the dog. One spring day in 2018 a well-dressed woman the man had never seen before was also walking her dog. She objected to the man's dog being off the leash; when he tried to explain what he was doing, she unleashed a verbal tirade. When the man tried to deescalate the situation by saying that she did not have to yell or curse to communicate about the dogs, she became angrier and more abusive. Another time, he and his wife were walking their dogs on a quiet trail, whose tranquility was shattered

---

171. "Mission Statement," Japanese American Citizens League, http://www.omahajacl.org.
172. Angie Brunkow, "For Growing Hindu Community, Temple is a Dream Come True," *Omaha World-Herald*, May 21, 2003, 15.
173. "Chancellor Li Among Six AAPI Leaders Recognized by Congressman Don Bacon," University of Nebraska Omaha, May 3, 2023, https://www.unomaha.edu/news/2023/05/chancellor-li-among-six-aapi-leaders-recognized-by-congressman-don-bacon.php.

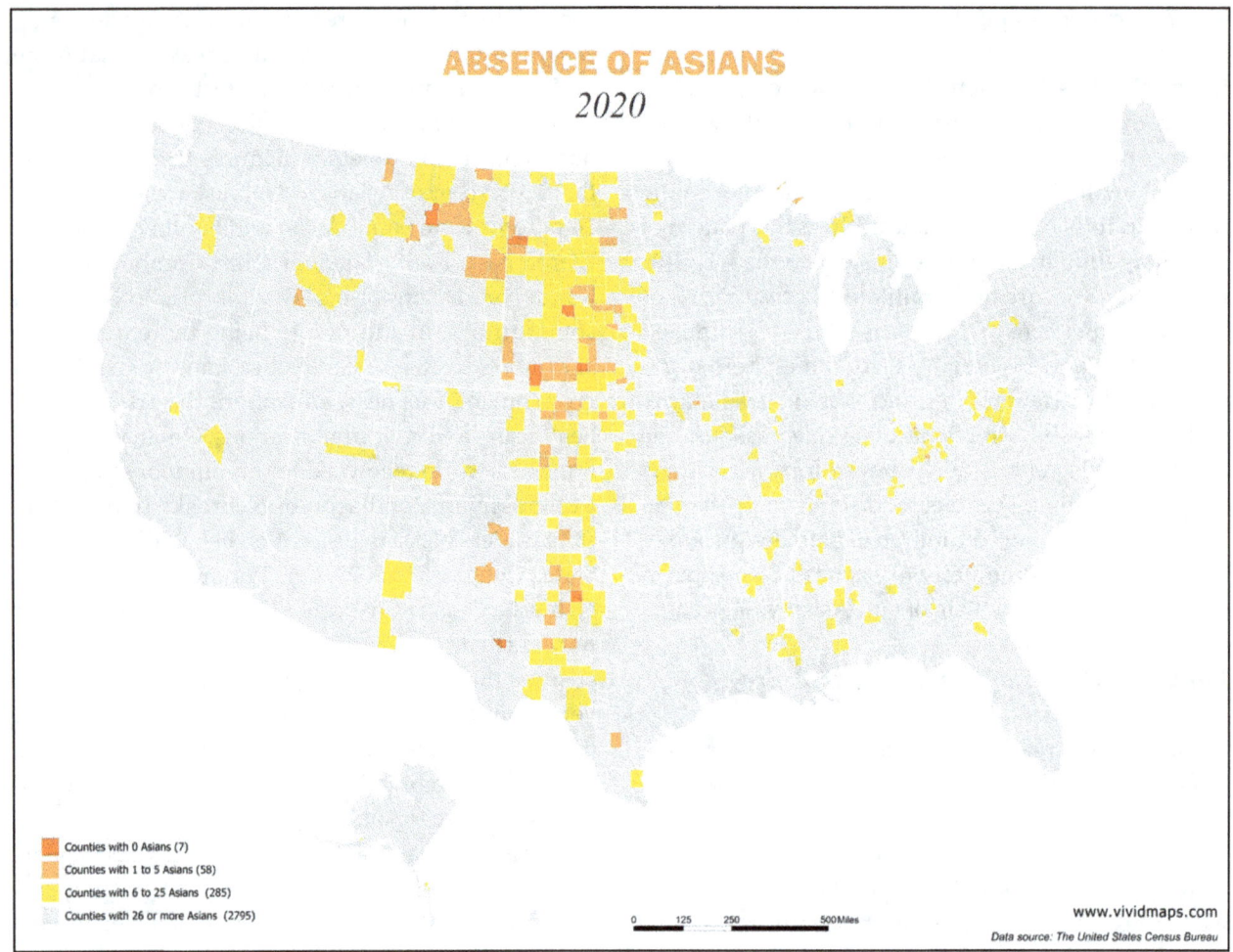

Map showing "Absence of Asians" 2020. https://vividmaps.com/us-asian-population-by-county/ . Used by permission of Alex Egoshin, vividmaps@gmail.com.

when someone passed them on a bicycle, screaming, "Go back where you came from!" The memory of Vincent Chin is not so far in the past as not to be terrifying to any Asian person targeted for somebody's anger or hatred in a time of national distress.[174]

A national report issued by Stop AAPI Hate in 2022 documented nearly 11,500 racially motivated anti-Asian attacks since March 2020, when then-President Donald Trump declared the outbreak of COVID-19 a national emergency.[175] Underscoring the virus's origin in Wuhan, China, many Americans – including the president – associated this deadly scourge with all Asian people. The number of mentions of the "China virus" increased 650 percent on Twitter on March 8, 2020, and 800 percent on conservative media outlets the next day.[176] It is possible that men who thought of themselves as an Omaha dog owner or CEO were cast by their assailants as the cause of the "Kung Flu." The head of the Omaha field office of the FBI reported a 21 percent increase in hate crimes including an attempt by a woman in Des Moines to run over two children with her car – one who she thought was Mexican, the other who she thought was part of the Islamic State.[177]

174. Anonymous, interviewed by Sharon Ishii-Jordan, September 6, 2023.
175. Shirelle Moore, "Anti-Defamation League Concerned over Anti-Asian Incidents in Omaha," KPTM News, March 17, 2021, https://fox42kptm.com/newsletter-daily/anti-defamation-league-concerned-over-anti-asian-incidents-in-omaha.
176. Sean Darling-Hammond, Eli K. Michaels, Rucker C. Johnson, et.al, After "The China Virus" Went Viral: Racially Charged Coronavirus Coverage and Trends in Bias Against Asian Americans. *Health Education & Behavior*, 47: 6 (2020), 870–879, https://doi.org/10.1177/1090198120957949
177. FBI: Nebraska, Iowa see jump in hate crimes in recent years, Associated Press, July 9, 2021, https://apnews.com/article/religion-crime-race-and-ethnicity-racial-injustice-iowa-98212d8146da9288e23b2b2d1c1cb3c7.

In 2019, the Omaha man from the Joslyn Castle neighborhood was driving on a busy main street when a young white man raised his middle finger at him for no apparent reason. Ignoring the insult, though making note of the bumper sticker reading "F### Black Lives Matter," the man turned the corner thinking a momentary unpleasantness had just ended. Instead, the young man followed him, alternately pulling up beside him or tailing very close to his rear bumper, shouting obscenities, raising his middle finger through the sunroof, and cutting the man off at a traffic light so he could not make a turn – only to speed away when the man took out his phone to get a photo of the license plate and bumper sticker before calling the Omaha police. An officer took the information and said very little. The man made some follow-up calls but, in line with much of the history of anti-Asian hate crimes, there was no significant action on the part of law enforcement. Equally disheartening, if not more, he said, is that since the COVID-19 pandemic, people in his neighborhood who used to say hello to him no longer engage.[178]

Alan Wang, executive director of Prairie STEM, a nonprofit organization specializing in STEM education for children, could never be certain of when or where he would be the target of verbal abuse or physical violence. As a Nebraskan of Chinese descent, ordinary daily activities carried some risk. A trip to the hardware store in 2020 was met with a verbal and physical assault. Driving on a busy street in 2021 grew exceedingly dangerous when a group of white teenagers in another car yelled racial slurs while attempting to throw things into Wang's open car window. While walking down the aisle in an Omaha grocery store in 2023, Wang became the target of more racial slurs and the all-too-common refrain "return to China."[179]

The increase in the number and severity of incidents of Asian hate prompted a Nebraska State Legislature committee to conduct hearings in both 2021 and 2023 to create a Commission for Asian American Affairs to research, educate, and advise Nebraska officials on solutions to problems that are common to Nebraskans of Asian descent, as there already existed commissions for Native American, Hispanic American, and African American populations.

Susanne Swanson, a Korean American, testified that racial hostility has been part of her life in Nebraska, and she has been told to "go back to China." She saw the pattern of anti-Asian racism to be so pervasive that the work of the proposed commission was needed to break it: "Without this commission" she said, "these incidents like I've experienced will continue."[180]

Invisibility: 21st century exclusion

Stereotyping, scapegoating, shrugging off violence, and treating Asians as "all the same," are, like restrictive laws, forms of Asian exclusion. Instead of excluding Asians by running them out of town like Sin Goon, or subjecting them to alien land laws, Asian people and their concerns have been made invisible. Omaha artist Lindsey Yoneda says of her present-day experience that "[r]acism towards Asians has been very under the radar, for most of my life anyway, from what I've experienced. It's always been there but it's never been talked about, it's never been on the front of people's minds." Yoneda designed T-shirts during the COVID-19 pandemic to raise money for Stop AAPI Hate. The graphic features a daruma: the round Japanese wish doll that is made without eyes. As one makes a wish, they fill in one eye of the daruma. When the wish is granted, the daruma will have both of its eyes. Alongside Yoneda's one-eyed daruma is the Japanese proverb: "Fall seven times, get up eight."[181] It suggests that surviving anti-Asian racism has been a quiet, solitary pursuit of a wish that is not yet fulfilled.

Daruma image from t-shirt design by Lindsey Yoneda. Courtesy of Lindsey Yoneda.

---

178. Anonymous, interviewed by Sharon Ishii-Jordan, September 6, 2023.
179. Alan Wang, interviewed by Sharon Ishii-Jordan, September 7, 2023.
180. "Legislative Commission Proposed," Unicameral Update, March 3, 2021, http://update.legislature.ne.gov/?p=29553.
181. Mario Lundak, Omaha artist combats Asian hate one T-shirt at a time, WOWT Television News broadcast April 21, 2021, https://www.wowt.com/2021/04/21/omaha-artist-combats-asian-hate-one-t-shirt-at-a-time/.

Now, as in the past, invisibility remains a danger to Nebraskans of Asian descent. Stop AAPI Hate found that discrimination and violence against Americans of Asian descent is widespread but rarely meets the criteria for being prosecuted as a crime. While this could appear to be a form of Asian-American privilege on the surface, the regularity with which people of Asian descent are targets of silent forms of violence has normalized the conditions that lead to deadly hate crimes. The report classified approximately two-thirds of the 11,500 incidents of anti-Asian violence as acts of harassment involving verbal, written, or gestural hate speech. Physical assaults took place in 17 percent of the incidents and acts of "avoidance or shunning" in another 16 percent.

Hate crimes classifications are not the only structures that obscure anti-Asian violence. Census categories historically, and today, define Asian people variously, making it just as difficult at times to classify who an "Asian person" is as it is to define an "anti-Asian hate crime." For many years, Americans understood race as meaning Caucasian or Black. This narrow understanding meant that criminologists and historians did not investigate the consequences of racism against people of color who were not part of the United States' most visible racial conflicts rooted in slavery and Reconstruction. It remains today a form of exclusion by way of invisibility.

A 2022 study showed that Asian Americans are among the least likely to feel that they completely belong and are accepted in the U.S. and that the U.S. population in general were less likely to trust the loyalty of Asian Americans, who many blamed for the COVID-19 pandemic. One-third of Americans were unaware that anti-Asian violence was increasing, and most could not name a prominent Asian American at all – the most common responses were actors in martial arts films from the late twentieth century. When describing Asian Americans, most respondents referred to stereotypes and villain roles in popular culture.[182] Monica Lu, whose family moved from Singapore to Nebraska when she was five years old, was excited to start school and felt she was adjusting well. She was one of two Asian students in the school. The other kids liked Lu because she was different. Sometimes, though, they made fun of her facial features. The comments were hurtful, she said, because "even though I've learned to love my culture and where I came from, I still felt insecure about being different." Determined not to let these stereotypes define her, Lu followed her mother's example of standing up to every encounter with racism. She now serves as a role model to other Asian-American women who refuse to be defined by stereotypes.[183] While her success is inspiring, it is important to account for the time and energy that Asian Nebraskans like Lu have had to expend just to be seen and accepted that their white counterparts do not.

The creation of the Nebraska Commission on Asian American Affairs represents a break in the long pattern of Asian American exclusion in this state. Sen. Rita Sanders of Bellevue introduced the bill, which Gov. Jim Pillen signed into law in April 2024. The commission's existence recognizes Asian Nebraskans as Americans, and as neighbors with just as much a place in the Good Life as all other Nebraskans. One committee cannot shift a deep current of history on its own. All Nebraskans who know this history of exclusion can see this pattern when it crops up in their own workplace, school, neighborhood, church, or family and friend group – and in themselves. Through seemingly small things like looking past stereotypes to see the unique individuals behind them and finding ways to be more inclusive than exclusive, Nebraskans can work together to uproot the patterns of the past and to choose a future where all Nebraskans can live with liberty and justice for all.

---

182. Jennifer Lee, "Confronting the Invisibility of anti-Asian Racism," Brookings Institution, May 18, 2022, https://www.brookings.edu/articles/confronting-the-invisibility-of-anti-asian-racism/ ; Monica Mong Trieu, *Fighting Invisibility*, 11-14.
183. Monica Lu interviewed by Jess Katz, "Singapore to Nebraska to New York: My Experience As an Asian American Woman in Tech," MongoDB (May 29, 2020), https://www.mongodb.com/blog/post/singapore-to-nebraska-to-new-york-my-experience-as-an-asian-american-woman-in-tech.

Recent Arrivals: Refugee Resettlement in Nebraska

By Emira Ibrahimpašić and Julia Reilly

I. Introduction

One of the stories Nebraskans tell themselves is that the story of Nebraska is a story of immigration. One of the most recent versions of this story is that Nebraska is one of the best and most welcoming places in the country to be a resettled refugee. In many respects, this narrative is true, but as with all narratives, reality is more complicated.

This chapter attempts to paint a fuller picture by providing a detailed history of the foundation of Nebraska's refugee resettlement program, and an overview of five of the most populous refugee communities in Nebraska. First, we survey the early history of immigration in Nebraska, show how policymakers tried to draw European immigrants here to settle the land, and discuss how national laws created a system that profoundly favored white, abled immigrants. Second, we detail national efforts to make immigration more racially equitable, which coincided with the first extensive efforts to resettle refugees after the Second World War. Third, we discuss the beginnings of the refugee resettlement system in the United States, and how this looked in Nebraska. Here, we detail how the demands for refugee resettlement after the Vietnam War led to the creation of the refugee resettlement system we have today, and how Nebraskans interacted with these developments.

We then turn to a discussion of refugees' experiences in and impacts on Nebraska. In our fourth section, we use data compiled from twenty years of Congressional reports[1] to give the fullest descriptive, quantitative picture to date of the refugees who have been resettled in Nebraska. Then, we write about five of Nebraska's largest and most influential refugee populations: Vietnamese, Yugoslavs, Iraqis, Burmese, and Sudanese. The sixth section discusses the essential economic contributions refugees have made to Nebraska's economy, and the seventh section details three ongoing challenges that Nebraska's refugees face: state government statements and actions, a lack of resources to support refugees after the first ninety days of resettlement, and English language barriers. The eighth section concludes this chapter.

---

1. The Office of Refugee Resettlement (ORR), which is housed in the US Department of Health and Human Services, collects and publishes annual data on refugee resettlement in the United States. These data are published in Congressional Reports, among other venues. We accessed them either directly though the ORR's website, or in their annual reports to Congress.

In *Roots of Justice: A History of Race and Racism in Nebraska*. Edited by Kevin Abourezk, with an Introduction by M. Dewayne Mays and Paul A. Olson (Lincoln, Nebraska: Truth and Reconciliation Nebraska, 2025). Copyright © 2025 by the authors; CC-BY. DOI: 10.32873/unl.dc.rj7

II. Early Immigration in Nebraska

What we know today as Nebraska was populated by various indigenous populations including Pawnee, Ponca, Oto-Missouria, Omaha, Dakota, Lakota, Arapaho, Cheyenne, and Kaw Peoples, as well as the relocated Ho Chunk (Winnebago), Iowa, and Sac and Fox Peoples for nearly 10,000 years. It was not until the European colonization that we saw large-scale migration to the area. The first colonizers settled in this territory in the late 1700s: they first established a trading post, which they expanded into a larger settlement in the early 1800s. The Homestead Act of 1862 contained significant incentives to attract Americans from the East Coast and immigrants from Europe to the then-territory of Nebraska (Kinbacher and Thomas 2008, 193). This was a crucial mode of colonization, which was "well planned, well promoted, and amazingly rapid" (Ibid). To accelerate colonization and connect the coasts, the federal government invested in building railways. Funded by land grants, and supported by local and national governments, the construction of the Burlington and Missouri River Railroads and the Union Pacific Transcontinental Railroad allowed the increased commercialization of agriculture, which increased the economic draw of Nebraska for migrants (Kinbacher and Thomas 2008, 192).

When Nebraska become a state, it had to follow existing American laws on immigration and citizenship: only someone who was considered "a free white person...of good character," or their child, could become a citizen after immigrating to the United States (U.S. House of Representatives 1790). This meant that only white immigrants could hope to attain American citizenship.

Nebraskan policymakers proved adept at working within these constraints. In February 1870, the Unicameral created the State Board of Immigration, tasked with making "known the advantages and resources of the State, and of inducing immigration" (Nebraska State Board of Immigration Collection). Nebraska invested in advertising so-called "free land," to attract immigrants. Of course, this was not "free land," but land that had been forcefully taken from indigenous populations, including the Pawnee, Ponca, Oto-Missouria, Omaha, Dakota, Lakota, Arapaho, Cheyenne, and Kaw Peoples. Further, the railroads deployed immigration agents to communities throughout northern and central Europe, advertising cheap land and job opportunities (When Railroads Promoted Immigration). Securing this "free land" hinged on "intention to declare citizenship," an opportunity that was only available to "free white" people "of good character" — hence, Nebraska's considerable efforts to attract immigrants to populate and develop the land were explicitly limited to white, European immigrants. The "intention to declare citizenship" requirement functioned as an effective ban on land ownership for any immigrant — or descendant of an immigrant — who was not white.

Seven years after Nebraska became a state, the first federal restriction on immigrant arrivals passed: the Page Act of 1875 (Marinari 2022). It prohibited Asian immigrants from several professions, which were selected with the goal of keeping Asian women out of the United States (Ibid.). Seven years later, the infamous Chinese Exclusion Act and Immigration Act of 1882 followed. The Immigration Act of 1882 barred anyone who could be considered a "convict, lunatic, idiot, or any person unable to take care of himself or herself without becoming a public charge." (Ibid., 274). The legal language and broader idea of preventing migrants from becoming public charges continues to be deeply influential in discussions about welcoming new Americans.

Despite these restrictions, Nebraska's population continued to grow, aided by European immigrant arrivals. Between 1860 and 1920, Nebraska's population increased from about 30,000 to 1,296,000 (Wunder 2008). By 1870, a quarter of Nebraskans were foreign-born (Gouveia 2018). These immigrants came overwhelmingly from central and northern Europe: Czechs and Germans made up the largest immigrant populations, and there were significant populations of Danes, Swedes, and Irish (Ibid.). As the decades passed, the immigrant population became more eastern and southern European, with small Mexican and Japanese communities (Ibid.).

Congress passed restriction after restriction over the next four decades. In 1917, Congress overrode an attempted veto from President Woodrow Wilson — a display of how united and committed legislators were on the legislation — to pass the Immigration Act of 1917, which expanded the list of people prohibited entry into the United States to include anyone from Asia, as well as "idiots," "feeble-minded persons," "epileptics," "insane persons," "alcoholics," "professional beggars," and anyone "mentally or physically defective" (Sohi 2022, 209). It also added a literacy test for immigrants, which anti-immigrant legislators were sure would further prevent hopeful migrants; this did not work, as immigrant arrivals passed the test at such high rates (Yang 2020, 30-32).

The Immigration Act of 1917 was followed by the Immigration Act of 1924, which implemented the "national origins" quota system — a scheme of limits on immigrant arrivals from each country in the world that was explicitly designed to preserve the racial composition of the United States' population to its exact 1890 proportions (Diamond 2020). Senator David Reed, the chief sponsor of the bill, wrote a *New York Times* op-ed upon passage of the law, gloating, "The racial composition of America at the present time thus is made permanent." (Reed 1924) The Immigration Act of 1924 ultimately failed on that front but succeeded at dramatically limiting immigration. Immigrant arrivals dropped 58 percent in one year, from 700,000 in 1924 to 300,000 in 1925 (Yang 2020, 60). By 1931, more people left the United States than entered it (Yang 2020, 73).

The Immigration Act of 1924 also made it much harder for refugees to enter the United States, because they would be counted as immigrants who needed highly limited quota spots. The next section discusses the efforts of advocates to overturn these effects, to de-couple American immigration policy from ethnonationalist goals, and to therefore make it easier for refugees to arrive and resettle in the United States.

III. Advocates create change: Refugee resettlement from 1924 to 1975

Immediately upon the passage of the Immigration Act of 1924, advocates began working to overturn it. This victory would come almost forty years later, with the Immigration Act of 1965, a signature and resounding victory of civil rights-era activism. The interim years, however, saw deep challenges for those — especially refugees — hoping to make lives in the United States. This era also saw the creation and galvanization of unlikely and savvy coalitions of activists and concerned citizens who remained committed to welcoming newcomers.

The fact that the Immigration Act of 1924 included refugees in the national origins quotas meant that, to admit refugees into the United States, bureaucrats needed to decide to prioritize them over other entry applicants or policymakers needed to create new pathways for them to enter. Therefore, refugee policy making became ad hoc, piecemeal, and comprised largely of temporary executive orders and legislation.

The end of World War II incentivized the creation of many such refugee policies, as the national origins quotas were far too low to allow the United States to have a significant refugee resettlement program. For context, the Immigration Act of 1924 allowed for only 13,000 new arrivals from eastern Europe per year (Yang 2020, 106), while, even after the end of massive efforts to return displaced Europeans to their homelands, 1.2 million eastern Europeans remained displaced by the end of 1945 (National World War II Museum).

One of the first significant short-term refugee policies passed during this period was an executive order known as the Truman Directive (White House 1945). In terms of numbers of refugees resettled, it barely made a dent, as it only mandated that people displaced by war be given preferential treatment in the national origins quotas (Yang 2020, 107). However, it set enduring precedents for refugee resettlement in the United States. It created a system in which sponsoring humanitarian organizations could agree to help resettle refugees — to do so, these organizations needed to guarantee that refugees would not become public charges, pay for the cost of their travel to the United States, and logistically and financially facilitate their resettlement and integration into an American community (Yang 2020, 105). This was the first step in the creation of the voluntary organization system of refugee resettlement we use today. President Truman, and the coalescing circle of largely Jewish refugee advocacy groups, knew that this was not nearly enough. In his State of the Union speech in 1947, Truman said,

> insofar as admitting displaced persons is concerned, I do not feel that the United States has done its part. Only about 5,000 of them have entered this country since May, 1946. The fact is that the executive agencies are now doing all that is reasonably possible under the limitation of the existing law and established quotas. Congressional assistance in the form of new legislation is needed. (Truman 1947)

On February 4, 1948, Governor Val Peterson formed the Nebraska Committee on Displaced Persons. Its purpose was to assist with the relocation of European refugees throughout the state (Kelly 2023).

In April 1947, Representative William J. Stratton, a Republican from Illinois, introduced legislation to admit 400,000 displaced persons into the United States (Yang 2020, 110). The bill language was written by the Citizens' Committee on Displaced Persons, a newly founded coalition of Jewish activist organizations, which raised a million dollars to get it passed (Ibid.). A version of the bill that had been amended almost beyond recognition passed on June 25, 1948, as the Displaced Persons Act of 1948 (Ibid., 114). The bill authorized the admission of 200,000 displaced persons; however, crucially, only displaced Europeans who had entered Germany, Austria, or Italy before December 22, 1945, were eligible for admission (Ibid.). By the president's estimate, this excluded 90 percent of displaced Jews in Europe, as the vast majority of those who survived the Nazi camps — which were largely concentrated in eastern Europe — would not have arrived at the designated three countries by the deadline (Ibid.).

Truman signed the bill "in order not to delay further the beginning of a resettlement program," (Yang 2020, 114) but roundly criticized it as an "anti-Semitic, anti-Catholic law." (Ibid., 117) Two years later, Truman signed into law a follow-up bill that admitted 400,000 refugees, most of whom ended up being eastern Europeans displaced by World War II, and Soviet citizens escaping communism (Ibid., 139). Indeed, the two earliest refugee resettlement agencies in Nebraska—St. Joseph's Church in Kimball and United Catholic Social Services in Lincoln and Omaha—primarily resettled Soviet refugees (Indochina Refugees—Interagency Task Force).

Shortly thereafter, the international community leapt forward in international cooperation to support refugees. The nascent United Nations realized the world would need a permanent legal and institutional framework to deal with the global problem of forced displacement (Jaeger 2001, 732-736). In 1950, the UN General Assembly voted to create the United Nations High Commissioner for Refugees (UNHCR), which was originally meant to be a three-year-long position to resettle Europeans displaced by World War II (Loescher, and Milner 2013, 20). As the UNHCR began its work, diplomats negotiated the creation of the 1951 Convention Relating to the Status of Refugees, which defined a refugee as

> [a person who], owing to well-founded fear of persecution for reasons of race, religion, nationality, membership of a particular social group or political opinion, is outside the country of his nationality and is unable or, owing to such fear, is unwilling to avail himself of the protection of that country; or who, not having a nationality and being outside the country of his former habitual residence as a result of such events, is unable or, owing to such fear, is unwilling to return to it (UN General Assembly 1951, Article 1, Section 2).

Since then, the UNHCR has determined whether individuals meet the criteria for legal refugee status, either on its own or by overseeing countries' internal processes of refugee status determination. Every person who is resettled in the United States as a refugee has been determined to fit this legal definition, either by the UNHCR itself, or by a country working in consultation with the UNHCR and according to the definition quoted above. Once a person is legally determined to be a refugee, the UNHCR plays a key role in finding them a lasting home. If a refugee is unwilling to go back to the country they fled, and if they are not welcome in the country where they sought refuge, the UNHCR may help them resettle in a third country that is willing to offer them permanent residence. Most of the refugees the United States has resettled had an application for resettlement submitted by the UNHCR.

Alarmed by the 600,000 refugee admissions spots created in 1947 and 1948, anti-immigration lawmakers and advocacy groups mobilized to pass legislation that would reinforce the Immigration Act of 1924. This nativist coalition countered the charge of being racially exclusionary by including a key provision in the new bill: the abolition of race-based barriers to becoming a naturalized American citizen (Silverman 1980, 28). This provision had become deeply important to Japanese-American advocacy groups, especially considering the remarkable service and sacrifices Japanese-American soldiers had given during World War II, even as members of their communities were forcibly detained in internment camps.[2]

Beyond the abolition of the barrier to naturalized citizenship for people of color, the bill retained the national origins quota system almost exactly as it had been created in 1924, but slightly increased the quotas given to many Asian countries — most of which had been given a quota of *zero* in the 1924 legislation — and commensurately decreased the quota slots given to African and Caribbean countries (Yang 2020, 170-171). In a show of anti-immigrant legislators' determination and the American public's uneasiness about immigration, the House and Senate voted to override Truman's veto, and the Immigration and Nationality Act of 1952 became law (Ibid., 171). Those who wanted to welcome immigrants and refugees had a new hurdle to overcome.

In 1953, President Eisenhower signed a law designed to admit 200,000 more refugees, but the man put in charge of administering refugee admis-

---

2. For an excellent discussion of this, see Yang 2020, 161-165.

sions was well-known for his anti-immigrant sentiment, so the pace of refugee admissions was predictably glacial (Yang 2020, 201-202). The subsequent decade saw three more laws passed by Congress around refugee policy — in August 1957, July 1960, and June 1962 — but these laws mostly adjusted legal definitions and bureaucratic procedures for refugee resettlement and resulted in only a few thousand additional resettled refugees.

The Democratic Party took aim at the national origins system in its 1960 election platform, which read, "The national-origins quota system of limiting immigration contradicts the founding principles of this nation. It is inconsistent with our belief in the rights of man." (Democratic Party Platforms) President Kennedy took up this torch in the summer of 1963, a year known for civil rights activism and calls for racial inclusion, when he asked Congress to eliminate the national origins quota system (Yang 2020, 206). A few months later, President John F. Kennedy was assassinated, and President Lyndon B. Johnson, a legendarily effective legislator, succeeded him. Immediately upon hearing this news, one of the most committed anti-immigration senators said, "Good God, Lyndon's President. He's gonna pass a lot of this damn fool stuff" (Yang 2020, 229).

The Johnson administration and pro-immigrant advocates went to work on immigration reform almost immediately. Their efforts coincided with the anti-immigration coalition's growing discontent with the national origins quota system. This was not because of any ideological change but because they had figured out it failed to keep immigrants out. The reformulated Immigration and Nationality Act of 1952 should have allowed 2 million immigrants into the country by 1965, and the vast majority of them should have been white (Yang 2020, 249). However, between 1952 and 1962, 3.5 million newcomers came to the United States (Ibid.). This is because the national origins quota system, coupled with the fact that it did nothing to accommodate the exceptional circumstances of refugees, incentivized politicians to create a series of executive orders and laws to create more slots to admit newcomers, many of whom were refugees.

The anti-immigration contingent decided it would be more effective to fight to prioritize family reunification over skills as criteria for admission in a new immigration system. Their logic was that since existing immigrant populations in the United States were still overwhelmingly white, family reunification was a better bet to preserve whiteness in the United States, whereas prioritizing immigrants with skills that would contribute to the country would more likely lead to more immigrants of color entering the United States (Yang 2020, 250). They also wanted, for the first time in American history, a cap on the number of immigrant arrivals from the Western Hemisphere (Yang 2020, 250). They agreed to immigration reform if these priorities were met, and they are enshrined in the final version of the bill.

On October 9, 1965, the Immigration and Nationality Act of 1965 became law. It eliminated the national origins quota system and replaced it with a system that prioritized family reunification, the admission of immigrants with special skills, and refugees (Silverman 1980, 28). It also, for the first time, created a permanent legal basis for admitting refugees, which it defined as "those persecuted on account of race, religion, or political opinion; those uprooted by natural calamity; those fleeing communist or communist-dominated countries; and those fleeing the Middle East" (Garcia 2017, 4). This explicitly linked the United States' refugee policy to its Cold War ideology and foreign policy imperatives.

IV. The Vietnam War changes refugee resettlement

With the opening of immigrant and refugee admissions facilitated by the Immigration and Nationality Act of 1965, there was a commensurate increase in immigration to Nebraska during the 1970s (U.S. Senate 1975). This period also marks the creation of refugee resettlement hubs in Nebraska.

Faced with a declining population, especially rapidly shrinking rural populations, brain drain, and encouragement from the federal government, Nebraska, much like its neighbors, opened its doors to new arrivals. While there was a steady stream of refugees and immigrants who had made Nebraska their home in the post-WWII period, it was the Vietnam War's end that played an important role in Nebraska's immigration story. Despite polls indicating a majority of Americans at the time were against resettling Vietnamese refugees, close to 590,000 Indochinese were eventually resettled in the U.S. (DeSilver 2015).

In May 1975, Congress passed the Indochina Migration and Refugee Assistance Act, which set aside $455,000,000 (in addition to amounts otherwise available) to help evacuate refugees from South Vietnam and Cambodia and provided legal protections and financial assistance to resettle over 130,000

Vietnamese and Cambodians in the United States (U.S. Senate 1975). In late 1975, President Ford asked Congress to support him in helping resettle thousands of refugees who fled Vietnam after American troops withdrew (U.S. Senate 1975). By 1976, approximately 130,000 of these refugees lived in the United States (HEW Task Force for Indochina Refugees 1976, 1a). By the end of 1975, the Nebraska Unicameral endorsed and supported the organizations that sought to bring Vietnamese and Cambodian refugees ("Resolution Revived" 1975).

The Vietnamese arrivals were culturally, linguistically, and racially different from other immigrant groups in Nebraska. Most Americans were disenchanted by the length and death toll of the Vietnam War and disinterested in accepting so many refugees (Kneeland 1975). A national Gallup Poll asked 1,491 adults in 300 locations across the United States "whether evacuated South Vietnamese should be permitted to live in the United States"; 36 percent of Americans said yes, and 54 percent said no (Kneeland 1975). Many feared the refugees' arrival would further exacerbate the country's high unemployment rate, which at the time was 8.7 percent (Kneeland 1975).

V. The Refugee Act of 1980 and the Creation of the Office of Refugee Resettlement

It is clear by this point that until the Vietnam War, the American approach to refugee admissions was ad hoc and piecemeal. Various parts of the government would create specific, short-term policies to deal with individual refugee crises. The displacement generated by the Vietnam War — and the very appropriate responsibility some American citizens and policymakers felt to respond to that displacement — showed the necessity of a comprehensive, permanent refugee admissions program. This program was created with the passage of the Refugee Act of 1980. (Refugee Act of 1980).

Groundwork for the current United States' refugee admissions program was laid in 1975, when the State Department contracted with nine major nonprofit organizations — known as voluntary organizations, or VOLAGS, in the refugee admissions community — to resettle Vietnamese refugees (Silverman 1980, 29). At first, the State Department paid VOLAGs $500 for every Vietnamese refugee they resettled; this was meant to cover basic costs of living for the first two months of resettlement (Ibid., 30). The following year, as it became clear that VOLAGs resettled many refugees who were displaced by conflicts other than the Vietnam War, the State Department altered the policy — it would pay $250 per refugee resettled, regardless of their origin (Wright 1981, 161). This $250 was meant to cover the same costs, for the same period that the previous year's $500 had. This discrepancy exemplifies an ongoing tension — on the one hand, there are increasing demands and ambitions to resettle and integrate refugees, but on the other hand, there are consistent imperatives to do the work of resettlement with financial support that remains stagnant, or even shrinks, despite rising resettlement needs.

In response to the challenges and opportunities of resettling Vietnamese refugees, a national coalition of refugee resettlement organizations called the National Coalition for Indochinese Refugee Resettlement was formed (Silverman 1980, 33). Throughout the 1970s, the coalition advocated for federal legislation and funding to meet the resettlement needs created by the Vietnam War (Ibid., 33-34). Coalition members' experiences lobbying for ad hoc legislation and funding convinced them of the need for a permanent refugee resettlement program, and they turned their advocacy toward that goal (Ibid.).

At the same time, Nebraskans who were committed to welcoming refugees worked to respond to the massive need created by the Vietnam War. In September 1975, Governor J. James Exon was asked to accept 300 refugee families, or around 1,600 individuals. The federal government promised to reimburse states for all costs of welfare, medical, and social services for Vietnamese and Cambodian refugees (States Refugee 1975). Still, Exon initially rejected the federal request, saying he did not want the refugees to be jammed "down the throats of Nebraskans" ("Exon rejects" 1975). By that fall, Exon had changed his stance and challenged Nebraskans to help empty the refugee camps by taking in the 300 families (Exon: Refugee Volunteers Best 1975).

In February 1979, the first version of the Refugee Act was introduced in Congress (Silverman 1980, 34). Iowa politicians played a leading role in advocating for its passage. In response to advocacy from the Coalition, President Carter appointed former Iowa Senator Dick Clark to be Ambassador-at-Large and Coordinator of US Refugee Affairs (Ibid., 40). Governor Robert Ray of Iowa wrote impassioned letters to other governors asking them to accept more refugees. Nebraska Governor Charles Thone responded that he would have the State Office of Planning and Programming look into it. (Accepting the refugees 1979)

At the same time, some Nebraskan citizens increased their efforts to help resettle refugees. During the fall of 1979, they founded the Nebraska Interchurch Refugee Task Force to coordinate ongoing resettlement activities (First of Viet 1979), and an assembly representing 42 Lincoln churches voted to establish the Lincoln Refugee Committee (Church Fellowship 1979).

On March 17, 1980, the Refugee Act was signed into law, and our current system of refugee resettlement was born. The act defined a refugee as

> any person who is outside any country of such person's nationality or, in the case of a person having no nationality, is outside any country in which such person last habitually resided, and who is unable or unwilling to return to, or is unable and unwilling to avail himself or herself of the protection of that country because of persecution or a well-founded fear of persecution on account of race, religion, nationality, membership in a particular social group or political opinion (Refugee Act of 1980).

The definition clearly used the concept outlined in the 1951 Refugee Convention (UNHCR "Refugee Convention, 1951," [7]; UN General Assembly 1951, Article I). It created government infrastructure to admit and resettle people who met this definition and authorized funds for temporary assistance to help refugees integrate socially and become economically self-sufficient.

The refugee resettlement system created by the Refugee Act works as follows. Every year, the president sets an annual refugee resettlement ceiling. This number functions as both a limit and a goal for the number of refugees that the United States will resettle the following year. The UNHCR first identifies refugees who would be strong candidates for resettlement, and then the United States government and NGOs assist in an extremely extensive process of vetting to choose among the resettlement applications submitted by the UNHCR (U.S. Citizenship and Immigration 2025; United States Refugee Admissions 2025). As of 2025, refugees applying to be resettled in the United States undergo multiple security screenings (Ibid.). The process can take many months or years.

Once a refugee is approved for admission into the United States, they are matched with one of 10 VOLAGs (voluntary organizations). The assigned VOLAG coordinates with its local affiliates to ensure the refugee is welcomed when they land at an airport on a flight for which they are expected to reimburse the State Department once they achieve economic self-sufficiency (Almy 2025). Failure to pay off their airfare debt has been used as evidence of "lack of character" to deny refugees' applications for citizenship (Ibid.). Then, the VOLAG provides the refugee with transportation to a home, economic assistance, the public benefits to which they are entitled, and the cultural, language, and employment training they will need to begin integrating into their new community. The day-to-day work of helping individual refugees resettle is done entirely by VOLAGs' local offices and staff members, as well as community members who care.

Upon passage of the Refugee Act, Nebraskans organized to enhance their capacity to support the local, hands-on work of refugee resettlement. On June 10, 1980, the Interchurch Ministries of Nebraska founded the Refugee Coordinating Council of Nebraska (Refugee Council 1980). The council received $118,000 in federal funding for English and job training courses for refugees and was promised an additional $280,986 to create an information and resource center for refugees, which was created in July of that year (Fussell 1980). However, in another instance of the ongoing mismatch between resettlement needs and government funding, the resettlement center shut down during the fall of 1980, due to a hiring freeze imposed by the governor and a lack of promised funding from the state welfare department (Welfare officials 1980).

Shortly after passage of the Refugee Act, there was a shortfall of federal funds to support refugee resettlement, and by April 1981, the federal government had recalled all refugee resettlement funds (Shortfall 1981). As a result, by the end of the spring of 1981, Nebraska was poised to run out of money to meet refugees' most basic needs (Ibid.).

Economic pressure on refugees increased over the next two years with two key policy changes. First, Congress passed legislation that made refugees' receipt of benefits contingent on their employment, which meant refugees would need to get jobs much more quickly upon resettlement (Brown and Scribner 2014, 106). Second, the federal government reduced the period for which refugees would be eligible for cash and medical assistance (Ibid.). Both changes coincided with increased suspicion of policies that were perceived as social welfare, which led both American citizens (Haines and Rosenblum 2010) and policymakers (Holman 1996, 22-24) to see refugee assistance as fostering unhealthy dependence on the government, the latest manifestation of the very old "public charge" concern.

National VOLAG	Nebraska Affiliates
Bethany Christian Services	None
Church World Service	None
Episcopal Migration Ministries	None
Ethiopian Community Development Council	Omaha: Refugee Empowerment Center
HIAS	None
International Rescue Committee	None
Lutheran Immigration and Refugee Service	Lincoln: Lutheran Family Services of Nebraska, Inc. Lexington: Lutheran Family Services of Nebraska Omaha: Lutheran Family Services
US Committee for Refugees and Immigrants	None
United States Conference of Catholic Bishops	Lincoln: Catholic Social Services
World Relief	None

National and Nebraska VOLAGs. Chart created by Emira Ibrahimpašić and Julia Reilly.

V: Country Case Studies

Country Case Selection

Since the passage of the Refugee Act of 1980, Nebraska has resettled about 24,000 refugees. They hail from Afghanistan, Albania, Bhutan, Burma, Burundi, Cambodia, the Republic of the Congo, Cuba, Czechoslovakia, the Democratic Republic of the Congo, El Salvador, Eritrea, Ethiopia, Guatemala, Haiti, Hungary, India, Iran, Iraq, Laos, Lebanon, Liberia, Libya, Mauritania, Nepal, Nigeria, Palestine, Poland, Sierra Leone, Somalia, South Sudan, the Soviet Union, Sudan, Syria, Thailand, Togo, Ukraine, Vietnam, Yugoslavia, and Zimbabwe (For sourcing information, see footnote 1, page 259).

It is impossible to discuss all these refugee groups, and their experiences in Nebraska, in a single chapter, so we have chosen to focus on five: Vietnamese, Yugoslavs, Iraqis, Burmese, and Sudanese. We chose these five groups because they all have comparatively high populations who resettled in Nebraska; combined, they comprise 64 percent of refugees resettled in Nebraska. We also chose them for their geographic diversity, and because their arrivals coincide with distinct eras in Nebraska's history of refugee resettlement. As the graph below shows, during the 1980s, the predominant group of refugees arriving in Nebraska were Vietnamese (red line). Then, during the middle of the 1990s, refugees from Iraq (yellow line), then Yugoslavia (blue line), and then Sudan (green line) began to arrive in large numbers. In the early 2000s, there was an uptick in the arrival of Sudanese refugees; in the mid-2000s and early 2010s, there was a significant increase in the arrival of Burmese refugees (orange line); and in the mid-2010s, there was an increase in the arrival of Iraqi refugees.

A HISTORY OF RACE AND RACISM IN NEBRASKA

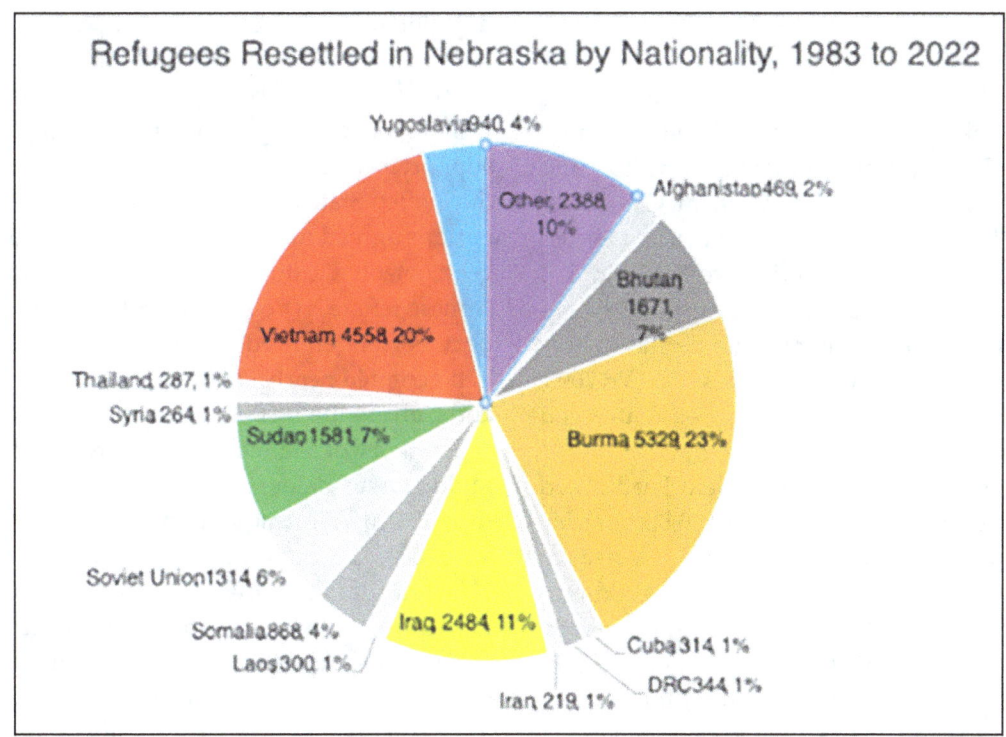

Refugees Resettled in Nebraska by Nationality, 1983 to 2022.

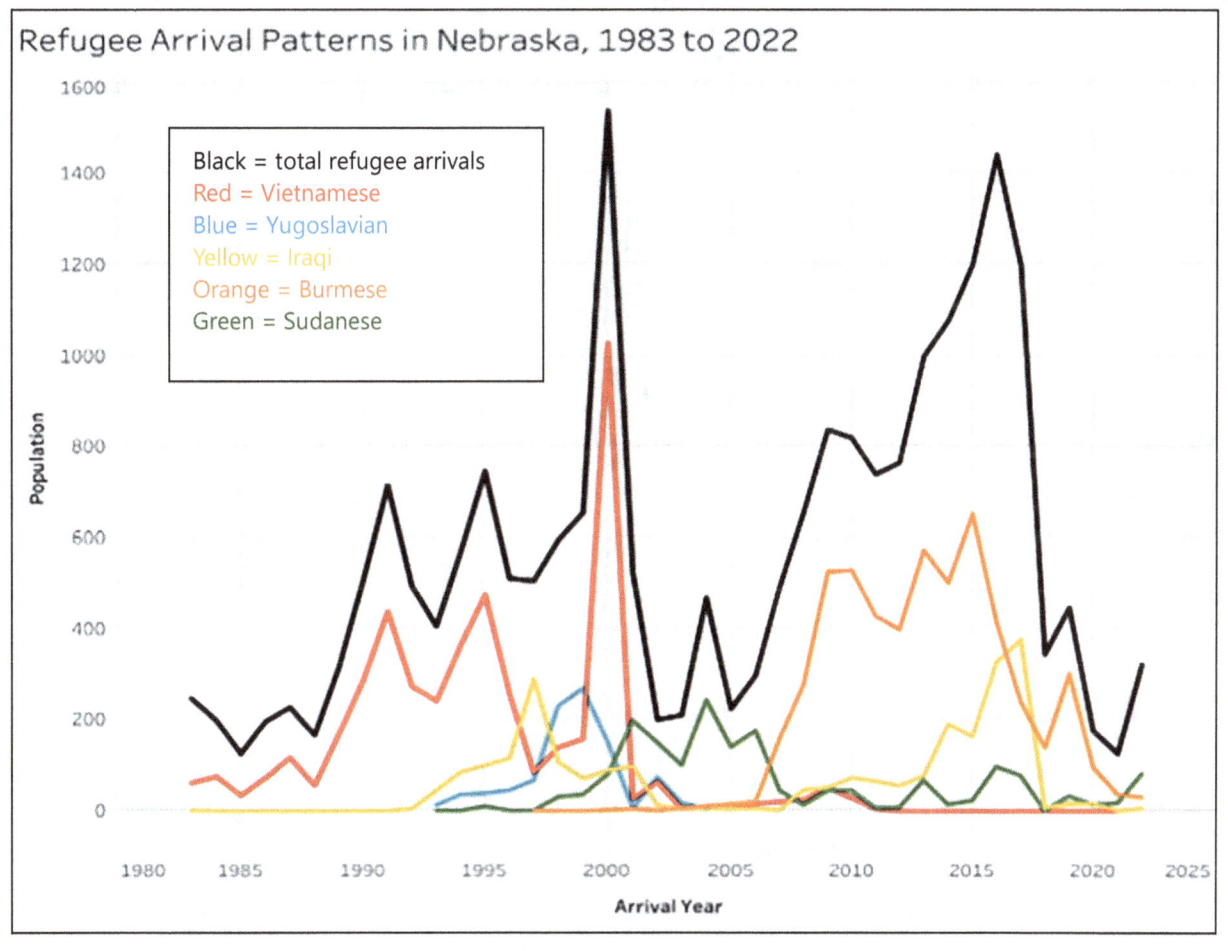

Arrivals in Nebraska by Group and Dates. Graph created by Emira Ibrahimpašić and Julia Reilly

Vietnam

The end of the war in Vietnam created one of the largest humanitarian crises the world had seen since World War II. It is estimated that between 1975 and 1995, over 3 million people fled Vietnam, Cambodia, and Laos (Vo 2006, 2). While many made it across to safety in neighboring countries like Thailand and Singapore, others escaped on boats towards Malaysia and Japan. There are no accurate numbers as to how many perished at sea trying to get to safety (Vo 2006, 2). Those that remained behind were persecuted and at times tortured.

As mentioned previously, President Ford asked Americans to open their doors to 130,000 people fleeing Vietnam and Cambodia. Despite his pleas to do something about the crisis, constituent communication to the White House and Congress mostly opposed assisting the Vietnamese (Binder 1975). In a closed-door session with Congress, then Assistant Secretary of State Philip Habib said the United States planned to evacuate 17,600 Vietnamese people who worked for the United States government, and the number would likely rise to 130,000 if their dependents were also accepted (Vo 2006, 64). Despite knowing the communists would likely commit mass murder, the Department of State would simply "ignore the rest of the population" (Ibid.). The lack of support toward Vietnamese refugees was not only in the United States, but across the globe. Neighboring nations agreed to accept very few Vietnamese refugees; notably, Australia agreed to accept only 100 Vietnamese refugees (Vo 2006, 124.) To garner public support, Ford referenced the fact that the United States had accepted nearly 700,000 refugees from Hungary and Cuba in the 1950s and 1960s.

The story of Vietnamese Americans is one of very rapid growth. Before the evacuation, there were fewer than 15,000 Vietnamese Americans (Zhou and Bankston 2000, 1). According to the U.S. Immigration and Naturalization Services, the United States admitted only 4,561 Vietnam-born persons between 1961 and 1970; most were exchange students, trainees, or diplomats on nonimmigrant visas (Skinner, 1980; Zhou and Bankston 2000, 1). There were a few wives of United States servicemen, and almost no children (Ibid.) After the fall of Saigon in 1975, Vietnamese people became one of the United States' largest ethnic groups

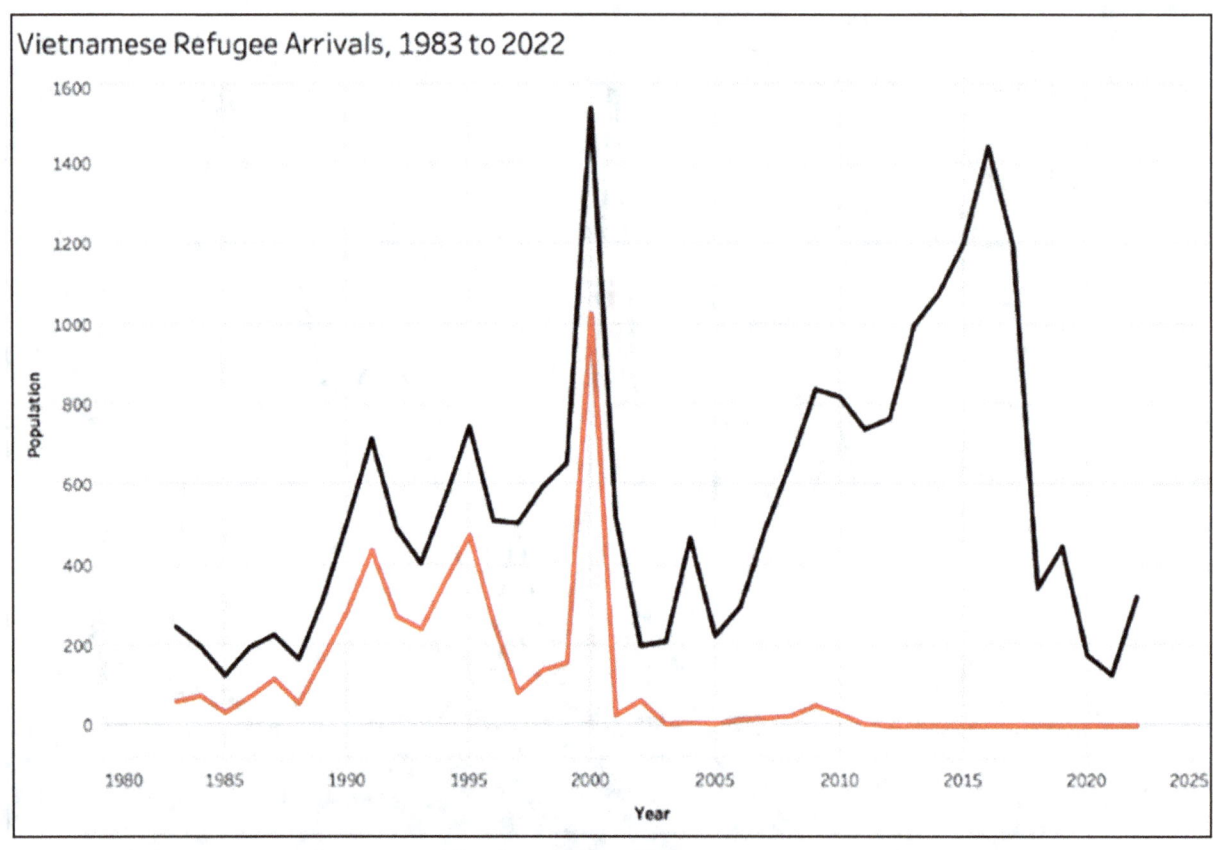

Vietnamese Refugee Arrivals, 1983 to 2022. Graph created by Emira Ibrahimpašić and Julia Reilly.
Black = total refugee arrivals in Nebraska

and thus had heightened visibility (Zhou and Bankston 2000, 1). By 1990, the Vietnamese numbered, by official figures, over 615,000 people, which is a dramatic underestimation as it excludes about 200,000 Sino-Vietnamese people (Rumbaut 1995a, cited in Zhou and Bankston 2000, 1). As of 2009, there were approximately 652,000 Vietnamese Americans living in the United States (Fix, Hooper and Zong 2017, 12).

Those refugees who made it to the United States were first housed at various military bases. Four reception centers were opened: Camp Pendleton in California, Fort Indiantown Gap in Pennsylvania, Eglin Air Force Base in Florida, and Fort Chafee in Arkansas (Vo 2006, 78). The first wave of refugees did not stay at the camps long; indeed, many were resettled by December 1975 (Vo 2006, 81). Some of these first refugees made their way to Nebraska. Among the first were medical doctors and their families.

Soon after refugees began arriving to United States, three Nebraska legislators, including Senator John W. De Camp of Neligh (District 40), Senator Richard H. Maresh from Milligan (District 32), and Senator Thomas C. Kennedy from Newman Grove (District 21) went to Camp Pendleton to recruit medical doctors to resettle in Nebraska (Nebraska Legislature. Transcripts. May 11, 1977). They were quickly granted authorization by the Legislature Executive Board to travel because they were worried Australia and Canada, which were already sending planes to Camp Pendleton to get physicians, would beat them to it (Doctor Hunt 1975). They were given $50,000 for travel and various recruitment events over the year. Their efforts were successful, and around 28 Vietnamese physicians relocated to Nebraska. They were primarily intended for rural parts of the state that at the time were facing a significant physician shortage, with an estimated 53 out of 93 Nebraska counties lacking medical doctors (Scramble for medics 1975). Twenty-eight communities submitted a request for a doctor (Viet Refugees 1975). A story of the first Vietnamese doctor arriving in Albion, Nebraska, even made national news (NBC News Archive 1975). Within a year and a half of their arrival in Nebraska, nearly all the physicians passed their national and state exams, including language proficiency exams, and all were practicing across rural areas of Nebraska (Nebraska Legislature. Transcripts. May 11, 1977). The first two Vietnamese doctors arrived in May 1975 in Beatrice (Mayor accepts 1975). They were a husband-and-wife team: Dr. Bao and Dr. Phuong (Ibid.).

By February 1976, 1,219 Vietnamese refugees had resettled in Nebraska (1,219 Refugees 1976). In addition to the physicians program, Nebraskan communities began sponsoring other Vietnamese refugees. Nebraska had a strong pull because of job abundance and many employers' willingness to train refugees despite language barriers. Moreover, local churches worked to equip refugees' new homes with furniture and other necessities. Volunteers organized English language classes as well as job preparation classes. By 1979, the Catholic diocese created a Vietnamese parish in Lincoln to accommodate the 30 Vietnamese Catholic families in Lincoln (Reeves 2004). Today, there is also a Protestant Vietnamese congregation at the Vietnamese Alliance Church, and the Linh Quang Buddhist Temple hosts a large Vietnamese community.

With the passage of time, the sympathy and financial support for arriving refugees began to wane across the nation and in Nebraska. An August 1977 poll reported most Americans opposed admitting 15,000 Southeast Asian refugees (Americans oppose 1977). Survey respondents felt the resettlement of the initial wave of refugees had been too difficult and refugees struggled to integrate into American society, with many references to refugees who remained on welfare (Ibid.). Most importantly, on June 30, 1977, federal support for refugees ended, which meant around 115 Nebraskan refugee families would no longer qualify for aid and would practically be left destitute (Wirth 1977). Despite the national feelings about Vietnamese integration, those who had resettled in Lincoln seemed to have integrated well in 1977, with only a few incidents of tensions, mainly among high school students (Camden 1977). However, not all refugees were doing well: some found themselves in extreme poverty with little resources and help from agencies. For example, a family of 14 recently arrived Vietnamese refugees was found to be living on very little money, with ill-fitting clothes and broken furniture (Dittrick 1978). Little had been done to help them.

Despite the polls, interest in sponsoring more refugees in Nebraska remained steady because of their impact on communities. Far more Vietnamese doctors than expected remained after their obligation under the resettlement program, and small communities across the state continued to ask to sponsor more refugees (Wirth 1979). Resettlement agencies reported a surge of interest and expanded their operations from resettling two families per month to eight to ten families per month (Wirth 1979). Leaders of resettlement efforts did not have issues finding sponsors for resettled refugees (Fussell 1979). As a result, by the summer of 1979, around 1,800 refugees had been resettled across Nebraska. While Nebraska did not have a centralized, federally funded program like Iowa's, there was interest in creating a similar program because funds to help resettle refugees were running out. Partially to that end, the Nebraska Interchurch Refugee Task Force was established in September of 1979 to ramp up the refugee resettlement efforts (First of Viet 1979).

As more refugees arrived in small communities across Nebraska, tensions arose, and there were reports of discrimination and harassment. In Tecumseh, where 57 Indochinese refugees settled to work at Campbell's Soup Company, they received little welcome and struggled with mistreatment and poor living conditions (Mulvey 1983). Similar situations were reported across the state, where there were reportedly 2,400 Indochinese refugees by 1983 (Ibid.).

By the end of 1980s, most Vietnamese refugee resettlement programs were scaled down, and many refugees found themselves in nearby countries that were no longer as welcoming as they once had been (Eng 1989). This also slowed the arrival of Vietnamese refugees to the United States and Nebraska (Ibid.). Racism remained a persistent challenge; for instance, in November of 1990 there were reports of threatening letters sent by the Ku Klux Klan of Nebraska to the Vietnamese National List Association in Omaha (Kelly 1990). We could find little news coverage of this incident, nor any evidence that anyone was held accountable.

In 1992, it was estimated that Lincoln's Southeast Asian population was 3,500 to 4,500 individuals. Lincoln was a prime resettlement city because of the availability of jobs, good schools, and adult education programs (Reeves 1992). The arrival of the Vietnamese in Lincoln meant many Asian-owned businesses opened, including grocery stores and restaurants (Ibid.). Local churches started services in Vietnamese, and the Lincoln Police Department hired two Vietnamese police officers (Ibid.). Since the 1990s, the Vietnamese and broader Southeast Asian refugee population of Nebraska has prospered. Their stories exemplify resilience, hard work, and a desire to build better futures for themselves and their families. Today, there are an estimated 9,000 people from Vietnam or of Vietnamese descent in Nebraska (Edwards 2013). Their contributions and successes can be found everywhere. They own multiple businesses that have revitalized north Lincoln (Edwards 2013). They have opened an Asian Community and Cultural Center (Who We Are...Asian 2023) in Lincoln that now serves refugees and immigrants from around the world, and they serve their community as physicians and other professionals (Bich Chau 2023).

Yugoslavia

The breakup of Yugoslavia began in the early 1990s because of political instability brought on by the death of President Josip Broz Tito, who failed to leave a successor but did leave economic instability and rising inflation. The political and economic instability, along with ethnoreligious differences and calls to ancient intergroup conflicts, were exploited by politicians to ensure their parties' political dominance. Nationalist rhetoric became part of daily life, fueling mistrust among people who had lived next to each other in harmony before and during Tito's reign. The dissolution of Yugoslavia took some time: Slovenia and Croatia declared independence on June 25, 1991, followed by Macedonia on September 8, 1991, then Bosnia and Herzegovina on March 3, 1992, and ending with the secession of the once Autonomous Region of Kosovo on February 17, 2008. Despite international recognition of these newly independent states, the central Yugoslavian government, which had been seated in Belgrade[3] since 1945, refused to let the partition occur and called on the National Army to intervene. The military intervention was unsuccessful, and after only a few days of fighting, Slovenia expelled the Belgrade-supported forces.

The situation was not as easy in neighboring Croatia, which had a relatively large Serb population, accounting for over 30 percent of the total population. With the support of the National Army and Belgrade, the Serb minority gained significant ground in the early part of the war. However, the newly acquired territories, which were now declared a proto-state within Croatia's borders called Srpska Krajina, came at a steep cost in human lives and property. Some of the earliest ethnonational cleansing occurred at the hands of Serb nationalist forces in places such as Vukovar, where thousands were murdered and the city was nearly leveled. The atrocities and destruction taking place across Croatia were soon to find their way across the border in Bosnia-Herzegovina.

---

3. Belgrade is now the capital of Serbia. Although, at the time, it was the capital of the central Yugoslavian government, it is a historically Serbian city, and a power center for the Serbian population.

A HISTORY OF RACE AND RACISM IN NEBRASKA

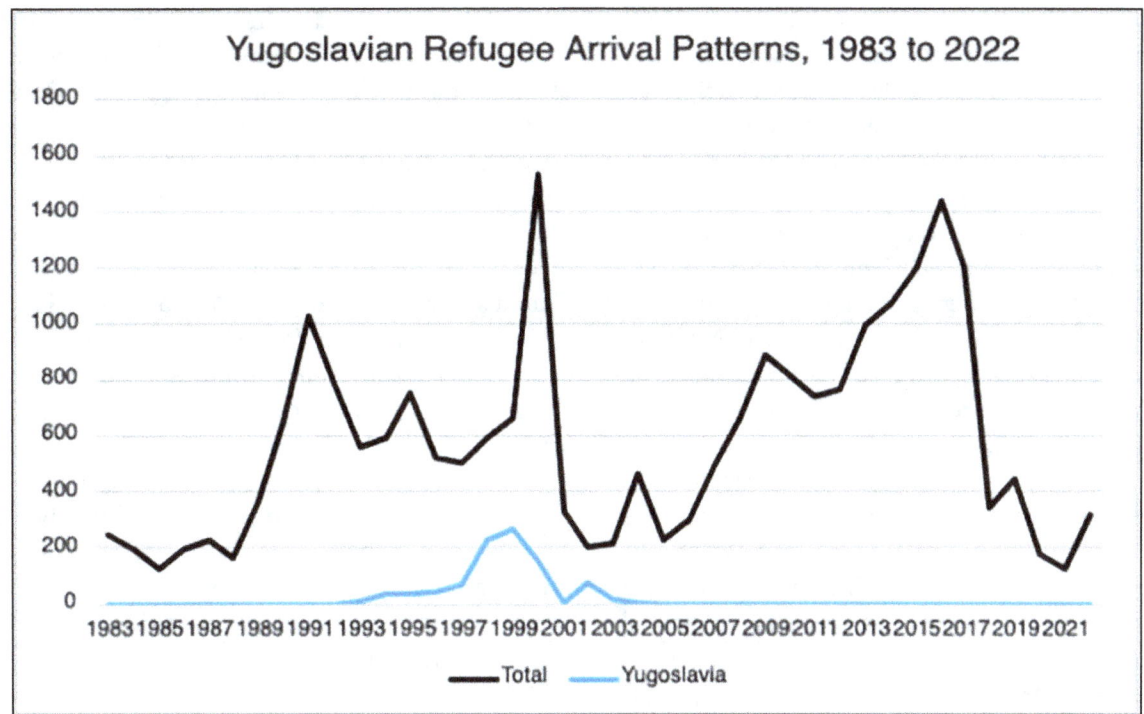

Yugoslavian Refugee Arrivals Patterns, 1983 to 2022. Graph created by Emira Ibrahimpašić and Julia Reilly. Black = total refugee arrivals in Nebraska

At the start of the war, Bosnia-Herzegovina was Yugoslavia's most diverse republic. The 1991 census indicated 43.5 percent of the population identified as Muslim, 31 percent as Serb, 17.4 percent as Croat, and the remaining 8 percent split between those who identified as Yugoslav or one of the many different ethnic groups that made Bosnia their home over the centuries, including Montenegrins, Roma, Albanians, and others. It was precisely this diversity that led to the outbreak of one of the bloodiest wars in Europe's modern history, in which ethnic cleansing and genocide were part of the strategy. The war left the country with close to 100,000 people dead, and 2.2 million people displaced ("Bosnia War Dead Announced" 2007; Internal Displacement Monitoring Centre, 2020). Many displaced Bosnians ended up in nearby states like Croatia, Serbia, Slovenia, and Hungary, while hundreds of thousands dispersed across western and northern Europe (Valenta and Strabac 2013).

The first Yugoslav refugees began arriving in the United States in 1991, with over 300,000 — primarily from Bosnia-Herzegovina — making their way to the United States in the 1990s. While it is often assumed most Bosnian refugees who made their way to the United States came in the early 1990s, that is not the case. It was in fact European repatriation policies that forced many to seek another move, leading to most Bosnian refugees arriving in the United States in the late 1990s.[4]

---

4. Refugee status is temporary by design, and there are three ways for a person to stop being a refugee: they can be resettled into a third country, like the United States; they can be reintegrated into the country to which they initially fled; or they can be repatriated or sent back to their country of origin. According to section 1c1 of the Refugee Convention, repatriation back to the country of origin should be voluntary. However, section 1c5 of the Refugee Convention indicates it is possible to force a refugee to return to their country of origin — and therefore revoke refugee status — if "the circumstances in connection with which he has been recognized as a refugee have ceased to exist" and if they no longer are deemed to have a well-founded fear of persecution.

In practice, it is left up to governments and international institutions to make the final determination as to whether a refugee still has well-founded fear of returning to their country of origin. Therefore, host countries — such as Germany in the 1990s — can claim the situation that created the forced displacement has been improved to the extent it is legal to compel refugees to repatriate. Indeed, in late 1996, Germany began repatriating Bosnian refugees after 16 German states complained they could not economically support resettlement (Drozdiak 1996). These repatriations included forced deportations (Ibid.). In this case, as in many others, arguments for repatriation were about reducing the economic burden of refugee resettlement, and not about the rights or well-being of the refugees themselves (Black 2002).

Yugoslav refugees had been arriving in the United States since the start of the Cold War. Those that came prior to 1991 requested asylum and protection from communism. However, a mass influx did not occur until the 1990s. At first the United States was reluctant to accept any refugees, but by the summer of 1992 the government agreed to accept those who escaped concentration camps and their families (U.S. to let 1992). While Croatia experienced a mass exodus of people during the war, none made their way to Nebraska; therefore, this section will focus on the Bosnians and Kosovars who were resettled in Nebraska.

The first recorded refugees from Bosnia-Herzegovina in Nebraska arrived in November 1992 in Wynot. Two teenagers, one of whom had been an exchange student, were forced to return to Nebraska after the war broke out (Allan 1992). The children and their mother were welcomed back to Wynot by the daughter's host family. No other refugees from the Yugoslav wars arrived again until later that year. Iowa, again, led the charge in refugee resettlement and began receiving refugees who escaped Bosnia's concentration camps in 1993 (Bosnians Head 1993). In 1993 large numbers of refugees left Bosnia, seeking shelter across Europe. Largely in response to rising anti-immigrant sentiments and rising animosity against foreigners, European countries increased restrictions on refugee arrivals (European Restrictions 1993). At the same time, to streamline refugee resettlement, the Lincoln Refugee Assistance Program overhauled its programming to help refugees better adjust to their new lives. The goal of the streamlined services was for refugees to stop using refugee services within three years of their arrival (Mabin 1994). These changes were supervised by the Nebraska State Refugee Coordinator.

On September 15, 1993, the first Bosnian refugees arrived in Lincoln. Emsud Deumić and his family were sponsored by First Plymouth Congregational Church of Lincoln (Leftin 1993). What made their resettlement easier was the fact that an exchange student from Bosnia who was studying at the University of Nebraska-Lincoln stayed when the war broke out. She was instrumental in helping welcome some of the first families to Lincoln.

Bosnian refugees continued to come to Nebraska, and by 1995 there were 71 Bosnian refugees that had been resettled, mainly in Lincoln and Omaha (Reeves 1995). However, the largest numbers of Bosnian refugees did not begin arriving until after the war ended in 1995. Most of the Bosnian refugees were successful in settling into their new lives in Nebraska, as most were provided with necessities and financial help (Hicks 2001).

Following the end of the war in Bosnia, the conflict extended into Kosovo. In 1999, with the war in Kosovo in full swing, Nebraska began to resettle ethnic Kosovars. By July, nearly 80 Kosovars were resettled in Nebraska, with more expected later in the year (Heinzl 1999). Most Bosnian and Kosovar refugees were Muslim, which was often discussed in the media (Muslic 2018). Their religious diversity provided an opportunity for Nebraska to establish itself as a welcoming space for all. The arrival of Bosnians and Kosovars, as well as Iraqis and other refugees from Muslim-majority countries, helped diversify the state's religious landscape. The Bosnian community organized, and throughout the next several years over 500 Bosnian refugees came to call Nebraska home.

Bosnians in Nebraska have settled across the state, and their contributions can be seen everywhere. Emsud Deumić, Lincoln's first Bosnian refugee (Andersen 2013), who survived a concentration camp, made a life in Lincoln that now includes a highly successful tailoring business called Emsud's. Bosnian youth opened a Bosnian Islamic Cultural Center called Sabah in 2008 (Younis 2013). Bosnians, such as Professor Lana Obradović, became university professors and community organizers (Konnath 2017) who now bring young people from Bosnia to learn about civic engagement and leadership at our universities through the University of Nebraska at Omaha's BOLD initiative (University of Nebraska at Omaha).

Iraq

Iraqis arrived in Nebraska during two main periods: the late 1990s and the mid-2010s. Their arrival was precipitated by distinct periods of upheaval and danger in Iraq, which tended to displace slightly distinct populations of Iraqis.

The first wave of Iraqis to arrive had been displaced due to brutal, violent government crackdowns that occurred throughout the late 1980s and 1990s. One such campaign, which forcibly displaced hundreds of thousands of Iraqi Kurds, began in 1988 and was known as the Anfal (Iraqi Anfal 1993). The Ba'athist regime in Iraq, led by Saddam Hussein, executed a violent militarized campaign whose stated purpose was to eliminate Kurdish rebel groups in northern Iraq. However, civilians were targeted to such an extent that Human Rights Watch characterized it as a genocide (Ibid.). Most of those displaced by the Anfal and its aftermath were Kurds, members of an ethnic and linguistic group that spans southwestern Turkey, northern Iraq, northeastern Iran, and northern Syria. Some of the people displaced were resettled

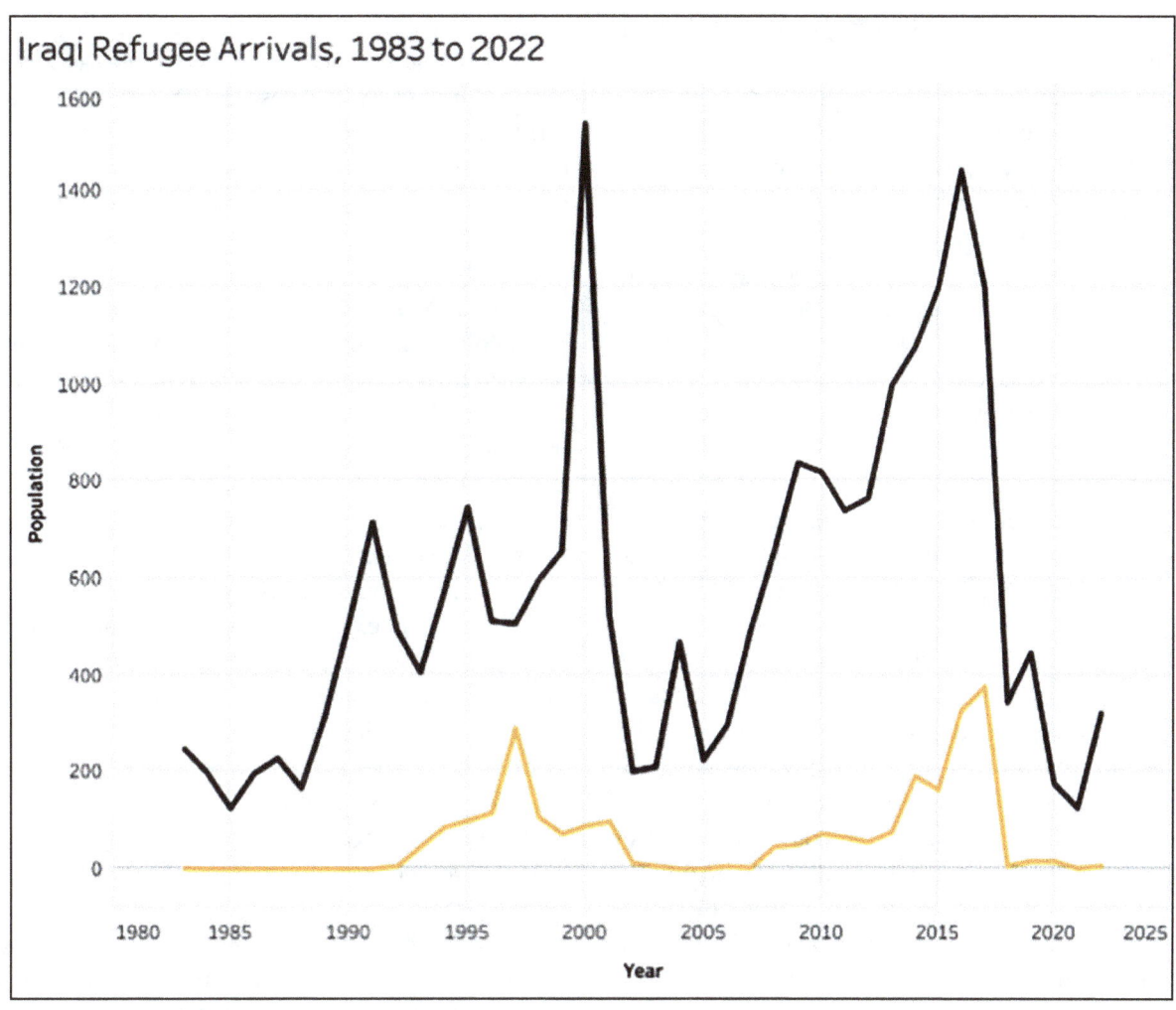

Iraqi Refugee Arrivals, 1983 to 2022. Graph created by Emira Ibrahimpašić and Julia Reilly.
Black = total refugee arrivals in Nebraska

as refugees in Nebraska, where there is a significant Kurdish community of about 100 families (Pembrick 2019).

Another significant era of persecution that displaced Iraqi families came in 1991. At the end of the Iran-Iraq War, opponents of the Ba'athist regime believed it was vulnerable to overthrow. A diverse array of ethnic and religious groups organized and, in many cases, took up arms against the regime, leading to a period of unrest in March and April 1991. These uprisings failed, and the government brutally punished the participants. The government's reprisals sent many families into hiding, or into refugee camps in Saudi Arabia and Jordan. Some of these families were eventually resettled in Nebraska (Loeb 2000; Hovey 2007).

The first few of these families arrived in 1994. The time lag between 1991 and 1994 reflects the fact that refugee journeys are long not only in terms of distance but in terms of time — many resettled refugees spend years in camps before they apply to be resettled in the United States (Burleigh 2010). As the first Iraqi refugees made lives and community in Lincoln, instability and displacement in Iraq continued. In May 1994, the Iraqi Kurdish Civil War began, when two Kurdish political parties — each with an armed group — fought against each other (Gunter 1996). This conflict displaced tens of thousands of civilians throughout the mid-1990s (Patriotic Union 2023).

By the early 2000s, the first wave of Iraqi refugees arriving in Lincoln subsided. They were largely Kurdish families, or families of those who had participated in the uprisings against Saddam Hussein's regime. By the end of 2000, there were about 1,000 such people in Lincoln, and they had begun forming a strong Iraqi community, including two Middle Eastern grocery stores and two mosques (Loeb 2000).[5] September

---

5. There are now three mosques in Lincoln: the Islamic Foundation of Lincoln, the American Islamic Center, and the Nebraska Islamic Foundation.

11, 2001, sent shockwaves through Nebraska's Iraqi refugee community and through Nebraska's broader Muslim communities, with many afraid to leave their homes for fear of persecution (Almy 2025). Women in the Lincoln Interfaith Council coordinated volunteers to accompany Middle Eastern women on public errands to make them feel safer (Ibid.).

The second wave of Iraqi refugees began arriving in Nebraska in 2008, after the State Department selected Lincoln as one of 10 target sites for resettling 7,000 Iraqi refugees with no known relatives in the United States (Hovey 2007). The strength of Lincoln's Iraqi community and refugee resettlement infrastructure enhanced the State Department's confidence that these refugees could find the support they needed. Reflecting this growth, in 2012, the Islamic Foundation of Lincoln began plans to build a new mosque (Bauer 2022).

These Iraqis had been displaced by the Second Gulf War, which began with the United States-led invasion of Iraq in 2003. This invasion led to widespread violence and instability — the United States-led coalition forces quickly overthrew the Ba'athist regime, but remnants of the regime included tens of thousands of men who had served in the Iraqi military who quickly joined anti-invasion insurgent forces. Islamic extremist terror organizations took advantage of the chaos to establish military presences in Iraq and try to recruit insurgents to their cause; their success in doing so, and the intensity of the resistance mounted by this ever-evolving constellation of armed groups, meant the war lasted many years longer than the United States had planned. Throughout, Iraqi civilians were displaced, and many arrived in Lincoln.

During this time, another important group of forcibly displaced Iraqis began to arrive in Nebraska: those who had worked as translators or interpreters for United States troops and who were unsafe in Iraq because of this work (U.S. Department of State Bureau of Consular Affairs). These men and their families arrived under a Special Immigrant Visa (SIV) program created for them. Congressman Jeff Fortenberry of Nebraska's First Congressional District was a key proponent of the creation of the SIV and helped usher its founding legislation through Congress (Martin 2017). The work of these interpreters was crucial in keeping American soldiers safe; as Lt. Colonel Michael Dosland wrote in a letter supporting the permanent residency application of his interpreter, "These individuals risked their lives for us. We trusted them implicitly, and they filled a very valuable role. My soldiers would have been paralyzed on the battlefield if it had not been for the sacrifices of Majid" (Hovey 2007). These new Nebraskans began arriving as part of the second wave of Iraqis but are not reflected in the graph above, which only shows people who first resettled in Nebraska as part of the United States' refugee resettlement program.

One of the radical insurgent groups created in the chaos that followed the United States-led invasion of Iraq evolved into the Islamic State of Iraq and Syria (ISIS). In the years after the United States declared the war over, ISIS gained considerable military strength in Iraq and Syria, and on August 3, 2014, ISIS troops stationed in northern Syria crossed the border into northern Iraq and began a campaign of genocide against the Yezidi people.

The Yezidis are a minority ethnic and religious group that has existed in northern Iraq for 4,000 years. They have experienced severe persecution, including scores of genocides, throughout their history ("Yezidis" Minority Rights Group). Many served as interpreters for American-led forces during the Iraq War, because they were likely to be targeted by Islamic insurgent groups for their faith, and because well-educated Yezidis tend to speak several languages.

When ISIS raided their villages in 2014, there were about 500,000 Yezidis living in northern Iraq. When ISIS began its genocide, about 200,000 of them were forcibly displaced. By 2018, more than 3,000 of them lived in Lincoln, Nebraska, which has the largest Yezidi community in the United States (Selby 2018; Wiltsey 2021). They constitute the majority of the second wave of Iraqi refugees in Nebraska, and the strength of the Yezidi community here has drawn Yezidis who had first resettled in other parts of the country to move to Nebraska. As Gulie Khalaf, the director of Yezidi programs for St. Matthew's Church, says, "Even though the resettlement office settles Yazidis elsewhere, they end up a year later or even six months later, giving up whatever they have collected and they end up coming to live here in Nebraska" (Williams 2017). More broadly, the Good Neighbor Community Center consistently estimates that 40 percent of the clients of its Middle East and North Africa Hope Project are refugees who moved to Lincoln after initially being resettled elsewhere (Almy 2025).

The Yezidis who come to Nebraska find not only strong social networks but key institutions the Yezidi community has built from the ground up. In 2017, they established a national cemetery for the Yezidi people in Malcolm, Nebraska (Bergin 2017; Conway 2017), a clear sign Nebraska had become a home (Pir 2019; Qassim 2019). At first, they met with resistance from the local community (Fox 2021), who feared a mosque would be built on the land, but diffused it with open conversations, in which Yezidi community members generously educated the local community on their faith and the role the cemetery would play (Qassim 2019).

Another significant challenge Iraqi refugees in Nebraska face is health. State surveys show Iraqi refugees report significantly poorer health than any other refugee group. While 30 percent of refugees overall reported health that was not good, 50 percent of Iraqi refugees did (Nebraska Office of Health Disparities and Health Equity 2020, 46). Further, health issues were much more likely to limit their lives: while 5 percent of refugees reported poor health had recently kept them from doing things they wanted, 41 percent of Iraqi refugees did (Ibid., 54).

They find home here not only in each other and in the community institutions they have built, but in Nebraska's landscape, which can physically resemble that of northern Iraq. As Hasan Khalil, a barbershop owner, said, "It's kind of like back home. It's smaller. You know, we lived in farms back in Syria. It looked, like, really safe. And that's what attracted me the most, besides the Yezidi community that we knew from back home" (Terrorized by ISIS 2021).

Iraqi refugees have formed communities, created institutions, and built careers that have made important contributions to Nebraska and the United States. In 2014, in the wake of the ISIS genocide, Yezidi activists from Lincoln who came together to stop the genocide formed Yazda, an international non-governmental organization that advocates for the preservation and protection of religious minority cultures in the Middle East, and justice and restoration for the Yezidi people (Krajeski 2018). Yazda created a Yazidi Cultural Center in Lincoln (Yazda), which coordinates community events, provides English classes, civics classes, financial assistance, immigration assistance, and general assistance adapting to American life (Hummel 2021). For youth, they offer Kurmanji classes (Khoudeida 2019), classes on Yezidi culture (Hummel 2021), and coordinate after school programs (Khoudeida 2019). Iraqi refugees also played a key role in establishing and growing the Islamic Foundation of Lincoln, which now provides vital language and community support to other Muslim refugees in Lincoln.[6] Iraqi refugees have also gone on to have extraordinary careers and make globally impactful contributions. For example, Wessam Al-Badry, a refugee from Iraq who was resettled in Lincoln, grew up to be an internationally recognized photojournalist whose work has shed light on human rights issues both in Nebraska (Estrin 2019) and around the world (Al-Badry).

Burma

The largest group of recently resettled refugees in Nebraska are ethnic minorities from Burma who have suffered decades of persecution by the government. To make their history clear, it is necessary to begin with a brief, hopefully clarifying, discussion of terminology. They come from a country officially called Myanmar, which is also called Burma. In this chapter, we will refer to it as Burma, as Myanmar was a name imposed in 1989 by the regime that is responsible for much of the suffering that Burmese Nebraskans have experienced.[7] Within the country, there are 135 ethnic groups that have been grouped by the government into eight "major national ethnic races" ("Composition of the Different..."). One of these is the Bamar ethnic group, which comprises about 68 percent of the country's population ("Burma" 2023). It is often transliterated into English as "Burman"; therefore, while "Burmese" refers to anyone from the country of Burma, "Burman" refers to a person of the majority ethnic group in the country.

Most of Nebraska's Burmese refugees are Karen, an umbrella term for an array of ethnic groups.[8] There are about 5,500 Karen refugees in Nebraska, as well as about 300 refugees from other ethnic groups, and most of them live in Omaha ("About Us" Karen Society of Nebraska). Traditionally, most Karen people lived in the eastern region of Burma, along the border with Thailand ("Karen" Minority Rights Group). When the British began colonizing Burma in 1826, they used their strategy of "divide and rule" by extending somewhat favored status to the Karen

---

6. This knowledge comes from the authors' conversations with refugees in Lincoln.
7. Burma is also the name the U.S. government uses, so this choice keeps our language consistent with the language used to record data on these refugees.
8. Population estimates regarding Burma's ethnic minorities are highly controversial and politicized; see this report for an excellent history: https://www.tni.org/en/publication/ethnicity-without-meaning-data-without-context.

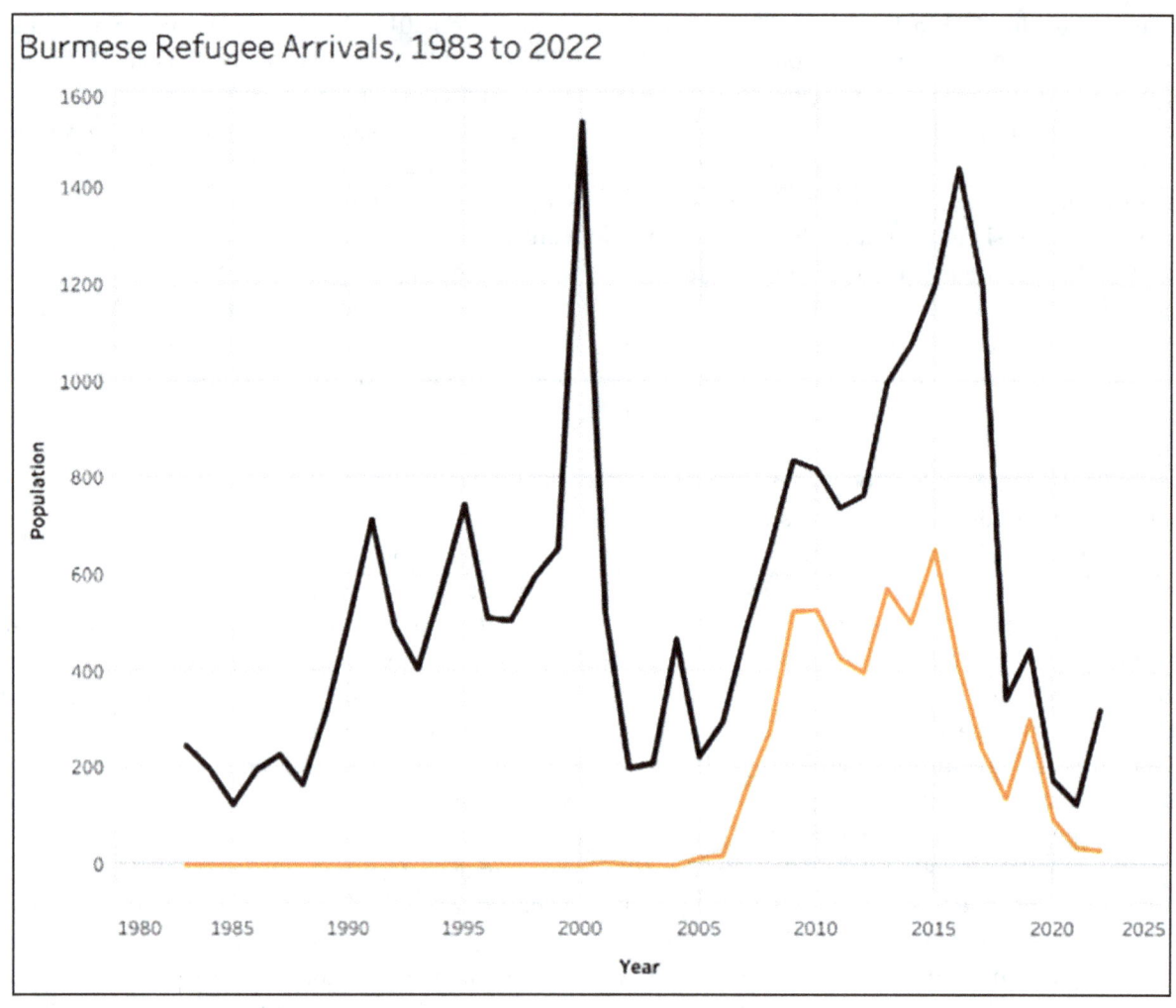

Burmese Refugee Arrivals, 1983 to 2022. Graph created by Emira Ibrahimpašić and Julia Reilly.
Black = total refugee arrivals in Nebraska

people (Ibid.). Thus, ethnically-motivated attacks on the Karen first began in the 1940s, at the end of the colonial era, and were carried out by anti-British, anti-colonial armed groups (Ibid.).

Burma became an independent state in 1948, and in 1949, the world's longest-running civil war began. In response to the first Burmese President U Nu's attempts to make the national army more Burman, two Karen armed groups — the Karen National Union and the Karen National Liberation Army — began a rebellion against the Burman-dominated government ("Karen" Minority Rights Group). Throughout the next two decades, more ethnic minority groups took up arms against the government, and the war raged on (Ibid.).

In 1988, many of the ethnic groups resisting the government joined with the National League for Democracy, the political party led by Aung San Suu Kyi, in a series of pro-democracy uprisings that took place throughout the country ("Karen" Minority Rights Group). These uprisings failed, and a group that called themselves the State Law and Order Restoration Council took over, built up the country's military, and redoubled the militarized campaign against both armed and civilian ethnic minority groups (Ibid.). This marked the beginning of a protracted refugee crisis[9] for the millions of ethnic minority civilians who were forced to flee this violent government onslaught. Within four years, there were 31 refugee camps filled with ethnic minority refugees from

---

9. According to the UNHCR, "A protracted refugee crisis is one in which refugees find themselves in a long-lasting and intractable state of limbo. Their lives may not be at risk, but their basic rights and essential economic, social and psychological needs remain unfulfilled after years in exile. A refugee in this situation is often unable to break free from enforced reliance on external assistance" (UNHCR, EC/54/SC/CRP.14 10 June 2004, II. 3).

Burma on the Thai border (Meigs and Baw, 2021). Even as they were living in refugee camps, Karen and other ethnic minority refugees were not safe from the war because Burmese armed groups frequently crossed the border to attack refugee camps (Loescher and Milner 2013, 71). Further, their access to services and resources was limited, as the Thai government restricted the United Nations High Commissioner for Refugees (UNHCR) from accessing the camps, as they deemed the decades-long displacement temporary (Loescher and Milner, 66). As a result, overcrowding, underemployment, lack of education, malnutrition, and lack of basic healthcare are endemic in these camps (Harkins 2012, 186).

It is not uncommon for children to be born in these refugee camps, and to have lived their entire lives there well into adulthood (UNHCR 2004). Indeed, an entire generation of Karen and other ethnic minority children were born and raised in refugee camps (Harkins 2012, 186). As Pew Bway Htoo, a Karen woman who was born in a Thai refugee camp and eventually resettled in Omaha, says, "In a refugee camp, you don't have no future. You just try to survive day by day" (Caracta 2023).

A key, if unlikely, turning point came in late 2004. The Thai government decided it would no longer allow the UNHCR to process applications for refugee status from people crossing the Burma-Thailand border (Nyce and Shukla 2005). Instead, they would have provincial-level Thai officials make these determinations (Ibid.), a setup that was prone to mismanagement and corruption. In response, the United States and other governments offered to resettle the Burmese refugees (Ibid.). Thus, in 2005, the Department of State began a special initiative to resettle some of the 150,000 ethnic minority refugees from Burma who had been living in the Thai border camps, often for many years (Meigs and Baw 2021). From then until 2017, almost 110,000 of these refugees were resettled, and over half of them were resettled in the United States (Camps in Thailand). The first of these refugees arrived in Nebraska in 2005.

Karen refugees began creating infrastructure for their communities very quickly upon their arrival in Nebraska. By 2008, the Karen Society of Nebraska was founded ("About Us" Karen Society), and it continues to play a crucial role in supporting and advocating for the needs of Karen people in Nebraska. Karen groups have successfully collaborated with many community organizations, especially in Omaha, to support the resettlement and integration needs of the Karen community. The Yates Community Partnership offers federally funded sewing, cooking, English, and computer classes to Burmese refugee women (Burbach 2010). In Lincoln, Karen students participated in a project with The Quilted Conscience to create a quilt and corresponding traveling museum exhibition to share their experiences of displacement and resettlement (Fleig 2014). They have collaborated with Omaha Public Schools to create and publish children's books written in Karen and English; previously, there were very few children's books available in Karen (Duffy 2015).

Churches play an especially vital role in Nebraska's Burmese communities. In Burma, roughly one third of Karen people are Christian and roughly two thirds are Buddhist ("Karen" Minority Rights Group). In the United States, many Karen refugees are Christian. Karen refugee communities have started two thriving churches in Nebraska: the Lincoln Karen Baptist Church and the Karen Christian Revival Church in Omaha. Other Burmese refugees have found community in existing faith institutions in Nebraska. For example, most of Nebraska's Karenni refugees are Catholic, and they have found community worshiping at Catholic services in Omaha ("We are neighbors in Omaha" 2018).

A key indication of the Karen community's success in organizing themselves and in gaining economic self-sufficiency was the Karen Christian Revival Church's construction of a new church building in 2013 (Burbach 2013). Less than a decade after the first Karen refugees arrived in Omaha, the church community raised $2.5 million — almost exclusively from Karen congregants — for the project, and church leaders estimated 300 Karen families in their congregation had bought homes (Ibid.). Crucially, they saw the project as a center for not only the Karen community but for anyone who wanted to worship with them; Saw Khu, a church elder, told the *Omaha World-Herald*, "Anybody can come and join, not only Karen, but Black, white, everyone" (Ibid.). In 2021, this vision was realized, and the church opened its doors (Curtis 2021).

A particularly significant and painful event for the Karen community in Nebraska was the city of Omaha's evacuation of the Yale Park Apartments on September 20, 2018. The Yale Park Apartments are a low-cost apartment complex whose residents were almost entirely Burmese refugees (Duffy September 22, 2018). The city of Omaha received over 90 complaints from residents about the living conditions in the apartments, and upon inspection, the city found that 90 percent of the units had multiple code violations and the building was unsafe for habitation (City finds horrid 2018). Residents were evacuated and put into temporary housing centers (Duffy September 22, 2018), which evoked their painful past of forced displacement in Burma and Thailand. As Mander Baw said, "It brought up a lot of bad memories. We have all gone through this before, and then it was happening again. It took several months for everyone to find new housing" (Meigs and Baw 2021). This time, however, their displacement was caused by poverty and the fact that public systems and policies do not do enough to protect families of limited means from housing precarity and exploitation. Myint Sein put it more succinctly: "If we had money, we'd live somewhere else" (Duffy September 25, 2018).

The Karen community and some members of the broader Omaha community stepped up to support the displaced residents of Yale Park (Duffy September 25, 2018). The disaster also led to lasting policy changes: refugee assistance organizations and other public service organizations in Omaha created structures to enhance collaboration (Duffy 2019), and Omaha philanthropists commissioned a study that revealed a dire lack of affordable housing in the area (Omaha Foundation 2021). At the time of this writing, an Omaha nonprofit recently won a $130,000 grant to study how to better place recently arrived refugees in safe housing (Caracta 2023). It was clear to concerned observers that what the refugee residents of Yale Park had experienced could have happened to other Nebraskans who did not have the resources to advocate for themselves in the face of exploitation, and that reforms were necessary to prevent recurrence. In this respect, the experiences of the Burmese refugees — and the courage of the 90 Yale Park residents who filed the initial complaints — stand to benefit the broader community.

Burmese refugee communities mobilized once again in the face of the coronavirus pandemic. Many Burmese refugees work in meatpacking plants (Meigs and Baw 2021), where the spread of the virus was especially rampant and unchecked (Stella 2020). The Karen Society of Nebraska worked to share COVID-19 prevention information to Karen communities (Meigs and Baw 2021), and Restoring Dignity — a refugee support organization largely staffed by Karen refugees (Our Staff 2016) — teamed up with the state Department of Health and Human Services and the Douglas County Health Department to educate the Karen community about vaccines (Facebook Live Town Hall 2021).

Sudan

Nebraska's Sudanese refugees were displaced by civil conflict and ethnic marginalization. Sudan was a British colony, and the British administered northern and southern Sudan separately: northern Sudan was administered as an Arab-dominated area, while southern Sudan was administered as an African colony. At the very end of the colonial era, the British imposed Arabic as the language of both the north and the south, even though elite southerners spoke English, and upon decolonization, the British granted most power to northern elites. This began decades of often violent political conflict between the central government, which was dominated by Arabic-speaking elites, and ethnic groups that were excluded and marginalized by the government, which often sought to impose the Arabic language and sharia law on all citizens, regardless of their culture or faith (Johnson 2011, 4-5).

The graph on page 267 appears to show two waves of Sudanese refugees, but this is misleading. The halting of resettlement of Sudanese refugees in 2002 happened due to the United States government's drastic contraction of the refugee program after 9/11, and the increased security focus on refugees that came from Muslim-majority countries. This affected the resettlement of Sudanese refugees in Nebraska. Although many Sudanese refugees are not Muslim, and many non-Muslim Sudanese refugees were targeted for Sudanese government persecution partially because of this fact, all Sudanese refugee resettlement applicants were targeted with increased American government scrutiny because they came from a Muslim-majority country. When this United States-imposed halt is considered, it is clear Sudanese refugees have been arriving in Nebraska since the late 1990s.

Most of the first Sudanese refugees to arrive in Nebraska in the late 1990s were displaced by the Second Sudanese Civil War, which lasted from 1983 to 2005. The war began when an armed group, then called the Sudan People's Liberation Army (SPLA), formed and fought, first for a united and secular Sudan, and later for an independent South Sudan. The war ended in 2005, with a peace agreement that created a complex system of power-sharing between northern and southern interests and installed southern Sudanese leaders as vice president (Ottaway and Hamzawi 2011).

However, while Sudanese government leaders were talking peace with the SPLA, they were fighting a genocidal war in Darfur. Darfuri rebels began attacking Sudanese military installations in 2002

(Flint and De Waal 2008), and the government retaliated with genocide. This conflict displaced about 2.5 million people, about 240,000 of whom became refugees in Chad (Amnesty International 2008, 2). A few of these refugees were resettled in Nebraska, where they created a community of Darfuris, including two Darfuri community organizations in Nebraska (Darfur genocide 2010).

South Sudan became the world's newest country in 2011, after a referendum in which 99 percent of voters voted to secede from Sudan (Smith 2011). As of 2011, the graph above includes refugees from both Sudan and South Sudan. Less than three years later, however, South Sudan descended into its own civil war when its president, Salva Kiir, fired his entire cabinet, which had many figures who represented key ethnic groups in South Sudan politics (Al Jazeera 2013). As of 2019, this conflict has created 2.3 million refugees ("South Sudan Refugee Crisis"), some of whom have found their way to Nebraska.

Indeed, most of Nebraska's Sudanese refugees are from the south, with several tribes represented (*World-Herald* editorial 2014). The Nuer is the single biggest Sudanese tribe in Nebraska, but there are also Dinka, Bari, Azande, and Maban people in Nebraska (Ibid.). There are also Nebraskans who originate from Sudan's central provinces and Darfur (Ibid.). South Sudanese leaders estimate Omaha has the largest concentration of South Sudanese people in the United States (Liewer 2019).

The South Sudanese community in Nebraska has been profoundly affected by political events in South Sudan, and since the community is so large, they also play a significant role in the South Sudanese diaspora. In 2006, the now-president of South Sudan and then-head of the SPLA, Salva Kiir, visited Omaha to promote the peace agreement that ended the Second Sudanese Civil War ("Salva Kiir" 2006). When the vote for South Sudanese independence took place, citizens in the diaspora were included. There were eight polling sites in the United States, and one of them was in Omaha (Liewer November 1, 2015).

When a peace agreement was signed to end the South Sudanese Civil War in 2015, the former vice president of South Sudan and leader of the Nuer side of the conflict, Reik Machar, came to Omaha to promote the peace agreement to the community there (Liewer October 6, 2015). He spoke of the opportunities Nebraska promised for South Sudanese youth, saying, "I am impressed by what I have heard from these young people. They should live their lives here, make the opportunities. Some will be scientists, some will be basketballers, some will be entrepreneurs. It's time for them to come together, to leave behind the bitterness. It's happening." (Ibid.) He said these opportunities situated South Sudanese youth in Nebraska to be tomorrow's peacemakers: "A good number of South Sudanese have accepted to live in Nebraska — maybe because of the description of 'Welcome to Nebraska, The Good Life.' We want them this time to be peacemakers. If we don't come and inform them, they will be detractors" (Ibid.).

Sudanese Nebraskans have consistently mobilized to try to promote peace in their country of origin. One of Reik Machar's top aides, Miyong Kuon, lives in Papillion and played a critical role in attempting to implement the 2015 peace agreement (Liewer November 1, 2015). South Sudanese Nebraskans have also held demonstrations to commemorate atrocity crimes committed during the conflict (Stoddard 2017) and coordinated to pressure the United States government to help find South Sudanese Nebraskans who had gone missing during the conflict (Liewer 2014). Nebraskans from Darfur have also participated in efforts to hold the perpetrators of the genocide in Darfur accountable in the International Criminal Court ("Darfur genocide demands action" June 7, 2010).

Sudanese refugees have created strong community organizations to support recently arrived immigrants and refugees. Refugees from Darfur created the Darfur Community Organization of Nebraska and the Darfur Organization of Nebraska ("Darfur genocide" 2010). In 2013, South Sudanese leaders created the New Life Family Alliance to connect families with community resources, especially to help with employment, legal support, finances, healthcare, and education (New Life Family Alliance). In 2018, South Sudanese refugees created a task force of refugee support organizations to enhance and coordinate support for South Sudanese refugees in Omaha, and this task force expanded to improve support for all refugees in Omaha ("Grace: Omaha Refugee" January 22, 2018).

Several remarkable young leaders have emerged from the Sudanese refugee communities in Nebraska. They do vital work in strengthening Nebraska's Sudanese communities, educating Nebraskans about the contributions of immigrants and refugees to the state, and building vital institutions in South Sudan. Buey Ray Tut started Aqua Africa, a nonprofit that provides access to clean water, sanitation, hygiene, and energy to communities in South Sudan and helps form institutions to ensure good community management of these resources ("Who We Are" Aqua Africa). He was named one of Ten Outstanding Young Omahans in 2020.[10] Jacob Maluak Manyang, one of the Lost Boys, started Education Refuge after resettling in Omaha (McDermott 2019). Education Refuge supports refugee-led education programs in the Kukuma Refugee Camp in Kenya ("Education Refuge"), which was founded by Lost Boys and hosts over 100,000 South Sudanese refugees (UNHCR 2019). Jacob Idra founded Republic of South Sudan (ROSS) Leaders in Omaha ("Jacob Idra" ROSS Leaders) to provide academic support, career exploration, health and wellness, and cultural engagement resources to youth from the South Sudanese community ("Our Programs" ROSS Leaders). ROSS Leaders has since expanded to Lincoln and Manchester, New Hampshire. In 2022, they collaborated with Wenyen Gabriel of the LA Lakers to launch basketball camps in the United States and South Sudan (Robidoux 2022). Indeed, many Sudanese Nebraskans have reached remarkable athletic heights, and athletics have become a key vehicle for engaging Sudanese youth and gaining access to education. Akoy Agou (Grosbard 2018), Koang Doluony, and Omaha Biliew are a few Sudanese basketball players from Nebraska who went on to achieve national profiles as college players.

Economic Impacts

Nebraska's refugees have made resounding economic contributions to the state, showing that concerns that refugee resettlement is an economic drain are misinformed. This section establishes the proportion of Nebraska's labor force that all migrants constitute, as well as refugees specifically. Conclusions from studies of the United States as a whole and the Midwest as a region demonstrate refugees' economic contributions. This section then reviews the specific economic contributions of Nebraska's refugees, spanning their role in the state's powerful meatpacking industry, their contributions to rural economic revitalization, and their entrepreneurship as small business owners. Finally, the section closes by discussing how underemployment prevents Nebraska's refugees from contributing all they can to the state economy.

Until recently, Nebraska had a growing foreign-born population (Kotkin 2021), and they have made vital contributions to our economy. Over 145,000 immigrants and refugees live in Nebraska, making up 9 percent of the state's labor force (Gonzalez 2023) and 7.4 percent of the state's population.[11] They have a higher labor force participation rate than native-born Nebraskans (Ibid.). Refugees make up an important and numerous subset of Nebraska's foreign-born population and labor force. Nebraska resettles more refugees per capita than any other state, resettling 379 refugees per 100,000 residents (Kallick 2023).

While refugees need economic support immediately upon arrival, they eventually become self-supporting and contribute to the economy. For their first eight years in the United States, refugees receive more in benefits than they pay in taxes, but by their eighth year of resettlement, the average refugee has paid more in taxes than they have received in benefits (Evans and Fitzgerald 2017, 6-7). After 20 years in the United States, the average refugee has paid $21,000 more in taxes than they have received in benefits (Ibid.). After 25 years in the United States, the average refugee household generates more income than the average American household: the median income for refugee households at this point is $67,000, compared to the national average of $53,000 (Chanoff 2016).

Initial investments in refugee resettlement not only pay dividends for refugees themselves, but for the broader economy. For example, a study of refugee resettlement programs in Cuyahoga County, Ohio, showed refugees generated 10 times the economic activity as was first invested in them in resettlement programs: an annual $4.8 million of mostly federal funding generated $48 million in total annual economic activity (Chmura Economics and Analytics 2013, 34). Economic models suggest Nebraska's refugee resettlement program generated $1.7 million for the state's economy in 2020 alone (New American Economy 2019).

Nebraska's immigrants and refugees constitute a vital labor force for the state's key industries. They often work in jobs with challenging working conditions that are essential to our state's economy. Nebraska's foreign-born workers are particularly likely to work low-wage jobs; Nebraska is among the 10 states with the largest share of these workers who make less than two-thirds of the median wage (Gonzalez 2023). Refugees and immigrants play a key role in

---

10. See TOYO! Ten Outstanding Young Omahans: Buey Ray Tut. https://www.youtube.com/watch?v=6ouVBVzSZI.
11. This figure was calculated using the US Census Bureau's 2021 figure for Nebraska's population, available here: https://datacommons.org/place/geoId/31/?utm_medium=explore&mprop=count&popt=Person&hl=en#.

the meatpacking industry, which is vital to Nebraska's economy. Nebraska leads the country in beef exports, exporting $1.64 billion annually ("Where's the Beef" 2023). Immigrant and refugee Nebraskans are crucial to making this possible, as national-level data show the meatpacking industry is powered by a labor force that is 66 percent foreign-born (Associated Press 2020).

Despite challenging conditions, refugees especially tend to be excellent, loyal employees. A national survey of businesses that employ refugees — including several businesses in Nebraska — revealed refugees have lower turnover than other new hires (Kallick and Roldan 2018, 12). In the meatpacking sector, refugees had a 15 percent lower turnover than other workers (Ibid., 9). Managers reported that refugee workers were loyal and diligent. One said, "Once you've fully trained people, they may go work for someone else, but with refugees there was a sense of loyalty there" (Ibid., 42). Another reported, "We've found refugees are willing to learn, not afraid to work hard, and they're very loyal because this company helps them" (Ibid., 25). They also reported that once their firm had put in a small initial investment to attract refugees, there were recruitment benefits, as refugee workers tend to attract others from their community to apply for jobs (Ibid., 12).

Refugees and immigrants make contributions to rural communities, especially communities that have meatpacking plants. For example, Schuyler and Fremont have been revitalized by refugees and immigrants and by the establishment of industries powered by their labor (Mathema, Svajlenka, and Hermann 2018). In another example, the population of Grand Island — known for its meatpacking plants and immigrant communities — has increased by 66 percent since 1970 (Kotkin 2021, 52). This is particularly striking since Nebraska's overall population growth rate over the same time period was only 22 percent, compared to the national average of 51 percent (Kotkin 2021, 32).

In recent years, however, Nebraska's economic growth has been hampered by a decrease in immigration. The drastic contraction of refugee resettlement from 2018 to 2021, shown in Figure 3, coupled with the pandemic's effects, have led to slower labor force growth for Nebraska. Historically, the largest plurality of people who move to Nebraska have been immigrants or refugees (Kauffman and McCoy 2023). Starting in 2017, immigration to Nebraska began to steadily fall (Ibid.), and as the graph on page 267 shows, refugee resettlement to Nebraska drastically fell in 2018. Had this immigration-fueled population growth continued, at the time of this writing, Nebraska would have 19,000 more people (Gonzalez 2023).

This decline in immigration and refugee resettlement corresponds to a remarkable labor force shortage. As of this writing, an estimated 80,000 jobs are unfilled in Nebraska (Gonzalez 2023), which translates to roughly 2.8 job openings per unemployed person in Nebraska (Kaufman and McCoy 2023). These vacancies are concentrated in low-skilled, low-paying jobs (Gonzalez 2023) — exactly the jobs Nebraska has historically relied on its immigrants and refugees to fill. Revitalized inclusion of refugees and immigrants in Nebraska's economy will be key to reversing this trend. As Bryan Slone, the president of Nebraska's Chamber of Commerce and Industry, puts it, "As we go forward, diversity and inclusion is not an option; it's not something nice — it's fundamental to the economic development of our state" (Kotkin 2021, 32).

Beyond making vital contributions to Nebraska's labor force, immigrants and refugees wield considerable spending power that bolsters Nebraska's economy. Immigrants and refugees, although they comprise 7.4 percent of the state's population, contribute 8 percent of the state's earnings (Gonzalez 2023). Refugees comprise an essential part of this; as of 2019, Nebraska's 25,297 refugees wielded $410.8 million in spending power (Immigrants in Nebaska 2023). This spending power translates to important tax revenue. In 2019, Nebraska's refugees paid $111.4 million in taxes, including $52.9 million in state and local taxes (Ibid.).

New Americans create economic growth through entrepreneurship that creates jobs and revitalizes communities. While 9 percent of native-born Americans start businesses, 11 percent of immigrants, and an even higher 13 percent of refugees, do (Refugees 2016). Some of these businesses become essential to American life and culture; indeed, 45 percent of American Fortune 500 countries have at least one founder who is an immigrant or refugee (Ewing 2019). In Lincoln and Omaha alone, refugees have led to the creation or retention of 500 jobs (McDermott 2019). Through the jobs they have created and the productivity they have generated, refugees create $0.60 of indirect economic activity for every $1.00 of direct economic activity they produce (Ibid.).

Refugee entrepreneurs can be found all around Nebraska. In Lincoln, the Deumić family, who resettled in 1992 from Bosnia-Herzegovina, opened Emsud's Clothiers, which has consistently been recognized by the Lincoln's Choice Awards (Jordon

2016). Thuy Nguyen is something of a legend in Lincoln, where she has built and owns Little Saigon Plaza, which includes a restaurant and grocery store (Case 2018). In Omaha, Mohamad Rahmanzai, a refugee from Afghanistan, built a real estate business and owned multiple properties, in addition to holding a full-time job (Jordon 2016). In Lexington, where there are now over 900 Somalis, Nuridin Nur has opened a restaurant that brings the community together (McElmurry 2018).

Immigrants and refugees face significant barriers to maximizing their economic potential. One of these is the job market mismatch problem: the fact that highly skilled immigrant and refugees' professional credentials often do not translate to the American labor market, leading to widespread underemployment for highly skilled immigrants and refugees (Lu and Hou 2020). Racism in America can hamper the economic contributions of refugees of color, especially black refugees. African refugees, and especially male African refugees, have earned less than all other groups of refugees for the past four decades, and researchers believe this is due to limited social mobility (Tesfai 2023). Further, the issues of racism and underemployment for highly educated new Americans can intersect: compared with all foreign-born populations, highly educated black Africans experience the most disadvantage in the labor market (Tesfai 2017).

In general, much of the opposition to continued or increased refugee resettlement to the United States often centers around cost, but the economic contributions of refugees demonstrate such concerns are misplaced. Refugees' economic successes could be attributed to the fact that most refugee resettlement efforts center on economic self-sufficiency. Whatever the reason for their overall economic success, investing in refugees is just a smart business. Any state that may be facing decreased population growth and many unfilled jobs might find that participating in refugee resettlement may be their best solution in addressing those challenges.

Current Issues and Future Outlook

Events of the past decade, as well as structural features of the American approach to refugee resettlement, present pressing issues that stand to impact the future of refugee resettlement and refugee communities in Nebraska. This section will detail three issues that the authors find to be especially concerning: government actions that do not match the welcoming spirit shown by so many Nebraskans, a shortage of resources available for refugees after the crucial first 90 days of resettlement, and language barriers.

While Nebraska nonprofits and concerned citizens have maintained consistent support for refugees, the state government has been at best distant from and at worst hostile to refugee resettlement. When we tell the story of Nebraska being an excellent place for refugees, it is the story of committed groups of Nebraskans whose individual contributions often go unsung, not the story of the state government or state policymakers. This has been especially true in the past decade. In 2015, then-presidential candidate Trump began making a series of statements that were highly critical of the United States' refugee resettlement program (Donald Trump: I would send 2015; Haberman 2015; Kopan 2015). Shortly thereafter, state legislators and governors followed suit by attempting to change refugee resettlement policy on the state level, and when Trump was elected, his administration began implementing federal policy changes that made refugee resettlement significantly more difficult.

In November 2015, closely following then-candidate Trump's call to send Syrian refugees back to Syria (Kopan 2015), Nebraska Governor Pete Ricketts joined 31 other governors (Fantz and Brumfield 2015) in calling for a halt to refugee admissions to the United States and ordered state government officials to work to stop any current efforts to resettle Syrian refugees in Nebraska (Syria 2015). One Nebraska refugee resettlement agency said it would comply with the governor's wishes to stop the resettlement of Syrian refugees, while two others said they would proceed as usual (Ibid.).

The next two legislative sessions saw the introduction of two bills that would make refugee resettlement in Nebraska significantly more difficult and costly. One of them, introduced in 2016, sought to make refugee resettlement agencies financially liable for any crimes committed by refugees they resettled if those refugees came from one of a list of 34 "high risk" countries (Our Staff 2016). The bill attempted to require resettlement agencies to pay $25 million for an insurance policy, or pay a $1,000 daily fine, to continue resettling any refugee from the bill's list of countries (Legislature of Nebraska January 14, 2016). The next year, a bill was introduced requiring refugee resettlement agencies to submit semi-annual reports to the state government about how many refugees they had resettled that year and how much these refugees had received in public benefits (Legislature of Nebraska January 18, 2017). Neither bill passed.

Shortly after he took the oath of office, on January 27, 2017, President Trump issued Executive Order 13769, which reduced 2017's refugee resettlement cap from the 110,000 refugees previously established by former President Obama to 50,000 refugees, imposed a 120-day halt to the resettlement process and issued a 90-day ban on issuing visas or refugee resettlement to anyone coming from one of seven specified Muslim-majority countries. Due to the last provision, it was widely known as "the Muslim ban." Several aspects of the executive order met numerous legal challenges (McGraw and Kelsey 2017), but the 60,000-person cut on the refugee resettlement ceiling stood. This reduction was followed by a further reduced refugee resettlement cap in 2018: a cap of 45,000 was set at the beginning of the year, and that September, the administration further lowered it to 30,000 (Hesson and Toosi 2018). In 2019, a member of the Trump administration leaked to the media that members of the administration were advocating for the refugee resettlement cap to be set to 0, which was resisted by Department of Defense officials who were concerned this would make it impossible to recruit local interpreters to support American troops (Mattis 2018). The cap was ultimately set at 18,000 (Shear and Kanno-Youngs 2019).

The 2019 refugee resettlement cap reduction was accompanied by Executive Order 13888, which required states and cities to provide written consent to resettle every refugee that the Office of Refugee Resettlement designated to be resettled in their territory. After first saying his office would review the order (Refugees December 1, 2019), about three weeks later, Governor Ricketts announced he would continue to allow Nebraska to resettle refugees (Stoddard 2019). He also joined other governments in sending a letter to Trump thanking him for the changes he had made to the refugee resettlement process (Ibid.).

The drastic reductions on the refugee resettlement cap rocked refugee resettlement agencies throughout the United States. By April 2019, 100 local refugee resettlement agencies around the country had closed, representing a loss of about a third of the entire refugee resettlement sector in the United States (Darrow and Scholl 2020, 378). This deeply impacted refugee resettlement in Nebraska. At the beginning of 2017, Nebraskan refugee resettlement officials were preparing for continued high rates of arrivals of refugees, especially Yezidi refugees. That May, Nebraska's refugee coordinator said Lincoln was slated to receive about 1,000 Yezidi refugees alone over the next two years (Grace May 7, 2017), but by November, only 10 refugees were expected to arrive in Omaha and 2 refugees — of any group — were expected to arrive in Lincoln (Grace: Omaha Refugee January 22, 2018).

These reductions meant Nebraska's refugee resettlement agencies received much less funding from the federal government, which caused Nebraska's refugee resettlement sector to shrink. In 2017, Lutheran Family Services cut 15 refugee resettlement workers from their roster — seven were reassigned to other parts of the agency, but the others lost their jobs (Grace: Fluctuating January 22, 2018). By December 2019, Catholic Social Services cut two staff positions (Refugees December 1, 2019).

The refugee resettlement cap was raised during President Biden's administration (White House, May 3, 2021; White House, September 27, 2022), but the ripple effects of the previous cuts remain in the reduced capacity of refugee resettlement organizations. Perhaps reflecting this lack of capacity, in 2023, the Biden administration launched Welcome Corps, a program that allows groups of five or more individuals, or community organizations, to sponsor a refugee's resettlement ("About" Welcome Corps). Members of the Welcome Corps create resettlement plans and raise the funds necessary to resettle one or more refugees, and the State Department then assigns them refugees to be resettled (Ibid.). Nebraskans reorganized to resettle refugees under the auspices of this program.

There is a gulf between the vibrancy of Nebraska as a hub for strong refugee communities and the resources available to support these communities. Much of this has to do with the fact that the federal government's refugee resettlement support lasts 90 days, a policy with roots in Nebraska. In 1991, Nebraska was the first state that proposed cutting aid to refugees from the current 12 months of aid back to three months ("Nebraska is only state…" February 14, 1991). In this respect, Nebraska was ahead of the national curve: today, 90 days is the default amount of support offered to resettled refugees upon arrival in the United States (Reception and Placement). As of 2023, the State Department paid resettlement agencies $2,375 per refugee to cover the costs of the first 90 days of resettlement (Ibid.). This amount is unlikely to cover the full costs of even this limited 90 days; for context, in 2008, an economic study conducted by the Lutheran Immigration and Refugee Service — one of the ten major organizations that contracts with the State Department to resettle refugees — estimated they paid $3,228 over 90 days to resettle a single refugee. That is equivalent to $4,665.96 at the time of this writing, about twice the amount the State Department covers.[12]

The case studies in this chapter show that the strong, vibrant refugee communities in Nebraska attract refugees long after the 90-day support period. Many of the refugees in Lincoln — especially Yezidi and South Sudanese refugees — were first resettled in other parts of the United States, where they received these 90 days of support, and then moved to Nebraska to participate in the strong communities here. When they move here, there is no government support waiting for them; the only support available is through community organizations, often founded by other refugees, and other nonprofits.

The current federal refugee resettlement policy, with its limited 90 days of support, leaves a huge gap for places like Nebraska, where extensive refugee communities continue to draw refugees from other parts of the country. Many Nebraskans have done transformative work to fill this gap. Organizations like Restoring Dignity in Omaha, Refugee Empowerment Center, the Asian Community and Cultural Center, Lincoln Literacy, ECHO Collective, Juniper Refuge, and initiatives like CareerLadder in Lincoln and Elevate in Grand Island do essential work, but refugees' needs remain great. Within government, the New Americans Task Force within the City of Lincoln performs a crucial coordinating function among the various organizations that work with refugee communities in Lincoln and was crucial to the creation of the CareerLadder program (Pitsch 2020). Lincoln Public Schools, which has students from 152 countries who speak 130 languages (Cultural Perspectives), created the Bilingual Liaisons Program, which employs members of Lincoln's immigrant and refugee communities. They enroll newly arrived students in Lincoln's public schools and educate both newly arrived families and LPS faculty and staff on relevant cross-cultural issues (Bilingual Liaisons).

English language literacy remains the biggest barrier to refugees' resettlement. Although there are many organizations doing essential work to support new Americans as they learn English, more needs to be done. This need is distinctly related to the limitations of the 90 days of support for resettlement, and the extent to which refugees report that lack of English language proficiency holds them back shows this issue is systemic. In a 2020 survey of Nebraska's refugees, all of whom had been resettled for over a year, 72.5 percent of participants reported low or non-existent English-speaking ability (Nebraska Office of Health Disparities and Health Equity 2020, 24), and 72 percent of participants said the lack of English ability was the biggest challenge they faced (Ibid., 17).

Language limitations impact all aspects of life. Limitations with English are the single biggest reason Nebraska's new Americans who were trained in skilled professions in their home country are blocked from practicing these professions in Nebraska.[13] For many refugees, whether they are trained in a profession, low English skills coupled with the 90-day limitation on resettlement aid can incentivize them to take survival jobs with low wages, tough working conditions, and little opportunity for advancement (Lumley-Sapanski 2021). The demands of these jobs make it difficult for refugees to carve out time to practice English, and without English, they have little hope of better employment, thus incentivizing them to remain in these survival jobs (Ibid.). Limited language proficiency can also impact health: in the same survey, 72.6 percent of refugees said they struggled to understand the information given to them by their healthcare provider (Nebraska Office of Health Disparities and Health Equity 2020, 58). Further, with new planned changes to the citizenship exam that will effectively require more English proficiency, language barriers stand to prevent refugees from becoming United States citizens (Ahmed 2023), and therefore from fully participating in our democracy.

Conclusion

This chapter relays the history of refugee resettlement in Nebraska. We began with three sections that survey the history of the creation of the refugee resettlement program, starting with the earliest days of immigration to Nebraska, moving through the imposition of racist immigration policies in the early 20th century and ending with how World War II and the Vietnam War shaped the evolution of the refugee resettlement program we have today.

---

12. The authors made this conversion by using the Consumer Price Index's Inflation Calculator, created by the US Bureau of Labor Statistics, available here: https://www.bls.gov/data/inflationcalculator.htm.
13. This claim is based on the authors' conversations with the leaders of the New Americans Task Force and professionals working in refugee resettlement in Lincoln.

We then turned to an exploration of the experiences of five major refugee groups in Nebraska: Vietnamese, Yugoslavs, Iraqis, Burmese, and Sudanese. The next sections broadened the lens to discuss the crucial economic contributions that refugees make to Nebraska and three ongoing issues that challenge those who work in refugee resettlement and refugees themselves.

Throughout this discussion, three important dynamics emerged. First, while Nebraska has earned a reputation for being a welcoming space for refugees, the reality is far more complicated: there are numerous examples of harassment, mistreatment, and neglect, and the broader history clearly shows that most of Nebraska's welcoming tradition can be attributed to the extraordinary generosity, creativity, and dedication of specific groups of concerned citizens. The actions and rhetoric of Nebraska's policymakers — especially state policy makers — tend to undermine this welcoming tradition more than they support it. Second, as the need for refugee resettlement increases, the resources available to support Nebraska's refugee communities do not increase to meet the need.

Third, especially after initial resettlement in the United States, much of the traditions of welcome and support for refugees that Nebraskans celebrate about themselves are carried out by members of refugee communities themselves. The studies of the five refugee groups in this chapter clearly show the most important organizations that support them were started by, and often remain primarily supported by, refugees who hope to help those who come after them. This suggests Nebraska offers an environment that makes self-help for resettled refugees possible more than it suggests Nebraskans as a whole are extraordinarily welcoming and generous.

Bibliography

"1,219 Refugees Now in State." *Omaha World-Herald*, February 22, 1976.

"About Us." Karen Society of Nebraska. Accessed July 16, 2023. http://karenksn.org/aboutus/index.html

"About." Welcome Corps. Accessed July 16, 2023. https://welcomecorps.org/about/

"Accepting the refugees." *The Lincoln Star*, July 3, 1979.

Ahmed, Trisha. "US citizenship test changes are coming, raising concerns for those with low English skills." *Omaha World-Herald*. July 9, 2023. https://omaha.com/news/nation-world/citizenship-test-changes-english-language/article_187eb9bb-6b6a-53c9-bfee-30e2c0e4c6b8.html

Al-Badry, Wessam. "Home" Accessed July 16, 2023. https://www.wesaamalbadry.com/

Allan, Tom. "Wynot Couple Opens Home to Bosnian Teens." *Omaha World-Herald*, November 22, 1992. https://www.newspapers.com/article/omaha-world-herald-lincoln-family-hosts/121231303/

Almy, Marvin. Review Memorandum to Emira Ibrahimpašić and Julia Reilly. May 1, 2025.

Amnesty International. "Sudan: Displaced in Darfur. A generation of anger." January 1, 2008. https://www.refworld.org/docid/4795a5692.html

Andersen, Erin. "Fulfilling their American dream: City's first Bosnian refugees celebrate 20 years in Lincoln." *Lincoln Journal Star*, September 16, 2013. https://www.newspapers.com/article/lincoln-journal-star-lincolns-first-bos/128151826/

"Archive: A refugee from Vietnam gets a new home; Albion, Nebraska gets a new doctor." NBC News Archive, May 28, 1975. https://www.msnbc.com/rachel-maddow/watch/archive-a-refugee-from-vietnam-gets-a-new-home-albion-nebraska-get-a-new-doctor-119290949597

Associated Press. 2020. "Nonprofit estimates two-thirds of Nebaska meatpackers are immigrants; worker shortage looms in industry." *Omaha World-Herald*, May 26 https://omaha.com/business/nonprofit-estimates-two-thirds-of-nebraska-meatpackers-are-immigrants-worker-shortage-looms-in-industry/article_29eb8b90-1dba-5384-950a-86abfac57119.html

Bauer, Will. "Lincoln's Sunni population has outgrown their mosque. They hope it will be ready next year." *Nebraska Public Media*, September 7, 2022. https://nebraskapublicmedia.org/en/news/news-articles/lincolns-sunni-population-has-outgrown-their-mosque-they-hope-it-will-be-ready-next-year/

Bergin, Nicholas. "Yazidi establish national cemetery near Malcolm." *Lincoln Journal Star*, June 10, 2017. https://journalstar.com/news/local/yazidi-establish-national-cemetery-near-malcolm/article_1f17beb9-29ee-5c14-8c6b-3ec4d479fddf.html

"Bich Chau, MD." BlueStem Health. Accessed on 12/4/2023. https://www.bluestemlincoln.com/provider/bich-chau/

Binder, David. "Ford Asks Nation to Open Its Doors to the Refugees." *The New York Times*, May 7, 1975.

"Bilingual Liaisons." Lincoln Public Schools Federal Programs. Accessed in 2025. https://home.lps.org/federal/bilingual-liaisons/

Black, Richard. "Conceptions of 'home' and the political geography of refugee repatriation: between assumption and contested reality in Bosnia-Herzegovina." *Applied Geography* 22, no. 2 (2002): 123-138.

"Bosnia War Dead Announced." BBC News, June 21, 2007. http://news.bbc.co.uk/2/hi/europe/6228152.stm

"Bosnians Head for New Homes in Iowa." *Omaha World-Herald*, February 22, 1993. https://www.newspapers.com/article/omaha-world-herald-iowa-bosnians-headi/121385057/

Brown, A. and T. Scribner. "Unfulfilled Promises, Future Possibilities: The Refugee Resettlement System in the United States." *Journal on Migration and Human Security* 2, no. 2 (2014): 101-120. https://doi.org/10.1177/233150241400200

Burbach, Christopher. "Classes help refugee women gain skills for life in a new land." *Omaha World-Herald,* June 21, 2010.

Burbach, Christopher. "Ethnic Karen refugees from Myanmar plan $2M church in north Omaha." *Omaha World-Herald*, December 20, 2013. https://omaha.com/news/ethnic-karen-refugees-from-myanmar-plan-m-church-in-north/article_a56d61b9-0a76-58fd-a284-792be8022cef.html

Burleigh, Nina. "Iraqis in America: 'We've Found Peace In This Land'" *Parade Magazine*, October 10, 2010. http://www.lacp.org/2010-Articles-Main/101210-IraqisInAmerica.htm

"Burma." *The World Factbook* (2023 ed.). Central Intelligence Agency. https://www.cia.gov/the-world-factbook/countries/burma/summaries/

Camden, Jim and Gordon Winters. "Viet refugees found adapting to the Midwest." *The Lincoln Star*, August 29, 1977. https://www.newspapers.com/article/the-lincoln-star-overview-of-asian-refug/120343118/

"Camps in Thailand." The Border Consortium. Accessed July 16, 2023. https://www.theborderconsortium.org/where-we-work/camps-in-thailand/

Caracta, Bella. "Omaha non-profit helping welcome, accommodate refugees." WOWT, July 13, 2023. https://www.wowt.com/2023/07/13/omaha-non-profit-helping-welcome-accommodate-refugees/

Case, Emily. "Lincoln business owner: 'I wanted to get freedom'" *Lincoln Journal Star*, September 2, 2018.

Certain Displaced Persons and Refugees in Europe (Washington, DC, December 22, 1945) https://www.trumanlibrary.gov/sites/default/files/TrumanDirective.pdf

Chanoff, Sasha. "Refugees revitalize American cities." *Boston Globe*, November 25, 2016. https://www.bostonglobe.com/opinion/2016/11/25/refugees-revitalize-american-cities/7Xe7PX6JbRq4sfE8D4pNyJ/story.html

Chmura Economics and Analytics 2013.

"Church fellowship forms refugee unit." *Lincoln Journal Star*, October 22, 1979.

"City finds horrid living conditions at Yale Park Apartments; residents evacuated." KMTV, Omaha, NE, Sept. 20. 2018. https://www.3newsnow.com/news/local-news/city-to-conduct-full-scale-inspection-of-yale-park-apartments

"Composition of the Different Ethnic Groups under the 8 Major National Ethnic Races in Myanmar" Embassy of Myanmar. Accessed on July 16, 2023. https://www.embassyofmyanmar.be/ABOUT/ethnicgroups.htm

Conway, Megan. "Yazidi national cemetery in southeast Nebraska." KLKN TV, June 12, 2017. https://www.klkntv.com/yazidi-national-cemetery-in-southeast-nebraska/

"Cultural Perspectives and the Role of LPS Bilingual Liaisons." Lincoln Public Schools News. February 23, 2022. https://www.lps.org/post/detail.cfm?id=14657

Curtis, Alyssa. "Myanmar refugees open doors to new church." 3 News Now KMTV Omaha, July 26, 2021. https://www.3newsnow.com/news/local-news/myanmar-refugees-open-doors-to-new-church

"Darfur genocide demands action." *Omaha World-Herald*, June 7, 2010.

Darrow, Jessica H., and Jess Howsam Scholl. "Chaos and confusion: Impacts of the Trump administration executive orders on the US refugee resettlement system." *Human Service Organizations: Management, Leadership & Governance* 44, no. 4 (2020): 362-380.

Democratic Party Platforms, 1960 Democratic Party Platform Online by Gerhard Peters and John T. Woolley, The American Presidency Project https://www.presidency.ucsb.edu/node/273234

DeSilver, Drew. "U.S. public seldom has welcomed refugees into country." Pew Research Center. November 19, 2015. https://www.pewresearch.org/short-reads/2015/11/19/u-s-public-seldom-has-welcomed-refugees-into-country/ [See section on "Indochina, 1970s."]

Diamond, Anna. "The 1924 Law That Slammed the Door on Immigrants and the Politicians That Pushed It Back Open." *Smithsonian Magazine*, May 19, 2020. https://www.smithsonianmag.com/history/1924-law-slammed-door-immigrants-and-politicians-who-pushed-it-back-open-180974910/

Dittrick, Paula. "Refugee families' first Lincoln Christmas will be bleak." *The Lincoln Star*, December 22, 1978. https://www.newspapers.com/article/the-lincoln-star-refugees-first-xmas/120957401/

"Doctor Hunt Isn't Official." *The Lincoln Star*, May 13, 1975.

"Donald Trump Calls for Surveillance of 'Certain Mosques' and a Syrian Refugee Database." *New York Times*, November 21, 2015. https://www.nytimes.com/2015/11/22/us/politics/donald-trump-syrian-muslims-surveillance.html?_r=0

"Donald Trump: I would send Syrian refugees home." BBC News. October 1, 2015. https://www.bbc.com/news/world-us-canada-34397272

Drozdiak, William. "Germany steps up expulsion of Bosnian refugees." *The Washington Post*, December 4, 1996.

Duffy, Erin. "Children in Omaha's large Karen community practice language skills in special classes." *Omaha World-Herald*, November 16, 2015. https://omaha.com/news/education/children-in-omaha-s-large-karen-community-practice-language-skills-in-special-classes/article_1ea63de1-934b-5b48-b651-751bbb3db6d2.html

Duffy, Erin. "500 refugees evacuated from Omaha apartments could be in new housing or hotel rooms by next week." *Omaha World-Herald*, September 22, 2018. https://omaha.com/news/metro/north-omaha/refugees-evacuated-from-omaha-apartments-could-be-in-new-housing/article_c2ca69bb-a1b3-5abc-897f-d93069ab6814.html?_gl=1*1tpftre*_ga*MTg5ODE3Njg5OC4xNjg4MDU5Njg2*_ga_1NLZ9C-MDMM*MTY4OTA5MzE3NS41LjEuMTY4OTA5NTM1NS41OC4wLjA

Duffy, Erin. "'They need our help': Omahans step up to help refugees evacuated from Yale Park apartments." *Omaha World-Herald*, September 25, 2018. https://omaha.com/news/local/they-need-our-help-omahans-step-up-to-help-refugees-evacuated-from-yale-park-apartments/article_02939701-bc71-5ad7-927c-1f308104d7af.html

Duffy, Erin. "1 year after Yale Park evacuation: What's happened to the tenants and apartments." *Omaha World-Herald*, September 15, 2019. https://omaha.com/news/local/1-year-after-yale-park-evacuation-whats-happened-to-the-tenants-and-apartments/article_ea9d6c23-8741-55f5-93d0-3d718bd80fe8.html

"The Economic Costs for U.S. States Who Opt Out of Refugee Resettlement." New American Economy, December 10, 2019, https://research.newamericaneconomy.org/report/state-fact-sheets-on-refugees/

"Education Refuge." Education Refuge. Accessed on July 16, 2023. https://www.educationrefuge.org/

Edwards, Jonathan. "Vietnamese businesses fueling neighborhood revitalization." *Lincoln Journal Star*, February 22, 2013. https://journalstar.com/special-section/new-directions/vietnamese-businesses-fueling-neighborhoods-revitalization/article_3626fc88-84b6-5fea-9157-28310449cbb8.html

Eng, Peter. "More Doors Closing to Vietnam's Boat People." *Omaha World-Herald*, January 15, 1989. https://www.newspapers.com/article/omaha-world-herald-vietnamese-refugees-s/117822729/

Estrin, James. "A Refugee's Story: 'No One's Family is Perfect but Mine is Perfect for Me'" *New York Times*, February 12, 2019. https://www.nytimes.com/2019/02/12/lens/refugee-iraq-family.html

"European Restrictions on Refugees." *Omaha World-Herald*, July 1, 1993. https://www.newspapers.com/article/omaha-world-herald-none-european-restr/121384404/

Evans, William N. and Daniel Fitzgerald. "The Economic and Social Outcomes of Refugees in the United States: Evidence from the ACS." *National Bureau of Economic Research Working Paper Series*, Working Paper 23498 (June 2017): http://www.nber.org/papers/w23498

Ewing, Walter. "Immigrants and Their Children Founded Almost Half of All US Fortune 500 Companies" *Immigration Impact*, July 30, 2019. https://immigrationimpact.com/2019/07/30/immigrants-half-fortune-500-companies/

"Executive Order 13769 of January 27, 2017, Protecting the Nation from Foreign Terrorist Entry Into the United States." *Code of Federal Register*, title 3 (2017): 8977-8982, https://www.federalregister.gov/documents/2017/02/01/2017-02281/protecting-the-nation-from-foreign-terrorist-entry-into-the-united-states

"Executive Order 13888 of September 26, 2019, Enhancing State and Local Involvement in Refugee Resettlement." *Code of Federal Register* (2019): 52355-52356, https://www.govinfo.gov/content/pkg/DCPD-201900669/pdf/DCPD-201900669.pdf

"Exon: Refugee Volunteers Best." *Omaha World-Herald*, September 18, 1975: 4.

"Exon rejects refugee plan." *Fremont Tribune*, August 29, 1975.

"Facebook Live Town Hall With Karen Refugee Community." Department of Health and Human Services. March 5, 2021. https://dhhs.ne.gov/Pages/Facebook-Live-Town-Hall-with-Karen-Refugee-Community.aspx

Fantz, Ashley and Ben Brumfield. "More than half the nation's governors say Syrian refugees not welcome." CNN, November 19, 2015. https://www.cnn.com/2015/11/16/world/paris-attacks-syrian-refugees-backlash/index.html

"First of Viet boat people arrives in Lincoln." *The Lincoln Star*, November 9, 1979.

Fix, Michael, Kate Hooper and Jie Zong. "How are Refugees Faring? Integration at U.S. and State Levels." Transatlantic Council on Migration, June 2017.

Fleig, Shelby. "Quilt created by Karen refugees in Lincoln showcases memories of homeland, dreams for future." *Omaha World-Herald*, April 24, 2014. https://omaha.com/news/quilt-created-by-karen-refugees-in-lincoln-showcases-memories-of-homeland-dreams-for-future/article_9bfc7b4a-52d2-5af7-8880-00fefcac2277.html

Flint, Julie, and Alex De Waal. *Darfur: A short history of a long war*. New York, NY: Zed Books, 2008.

Fox, Neva Rae. "Nebraska Parish, Yazidi in Thriving Relationship." The Living Church, November 16, 2021. https://livingchurch.org/2021/11/18/nebraska-parish-yazidi-thrive-in-long-term-relationship/

Fussell, Anita. "Refugee resettling success though poll shows opposition." *Lincoln Journal Star*, December 16, 1979. https://www.newspapers.com/article/lincoln-journal-star-refugees-settling-d/121013353/

Fussell, Anita. "Task force organizes refugee resettlement." *Lincoln Journal Star*, August 6, 1980.

Garcia, Maria Cristina. *The Refugee Challenge in Post-Cold War America*. New York, NY: Oxford University Press, 2017.

Gonzalez, Cindy. "Foreign-born Huskers contribute 8% of state economic input, report says." *Nebraska Examiner*, May 22, 2023. https://nebraskaexaminer.com/2023/05/22/foreign-born-huskers-contribute-8-of-state-economic-input-report-says/

Gouveia, Lourdes. "Immigrant Nebraska — Because we forget, we must tell the story all over again: Blog Post." UNO Latino/Latin American Studies (OLLAS) Other Publications. March 8, 2018. https://digitalcommons.unomaha.edu/latinamstudies_ollas_publications/23

Grace, Erin. "Grace: Omaha Refugee Task Force helps smooth newcomers' rough transition."

Omaha World-Herald, January 22, 2018. https://omaha.com/news/grace-omaha-refugee-task-force-helps-smooth-newcomers-rough-transition/article_6c981956-d2a6-5b59-b718-39f87380c89c.html

Grace, Erin. "Refugee resettlements pick up in Nebraska, could surge this fall." *Omaha World-Herald*, May 7, 2017. https://omaha.com/news/local/refugee-resettlements-pick-up-in-nebraska-could-surge-this-fall/article_e80a3de9-f516-57c3-8974-18278cdd1461.html

"Grace: Fluctuating number of refugees can be hard for agencies to handle." *Omaha World-Herald*, January 22, 2018.

Grosbard, Adam. "Flashback: Akoy Agau's journey from war-torn Sudan to SMU." *Dallas Morning News* (Dallas, TX), June 6, 2018. https://www.dallasnews.com/sports/smu-mustangs/2018/06/07/flashback-inside-akoy-agau-s-journey-from-war-torn-sudan-to-smu/

Gunter, Michael M. "The KDP-PUK conflict in northern Iraq." *The Middle East Journal* (1996): 224-241.

Haberman, Maggie. "Donald Trump Calls for Surveillance of 'Certain Mosques' and a Syrian Refugee Database." *New York Times*, November 21, 2015. https://www.nytimes.com/2015/11/22/us/politics/donald-trump-syrian-muslims-surveillance

Haines, David W., and Karen E. Rosenblum. "Perfectly American: Constructing the refugee experience." *Journal of Ethnic and Migration Studies* 36, no. 3 (2010): 391-406.

Harkins, Benjamin. "Beyond "temporary shelter": A case study of Karen refugee resettlement in St. Paul, Minnesota." *Journal of Immigrant & Refugee Studies* 10, no. 2 (2012): 184-203.

Harris, Louis. "Americans oppose refugees." *Fremont Tribune*, August 25, 1977. https://www.newspapers.com/article/fremont-tribune-no-ne-americans-oppose/120333713/

Heinzl, Toni. "Refugees to Come to Lincoln: First Wave of Up to 80 Kosovars Is Expected by Next Week." *Omaha World-Herald*, May 25, 1999. https://www.newspapers.com/article/omaha-world-herald-1999-refugees-to-linc/122611837/

Hesson, Ted and Nahal Toosi. "Trump administration to slash refugee cap." *Politico*, September 17, 2018. https://www.politico.com/story/2018/09/17/trump-refugees-limits-ceiling-826302

HEW Refugee Task Force. Report to the Congress. March 15, 1976. https://www.fordlibrarymuseum.gov/sites/default/files/pdf_documents/library/document/0204/1511799.pdf

Hicks, Nancy. "Refugee family makes new life in U.S., Lincoln." *Lincoln Journal Star*, December 25, 2001. https://www.newspapers.com/article/lincoln-journal-star-maidas-story-bos/122707898/

Holman, Philip A. "Refugee resettlement in the United States." *Refugees in America in the 1990s: A reference handbook*, 1996. 3-27.

Hovey, Art. "Iraqi refugees live in legal limbo." *Lincoln Journal Star*, September 23, 2007. https://journalstar.com/special-section/news/iraqi-refugees-live-in-legal-limbo/article_204c739f-4dc6-5fa0-8db1-73d7503b4cca.html

Hummel, Becca. "Yazidi Cultural Center provides resources to Yazidi immigrants and refugees." *Daily Nebraskan*, May 5, 2021. https://www.dailynebraskan.com/news/yazidi-cultural-center-provides-resources-to-yazidi-immigrants-and-refugees/article_9e014740-add4-11eb-8837-9f916c159f22.html

"Immigrants in Nebraska." American Immigration Council. Accessed on July 16, 2023. https://map.americanimmigrationcouncil.org/locations/nebraska/

Indochina Refugees—Interagency Task Force. "Directors of Diocesan Resettlement Committees 6-2-75," pp. 38, 40 in "Indochina Refugees - Interagency Task Force (1)," Theodore C. Marrs Files, Box 10, Gerald R. Ford Presidential Library. https://www.fordlibrarymuseum.gov/library/document/0164/1505189.pdf

Internal Displacement Monitoring Centre. Bosnia and Herzegovina: Displacement Associated with Conflict and Violence, Figure Analysis— GRID 2020, 2020. https://api.internal-displacement.org/sites/default/files/2020-04/GRID%202020%20-%20Conflict%20Figure%20Analysis%20-%20BOSNIA%20AND%20HERZEGOVINA.pdf

"Iraq Anfal." Human Rights Watch. 1993. https://www.hrw.org/reports/1993/iraqanfal/ANFALINT.htm

"Jacob Idra." ROSS Leaders. Accessed on July 16, 2023. https://www.rossleaders.com/team/jacob-idra

Jaeger, Gilbert. "On the history of the international protection of refugees." *International Review of the Red Cross* 83, no. 843 (2001): 727-738.

Johnson, Douglas Hamilton. *The root causes of Sudan's civil wars: Peace or truce.* Boydell & Brewer Ltd, 2011.

Jordon, Steve. 2016. "Refugees: opportunity in a new nation." *Omaha World-Herald*, March 10, 2016.

"Karen" Minority Rights Group. Accessed July 16, 2023. https://minorityrights.org/minorities/karen/

Kallick, David Dyssegard and Cyierra Roldan. Refugees as Employees: Good Retention, Strong Recruitment. (Tent and Fiscal Policy Institute, New York, NY: 2018), https://www.tent.org/wp-content/uploads/2021/09/TENT_FPI-Refugees-as-Employees-Report.pdf

Kallick, David Dyssegard. "Refugee Resettlement per Capita: Which states do the most?" Immigration Research Initiative, May 3, 2023. https://immresearch.org/publications/refugee-resettlement-per-capita-which-states-do-the-most/

Kaufmann, Nate and John McCoy. "Population Growth Needed To Address Labor Scarcity." Federal Reserve Bank of Kansas City, April 5, 2023. https://www.kansascityfed.org/omaha/nebraska-economist/population-growth-needed-to-address-labor-scarcity/

Kelly, Kevin. "Racist Letters Prompt Efforts To Tighten Law." *Omaha World-Herald* Dec. 4, 1990: 11.

Kelly, William. Nebraska and the resettlement of displaced persons after World War II, part 2 (Blog). This is the second of a three-part series. The entire article appeared in the Fall 2023 issue of *Nebraska History Magazine*. https://history.nebraska.gov/nebraska-and-the-resettlement-of-displaced-persons-after-world-war-ii-part-2/

Khoudeida, Laila. 2019. "Yazidi History Harvest." Transcript of interview at the Yezidi Cultural Center, Lincoln, NE, Fall 2019, https://www.youtube.com/watch?v=WZ1JaVt0wpg

Kinbacher, Kurt E., and William G. Thomas III., "Shaping Nebraska An Analysis of Railroad and Land Sales, 1870-1880," *Great Plains Quarterly* 28, no. 3 (2008): 191-207.

Kneeland, Douglas E., "Wide Hostility Found to Vietnamese Influx." *The New York Times*, May 2, 1975.

Konnath, Hailey. "'A light for freedom and for democracy' Crowd comes together at vigil to show support for refugees in Omaha, elsewhere." *Omaha World-Herald*, February 1, 2017. https://www.newspapers.com/article/omaha-world-herald-obradovic-on-refugees/128152091/

Kopan, Tal. "Donald Trump: Syrian refugees a 'Trojan horse'." CNN, November 16, 2015. https://www.cnn.com/2015/11/16/politics/donald-trump-syrian-refugees/index.html

Kotkin, Joel, et al. "The Emergence of the Global Heartland." *Heartland Forward*. Published May 26, 2021. https://heartlandforward.org/case-study/the-emergence-of-the-global-heartland/

Krajeski, Jenna. 2018. "The Daring Plan to Save a Religious Minority from ISIS." *New Yorker*, February 19. https://www.newyorker.com/magazine/2018/02/26/the-daring-plan-to-save-a-religious-minority-from-isis

"'The Last Million:' Eastern European Displaced Persons in Postwar Germany.'" National World War II Museum, Published April 4, 2022, https://www.nationalww2museum.org/war/articles/last-million-eastern-european-displaced-persons-postwar-germany

Leftin, Adeana. "Refugee family from war-torn Bosnia arrives to begin a new life in Lincoln." *The Lincoln Star*, September 16, 1993. https://www.newspapers.com/article/the-lincoln-star-first-bosnian-family-in/128213505/

Legislature of Nebraska. *Refugee Resettlement Agency Indemnification Act.* LB 966. 104th Legislature, 2nd Session. Introduced January 14, 2016. https://nebraskalegislature.gov/FloorDocs/104/PDF/Intro/LB966.pdf

Legislature of Nebraska. *Refugee Resettlement Notification Act.* LB 505. 105th Legislature, 1st Session. Introduced January 18, 2017. https://nebraskalegislature.gov/FloorDocs/105/PDF/Intro/LB505.pdf

Liewer, Steve. "'This community is suffering': In Omaha, South Sudan's former second lady joins prayers marking anniversary of deadly clash" *Omaha World-Herald*, July 18, 2019. https://omaha.com/news/local/this-community-is-suffering-in-omaha-south-sudan-s-former-second-lady-joins-prayers-marking/article_cd9002d6-1d05-5eab-99ac-2703c7543851.html

Liewer, Steve. "South Sudanese in Omaha mourn their losses this holiday season." *Omaha World-Herald*, December 20, 2014. https://omaha.com/news/local/south-sudanese-in-omaha-mourn-their-losses-this-holiday-season/article_e925f9df-1ee3-5805-84fb-f5b037e2ecb5.html

Liewer, Steve. "South Sudanese leader tells Omaha: Young people are key to future, and to peace." *Omaha World-Herald*, October 6, 2015. https://omaha.com/news/local/south-sudanese-leader-tells-omaha-young-people-are-key-to-future-and-to-peace/article_bf42d612-6aeb-11e5-af05-d36d877a814f.html

Liewer, Steve. "UNO grad shuttles between Omaha, South Sudan homeland for one cause: democracy." *Omaha World-Herald*, November 1, 2015. https://omaha.com/news/local/uno-grad-shuttles-between-omaha-south-sudan-homeland-for-one-cause-democracy/article_24367412-d041-545b-87cb-e1d758f69a4d.html

Loeb, Vernon. "Iraqi Dissidents' American Dream and Nightmare." *Washington Post*, December 28, 2000. https://www.washingtonpost.com/archive/politics/2000/12/28/iraqi-dissidents-american-dream-and-nightmare/aae0ac1a-056d-43ca-9cef-be2e153ff16e/

Loescher, Gil, and James Milner. *Protracted refugee situations: Domestic and international security implications*. New York, NY: Routledge, 2013.

Lu, Yao, and Feng Hou. "Immigration system, labor market structures, and overeducation of high-skilled immigrants in the United States and Canada." *International migration review* 54, no. 4 (2020): 1072-1103.

Lumley-Sapanski, Audrey. "The survival job trap: Explaining refugee employment outcomes in Chicago and the contributing factors." *Journal of Refugee Studies* 34, no. 2 (2021): 2093-2123.

Mabin, Butch. "Refugee services to be streamlined." *The Lincoln Star*, December 31, 1994. https://www.newspapers.com/article/the-lincoln-star-changes-in-the-refugee/121700224/

Marinari, Maddalena, "The 1921 and 1924 Immigration Acts a Century Later: Roots and Long Shadows," *Journal of American History*, Volume 109, Issue 2, September 2022, Pages 271–283, https://doi.org/10.1093/jahist/jaac232

Markowitz, Fran. "Census and Sensibilities in Sarajevo." *Comparative Studies in Society and History*, no. 49 (2007): 40-73.

Martin, Brent. "Congressman Fortenberry welcomes new exhibit, new immigrants." *Norfolk Daily News*, October 20, 2017. https://norfolkdailynews.com/congressman-fortenberry-welcomes-new-exhibit-new-immigrants/article_0860694a-b59f-11e7-8ad3-77dafabf1ef8.html

Mathema, Silva, Nicole Prchal Svajlenka, and Anneliese Hermann. "Revival and Opportunity: Immigrants in Rural America" Center for American Progress, September 2, 2018. https://www.americanprogress.org/article/revival-and-opportunity/

Mattis, James. *Memorandum for Assistant to the President for National Security Affairs*. U.S. Department of Defense, Washington, DC, 2018. https://www.politico.com/f/?id=0000016c-0709-dd54-a17d-7f8b31690002

"Mayor accepts refugee doctors, families for the City of Beatrice." *Beatrice Daily Sun*, May 21, 1975.

McDermott, Brandon. "Living the Dream in Nebraska, Returning the Wish to South Sudan" Nebraska Public Media, March 20, 2019. https://nebraskapublicmedia.org/en/news/news-articles/living-the-dream-in-nebraska-returning-the-wish-to-south-sudan/

McElmurry, Sara. 2018. "Proactive and Patient: Managing Immigration and Demographic Change in 2 Rural Nebraska Communities" Center for American Progress, November 14. https://www.americanprogress.org/article/proactive-and-patient/

McGraw, Meredith, and Adam Kelsey. "A Timeline of Trump's Immigration Executive Order and Legal Challenges." ABC News, March

16, 2017. http://abcnews.go.com/Politics/timeline-president-trumps-immigration-executive-order-legal-challenges/story?id=45332741

Meigs, Doug and Mander Baw. "Finding Refuge in Omaha: The Karen Community's Perseverance Through War, Displacement, and Pandemic." *Omaha Magazine*, February 15, 2021. https://www.omahamagazine.com/2021/02/15/347618/finding-refuge-in-omaha-the-karen-community-s-perseverance-through-war-displacement-and-pandemic

Mulvey, Mike. "Language, fear, ignorance keep newcomers, natives apart." *The Lincoln Star*, November 2, 1983. https://www.newspapers.com/article/the-lincoln-star-struggle-to-integrate-f/128302212/

Muslic, Hana. "Everybody is my brother or sister: Former pastor Bud Christenson helps refugees, inmates." *Lincoln Journal Star*, January 18, 2018. https://journalstar.com/news/local/everybody-is-my-brother-or-sister-former-pastor-bud-christenson-helps-refugees-inmates/article_9d1b359f-257a-55dd-98e4-326f14b71834.html

"Nebraska is only state to propose cutting aid." *The Lincoln Star*, February 14, 1991.

Nebraska Legislature. Transcripts. [Sen. DeCamp on bringing Vietnamese doctors to Nebraska] May 11, 1977, p. 04275. https://nebraskalegislature.gov/transcripts/view_page.php?page=04276&leg=85 ; p. 04276. https://nebraskalegislature.gov/transcripts/view_page.php?page=04277&leg=85

Nebraska Office of Health Disparities and Health Equity. "Nebraska Refugee Health Report 2020" (Lincoln, Nebraska Department of Health and Human Services, 2020). https://dhhs.ne.gov/Reports/Nebraska%20Refugee%20Health%20Report%202020.pdf

Nebraska State Board of Immigration Collection. State Government Records, History Nebraska, Lincoln, NE. https://history.nebraska.gov/wp-content/uploads/2017/04/doc_Immigration-State-Board-of-RG0024.pdf

New American Economy. "The Economic Costs for U.S. States Who Opt Out of Refugee Resettlement." December 10, 2019. https://research.newamericaneconomy.org/report/state-fact-sheets-on-refugees/

"New Life Family Alliance." New Life Family Alliance, accessed July 16, 2023, https://nlfaomaha.org/

"Nonprofit estimates two-thirds of Nebraska meatpackers are immigrants; worker shortage looms in industry" *Omaha World-Herald*. May 26, 2020. https://omaha.com/business/nonprofit-estimates-two-thirds-of-nebraska-meatpackers-are-immigrants-worker-shortage-looms-in-industry/article_29eb8b90-1dba-5384-950a-86abfac57119.html

Nyce, Sayre and Kavita Shukla. "Thailand: Complications in the resettlement of Burmese refugees." Refugees International Report, December 12, 2005. https://reliefweb.int/report/thailand/thailand-complications-resettlement-burmese-refugees

Omaha Foundation. "Housing Affordability in the Omaha and Council Bluffs Area." (Omaha, Omaha Foundation, 2021). https://omahafoundation.org/wp-content/uploads/2021/05/Housing-Affordability-Assessment-of-Needs-Priorities.pdf

Ottaway, Marina and Amr Hamzawy. "The Comprehensive Peace Agreement" Carnegie Endowment for International Peace, January 4, 2011. https://carnegieendowment.org/2011/01/04/comprehensive-peace-agreement-pub-42223

"Our Mission." New Life Family Alliance, accessed July 16, 2023. https://nlfaomaha.org/our-vision

"Our Programs." ROSS Leaders. Accessed on July 16, 2023. https://www.rossleaders.com/ross-programs

"Our Staff" Restoring Dignity. Accessed on July 16, 2023. https://rdomaha.org/our-staff/

Ozaki, Andrew. "New bill makes relocation agencies liable for refugee crimes." KETV Omaha, January 16, 2016. https://www.ketv.com/article/new-bill-makes-relocation-agencies-liable-for-refugee-crimes-1/7657505

"Patriotic Union of Kurdistan" Global Security. Org. Accessed July 16, 2023. https://www.globalsecurity.org/military/world/para/puk.htm

Pembrick, Jael. "Lincoln Kurdish community speak out about ISIS leader's death." KLKN TV, October 27, 2019. https://www.klkntv.com/lincoln-kurdish-community-speak-out-about-isis-leaders-death/

Pir, Hadi. 2019. UNL History Harvest. Transcript of interview at the Yezidi Cultural Center, Lincoln, NE, Fall 2019. Hadi Pir Interview https://history.unl.edu/yazidi-history-harvest .

Pitsch, Madison. 2020. "Nebraska non-profits vying for $125,000 grant from Google" 1011 Now, July 30. https://www.1011now.com/2020/07/30/nebraska-non-profits-vying-for-125000-grant-from-google-vote-here/

Qassim, Khedir. 2019. UNL History Harvest. Transcript of interview at the Yezidi Cultural Center, Lincoln, NE, Fall 2019. https://history.unl.edu/yazidi-history-harvest/

The Real Cost of Welcome: A Financial Analysis of Local Refugee Reception. Lutheran Immigration and Refugee Service. (Baltimore: Lutheran Immigration and Refugee Service, 2009).

"Reception and Placement." US Department of State. Accessed July 16, 2023. https://www.state.gov/refugee-admissions/reception-and-placement/

Reed, David A. "AMERICA OF THE MELTING POT COMES TO END; Effects of New Immigration Legislation Described by Senate Sponsor of Bill — Chief Aim, He States, Is to Preserve Racial Type as It Exists Here Today" *New York Times*, April 29, 1924. Section XX. Page 3. https://www.nytimes.com/1924/04/27/archives/america-of-the-melting-pot-comes-to-end-effects-of-new-immigration.html

Reeves, Bob. "State earns renown for its refugee aid." *Lincoln Journal Star*, December 24, 1995. https://www.newspapers.com/article/lincoln-journal-star-2-stories-lincoln/121725742/

Reeves, Bob. "Vietnamese find new life." *The Lincoln Star*, December 1, 1992. https://www.newspapers.com/article/the-lincoln-star-southeast-asian-populat/121380445/

Reeves, Bob "Vietnamese church celebrates 25 years" *Lincoln Journal Star.* June 18, 2004. https://journalstar.com/news/local/vietnamese-church-celebrates-25-years/article_916adf38-7b5b-5368-8e2d-5b9b3eef6bfa.html

Refugee Act of 1980. 94 STAT. 102 PUBLIC LAW 96-212 (1980) https://www.govinfo.gov/content/pkg/STATUTE-94/pdf/STATUTE-94-Pg102.pdf

"Refugee council is established." *The Lincoln Star*, June 10, 1980.

"Refugee Resettlement Workshop Set." *The Lincoln Star*, September 12, 1975.

"Refugee: 'The numbers will have to drop to a trickle very soon.' *Omaha World-Herald*, February 18, 2017.

"Refugees." *Omaha World-Herald*, December 1, 2019.

"Refugees." New American Economy, November 25, 2016, https://www.newamericaneconomy.org/issues/refugees/

"Resolution Revived: Senators Endorse Doctor Rule." *Omaha World-Herald*, May 14, 1975. https://www.newspapers.com/article/omaha-world-herald-neb-senators-endorse/125127193/

Robidoux, Carol. "Wenyen Gabriel: Building community—and hope—through global connections and basketball." *Manchester Ink Link* (Manchester, NH), August 14, 2022. https://manchesterinklink.com/building-community-and-hope-through-global-connections-and-basketball/

Rowan, Carl, "Bigotry Against Refugees is Familiar, Vintage Americanism." *Omaha World-Herald* (Omaha, NE), May 11, 1975. https://www.newspapers.com/article/omaha-world-herald-bigotry-against-refug/127302484/

"Salva Kiir speech to Sudanese community in US Omaha." *Sudan Tribune*, July 24, 2006. https://sudantribune.com/article17283/

Schleicher, John. "UNMC History: Rallying to aid refugee physicians." May 14, 2014. https://www.unmc.edu/newsroom/2014/05/14/unmc-history-rallying-to-aid-refugee-physicians/ [For a more detailed story on two such physicians, see the Stevens article.]

Stevens, William K. "Nebraska Recruits Vietnamese Doctors," The *New York Times*, June 17, 1975. https://www.nytimes.com/1975/06/17/archives/nebraska-recruits-vietnamese-doctors.html

"Scramble for medics." *Beatrice Daily Sun*, May 20, 1975.

Selby, Daniele. "Yazidi Refugees Fleeing ISIS Have Found Home in This Surprising US City." Global Citizen, January 16, 2018. https://www.globalcitizen.org/en/content/yazidi-refugee-isis-nebraska-lincoln-iraq-us/

Shear, Michael and Zolan Kanno-Youngs. "Trump Slashes Refugee Cap to 18,000, Curtailing U.S.

Role as Haven." *New York Times*, September 26, 2019. https://www.nytimes.com/2019/09/26/us/politics/trump-refugees.html

"Shortfall of welfare money for state refugees predicted." *Lincoln Journal Star*, May 20, 1981.

Silverman, Edwin B. "Indochina legacy: The refugee act of 1980." *Publius* 10, no. 1 (1980): 27-41.

Skinner, Kenneth A. "Vietnamese in America: Diversity in Adaptation." California Sociologist. 3 (Summer 1980): 10324.

Smith, David. "Sudan referendum result confirmed." *Guardian*, February 7, 2011. London, UK. https://www.theguardian.com/world/2011/feb/07/sudan-referendum-result-confirmed

Sohi, Seema. "Barred Zones, Rising Tides, and Radical Struggles: The Antiradical and Anti-Asian Dimensions of the 1917 Immigration Act." *Journal of American History* 109, no. 2 (2022): 298-309.

"South Sudan president fires cabinet" *Al Jazeera*. July 24, 2013. https://www.aljazeera.com/news/2013/7/24/south-sudan-president-fires-cabinet

"South Sudan Refugee Crisis" USA for UNHCR. Accessed July 16, 2023 https://www.unrefugees.org/emergencies/south-sudan/

"State Explores Options to Assist Boat People." *Omaha World-Herald*, July 29, 1979.

"States Refugee Costs to Be Reimbursed." *Lincoln Journal Star*, June 11, 1975.

Stella, Christina. "COVID-19 Cases at Nebraska's Meatpacking Plants More Than Double." Nebraska Public Media, May 18, 2020. https://nebraskapublicmedia.org/en/news/news-articles/covid-19-cases-at-nebraskas-meatpacking-plants-more-than-double/

Stoddard, Martha. "Gathering at State Capitol commemorates anniversary of mass killing in South Sudan." *Omaha World-Herald*, December 15, 2017. https://omaha.com/state-and-regional/gathering-at-state-capitol-commemorates-anniversary-of-mass-killing-in-south-sudan/article_c32c02f4-e1f3-11e7-83fc-2357a563a5ee.html

Stoddard, Martha. "Gov. Pete Ricketts says he'll consent to refugees continuing to resettle in Nebraska." *Omaha World-Herald*, December 19, 2019. https://omaha.com/state-and-regional/gov-pete-ricketts-says-hell-consent-to-refugees-continuing-to-resettle-in-nebraska/article_e1028a2e-1d9c-5ba9-a569-00b5ec3419e5.html

"Syria: Agency confident in screening of refugees." *Omaha World-Herald*, November 20, 2015.

"Terrorized by ISIS, Yazidi refugees find welcoming community in Nebraska." PBS NewsHour. January 15, 2021. https://www.pbs.org/newshour/show/terrorized-by-isis-yazidi-refugees-find-welcoming-community-in-nebraska

Tesfai, Rebecca. "Racialized labour market incorporation? African immigrants and the role of education-occupation mismatch in earnings." *International Migration* 55, no. 4 (2017): 203-220.

Tesfai, Rebecca. "Success or Self-Sufficiency? The Role of Race in Refugees' Long Term Economic Outcomes." *Journal of Refugee Studies* 36 no. 1 (March, 2023): https://doi.org/10.1093/jrs/feac066

Truman, Harry S. *Annual Message to the Congress on the State of the Union* January 6, 1947. Online by Gerhard Peters and John T. Woolley, The American Presidency Project https://www.presidency.ucsb.edu/node/232364

UN General Assembly. "Convention Relating to the Status of Refugees." July 28, 1951. https://www.un.org/en/genocideprevention/documents/atrocity-crimes/Doc.23_convention%20refugees.pdf

UNHCR. 2004. Executive Committee of the High Commissioner's Programme, "Protracted Refugee Situations", Standing Committee, 30th Meeting, UN Doc. EC/54/SC/CRP.14 10 June 2004.

UNHCR. 2019. "Kakuma Camp and Kalobeyi Settlement Briefing Kit." United Nations High Commissioner for Refugees, May 2019. https://www.unhcr.org/ke/wp-content/uploads/sites/2/2019/06/Briefing-Kit_May-2019-approved.pdf

UNHCR. 1951. "The Refugee Convention, 1951." https://www.unhcr.org/sites/default/files/legacy-pdf/4ca34be29.pdf

U.S. Citizenship and Immigration Services. "Refugee Processing and Security

Screening." 2025. https://www.uscis.gov/humanitarian/refugees-and-asylum/refugees/refugee-processing-and-security-screening

U.S. Department of State Bureau of Consular Affairs. "Special Immigrant Visas (SIVs) for Iraqi and Afghan Translators/Interpreters." Accessed July 16, 2023. https://travel.state.gov/content/travel/en/us-visas/immigrate/siv-iraqi-afghan-translators-interpreters.html

United States Refugee Admissions Program (USRAP) [Flow chart of the processes in the program.] https://www.uscis.gov/sites/default/files/document/charts/USRAP_FlowChart.pdf

U.S. House of Representatives. *A bill to establish a uniform Rule of Naturalization, and to enable Aliens to hold Lands under certain Restrictions.* (H.R. 40, March 9, 1790) https://www.visitthecapitol.gov/artifact/h-r-40-naturalization-bill-march-4-1790

U.S. Senate. Indochina Migration and Refugee Assistance Act of 1975. (S. Rpt. 94-119).

"U.S. to Let Bosnians Immigrate: Policy Opens Doors to 1,000 Refugees." *Omaha World-Herald*, October 27, 1992. https://www.newspapers.com/article/omaha-world-herald-none-usa-to-let-bos/121380754/

University of Nebraska at Omaha. "BOLD (Balkan Youth Leaders) Civic Engagement Fellowship Program." Accessed July 16, 2023. https://www.unomaha.edu/college-of-arts-and-sciences/political-science/community-engagement/bold.php

Valenta, Marko, and Zan Strabac. "They dynamics of Bosnian refugee migrations in the 1990s, current migration trends and future prospects." *Refugee Survey Quarterly* 32, no. 3 (2013): 1–22. http://www.jstor.org/stable/45054962

"Viet Refugees 'Want to Work'." *Lincoln Journal Star*, May 16, 1975.

Vo, Nghia M. *The Vietnamese Boat People, 1954 and 1975-1992*. McFarland & Co., 2006.

"'We are neighbors in Omaha': Meet the city's Karenni community." *Omaha World-Herald*, December 21, 2018. https://omaha.com/sponsored/creighton/we-are-neighbors-in-omaha-meet-the-citys-karenni-community/article_321d1050-3abf-5537-8ab2-9fd19e54bacb.html

"Welfare officials are the cause of the refugee center being closed down." *The Lincoln Star*, October 8, 1980.

"When Railroads Promoted Immigration." History Nebraska. Accessed July. 16, 2023. https://history.nebraska.gov/when-railroads-promoted-immigration/

"Where's the Beef Trade?" Nebraska Farm Bureau, May 9, 2023. https://www.nefb.org/05/09/2023/wheres-the-beef-trade/

White House, *Memorandum on Presidential Determination on Refugee Admissions for Fiscal Year 2023* (Washington, DC, September 27, 2022) https://www.whitehouse.gov/briefing-room/presidential-actions/2022/09/27/memorandum-on-presidential-determination-on-refugee-admissions-for-fiscal-year-2023/

White House. "The Truman Directive. Statement and Directive by the President on Immigration to the United States of Certain Displaced Persons and Refugees in Europe." December 22, 1945. Harry S Truman Presidential Library and Museum. https://www.trumanlibrary.gov/sites/default/files/TrumanDirective.pdf

White House. *Statement by President Joe Biden on Refugee Admissions* (Washington, DC, May 3, 2021) https://www.whitehouse.gov/briefing-room/statements-releases/2021/05/03/statement-by-president-joe-biden-on-refugee-admissions/

"Who We Are." Aqua Africa. Accessed on July 16, 2023. https://aqua-africa.org/who-we-are/

"Who We Are: Mission & History." Asian Community & Cultural Center. Accessed on July 14, 2023. https://www.lincolnasiancenter.org/who-we-are/mission.html

Williams, Jack. "Yazidis from Iraq Find Welcome Refuge in Nebraska. Nebraska Public Media, December 14, 2017. https://nebraskapublicmedia.org/en/news/news-articles/yazidis-from-iraq-find-welcome-refuge-in-nebraska/

Wiltsey, Ellis. "Lincoln Yezidi community remembers 74th genocide." 1011 Now, August 3, 2021. https://www.1011now.com/2021/08/04/lincoln-yazidi-community-remembers-74th-genocide/

Wirth, Eileen. "Nebraska Feels Impact of Indochina Refugees." *Omaha World-Herald*, July 29, 1979. https://www.newspapers.com/article/omaha-world-herald-refugees-helping-ne-1/121005772/

Wirth, Eileen. "Refugees Losing Special Aid." *Omaha World-Herald*, May 22, 1977. https://www.newspapers.com/article/omaha-world-herald-refugees-to-lose-aid/120338619/

"*World-Herald* editorial: Sudan isn't so far away." *Omaha World-Herald*, January 13, 2014. https://omaha.com/opinion/editorials/world-herald-editorial-sudan-isn-t-so-far-away/article_2a43acca-08e3-538b-bd4d-818786fee38f.html

Wright, Robert G. "Part IV: Resettlement: Voluntary Agencies and the Resettlement of Refugees." *International Migration Review* 15, no. 1-2 (1981): 157-174.

Wunder, John, "Re-Inventing the Wheel: Nebraska's Immigration History," in Immigration in Nebraska. *Strategic Discussions for Nebraska*. 3 (2008): 8-9. http://digitalcommons.unl.edu/sdn/3

Yang, Jia Lynn. *One Mighty and Irresistible Tide: The Epic Struggle Over American Immigration, 1924-1965*. WW Norton & Company, 2020.

"Yazda." Yazda. Accessed July 16, 2023. https://www.yazda.org/yazda

"Yezidis" Minority Rights Group. Accessed July 16, 2023 https://minorityrights.org/minorities/yezidis/

Younis, Layla. "Bosnian mosque offers a welcoming state for immigrants, Muslims." *The Daily Nebraskan*, November 18, 2013. https://www.dailynebraskan.com/culture/bosnian-mosque-offers-a-welcoming-space-for-immigrants-muslims/article_29241848-5009-11e3-9c59-0019bb30f31a.html

Zhou, Min and Carl L. Bankston, III. (2000). *Straddling Two Social Worlds: The Experience of Vietnamese Refugee Children in the United States*. Urban Diversity Series No. 111. https://files.eric.ed.gov/fulltext/ED439180.pdf

Contributors

Kevin Abourezk, an award-winning journalist, played a dual role in the history, as overall editor and as co-writer of the Native American section. He is managing editor of *Indian Country Today* and was a reporter and editor for *Lincoln Journal Star* for 18 years. A member of the Rosebud Sioux Tribe, Abourezk has spent his career documenting the lives, accomplishments and tragedies of Native American people. He holds a bachelor's degree in English from the University of South Dakota and master's in journalism from the University of Nebraska-Lincoln.

Gabriel Bruguier, Ph.D., is an Assistant Professor and Teaching and Learning Librarian at University of Nebraska-Lincoln Libraries. He is an enrolled member of the Yankton Sioux Tribe and grew up in Vermillion and Sisseton, South Dakota. He holds M.A. and Ph.D. degrees in philosophy from the University of Nebraska--Lincoln, a B.A. in philosophy from University of Minnesota Morris, and a Licentiate in International Relations from the Universidad de las Américas-Puebla. Bruguier was previously the Education and Outreach Coordinator at the Mid-America Transportation Center at Nebraska, where he oversaw three outreach programs. His efforts have been dedicated to helping Native American students gain spaces and be more visible and successful in higher education.

Heather Fryer, Ph.D., is a freelance writer, editor, and social and cultural historian of the 20th century U.S. West who was on the faculty at Creighton University from 2004 to 2022. She is the author of *Perimeters of Democracy: Inverse Utopias and the Wartime Social Landscape in the American West*, a biography of Father Edward J. Flanagan of Boys Town, and the PBS documentary "Shinmachi: Stronger Than a Tsunami." She is past executive editor of *Peace & Change: A Journal of Peace Research* and served on the advisory board for the Japanese Hall exhibit at the Legacy of the Plains Museum, Gering, Nebraska.

Emira Ibrahimpašić, Ph.D., is an Associate Professor of Practice and Assistant Director of Global Studies in the School of Global Integrative Studies at the University of Nebraska-Lincoln. She is the founding member of Nebraska Initiative for Migration Studies (NIMS) and holds a Ph.D. in cultural anthropology from the University of New Mexico and an M.B.A. from UNL. A dedicated advocate for human rights, Dr. Ibrahimpašić serves on the City of Lincoln Human Rights Commission. As a refugee from war-torn Bosnia and Herzegovina who found a new home in Lincoln, she brings a deeply personal commitment to projects that elevate the voices and experiences of immigrants and refugees. "Our voices, like those of other ethnic and racial minority groups, are often silenced, minimized, or simply forgotten," she said. She views this history project as a vital opportunity to amplify these stories and honor the rich contributions immigrants and refugees have made to Lincoln and to Nebraska as a whole.

Sharon Ishii-Jordan, Ph.D., is an emerita professor of education and former associate dean at Creighton University with a professional background in leadership and education (disabilities and English language learning). Besides Creighton, she has taught in Japan, the Omaha Public Schools, and UNL. She is a sansei whose grandparents immigrated from Japan. She conducts teacher workshops on the U.S. incarceration camps for Japanese during WWII, serves on the board of the Omaha chapter of the Japanese American Citizens League, and serves on the advisory board for the Japanese Hall historical project at the Legacy of the Plains Museum. She has also presented on Japanese American history, Asian American discrimination, and cultural diversity issues at museums, colleges, and school districts in 17 states.

Preston Love, Jr. is a former IBM marketing executive who teaches in the Black Studies Department of the University of Nebraska at Omaha, writes an editorial page column for the *Omaha World-Herald* and is the author of several books. He leads Black History tours to key civil rights sites and is a founder and director of the Institute for Urban Development 4Urban.org. He is the first vice president of NAACP Omaha. He earned a Bachelor of Science degree in economics at the University of Nebraska-Lincoln and a master's in professional studies from Bellevue University.

M. Dewayne Mays, Ph.D. in Agronomy, retired from the USDA Natural Resources Conservation Service after 39 years of service. Since his retirement he has volunteered with Malone Community Center, ACLU Nebraska, Nebraska Appleseed as board member and is president of the Lincoln Branch NAACP. He serves as co-chair of the Truth and Reconciliation Steering Committee.

Paul A. Olson, Ph.D., is Kate Foster Professor of English emeritus, University of Nebraska, where he was a medievalist and early modern specialist. For several decades, he worked extensively on teacher education reform, curricular reform, and issues of profundity, relevance, and prejudice in education. Throughout his life, he retained his interest in the creation of a productive and environmentally sound rural life as witnessed by his 40-year membership on the board of the Center for Rural Affairs and his late life work to make rural education central to the revival of rural communities. Olson was the founding director of the Center for Great Plains Studies at the University of Nebraska. In retirement, he continued his work on Great Plains, medieval, and early modern studies and his peace and justice efforts.

Julia Reilly, Ph.D., is an Assistant Professor of Practice in the University of Nebraska-Lincoln's School of Global Integrative Studies and Human Rights and Humanitarian Affairs Program. She holds doctorate and master's degrees in political science from UNL and a Bachelor of Arts degree from Colgate University in International Relations and Spanish. She is a founding member of the Nebraska Initiative for Migration Studies.

J.S. Onésimo (Ness) Sándoval, Ph.D., is a professor of demography and sociology at Saint Louis University whose work bridges demographic research and spatial data science. His research harnesses big data to uncover socio-economic and demographic trends in American cities, with a particular focus on how these patterns shape communities over time. He also authors a newspaper column, "Rediscovering America Through Demography," where he explores the evolving demographic landscape of the United States and its long-term implications. Through both his scholarship and public engagement, Sándoval aims to translate data into meaningful insights that inform policy and empower communities. He is the founder of two applied geospatial initiatives—Demography 4 Democracy and Coding for Spatial Justice—which equip residents with the tools to reimagine their neighborhoods and secure the resources to bring their visions to life. Sándoval is a founding member of the Taylor Geospatial Institute, and serves as Director of both the Ph.D. Program in Public and Social Policy and the Master's Program in Sociology at Saint Louis University.

Adam Fletcher Sasse is the author of #OmahaBlackHistory: African American People, Places, and Events from the History of Omaha, Nebraska; *North Omaha History* Volumes 1, 2 & 3 and four other books related to Omaha history; the editor of NorthOmahaHistory.com; the host of the North Omaha History Podcast; and an artist focused on North Omaha's built environment. His professional work includes organizational consulting for K-12 schools, nonprofit organizations and government agencies.

Acknowledgements

The authors wish to thank the NAACP Lincoln and Nebraskans for Peace Lincoln for their seminal role in sponsoring this book. The Truth & Reconciliation Nebraska Steering Committee and Paul A. Olson provided wise guidance throughout the effort.

Past and present Steering Committee members are: M. Dewayne Mays, Greg Rutledge, Marty Ramirez, Paul Olson, Colette Yellow Robe, Susana Geliga, Jackie Guzman, Jeannette Eileen Jones, Takako Olson, William Arfmann, Kathleen Johnson, Kathleen Rutledge.

Thanks go, too, for the financial support of a host of individual donors, plus churches and labor unions, and these charitable foundations: Lincoln Community Foundation, Weitz Family Foundation and Woods Charitable Fund.

The Center for Great Plains Studies, Nebraska Appleseed, UNL Digital Commons and University of Nebraska-Lincoln Center for Digital Research in the Humanities provided valuable services to the project, as did Patricia A. Saldaña. Many organizations and individuals in Lincoln, Omaha and elsewhere in the state helped conduct listening sessions that helped guide the vision for this history.

Authors were assisted in research by Genese Clark, Annabel Hazelton, Le Clara Gilreath, Portia Love, Emily Binder, Izchel Quintero, and Ellie Heinrichs, as well as many others. Thanks also to peer reviewers for each chapter, as well as Paul Royster, Emily Levine, Heather Fryer, Charlyne Berens, Kathleen Rutledge and Kathleen Johnson for their editorial assistance.

www.ingramcontent.com/pod-product-compliance
Lightning Source LLC
Chambersburg PA
CBHW080847010526
44114CB00017B/2386